Semantic Analy

OXFORD TEXTBOOKS IN LINGUISTICS

Semantic Analysis
A Practical Introduction

Second Edition
Cliff Goddard

OXFORD
UNIVERSITY PRESS

Great Clarendon Street, Oxford OX2 6DP

Oxford University Press is a department of the University of Oxford.
It furthers the University's objective of excellence in research, scholarship,
and education by publishing worldwide in

Oxford New York

Auckland Cape Town Dar es Salaam Hong Kong Karachi
Kuala Lumpur Madrid Melbourne Mexico City Nairobi
New Delhi Shanghai Taipei Toronto

With offices in

Argentina Austria Brazil Chile Czech Republic France Greece
Guatemala Hungary Italy Japan Poland Portugal Singapore
South Korea Switzerland Thailand Turkey Ukraine Vietnam

Oxford is a registered trade mark of Oxford University Press
in the UK and in certain other countries

Published in the United States
by Oxford University Press Inc., New York

British Library Cataloguing in Publication Data
Data available

Library of Congress Cataloging in Publication Data
Data available

Typeset by SPI Publisher Services, Pondicherry, India
Printed in Great Britain   by
Ashford Colour Press, Gosport, Hampshire

ISBN 978-0-19-956028-8

10 9 8 7 6 5 4 3 2 1

Contents

Preface

The main aim of this book, whose first edition appeared in 1998, is to give students and teachers a resource for developing their own practical skills in semantic analysis. It also aims to help students develop the knowledge and perspective to critically evaluate semantic analysis and argumentation in linguistics at large. As described shortly, the book has been thoroughly revised since the first edition.

Any introductory text must be selective. It must try to balance consistency and diversity of approach, breadth and depth of coverage. In this book, the main method used for describing and analysing meanings is the Natural Semantic Metalanguage (NSM) approach. Originated by Anna Wierzbicka, this is a rigorous but commonsense approach based on reductive paraphrase in natural language. Other significant figures that students will meet in the following pages, along with their distinctive treatments of particular semantic problems, include Ray Jackendoff, Ronald Langacker, Charles Fillmore, Leonard Talmy, Beth Levin, John Searle, Brent Berlin, Steven Levinson, George Lakoff, and William Labov. A key theme throughout the book is the relationship between semantics, conceptualization, and culture. Aside from English, languages drawn on for illustrative purposes include Arrernte, Chinese, Danish, Ewe, Jacaltec, Japanese, Malay, Polish, Spanish, and Yankunytjatjara.

The structure of the book can be sketched as follows. The first two chapters go over background concepts, issues, and research traditions. Chapter 3 introduces the NSM approach and compares and contrasts it with some other leading approaches. Then follows a series of case study chapters, beginning with three areas that are relatively abstract but at the same time full of human interest: emotion words, speech-act verbs, and discourse particles. The next three chapters also have something in common, dealing as they do with concrete areas of vocabulary: words for animals and artefacts, verbs of motion, and verbs for physical activities. The final two case study chapters, on causatives and grammatical categories, take us into grammatical territory. The final chapter reviews the research trajectory of the NSM approach, and explores its applications to language acquisition studies, to ethnopragmatics, and to non-verbal communication.

Though the chapters fit together into a loose thematic sequence, they have been written to be largely independent of one another in terms of content, so as to give students, teachers, and general readers greater flexibility in choosing a sequence of topics. Each chapter closes with a selection of exercises and discussion questions. Solutions for most of the exercises are provided at the end of the book.

The twentieth century was not a very friendly time for semantics, dominated as it was by the twin figures of Leonard Bloomfield, who believed that meaning lay outside the scope of scientific inquiry, and Noam Chomsky, who focused almost exclusively on abstract formal syntax. As the new century progresses, however, it is clear that times have changed. Linguists have rediscovered the lexicon and its centrality to grammar and revived their traditional interest in connections between language and mind, and, increasingly, they are rediscovering culture.

Meaning is moving back to centre stage in the linguistic enterprise.

Enjoy!

Cliff Goddard

University of New England
July 2010

Changes from the first edition

Many things remain the same from the first edition of this book, but there have also been a great many changes. Every chapter has been altered significantly, every explication revised. For the most part the revisions are due to refinements and improvements to the natural semantic metalanguage (NSM) (see sections 12.1 and 12.2), above all due to improved understanding of the metalanguage syntax. As acknowledged in the previous edition, cross-linguistic research into the syntax of semantic primes was in an early stage in 1998. After more than a decade of serious inquiry, the picture is now much clearer. Likewise, the theory of semantic templates has progressed greatly since the first edition. Each case study chapter of the revised edition includes a more focused discussion of the semantic templates that are appropriate for the area under attention. Only in recent years has the theory of semantic molecules firmed up to the point where it is possible, albeit provisionally, to standardize the semantic molecules used in explications for very complex concepts. This particularly affects Chapters 7–9 of the current edition.

In terms of coverage, the most notable change is that a new chapter on physical activity verbs (Chapter 9) has been added, but compensating for this, there is no longer a chapter on colour words (interested readers should see Wierzbicka 2005; 2008; in press a for developments in this area). New material has been added on frame semantics and cognitive linguistics in Chapter 3, on higher-level categorization in Chapter 7, on diminutive constructions in Chapter 11, and on non-verbal communication in Chapter 12. The NSM analyses of speech-act verbs in Chapter 6 have been thoroughly overhauled, with new semantic templates proposed. Less sweeping but significant changes have been implemented in the analyses for emotion terms, interjections, motion verbs, causative constructions, and pronominal systems.

Needless to say, references have been updated in every chapter, and where appropriate, the discussion has been adjusted to take account of new empirical studies and theoretical developments over the last decade or so.

The exercises and discussion questions are an important part of the book, so it is pleasing to report that they too have been revised and expanded. A number of new exercises have been added and some problematical ones removed. As well, many additional solutions have been provided.

Acknowledgements

Acknowledgements to the first edition

Many people have generously furnished criticisms and comments which have helped improve this book. I want particularly to thank my semantics students at the University of New England, and those people who have made detailed comments on the entire manuscript, especially Keith Brown, Anna Wierzbicka, David Wilkins, and several anonymous reviewers. My research assistant, Vicki Knox, provided me with invaluable help on technical and practical matters, and also with many insightful criticisms. For helpful discussions and/or information on particular topics, my thanks are also due to Timothy Curnow, Kumie Fujimori, Dan Gartner, Rie Hasada, Norlinda Hasan, Mee Wun Lee, Beat Lehman, Nick Reid, Verna Rieschild, and Malindy Tong.

Acknowledgements to the second edition

It has been my privilege to collaborate with Anna Wierzbicka on many semantic projects that have influenced the shape and content of this new edition. Anna has also provided specific comments and input on almost every chapter. Of the many other individuals who have contributed helpfully, I am particulary grateful to Carsten Levisen, who reviewed the entire first edition and made many thoughtful suggestions for revision. Christina Levisen and Helen Bromhead read and reviewed parts of the new edition. Other significant input has come from Anna Gladkova, Sandy Habib, Zhengdao Ye, and Sophia Waters. My research assistant, Vicki Knox, played an indispensable role in the revision process, both in helping to manage a shifting and difficult manuscript and in providing insightful advice and criticisms. I would also like to thank successive cohorts of students in my Meaning in Language units over the years. Semantics students never cease to amaze me.

Research for parts of the book was supported by the Australian Research Council.

Figures and map

Tables

Typographical conventions and symbols

- *Italics* are used for citing linguistic forms (words, sentences, or phrases) in any language, including English.
- 'Single inverted commas' are used (a) for glosses, translations, definitions, and for citing components of explications and (b) for drawing attention to a term, either because it is new or because there is something peculiar about it.
- SMALL CAPS are used (a) for proposed semantic primes, (b) for emphasis, and (c) for grammatical morphemes in interlinear glosses.
- **BOLD SMALL CAPS** are used when a key technical term is introduced for the first time.
- Square brackets are used to enclose 'literal' morpheme-by-morpheme glosses

The following symbols are used in interlinear glosses, without further explanation. Other interlinear symbols are either self-explanatory (e.g. PAST for past tense) or are explained at the time they are used. Generally speaking, I have retained the interlinear symbols used by the original authors.

1sg	first person singular (i.e. 'I')
2sg	second person singular (i.e. 'you')
3sg	third person singular (i.e. 'he/she')
SUBJ	grammatical subject
OBJ	grammatical object
DEF	definite
?	semantically odd or anomalous expression
*	unacceptable expression

1

Semantics:
the study of meaning

1.1 Language and meaning

Semantics, the study of meaning, stands at the very centre of the linguistic quest to understand the nature of language and human language abilities. Why? Because expressing meanings is what languages are all about. Everything in a language—words, grammatical constructions, intonation patterns—conspires to realize this goal in the fullest, richest, subtlest way. To understand how any particular language works, we need to understand how its individual design works to fulfil its function as an intricate device for communicating meanings. Equally, semantics is crucial to the goal of describing and accounting for linguistic competence—that is, the knowledge that people must have in order to speak and understand a language. Semantic competence is a crucial part of overall linguistic competence.

Another concern of semantics is to shed light on the relationship between language and culture, or more accurately, between languages and cultures. Much of the vocabulary of any language, and even parts of the grammar, will reflect the culture of its speakers. Indeed, the culture-specific concepts and ways of understanding embedded in a language are an important part of what constitutes a culture. Language is one of the main instruments by which children are socialized into the values, belief systems, and practices of their culture.

1.1.1 Meaning variation across languages

It's hard to believe the colossal variation in word-meanings between languages. You might assume, for instance, that since all human beings have the same kind of bodies, all languages would have words with the same meanings as English *hand* and *hair*. But no. In many languages, the word which refers to a person's hand can apply to the entire arm, as well as to the hand; the Russian word *ruka*, for example, is like this. In many languages, different words are used to refer to head-hair and to body-hair; for example, in Yankunytjatjara (Central Australia) *mangka* refers to head-hair and *yuru* to body-hair (as well as fur).

You might think that all languages would have words for environmental features like *trees*, *mountains*, and *clouds*. Well, in a loose sense this may be true. In any language one can say things about what (in English) we call trees, mountains, and clouds, but not necessarily using words which correspond precisely in meaning to the English words. For example, Yankunytjatjara does not have separate words corresponding to English *tree* and *bush* (one word, *puṇu*, covers both), nor does it have separate words for *mountain* and *hill* (one word, *apu*, covers both). Conversely, Yankunytjatjara has several words for different kinds of clouds but no general word like English *cloud*.

The same applies to words for events and actions as well. It is natural (in English) to think that 'breaking' is a single, simple event. But in Malay there are three words which can cover the range of the English word: *putus* for where the thing is completely severed or broken-off (like a pencil being broken in two), *patah* for when the break isn't complete (like a branch which is broken but not broken off completely), and still another, *pecah*, which is more like 'smash' (like what happens when you break a glass).

If even concrete 'physical' meanings are not necessarily universal but vary from language to language, just think of the variation that exists in relation to more abstract and culture-related meanings. How many languages would have words with the same meanings as English *privacy*, or *apologize*, or *work*? How many languages would draw a distinction, as English does, between *guilt* and *shame*? Obviously, we can't say precisely, but we can say that the number is much, much smaller than most non-linguists would ever imagine. In a similar fashion, every language has its own culture-specific meanings, which don't translate readily into English. Admittedly, each word in itself makes only a small contribution to the differences between languages, but when you sum up the meaning variation over 10,000 words, perhaps you can see why linguists sometimes say that every language represents a unique way of seeing and thinking about the world.

1.1.2 The role of meaning in grammar

In this book we are concerned primarily with semantics, not with other areas of language description such as morphology and syntax. Since many readers will have some familiarity with these other fields of linguistics, however, it is worthwhile mentioning the relevance of semantics to the broader domain of linguistic theory.

One of the main concerns of linguistic theory is to identify the governing principles that account for the regularity and orderliness of languages. In other words, to answer questions like: Why does language X have the grammatical rules it has? Why does language Y differ from language X in the way it does? What underlying principles apply to both X and Y?

For many years in the last century the orthodoxy was that semantics did not have much relevance to questions like these, because it was believed that the syntactic workings of language were independent of meaning. As Langacker (2010: 94) points out, this view depended in part on a particular attitude to meaning:

How linguists think about grammar is greatly influenced by how they think about meaning. Approaches to meaning that bypass the role of human conception—treating it in terms of formal logic, truth conditions, or correspondences to the world—resonate with the view of grammar as an autonomous formal system.

Since the mid-1980s, however, many linguists have begun to think differently. As Thomas Wasow (1985) pointed out (in Sells 1985: 204–5).

contemporary syntactic theories seem to be converging on the idea that sentence structure is generally predictable from word meanings . . . the surprising thing (to linguists) has been how little needs to be stipulated beyond lexical meaning.

Of course, to make good on the assumption that syntactic properties flow from word meaning (especially, from the meanings of verbs) linguists need to take the challenges of semantic description seriously, and it is questionable how well many syntax-oriented linguists have lived up to this requirement (Levin and Rappaport Hovav 2005). A more recent focus of interest is that in some contexts there can be an apparent fusion of lexical meaning and constructional meaning (Fillmore et al. 2010); but though this may well be true, to investigate this phenomenon requires a high standard of semantic description. In short, a well-developed approach to semantics is essential to the study of grammar.

1.2 The nature of meaning

Whether we are interested in exploring the connections between meaning and culture, or between meaning and grammar, or simply in exploring meaning for its own sake, the first thing we need is a consistent, reliable, and clear method of stating meanings—a system of semantic representation. Not surprisingly, the main theoretical controversies in semantics concern the nature of the optimal system of semantic representation.

The vexed question of the nature of meaning is easiest to approach indirectly, by first asking what meaning is not.

1.2.1 Meaning is not reference

People sometimes think that the meaning of an expression is simply—and merely—the thing that it identifies or 'picks out' in the world (the so-called REFERENT). This seems sensible enough in relation to names, for instance, *Barack Obama*, *the Sydney Harbour Bridge*, *London*, or definite descriptive noun phrases, such as *the President of the United States*. But to see that meaning is distinct from reference, we only have to think of words which do not refer to anything at all, such as *no one*, *empty*, *unicorn*, *and*, *usually*, *hello*. These words are not meaningless, so whatever the meaning of a word may be, it must be something other than what the word refers to.

Another argument against the view that meaning equals reference is that if this view were correct, expressions which referred to the same thing would have the same meaning. The most famous counter-examples are the expressions *The Morning Star* and *The Evening Star*, which clearly differ in meaning, even though objectively they refer to the same thing,

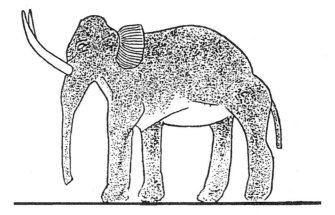

Figure 1.1 von Humboldt on the elephant. '[I]f in Sanskrit, for example, the *elephant* is now called the twice-drinking one, now the two-toothed one, and now the one equipped with a single hand, as many different concepts are thereby designated, though the same object is meant. For language never represents the objects, but always the concepts that the mind has spontaneously formed from them in producing language . . .' (Wilhelm von Humboldt 1988 [1836]: 84)

namely the planet Venus. A more prosaic, but very nice, example (from Allan 1986) is furnished by the two expressions *the man who invented parking meters* and *the man who invented the yo-yo*. I'm sure you will agree that these two expressions convey different meanings, and I don't expect your opinion will change if I tell you that as a matter of fact both refer to the very same man. A classical example is the expression *featherless biped*. Although this has the same referential range as the expression *human being*, as an explanation of meaning it clearly leaves a lot to be desired.

A final reason for rejecting the simplistic view that meaning is reference is that the property of 'making reference' is not something that belongs to words or expressions in themselves at all, but rather to the use of words on a particular occasion. For instance, the words *this*, *here*, *now*, and *I* can refer to any number of things, places, times, or persons depending on the context, but it would be foolish to say that such words had a different meaning every time they were uttered.

Of course, just because meaning is distinct from reference doesn't mean that the two are unrelated. Obviously, they are related: the reference made by the use of a particular expression on a particular occasion depends, at least in part, on the meaning of the expression. Linguists sometimes speak of the SENSE of a word, when they want to make it clear that they are interested in meaning as opposed to reference.

1.2.2 Meaning is not scientific knowledge

It is also wrong to think that meaning can be described in terms of scientific knowledge, a position advocated by the early American linguist Leonard Bloomfield. As a behaviourist, he believed that meaning should be treated as a stimulus-response relationship between a speech-form and objective aspects of the speaker's world. Bloomfield (1933: 139) wrote:

we can define the meaning of a speech-form accurately when this meaning has to do with some matter of which we possess scientific knowledge. We can define the names of minerals, for example, in terms of chemistry and mineralogy, as when we say that the ordinary meaning of the English word *salt* is 'sodium chloride (NaCl)', and we can define the names of plants and animals by means of the technical terms of botany and zoology, but we have no precise way of defining words like *love* and *hate*, which concern situations that have not been accurately classified.

Some dictionaries follow Bloomfield's prescription, supplying definitions like the following from the *Concise Oxford Dictionary*.

liver: large glandular organ in abdomen of vertebrates, secreting bile
water: colourless transparent tasteless odourless compound of oxygen and hydrogen in liquid state . . .
red: of or approaching the colour seen at the least-refracted end of the spectrum

Clearly, however, people use the words *liver*, *water*, and *red* quite happily and correctly without having any ideas about glands, chemical compounds, or the spectrum. Knowledge of everyday word meanings is part of people's linguistic competence, but scientific knowledge is not.

Another reason for rejecting the idea that meaning can be described in terms of scientific knowledge is that such an approach would not lead to a uniform account of meaning, since as Bloomfield concedes, it would only be applicable to a limited proportion of word meanings. How could it cope with words like *love*, *God*, and *hello*?

Finally, there is the point that technical terms, like *hydrogen*, *glandular*, and *spectrum*, are also words, and as such their meanings will ultimately need to be explained too. If you are going to use words to explain the meaning of other words, an important principle is that the definition or explanation must consist of simpler, more easily understood terms than the word being defined.

1.2.3 Meaning is not 'use'

Some people hold that the meaning of a word is 'its use in the language', a slogan taken from the work of the great twentieth-century philosopher Ludwig Wittgenstein. As with the reference theory, this view clearly has something going for it. Children learn most word-meanings simply by exposure to them in use, without much verbal explanation. There is no doubt that the meaning of a word is related to its use; in fact, it can be argued that the meaning of a word is the main determinant of its use. But for the purpose of accounting for linguistic competence, the 'meaning is use' theory must be rejected, or at least heavily modified. What we are after is an account of what people know about their language. Just to say that they know the use of all the words is not very helpful—we would have to go on to describe in each case what it is that they know about the use.

It is also hard to see how the 'meaning is use' view could account for the meaning of whole sentences or utterances.

In practice, scholars who subscribe to the 'meaning is use' slogan generally believe that the meanings of words and expressions cannot be pinned down at all by any form of systematic semantics. Instead they emphasize the interdependence of meaning and context and the importance of understanding the myriad of 'language games' (another phrase from Wittgenstein) within which meaning is created and negotiated.

1.3 Linguistic approaches to meaning

In this section, we briefly meet some views of meaning which are more relevant to modern linguistics.

1.3.1 Truth-conditional theories

Although the crude 'meaning equals reference' theory doesn't stand up for long, the basic notion that meaning is a relationship between an expression and a state of affairs in the world has given rise to more sophisticated versions of the same basic idea. One influential idea from the study of logic is that the meaning of a sentence is the conditions in the world which would have to be met for the sentence to be true. To understand a sentence like *Snow is white*, for instance, you have to understand how the world would have to be for that sentence to be true. Theories based on this approach are called TRUTH-CONDITIONAL. They say that the meaning of a word is the contribution it makes to the 'truth conditions' of sentences in which it appears (see section 2.3).

The main theoretical difficulty faced by truth-conditional approaches is raised by the question: How are the truth conditions themselves to be stated? Inevitably, in some language—or metalanguage, as a language used to describe another language is usually called. But how then are the meanings of the sentences in the metalanguage to be described? By stating their truth-conditions in terms of yet another metalanguage? Clearly the buck has to stop somewhere, or we will have what is called an infinite regress.

Another problem lies with what critics call the 'objectivist' attitude toward meaning—that is to say, the very idea that meaning resides in the relationship between a linguistic expression and aspects of an 'objective' world. For, clearly, there are innumerable expressions in any language whose meanings are inherently subjective and/or culture-bound and cannot be reduced to a correlation with features of the external world. How could moral, aesthetic, religious, or philosophical meanings be tied down to correlations with an objective world? Consider words like *unfair*, *beautiful*, *God*, and *rights*. It seems obvious that these meanings do not correspond to anything in external reality, and the same applies to a myriad of culture-specific words like *Monday*, *bar mitzvah*, *associate professor*, *second base*, or *fiancee* (Lakoff 1988: 135). In this book we will not consider truth-conditional semantics in any detail.

1.3.2 Conceptualist theories: classical

CONCEPTUAL THEORIES OF MEANING are closest to the commonsense view. They say that a meaning of a word is a structured idea, or 'concept', in the mind of the person using that expression. As children growing up in a culture, we acquire, in the form of word-meanings, a huge number of 'pre-packaged' concepts shared by those around us. Because these underlying ideas are shared, communication becomes possible. In its classical form, this view of meaning is often associated with the seventeenth-century English philosopher John Locke, who wrote:

[W]ords, in their primary or immediate signification, stand for nothing but the ideas *in the mind of him that uses them,* . . . When a man speaks to another, it is that he may be understood; and the end of speech is that those sounds, as marks, may make known his *ideas* to the hearer. (Locke 1976 [1690]: 208, emphasis in original)

Conceptual theories take various forms, especially as regards the following important question: If meanings are concepts or ideas, where do those ideas come from, how are they acquired? Locke believed that the human mind is analogous to a blank slate (*tabula rasa*) at birth, but that since we all share the same kind of sense organs and therefore experience the world in more or less the same way, we come, in time, to have more or less the same basic ideas about it; our complex ideas are then built up from these basic ideas derived from experience. This is called an empiricist position, because it emphasizes the importance of knowledge derived through the senses.

The alternative position is the rationalist one held by contemporaries of Locke's such as Gottfried Wilhelm Leibniz and René Descartes. This holds that the very simplest concepts are a natural or innate property of the human mind, which are activated by experience but not wholly and solely derived from it. One argument in favour of semantic rationalism is that it is hard to see how concepts like time, causation, and identity (sameness) could ever be derived from 'pure' sensory experience. Another argument comes from the vast complexity and intricacy of language. It seems implausible that children could acquire all this as reliably and effortlessly as they do without some innate predisposition. Modern conceptualist approaches are dealt with below.

1.3.3 Structuralist theories

Structuralism is a powerful intellectual tradition in modern thought, especially in literary studies and anthropology, as well as in linguistics. One of its pioneers was the great Swiss linguist Ferdinand de Saussure, who was fond of drawing an analogy between language and the game of chess. Just as the various chess-pieces, and their moves, can only be understood in terms of how they function together and in contrast with one another, so it is in language also: to understand the meaning of a word, for instance, we have to understand how it functions together with, and in contrast to, other, related words. According to a fully STRUCTURALIST THEORY OF MEANING, the meaning of any word is actually constituted by the totality of relationships this word has with the other words in the language.

Taken to its logical extreme, a structuralist view holds that meanings (and sounds also, for that matter) cannot be characterized in positive terms at all. A famous quotation to this effect comes from Saussure's *Course in General Linguistics* (1983 [1922]: 118):

> IN LANGUAGE ITSELF, THERE ARE ONLY DIFFERENCES. Even more important than this is the fact that, although in general a difference presupposes positive terms between which the difference holds, in a language there are differences, AND NO POSITIVE TERMS ... language includes neither sounds nor ideas existing prior to the linguistic system, but only conceptual and phonetic differences arising out of that system. (emphasis in original)

The favoured structuralist method is known as componential analysis (see section 2.4).

1.3.4 Extensionalist approaches

Although meaning cannot be identified with reference, some linguists argue that the best way to study meaning differences between words is to look at their range of reference or 'extension' (a term borrowed from philosophy). When the words are about aspects of the physical world, such an approach can seem to work rather well. For example, if we want to compare words for 'colours' across different languages, it seems very practical to employ a standardized set of samples of (such as the Munsell colour chips) and to ask speakers of each language to just point out which hues count as examples of a particular colour word in their language. If one is interested in words for spatial relationships or configurations, it can be helpful to use diagrams, models, or other props to elicit the range of use of particular words. Such methods have been greatly developed by the 'Nijmegen School' led by Stephen Levinson (2003; cf. Levinson and Wilkins 2006). They have even extended the extensionalist approach to the verbal arena, by devising sets of video clips of various actions and activities and asking speakers to label the video clips in the words of their own language.

The results of these procedures are often presented in the form of diagrams or 'maps' that display differing ranges of use. It takes just a short leap of logic (or illogic) to start speaking as if these diagrams or maps display the actual meanings of words, rather than just their range of use. In this way, the extensionalist approach comes to function as a kind of de facto theory of meaning.

Extensionalist approaches can be useful, but they are limited in their scope. They do not lend themselves well to non-concrete domains of the lexicon, such as words to do with feelings, thoughts, values, causation, logical concepts, and the like; nor to grammatical semantics. More seriously, extensionalist methods cannot give access to the conceptual or cognitive representations of speakers. The very same physical referents or activities (parts of the human body or bodily actions, for example) might be conceptualized differently in (or through) different languages, but extensionalist methods could not reveal this. This brings us back to conceptualist theories.

1.3.5 Conceptualist theories: modern

At a very general level, most contemporary linguists (and most psychologists) have a conceptualist approach to meaning; that is, they think of meaning as a mental phenomenon, as something that is in people's heads. If we were to apply the classical distinctions, we could say that George Lakoff and Ronald Langacker, for example, are conceptualists in the empiricist tradition, while Ray Jackendoff and Anna Wierzbicka are conceptualists in the rationalist tradition. The truth is, however, that there is a very wide range of approaches to meaning on the contemporary linguistic scene, and that proponents of different approaches are themselves not always very clear about—or very interested in—the philosophical underpinnings and precise theoretical commitments of their approaches. Unlike philosophers, linguists tend to have a rather practical bent of mind. Rather than debate the nature of meaning, they want to get down to the task of describing languages. Many descriptive linguists use—or even compile— dictionaries of various languages without troubling themselves greatly about their philosophical status. Others interested in specific linguistic problems in a particular language (for example, aspects of morphology or syntax) often devise their own systems for describing the aspects of meaning that they think are relevant to the problem at hand, and they do not feel obliged to explain how (if at all) their account fits into a bigger picture about the workings of the language as a whole.

The best way to get a grip on the range of conceptualist approaches in contemporary linguistics is to focus on the kind of issues that divide them. This is where we will go in the next section.

1.4 Issues in semantic theory

The 'irreducibility of the sign' was emphasized by Charles Sanders Peirce, the great American logician and philosopher. Peirce coined the term 'semiotics', which he envisaged as a new science devoted to the study of 'signs'. For our purposes a sign is just an expression, such as a word, which has a meaning. One of Peirce's (1932: 2.230f.) main contentions is that it is impossible to reduce a sign to any elements that are themselves not signs. For all intents and purposes, it is impossible to analyse or describe meanings except in terms of some other language—perhaps a more technical language consisting of special symbols, but a sort of language nonetheless.

But while it may be impossible to 'escape from language' in any ultimate sense, this does not mean that we cannot be clear and systematic about how we go about the task of using language to describe language. For this reason, it is useful to introduce the term METALANGUAGE. In general, a metalanguage simply means a language that is used to describe or analyse another language. For instance, in a bilingual Russian–English dictionary, where Russian words are defined or explained in terms of English words, the metalanguage is English; in an English–Russian bilingual dictionary, on the other hand, the metalanguage is Russian because it is the language in which the definitions are given. Another example: technical terms like *noun*, *verb*, *adjective*, *subject*, *object*, *active*, and *passive* are part of the grammatical metalanguage of linguistics—that is, they are words used to describe or analyse the grammatical relationships in ordinary everyday language. Of course, a metalanguage doesn't have to be a different language (or even a different register) from the one being described. A normal English dictionary uses English words to describe the meanings of other English words.

Now, any semantic theory needs some way to state the meaning of an expression. An object of any kind which states the meaning of an expression can be called a SEMANTIC REPRESENTATION of that expression. The terms in which the representation is composed make up the metalanguage of semantic representation (or just SEMANTIC METALANGUAGE, for short). There are many controversies about what is the best kind of semantic metalanguage.

1.4.1 Semantic primitives (primes)

If it is possible to analyse meanings at all, it would seem only logical that there must be a set of basic terms which cannot be defined or reduced further, which we would reach as the endpoint of all the analysis. Such elementary meanings are these days often called SEMANTIC PRIMITIVES or SEMANTIC PRIMES, though they were known to the rationalist philosophers of the seventeenth century as 'simple ideas'. For example, Arnauld wrote:

> I say it would be impossible to define every word. For in order to define a word it is necessary to use other words designating the idea we want to connect to the word being defined. And if we then wished to define the words used to explain that word, we would need still others, and so on to infinity. Consequently, we necessarily have to stop at primitive terms which are undefined. (Arnauld and Nicole 1996 [1662]: 64)

A conceptualist argument for elementary meanings is that without them, we would be unable to understand anything; because to understand anything, there must be something in terms of which it is understood. As Leibniz put it:

> Whatever is thought of by us is either conceived through itself, or involves the concept of another. Whatever is involved in the concept of another is again either conceived through itself, or involves the concept of another; and so on. So one must either proceed to infinity, or all thoughts are resolved into those which are conceived through themselves. If nothing is conceived through itself, nothing could be conceived at all. (Leibniz 1973 [1679]: 1)

Leibniz even began a programme of lexical investigation with a view to discovering the primitive notions and rules of composition from which all complex notions were composed (Ishiguro 1972: 36–48)—his *ars combinatoria* or 'universal characteristic'. Modern linguists who have taken a positive approach to universal semantic primitives include Manfred Bierwisch, Jerrold Katz, Ray Jackendoff, and Anna Wierzbicka.

1.4.2 Universality

On the face of it, it would seem only sensible to approach semantics with the aim of finding a universally applicable system for describing meaning wherever we find it; just as in phonetics, phonology, and syntax we seek frameworks and principles which are equally applicable to all the world's languages. As Noam Chomsky once remarked (1965: 160):

It is important to determine the universal, language-independent constraints on semantic features—in traditional terms, the system of possible concepts. The very notion 'lexical entry' presupposes some sort of fixed, universal vocabulary in terms of which these objects are characterized, just as the notion 'phonetic representation' presupposes some sort of universal phonetic inventory.

The possibility of translation between languages, and the ability that we all have to learn and understand new languages, also seem to indicate that there is some universal framework for understanding, which is shared by all human beings. The notion that there is a 'psychic unity' to humankind has a long history in philosophy, and more recently, in linguistics and anthropology.

Many modern linguists, however, doubt that a universal system for describing meanings is possible. For one thing, translatability is not always a simple matter if there are wide differences in culture and grammar to be reckoned with. Also, many linguists are daunted by the 'slipperiness' of meaning, and fear that it would be impossible to establish a universal inventory of semantic features because it would be too difficult to choose between competing analyses. Some modern linguists even claim that empirical studies have proven that there are no universals of meaning, while others assert the opposite.

1.4.3 Anglocentrism

ETHNOCENTRISM is a general term that originates in anthropology, where people are very mindful of the dangers faced when one tries to describe anything across a culture gap. The term refers to the distortions that can arise when the concepts, values, or practices of people of one culture are described through the prism of concepts from an alien culture (the culture of the investigators) that have no equivalents in the culture being described. Ethnocentrism is often unintentional (it is only natural, after all, to describe the unknown in terms of the known). In the modern world, with English approaching the status of a global lingua franca (certainly a scientific lingua franca), the most widespread and dangerous kind of ethnocentrism is ANGLOCENTRISM.

Unfortunately, many linguists (including many semanticists) are unaware that their own descriptive practices are deeply affected by Anglocentrism. How? Because they use English words uncritically as a metalanguage to describe meanings in other languages, disregarding (or unaware of) the fact that many of these English words do not have equivalents in the language being described.

1.4.4 Discreteness

Are the terms of semantic description discrete elements, each one clearly separate from the others (like words, for instance)? Or is it necessary to have a system with continuously varying dimensions, where a specification could be given as a number on a scale, for instance? This is the issue of discreteness.

One point upon which almost all semanticists agree these days is that there is a certain vagueness and subjectivity to the meaning of many (perhaps most) words, which makes it impossible to pin down the complete meaning in terms of a list of cut-and-dried objective features. Take the words *man*, *fruit*, or *red*. It isn't hard to think of situations where one wouldn't be quite sure if they are applicable or not. Is a male person aged 16 or 17 a *man*, or not? Is a *tomato* a *fruit*? When does *reddish-orange* become *red*? Obviously, it is hard to say. Some linguists have concluded from facts of this kind that the underlying components of meaning are 'fuzzy' rather than fixed and discrete.

The influence of Ludwig Wittgenstein, possibly the twentieth century's most brilliant philosopher, cannot be underestimated in this regard. In a famous passage, Wittgenstein came to the conclusion that the word *game* (or more precisely, the German word *Spiel*) could refer to so many different kinds of thing (board-games, card-games, ball-games, chess, noughts-and-crosses, tennis, ring-a-ring-a-roses, etc.) that it was inconceivable that its meaning could be captured in a specifiable set of common features. 'What is common to all of them?' he wrote,

Don't say: 'There must be something common, or they would not be called *games*'—but look and see whether there is anything common to all. For if you look at them you will not see something that is common to all, but similarities, relationships and a whole series of them at that. (Wittgenstein 1953: 31–2)

In place of the traditional notion of meaning, Wittgenstein introduced the notion of FAMILY RESEMBLANCE: 'a complicated network of similarities overlapping and criss-crossing'. The various uses of a word cannot be summed up in a single statement of meaning, he insisted, but overlap and criss-cross in much the same way as the various resemblances (build, features, colour of eyes, gait, temperament, etc.) between members of a family do. Although many have tried, however, no one has been able to adapt the family resemblances idea into a practical analytical system.

We will see later in this book that vagueness and subjectivity are not actually incompatible with the idea of discrete and specifiable meanings.

1.4.5 Linguistic vs. encyclopedic knowledge

Many linguists accept that in principle it is possible to draw some sort of line between our knowledge of a language and our other knowledge, that is, between linguistic knowledge and 'real-world' knowledge (ENCYCLOPEDIC KNOWLEDGE, as it is usually called). Thus, what we know about the meaning of the words *dog*, *hair*, and *light bulb* (for example) should be distinguishable in principle from our other factual knowledge about dogs, hair, and light bulbs. One argument in favour of this view is that linguistic knowledge is essentially shared between all the speakers of a language, whereas real-world knowledge is not. Dog-breeders, hair stylists, and electrical engineers, for instance, know a lot of specialized things about dogs, hair, and light bulbs which are not part of the shared meanings of the words.

So far so good. But what about 'common knowledge'—the kind of thing which almost everyone knows, for instance, that *dogs* have four legs, bark, and wag their tails? It is not always easy to decide whether such information should be regarded as a part of the meaning of a word or not. Geoffrey Leech (1981) expressed the minimalist view when he said that it is a matter of real-world contingency, and nothing to do with word-meaning, that an *elephant* has four legs rather than eighty. Jurij Apresjan and Anna Wierzbicka are associated with the maximalist view. Apresjan (1992 [1974]: 32–3) says that there is nothing less than a 'naive picture of the world hidden in lexical meanings', including a folk geometry, physics, psychology, etc. 'developed in the course of centuries and ... [which] reflects the material and spiritual experience of a people'. Wierzbicka (1985) argues that the full meanings of words like *dog*, *cat*, and *mouse* incorporate a great deal of folk knowledge; that the linguistic concept of *dog*, for instance, includes barking, tail-wagging, and much more besides.

An alternative view denies the existence of any boundary between real-world and linguistic knowledge. Theorists like Charles Fillmore and Ronald Langacker believe that knowledge of all kinds is integrated in the mind to such an extent that it doesn't make sense to partition it into two distinct realms.

1.4.6 Semantics vs. pragmatics

Linguists agree that when people are communicating, they do more than just attend to what is actually being said by way of words, grammatical constructions, and intonation patterns. They are also alert to what is implied—for example, by a speaker's choice of certain words rather than others, by what a speaker is not saying compared to what might have been expected, by the extralinguistic context in which the communication is taking place.

A distinction is often drawn between meanings which are encoded in the structure of the language, as opposed to meanings which can be derived or deduced from how language is used on a particular occasion, in a particular context. Semantics is usually understood to be the study of meaning in the first of these senses, that is, the study of the more or less stable, conventionalized meanings of linguistic signs. The study of how speakers and hearers interpret meanings in particular contexts—taking account of the physical and social situation, knowledge of each other's backgrounds, and cultural conventions, among other factors—is usually termed PRAGMATICS. Roughly speaking, semantics deals with meanings which are coded into linguistic forms, while pragmatics deals with the inferences people make from how linguistic meanings are used in particular situations. Even more roughly, semantics deals with words and sentences, while pragmatics deals with words and sentences as used on particular occasions, i.e. with utterances.

Distinctions like this may sound clear enough in theory, but when it comes down to practical applications there is often disagreement about where the line should be drawn. Much of it stems from disagreement about the criteria for stating and testing semantic meaning. Some linguists, such as Fillmore, Langacker, and Lakoff, argue that it makes no sense to draw a rigid distinction between semantics and pragmatics, just as it makes no sense (they say) to draw a rigid distinction between linguistic and real-world knowledge. In any case, even assuming that semantics and pragmatics are conceptually distinct fields of study, it is obvious that they must be very closely integrated if we are ever to achieve a satisfying theory of linguistic communication. There is also plenty of evidence from the study of language change and language acquisition which leads to the same conclusion.

In this book we stay largely within the realm of semantics, in the sense just described. It should be noted, however, that there is another use of the term pragmatics, employed by linguists whose approach to meaning is strongly influenced by the study of logic. As mentioned earlier, in the logical tradition (see also section 2.3) meaning is defined in terms of relationships (truth conditions) between sentences and an objective outside world. In this tradition, all aspects of meaning which cannot be stated in terms of truth conditions are regarded as part of 'pragmatics', as opposed to truth-conditional semantics. In this logic-based terminology (which we will not adopt), much of this book would be about pragmatics.

1.5 Semantic phenomena

As you can probably appreciate by now, semantics is such a controversial field that there isn't even consensus on what it should cover. To conclude this chapter, we take a look at some phenomena which are widely agreed to be semantic in nature—that is, at the kind of phenomena any reasonable semantic theory could be expected to cover.

1.5.1 Meaning relations

It is generally agreed that someone who knows the English language well knows that the words *hot* and *cold*, for example, are incompatible by virtue of their meanings. A thing cannot be *hot* and *cold* at the same time. Likewise, someone who knows English well knows, by virtue of the meaning of the word *terrier*, that *terriers* are *dogs*. These are examples of MEANING RELATIONS.

Perhaps the most familiar term referring to a meaning relation is SYN-ONYMY, which is supposed to mean simply 'sameness of meaning'. Diction-aries use the term synonymy fairly loosely, but linguistic textbooks usually make the point that true synonymy, i.e. precise sameness of meaning, is so rare as to be almost nonexistent. The usual examples are pairs like *father* and *dad*, or *couch* and *sofa*, but these are better termed 'near-synonyms' because it can be shown that they do not convey exactly the same meanings.

ANTONYMS are words which are 'opposite' in meaning. GRADABLE ANT-ONYMS, such as *good* and *bad*, and *hot* and *cold*, are so called because in principle there is an indefinitely large number of gradations in between one and the other. Things can be more or less *good* or *bad*, more or less *hot* or *cold*. COMPLEMENTARY ANTONYMS are pairs like *true* and *false*, *dead* and *alive*, which divide a particular domain into two mutually exclusive com-partments. Pairs of words like *buy* and *sell* are sometimes called 'relational antonyms', but they are not really opposites in any clear sense and are better termed CONVERSES.

INCOMPATIBILITY is a broader heading that takes in gradable and com-plementary antonyms, and various other kinds of mutually exclusive words as well. Many words fall into sets, sometimes called 'contrast sets', whose members are mutually exclusive. For example, if something is *red*, it cannot be *blue*, *green*, or *black*, but it would not make sense to say these other words were 'opposites' of *red*. Likewise, if something is a *dog*, it cannot be a *cat*, *horse*, *monkey*, etc.

A prominent but problematical term which often comes up in discus-sions of meaning relations is HYPONYMY. It is usually defined as 'where the range of one term includes that of another' or 'where one class or set of things is included in the class or set of another'. The more inclusive term is known as the SUPERORDINATE and the more specific term as the HYPONYM. The problem is that hyponymy defined in this fashion does not correspond to any particular meaning relation, because there are several semantically different kinds of superordinate; for example, taxonomic (based on the 'kind of' relation) and collective. This is explained in the next section.

Less well known than hyponymy but extremely important is the concept of PARTONOMY (sometimes called meronymy). This refers to the meaning relation based on 'part of'. Good definitions of the words *hands*, *mouth*, and *eyes*, for example, would include the specification that they are 'parts of someone's body'. Many words from the biological realm are partonomic in their meaning, e.g. *leaf, branch, wings, tail*.

Semanticists in the structuralist tradition have spent a great deal of time devising schemes for classifying different kinds of meaning relations. Why? Because the basic idea behind structuralism is that meanings do not exist 'in themselves', but only in relation to one another as part of an overall system of cross-cutting contrasts and similarities. Whether or not one accepts the structuralist approach, it is obvious that intuitive knowledge of such mean-ing relations is part of ordinary linguistic competence.

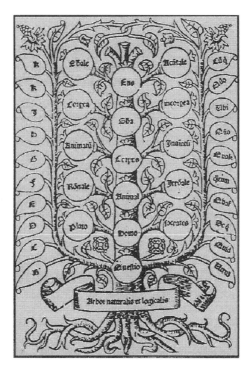

Figure 1.2 The Tree of Porphyry: a medieval diagram representing Aristotle's idea that all things can be arranged into multi-level hierarchies of taxonomic superordinates and hyponyms. Such schemes are not particularly plausible from a conceptual or linguistic point of view, but are still often used in computer science systems of knowledge representation

1.5.2 Taxonomic vs. collective superordinates

One of the most important meaning relations is called TAXONYMY. It is based on the 'kind of' relationship. *Magpies*, *robins*, and *eagles*, for example, are birds of different kinds. *Trout*, *salmon*, and *snapper* are fish of different kinds. Putting it another way, the word 'bird' (or more precisely, the meaning of the word 'bird') is included in the meaning of *magpie*, *robin*, and *eagle*. A good definition of each word would begin: 'a bird of one kind'. Likewise, a good definition of *trout*, *salmon*, *snapper*, etc. would begin: 'a fish of one kind'. Words like *bird* and *fish* can therefore be termed TAXO-NOMIC SUPERORDINATES. Aristotle believed that all things could be arranged into a vast taxonomic hierarchy (see Figure 1.2).

Many superordinate terms, for example, *furniture*, *vegetables*, *weapon*, are not taxonomic but COLLECTIVE SUPERORDINATES. Such words do not represent higher-level 'kinds'. Rather they are grouping words: words

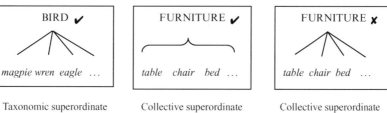

Taxonomic superordinate   Collective superordinate   Collective superordinate
                                                                    misconstrued as taxonomic

Figure 1.3 Diagrams representing correct and incorrect understandings of taxonomic and collective superordinates

that bring together things of different kinds that share a common function and origin (Wierzbicka 1985). *Furniture*, for example, designates various things such as tables, chairs, beds, and the like that people make for their homes and offices. *Vegetables* designates things like peas, carrots, and the like that grow in the ground and that can be eaten after some preparation, usually together with some other foods. *Weapons* are things like guns and swords that are made for the purpose of killing people.

The term 'hyponymy' is problematical principally because it glosses over the difference between taxonomic superordinates and collective superordinates. A second, more subtle problem is that the standard definitions are phrased in terms of set inclusion or referential range, and yet class inclusion is a referential (extensional) relationship, not a meaning relationship. Every *policeman*, for example, is somebody's *son*, but it would hardly make sense to regard *son* as a superordinate of *policeman*; nor is a *policeman* conceptualized as a 'kind of *son*'. A third difficulty with the term 'hyponymy' is that many writers extend it to verbs, without taking into account that semantic relationships between verbs can be quite different in nature to those between nouns. For example, some textbooks say that *sprint* and *jog* are hyponyms of *run*, yet it may be more accurate to say that *sprinting* and *jogging* designate certain 'ways of *running*' than to say that they are 'kinds of *running*'. In this book we will try to keep things clear by avoiding the term hyponymy.

1.5.3 Entailment, contradiction, and paraphrase

Strictly speaking, the term 'meaning relations' is reserved for relations between individual words, but speakers also have intuitive knowledge of certain relationships between single words and word combinations (phrases or sentences), and these too ought to be accounted for by an adequate theory of semantics. ENTAILMENT is a relationship that applies between two sentences, where the truth of one implies the truth of the other because of the meanings of the words involved. CONTRADICTION is where a sentence must be false because of the meanings involved.

Many obvious entailments come about because of inclusory relations between the meanings of words; for instance, because the meaning 'do something to' is included in *eat*, the sentence *Max ate the pizza* entails *Max did something to the pizza*. Similarly, many obvious contradictions come about because of incompatibility, as for instance, *It moved up and down at the same time* or *It was (all) blue and it was (all) red*. However, there are entailments and contradictions which are subtler than these. The contradictoriness of *I'm my own mother*, for instance, does not come from any special relation between *I* and *mother*. Likewise, if *I love her* entails *I want the best for her*, this is not on account of any obvious relation between individual words either.

The most important relationship for the whole enterprise of linguistic semantics is PARAPHRASE—the relationship between a word and a combination of other words with the same meaning. For instance, most people would probably agree that *to speak* means the same as 'to say some things to someone else with words' and that *loud* means something like 'can be heard from far away'. Ultimately, the whole project of describing or explaining word meanings depends on paraphrase because we must use words—or other equivalent symbols—to explain other words.

1.5.4 Homonymy

HOMONYMY designates a situation in which different words (homonyms) happen accidentally to have the same form; as for instance, *bank₁* (as in *She robbed the bank*) and *bank₂* (as in *We walked along the bank*), *left₁* (as in *Turn left*) and *left₂* as in (*He left*), *port₁* (as in *The ship left port*) and *port₂* (as in *He drank port*). Generally speaking, sameness of form is taken to refer to phonetic form. If it is necessary to distinguish terminologically between sameness of phonetic form vs. sameness of graphic form, one can use the terms HOMOPHONE and HOMOGRAPH, respectively. Because English spelling is not phonetically consistent, there are many English homophones which are not homographs (e.g. *two*, *to*, and *too*; *sight* and *site*; *sun* and *son*); and vice versa, there are some homographs which are not homophones (e.g. the written form *live* can be pronounced to rhyme with *give*, or with *strive*).

Defining homonyms as 'different words with the same form', as I have just done, does not take into account the fact that the term 'word' can be used in several different ways. Linguists often distinguish between 'word as lexeme' and 'word as word-form'. Lexemes are words thought of as items in the vocabulary of a language (roughly, the expressions one would expect to find listed in a dictionary); for example, *talk, think, go*. Word-forms are variant forms which lexemes adopt due to the grammatical rules of the language; for example, *talk, talks, talked*. Word-forms of the same lexeme can be quite dissimilar from one another (e.g. *think, thought*), or even completely unrelated in form (e.g. *go, went*). When we look at things from this point of view, we can see that it is possible to have partial homonymy: a situation in which some word-forms of two different lexemes are identical, but others are not (cf. Lyons 1995: 55–8). For example, the same word-form *found* can belong either to the lexeme *find* (as in, *I can't find my pen*) or to the lexeme *found* (as in *He founded the bank in 1922*). Since homonymy is not a meaning-based phenomenon, we will not pursue these complications here.

1.5.5 Polysemy vs. generality

POLYSEMY designates a situation in which a single word has a set of distinct but related meanings. Many—perhaps most—words are polysemous. For example, the noun *chip* can mean (i) a small piece of some hard substance which has been broken off from something larger, e.g. *a chip of wood/glass* (ii) a small cut piece of potato which is fried for eating, e.g. *Can I try one of your chips?* (iii) a small but vital piece of a computer, e.g. *It's got a faster chip than the old one*. The meanings are related because they all contain the component 'small piece'.

Polysemy (i.e. the existence of several distinct-but-related meanings) must be distinguished from semantic GENERALITY. This designates a situation in which a word has a single general meaning which can be used in different contexts. Consider, for example, the word *wrong* as used in these two sentences: *We thought that the war was wrong* and *It was wrong not to thank your host*. It would be easy to jump to the conclusion that there are two different meanings involved (roughly, 'immoral' vs. 'improper'), but closer thought will show that is possible to formulate a single meaning which is applicable to both contexts; roughly, saying it is *wrong* (to do such-and-such) means that 'if one thinks about it well, one can know that it is bad (to do such-and-such)'. It is not always easy to tell the difference between polysemy and generality.

A useful indicator that we are dealing with polysemy, rather than with generality, is the presence of different grammatical properties associated with the (proposed) different meanings. Consider the verb *to skip*, for instance: How many meanings are involved in the following sentences?

a. *The children skipped happily down the street.*
b. *We skipped the first chapter.*

Even without our intuitions as native speakers of English, we can tell that two distinct meanings are involved because *skip* is an intransitive verb in (a), but a transitive verb in (b).

Other diagnostics of polysemy are the existence of different derived forms or different meaning relations. For example, one piece of evidence that the word *faithful* is polysemous is the existence of two corresponding nouns, *faithfulness* and *fidelity*. To describe the quality exhibited by *a faithful friend*, *a faithful servant*, or *a faithful disciple* we would speak of this person's *faithfulness*, but to describe the quality designated by a husband or lover who is *faithful* we would speak of his or her *fidelity*. This suggests that *faithful* has two meanings, one more specialized than the other. Further support for this idea is that the word *unfaithful* relates only the more specialized, 'love-related' meaning; one may have *an unfaithful husband*, but not an **unfaithful friend*.

Even when it is clear that two distinct meanings are involved, it can be difficult to decide whether they are related closely enough to warrant being considered polysemic, particularly when one is working with a language which is not one's mother tongue. Ultimately the decision depends on being able to identify and state the related meaning components.

What would we want to say about *to skip*, for example? Is the meaning in (a) closely related to meaning in (b)? For someone who is not a native speaker of English they could seem quite unrelated. Let's analyse each meaning more closely. The (a) meaning (as in *skipping down the street*) involves a certain sequence of moving the feet: each foot touches the ground more than once before the other foot does, unlike the normal sequence in walking or running in which one foot touches the ground followed immediately by the other. That is, physically *skipping* involves missing out one of the usual 'steps'. The (b) meaning (as in *skipping a chapter* or *skipping a class*) also involves missing out one element in the normal or expected sequence. Now that we have analysed each meaning, we can see the connection between them more clearly and would have little hesitation in recognizing polysemy.

Another phenomenon which is often called polysemy concerns examples like *table₁* (noun, as in *on the table*) and *table₂* (verb, as in *Don't table that document*). Most linguists would say that even though *table₁* and *table₂* are identical in form and closely related in meaning, they must be different words because they belong to different part-of-speech categories. Strictly speaking, therefore, such a situation does not qualify as polysemy but you will sometimes see it designated as such; some linguists use the term 'heterosemy' instead. Other examples are *behind₁* (preposition, as in *behind the couch*) and *behind₂* (noun, as in *He kicked me in the behind*).

1.5.6 Prototype effects

PROTOTYPE EFFECTS were not recognized as a classical meaning phenomenon relation, but modern semanticists agree that any decent semantic theory must account for them. The term refers to the phenomenon, first studied by the cognitive psychologist Eleanor Rosch, whereby some members of a category appear to be more typical and more salient than others. Rosch (1977; 1978) asked people to rate to what extent particular items could be regarded as 'good examples' of certain category-words such as *furniture*, *fruit*, *vehicle*, *bird*, *toy*, and *clothing*. People were very definite that some things were good examples of the kind of thing in question—for instance, a *robin* was a 'very good' example of a *bird*, a *chair* was a very good example of *furniture*—but equally that other items were not good examples—for instance, a *pelican* was judged as a not very good example of a *bird*, a *telephone* as a not very good piece of *furniture*.

Other measures aside from direct subjective rating produced similar results. For instance, it was found that people list the high-rating members earlier than the low-rating members, and that they can make snap judgements about category membership faster and more accurately about the high-rating members than about the low-rating members. The general effect is well conveyed by Figure 1.4 (Aitchison 2003: 56).

The flip-side of prototype effects is the apparent 'fuzziness' around the boundaries of many meanings—or more precisely, around the range of reference or extension of many words. We've mentioned the examples of

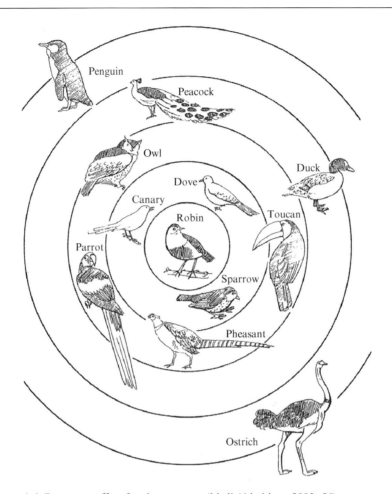

Figure 1.4 Prototype effect for the category 'bird' (Aitchison 2003: 56)

colour words already. Just as there are prototypical 'reds', i.e. hues that everyone will agree are definitely *red*, there is also a kind of fuzzy border zone where particular hues can be judged to be either *red* or *orange*, or both, or some intermediate hue (*reddish orange, orangy red*, etc.).

In the 1970s, some linguists concluded from the experiments on proto-types that such meanings could only be described using non-discrete modes of representation, such as scales and diagrams. However, it is faulty logic to jump from the existence of prototype effects to the conclusion that the underlying components of semantic representation are 'fuzzy'. For one thing, some 'prototype experiment' results are due to the experimental design and do not reflect people's conceptualization of meaning. After all, if people are asked to rank *robins*, *eagles*, *chickens*, *pelicans*, and *bats* on a seven-point scale of 'birdiness', naturally a scale of 'birdiness' emerges. Even so, people have clear intuitions that a *bat* is definitely not a *bird*, whereas a *pelican* definitely is. At the same time, people also have clear intuitions that some individual kinds of birds, such as *penguins* and *ostriches*, are definitely non-typical. We will see at many places in this book that typicality and salience effects of various kinds can be explained in terms of discrete verbal explications.

1.5.7 Connotations

What are 'connotations'? Unlike most of the technical terms of linguistics, *connotation* exists as a word in everyday English, where it means something like 'a subtle aspect of meaning'. In the strict linguistic sense, CONNOTATIONS are shifting and idiosyncratic associations which a word may have for some speakers but not for others (as opposed to the shared meaning of a word). For example, the words *feminist*, *school*, and *environment* tend to have very different connotations depending on a person's attitudes and experience.

Sometimes, however, even linguists slip up and use the term 'connotation' to refer to an aspect of word meaning which is, so to speak, subjective and value-laden. For instance, one textbook says that *stingy* and *thrifty* have the same basic meaning (presumably, something like 'reluctant to spend money') but that they differ in connotation: *stingy* sees the attitude toward money as bad and *thrifty* sees it as good. But—and this is the crucial point—these evaluational components are integral to the meanings involved and are therefore not connotations. People are judgemental creatures. It stands to reason that many word-meanings incorporate evaluational components.

Connotations in the strict sense of the word have only a minor place in semantic analysis, since they are idiosyncratic and not part of word-meaning. They are important in the study of semantic change and variation in the speech community, but we will not touch on these matters in this book.

1.5.8 Collocations and fixed expressions

The term COLLOCATION refers to a combination of words—usually, to a frequently found combination. A FIXED EXPRESSION, as the term suggests, refers to a collocation which is fixed to the extent that it could be listed in a good dictionary of the language. Some semantic theorists believe a complete semantic analysis of a word should provide a basis for understanding its appearance in at least some kinds of fixed expression. For instance, they would say the meaning descriptions of *snow* and *mouse* should help account for the expressions *white as snow* and *quiet as a mouse*. Most people find it easy to accept that the meaning of *snow* includes the component 'it is white', but many wouldn't go as far as saying that the meaning of *mice* includes reference to the fact that mice are quiet. Similarly, some semantic theorists believe that a complete explication of *rage* and *blue*, for instance, would help us see the sense in expressions like *a raging storm* or *having the blues*; but others disagree.

How far collocational possibilities follow from meaning is a contentious point and, like most interesting questions about meaning, one which cannot be resolved without a workable method for deciding on and stating meanings in the first place. In modern linguistics, the most detailed theory of collocation is that of the Russian linguists Jurij Apresjan, Igor Mel'čuk, and Aleksandr Žholkovskij.

The study of collocations has been greatly advanced by the development of computerized corpora (singular: corpus) of English, and of many other languages. A CORPUS is a large indexed archive of examples of real language use, usually consisting of millions or hundreds of millions of words. The data in a corpus can be searched and 'mined' in various ways to determine the relative frequencies of words and expressions, to identify fixed expressions and collocations, and to detect other patterns of language use.

Key technical terms

Anglocentrism	paraphrase
antonyms (gradable, complementary)	partonomy
collocation	polysemy
connotation	pragmatics
contradiction	prototype effects
converses	referent
corpus	semantic metalanguage
encyclopedic knowledge	semantic primitives (primes)
entailment	semantic representation

ethnocentrism

family resemblance

fixed expression

generality

homonymy (homonym)

hyponymy (hyponym)

incompatibility

meaning relations

sense

superordinates: taxonomic vs.
   collective

synonymy (synonym)

taxonomy

theories of meaning:
   conceptualist, truth-conditional,
   structuralist

Exercises and discussion questions

† next to a problem means that a solution or some commentary can be found at the end of the book.

1†. In daily life, people use the words *mean*, *meaning*, etc. in a wide variety of ways, including sometimes to indicate reference. In the following examples, mark whether what is intended is sense (S) or reference (R).

   a. *Extinguish* has the same meaning as *put out*. S/R
   b. When he said 'my ex', he meant Helen. S/R
   c. If you look out the window, you'll see who I mean. S/R
   d. What do you mean, you've been 'seeing' my sister? S/R

2†. Decide whether the following are examples of polysemy or of homonymy.

   a. *bark* (of a dog vs. of a tree)
   b. *fork* (in a road vs. instrument for eating)
   c. *tail* (of a coat vs. of an animal)
   d. *steer* (to guide vs. young desexed bull)

3†. The examples below show sentences in which a single written word-form is used in different ways. In each case, decide whether we have polysemy or homonymy. Explain your reasons. (For polysemy, say what the common element of meaning is or how one meaning is an extension of the other.)

   a. You've tried the *rest*. Now try the best.
      My aching limbs cried out for *rest*.
   b. I can't *see* the reason for it.
      What did you *see*?
   c. She chose a red and black *dress*.
      The dancers all wore national *dress*.
   d. Don't *patronize* me!
      I always *patronize* this place.

4. Consider the following pairs of sentences and decide in each case whether it is an example of homonymy or polysemy. In cases of polysemy, state clearly what the relationship between the meanings is.

   a. Lend me your *pen*.
      They put the pigs in the *pen*.
   b. I got a cut *lip*.
      The *lip* of the cup was chipped.
   c. She landed the first *punch*.
      We all got stuck into the *punch*.
   d. When I started, I couldn't even *drive* in a nail.
      Suzie decided that she'd better *drive*.

5. There is something odd about the following expressions. Say what it is in each case, and what it tells us about the meanings of the words involved:

   intentionally murder, accidentally chase, scrutinize carefully, wailed silently, circumnavigate around, male uncle

6†. Classify the following pairs as complementary antonyms, gradable antonyms, or converses:

   a. *cruel–kind*
   b. *win–lose*
   c. *landlord–tenant*
   d. *present–absent*
   e. *quickly–slowly*
   f. *serve–receive* (in tennis)
   g. *soft–loud*

7†. Consider the following items, which each show a superordinate term and several of its hyponyms. Decide in each case whether the superordinate is taxonomic or collective.

   a. *book: novel, dictionary, cookbook*
   b. *jewellery: earrings, necklace, bracelet*
   c. *game: tennis, chess, cricket*
   d. *snake: viper, adder, python*
   e. *tool: hammer, saw, screwdriver*
   f. *cutlery: knife, fork, spoon*

8†. The following data about Ewe, a language of West Africa, comes from Adzomada's (1969) *Dictionary of Ewe Homonyms*. Carefully consider each set of forms and put forward your own analysis. Options to consider are:

   • some are separate words with unrelated meanings, i.e. there is homonymy;
   • some are related meanings of a single word, i.e. there is polysemy;

- some are separate words because they belong to different parts of speech, but are closely related in meaning;
- for some forms, there is neither homonymy nor polysemy because the 'senses' given are not distinct; instead, there is a general meaning which is applicable to the various uses.

To give you a clear idea of what is involved, try your hand with the set of four forms *dzo* shown below.

dzo	fire
dzo	'juju' (i.e. sorcerous powers)
dzo	to fly (e.g. as a bird does)
dzo	to jump

Answer: This set of forms contains two unrelated words. The word dzo_1 is polysemous, with two meanings: (i) fire, (ii) sorcerous powers. The meanings of dzo_1 are related through the notions of danger and power. The word dzo_2 has a single general meaning, namely, 'move above the ground', which requires the English translations 'fly' or 'jump' according to context.

Now consider the data below. Take your time. This will need careful thought. There is some further information and advice after the data.

zɔ	clay container set in the ground, used for storing palm wine and water
zɔ	heel
zɔ	butt end
zɔ	to walk
nya	word
nya	to chase (away)
nya	to wash (clothes), to purge of dirt
nya	to knead
nya	to mould
to	ear
to	mountain
to	quarter, section (of a town)
to	clan
to	edge
to	father-in-law
to	to be in vogue
to	to pass through (e.g. I passed through Guyra before coming to Armidale)
to	to pound

Important notes: (i) Couples go to fathers-in-law for advice on married life and for mediation with their troubles. (ii) Washing of clothes is usually done by hand. (iii) A clan is made up of a lineage or a group of families with similar descent and migration histories, and they usually live together in the same part of the town or village.

2

Three traditions: lexicography, logic, and structuralism

In this chapter we look into three scholarly traditions which are important to linguistic semantics, namely, lexicography (i.e. dictionary-making), logic, and structuralism. These three traditions have adopted quite different approaches to the question of how to describe meanings. As we will see, each approach has certain deficiencies from the point of view of semantic theory.

2.1   The pitfalls of defining

A definition is an attempt to show the meaning of one word (or other linguistic expression) by means of some other words which 'say the same thing'. That is, definitions depend on the relation of paraphrase. The definitional approach goes back to Aristotle. Although he has rather a bad name with some people in semantics these days, Aristotle's treatise *On Definitions* is a clear and sophisticated work which still makes good reading. In it he was concerned not with semantic analysis for its own sake but with techniques for winning an argument, one of the easiest of which is to attack your opponent's definitions. 'It is the easiest of all things', he wrote, 'to demolish a definition, while to establish one is the hardest' (*Topica*: 7. 5. 155[a]15). Generations of lexicographers can testify that Aristotle was right on this point at least.

We now look at several ways in which definitions can go wrong. As we will see later, these problems are not confined to dictionaries, but afflict most approaches to meaning.

2.1.1 Obscurity

Any explanation of a word-meaning worth its salt must be framed in terms of simpler, more easily understood words. If not, it is an OBSCURE DEFINITION. As Aristotle put it (*Topica*: 6. 4. 141[a]25): 'we make things known by taking not any random terms, but such as are prior and more intelligible . . . a man who does not define through terms of this kind has not defined at all.'

It is easy to find examples of obscure definitions in dictionaries. For instance, *The Macquarie Dictionary* defines the verb *demand* as follows:

demand /dəˈmænd, -ˈmand/, *v.t.* **1.** to ask for with authority; claim as a right: *to demand something of or from a person.*

Are the words in this definition 'prior and more intelligible' than the word whose meaning is being explained in the first place? For instance, if a person didn't have enough command of the English language to understand *demand*, is it likely that they would be able to understand words like *authority* or *claim*? Presumably not.

Here are some other examples from various dictionaries. In each case, the words in the definition are no simpler than those being defined.

take: accept or receive possession of
make: to produce by any action or causative agency
fire: state of combustion
harm: injury; damage; hurt
pepper: a pungent condiment obtained from the dried berries of various plants either whole or ground
hiccup: involuntary spasm of respiratory organs, with sudden closure of glottis and characteristic sound

Definitions can also be obscure in a more subtle fashion, if they employ ordinary-looking words in a semi-metaphorical way; for example, in the following definitions *come* and *bring* are not being used in their ordinary meanings.

become: come into being
find: to come upon by chance
finish: to bring to an end

Two further types of obscure definition are unusual phrases and scientific definitions. By unusual phrases I mean the kind shown in (a) below, which one can hardly imagine an ordinary person ever saying. Examples of scientific definitions are given in (b).

a. *love*: a settled good-will
   gather: to bring together in one company or aggregate
   distress: severe pressure of pain, sorrow, etc.
b. *air*: a mixture of oxygen, nitrogen and other gases which surrounds the earth and forms its atmosphere
   water: a compound of hydrogen and oxygen H_2O, freezing at 0°C, and boiling at 100°C
   circle: a closed plane curve every point of which is equidistant from the given fixed point, the centre. Equation $(x–h^2) + (y–k)^2 = r^2$ where r is the radius and (h, k) are the coordinates of the centre

Aside from the obscure wording, scientific definitions can be faulted as containing information which is not part of ordinary linguistic competence and which is not shared by every member of the speech community. Conversely, they omit information which is part of the everyday concept, e.g. that people need to breathe *air* to live and that *water* is drinkable.

Above all, obscure definitions are futile. They may appear to explain something—for instance, you may agree that *demand* means 'to claim as a right' or that *fire* means a 'state of combustion'—but that impression is due to the fact that you already understand the meaning of the words in the first place. The definition in itself is failing in its task of making the meaning explicit and intelligible. At best, an obscure definition is just putting off the necessary explanatory work—it replaces the job of understanding one obscure or unknown term by the job of understanding another. Commenting on this aspect of obscure definitions, Leibniz wrote:

I will illustrate this by a simile. Suppose I offer you one hundred crowns, to be received from Titus; but then Titus sends you to Caius, and then Caius to Maevius. If you are perpetually sent on in this way, you will never be said to have received anything. (Leibniz 1973 [1679]: 2)

2.1.2 Circularity

Sometimes we see a blatantly CIRCULAR DEFINITION, as in Palmer's (1981) definition of *salt* as *the stuff we add to salty food*. More commonly, circularity only shows itself after a little research, often coming to light when one seeks out the definitions of obscure terms in a definition. For instance, suppose we look up the definition of *claim* in *The Macquarie Dictionary*. As you can see, *claim* is defined in terms of *demand*, even though *demand* was defined in terms of *claim*. Incidentally, if you look up the expression *ask for*, you will find it defined as *to demand; expect*—another instance of circularity.

claim /kleim/ v.t. **1.** to demand by or as by virtue of a right; demand as a right or due.

Aristotle gives a nice example of an unwittingly circular definition: *sun = star that appears by day* (*Topica*: 6. 4. 142^{b}35). The problem here is that the definition of *day* will probably have to involve *sun*. Some examples of circular dictionary definitions are given below and in Figure 2.1. As you can see, it

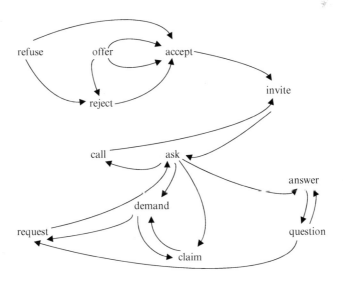

Figure 2.1. Some circularities in the *Oxford Paperback Dictionary* (Wierzbicka 1996a: 277)

sometimes takes several steps before the circle closes: A is defined via B, B via C, then C via A. Or there may be large webs of interconnections between the multiple senses of the words involved.

fate: a person's destiny
destiny: that which happens to a person or thing thought of as determined by fate
receive: accept delivery of; take into one's hands
accept: consent to receive
take: accept or receive possession of
appropriate: suitable or fitting for a particular purpose
fitting: suitable or appropriate
suitable: such as to suit; appropriate, fitting

How can circularity be avoided? As Leibniz well recognized, the only way to avoid circularity in semantic analysis is to insist that all definitions be phrased in terms that are simpler than the original words that are being defined. Carried to its logical conclusion, this means that there must be some terms that are so simple and basic that they cannot be defined (without circularity) at all. As you know already, such terms are known as semantic primes.

2.1.3 Superfluous components and disjunctions

As Aristotle put it, a superfluous component is one 'upon whose removal the remainder still makes the term that is being defined clear' (*Topica*: 6. 3. 140^{b}35). For example, the *Longman Dictionary of Contemporary English* (1978) defined *weapon* as follows:

weapon: an instrument of offensive or defensive combat; something to fight with

The first component was not only obscure (the words *offensive*, *defensive*, and *combat* are no simpler than *weapon*), but superfluous, because the second component does the same job.

DISJUNCTION means using *or*. Using *or* lets the dictionary-maker off the hook. By saying 'A *or* B' we don't have to state explicitly what A and B have in common. As well, most disjunctions in dictionaries seem to introduce inaccuracy or else to be superfluous. For instance, *The Oxford Australian Junior Dictionary* (1980) defines *succeed* as 'to do or get what you wanted to do or get'. But *succeeding* always implies having done something—simply 'getting' something you want, e.g. a nice present, isn't *succeeding*. The *Oxford Paperback Dictionary* (1979) defines *tempt* as follows:

to tempt: to persuade or try to persuade (especially into doing something wrong or unwise) by the prospect of pleasure or advantage.

The first disjunct is superfluous and can be dispensed with entirely. It is enough to say 'try to persuade'. The second disjunction ('something wrong or unwise') can be simplified to 'something bad' and the prospect of 'pleasure or advantage' can be simplified to 'something good (for this person)'.

2.2   Accuracy in a definition

There is no universal agreement about how accurate one is entitled to expect a definition to be. In this book, we will assume that we are entitled to expect that an accurate definition (or, in the cases of a polysemous word, a set of accurate definitions) will predict the appropriate range of use of a word. Putting it another way, the reader should be able to trust that the definition is a reliable guide to how to use the word; such a definition is said to be 'descriptively adequate'. Many dictionary definitions, unfortunately, do not reach this level of accuracy.

Inaccuracy may take many forms. A definition may be too broad—that is, it may cover the whole range of use of the word itself and more besides. It may be too narrow—that is, the uses it predicts are legitimate but too limited. It may predict only a part of the correct range of use. Let's see some examples of each kind.

2.2.1 Too broad

A simple example of a definition which is too broad is the old stand-by '*bachelor*: an unmarried man'. It is easy to see that there is more to being a *bachelor* than just being 'an unmarried man', since *priests* are not *bachelors* although they are unmarried men. Sometimes people think this criticism is a bit unfair. 'Of course, it doesn't mean that kind of unmarried man.' But this is just the point. You have the semantic competence of a native speaker of English; you don't need the dictionary to specify what kind of unmarried man is intended. But someone who doesn't genuinely know the meaning of the word would be misled.

Here are some other examples of dictionary definitions which are too broad:

cashier: person in charge of cash
tongs: implement consisting of two limbs connected by a hinge
sleazy: shabby, shoddy, untidy, grubby

2.2.2 Too narrow

Definitions which are too narrow are probably rarer. For an example from *The Macquarie Dictionary* (1987), we can go back to *demand*, which you'll recall was defined as 'ask for with authority; claim as a right'. Suppose a bank robber says to the teller *Give me all your cash or you're dead*. It seems to me that this qualifies as *demanding* (do you agree?)—but this is not predicted by the *Macquarie Dictionary* definitions. We could hardly say that the robber was asking 'with authority' (or even 'asking' at all); or that he was 'claiming the money as a right'. By not accounting for this use, the definition falls short of complete descriptive adequacy. In this case, we say the definition is too 'narrow'.

Again, it is missing the point to say 'but metaphorically the gun was his authority'. Even if this makes sense, how is someone relying on the definition alone supposed to know it? (To be fair I should point out that the *Macquarie Dictionary* depicts *demand* as a polysemous word, giving as its second meaning 'to ask for peremptorily or urgently'. Presumably this second meaning would be invoked to cover the bank robber case. This definition, however, is flawed by the obscurity of the word *peremptorily*, as well as being too broad—there are many situations where one could 'ask urgently' without being said to *demand*.)

Here are two other examples of narrow definitions. Can you see why these are too restrictive?

browse: to glance at random through a book or books
appointment: a time when you have arranged to go and see someone

Sometimes a definition looks too narrow, but turns out on closer inspection to be more inaccurate than it first seemed. For instance, consider this definition of *smog* given in the *Oxford Advanced Learner's Dictionary* (1995): 'a mixture of smoke and fog'. Of course, the origin of the word *smog* as a blend of the words *smoke* and *fog* is well known, at least to lexicographers. But etymology is never a good guide to current meaning. It is not difficult to think of contexts where one would speak of *smog* without fog being involved, for instance, the *smog* that hangs over Los Angeles or Sydney in mid-summer. Thus, it would appear that the definition above is too narrow. But if we remove *fog* from the definition, *smog* would then become identical in meaning to *smoke*. In fact, it is probably better not to use either *smoke* or *fog* in the definition but to rephrase it from scratch in simpler terms; for example, as 'something in the air, because of things that people do in that place (i.e. because of human activities); people can see it; it is bad for people to breathe.'

2.2.3 False components

There are many cases where an inaccurate definition apparently predicts a range which overlaps with that of the word it is out to define. When looked at more closely, however, it usually turns out in most cases that the apparent overlap is actually an illusion, and that in reality the definition is, so to speak, 'close' but wrong. For example, let's consider this definition of *sure* from *The Australian Concise Oxford Dictionary* (1987): 'having or seeming to have adequate reason for belief'. At first, this seems basically correct. For instance, if someone asks you *Are you sure?* it seems reasonable to think they are asking whether you have 'adequate reason' for your belief. But counter-examples are not difficult to find. For instance, when playing a game of chance such as poker one can often be *sure* that something is going to happen without having any clear reasons for the belief. Conversely, one can have very good reasons for thinking something will happen, but still not be *sure* about it. In other words, having 'adequate reasons' is neither necessary nor sufficient for being *sure* of something.

2.2.4 Open-ended (non-predictive) definitions

By open-ended definitions we mean definitions which rely on vague terms such as 'etc.' and 'esp.' (i.e. especially). Examples can be found on the page of any dictionary. By resorting to 'etc.' the lexicographer makes the definition untestable. Presumably, 'etc.' is intended to mean 'and other similar things', but because no criterion for similarity is made explicit, and because almost anything can be viewed as similar to something else in some respect, the definition becomes non-predictive. 'Etc.' has rightly been called 'the lexicographer's security blanket'.

2.2.5 Not distinguishing polysemy from generality (or vice versa)

So far we have looked at (and criticized) attempts by dictionaries to define individual senses of a word; but a typical dictionary entry contains not one but several related senses, set off from one another by numbers and/or by semicolons. Different numbering usually indicates distinct senses, while the semicolon usually indicates alternative renditions of a single meaning (or sometimes supposed 'subsenses' of one meaning). Although lexical polysemy is a fact of life, dictionaries generally speaking posit excessive polysemy. They posit a set of distinct, overly specific meanings because they have failed to identify a plausible general meaning that will 'work' across a range of contexts. For example, consider the English verb *love* in contexts such as the following (where the grammatical 'object' designates a person):

What mother doesn't love her children?
He loved her passionately.
I love you.

How many meanings are we dealing with? (Notice that the choice of syntactic frame excludes uses such as *She loves music*, which has a non-personal object. This is, clearly, a distinct polysemic meaning. Also, note that we are not concerned with the expression *in love (with)*, which has a much narrower range of use than the verb *love*, and a much more specific meaning.)

The striking fact about the verb *love* (and the corresponding noun, to some extent) is that it can be used in connection with a very broad range of human relationships: between family members, between sweethearts, between husband and wife, between close friends. Speakers of English generally recognize that there are many different 'kinds of love'; and distinctions such as 'familial love' vs. 'erotic (romantic, sexual) love' vs. 'Platonic (fraternal) love' are common in Biblical scholarship and moral philosophy. But does all this mean that the word *love* has more than one meaning?

According to most dictionaries, the answer is yes. For example, *Webster's Third New International Dictionary* (1971) defines the verb *love* as 'to feel love for', and since it recognizes various senses for the noun *love* the implication is that the verb too is polysemous. The relevant definitions are the following:

1. a deep and tender feeling of affection for and attachment or devotion to a person or persons
5a. a strong, usually passionate, affection for another person, based in part on sexual attraction

Similarly, the *Longman Dictionary of Contemporary English* (1987) distinguishes two senses of the noun *love*, and defines the verb as 'to feel love, desire, or strong friendship (for)', again implying polysemy. For example, consider the English verb *love* in contexts such as the following, where the grammatical 'object' designates a person (Goddard 2000):

1. a strong feeling of fondness for another person, esp. between members of a family or close friends
2. fondness combined with sexual attraction

These definitions show the usual shortcomings (disjunctions, complex terms, etc.), but these faults aside, how plausible is the polysemy which is posited by both dictionaries? Even granted that in the real world of human relationships there are 'different kinds of love', it doesn't follow that the word *love* has several different meanings. After all, there are also many different kinds of tree, and many different kinds of car, yet this doesn't mean that the words *tree* and *car* have multiple meanings.

Actually it does not seem impossible to draft a single explication that would span all the uses of *love* (in relation to a person), roughly as below. According to this, *loving* someone is constituted by an amalgam of thoughts, intentions, and recurrent feelings toward that person. It includes having good feelings towards this person, having a 'favourable' view of them, wanting to 'benefit' them (i.e. to do good things for them), and 'wanting the best' for them (i.e. wanting good things to happen to them).

> *Someone X loves someone Y*: X feels something good towards Y, thinks good things about Y, wants to do good things for Y, and wants good things to happen to Y.

Though false polysemy is a common fault in dictionaries, in some linguistic arenas, especially in theoretical linguistics, there is a tendency to underestimate polysemy. In the end, the most important thing is that we have a procedure for deciding the question of generality vs. polysemy.

One general meaning or two more specific meanings? In principle the distinction is clear enough, and so is the procedure to be followed. In the interests of economy and simplicity one should assume, to begin with, that there is but a single meaning, and attempt to state it in a clear and predictive fashion. Only if persistent efforts to do this fail should polysemy be posited. The next hypothesis will be that there are two distinct meanings, and attempts should be made to state both in a clear and predictive fashion. And so the process goes, until the full range of application of the word can be captured within the specified range of meanings. Of course, this procedure can only be implemented if the principles of good definition are followed (especially avoidance of obscurity and open-ended hedges like 'etc.' and 'esp.').

2.2.6 Diagrams in dictionaries

Some dictionaries include diagrams (line illustrations) and these can indeed be very helpful, especially if the verbal definition is faulty. But even when a word designates a type of physical object that lends itself to visual depiction, there are serious limitations to what a diagram can do. As we will see in Chapter 7, the meanings of words for artefacts (tools, implements, and other manufactured objects) involve a reference to their function, as well as to their physical structure and appearance, and a diagram cannot easily depict functions. Names for species of animals and plants often include culture-related information about their potential usefulness for humans and/or about people's attitudes towards them. Finally, even in relation to physical appearance, a single diagram cannot indicate much about the range of variation in physical appearance.

We can illustrate these points with the *Longman Dictionary of Contemporary English* (1987) diagram reproduced in Figure 2.2. It is provided to supplement the following definition of *cup*.

> CUP: a small round container, usu. with a handle, from which liquids are drunk, esp. hot liquids such as tea or coffee: *a cup and saucer*—compare MUG

The difficulty with Figure 2.2 is that *cups* actually come in various proportions (height-to-width ratios) and often they have tapering sides, not straight sides as shown in the Longman diagram. Merely adjusting the illustration so that it depicted more typical (or prototypical) cups wouldn't

Figure 2.2. *Longman Dictionary of Contemporary English* (1987) cup–mug illustrations

solve the basic problem, which is that a single static diagram cannot capture a range of possible shapes and sizes.

We will be studying the meanings of *cup* and *mug* in some detail in Chapter 7.

2.2.7 Prospects for improvements in dictionary-making

It would be wrong to give the impression that lexicographers don't know or don't care about the kind of problems we have been canvassing. One major series of dictionaries, the *Cobuild* dictionaries, has banned 'etc.' from its definitions. Another major dictionary, the *Longman Dictionary of Contemporary English*, employs a 'controlled defining vocabulary' of about 2,000 common and relatively simple words with the goal of ensuring that 'definitions are always written using simpler terms than the words they describe' (1978: viii–ix). Children's dictionaries and dictionaries for language-learners also make efforts to keep the defining language relatively simple. In general, however, lexicographers believe that using a fixed defining vocabulary leads to awkward phrasing or makes it too difficult to get the meaning right within the limited space available.

Though we have examined dictionaries in the harsh light of semantic theory, the reality is that dictionaries are first and foremost commercial publishing ventures, not scientific or scholarly projects. Though they certainly have a scholarly dimension, they are essentially products created by a publishing house to sell in a competitive market. The publisher's budget affects the length of the dictionary, the time that can be spent on production, the size of the team involved, the compiling process, and many other lexicographical decisions. Furthermore, the so-called 'general purpose' dictionary must meet a diversity of market expectations—not only as a guide to meanings, but as a spelling checker, as an aid for crosswords and other word-games, as a resource for language-learners, as a guide to 'proper usage', as a source of encyclopedic information, and so on (cf. Atkins 1992/93; Béjoint 1994; Ilson 1986).

In short, dictionaries are the products of a whole complex of factors—commercial, historical, technical, and scholarly. I don't want to imply that we cannot (or should not) expect further improvements in dictionary-making, but given the commercial realities, such improvements will probably be slow in coming. In the end, it may be unrealistic to hope any such dictionary could be both theoretically satisfying and commercially viable.

2.3 The logical tradition

Aside from dictionary-making, another tradition which has concerned itself with meanings is philosophical logic. Logic is basically about reasoning. It seeks to devise procedures for distinguishing valid chains of inference from invalid ones. Though the two disciplines are quite different in their goals, logic continues to exert an influence on linguistic semantics.

2.3.1 Truth and meaning

To a linguist, the key concept in semantics is that of meaning: linguistic semantics is about meaning. To a logician, however, the key concept is truth. Naturally enough. The 'mission' of logic is to investigate and understand the nature of valid reasoning and valid reasoning is that which leads from true premises to true conclusions. Many logicians even define the concept of 'meaning' in terms of truth, though this is quite dubious from a linguistic point of view. But we are getting ahead of ourselves. To begin with, we have to go through some terminology, beginning with the concept of a proposition. As logicians use the term, a PROPOSITION is (roughly) something said about something. A proposition can be true or false, and can be the premise or conclusion of a chain of inference.

Propositions are not the same as sentences, though sentences can express propositions. Consider, for instance, the sentence *It's Saturday today*. To decide whether the proposition this expresses is true or false we have to know when the sentence was said; or, putting it another way, the sentence expresses different propositions depending on which day it is uttered. The same applies to the sentence *I wear glasses*. The meaning remains the same, but different propositions are expressed depending on who utters it. Similarly for *Paris is far from here*, for which the place of utterance is important. Expressions like *I*, *today*, and *here* are known as INDEXICAL EXPRESSIONS, because what they refer to depends on the circumstances in which they are said.

Could we say, then, that a proposition is a sentence supplemented by information about the reference of any indexical expressions it contains? Roughly, yes—provided we agree to exclude the many sentence types which it doesn't make sense to call true or false, such as imperatives (*Stop it at once!*), questions (*Where's the station?*), wishes (*If only I had a car like that!*), and so-called 'performatives' (*Bet you it'll rain*, *I apologize*, *I bid three clubs*).

What does it mean for a proposition to be true (or false)? Most of us would probably say that it depends on whether what is being said corresponds (or doesn't correspond) with reality, with the way things are in the real world. The propositions expressed by *Tokyo is the capital of Japan* and *New York is the capital of Japan* have the 'truth-values' that they do (namely, true and false, respectively) on account of the way the real world is.

The idea of truth being a relationship with reality is a very important one for logic, but it doesn't apply to all true propositions. For instance, the following are true regardless of any facts about the world: *It's either Saturday today or it's not*; *A square has four sides*; *A sparrow is a bird*. Propositions like these (which are called ANALYTIC) are true because of certain relationships between the meanings of the words involved. This (of course) brings us back to meaning. Though logicians are primarily interested in truth and reasoning, they must inevitably get involved in meaning analysis to determine the truth of some propositions and whether the links between certain propositions are or are not valid.

2.3.2 Logic-based concepts of meaning

According to many logicians, the meaning of a sentence (or, more precisely, a proposition) is, in essence, the conditions under which that sentence is true—its truth conditions. To offset the counter-intuitive effect of this proposal, it is usually pointed out that, after all, one could certainly not be said to know what, say, *Snow is green* means unless one understood how the world would have to be in order for that sentence to be true.

Logicians have formalized a way of speaking about 'how the world would have to be' by means of the concept of a 'possible world'. A possible world is a complete and total way that the world could be. The actual world is one possible world, but there are many things about the actual world which needn't be the way they are. For instance, Tokyo needn't be the capital of Japan now. It just happens that it is. On the other hand, a *square* must have four sides in all possible worlds (because otherwise we couldn't call the shape a *square*). These ideas lead to what logicians call 'possible worlds semantics'. The meaning of a sentence, in such a system, is a class of possible worlds. The meaning of a word is the contribution the word makes to determining the class of possible worlds associated with sentences in which the word appears. A more recent version of this kind of approach is called 'situation semantics'. A 'situation' in this theory is like a part of a possible world. Both kinds of approaches can be described as 'formal semantics' or as 'model-theoretic semantics'.

Now I don't blame you if this all sounds mystifying and obtuse. Surely no one could seriously propose that everyday semantic competence involves such arcane concepts as truth conditions and possible worlds. As a matter of fact, some linguists do subscribe to a version of this view, though usually they explain that they are interested not in the ordinary (pre-theoretical) notion of meaning but in some more specialized notion such as 'informational significance'. One textbook explains this concept as follows (notice the reference to truth as a 'nonlinguistic' notion):

Informational significance is a matter of aboutness, of connections between language and the world(s) we talk about. Informational significance looks outward to a public world and underlies appraisal of message in terms of objective nonlinguistic notions like truth. (Chierchia and McConnell-Ginet 2000: 11)

In contrast, the same writers continue, there is another kind of meaningfulness which they call 'cognitive significance':

Cognitive significance involves links between language and mental constructs that somehow represent or encode speakers' semantic knowledge. Cognitive significance looks inward to a speaker's mental apparatus and does not confront issues of the public reliability of linguistic communication.

The view adopted in this book is that linguistic semantics should deal with (or at the very least start with) cognitive significance. This is, essentially, the traditional linguistic concept of meaning. Formal semantics, with its concern for informational significance and for the connections between language and the world, is more closely aligned with the logical tradition. If you are interested in pursuing formal semantics, Cann (1993) and Blackburn and Bos (2005) are good textbooks.

2.3.3 Some logical concepts used in semantics

Though formal semantics is outside our scope, it is necessary for us to gain basic familiarity with a number of terms borrowed from a branch of logic known as the predicate calculus, which is a system for analysing the internal structure of propositions. They include the following:

PREDICATES and ARGUMENTS. The basic idea is that a proposition consists of something being said (the predicate) about one or more other things (the argument or arguments). Often the arguments will be indicated by means of referring expressions (roughly, noun phrases); for instance, in the expression *The cat died*, the argument is *the cat* and the predicate is *died*.

Die is what logicians call a 'one-place predicate', i.e. it goes with one argument only. Other predicates, e.g. *have*, *eat*, and *see*, may have two arguments and are called 'two-place predicates'. There are even three-place and four-place predicates, such as *give* and *sell*, respectively. In *X gave Y to Z*, for instance, *X*, *Y*, and *Z* are all arguments of *gave*; in *A sold B to C for D* the expressions *A*, *B*, *C*, and *D* are all arguments of *sold*. The predicates *gave* and *sold* say something about all the arguments simultaneously—or, to put it another way, they say something about the relationship between the arguments. As you can see, the term 'predicate' has a different meaning in logic to the meaning it has in traditional grammar, where 'predicate' contrasts with 'subject'. Also, 'argument' is not identical with the grammatical concept of 'subject' except in the case of one-place predicates.

In natural language, propositions sometimes function as arguments. For instance, in *Max caused the cat to die* both *Max* and *the cat to die* are arguments of the predicate *cause*, even though *the cat to die* is itself a proposition with a predicate–argument structure of its own.

Logicians traditionally put the symbol for a predicate (usually an upper-case letter) in front of the symbols for the arguments (shown by lower-case letters). So *Fxy* stands for a proposition where predicate *F* is applied to arguments *x* and *y*. Linguists sometimes follow this convention, leading to notations like this: CAUSE *x* (DIE *y*). That is, the predicate CAUSE has two arguments, namely *x* and (DIE *y*), and the second argument is itself a proposition consisting of predicate DIE with a single argument *y*. However, many linguists disregard the logic-based 'predicate first' convention, so one also sees the same representation written as: *x* CAUSE (*y* DIE).

CONNECTIVES are intended to represent certain types of logical connection between propositions. They are analogous to words like *and*, *or*, and *if*. In line with their general push to reduce meaning to truth, logicians normally define the meanings of logical connectives by means of a so-called 'truth table'. For instance, the table below gives a 'definition' of the meaning of the symbol ∨. It works by stipulating the truth outcome of joining two propositions A and B together using ∨, for all possible truth-values of A and B. This is called a 'truth-functional' definition.

A	B	A∨B
True	True	True
True	False	True
False	True	True
False	False	False

You read such a table like this. The first line says that if A is true and B is true, then A∨B is also true. The second and third lines say that if A is true and B is false or vice versa, then A∨B remains true. The final line says that if both A and B are false, then A∨B is false. From this you can probably guess that ∨ corresponds roughly to ordinary English *or*.

At this point, it's a good exercise to figure out for yourself the truth table for English *and*. Start by selecting four unrelated propositions, two of which are true and two of which are false. Then put them together in pairs, joining each pair with *and*, and see how the truth-value of each pair is determined by the truth-values of the component propositions. If all goes well, you should arrive at the table below (but try it for yourself before looking closely!). Notice that ∧ is the logical symbol closest in meaning to *and*.

A	B	A∧B
True	True	True
True	False	False
False	True	False
False	False	False

The symbols for some other logical connectives are ∼, which corresponds to *not*, and ⊃, whose closest English translation is *if... then*. Admittedly, *not* isn't strictly a connective in the linguistic sense, but we can let that pass.

Just now I referred to *If... then* as the 'closest English translation' for the connective ⊃. It's instructive to see why. The table below gives the usual truth-functional definition of ⊃. If you examine this table carefully, and think about what it means, I think you'll agree that it makes some peculiar claims, if we think of A⊃B as basically meaning *If A, then B*.

A	B	A⊃B
True	True	True
True	False	False
False	True	True
False	False	True

According to line one of this table, the proposition '6 is an even number ⊃ Tokyo is the capital of Japan' counts as true, but it would sound pretty strange to say that *If 6 is an even number, then Tokyo is the capital of Japan* is a true statement. Similarly, according to line three of the table '6 is an odd number ⊃ Tokyo is the capital of Japan' is also true, but it would sound strange to make this claim about *If 6 is an odd number, then Tokyo is the capital of Japan*.

The moral of this story is that the logical connective ⊃ doesn't really correspond to *if... then* at all (or to any connective in ordinary language). In fact, when we look into it more closely, even ∧ and ∨ don't correspond perfectly to ordinary *and* and *or* either (cf. Allwood, Andersson, and Dahl 1977: 26–41). For example, although the propositions A∧B and B∧A are logically equivalent, in ordinary English sequencing two sentences with *and* often conveys the order in which two events occurred. *Gunnar lay down on the bed and died* doesn't mean the same as *Gunnar died and lay down on the bed*. So why have I taken you through all this business about logical connectives? Because, as I said at the onset, you will often find connective symbols like ⊃, ∧, and ∨ used in semantic discussions in the literature.

QUANTIFIER is another logical term which is often used in linguistics. In linguistics, this basically means any word which says how many or how much of something is being referred to. For example, words like *many*, *much*, *some*, *all*, and numerals like *one*, *two*, and *three* are all routinely called quantifiers. In logic, it is usual to recognize just two basic quantifiers:

∀ the 'universal quantifier': roughly, *all*
∃ the 'existential quantifier': roughly, *(there are) some* or *(there is) a*

The qualification 'roughly' has to be taken seriously, however, for neither symbol corresponds precisely with any element of ordinary English. In particular, ∃ cannot be given any single equivalent in English, if only because English distinguishes between singular and plural reference whereas ∃ does not.

Quantifiers cannot refer to anything by themselves. It is always necessary to have some kind of thing in mind: we can't just talk about *all* or *many*, but we can talk about *all people* or *many horses*. An expression like *people* or *horses* used in this way is said to specify the domain of the quantifier. In logic, it is common to think of the domain in terms of a 'set', which enables mathematical set theory to be applied to the interpretation of quantified expressions.

SETS. Basically a set consists of members which all share some property; for instance, one could speak of the set of even numbers, the set of female people with one arm, the set of things which are edible, or whatever. The reference (or extension) of a word like *red* or *heavy* can be described as the 'set of red things' or 'the set of heavy things'. Some logicians who subscribe to a referential theory of meaning would even define the meaning of *red* and *heavy* in this way (of course, from a semantic point of view, this isn't very helpful since the 'definition' contains the very word it is purporting to define; but we can let that pass here).

There are various operations which can be performed on sets. For instance, the operation of SET UNION combines the members of two sets A and B, creating a new set denoted A∪B; the operation of SET INTERSECTION creates a new set, denoted A∩B, consisting of the elements shared between A and B.

Thus, the extension of the expression *heavy red things* can be described as the intersection of the 'set of heavy things' and the 'set of red things'.

One obvious difficulty with applying set theory to words like *red* and *heavy* is that membership of a set is an all-or-nothing matter (that is, something either is a member or it is not), whereas the application of words like *red* and *heavy* is not always clear-cut: things can be more or less *red*, or more or less *heavy*. This difficulty is more apparent than real, however, because it is perfectly simple from a mathematical point of view to allow for set-membership to be partial. We can define membership as a fraction which may range between 0 (non-membership) to 1 (complete membership), with the in between values indicating the degree of partial membership. This innovation, pioneered by mathematician and computer scientist Lotfi Zadeh (1965), is the basis of what is called 'fuzzy set theory'. Fuzzy sets enjoyed popularity with logically minded linguists in the 1970s and 1980s, though they have since gone out of fashion in linguistics.

2.4   Classical componential analysis (CA)

As mentioned in Chapter 1, structuralism was one of the influential trends in twentieth-century linguistics. Applied to meaning, structuralist thinking says that word-meanings do not exist 'in themselves', as it were, separately from other words: rather they only exist in relation to one another, as parts of an overall system. On this view, the sense of an expression is the totality of its possible relations with all other words. Semantic analysis therefore consists of systematically comparing and contrasting related words (known as a semantic field or domain), and summarizing the similarities and contrasts in the most economical way. The procedure most closely associated with this point of view is known as COMPONENTIAL ANALYSIS. Componential analysis of meaning can be compared with distinctive feature analysis in phonology.

2.4.1 Distinctive features in phonology

Distinctive feature analysis compares the phonetic characteristics of the phonemes in a language, seeking out the smallest number of dimensions of contrast at work in the system. For instance, the eight English consonants

/p, b, t, d, f, v, s, z/ can be arranged into two sets of exactly parallel contrasts as shown below:

The horizontal lines designate a contrast in voicing (whether the vocal cords are vibrating as the sound is produced). In the case of /p, t, f, s/ there is no voicing, whereas with /b, d, v, z/ there is voicing. The vertical lines designate a contrast between 'stop' sounds (where the airflow through the vocal tract is momentarily blocked during the articulation) and continuant sounds which involve no such blockage: /p, b, t, d/ are stops and /f, v, s, z/ are continuants.

The contrasts within each set can be summarized by using a pair of binary features, namely, ±VOICED and ±CONTINUANT:

/p/	−VOICED, −CONTINUANT		/t/	−VOICED, −CONTINUANT
/b/	+VOICED, −CONTINUANT		/d/	+VOICED, −CONTINUANT
/f/	−VOICED, +CONTINUANT		/s/	−VOICED, +CONTINUANT
/v/	+VOICED, +CONTINUANT		/z/	+VOICED, +CONTINUANT

An additional feature is needed to capture what all the sounds on the left have in common, as opposed to those on the right. Since the ones on the left are all pronounced using the lips we might consider +LABIAL for this purpose.

On comparing all eight of these sounds with others in the English phoneme inventory we would decide that still more features are called for, such as ±CONSONANTAL and ±NASAL, among others, but in the end we wind up with a couple of dozen binary features which can capture the systematic contrasts and similarities that exist among 40-odd phonemes. Not only is this a gain in economy, it turns out that the same phonological features can describe many other facts about the English language, for instance, facts about which sequences of sounds can and can't occur in a word; for example, that *blik* and *zil* are possible words of English but *bkli* and *zli* are not. To top it all off, when the same approach is applied to other languages it is found that a relatively small set of features is sufficient to describe any phonological system found in the world. Many phonologists believe that there is a universal stock of phonetic features, which individual languages select from, so to speak, to tailor their individual sound systems.

2.4.2 Distinctive features in semantics

The vocabulary of a language differs enormously from its stock of phonemes. There are thousands upon thousands of words. But even so, the success of the distinctive feature approach in phonology has impelled linguists of many persuasions to apply the same approach to meaning analysis.

Sometimes it seems to work, if the set of words is a small and tightly organized semantic field. If we consider the sets of words below, it is easy to see how.

Within each set, the horizontal contrasts are male vs. female and the vertical contrasts are adult vs. young. The left-hand set applies to humans and the right-hand set to horses.

Thus, within each set one could posit an analysis such as:

man:	+MALE, +ADULT	*stallion*:	+MALE, +ADULT
woman:	−MALE, +ADULT	*mare*:	−MALE, +ADULT
boy:	+MALE, −ADULT	*colt*:	+MALE, −ADULT
girl:	−MALE, −ADULT	*filly*:	−MALE, −ADULT

The left-hand set would all contain the common component +HUMAN and the right-hand set the component +HORSE (or, for a technical sound +EQUINE).

Of course, there are a couple of debatable steps involved in this analysis. In the pursuit of binary features, we are forced to choose between ±MALE or ±FEMALE (it would have been uneconomical to have both) and though most analysts select ±MALE without flinching, the choice can be questioned on various grounds. Also, though the feature ±HUMAN may seem plausible enough (it is easy to foresee a use for −HUMAN, for instance, to refer to supernatural beings like *angels* or *goblins*), the feature ±HORSE seems faintly ridiculous.

Proponents of CA have answers to these objections. First, they point out, feature analysis is not intended to be a complete account of the meaning of words, merely of those aspects which are in systematic opposition to the other words in the set. Second, a feature like ±HORSE is purely provisional and will no doubt be replaced by more plausible features once more and more other sets of words are brought into the analysis. For instance, once other domesticated and wild animals are included we might see a set of features like ±ANIMAL, ±DOMESTICATED, ±QUADRUPED, ±HERBIVORE, and so on. Third, it is often claimed that the features should not be confused with the meanings of the English words by which they are designated; for instance, the feature ADULT should not be completely equated with the meaning of the ordinary word *adult*.

Because it does not seek to be exhaustive, but aims only to account for the meaning relations in the semantic field at hand, a componential analysis changes as the field is expanded or contracted. For instance, Pottier (1963) used the six features shown below for the French equivalents of *chair*, *armchair*, *stool*, *sofa*, and *pouf*. When in a later work he excluded *pouf* from consideration, the feature s_6 became unnecessary.

s_1 'with a back support', s_2 'with legs', s_3 'for one person', s_4 'for sitting on', s_5 'with arms', s_6 'made of rigid material'

The attractions of CA are that it allows a highly explicit and economical account of meaning relations such as hyponymy and incompatibility (cf. section 1.5). In CA terms, hyponymy is the situation in which all the features of word A are included in those of word B; for instance, the features of the word *human* are included in the words *man* and *woman*. Incompatibility comes about when features have conflicting values. For instance, *female man* is a contradiction because of the clash between −MALE (in the word *female*) and +MALE (in the word *man*).

2.4.3 Relational predicates

A necessary refinement to CA is a way of specifying what individual features apply to (are predicated of). A simple example of the need for this comes from a word like *father*. An analysis like *father* = [PARENT] [MALE] doesn't say anything about the direction of the fatherhood, so to speak. We need some way of specifying that fatherhood is a relation between two individuals (call them X and Y) such that *X is male* and *X is parent of Y*. Such predicates are called RELATIONAL PREDICATES. Without a way of specifying what predicates apply to, there would be no way of distinguishing between pairs of converses, such as *give* and *take*.

A good example of the use of relational features is the componential analysis of kinship. (This is historically important too: CA was pioneered, and is still held by many people to be more or less successful, in this domain.) If we consider English kin terms like those below, it is obvious that gender is important. Once the ± MALE feature from *father* and *mother* is extracted, what is left? Presumably, only the relation of parenthood. This gives rise to analyses like these for kin relations between individuals X and Y across a single generation:

X is *father* of Y:	X +MALE, X IS PARENT OF Y
X is *mother* of Y:	X −MALE, X IS PARENT OF Y
X is *son* of Y:	X +MALE, Y IS PARENT OF X
X is *daughter* of Y:	X −MALE, Y IS PARENT OF X

If we make use of bracketing and an additional semantic relationship of 'sameness' of reference (symbolized in the analysis by =), this analysis is readily extended to kin terms for relatives within the same generation and across two generations.

X is *brother* of Y:	X +MALE, PARENT OF X = PARENT OF Y
X is *sister* of Y:	X −MALE, PARENT OF X = PARENT OF Y
X is *grandfather* of Y:	X +MALE, X IS PARENT OF (PARENT OF Y)
X is *grandmother* of Y:	X −MALE, X IS PARENT OF (PARENT OF Y)

Another commonly cited example of CA applies to kinship terms in languages with so-called 'classificatory' systems, as in many Australian Aboriginal languages. In the Pitjantjatjara language of Central Australia, for instance, the word *mama* applies not just to your biological father, but also to your father's brother; and the word *ngunytju* takes in not only your mother but also your mother's sister. And it doesn't stop there. *Mama* includes your father's male cousins and your mother's sister's husbands, and *ngunytju* your mother's female cousins and your father's brother's wives.

Obviously there is some logical principle at work here. But how could it be stated? The cognitive anthropologist Scheffler (1978: 102) proposed the formulas below as a 'componential definition of the primary sense' of the words *mama* and *ngunytju*.

mama: K.L.G1.+. ♂
ngunytju: K.L.G1.+.♀

where K stands for 'kinsman', L for 'lineal', G1 for 'one generation removed', + for 'senior', ♂ for 'male', and ♀ for 'female'. These 'definitions', by the way, are not intended merely to represent the facts of usage as they appear to an outside observer such as an anthropologist; they are intended to represent the conceptualization (perhaps only semi-conscious or unconscious) of the Pitjantjatjara people themselves.

2.4.4 Diagnostic vs. supplementary components

Eugene Nida is one of the main exponents of componential analysis. Nida (1975) draws a distinction between diagnostic and supplementary components. DIAGNOSTIC COMPONENTS are those which are relevant to distinguishing between the meanings involved. The diagnostic components (also called 'markers' and 'classemes') specify just that part of the meaning which is necessary to account for the meaning relations that the word has with the other words in the semantic field. SUPPLEMENTARY COMPONENTS (also called 'distinguishers' and 'semes') are 'additional features which may be very important for an extensive definition of a meaning but which are not diagnostic in specifying basic differences' (Nida 1975: 112). For instance, in Nida's componential analysis (see below) of *run*, *walk*, *hop*, *skip*, *jump*, and *crawl* the component <speed> is not diagnostic, but it is an important supplementary component.

2.4.5 Non-binary features

To make CA more flexible, Nida drops the stipulation that features must be binary and allows multi-valued features when economy seems to demand it. For instance, he proposed the following analysis for the set of motion verbs just mentioned. Grouping the components in terms of the limbs involved, the order of movement, and the relationship to the surface, produces a more economical and revealing analysis than would be possible with exclusively binary components; see Table 2.1.

Nida (1975: 120) also draws attention to the existence of 'well-defined structural relationships between the components', based either on the logical interrelationships between components or on the temporal structure, i.e. how the component events unfold in sequence. For instance, if we

Table 2.1.   Nida's (1975) analysis of several English verbs of motion

	run	*walk*	*hop*	*skip*	*crawl*
LIMBS INVOLVED	pedal	pedal	pedal	pedal	four limbs
ORDER OF MOVEMENT	121212	121212	111 or 222	11221122	1–3, 2–4
					1–3, 2–4
RELATION TO SURFACE	one foot	one foot	one foot	one foot	two limbs
	not always	always	not always	not always	always
	on surface	on surface	on surface	on surface	on surface

analyse the relationships of the components of *run*, including the common components as well as the diagnostic ones, we find the following relations:

   1. movement
      2. through space
         3. by a human being
            4. using the lower limbs
               5. in 121212 order
                  6. with recurring movements when neither foot touches the ground

As Nida remarks, once all the components of a meaning, common and diagnostic, are arranged in the logical order of their dependency, the result is a definition. He continues:

It may therefore be asked just what componential analysis does which good definitions have not already done. In a sense, nothing; but there is an appalling lack of good definitions of meanings, that is, definitions which contain all the necessary and sufficient components to place the meaning in a domain and to distinguish it from all the other meanings which compete for similar or related semantic space. (Nida 1975: 120)

2.4.6 Shortcomings of componential analysis

Componential analysis easily falls prey to obscurity. For an example, let's reconsider the analysis of *father* and *mother* as, effectively, *male parent* and *female parent*. Is it reasonable to say that *parent* is a 'prior and more intelligible term' than *father* or *mother*? On the contrary, one can well imagine a language-learner asking for an explanation of a sentence like *Children should obey their parents*. What answer could one give? Presumably, that it means *Children should obey their father and mother*. What this brings home is that *parent* is a more complex and obscure term than either *father* or *mother*, and that it will need to be itself analysed using the terms *mother* and *father*. But if this is so, the analyses above are all circular. You cannot use *parent* to explain *mother* and *father*, and then use *father* and *mother* to explain *parent*.

The componential analysis of Pitjantjatjara kin terms (such as *mama* = K.L.G1.+.♀ = 'kinsman, lineal, one generation removed, senior, male') is even more obviously obscure. From a semantic point of view, technical terms like 'lineal' and 'one generation removed' stand in need of explication. In fact, in order to explain them it is necessary to draw on the concepts of *father* and *mother*. Henry Lewis Morgan (1871: 17), one of the founders of modern anthropological studies of kinship, explained the term 'lineal' by way of a chart or table detailing a person's family relationships; you start by putting yourself in the central place, and are yourself in 'the lineal line':

In a chart of relationships this line is vertical. Upon it may be inscribed, above and below any given person, his several ancestors and descendents in a direct series from FATHER TO SON, and these persons will constitute his right lineal male line. (Emphasis added.)

Other criticisms of CA are that it makes no attempt to standardize the inventory of semantic features or to constrain its size, and that it seems highly unlikely that a strict componential technique could ever achieve comprehensive analysis of the entire vocabulary, because it is doubtful that all lexical meanings could be assigned to clearly delimited semantic fields.

Classical componential analysis has also come under attack for the assumption (evident in the quotation from Nida above) that it is possible to reduce meaning to a set of 'necessary and sufficient conditions'.

2.5   Componential analysis in generative grammar

In the 1970s there was a semantic boom of sorts, as different types of generative grammar competed about how semantics could be integrated with the exciting new studies into syntax being pioneered by Noam Chomsky (cf. Harris 1993). Jerrold Katz was one of the main figures to introduce lexical decomposition into generative linguistics (cf. Katz and Fodor 1963; Katz and Postal 1964; Katz 1972). Later, George Lakoff and James McCawley introduced divergent trends in the form of the so-called 'generative semantics' movement, now defunct (cf. Lakoff 1972; McCawley 1970; 1993). The most prominent semanticist in generative linguistics today is Ray Jackendoff, whose work we will look at in Chapter 3.

Lexical decomposition in generative linguistics isn't driven directly by structuralist philosophy, and, for the most part it hasn't concerned itself greatly with delineating the structure of lexical fields. Instead, it is syntax-oriented. The priority is to discover those aspects of word-meaning which are relevant to grammatical properties and processes, and to capture these in a framework which dovetails with formal models of syntax. Even so, the very fact that Katz, Lakoff (in his generative semantics phase), and Jackendoff pursue only a partial description of word-meaning constitutes one affiliation with classical CA. When we consider some of their analyses, the resemblance can be seen to be quite marked.

The simple analyses below come from works by George Lakoff and James McCawley published in the 1970s. (a) shows some verbs in the natural class of 'causative-inchoatives' (see section 10.4). This analysis makes explicit the fact that the verbs *kill*, *liquify*, and *open* are related, respectively, to the adjectives *dead*, *liquid*, and *open*. The interesting thing is that the same semantic relationship appears to apply even though the morphological relationships differ markedly, e.g. *liquify* is morphologically related to *liquid*, but *kill* is not morphologically related to *dead*. (b) makes explicit some of the semantic and argument-structure properties of the converses *give* and *take*. (c) is supposed to describe the polysemy of the verb *persuade*.

a. x *kill* y: x CAUSE [COME ABOUT [y DEAD]]
    x *liquify* y: x CAUSE [COME ABOUT [y LIQUID]]
    x *open* y: x CAUSE [COME ABOUT [y OPEN]]

b. x *give* y to z: x [CAUSE [z HAVE y]]
    x *take* y from z: x [CAUSE [z NOT-HAVE y]]

c. x *persuade* y to do z: x CAUSE [COME ABOUT [y INTEND [DO z]]]
    x *persuade* y that z: x CAUSE [COME ABOUT [y BELIEVE z]]

Jerrold Katz's style of semantic analysis is characterized by a much richer formal structure of hierarchically grouped category types, designed to allow an interface with the syntactic part of the grammar. Figure 2.3 presents an annotated 'tree diagram', similar to those used in generative grammar to display phrase structure. Katz (1987: 186) calls this a 'representation of the conceptual structure' of *chase*.

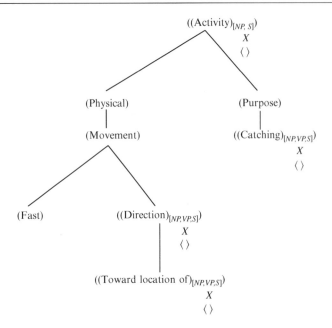

Figure 2.3. Katz's (1987) analysis of English *chase*

As we will see in the next chapter, Ray Jackendoff's ideas have passed through several stages of development, and continue to develop. The examples below show the style of analysis he was using in the mid-1980s. A fundamental principle for Jackendoff is the 'principle of correspondence' according to which every major syntactic constituent of a sentence (NP, AP, PP, etc.) corresponds with a major conceptual constituent (such as Event, Thing, Place, and Path). For example, a sentence like *John ran into the room* could be analysed syntactically as in (a) below, and conceptually as in (b), with the categories labelled by subscripts to the brackets.

a. [$_S$ [$_{NP}$ John] [$_{VP}$ ran [$_{PP}$ into [$_{NP}$ the room]]]]

b. [$_{Event}$ GO ([$_{Thing}$ JOHN], [$_{Path}$ TO ([$_{Place}$ IN ([$_{Thing}$ ROOM])])])]

Implicit in (b) are the following conceptual decompositions for the verb *to run* and for the preposition *into*:

run: [$_{Event}$ GO ([$_{Thing}$]$_i$, [$_{Path}$]$_j$)]

into: [$_{Path}$ TO ([$_{Place}$ IN ([$_{Thing}$]$_j$)])]

Similar decompositions for some other, more complex transitive verbs are shown below (Jackendoff 1990: 76, 53, 61):

climb: [$_{Event}$ GO([$_{Thing}$]$_i$, [$_{Path}$ TO ([$_{Place}$ TOP-OF [$_{Thing}$]$_j$])])]

drink: [$_{\text{Event}}$ CAUSE([$_{\text{Thing}}$]$_i$, [$_{\text{Event}}$ GO ([$_{\text{Thing}}$ LIQUID]$_j$,

[$_{\text{Path}}$ TO ([$_{\text{Place}}$ IN ([$_{\text{Thing}}$ MOUTH OF ([$_{\text{Thing}}$]$_j$)])])])])]

Decompositional methods have also been used in some typological studies into the lexicon, such as Leonard Talmy's work on the different patterns which languages use to 'package' lexical meaning. Talmy (1985a; 2007) shows that English motion verbs, for instance, typically incorporate a 'manner' component (e.g. *run, swim, fly, roll*), whereas Spanish motion verbs incorporate a 'path' component (e.g. *entrar* 'move in', *salir* 'move out', *pasar* 'move through', *volver* 'move back'). We will look at this work in Chapter 8.

Key technical terms

analytic	predicate
argument	proposition
circular definition	quantifier
componential analysis	relational predicate
connective	set intersection
diagnostic component	set union
disjunction	sets
indexical expression	supplementary component
obscure definition	

Exercises and discussion questions

† next to a problem means that a solution or some commentary can be found at the end of this book.

1. Go through a recent edition of any major dictionary and find two examples of each of the following: (a) a group of definitions which are circular, (b) a definition of a common word which includes scientific or technical knowledge, (c) a definition which is either too broad or too narrow

2†. Consider the following definitions of English words, and assess them on the criteria of circularity, obscurity, and descriptive adequacy (i.e. accuracy).

courageous: brave
bold: courageous
brave: able to face and endure danger and pain.

Figure 2.4. Man, cow, bird, tiger

3†. Below is a set of dictionary definitions for the verb *chase*, and some related words. Comment on them from the point of view of: (a) how well they avoid obscurity and circularity, (b) the descriptive adequacy of the definitions for *chase* and *pursue*. Ignore figurative and metaphorical uses; just deal with the basic, motional senses of the words.

   chase: to pursue in order to seize, overtake, capture, kill, etc.
   pursue: to follow with a view to overtake, capture, kill, etc.
   follow: to go or come after; move behind in the same direction

4†. Investigate the definitions of the word *party* (as in *I went to a great party last night*) in a recent edition of any major dictionary. Assess the definitions from the point of view of: (a) descriptive adequacy, (b) obscurity, (c) circularity. Can you suggest any improvements in the definitions?

5†. How would you capture the difference in meaning between the words *evening* and *night*? How does the meaning difference fit in (if at all) with the difference between saying *Good night!* and *Good evening!*?

6†. Draw up a truth table for the English connective *but*, and compare it with the truth table for ∧ (*and*). Are there any differences between the two truth tables? What does this exercise show about truth tables and meaning?

7†. Study the drawings above (modified from Hurford and Heasley 1983: 81). Devise an economical set of binary semantic components that would allow us to distinguish each object from all the others. Give the componential analysis for each object, according to your system. There are several possible solutions.

8. Devise an economical set of binary features to capture the similarities and differences in the meanings of the following sets of words: (a)† *mist, smog, haze, fog* (b) *babble, sing, murmur, hum.*

9†. (a) Using componential analysis, how would you analyse the word *cousin*? (b) How would you analyse the meaning of *nephew*? (Hint: Figure out how to analyse *sibling of* first.)

10†. Critically discuss the following analyses (Cruse 1986: 195):

   mountain: extremely large earth-protuberance
   hill: very large earth-protuberance
   hillock: fairly large earth-protuberance
   mound: moderately large earth-protuberance

11†. Critically discuss the following analyses of cooking terms, adapted from Lehrer (1969). (Note that the feature +LIQUID is intended to cover only liquids other than fat.)

   boil: [+LIQUID] [+VIGOROUS ACTION]
   fry: [−LIQUID] [+FAT] [+FRYING PAN]
   steam: [+LIQUID] [−FAT] [+VIGOROUS ACTION] [+RACK, SIEVE, ETC.]
   poach: [+LIQUID] [−FAT] [−VIGOROUS ACTION] [+TO PRESERVE SHAPE]

3

NSM and other contemporary approaches

This chapter introduces the reductive paraphrase or Natural Semantic Metalanguage approach to semantic analysis used throughout this book and compares it with some of the other cognitively oriented systems in current use: the Conceptual Semantics approach of Ray Jackendoff, FrameNet semantics as originated and inspired by Charles Fillmore, and the Cognitive Linguistics movement. The chapter concludes with some advice and guidelines on how to do reductive paraphrase explications.

3.1 The Natural Semantic Metalanguage approach

The REDUCTIVE PARAPHRASE or Natural Semantic Metalanguage (NSM) approach is founded on the principles of maximum clarity and universality. Its originator is Anna Wierzbicka. Though Polish by birth, Wierzbicka has been based at the Australian National University (Canberra) since the 1970s. Some historical notes on the approach are given in section 12.1.

An ideal NSM semantic analysis—often called an EXPLICATION—is a paraphrase composed in the simplest possible terms, thus avoiding circularity and obscurity. No technical terms, 'fancy words', logical symbols, or abbreviations are allowed in explications, which should contain only simple expressions from ordinary natural language (e.g. I, YOU, SOMEONE, DO, HAPPEN, THINK, KNOW, GOOD, BIG, BECAUSE). As a true paraphrase, the explication should be exhaustive; that is, it should faithfully portray the full meaning of the expression being analysed. It is also expected that an explication couched in semantically simple terms will be readily translatable across languages.

One reason for the reliance on natural language is that, as John Lyons (1977: 12) once put it: 'any formalism is parasitic upon the ordinary everyday use of language, in that it must be understood intuitively on the basis of ordinary language'. In a sense therefore, the NSM approach merely makes a virtue of necessity in seeking a system of representation based on natural language.

The NSM approach accepts a stringent standard of descriptive adequacy—the test of SUBSTITUTABILITY without change of meaning. This means that the ultimate test of a good explication is that native speakers will agree that the explication expresses the same meaning as the original expression in context. This is another reason to formulate explications in straightforward, non-technical terms: they must be intelligible to ordinary language users.

3.1.1 Semantic primes

Once we adopt the principle of reductive paraphrase it follows that there ought to be a set of expressions—a kind of semantically minimal 'core'—that remains even after a completely exhaustive semantic analysis has been carried out. These are semantically basic expressions—expressions that cannot be defined any further.

Of all the modern proponents of semantic primitives, Anna Wierzbicka has been at once the most persistent, and the most insistent that semantic

Table 3.1.   Semantic primes: English exponents, grouped into categories

I, YOU, SOMEONE, SOMETHING~THING, PEOPLE, BODY	Substantives
KIND, PART	Relational substantives
THIS, THE SAME, OTHER~ELSE	Determiners
ONE, TWO, MUCH~MANY, SOME, ALL	Quantifiers
GOOD, BAD	Evaluators
BIG, SMALL	Descriptors
THINK, KNOW, WANT, FEEL, SEE, HEAR	Mental predicates
SAY, WORDS, TRUE	Speech
DO, HAPPEN, MOVE, TOUCH	Actions, events, movement, contact
BE (SOMEWHERE), THERE IS, HAVE, BE (SOMEONE/ SOMETHING)	Location, existence, possession, specification
LIVE, DIE	Life and death
WHEN~TIME, NOW, BEFORE, AFTER, A LONG TIME, A SHORT TIME, FOR SOME TIME, MOMENT	Time
WHERE~PLACE, HERE, ABOVE, BELOW, FAR, NEAR, SIDE, INSIDE	Space
NOT, MAYBE, CAN, BECAUSE, IF	Logical concepts
VERY, MORE	Intensifier, augmentor
LIKE~WAY	Similarity

Notes: Primes exist as the meanings of lexical units (not at the level of lexemes). Exponents of primes may be words, bound morphemes, or phrasemes. They can be formally complex. They can have language-specific combinatorial variants (allolexes, indicated with ~). Each prime has well-specified syntactic (combinatorial) properties.

primitives can and must be embodied in expressions (words, bound morphemes, or fixed phrases) from ordinary, natural language. In all her studies, Wierzbicka has attempted to work with a small inventory of hypothesized semantic primitives in mind, with a view to testing the adequacy of the set as a whole. In 1972, with the publication of her first book, *Semantic Primitives*, the proposed set numbered a mere fourteen. Since then, the list has been expanded to 63 items. They are listed in Table 3.1. Notice also that there has been a slight shift in terminology—from semantic primitives to SEMANTIC PRIMES.

The main 'discovery method' which has led to the current NSM inventory has been experimentation (trial and error) with trying to define a wide variety of expressions. All the proposed primes have proved themselves to be, on the one hand, very useful and versatile in framing explications and, on the other, themselves resistant to (non-circular) explication. Ultimately, the only way to show that something is not an indefinable element is to succeed in decomposing it. It is never possible, strictly speaking, to absolutely prove that something is indefinable. The best we can say is that as various attempts are made and are seen to fail the claim to indefinability becomes stronger and stronger.

3.1.2 Semantic primes as universals

An important NSM principle is that a semantic prime ought to be a so-called LEXICAL UNIVERSAL, in the sense that it should have a lexical equivalent in every human language. An expression that represents a prime in a given language is known as the EXPONENT of the prime. It has to be stressed, however, that the term 'lexical' is used in a broad sense to include not only words but also bound morphemes and fixed phrases. In many languages some primes are expressed by bound morphemes, rather than by separate words. For example, in Pitjantjatjara/Yankunytjatjara the prime BECAUSE is expressed by the ablative suffix -nguru (see section 10.5). In some languages, there are primitive meanings expressed by means of fixed phrases (also known as phrasemes) composed of several words. The English expression *a long time* provides a convenient example: notice that the meaning cannot be broken down into the words *a*, *long*, and *time* in their ordinary senses. In many (perhaps most) languages the meaning A LONG TIME is conveyed by a single word; for example, Malay *lama*, Pitjantjatjara/Yankunytjatjara *rawa*, Lao *don*.

Even when exponents of semantic primes do take the form of single words, there is no need for them to be morphologically simple (though very often they are). For example, in English the words *someone*, *maybe*, and *inside* are morphologically complex. But—and this is the crucial point—their meanings are not composed from the meanings of the morphological 'bits' in question. That is, *someone* ≠ *some+one*, *maybe* ≠ *may+be*, and *inside* ≠ *in+side*.

Exponents of semantic primes may have variant forms (allolexes or allomorphs). This is the phenomenon of ALLOLEXY. The 'double-barrelled' items in Table 3.1 indicate English allolexes. For example, 'other' and 'else' express the same meaning but they occur in different contexts: e.g. *another place*, *somewhere else*. Likewise, in some combinatorial contexts the word *thing* is equivalent in meaning to *something*. In ordinary English it sounds odd to directly combine SOMETHING with determiners or quantifiers

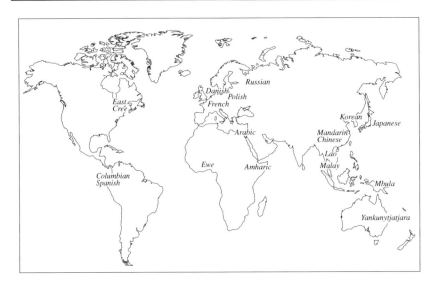

Map 3.1 Sample of non-English languages studied intensively in the NSM framework up to 2010

(e.g. *this something, one something*), but the relevant meaning combinations can be expressed quite naturally if the word *thing* is used in place of *something* (e.g. *this thing, one thing*). Another kind of allolexy found in English involves the pronoun *I*, which occurs post-verbally as *me*, because of a language-specific rule of English whereby most pronouns have post-verbal variants (*I/me, he/him, she/her, they/them*, etc.). NOT also has several allolexic variants, including *don't* (as in *I don't know*). Patterns of allolexy are language-specific, i.e. they vary from language to language.

All these factors, as well as the fact that exponents of semantic primes are often polysemous, mean that identifying exponents of primes across languages is no straightforward matter. Research on this has been going on since the mid-1990s in a variety of languages (cf. Goddard and Wierzbicka 1994; 2002; Goddard 1997c; 2008; Peeters 2006). The existence of lexical exponents for the NSM primes has been confirmed for languages as diverse as Russian, Polish, French, Spanish, Malay, Lao, Ewe, Amharic, Japanese, Chinese, Korean, East Cree, Arabic, Danish, and Yankunytjatjara (see Map 3.1). A few problematical cases have been identified and these require further investigation, but it is safe to say that the NSM primes are much more translatable than the vast majority of other words.

3.1.3 A natural semantic metalanguage

The set of semantic primes should contain only those expressions which are indefinable without circularity, and it should contain all such expressions, making it powerful enough to take on the full range of complex meanings capable of being expressed in the language as a whole. The primes constitute a kind of 'mini-language' with the same expressive power as a full natural language, hence the term NATURAL SEMANTIC METALANGUAGE (NSM).

A full account of the metalanguage of course includes an explicit description of its syntax as well as of its lexicon. That is, along with a mini-lexicon there is also a mini-syntax. In practical terms what this means is simply that certain patterns of combination of primes are (or are hypothesized to be) found universally. For instance, given the primes SOMEONE, SOMETHING, SAY, BAD, and YOU, it is hypothesized that one could put them together to say, in any language, the equivalent of 'someone said something bad about you'. Likewise, given the primes I, YOU, SOMETHING, WANT, DO, GOOD, it is hypothesized that one can put them together, in any language, to say the equivalent of 'I want to do something good for you'.

We need not explore the syntax of the NSM metalanguage in any great detail at this point, but it is necessary to draw attention to two points. The first is the idea that semantic primes may have optional or alternative VALENCY OPTIONS. For example, it is assumed that DO, in addition to its obligatory 'agent' and complement, may also take an optional 'patient' and a further optional 'instrument'. In other words, from the point of view of their realization in English, it is proposed that DO, DO TO, and DO WITH are all manifestations of a single prime; or, to put it slightly differently, that the prime DO can be used in several different configurations.

someone did something	[minimal frame]
someone did something to someone else	[plus 'patient$_1$']
someone did something to something	[plus 'patient$_2$']
someone did something to something with something	[plus 'instrument']

The prime SAY also has an array of valency options. Its minimal frame has an obligatory 'speaker' and complement, or, alternatively, there is a direct speech frame. But the minimal frame can be expanded by adding an 'addressee' and/or a 'locutionary topic'. That is, in an English-based NSM, SAY has extra valency options SAY TO and SAY ABOUT.

someone said something   [minimal frame]
someone said: '– – –'   [direct speech]
someone said something to someone   [plus 'addressee']
someone said something about something/someone [plus 'locutionary topic']

DO and SAY are not the only primes with valency options. For instance, GOOD has a 'beneficiary' option (GOOD FOR); HAPPEN has an 'undergoer' (HAPPEN TO) and 'locus' options (HAPPEN IN THIS PLACE); and (like SAY), THINK and KNOW have 'topic' options (THINK ABOUT, KNOW ABOUT). Other kinds of valency option are also attested. For example, a 'subset' or 'partitive' option is available to certain quantifiers: ONE OF . . . , TWO OF . . . , SOME OF . . . .

The idea that semantic primes have individual valency options is akin to the influential notion (descending from Gruber 1970; Fillmore 1968; 1977), that all languages make use of a universal set of 'participant roles', such as 'agent', 'patient', 'instrument', 'theme', 'experiencer', and 'beneficiary'. In general linguistic theory, however, participant roles (also known as semantic cases, semantic roles, thematic relations, or thematic roles) are regarded as free-floating, so to speak, i.e. as having an independent existence. They are also usually described in rather abstract terms; for example, the 'instrument' role has been described as 'an inanimate object or force which is "causally involved" in carrying out an action or event, but which is not a causer per se' (Fillmore 1968).

In the NSM approach, on the other hand, valency options belong to specific semantically primitive predicates. The idea of an instrument, for example, is tied to the idea of 'doing something': it only makes sense in terms of DO. One could say that in the NSM approach, semantic roles are characterized as the argument slots of semantically primitive predicates. (A similar proposal has been made by Jackendoff 1990: ch. 2, except that his primitive predicates are highly abstract, not words of ordinary language.)

The second point about the syntax of the metalanguage is that it allows complex clauses to be combined in various ways. Some primes, such as WANT, THINK, and KNOW, can take propositional or quasi-propositional complements, in structures like the following:

I want you to do (know, say, etc.) something
this someone knows (doesn't know) that . . .
this someone thinks like this: '—'

As well, a powerful clause linking strategy is made possible by the capacity of the element THIS to refer back to the content of a preceding clause. This enables entire clauses to function as temporal adjuncts (e.g. AFTER THIS, BEFORE THIS), and also to participate in causal adjuncts (BECAUSE OF THIS). There is one purely interclausal construction in the current NSM metalanguage: conditional IF. All sorts of other variations and nuances can be introduced using the NSM 'operators' and connecting elements, such as CAN, NOT, LIKE, and BECAUSE.

This has been only a thumbnail sketch of the natural semantic metalanguage, but the basic claims should be clear enough: that there are correspondences between the semantic primes of all languages, and also between certain combinations of primes, so that, essentially, anything that can be said in one NSM can be equally well expressed in any other. The viability of a universal semantic metalanguage is an empirical question, but not one we can delve into deeply here. In this book we use the reductive paraphrase approach primarily for its practical and heuristic value. There is more information about the NSM theory and issues of translatability and universality in Chapter 12.

3.1.4 Semantic molecules

Not all concepts can be resolved 'in one go', as it were, into an explication consisting exclusively of semantic primes. For some areas of the lexicon, explications must also include certain non-primitive meanings that function, alongside the semantic primes, as conceptual building blocks in the meaning structure of other, yet more complex words. Such meanings are called SEMANTIC MOLECULES. The notion is similar to that of 'intermediate-level concepts' in the Moscow School of Semantics (Apresjan 1992 [1974]; 2000; Mel'čuk 1989), but with the important additional constraint that NSM semantic molecules must be meanings of lexical units in the language concerned.

From a cognitive point of view, the claim is that some complex concepts are semantically dependent on other less complex, but still non-primitive, concepts. For example, semantic explications for words like *sparrow* and *eagle* include 'bird' as a semantic molecule; the cognitive claim is that the concept of *sparrow* includes and depends on the concept of 'bird'. In this case, the relationship is taxonomic: *sparrows* and *eagles* are both 'birds [m] of one kind' (molecules are marked in explications with the notation [m]). Many semantic molecules are taxonomic superordinates, but semantic molecules can enter into semantic structures in many other ways. For example, explications for *walk* and *run* include 'feet [m]' and 'ground [m]', where the relationships are, roughly, body-part instrumental and location, respectively. Explications for *cut* and *chop* include 'sharp [m]', where the molecule characterizes the nature of a physical instrument. Explications for *cup*, *glass*, and *mug* include 'drink [m]', where the relationship relates to intended purpose or function.

Research on semantic molecules is still in an early stage, but it is already clear that many semantic molecules in any given language are language-specific. It is possible that a small number of semantic molecules, perhaps 20 or so, may be universal or near-universal; for example, 'hands', 'head', 'men', 'women', 'children', 'mother', 'water', 'fire', 'sky', and 'ground' (Goddard 2010a; 2011a).

Whether or not a word (strictly speaking, a word-meaning) is or isn't a semantic molecule is not a matter of the analyst's convenience. It is an empirical question which can only be determined by detailed semantic analysis. It is important to stress that one's immediate intuitions and/or the availability of a ready-to-hand near-paraphrase can be misleading. For example, verbs like *punch*, *slap*, and *kick* are often referred to by linguists as 'verbs of hitting', and native speakers will sometimes volunteer paraphrases like 'hit with the fist' for punch or 'hit with the foot' for *kick*. However, semantic analysis shows that *punch*, *slap*, *kick*, and so on do not require 'hit' as a semantic molecule, and furthermore that *hit* contains some semantic components that would make it unsuitable for this purpose (Sibly 2008; 2010).

We will be using semantic molecules extensively in Chapters 7–9, and considering the theory behind them and their cross-linguistic status in more detail in Chapter 12.

3.1.5 Cultural scripts

The NSM approach has a pragmatic 'sister theory' in the form of the theory of cultural scripts (Wierzbicka 2003a; Goddard and Wierzbicka 1997; 2004; Goddard 2006a). We will look briefly into this theory and some of its applications in Chapter 12. The best way to indicate the main idea behind it is probably to refer to the field of study known as the ethnography of communication (Hymes 1968; Carbaugh 2005). The main insight of this field is that people's ways of speaking, i.e. their ways of using language, are profoundly influenced by cultural factors. In any particular speech community there are certain tacitly shared understandings about how it is appropriate to speak in particular, culturally construed situations. Different researchers have termed these 'norms of interpretation', 'rules of speaking', or 'discourse strategies'. Essentially, a CULTURAL SCRIPT is a way of stating such norms, rules, or strategies using the metalanguage of semantic primes. That is, instead of using complex and English-specific terms such as 'politeness', 'directness', 'formality', and so on, we try to capture the shared understandings of speakers using simple words that have equivalents in the language of the people concerned. Cultural scripts are very important for understanding (from an 'insider perspective') what is going on in actual communicative events, but they are not semantic explications. Rather than decoding and articulating the content of words and other linguistic expressions, they are a way of tapping into cultural assumptions and expectations.

3.2 Ray Jackendoff's conceptual semantics

Ray Jackendoff is the major semantic theorist associated with the dominant school of generative grammar. He has been a staunch defender of a conceptualist approach to semantics; that is, he believes that word meanings should be thought of as composed of what 'ordinary language calls concepts, thoughts or ideas' (1990: 1). Like Wierzbicka, he sees the 'indefinitely large' stock of possible word meanings (lexical concepts) as built up from a finite set of 'conceptual primitives' and principles of combination (Jackendoff 1983; 1991; 2002; 2007; 2010). Unlike Wierzbicka, however, Jackendoff does not see conceptual primitives as anchored in the meanings of ordinary words. His system can be seen as an abstract semantic metalanguage.

3.2.1 Developments in Jackendoff's conceptual semantics

Jackendoff (1983) proposed that among the innate concepts is a set of conceptual categories which are 'semantic parts of speech'. These include Thing, Event, State, Action, Place, Path, Property, and Amount. Each of these can be elaborated into a function–argument organization, by means of 'conceptual functions' such as GO, STAY, TO, FROM, VIA, and CAUSE, among others. For example, the rule in (a) below says that a constituent which is an Event can take the form of either of the two Event-functions GO ('motion along a path') or STAY ('stasis over a period of time'). Each of these functions takes two arguments, the first of which is in both cases a Thing. The second is a Path in the case of GO (*Bill went to New York*) and a Place in the case of STAY (*Bill stayed in the kitchen*). An Event can also be constituted by the function CAUSE, as shown in (b). Similar rules stipulate how each of the other constituent types (Thing, State, Action, Place, Path, Property, and Amount) can be elaborated.

a.

$$[\text{EVENT}] \rightarrow \left\{ \begin{array}{l} \left[_{\text{Event}} \text{GO}([\text{THING}], [\text{PATH}]) \right] \\ \left[_{\text{Event}} \text{STAY}([\text{THING}], [\text{PLACE}]) \right] \end{array} \right\}$$

b.

$$[\text{EVENT}] \rightarrow \left[_{\text{Event}} \text{CAUSE} \left(\left[\left\{ \begin{array}{l} \text{THING} \\ \text{EVENT} \end{array} \right\} \right], [\text{EVENT}] \right) \right]$$

Jackendoff has subsequently moved in the direction of a more abstract, feature-based metalanguage. Whereas in 1983 he viewed functions like GO, STAY, and CAUSE, and categories like Thing, Path, and Place, as conceptual primitives, he now sees value in decomposing them further. The stage illustrated above, he now says, can be compared to that stage in the history of chemistry in which the elements had been identified, but before the internal structure of the atom had been described. For instance, the category Thing as used above is intended to denote individuals only. Jackendoff (1991; 1996; 2010) argues, however, that individuals need to be brought under a larger super-category which also takes in groups, substances, and aggregates. He proposes to call the super-category Material Entity (Mat for short), and to recognize two binary features, +b (bounded) and +i (internal structure), so as to decompose the notions of individual, group, substance, and aggregate as follows:

Mat, +b, −i: individuals (e.g. *a pig, someone*)
Mat, +b, +i: groups (e.g. *a committee*)
Mat, −b, −i: substances (e.g. *water*)
Mat, −b, +i: aggregates (e.g. *pigs, people*)

The earlier primitives Place, Path, State, and Event are also regarded as decomposable. Place and Path are now seen as instances of the super-category

Space, and State and Event are seen as instances of the super-category Situation. The discrimination between them is achieved by a feature for 'directionality' (DIR); for instance, Paths have directionality but Places do not.

In the same work Jackendoff introduced a swag of new and more abstract 'conceptual functions' such as PL (Plural), ELT (Element of), COMP (Composed of), CONT (Containing), PART (Partitive), and GR (Grinder, a function which maps +b arguments onto −b ones). Another innovation is a formalism for specifying dimensionality, and in conjunction with this a pair of functions that relate boundaries to what they bound: BD (Bounded) and BDBY (Bounded By). This enables him to decompose earlier functions such as TO and VIA, as follows:

$$\text{TO } X = \begin{bmatrix} +b, \ -i \\ \text{DIM 1d DIR} \\ _{\text{Space}}\text{BDBY}^{+}([_{\text{Thing}}/_{\text{Space}}X]) \end{bmatrix}$$

$$\text{VIA } [_{\text{Place}}X] = \begin{bmatrix} -b, \ -i \\ \text{DIM 1d DIR} \\ _{\text{Space}}\text{CONT}([_{\text{Space}}X]) \end{bmatrix}$$

Decoding the TO X formula above, Jackendoff (1991: 36) writes: 'That is, TO specifies a 1-dimensional bounded directed Space (i.e. a bounded Path), bounded on its positive end by the Goal.'

An important part of Jackendoff's thinking, which we cannot consider in any detail here, is that many meanings incorporate a 3D visual-spatial representation 'that encodes geometric and topological properties of physical objects', in addition to their conceptual content (Jackendoff 1990: 33; 1996).

3.2.2 The weaknesses of abstract metalanguages

Jackendoff's metalanguage of conceptual functions is subject to a serious critique which emerges once we ask the question: What is the relationship between this metalanguage and ordinary English? A semantic metalanguage can serve its function only if it is intelligible; and the only way we can understand formulas like those above is via our knowledge of the meanings of English words. Any abstract metalanguage is therefore, in Keith Allan's phrase, 'a degenerate form of a natural language' (Allan

1986: 268). To understand the formula we have to mentally turn it back into ordinary English, undoing the 'deformation' that has been involved in turning it into a technical formula in the first place.

It is not hard to see that Jackendoff-style formulas are open to the charge of obscurity. For example, we can only make sense of a formula like:

drink:

$$[_{Event}CAUSE([_{Thing}]_i, [_{Event}GO([_{Thing}LIQUID]_j,$$
$$[_{Path}TO([_{Place}IN([_{Thing}MOUTH\ OF([_{Thing}]_i)])])])])]$$

by mentally translating it into something like this: 'drinking is an event in which something causes liquid to go into its own mouth'.

As usual, in tandem with obscurity comes circularity, which can be more or less explicit. Consider a representation like the following (Jackendoff 2007: 205), which is supposed to represent *X sees Y*:

$$\begin{bmatrix} X\ SENSE_{visual}\ Y \\ X\ EXP\ Y \end{bmatrix}$$

Effectively this glosses *see* as 'sense visually'; but *visual* is clearly a more complex word than *see*, and (obviously) one whose meaning depends on *see*. There is nothing to be gained by substituting 'visual' for *see*, 'auditory' for *hear*, and so on.

---

open [+ —— NP, . . .] ; (

	[NP, S]	
	X	(Causes)
	⟨(Physical object) ∨ (Physical event)⟩	

(((Condition) (Positioned to prevent passage between inside and outside

	[NP, Prep P, VP, PP, S]		[NP, VP, PP, S]
of	X	) of	X
	⟨(Enclosure)⟩		⟨(Barrier)⟩

	[Tense, Aux, PP, S]			[Tense, Aux, PP, S]	
at	X	/H₁, H₂, H₄,), . . . ,(. . .		X	/H₃, H₂, H₅,), . . . ,
	⟨(. . . t . . .)⟩			⟨(. . . t . . .)⟩	

((Condition) (Positioned to allow passage between inside and outside

	[NP, Prep P, VP, PP, S]		[NP, VP, PP, S]	[Tense, Aux, PP, S]	
of	X	) of	X	at X	/H₆)))
	⟨(Enclosure)⟩		⟨(Barrier)⟩	⟨(. . . t . . .)⟩	

Figure 3.1. Katz's (1972: 358) analysis of *open*

Similar charges apply to Katz's semantic representations. For instance, Katz (1972: 336) proposed the analysis for the verb *to open* shown in Figure 3.1.

Neglecting the details concerned with the time-structure of the event, the guts of this analysis may be paraphrased as follows:

something causes a condition in which there had been a barrier positioned to prevent passage from inside to outside of some enclosure to change to a condition where the barrier is no longer positioned in that way.

Clearly the words *barrier*, *passage*, and *enclosure* are more complex than is *open* in the first place. There is also a lot of redundancy in this account; for example, what is a *barrier* except something that *prevents passage*?

Sometimes advocates of abstract metalanguages claim that the terms they use are not really those of ordinary language but represent more 'abstract' meanings; for instance, it might be claimed that CAUSE and LIQUID don't really necessarily mean exactly the same as the English words *cause* and *liquid*. However, as emphasized by various critics (e.g. Kempson 1977; Lyons 1977; Wierzbicka 1980a: ch. 1), a semantic analysis can only be tested and improved on the assumption that it bears a straightforward relationship with natural language.

To see this, let us suppose that someone were to analyse *kill* as: [INTEND] X ([CAUSE] X ([DIE] Y)). The evidence of ordinary usage would be against this because it is not contradictory to say *John killed Bill without intending to*. That is, we can test and disconfirm the proposed analysis by reference to what is and isn't acceptable in ordinary English. On the other hand, if the elements of a semantic analysis are regarded as 'merely abstract constructs' then we deprive ourselves of the simplest way of testing the analysis.

We can illustrate further with another example involving *kill*, this time a real one. In the 1970s, linguists such as James McCawley and George Lakoff proposed the analysis *kill* = X CAUSE (Y DIE). It was quickly pointed out by critics that *cause to die* doesn't necessarily mean *kill*. Katz (1970: 253) made up a little tale about a Wild West sheriff whose six-shooter is faultily repaired by the local gunsmith, as a result of which the weapon jams at the last moment and he is gunned down. Clearly the gunsmith caused the death of the sheriff, but equally clearly, the gunsmith did not *kill* him, showing that the causative relationship inherent in *kill* must be somehow 'direct'. Fillmore (1970) pointed out that *Peter killed the cat in the attic* and *Peter caused the cat to die in the attic* were not synonymous, highlighting the fact that some 'unity of place' is required. Fodor (1970) pointed out that unity of time was also required. It is OK to say *John caused Bill to die on Sunday by stabbing him on Saturday*, but there is no way that the two time specifications can be indicated using *kill*.

These objections should have led to the original analysis being revised, but instead McCawley (1972) proposed that there were two underlying 'abstract' semantic components CAUSE$_1$ and CAUSE$_2$, corresponding roughly to direct and indirect causation respectively. Neither, he said, could be identified with the English word *cause*; nor could they be understood as *directly cause* and *indirectly cause* either. I hope you can see how this manoeuvre makes the analysis completely unverifiable. Whenever a counter-example is pointed out, the analyst can just say, 'Oh, I didn't mean that. That component is abstract, you see. It doesn't mean the same as any English word.'

3.3 Charles Fillmore's frame semantics and the FrameNet project

Charles Fillmore is the main theorist behind the development of what is generally called FRAME SEMANTICS. In recent years it has given rise to a specific ongoing project called FrameNet. Fillmore's work started from the conviction that semantic theory must be linked directly to people's comprehension processes, that is, to how we understand real discourse in context. This implies finding ways of integrating information about a word's meaning, grammatical properties, and knowledge about the world.

According to frame semantics, the meaning of a word can only be understood against a background frame of experience, beliefs, or practices that 'motivate the concept that the word encodes'. One of Fillmore's favourite examples is the set of verbs *buy*, *sell*, *charge*, *pay*, *cost*, and *spend*. To understand any of these calls for an understanding of a complete 'commercial transaction frame':

... in which one person acquires control or possession of something from a second person, by agreement, as a result of surrendering to that person a sum of money. The needed background requires an understanding of property ownership, a money economy, implicit contract, and a great deal more. (Fillmore and Atkins 1992: 78)

For another example, consider the names for the days of the week (*Monday*, *Tuesday*, *Wednesday*, and so on). Fillmore sees their meanings as depending on a whole set of interconnected notions, including knowledge about the natural cycle created by the daily movement of the sun across the sky, the standard means for reckoning when one day begins and another ends, the existence of a conventionalized calendric cycle of seven days, with a subconvention for specifying the beginning member of the cycle, and the practice in our culture of assigning different portions of the week to work and to non-work.

3.3.1 FrameNet

Inspired and led by Fillmore, the FrameNet programme has been steadily documenting the English lexicon in line with the assumptions of frame semantics (Ruppenhofer et al. 2006). The programme has extended to several other languages, including Spanish, German, and Japanese (Boas 2009b). FrameNet is radically different to most approaches to linguistic semantics because its architecture depends crucially on identifying frames of real-world knowledge. The number of posited frames is very large, and they exist at different levels of generality. Any given word or set of words will belong to a rather specific frame, such as INGESTION, CUTTING, or TRAVEL, and to various higher-level frames, such as INTENTIONALLY_ACT. Lower-level frames are said to 'inherit' higher-level frames. Frames are characterized by a set of frame-specific Frame Elements and a statement (a Frame Definition) about how they are interrelated. At the lowest level, the Frame Elements are highly situation-specific (in effect, situation-specific semantic roles), but higher-level frames employ rather generic Frame Elements, such as Agent, Patient, and Instrument. There are also numerous so-called extra-thematic frame elements, such as Manner, Time, Reason, Duration, Circumstances, and Reciprocation.

As mentioned, Frames are supposed to be extra-linguistic in nature. Petruck (1996: 2) characterizes the Frame as 'a cognitive structuring device, parts of which are indexed by words associated with it'. It seems to me, however, that in practice FrameNet analysts often proceed as if Frames and Frame Elements were linguistic meanings, especially at the higher-levels. Be that as it may, what is distinctive about the FrameNet approach is that:

words or word senses are not related to each other directly, word to word, but only by way of their links to common background frames and indications of the manner in which their meanings highlight particular elements of such frames. (Fillmore and Atkins 1992: 76–7)

As one might expect on these assumptions, FrameNet analysts are not much interested in individual word-meanings. Where definitions for individual words are given, they are often just taken from the *Concise Oxford Dictionary* and exhibit all the usual faults of conventional definitions (circularity, obscurity, inaccuracy, etc.). For example: *walk*: 'move at a regular and fairly slow pace by lifting and setting down each foot in turn'; *drink*: 'take (a liquid) into the mouth and swallow'; *chop*: 'cut with repeated sharp, heavy blows of an axe or knife'. Some words, such as *cut*, receive no separate definition because they are in effect lexical instantiations of a Frame (in the case of *cut*, the CUT Frame). The character of low-level Frame Descriptions can be indicated with the INGESTION Frame, which includes *drink* and *eat*, and the CUT Frame, which includes *cut, chop, slice, mince*, and a number of others. The capitalized words represent Frame Elements.

> INGESTION Frame: An Ingestor consumes food or drink (Ingestibles), which entails putting the Ingestibles in the mouth for delivery to the digestive system. This may include the use of an Instrument.

> CUT Frame: An Agent cuts an Item into Pieces using an Instrument (which may or may not be expressed).

The INGESTION Frame and the CUT Frame both inherit the higher Frames INTENTIONALLY_ACT, TRANSITIVE_ACTION, and INTENTIONALLY_AFFECT. In addition, the INGESTION frame inherits MANIPULATION.

The initial goal of FrameNet was to document the lexicogrammar of English, and especially to capture the complex interrelationships between lexical units (word-senses) and their valence patterns. However, since Frames are supposed to be conceptual structures not tied to any particular language, and given the great amount of work that has already been devoted to identifying numerous frames and their interrelationships, they may seem to provide a valuable platform for cross-linguistic comparison. The Spanish, German, and Japanese FrameNet projects now under way have taken the existing (English-derived) Frames as a starting point: '[this] means that non-English FrameNets do not have to go through the entire process of frame creation' (Boas 2009a: 73). It is recognized that new frames may need to be invented where necessary, especially in highly culture-specific domains, but the general assumption is that the English-derived Frames will provide a solid foundation for cross-linguistic work.

Unfortunately, from an NSM vantage point this assumption seems quite unrealistic. Because the Frame elements and definitions are constructed in a technical English-based terminology, one would expect there to be major problems ahead with implementing the cross-linguistic programme. Even in its English work, the FrameNet 'workflow' has shown little concern with metalanguage issues, apparently identifying and constructing frame descriptions on a rather ad hoc basis. The result is a maze of complex interrelated notions that will require a great deal of interrogation and reinterpretation before they reach a form in which they can be unproblematically mapped across to other languages. FrameNet practitioners are becoming aware of these problems. Boas (2009a: 92–3) states that the 'applicability of semantic frames as a cross-linguistic metalanguage' remains to be tested, and that 'to determine the feasibility of a truly independent metalanguage based on semantic frames for connecting multiple FrameNets [in different languages is]... not an easy task'.

For example, in the Japanese FrameNet, it was found necessary, in order to capture differences between Japanese verbs of motion (*wataru* 'go across' and *koeru* 'go beyond'), to divide the Frame Element PATH into two sub-categories: ROUTE and BOUNDARY (*wataru* can occur with both, but *koeru* only with BOUNDARY). The danger is that this kind of 'splitting' procedure will lead to ever more sub-categories with ill-defined relationships to each other and to the higher frames and frame elements.

3.4 Semantics in cognitive linguistics

The past 15–20 years have seen a steady rise of a broad approach to language known as COGNITIVE LINGUISTICS. It is better thought of as a coalition or 'movement' than as a single approach, because cognitive linguists generally agree that is no single unifying theoretical doctrine (Geeraerts and Cuyckens, 2007a: 9). What unites many otherwise disparate scholars is the drive to make cognition central to the study of languages. This means undoing a pervasive way of thinking according to which language is seen as a self-contained system, separate from other faculties or aspects of the human mind. As Langacker (2010) puts it, in cognitive linguistics, language is seen as an integral facet of cognition, emerging from more general phenomena (e.g. perception, attention, categorization) rather than being separate and autonomous. (Langacker 2010: 89)

On some accounts, NSM semantics can be counted as part of the cognitive linguistics movement, or at the least, as a 'fellow traveller' (Peeters 2000a: 14; Goddard 1998). Certainly in the 1970s and 1980s Anna Wierzbicka was one of the few linguists who upheld the centrality of meaning in the conceptualist sense, against the then dominant 'object-ivist' approach to meaning. 'In natural language', she wrote,

meaning consists in human interpretation of the world. It is subjective, it is anthropocentric, it reflects predominant cultural concerns and culture-specific modes of social interaction as much as any objective features of the world 'as such'. (Wierzbicka 1988: 2)

Wierzbicka's work on prototypes and the meaningfulness of grammar was at the leading edge of cognitive linguistic thinking in those decades. Her 1988 book *The Semantics of Grammar* (some chapters of which had appeared as early as 1979) anticipated by many years key ideas in what is now known as Construction Grammar (counted by some as part of cogni-tive linguistics). On the other hand, in its commitment to semantic univer-sals and to reductive paraphrase as a mode of semantic analysis, the NSM programme diverges from the cognitive linguistics mainstream. To quote Langacker again:

lexical meaning is therefore viewed in CG [cognitive grammar] as being fuzzily delimited, non-distinct from other knowledge, and only partially determined conventionally. (Langacker 2010: 97)

Some prominent cognitive linguists have been constructing a picture of cognitive linguistics in which NSM semantics hardly rates a mention (as, for example, in Geeraerts and Cuyckens 2007b). Given that the term 'cognitive linguistics' is open to wider and narrower interpretations, it is perhaps not going too far to suggest that there is something of a struggle going on to control the 'brand' and it will be interesting to see how this plays out over time.

In this section, we will briefly review some of the most prominent con-cepts employed in mainstream cognitive linguistics, including prototypes, scenarios, conceptual metaphor, and image schemas, and ask how they figure in relation to NSM thinking.

3.4.1 Prototypes

As mentioned in Chapter 1, prototype effects are now generally recognized as phenomena that must be accounted for by any adequate semantic theory, and it is true to say that cognitive linguists (and cognitive psychologists) have played a major role in promoting the importance and pervasiveness of prototype effects. How prototype effects are best conceptualized and explained is another question, however, and one about which there is a wide range of views, even within cognitive linguistics (Taylor 2003). One popular idea is George Lakoff's (1987) notion of the Idealized Cognitive Model (ICM). The basic idea is that the cognitive categories (cognitive linguists often talk about word-meanings in terms of 'categories') that underlie and explain word use are not defined in terms of a fixed set of necessary and sufficient conditions, but rather take the form of an idealized 'central' concept from which various extensions and adaptations are possible. For example, the ICM behind the word *mother*, according to Lakoff, is based on biological reproduction and birth, but the concept can be extended to embrace a network of concepts (*stepmothers, adoptive mothers, mothers-in-law, mother superiors*, etc.), in what he terms radial polysemy.

Another idea is that the core of a category (for some categories at least) is not idealized in any sense, but is rather constituted by particular actual sub-categories which enjoy high conceptual salience. For example, for the concept of *bird*, the subcategories of (say) *robin* and *wren* can be regarded as the central members of the category, with sub-categories such as *penguin* and *ostrich* being regarded as peripheral members.

A third notion has it that not only are categories non-discrete, but that the same applies to their constituents or components. Rather than thinking of semantic components as units that must be either present or absent, we should think instead of them being present to a greater or lesser extent (like ingredients in a recipe). This way of thinking can be formalized using so-called fuzzy set theory, which allocates a scalar value to set membership, so that something can be considered as wholly included in a particular set (with a value of 1.0) or as only 50 per cent included (with a value of 0.5), 25 per cent included (with a value of 0.25), or whatever. This can be illustrated by an example devised by Allan (1986: 109–10). He took test results from Battig and Montague (1969), who had elicited the most salient examples of the category Vegetable among American university students.

The ranking turned out to be as follows: carrot, pea, corn, bean, potato, tomato, lettuce, spinach, asparagus, broccoli. Allan explains:

a sparrow is absolutely not a member of the category Vegetable, so we assign it a value of 0. A carrot seems to be the best instance of a vegetable, so it should be assigned a value of 1. Using Battig and Montague's figures, and giving carrot a value of 1, asparagus [h]as a value of 0.43, celery 0.3, onion 0.14, parsley 0.04, and pickle only 0.006. (Allan 1986: 110)

As Fillmore (1975b: 128) pointed out, fuzzy set formulations are merely statistical models of the experimental data and are unconvincing from a cognitive point of view.

As mentioned, prototypicality effects have been concerning NSM semanticists for decades, and we will see many examples in later chapters of how such effects can arise from particular semantic structures. The basic point, on the NSM view, is that many elements of human thinking are inherently subjective and therefore that people may differ in their judgements about how a particular concept applies in real-world situations. For example, many concepts involve evaluational components, i.e. components like 'it is bad (good, not good, etc.) if someone does something like this'. Many contain dimensional terms such as NEAR, FAR, A LONG TIME, or A SHORT TIME—terms whose application to a particular context is a matter of interpretation. Many contain components based on likeness (using semantic prime LIKE) or components characterizing something as 'of one kind'. On the NSM view, therefore, prototypicality is not a uniform phenomenon and it doesn't have a single origin or explanation.

3.4.2 Scenarios

The term SCENARIO (or 'script') is best reserved for representations with a dynamic, time-based structure. A classic example is Lakoff and Kövecses's (1987: 213f.) five-stage scenario for *anger*, which opens as follows:

Stage 1, Offending Event: Wrongdoer offends S. Wrongdoer is at fault. The offending event displeases S. The intensity of the offense outweighs the intensity of the retribution (which equals zero at this point), thus creating an imbalance. The offense causes anger to come into existence.

Stage 2, Anger: Anger exists. S experiences physiological effects (heat, pressure, agitation). Anger exerts force on the Self to attempt an act of retribution.

Subsequent stages portray an attempt to control the anger, a loss of control leading to an outbreak of 'angry behaviour', and a final stage of retribution such that the intensity of the retribution balances that of the offence and the anger disappears. This formulation leaves a good deal to be desired (for example, the expressions *offending event* and *retribution* are just as complex as *anger* itself, and the use of *angry behaviour* is circular), but it does seem appealing to view the meaning of *anger* in terms of a prototypical scenario involving someone else doing something (seen as) bad and the consequent desire to do something bad in return. Prototypical cognitive scenarios have been used in the NSM analyses of emotion words for many years. We will see examples of current work in Chapter 4.

3.4.3 Conceptual metaphor

Metaphor has been a central topic in cognitive linguistics since the field was born in the early 1980s, impelled especially by George Lakoff (whose 1987 book *Women, Fire and Dangerous Things* was an intellectual bestseller), Zoltán Kövecses, Joseph Grady, and others. From the beginning, a key element in this work was the idea that metaphor is not merely a matter of superficial linguistic expression, but a deep-seated pattern of thinking or even a 'cognitive faculty'. Theorists such as Antonio Barcelona (2003) and Klaus-Uwe Panther and Günter Radden (1999) have claimed that the same applies to metonymy, and to other figurative modes of thought and expression.

Many scholars have been inspired by the way these ideas have liberated semantic analysis from the strictures of componential analysis and formal semantics, and have brought imagination and bodily experience back into semantics.

To go back to the source, in their widely read book *Metaphors We Live By*, Lakoff and Johnson (1980; 2003) pointed to the pervasiveness of what they called 'systematic metaphor' in our way of talking about—and, they argued, thinking about—countless abstract domains.

[W]e have found that most of our conceptual system is metaphorical in nature. And we have found a way to begin to identify in detail just what the metaphors are that structure how we perceive, how we think, and what we do. (Lakoff and Johnson 1980: 4)

The key concept is that of the CONCEPTUAL METAPHOR. This was defined as an underlying identification of an abstract concept with a more basic or concrete concept, or, in a more elaborate formulation, as a mapping or set of correspondences between elements in a concrete source domain and elements in an abstract target domain. Conceptual metaphors are invoked to explain the coherence between whole sets of ordinary language expressions. For example, much of our language about language is expressed through the so-called 'conduit metaphor' (Reddy 1979), which can be broken down into three component metaphors: (i) IDEAS ARE OBJECTS, (ii) LINGUISTIC EXPRESSIONS ARE CONTAINERS, and (iii) COMMUNICATION IS SENDING. Reddy documented more than 100 English expressions which all seem to reflect or to instantiate the conduit metaphor, including:

It's hard to get that idea across to him.
I gave you that idea.
His words carry meaning.
It's difficult to put my thoughts into words.

Some other examples of 'classic' conceptual metaphors, and the kind of everyday expressions which are supposed to evidence them, are shown below (Lakoff and Johnson 1980: 4, 44; Lakoff and Kövecses 1987):

THEORIES ARE BUILDINGS:
We will show that this theory is without foundation.
We need to buttress that argument with more support.
Some of the arguments are well constructed.

ARGUMENT IS WAR:
Your claims are indefensible.
He attacked every weak point in my argument.
His criticisms were right on target.

As work on conceptual metaphors advanced, certain problems became apparent. On the one hand, the correspondences between source and target domains are not comprehensive; one cannot, for example, speak of a *theory* having walls or a roof, or as having inhabitants. On the other hand, many attested correspondences are not specific to particular source domains or target domains. Rather, the mappings are many-to-many. Grady (1997) proposed that the correspondences be reformulated in terms of broader and more general metaphorical mappings, such as those below. A similar proposal was made by Kövecses (1995: 326–8; cf. 2002).

ORGANIZATION IS PHYSICAL STRUCTURE
PERSISTING IS REMAINING ERECT

From the point of view of the language of representation, however, these proposed metaphors are framed in terms which are abstract and remote from ordinary usage. If these terms were supposed to have a privileged theoretical status this could be problematical, but Grady (1997: 274) regards them as merely 'shorthand'. The term 'structure', he explains, is to be understood as implying 'a complex entity composed of arranged parts'. The 'parts' of a *theory* (such as its premises, claims, arguments, and supporting facts) can be seen as 'arranged in certain logical relationships' in an analogous fashion to the arrangements of the physical parts of a complex physical object. In similar fashion, Kövecses (1995: 328) explains that 'complex systems' (which include *theories*, *society*, and interpersonal relationships such as *marriage* and *friendship*) resemble complex objects in the following ways: 'they are made for a purpose; they have a function; they have a large number of parts that interact with each other; they require effort to make and maintain; the stronger they are the longer they last.'

This kind of conceptual unpackaging is moving in the right direction: resolving complex notions into simpler ones and in the process making semantic relationships more explicit; as, for example, when Grady and Kövecses identify two key components of 'structure' as 'having many parts' and being 'made by people'. Once this unpackaging has been done, it becomes much easier to understand how certain concrete physical objects and certain abstract objects can be viewed as analogous to one another, such that conceptual schemas and associated ways of speaking that come from the concrete domain can be transferred to the abstract domain.

If we follow this path of reasoning, however, along the way some of the more extreme tenets of the Conceptual Metaphor Theory no longer appear sustainable. It no longer appears, for example, that abstract concepts are literally created or constituted from concrete ones. Rather, the relationship is 'elaborative': the concrete domain provides a source of analogies and phraseology for the abstract. Further, the basic 'metaphors' (if that is still the correct word) are themselves no longer particularly grounded in familiar concrete concepts. For critiques of Conceptual Metaphor Theory, see Haser (2005) and Kertész and Rákosi (2009).

A final point about metaphor, at least in the sense of a linguistic mode of expression, is that languages and cultures differ considerably in how much they employ 'metaphorizing'. In English and other European languages, the use of active metaphor is valued and even cultivated as a feature of colourful and artful speech, in a tradition that can be traced back to classical Greece. Many languages and cultures make less use of active metaphor (Goddard 2004a).

3.4.4 Image schemas and embodiment

Conceptual metaphors, as originally proposed, did not break completely with the classical tradition insofar as they were composed of discrete (word-like) elements. But by the late 1980s, Johnson (1987), Lakoff (1987), and other theorists such as Ronald Langacker (1987), were rejecting propositional representation entirely. They proposed that even the most general and abstract concepts such as time, cognition, and causation are constituted by 'imaginative projection' from concrete experiences of move-ment, perception, and 'force dynamics' (the bodily experience of pressure, e.g. in pushing, pulling, weight; cf. Talmy 1988; 2000). In these writings, 'metaphor' no longer refers to a mental faculty which crystallizes articulate concepts from bodily experiences.

Such bodily experience is not, however, unstructured 'raw sense data'. On the contrary, it has its own structure shaped by the physical realities of the human body. Thus we are led to the novel notion of kinaesthetic IMAGE SCHEMAS (or schemata). These theorists believe that semantic (including grammatical) structure derives from the pre-conceptual structuring of bodily experience and from perceptual processes such as 'scanning' and figure–ground organization. It is impossible to represent this experiential structuring in verbal terms.

The concepts *in* and *out*, for instance, are said to have their origin in our kinaesthetic apperception of the body as a container as we ingest, excrete, inhale, and exhale. This 'embodied understanding' is imaginatively pro-jected into conceptual terms, giving rise to the myriad uses of *in* and *out*, many of which are of an abstract nature, as in particle–verb constructions like *figure out* and *freak out*. The usual method for depicting kinaesthetic image schemas is the use of diagrams. The examples in Figure 3.2 are adapted from the work of Susan Lindner (1983), who identified these

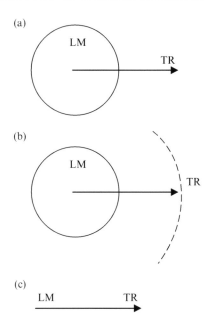

Figure 3.2. (a) Image schema for *out₁*, e.g. *John went out of the room, Pick out the best theory, Drown out the music.* (b) Image schema for *out₂*, e.g. *Pour out the beans, Send out the troops, Write out your ideas.* (c) Image schema for *out₃*, e.g. *The train started out for Chicago, He set out on his long journey.* From Johnson (1987)

three basic image schemas for the English verb-particle *out*. The label 'TR' designates a 'trajector' which moves or is oriented with respect to a 'landmark' ('LM'), concepts said to be generalizations of the psychological notions of figure and ground.

Aside from the CONTAINER schema, other important image schemas which have been proposed include the following: BLOCKAGE, ENABLEMENT, PATH, CYCLE, PART–WHOLE, FULL–EMPTY, ITERATION, SURFACE, BALANCE, COUNTERFORCE, ATTRACTION, LINK, NEAR–FAR, MERGING, MATCHING, CONTACT, OBJECT, COMPULSION, RESTRAINT REMOVAL, MASS–COUNT, CENTRE–PERIPHERY, SCALE, SPLITTING, STRAIGHT, SUPERIMPOSITION, PROCESS, COLLECTION (Johnson 1987: 126; Lakoff 1987; Cienki 1998).

It must be remembered, however, that these terms are intended to be merely convenient labels for embodied pre-conceptual 'experience structures', which can be better (though still not perfectly) represented by diagrams such as those in Figure 3.3.

Image schema theorists contend that schemas can be interwoven and superimposed upon one another, and elaborated by the operation of con-

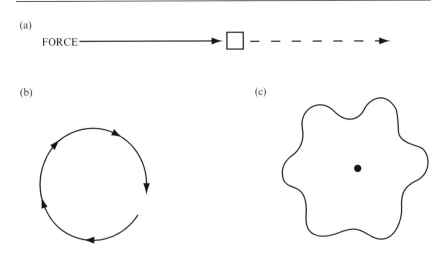

Figure 3.3. Image schema diagrams for (a) Compulsion, (B) Cycle, and (C) Center–Periphery (after Johnson 1987: 2, 120, 124)

ceptual metaphors at different levels. They are held to pervade not only the fabric of our experience, but also the fabric of our conscious understanding, including the semantic structure of language. Needless to say, these are far-reaching claims.

In NSM semantics, which is focused purely on paraphrasable conceptual content, there is nothing comparable to experiential schemas. On the other hand, there is nothing in the NSM approach that is incompatible with their existence either. NSM theorists certainly deny that conceptual meaning can be reduced to experiential schemas, but this does not necessarily mean denying their existence or their possible importance. One may very well accept that embodied, pre-conceptual experiential schemas underlie, constrain, and support the emergence of conceptual meaning without accepting that conceptual meaning is reducible to experiential schemas. Mark Johnson (1987: 5) himself expressed a similar view, though from the opposite perspective:

I am perfectly happy with talk of the conceptual/propositional content of an utterance, *but only insofar as we are aware that this propositional content is possible only by virtue of a complex web of non-propositional schematic structures that emerge from our bodily experience.* (Johnson 1987: 5, emphasis in original)

From a theoretical point of view, therefore, the two approaches could coexist, each with its distinct aims and methods. There is, however, one point on which the NSM theory necessarily has to take issue both with image schema theorists and with many others in cognitive linguistics, and this concerns their reliance on diagrammatic representations.

3.4.5 Diagrammatic representation in cognitive linguistics

Many cognitive linguists, not only image schema theorists but also those working in Ronald Langacker's (related) Cognitive Grammar approach, make heavy use of diagrams. Sometimes these diagrams are simple and schematic, like those in Figures 3.2 and 3.3. Sometimes they are much more complex, like the force-dynamic diagrams we will see later, in Chapter 10.

The primary point to be made here is that even apparently simple and transparent visual depictions are not as semiotically 'pure' as they may seem. They cannot do their intended job without the assistance of verbal captions and explanations (Goddard 1998).

Consider Figure 3.3(a), for example. Without verbal explanation I doubt very much if anyone would interpret it as depicting 'compulsion'. We need the caption and the accompanying explanation:

In such cases of compulsion, the force comes from somewhere, has a given magnitude, moves along a path, and has a direction. We can represent this image-schematic gestalt structure with the visual image below. Here the dark arrow represents an actual force vector and the broken arrow denotes a potential force vector or trajectory. (Johnson 1987: 45)

Even apparently self-explanatory diagrams are not necessarily as simple as they look. It is not clear, for example, that most people would recognize the standard cognitive linguistic diagram in Figure 3.4(a) as representing 'containment' if it were not for the aid of the caption. The diagram is open to various interpretations. Interestingly, the very similar diagram shown in Figure 3.4(b) was employed by Hawkins (1984) to designate not IN (or 'containment'), but ON. Hawkins' diagram makes sense within his own set of conventions, because these include adopting the ellipse shape

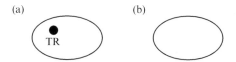

Figure 3.4. (a) IN (containment) (b) ON (profile only)

as representing SURFACE. The point is that the captions play a vital interpretive role.

None of this is to say that diagrams are perfectly equivalent to the verbal glosses of what they mean. No doubt diagrams have the capacity to convey gestalt or figural properties in a way which cannot be duplicated in words, and it may well be that properties of this kind are important for our understanding of how language works as part of the overall cognitive system. Nevertheless, since diagrams cannot achieve their purpose without verbal support, it is incumbent on cognitive linguists to have some theory about the nature of these verbal items. It can hardly be satisfactory to lumber supposedly transparent diagrams with complex, opaque, and Anglocentric terminology.

There is a further point. Even simple cognitive linguistic diagrams often—if not always—rely on western iconography and interpretive conventions. These can seem so natural to the encultured person that their artificiality is seldom noticed. For example, it seems natural to westerners that moving from left to right across the page can represent the passage of time (because European languages are read sequentially from left to right). It seems very natural that the 'top' of the page (i.e. the side canonically held furthest from the body) can represent a higher position than the 'bottom' of the page. Furthermore, the institutions of representational art and photography have entrenched the convention that, all other things being equal, images will be read as representing shapes viewed from one side and 'in perspective'.

The culture-specific nature of these conventions becomes clearer when we consider cultures that lack literacy and representational art. In the traditional Aboriginal cultures of the Australian Western Desert, for example, visual representations are usually made on the ground (as sand-drawings) or on the human body (as ceremonial designs). The usual viewpoint is from above (an aerial view), rather than from one side. In sand-drawings the placement of elements is usually done with respect to an absolute, external frame of reference; for example, a figure placed on the east side of the drawing represents someone who is on the east in the scene depicted.

Figures 3.5 and 3.6 show some figures from typical Western Desert sand-drawings (Bardon 1979; Munn 1973). In their own cultural context, figures such as the U-shape and the concentric circles are instantly recognizable as depicting human figures and camp or waterhole, respectively. Similarly,

Figure 3.5. Two people in camp

Figure 3.6. (a) kangaroo track, (b) emu track, and (c) dingo track

depictions of animal tracks (such as kangaroo, emu, and dingo) are instantly recognizable as indicating the presence or movements of those animals.

These considerations dramatize the fact that something like the 'arrow' symbol (→) of Western iconography, which is heavily relied upon in cognitive linguistic diagrams, is by no means a transparent and purely iconic sign of movement or directionality. For someone raised in the traditional Central Australian cultures, for example, it looks more like an emu track than anything else.

A final point about diagrams is that they struggle to represent concepts that lack physical or perceptual correlates. For example, how could one represent evaluational notions (GOOD and BAD) in a purely visual medium? How could one depict the difference between THINKING that something is the case and KNOWING that it is the case? How to depict the relationship of similarity (LIKE) or the notions of potentiality (CAN) or possibility (MAYBE)? It would of course be a simple matter to set up symbolic conventions that could enable us to express such concepts in a visual mode; for example, designating GOOD by a tick (✔) and BAD by a cross (✗), but these would be just visual substitutes (ciphers) for the words whose meanings they represent.

In summary, this section has raised three issues with diagrammatic representation, which challenge unexamined assumptions in much cognitive linguistic work. The first point is that diagrams cannot stand alone without verbal support. The second is that cognitive linguistic diagrams often rely on culture-specific iconographic conventions, which are 'smuggled in' without acknowledgement or explanation. The third is that diagrams cannot model concepts that lack perceptual correlates.

3.4.6 A cautionary note

Despite the valuable work being carried out under the banner of cognitive linguistics, cognitive linguistic approaches to meaning face significant challenges. Mainstream cognitive linguistics continues to underestimate metalanguage issues, with the result that many analyses fall prey to obscurity, circularity, and Anglocentrism. It remains to be seen whether the profusion of cognitive linguistic theoretical concepts can be melded together to form the basis of a comprehensive and verifiable system of cross-linguistic semantic analysis.

3.5 Back to reductive paraphrase

In the remainder of this book we will be using the tool of reductive paraphrase as we explore meaning in different realms of vocabulary and grammar. In the Exercises at the end of each chapter you will be invited to use this method yourself for solving semantic problems and, ultimately, for writing full semantic explications. Learning how to produce a viable expli- cation is a complex business which involves many component sub-skills. As you make your way through this book, working through the Exercises along the way, you will be able to develop these skills. For the moment, here are a few words of advice.

It is usually helpful to work on a group of related words at the one time, because this helps sensitize you to the subtleties of meaning involved. Collect examples of different uses of the words you are interested in, either from corpora or from personal observation. It is usually very helpful to find some contexts where a word cannot be used felicitously. You then begin to draft paraphrases, checking to see if they can be substituted into the examples in an intuitively satisfying way, and producing the right entailments. Equally important is to ensure that the explication is incom- patible (as it should be) with contexts where the word CANNOT be used. Usually many drafts and redrafts will be necessary before a satisfactory explication is found. The challenge is twofold: to find the optimal set of semantic components and to frame them in terms of correct NSM.

To safeguard against circularity, it is important to avoid using any non-primitive words unless you can be sure (at least, reasonably sure) that these are simpler than the word being defined. Many areas of the lexicon can be explicated directly into semantic primes, and it is always safer to try this in the first instance. Some semantic fields, such as emotions, speech-act verbs, and value words, seem to have a direct foothold in the inventory of primes. Emotion words like *sad*, *angry*, and *homesick*, for instance, all include components based on FEEL, THINK, and WANT. Speech-act verbs like *demand*, *promise*, and *complain* include comparable components with SAY and WANT. For areas of the lexicon that resist explication solely in terms of primes, try in the first instance to use only those semantic molecules that have been established as plausible building blocks. (There is more detail on this in later chapters.)

Usually, explications for words of a similar semantic type will share a similar overall structure or semantic template. Finding out about existing NSM work in a given area will often help, either by supplying a viable template or by providing ideas about the likely template structure in your area of interest.

When we try to follow these procedures, it turns out that it is still quite possible to work out definitions and they are often more descriptively adequate than definitions using obscure terms. However, they are usually very much longer, often running to a dozen or more component clauses. Even quite simple-sounding words often turn out to have complex meaning structures.

Key technical terms

allolexy	lexical universal
cognitive linguistics	natural semantic metalanguage (NSM)
conceptual metaphor	reductive paraphrase
cultural script	scenario
explication	semantic molecule
exponent	semantic prime
frame semantics	substitutability test
image schema	valency options

Exercises and discussion questions

† next to a problem means that a solution or some commentary can be found at the end of this book.

1†. Compare the sentences *This is unusual* and *This is abnormal*. Can you capture (in a simply phrased component) a part of the meaning of *abnormal* which is not shared by *unusual*?

2†. Below there are two pairs of words whose meanings are similar but not identical. For each pair, find an example of a sentence where one of the words would be acceptable ('make good sense'), but the other would be unacceptable. Stick to ordinary, straightforward uses, avoiding metaphorical uses. In your own words, comment on one aspect of the meaning difference between the two words. Try to do this in a clear, simple way.

   a. *cried – wept*
   b. *horrified – terrified*

3†. Consider the words *know* and *good*. These have been proposed as semantic primes, which means that it is claimed that it is impossible to explain their meanings using simpler words. Experiment. See if you can come up with any possible ways of defining the meanings of *know* and *good* as used in sentences like these:

   I don't know.
   I know where she is.
   Something good happened to me.
   He is a good person.

4†. Assess the following set of definitions, based on the *Oxford Paperback Dictionary*, from the point of view of obscurity and circularity, and of descriptive adequacy. (Don't worry about other meanings of the same words, e.g. *glare* as in *the glare of the sun*.)

   gaze: to look long and steadily
   glare: to stare angrily or fiercely
   stare: to gaze fixedly with the eyes open, especially in astonishment
   watch: to look at, to keep one's eyes fixed on, to keep under observation

5†. Consider the meanings of the verbs *swing*, *wave*, and *wag* as used in the sentences below and answer the questions. Frame your answers as clearly and simply as you can.

   John swung the bat.
   Maria waved the flag.
   Fido wagged his tail.

a. What are the similarities between the situations depicted in these sentences? Consider both the movements of the bat, flag, and ball, and the actions being performed by John, Maria, and Fido.

b. What are some of the differences between the actions being performed?

c. What is the typical purpose of *swinging* something? What is the typical purpose of *waving* something?

d. Of the three verbs, *wag* is the most restricted. A fish could *wiggle* its tail, but it couldn't *wag* it. Horses and elephants can move their tails, for instance to get rid of flies, but this isn't called *wagging* either. How can you explain this?

6†. One of words most discussed in connection with prototypes is *game*. Consider the meaning of this word as used in expressions like *play a game, a game of tennis*, or *a kids' game*. Suppose that a dictionary attempted to explicate the meaning of *game* as follows.

1. an amusement or pastime e.g. *a children's game*;
2. a contest for amusement in the form of a trial of chance, skill or endurance, according to set rules, e.g. *games of football, golf*, etc.

Assess these definitions from the point of view of obscurity and descriptive adequacy. For each criticism you make, suggest an improvement. Do you think it is possible to produce a single definition which will cover all the activities we call *games*?

7. Consider the drawings in Figure 3.7. Rank the objects shown in terms of how well they correspond to your idea of a *cup*. Get a couple of your friends or family members to do the same exercise for you. Do you think that people agree in their intuitions about what is an ideal or prototypical *cup*? What are some of the factors that seem to characterize the prototypical *cup*?

8†. In Lakoff and Johnson (1980: 47) the following sets of expressions are grouped together as instances of a single conceptual metaphor about ideas. See if you can formulate an intuitively plausible conceptual metaphor (of the form IDEAS ARE ——) to cover all these examples. You may find that one or more of the examples don't really seem to fit well into your proposed metaphor; if so, what would you do about this?

The theory of relativity *gave birth* to an enormous number of ideas in physics. He is the *father* of modern biology. Whose *brainchild* is that? Look at what his ideas have *spawned*. Those ideas *died off* in the Middle Ages. Cognitive psychology is still in its *infancy*. That's an idea that ought to be *resurrected*. Where'd you *dig up* that idea? He *breathed new life* into that idea.

9. The main character in Naomi Mitchison's (1985 [1962]) novel *Memoirs of a Spacewoman* is a communications officer, whose job is establishing communication with life-forms on other planets. She describes the inhabitants of one world as follows:

Figure 3.7. Cups, mugs, and similar objects

in Lambda 771 the inhabitants evolutionary descent had been in a radial form, something like a five-armed starfish, itself developing out of a spiral...[they had] arms of a kind that could be partially retracted, flattened and so on, and which were studded with suckers which could be used to hold tools [p. 20]...Their main organs were, of course, central and not oriented in any direction [p. 23]...These creatures had a definite top and bottom, necessary above all for gravitation. But the radial pattern which had developed out of the budding spiral had remained throughout evolution and completely dominated all mental and psychic processes [p. 20].

Cognitive linguistic theorists also stress that the physical form of the human body profoundly influences human experience and, therefore, human mental processes. Use the Lambda 771 scenario as a springboard for discussion. How do you think the minds of the 'radial beings' of Lambda 771 might differ from our own minds?

4

The semantics of emotions

We now change gears, moving from an overview of issues and controversies into detailed case studies in a range of different semantic fields. Not that issues and controversies will cease to concern us. On the contrary, we are studying emotions and speech acts, for instance, precisely because they highlight and sharpen theoretical and methodological conflicts in semantics, and because they illustrate how the study of linguistic semantics is influenced by the other human sciences, and how linguistic semantics can influence them.

4.1 Approaches to the emotions

Emotions are a subject which seems to interest most people, I suppose because most of us are interested both in our own feelings and in those of others. In the last twenty years or so, the nature of emotions and the meaning of emotion terms have been much discussed in anthropology and psychology, as well as in semantics. To begin with, then, a few words on this background. One of the perennial issues is the relationship between emotions and the body.

The strongest position is that emotions are essentially physical, i.e. bodily, in nature. This was the view of the early American psychologist-philosopher William James (cf. Solomon 1984), who advocated a PHYSICALIST theory of emotion. James thought that fear, for instance, more or less consisted of the bodily symptoms of trembling, excitement, and so on, together with our awareness of them. While this idea has a certain appeal, it is open to many objections. For instance, there are some emotions, such as happiness, that don't seem to have any characteristic (or prototypical) bodily signs associated with them. It is also hard to imagine that physical descriptions alone could capture distinctions as fine as those between *distressed*, *miserable*, *downhearted*, and *despondent*.

Many psychologists believe that emotions are, if not physical in the Jamesian sense, then at least physiological—because (they believe) certain BASIC EMOTIONS are inbuilt as part of human neurophysiology (Izard 1977; 2009; Ekman 1992; 2004). 'Anger', 'fear', 'surprise', 'sadness', 'joy', and 'disgust' are the most widely accepted candidates. Other emotions are explained as amalgams of these, e.g. *delight = joy + surprise*. Proponents usually place great reliance on the claim that each supposed basic emotion has its own specific facial expression, which can be accurately identified (i.e. matched with the appropriate emotion) across language and culture barriers (see section 12.5 for a critical view). Though still common in introductory psychology textbooks, the basic emotions position has come under criticism, even within psychology, for its assumption that emotional variation across cultures is fairly limited and for methodological failings in the experiments on facial recognition, among other reasons (cf. Ortony and Turner 1990; Russell 1991; 1994; Shweder 2004; Barrett et al. 2007).

The view that emotional experience differs relatively little across cultures has also been assailed by anthropologists, who have documented surprising diversity in the emotional lives of people in other cultures. Landmark studies include Briggs (1995; 2000) on the Inuit, Lutz (1988) on the Ifaluk people of Micronesia, Rosaldo (1980) on the Ilongot (Philippines), and Overing and Passes (2000) on Amazonian cultures. Psychological and literary studies on bilingualism and the bilingual experience testify in the same direction (Pavlenko 2005; Besemeres and Wierzbicka 2007). NSM linguists have contributed many studies which demonstrate cross-linguistic differences in the meanings of emotion words, and at the same time show that many languages lack any words whose meanings match those of the supposed basic emotions (Wierzbicka 1999; Harkins and

Wierzbicka 2001; Enfield and Wierzbicka 2002; Goddard 1996a; 2010b; Gladkova 2010a; 2010b; 2010c; Levisen 2010).

Two well-known rival positions to the basic emotions theory are the cognitive and social constructivist approaches. The so-called COGNITIVE APPROACH to emotions (Averill 1980; Oatley and Johnson-Laird 1987; Ortony, Clone, and Collins 1988; Power and Dalgleish 2008) holds that emotions depend in large part on cognitive processes (appraisals). For example, it holds that *anger* is evoked and partly constituted by the thought that one has been wronged, together with an urge to retaliate; that *sadness* is evoked and partly constituted by an appraisal of 'loss'. The SOCIAL CONSTRUCTIVIST APPROACH (Harré 1986) stresses the cultural aspect of emotions, saying that social judgements, cultural values, and other cultural practices actually shape and create emotions; in the words of Clifford Geertz (1975: 81), that emotions are 'cultural artifacts', embodying shared understandings of human nature and social interaction.

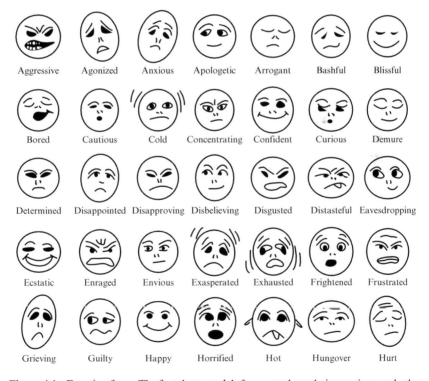

Figure 4.1. Emotion faces. The fact that people's faces can show their emotions and other feelings has given rise to many creative and amusing illustrations and t-shirt designs. The famous 'happy face' Smiley was devised by Harvey Ball in 1963. It paved the way for the many 'emoticons' used in texting, blogs, and so on (Hollier, Murray, and Cornelius 2008)

Trying to tackle the meaning of emotions across cultural divides raises the dilemma of how to ensure our inquiries are not distorted by ETHNOCEN- TRISM (i.e. culture bias). One source of ethnocentrism in studies of emotion is the practice of using complex and English-specific terms as though they were part of a universal, culture-free metalanguage. Obviously, it is no good 'explaining' the meanings of words like Ilongot *liget* or Ifaluk *song* in terms of 'anger' if these languages do not have equivalents to 'anger' in the first place. That would be imposing an English point of view.

How then can we proceed at all, if we can't use culture-specific, English words without biasing the whole procedure? The most promising avenue is to resort to simpler English words, which evidence suggests have counter- parts in most, if not all, other languages (Wierzbicka 1999; 1986a; Goddard 2007). These include the semantic primes FEEL, THINK, WANT, KNOW, GOOD, and BAD. So let us make a start exploring the linguistic semantics of emotion words, in English and in other languages.

4.2 Semantic components of emotion words

Remember that from a semantic point of view, our interest is not so much in the 'reality' of emotional experience (if we could ever access that), but rather in the meaning of the words by which people discuss and describe emotions.

4.2.1 Iordanskaja's work on Russian emotions

Some of the earliest semantic work on the meaning structure of emotion words was done by Lidija Iordanskaja (1974) on Russian. Iordanskaja sees the fundamental requirement of semantics as 'standardizing the semantic description of language units', and accepts the need to formulate defin- itions in terms which are as uniform as possible and do not fall into circularity. Essentially, she sets out to develop paraphrase-style definitions, though she tolerates a fair bit of technical-sounding language.

The following summary of Iordanskaja's proposals may be a little hard to follow at times. You may sometimes have the feeling that you don't really know what these Russian words mean. I hope this may have a sobering, even a salutary effect—helping to bring you to a clear realization of two points. First, that the emotion terms of different cultures really do not match up. And secondly, that the challenge for semantic description is to analyse the meanings in question in a clear and complete way, accessible to a cultural outsider.

Iordanskaja's main proposal is that, in general, the definition of an emotion term should consist of two kinds of component: an 'internal description of the emotional state' and 'the reason for its occurrence'. The internal description takes in such things as whether the feeling is positive (a good feeling) or negative (a bad feeling), and whether or not it is 'active' or 'passive', i.e. whether or not it is coupled with a desire to do anything. For instance, *vosxiščenie* 'delight, rapture' is a positive active state, *ogorčenie* 'grief' is a negative, passive state, and *gnev* 'anger, rage' is a negative, active state. (All these English glosses are, of course, approximate.)

This type of characterization alone could hardly provide enough detail to differentiate the various emotion terms from one another. The principal part of an emotion definition, as Iordanskaja sees it, gives the reason or typical conditions for its occurrence:

Such a reason is always an evaluation of some event by the subject of the emotion, that is, an aggregate of opinions on this event, its evaluation from the point of view of its desirability, and for active states, a wish in connection with this event. (Iordanskaja 1974: 90)

Of course, the 'event' need not actually have occurred, so long as the person thinks it has occurred (or that it will or might occur, as the case may be).

Iordanskaja was able to classify Russian emotion words into six groups—*radost'* 'joy', *gnev* 'anger, rage', *ogorčenie* 'grief', *strax* 'fear', *nadežda* 'hope', and *udivlenie* 'surprise'. The main features she used for this classification were: the experiencer's assessment of the likelihood of the triggering event, whether the experiencer evaluates the event as good or bad, and whether or not the experiencer wants to do anything in relation to the trigger event.

In the *strax* 'fear' and *nadežda* 'hope' groups, the experiencer (let's call him or her X) thinks that a future event is probable, but the two groups differ according to whether or not X wants it to happen. The other groups concern an event which the experiencer is sure has already taken place. The *radost'* 'joy' group is characterized by that event being desirable for X. The *gnev* 'anger, rage' and *ogorčenie* 'grief' groups, on the other hand, share the contrary component, i.e. that the event is not desirable for X. Where they differ is on whether or not X wants to do something on account of what has happened—*gnev* 'anger, rage' feelings are active and motivating, whereas *ogorčenie* 'grief' feelings are passive.

Within each group there are from one to twelve individual words, which must be differentiated by further and subtler specifications. For example, within the *radost'* 'joy' group, the words *vosxiščat'sja* 'be delighted with' and *radovat'sja* 'be glad of' differ in that the former implies an absolute judgement of value whereas the latter only implies that something has happened which the experiencer wants. For instance, to describe X's reaction to a remark someone else made in a conversation in terms of *vosxiščat'sja* implies that X believes that the remark was a very good thing to say in itself, whereas to describe X's reaction in terms of *raduetsja* merely implies that the remark moved the conversation in the direction X wanted.

To take a second example, within the *gnev* 'anger, rage' group one important difference is between the 'noble' and the merely personal emotions. In the case of the former (like *vozmuščenie* and *negodovanie* 'indignation'), the experiencer is moved by a judgement about how people in general should act, whereas with the latter (like *gnev* 'anger, rage', *dosada* 'vexation, annoyance', and *zavist'* 'envy') the experiencer's concern is with the adverse effect on him or herself. Also, *gnev* 'anger, rage' implies a desire to do something to the person who has done something which the experiencer thinks is bad and doesn't want; but *vozmuščenie* and *negodovanie* 'indignation' are not necessarily focused on particular persons—rather, the experiencer's objective is to counteract the objectionable event.

4.2.2 Wierzbicka on emotion concepts

From her earliest work on emotions, Wierzbicka (1972) has employed the concept of a prototypical scenario, taking her cue in this regard from literature. In Tolstoy's *Anna Karenina* the author conveys a great variety of subtle emotions by means of ingenious hypothetical scenarios. For example: (i) Kitty is awaiting a decisive visit: 'From after dinner till early evening, Kitty felt as a young man does before a battle'; (ii) Hitherto his wife's soul had been open to Karenin: 'He felt now rather as a man might do returning home and finding his own house locked up'; (iii) At the station, Vronsky catches sight of Anna's husband: 'Vronsky...had such a disagreeable sensation as a man tortured by thirst might feel on reaching a spring and finding a dog, sheep, or a pig in it, drinking the water and making it muddy.'

References to imaginary situations of this kind, while highly evocative, are essentially individual and do not have the force of generalizations. Wierzbicka's insight was that the emotion words of ordinary language work in a similar fashion, except that instead of linking feelings with illustrative situations they link them with prototypical cognitive scenarios involving thoughts and wants. For instance, *sadness* is a bad feeling linked with thinking 'something bad happened', *remorse* is a bad feeling linked with thinking 'I did something bad', *joy* is a good feeling linked with thinking 'something very good is happening now'. There is an obvious similarity with Iordanskaja's notion that emotions are largely distinguished from one another by the (subjective) 'reasons' for the occurrence.

4.2.3 Semantic templates for emotion words

As mentioned in Chapter 3, an important observation about lexical semantics in general is that explications for words of a similar kind conform to a common structural pattern. Emotion words are no exception in this respect. In earlier NSM work, the term 'format' was used to refer to this aspect of the explications, but more recently the term SEMANTIC TEMPLATE has been adopted.

Over the years, Wierzbicka and other NSM researchers have experimented with slightly different semantic templates for emotion words. Current work favours the following template for expressions like *She/he was happy*, *She/he is angry*, *She/he will be disappointed*, etc.; that is, expressions that use an emotion adjective in combination with the copular verb 'to be', in one of its forms. The basic idea is that being *happy*, *angry*, *disappointed*, or whatever, means being in a certain state of mind and because of that experiencing a certain kind of feeling which is seen as normally linked with such a mental state.

Semantic template for English emotion adjectives with verb 'to be'; e.g.,
Someone X was happy/angry/disappointed (etc.) at this time.

a.   someone X thought like this at this time:

   '_ _ _ _

   _ _ _ _'

b.   because of this, this someone felt something (very) good/bad at this time
c.   like someone can feel when they think like this

This template has three parts, which for convenience are labelled here (a), (b), and (c). Part (a) is introduced by the line 'someone X thought like this at this time', and after this follows the PROTOTYPICAL COGNITIVE SCENARIO. This usually constitutes the bulk of the explication. After the scenario, in the component labelled (b), comes the statement that the individual feels something as a result; usually the 'feeling tone' is specified as 'good' or 'bad' (or as 'very good' or 'very bad'). Finally, in the component labelled (c), this feeling is characterized as (so to speak) typical of how people feel when they have such thoughts.

A different template is used for expressions like *She/he felt happy*, *He/she feels angry*, *He/she feels disappointed*, etc.; that is, where an emotion adjective is used in combination with the verb 'to feel', in one of its forms.

Semantic template for English emotion adjectives with verb 'to feel'; e.g.,
Someone X felt happy/angry/disappointed (etc.) at this time.

this someone felt something (very) good/bad at this time
like someone can feel when they think like this:

   '_ _ _ _

   _ _ _ _'

The idea is that using an emotion adjective with the verb 'to feel' highlights the 'feeling aspect'. In effect, the relative priority of the feeling state and the cognitive state are swapped around. Incidentally, the structure of this template explains why it is possible to 'feel' some emotions (for instance, to *feel sad* or to *feel happy*) without necessarily being aware of the cause. Saying that someone *feels joy*, for instance, is not saying that the experiencer necessarily thinks 'something very good is happening now'. Rather, it is saying that this person feels something very good like someone can feel who is thinking that thought.

In this book, we will stick mainly to examples of *being happy/angry/disappointed*, etc., so we will be using the first of the two templates. It should also be pointed out that some emotion terms (both in English and in other languages) will require other templates, in order to accommodate subtle differences between different sub-classes of emotion meanings, but there is no need for us to go into these complications here.

4.2.4 Pleased, contented, *and* delighted

Let's have a quick look at what different kinds of components can be found in emotion templates, by comparing a group of English words: *pleased, contented,* and *delighted.* The treatment follows Wierzbicka (1999). All three are obviously good feelings, but *delighted* conveys a 'stronger' feeling than the other two. We can capture this difference by positing for *delighted* the component 'this someone felt something very good at this time', while the corresponding component for the more moderate words can be simply: 'this someone felt something good at this time.' Of course this only accounts for a small part of the difference between the three words. The main burden of discriminating between them falls on their respective prototypical cognitive scenarios.

Based on Wierzbicka's discussion, we can posit for *pleased* a fairly simple prototypical thought, along the following lines: 'something good happened before, I wanted this.' The component suggests someone who is, so to speak, reviewing a particular past event. For *contented,* on the other hand, the experiencer's mind is focused on the present, i.e. on what is happening now, and it is also focused on oneself. The prototypical thought can therefore be characterized: 'something good is happening to me now, I want this.' In addition, the word *contented* implies that one's wishes are fully met, at least for the present, so we should add the component: 'I don't want anything else now.'

The explications for *pleased* and *contented* would therefore look as follows. Notice how slight variations in the phrasing allow us to portray subtle differences in the effect conveyed by one word, as opposed to the other.

Someone X was pleased at this time:

someone X thought like this at this time:
  'something good happened before
  I wanted this'
because of this, this someone felt something good at this time
  like someone can feel when they think like this

Someone X was contented at this time:

someone X thought like this at this time:
  'something good is happening to me now
  I want this
  I don't want anything else now'
because of this, this someone felt something good at this time
  like someone can feel when they think like this

Now let's bring a third word into the picture. As with *pleased*, the cognitive scenario for *delighted* is connected with knowing that something good (in fact, very good) has happened, but *delighted* implies something more immediate. To capture this effect, we can begin its prototypical cognitive scenario with the component 'something very good happened a short time before': the temporal adjunct 'a short time before' indicates that the triggering event is seen as recent. Furthermore, unlike as with *pleased*, *delighted* suggests something akin to *surprise*. How can this be captured? Arguably, the key component in concepts such as *surprise*, *amazement*, and the like, concerns the experiencer's knowledge state. Roughly speaking, we feel *surprise* when something happens that we did not know would happen (Goddard 1997a). This suggests that we add to the prototypical cognitive scenario for *delighted* a component like this: 'I didn't know that this would happen.' The overall explication therefore becomes:

Someone X was delighted at this time:

someone X thought like this at this time:
   'something very good happened a short time before
   I didn't know that this would happen'
because of this, this someone felt something very good at this time
   like someone can feel when they think like this

Perhaps it is worth noting at this point that it is no coincidence that we have chosen to explicate these emotion words in a third-person frame, i.e. in sentences whose subject is 'someone', rather than 'I'. The reason is that many emotion adjectives appear in conventionalized first-person formulas, such as *I'm delighted (to)*, *I'm afraid (that)*, and the like. Formulas like these need to be treated separately, because in the context of the formula the emotion word does not have the same significance as it has in its 'free' uses. For example, though one often hears someone welcome a speaker to the stage with a formula like *I'm delighted to introduce (so-and-so)*, one could not normally say about the person making such an introduction: *?He/she was delighted to introduce (so-and-so)*. (Here, as elsewhere in this book, a raised question mark indicates that the expression is semantically odd or anomalous.) Likewise, someone who 'softens' a refusal by saying *I'm afraid that's not possible* can hardly be described as being *afraid*. As these examples suggest, when in doubt about whether a particular first-person usage of an emotion word is or isn't a formulaic one, a simple test is to transpose the sentence into the past tense or to substitute a non-first-person subject. In the following, we will only concern ourselves with non-formulaic uses of emotion terms.

4.3 Some English emotion words

Let's start with English *happy* and *happiness*. Both are very common words and highly salient ones too. *Happiness* is, after all, one of the ideals of modern Anglo life (as reflected in its place in, among other things, the American Declaration of Independence, with its goal of 'the pursuit of happiness'). Nevertheless, the concept of *happiness* is not as simple as it may seem, both because the frame of mind linked with being *happy* is fairly general and abstract, and also because the English word *happy* is polysemous.

4.3.1 Happy *and* happiness *in English and in broader European perspective*

Consider sentences with *happy*, such as *I'm happy, Are you happy?, He/she was happy*. One thing such sentences no doubt convey is that the subject is feeling something good for some time. But what is the associated frame of mind? Wierzbicka (2010b; forthcoming) proposes that it is more 'generic' than related words like *pleased* and *contented*—rather than being a response to actual events, it is more a response to the experiencer's general assessment of his or her situation. She suggests that the prototypical cognitive scenario includes the following thoughts:

'many good things are happening to me now as I want
I can do many things now as I want
this is good'

This represents a significant change from the analysis presented in the first edition of this book, notably in its focus on the present situation ('now') and on the experiencer's sense that he/she is, as it were, free to do as he or she wants ('I can do many things now as I want'). The idea is that describing someone as *happy* means portraying that person as focusing on and appreciating the good things that are happening to him/her, and on that person's sense that they can do as they wish.

As just mentioned, one of the complications with English *happy* is that it has several polysemic meanings. One of the most characteristic is in the expression *happy with*, as in examples like:

I'm happy with my results.
I'm happy with the outcome.

Arguably, the same meaning can also occur without any accompanying 'with-phrase'; for example:

I'm happy where I am.
He seems happy enough.

Examples like these can be converted to equivalents phrased with a '*with-*phrase', e.g. *I'm happy with my present situatio*n. The point is that the word *happy* has a second meaning which can be linked with the expression *happy with*. Intuitively, this meaning differs from the emotional meaning of *happy*, in that it does not express *happiness*. Another indicator that this is a separate meaning to 'emotional *happy*' is that the former has its antonyms in *unhappy* and *sad*, whereas the latter has its antonym in *not happy*.

This extended meaning of English *happy* has no counterparts in other European languages. For example, one can say in English *I am happy with his answer*, but one could not use German *glücklich* or French *heureux* in this way. Instead one would have to use quite different words, such as *zufrieden* or *satisfait/content* (roughly, 'pleased'):

— *Ich bin zufrieden (*glücklich) mit seiner Antwort.* [German]
'I am pleased with his answer.'
— *Je suis satisfait (*heureux) de sa réponse.* [French]
'I am happy with his answer.'

Returning to the emotional meaning of English *happy*, if we embed the proposed prototypical thoughts into our normal semantic template, we arrive at the following explication:

Someone X was happy at this time:

someone X thought like this at this time:
    'many good things are happening to me now as I want
    I can do many things now as I want
    this is good'
because of this, this someone felt something good at this time
    like someone can feel when they think like this

According to Wierzbicka (2010b), the meanings of the English words *happy* and *happiness* have shifted over the last few centuries. Before the eighteenth century, they referred to a more intense, more exceptional, and more short-lived feeling, linked with something like good luck or good fortune. In a series of semantic shifts, English *happiness* has morphed into its present milder and more generic meaning. In many other European languages, however, words corresponding to *happy* are closer in meaning to the earlier English meaning (a short-lived, exceptional, very good feeling). For example, the following explication has been proposed for German *glücklich* and French *heureux*:

> *Someone X was* glücklich (heureux) *at this time:*
>
> someone X thought like this at this time:
>   'something very good is happening to me now
>   this is very good
>   things like this don't often happen to people
>   I can't want anything more now'
> because of this, this someone felt something very good at this time
>   like someone can feel when they think like this

German *glücklich* and French *heureux* are closer to English *joyful* than to *happy*, both in the first component in the cognitive scenario ('something very good is happening to me now') and in designating a 'very good' feeling (not merely a 'good' one, as with *happy*). The component 'I can't want anything more now' is a little like one that we saw for *contented* ('I don't want anything else now'), except that for *glücklich/heureux* the component is much 'stronger' ('I can't want' vs. 'I don't want'). One component of the *glücklich/heureux* explication is quite different, however, from anything we have seen so far: namely, the thought that 'things like this don't often happen to people'. Such a thought links these feelings with concepts such as 'luck' and 'good fortune'.

Many other European languages have common words which are similar (if not identical) in meaning to that of *glücklich/heureux*; for example, *felice* in Italian, *sčastliv* in Russian, *szczęśliwy* in Polish. English seems to be the odd one out with its relatively bland word *happy*. It might well be observed that the comparatively muted quality of most English words for good feelings is consistent with the traditional Anglo-Saxon distaste for extreme emotions.

4.3.2 Sad *and related words* (unhappy *and* depressed)

Returning to English, let us ask: What's the difference between 'being *sad*' and 'being *unhappy*'? Conventional dictionaries cannot shed much light on this question, because their definitions are flawed by circularity, reliance on more obscure terms than the ones being defined, and other lexicographic problems. For example, the *Australian Oxford Dictionary* defines *sad* as 'unhappy, feeling sorrow or regret', *unhappy* as 'not happy, miserable', and *miserable* as 'wretchedly unhappy or uncomfortable'. On this account, the words *sad* and *unhappy* would be pretty much the same in meaning, but this does not tally with the intuitions of native speakers or with the evidence of usage. There are contexts in which one could use one word but not the other, or where the choice of one word or the other would lead to different implications, as suggested by the examples below. These examples, and the explications that follow, are based on Wierzbicka (1999: 60–3).

a. *I miss you a lot at work . . . I feel so sad (*unhappy) about what's happening to you.*
    [said to a colleague in hospital who is dying of cancer]
b. *I was unhappy at work.* [suggests dissatisfaction]
c. *I was sad at work.* [suggests depression, sorrow, etc.]

One difference is that one can be *sad* in response to a much broader range of events: for instance, if my neighbour's close friend dies, or if my cat dies, I am more likely to be *sad* than *unhappy*. As well, being *unhappy* suggests a more active frame of mind than *sad*. If someone says *I am unhappy about it*, they may be indicating that they intend to do something about it, or at least that they are considering it. To a large extent, these differences can be captured in the explications below.

First let's consider *sad*. The explication contains components suggesting something like resignation and acceptance.

Someone X was sad at this time:

someone X thought like this at this time:
  'I know that something bad happened
  I don't want things like this to happen
  I can't think like this: I can do something because of this
  I know that I can't do anything'
because of this, this someone felt something bad at this time
  like someone can feel when they think like this

The following explication for *unhappy* differs in several ways. The cognitive scenario starts with a more personal event ('some bad things happened to me'), and it suggests an unaccepting and potentially active response.

Someone X was unhappy at this time:

someone X thought like this at this time:
   'some bad things happened to me
   I wanted things like this not to happen to me
   I can't not think about it'
because of this, this someone felt something bad at this time
   like someone can feel when they think like this

It is a testimony to the influence that psychology and therapy have had on how we view ourselves that the word *depressed* is in common use in everyday life. As it happens, it too is a strikingly English-specific word, lacking equivalents (even near-equivalents) in many languages. The following explication shows how its meaning can be unpacked in terms of semantic primes. It differs from the other 'sad' words we've looked at in including a judgemental, quasi-clinical perspective ('it is bad for someone if this someone thinks like this').

Someone X was depressed at this time:

someone X thought like this at this time:
   'good things can't happen to me
   if I want to do anything good, I can't do it
   I can't do anything'
because of this, this someone felt something bad at this time
   like someone can feel when they think like this
it is bad for someone if this someone thinks like this

4.4 Culture-specific emotions

In a sense, all emotion terms are somewhat culture-specific. The emotion meanings of any language provide its speakers with an interpretive framework through which to categorize and understand their own and other people's feelings. In this way the emotion lexicon actually helps constitute the culture, a point which has been stressed by the psychologist Jerome Bruner (1990: 35) in his important book *Acts of Meaning*. Bruner draws attention to the fact that every culture has a somewhat different FOLK PSYCHOLOGY, and that we wind up as we are partly through having been socialized according to the view of human nature embodied in our folk psychology.

All cultures have as one of their most powerful constitutive instruments a folk psychology, a set of more or less connected, more or less normative descriptions of how human beings 'tick', what our own and other minds are like, what one can expect situated action to be like, what are the possible modes of life, how one commits oneself to them, and so on. We learn our culture's folk psychology early, learn it as we learn to use the very language we acquire and to conduct the interpersonal transactions required in communal life.

The inventory of emotions labelled by the words of any language are one of the most important components of its folk psychology. We now look briefly at three particularly clear examples of emotions which can be directly related to the values and priorities of a culture.

4.4.1 Japanese amae

The concept of *amae* has been characterized as a 'peculiarly Japanese' emotion. It was made famous by the Japanese psychiatrist Takeo Doi in his long-standing best-seller *Amae no Kōzō* (1971; translated as *The Anatomy of Dependence* 2002 [1973]). Doi claimed that *amae* is 'a key concept for the understanding not only of the psychological makeup of the individual Japanese but of the structure of Japanese society as a whole' (p. 28). According to Doi, Japanese people find it hard to believe that English and other Western languages lack a word for the (to them) seemingly universal concept of *amae*. As one of Doi's colleagues remarked, 'Why, even a puppy does it' (p. 15).

Doi's book is over three decades old now. In the meantime, *amae* has become something of a sensitive and contested concept in the ongoing discourse about 'Japanese-ness' and modernity. Some now insist that Doi's portrayal of the '*amae* syndrome' was always exaggerated and distorted (Dale 1986); others say that although it was once appropriate, times have changed. Be that as it may, from a semantic point of view, the challenge remains: What exactly does it mean to *amaeru*?

Kenkyusha's New Japanese–English Dictionary (1974) defines the verb *amaeru* as 'to presume upon (another's) love' and 'to take advantage of (another's) kindness)'. Doi gives glosses like: 'to depend and presume on another's benevolence' (1974: 145) and 'presuming on some special relationship' (2002: 29). Some Japanese–English dictionaries list it as 'coaxing'.

Kojima and Crane's *A Dictionary of Japanese Culture* (1987) explains it as 'to indulge in a feeling of security as a child feels with its loving mother'.

This last explanation relies on the fact, highlighted by Doi, that the psychological prototype for *amae* is the way an infant feels for his or her mother. Interestingly, Doi notes that a baby cannot *amaeru*, as the feeling depends on conscious awareness: 'the seeking after the mother that comes when the infant's mind has developed to a certain degree and it has realised that its mother exists independently of itself' (2002: 74). According to traditional Japanese values, however, the desire to *amaeru* is not necessarily seen as childish but can be expected (and respected) in a range of adult relationships, for example, between husband and wife, and in formal relationships of dependency and support, such as between teacher and student, and doctor and patient.

The explication below, adapted somewhat from Wierzbicka (1992a: 136–7), is for the noun *amae*. It presents it as a good feeling that follows from recognizing that there is someone (Y) powerful and well-intentioned ('Y can do good things for me', 'Y wants to do good things for me') with whom one is completely protected ('when I am with Y, nothing bad can happen to me'). Naturally then, the experiencer wants to be with Y.

Someone X feels amae *(towards Y) at this time:*
someone X thinks like this at this time (about someone Y):
  'this someone can do good things for me
  this someone wants to do good things for me
  when I am with this someone, nothing bad can happen to me
  I want to be with this someone'
because of this, this someone feels something good at this time
  like someone can feel when this someone thinks like this

Cross-cultural commentators often point out that Japanese culture places positive value on 'dependency' or 'interdependency' (rather than on independence and autonomy, as in the West). This has been linked with Japanese child-raising, which is characterized by intimate contact with the mother. One linguistic barrier to cross-cultural appreciation is the lack of match-up between words for Japanese and English cultural concepts. The word 'dependence' is particularly unhelpful in this regard, given its strong negative connotations in English. Wierzbicka concludes her discussion of *amae* with the hope that semantic explications can help make this concept 'a little more intelligible to the cultural outsider' (1992a: 137).

4.4.2 Polish tęsknić

The Polish words *tęsknić* (verb) and *tęsknota* (noun) have no exact equivalents in English, though in different contexts they could be translated as *homesick, missing, longing, pining*, or *nostalgic* (Wierzbicka 1992a: 121–3; Goddard and Wierzbicka 2008). For example, if a teenage daughter leaves the family home and goes to study in a distant city, the emotion felt by her Polish parents could be described using the verb *tęsknić*, but one could not say that they were *homesick* for her, or that they felt *nostalgia* for her, or that they were *pining* for her. One could say in English that they *missed* her, but *missed* implies a less intense—and less painful—feeling. Also, one can *miss* someone who has died (e.g. *My grandmother died recently. You have no idea how much I miss her*), but one could not use Polish *tęsknić* like this, because it implies a real separation in space. Probably the best short English gloss for *tęsknić* is 'the pain of distance'.

The following explication is for the verb *tęsknić* when used about a person. In Polish, one feels this way *do* 'towards' someone. (A slightly different explication will be needed when *tęsknić* is used about a place. Can you see what adjustments to make?)

Someone X tęskni *('feels* tęsknota*') (do 'towards' Y) at this time:*

someone X thinks like this at this time (about someone Y):
    'this someone is very far from the place where I am now
    because of this, I can't be with this someone now
    when I was with this someone before, I felt something good
    I want to be with this someone now'
because of this, this someone feels something very bad at this time
    like someone can feel when this someone thinks like this

Wierzbicka (1992a) explains the cultural salience of the words *tęsknić* and *tęsknota* in terms of the history of the Polish people. Before the eighteenth century these words designated a kind of vague sadness, as the related Russian word *toska* does to this day. It was only after the partitions of Poland at the end of the eighteenth century, and especially after the defeat of the Polish Uprising in 1830, that *tęsknić* and *tęsknota* began to develop their present-day meanings. It was in this period that the best, and most influential, Polish writers were in political exile abroad, separated from relatives, friends, and from their beloved homeland. Naturally they, and their writings, soon became consumed with nostalgia, or rather, with *tęsknota*.

4.4.3 Malay marah

One of the emotion concepts of the Malay people which has most confused Western observers but which at the same time is central to ordinary Malay interaction is *marah*. It is often glossed as 'angry'. But though English *angry* and *marah* are both unpleasant reactions to the perception that someone else has done something wrong, the nature of the prototypical responses is so different that English terms like 'offended' and 'resentful' are semantically closer to *marah* than is 'angry'. From a Western point of view, one of the most salient things about the *marah* response is its muted, restrained nature. Malays are known, on the one hand, for the ease with which they take offence and, on the other, for their reluctance to express it explicitly. Rather than the outburst of hostile words and physical symptoms characteristic of 'anger', there is a lingering period of sullen brooding, described by the verb *merajuk*, which may last for days, weeks, or months before subsiding.

Among friends and family, one may candidly ask or comment on whether another person is *marah*. The accusation that someone is *marah* is also found in teasing and mockery. Such explicit mentions of *marah* are very often linked with observations about tone of voice and facial expression. In literature, the attribution of *marah* is often accompanied by a comment on the demeanour of the character, as in the example below:

> '*Awak ni Anum, marah awak masih tak padam-padam pada si Hafiz tu. Buruk baiknya dia tetap anak kita,' tingkah Encik Eman bila dilihatnya muncung isterinya itu semakin panjang.* (Nasir 1989: 5)
> ' "What's with you Anum, you're still angry with Hafiz. Good or bad, he's still our child," retorted Encik Eman when he saw his wife's face becoming long.'

As for the prototypical cognitive stimulus for *marah*, at first it appears to be the same as for English 'angry', viz. the thought that 'someone did something bad'. But closer inspection suggests that there is something more personal about *marah*, more akin to English 'offended' than to 'angry'. Typical examples would be the reaction to being teased or embarrassed in front of others. People are often described as *marah* as a result of having been shabbily treated, or as a reaction to a family member or friend being so treated. 'Taking it personally' is an important aspect of the prototypical scenario for *marah*. Interestingly, one could not speak of protesters as being *marah* about the destruction of the rainforests, in the way that one could use English *angry*; in this situation, *panas hati* (lit. 'hot-hearted') would be more appropriate.

These observations lead to the explication below (Goddard 1996a). The first component of the cognitive scenario shows an important similarity between *marah* and *anger*—in both cases, the prototypical antecedent is the thought that someone has done something bad. The 'feeling tone' component is also the same as for *anger*—both are 'bad feelings'. But this is where the resemblance ends. A key feature of the scenario for *marah* is the experiencer's sense of personal affront. One experiences *marah* most sharply and clearly when one believes that the other person has knowingly disregarded one's wishes. Unlike *angry*, Malay *marah* has no component which seeks retaliation or retribution. Rather, as set out in the final two components of the cognitive scenario, what the experiencer wants is for the other person to recognize the hurt feelings which he or she has caused—without the experiencer having to explicitly say anything about it. That is, if I am *marah* I want the other person to deduce from my non-verbal reactions that there is something wrong, and to examine his or her conscience for the cause.

> *X* rasa marah *('feels* marah*')* (pada *'towards'* Y) *at this time:*
>
> someone X feels something bad (towards someone else Y) at this time
>   like someone can feel when they think like this about someone else:
>   'this someone did something bad
>   this someone knows that I do not want him/her to do something like this
>   I feel something bad because of this
>   I don't want to say something about it to this someone with words
>   at the same time I want this someone to know how I feel
>   I want this someone to do something because of it'

4.5 Three 'anger words' in Yankunytjatjara

In this section, we look at methods that can help draw out the similarities and differences between closely related words in an unfamiliar language. Yankunytjatjara is a dialect of the Western Desert Language spoken in the interior of Australia (Goddard 1991b). In this language, there are three expressions that could be used to translate the English expression *He got angry at me.*

$$Paluru\ ngayuku \begin{cases} pika & -ri & -ngu. \\ mirpan & -ari & -ngu. \\ kuya & -ri & -ngu. \end{cases}$$

he/she 1sgPURP   -INCHO-PAST
'He/she got angry at me.'

All three verbs are formed with the aid of the so-called INCHOative (or 'happening') suffix *-ri/-ari*. The roots—*pika, mirpan,* and *kuya*—can function as separate words: *pika* and *mirpan* may be active adjectives, meaning (roughly) 'angrily'; and *kuya* is a stative adjective 'bad'. The person or thing at which the emotion is directed appears in the PURPosive case, marked by *-ku/-mpa*. (Incidentally, the underlining beneath some letters in Yankunytjatjara words is a diacritic representing retroflex pronunciation.)

4.5.1 Pikaringanyi

Semantically, *pikaringanyi* involves little more than the urge or readiness to fight or inflict pain; so, strictly speaking, it should not be regarded as an emotion at all. English words like 'hostile, aggressive, feisty, combative' often provide appropriate translation equivalents.

> X pikaringanyi (Y-ku) *(at this time)*:
> ≈ *X wants to fight/cause pain (to Y) at this time*
>
> X feels something bad towards Y at this time
> because of this, X wants to do something bad to Y's body at this time
> X wants Y to feel something bad because of it

The first piece of evidence for this structure comes from polysemy. The root *pika* can function as a noun with the possible meanings 'a sore', 'pain', or 'a fight'.

a. *Pika ala* 'a wound' (*ala* 'opening'); *pika warutja* 'a burn' (*waru* 'fire')
b. *Kututu pika ngarala, nyangakutu tjunkupai.*
   'If there's chest pain, you put (ointment) on here.'
c. *Pika nyaakun nyangatja ngarala nyanganyi?*
   'Why are you just standing here watching the fight?'

The hypothesis that the urge to fight or hurt someone is crucial to *pikaringanyi* is supported by examples which involve anger, in the English sense of the word, but without physical confrontation. If a sorcerer has a grievance and is angry enough to set his internal spirit forces upon me, this action cannot be described as due to his having become *pika*, though either of the other 'anger' words is possible. (Note that in this example, the emotion words occur with a special ending, in the so-called 'serial form'. Serial verbs, depicting a prior or simultaneous action, may be included in the same clause as the final, finite verb, without the need for any intervening conjunction.)

Wati ngangkaringku ngayinya $\left\{ \begin{array}{l} *pikaringkula \\ mirpa\underline{n}arira \\ kuyaringkula \end{array} \right.$ *wankangka iritujunu.*

'The sorcerer got angry and set upon me with his spirit forces.'

If a person gets frustrated with an inanimate object, such as a tool that won't work properly, or a shade-shelter that refuses to go up correctly, *pikaringanyi* is not a suitable word to describe this state. The reason is presumably that it makes no sense to think of fighting or causing pain to inanimate objects.

Pu\underline{t}u palya\underline{r}a palya\underline{r}a ngayulu $\left\{ \begin{array}{l} *pikaringu, \\ \\ mirpa\underline{n}aringu, \end{array} \right.$ *munu\underline{n}a atu\underline{r}a minya — minya\underline{n}u.*

'After trying and trying to fix it, I got really annoyed, and I smashed it to pieces.'

Something similar applies in respect of children: though they may *pikar-inganyi* among themselves, the angry reaction of an adult towards a child is unlikely to be described as *pika*. One does not usually want to 'fight' a child. Nor can one speak of becoming *pika* towards oneself, though *anger* at oneself on account of doing something stupid or self-defeating may be described with either of the other 'anger' words. Animals and young babies are capable of *pikaringanyi*, implying that judgement or appraisal is not a necessary component of its meaning (notice that the opposite is the case for *mirpa\underline{n}arinyi*).

Papa/nantju palatja $\left\{ \begin{array}{l} pikaringanyi! \\ *mirpa\underline{n}arinyi! \end{array} \right.$

'(Look out!) That dog/horse is getting aggressive.'

In sum, the evidence from polysemy and from contextual restrictions on distribution converges on an interpretation of *pikaringanyi* that does not involve any imputed act of judgement or evaluation, but merely the urge or tendency to be hostile.

4.5.2 Mirpaṉarinyi

The proposed explication for *mirpaṉarinyi* is set out below. We can see at once that it differs markedly from *pikaringanyi* in originating with an appraisal that 'this someone is someone bad'. This appraisal leads to two complementary urges—first, not to oblige Y in any way, e.g. by talking to him or her, cooperating, caring; and second, to actively do Y some wrong. Accordingly, we sometimes find that better translation equivalents are provided by expressions such as 'aggrieved', 'offended', 'having something against (him/her)'.

X mirpaṉarinyi (Y-ku) *('X is hostile/aggrieved/annoyed at this time'):*

someone X thinks (about someone else Y) like this at this time:
  'this someone is someone bad
  I don't want to do anything good for this someone
  I want this someone to feel something bad
   because of this, I want to do something bad to this someone at some time'
  because of this, this someone feels something bad (towards Y) at this time
   like someone can feel when this someone thinks like this

Let us now see how each of these components can be supported. Consider first the example below, which is from a text of girlhood reminiscences. It describes an incident that arose after the girl's classificatory grandmother arrived back in camp to discover that her classificatory son (the speaker's father) had not saved any meat for her from a kill of kangaroo. She reproaches him, and becomes *mirpaṉ* toward the speaker's mother—i.e. the hunter's wife—because she ought to have intervened with her husband to ensure that meat was set aside, and probably also because it is dangerous for a woman to confront a man directly on such a matter. In this, and the remaining Yankunytjatjara examples, bolding is used to draw attention to the word at issue. There is some variation in the forms of the words, which is due to the fact that they appear in different grammatical contexts, but this variation can be ignored for our purposes.

> *'Nyuntu nyaaku kuka ngayuku tjunkunytja wiya? Wati katjangkumpaṉi kuka ungama!' Ka **mirpaṉaringu**, ngayuku ngunytjuku. Munu pulanku pikangku pungangi, kukanguṟu.*
> ' "Why didn't you save any meat for me? A son ought to give me meat". She got really angry at my mother. And the two of them fought, over meat.'

The example above is typical of adult uses of *mirpaṉarinyi* in that it focuses on a kin-based grievance which leads to a fight. Neither of these characteristics, however, is necessary. The next example, from another text of girlhood reminiscences, relates how the girl's grandmother reacted to her childish greed for goanna eggs. After the girl had tried to keep them all for herself, the grandmother retaliated by ignoring her pleas, and breaking the eggs.

> *Ka ngayuku kami pulkaṟa* **mirpaṉaringu**. *Paluṟu pulkaṟa tungunpung-kupai munu ngampu kaṯanankupai.*
> 'My grandmother got really annoyed. She ignored me and would break the eggs.'

There is no semantic component in *mirpaṉarinyi* that implies a real or anticipated fight. This is confirmed by the next example, which comes from a folktale telling how a jealous husband becomes suspicious that his wife is carrying on an affair with his brother. The story goes on to relate how the husband plots to trap the brother on a high mesa and abandon him there.

> *'Kuwari mulapa pula mungaringu. Pula kaḻaḻa pitjapai.' Munu kunyu* **mirpaṉpa** *nyinangi.*
> ' "This time they've stayed out till after dark. They usually come back in daylight," (he thought.) And he felt aggrieved and vengeful.'

The example above also shows that *mirpaṉ* can be a state, extended in time. In fact, one of its uses is to describe a situation of someone harbouring a grudge or grievance. During this time, they are typically uncommunicative and unsmiling (*mulyara* 'sullen') and uncooperative. The example below makes reference to this possibility, and sheds light on the contrast between *mirpaṉarinyi* and *pikaringanyi*.

> *Ka kunyu ngunytjilta* **pikaringanyi**. *Ngunytji—panya paluṟu* **mirpaṉ** *ngaṟala. Paluṟu tjukutjukunguṟu,* **mirpaṉ** *nyinara nyinarampa* **pikaringanyilta**.
> 'He'll get mad for no good reason. For no real reason—because he's been brooding over something. After brooding angrily for some time, he'll get mad over something small.'

One might get the impression that *mirpaṉ* is necessarily an extended state—something like holding a grudge. This is, however, far from the case, as was explained to me as below. In relation to people, any act of getting aggressive, combative, or feisty (*pika*) is held to originate in a prior, internal act of *mirpaṉarinyi*. Unlike dogs or horses, people do not become aggressive without reason—they first *mirpaṉarinyi*, that is to say, form an intention based on a grievance.

> *Aṉangu mirpaṉ ngarala,* **pikaringanyi.** **Mirpaṉ** *wiya,* **pikaringkunytja** *wiya.*
> *Kalypa.*
> 'If a person's angry, they get aggressive. If they're not angry, they don't get aggressive. They stay peaceful.'

Let's review. It is clear that the capacity to *mirpaṉarinyi* is restricted to persons. This suggests that the exercise of judgement or appraisal is required, in the form of a simple act of evaluation, that 'this someone (Y) is someone bad'. I have proposed that the resulting intentions take a two-sided form: on the one hand, wanting not to oblige Y in any way, for example, by talking to him or her, cooperating, caring; and on the other, actively wanting to do Y some wrong. This formulation allows for the possibility of a delayed outburst, preceded by the sullen *mulyara* phase. It also allows that the eventual action may be sorcery, betrayal, character assassination, or some other form of indirect retaliation, rather than a physical confrontation, as implied by *pikaringanyi*.

4.5.3 Kuyaringanyi

It is suggestive that the root *kuya* when used alone means 'bad'. Significantly, the expression *(kurun) unngu kuyaringanyi* 'going bad inside (one's spirit)', is often used to help explain the meaning of *mirpaṉarinyi*. These facts suggest that the explication for *mirpaṉarinyi* already fully contains *kuyaringanyi*, for which we can propose the explication below.

According to this, *kuyaringanyi* involves a negative appraisal of someone, leading to a disinclination to assist them, but it stops short of the active hostility of *mirpaṉarinyi*. Appropriate translation equivalents include 'resent, go off, be pissed off with'.

X kuyaringanyi (Y-ku) *('X was in a bad mood towards Y at this time'):*

someone X thinks (about someone else Y) like this at this time:
  'this someone is someone bad
  I don't want to do anything good for this someone'
because of this, this someone feels something bad (towards Y)
  at this time like someone can feel when this someone thinks like this

Some examples follow. In the first, an ex-boyfriend is approached by someone with a message from his old girlfriend, who wants to talk with him. From his reply, it is clear that *kuyaringanyi* need not imply any aggressive intentions: it may simply be a matter of not wanting to oblige.

> A: *Piyuku kunyu wangka!*
> B: *Wiya. Ngayulu palumpa **kuyaringanyi**. Wangkanytjakuna wiya ngaranyi.*
> A: 'She says for you to talk (to her).'
> B: 'No. I've gone off her. There's nothing I need talk to her about.'

The next example relates the consequences of a boss favouring one of the lads working for him over the others. Here *kuyaringanyi* covers something like English 'resent'. As things turned out, the others later decided to ambush the favoured one and beat him up. It was explained to me that 'after being resentful for some time, they got angry' *kuyaringkula, kuyaringkula mirpanaringulta*. In other words, *kuyaringanyi* may well lead to *mirpanarinyi*, as displeasure turns to active hostility.

> *Mayatjangku tjitji kutju wirura kanyilpai, warkiwiyangku. Ka tjitji kutjupa tjuta palumpa **kuyaringkupai**.*
> 'The boss only treated one of the lads well, not swearing at him. So the other lads used to resent him.'

If our explications successfully capture the difference between the two words, we might expect *kuyaringanyi* to be well-suited as a euphemism or understatement for the stronger, more positively hostile feeling of *mirpanarinyi*. This is in fact the case. *Kuyaringanyi* is often used in preference to the more explicit *mirpanarinyi*. This is exemplified below, in a husband and wife exchange.

> A: *Nyaaku nyuntu ngayuku yulytja paltjintja wiya? **Kuyaringanyin** ngayuku?*
> B: *Wiya. Kuyaringkunytja wiyana. Minana paku.*
> A: 'Why haven't you done my washing? Are you annoyed with me?'
> B: 'Oh no. I'm not annoyed. It's just that my arms are tired.'

Key technical terms

approaches to emotions: cognitive, physicalist, social constructivist
basic emotions
ethnocentrism
folk psychology
prototypical cognitive scenario
semantic template

Exercises and discussion questions

† next to a problem means that a solution or some commentary can be found at the end of this book.

1†. Consider the English terms *pride*, *admiration*, *contempt*, and *shame*. See if you can come up with a componential analysis (CA) for them; that is, try to isolate the dimensions of contrast between the four terms using binary features.

2†. Consider the explications (a)–(c) below (adapted from Wierzbicka 1990b) for the words *afraid*, *terrified*, and *frightened*. Can you match the explications with the words they are intended to define? Discuss your reasons.

a. someone thinks like this at this time:
   'something bad can happen
   I don't want this
   I don't know what I can do'
   because of this, this someone feels something bad
      like someone can feel when this someone thinks like this

b. someone thinks like this at this time:
   'something bad can happen to me now
   I don't want this
   because of this, I want to do something
   I don't know what I can do'
   because of this, this someone feels something bad
      like someone can feel when this someone thinks like this

c. someone thinks like this at this time:
   'something very bad is happening now
   because of this, something very bad can happen to me now
   I don't want this
   because of this, I want to do something
   I can't do anything'
   because of this, this someone feels something very bad
      like someone can feel when this someone thinks like this

3†. Can you tell what emotion word goes with the following explication? Discuss the reasons for your judgement.

someone thinks something like this at this time:
   'something good happened to this other someone
   it didn't happen to me
   I want things like this to happen to me'
   because of this, this someone feels something bad towards this other someone

4†. *Jubilant.* Below you will see a set of possible components that could go into a plausible prototypical cognitive scenario for the word *jubilant*.

a. something very good happened now
b. I did something very good now
c. someone did something very good now
d. I wanted this for some time
e. I wanted this very much
f. I thought before that maybe this someone couldn't do it
g. some people thought before that I couldn't do it
h. I feel something very good now
i. other people here feel the same
j. I want other people to know it
k. I want other people here to know how I feel

Consider the six possible combinations shown below and choose the most suitable one. You will have to do some research into common uses of the word *jubilant*. You may have the feeling that some components are not perfectly appropriate. Nevertheless, choose the best available combination.

(i) b, d, g, h, j
(ii) a, d, h
(iii) c, e, f, h, i
(iv) a, d, f, k
(v) a, e, i, j
(vi) a, h, k

5†. *Ashamed* and *embarrassed* are unpleasant emotions which are rather similar in some ways, but differ in others. English makes a distinction between *ashamed* and *embarrassed*, whereas many languages have a single, less specific concept that in a sense covers both situations. Compare examples of usage. Using a selection of the components listed below, devise prototypical cognitive scenarios for (a) *Someone X was ashamed at this time* and (b) *Someone X was embarrassed at this time*.

something is happening to me now
people can know something bad about me
people know something about me
I now know: I did something bad
because of this, someone here is thinking about me
because of this, people here are thinking something bad about me
if people know this, they can think something very bad about me
if people know this, they can't not think something very bad about me
I don't want this
I can't not think the same

6†. The following are intended to be components in explications for emotion words. Rewrite them so that they are phrased entirely in semantic primes and conform to the rules of NSM syntax.

a. it makes this person feel bad
b. I feel good about this someone

7†. Consider the meaning of the three English words *surprised*, *amazed*, and *shocked*, as used in sentences like the following:

She was surprised to find he was still there.
They were amazed by her success.
He was shocked at what he saw.

Present and justify reductive paraphrase analyses for *Someone X was surprised*, *Someone X was amazed*, and *Someone X was shocked*. In each case, begin by stating the full paraphrase. Then briefly discuss each of its components, giving evidence to justify its presence in the explication. Your paraphrases must be phrased exclusively in terms which are simpler and easier to understand than the words being defined. They should not make use of any other emotion terms, though it is alright to use FEEL and the other mental primes WANT, THINK, KNOW, and SAY. You may find it useful to consult some dictionaries, but do not appeal to what they say as evidence, and (as ever) be wary of relying on the kind of wording they employ in their definitions.

8†. Write explications for *Someone X feels disappointed* and *Someone X feels relief*.

9†. *Mut(to)* and *kat(to)* are Japanese emotion terms. Japanese–English dictionaries distinguish the two in terms of the difference of intensity of feeling (e.g. 'get angry' vs. 'be stirred into passionate anger'), but there is more to it than this. Study the examples below and propose explications for 'X feels MUT' and 'X feels KAT', phrasing them as simply and clearly as you can. Do not use any English emotion terms in the explications. For each word, present your analysis as follows: first state your explication, numbering each component, then argue for each component in turn referring to the example sentences. If you are unable to decide on a particular point, say so, and say what evidence would be needed to resolve the issue.

Mut(to) can also refer to the physically stifling feeling of being engulfed by heat or stench. *Kat(to)* can refer to the physical feeling of strong heat. These sensory meanings do have a bearing on the emotional meanings, but for this exercise, do not attempt to incorporate any sensory images or situations into your explications.

i. *Nibe mo naku kotowarare MUT to shita ga, bashogara osaeru koto ni shita.*
'He turned me down and I was thoroughly annoyed [i.e. felt MUT], but out of regard for the occasion I decided to suppress my anger.'

ii. *Hahaoya ga jibun no shoorai o shinpai shitekurete iru no wa arigatai ga, amari kanshoo sareru to MUT to suru.*
'Although I am grateful that my mother is concerned about my future, I feel MUT when she meddles in my affairs too much.'

iii. *Namae o kiita dake na no ni, MUT to oshidamatte, itte shimatta.*
'When I just asked his name, he kept his mouth shut feeling MUT and went away.'

iv. *Sekkaku bijutsukan ni itta noni, kyuukan de MUT to shita yo.*
'I felt MUT when I found the art gallery closed, after having gone there especially.'

v. *Jooshi ga boku no gaarufurendo no koshi ni te o ateta node, MUT to shita.*
'I felt MUT when my boss put his hand on my girlfriend's waist.'

vi. *Kare no hitokoto ni MUT to shita node, nanika itte yaroo ka/*tataite yaroo ka to omotta.*
'Since I felt MUT towards his words, I felt like saying something back to him/*hitting him.'

vii. *Nanika ni tsukete chichi wa kogoto o itta no de, watashi wa KAT to natta.*
'I got mad [i.e. became KAT] because my father found fault with everything.'

viii. *Kono aida wa, KAT to natte, aisumimasen deshita.*
'I'm sorry I lost my temper [i.e. became KAT] the other day.'

ix. *Kare wa tachishooben o togamerareta koto ga kikkake de, KAT to natte sono josei o sashi-koroshita.*
'Being admonished (by the woman) for urinating in the street made him go mad with rage [i.e. become KAT] and he stabbed the woman to death.'

x. *Otokotte, KAT to naru to, tsui te ga deru mono desu kara nee.*
'We men tend to hit (our wives) when we become KAT (with them).'

xi. *Dara no shiwaze ka wakaranai ga, watrashi no hanabatake ga fumiarasarete iru no o mitsuketa toki wa, KAT to natta.*
'I didn't know who did this, but I became KAT when I found my flower garden was trampled down.'

xii. *Doa no mukoo de dareka ga watashi no sonkei suru hito no warukuchi o itte iru no ga kikoe, watashi wa KAT to natta.*
'I became KAT when I heard somebody near the door speaking ill of the person I respect very much.'

5

Speech-act verbs

'Speech-act verbs' are words like *ask, promise, thank, boast, insist, exclaim, hint*, and *bet*. The English language contains an unusually large number of them, making it possible in English to easily categorize people's 'acts of saying' with great subtlety. Some languages, however, have only a handful of such verbs (though, as far as we know, all have an equivalent to the most basic speech-act verb of all, namely, 'say'). In this chapter we investigate the semantic structure of speech-act verbs and ask to what extent they reflect the cultural priorities of a people.

The study of speech acts is an important interdisciplinary area between linguistics and philosophy. One of the most influential modern works on the topic was the English philosopher J. L. Austin's (1975 [1962]) book *How to Do Things with Words*. Austin's work has been extended and refined greatly by the American philosopher of language John Searle.

5.1 What is a speech act?

What makes a speech act a 'speech act', and what is the relationship between speech acts and speech-act verbs?

5.1.1 Speech-act verbs

A SPEECH-ACT VERB is a label for something that you can do in or by saying something. Sometimes this involves expressing a message of a certain kind that can be more or less specific. For example, to *promise* you have to say something like *I promise I'll do it* or *I'll do it for sure, you can count on me*; to *insult* you have to say some very bad things about someone else. Sometimes, though, no particular message is implied, as for example, with *hint*— the very nature of *hinting* is that you avoid saying something in the way that might be expected. If X is a speech-act verb, it is always possible to formulate a sentence like 'In saying that, I was X-ing' or 'When he/she said that, he/she was X-ing'. This provides us with a test for identifying speech-act verbs.

Thus, *promise* and *hint* qualify as speech-act verbs because it makes sense to say 'In saying what I said, I was promising/hinting'. On the other hand, *yell* and *whisper* are not speech-act verbs, even though they involve the voice, because they describe how you say something, rather than categorizing what you are doing as you speak. And so it sounds odd to say 'In saying that I was yelling'.

Bear in mind, however, that a speech act may be labelled by a multi-word expression rather than a single word. For instance, *to put someone down, to tell someone off, to point out, to give one's word* are English speech-act expressions. In some languages, the majority of speech-act expressions are like this.

Of course, merely being able to identify a class of verbs (in this case, speech-act verbs) is a far cry from understanding why they constitute a class. As we will see shortly, analysts generally agree that the 'impact' of a speech act comes from the fact that there is an amalgam of intentions, assumptions, and feelings involved along with the act of saying something. Before that, however, we should acquaint ourselves with an interesting subclass of speech-act verbs known as 'performative verbs'.

5.1.2 Performative verbs

Some speech-act verbs have the peculiarity that using them in the first-person 'present tense' frame—i.e. *I verb (you)* . . . —can actually perform or carry out the speech act. For example, to say *I object* is to *object*, to say *I bet you it will rain tomorrow* is to make a *bet*. Often it is possible to insert the word *hereby* into a performative sentence, emphasizing the 'doing-it-by-saying-this-now' effect.

Such so-called PERFORMATIVE VERBS have played a big part in the history of the study of speech acts, for it was performative verbs which first caught the eye of the Oxford philosopher J. L. Austin in the late 1930s. This was a period in which many philosophers were attracted to a doctrine called 'positivism', according to which the meaningfulness of a sentence depends on the possibility of being able to test its truth or falsity (this might remind you of the truth conditional approach to meaning: cf. section 2.3). What attracted Austin's attention was that the concepts of truth and falsity don't seem applicable to performative utterances. That is, it doesn't seem to make sense to ask whether *I object* or *I bet you it will rain tomorrow* is true or false. Performative utterances thus seemed fundamentally different from statements, assertions, and other similar utterances (which he termed 'constatives'). This seemed all the more strange because superficially there isn't much difference between the grammatical structure of a performative utterance (to use another example, *I promise I'll be there on time*) and an ordinary present-tense declarative statement with a first-person subject (for example, *I live in Auckland*).

Though falsity cannot be the downfall of a performative utterance, it can still 'go wrong' in various ways. Austin coined the term FELICITY CONDITIONS to designate the conditions that must apply if a particular performative is to work as it should. Felicity conditions can be of several different kinds. Many performatives, such as *pronouncing* a couple as married, *naming* a ship, *baptizing* a child, *finding* a defendant guilty, presuppose various institutional arrangements and conditions. Unless these conditions are met, the performative procedure will 'misfire'. For example, to *pronounce* a couple as married the speaker must be legally entitled to do so (being an authorized marriage celebrant, a priest, a ship's captain, etc.), the couple must both be unmarried and over a certain age, and (in most places in the world) must be of opposite genders. These conditions have to do with the participants. Further, the speaker must have seen the couple perform certain other speech acts (the marriage vows), a condition having to do with the procedure itself.

Many performatives, however, don't require any institutional framework and people don't have to be in any particular formal relationship to undertake them. For example, *thank, promise, apologize, bet,* and *dare*. Even so, most 'ordinary' performatives still imply that the speaker has, in Austin's (1975 [1962]: 39) phrase, certain requisite 'thoughts, feelings or intentions'. If these are not satisfied, the speech act may still go through successfully but it will be, in a sense, an 'abuse'. For example, if I say *I promise you I will be there tomorrow*, but I have no intention of going there, or if I say *I apologize* without actually feeling sorry about what I did. Conditions of this kind are nowadays often called SINCERITY CONDITIONS.

Sincerity conditions apply to speech acts of all kinds, not just to those achieved by performative utterances. For example, to describe someone as *boasting* is to say that this person gives the impression of thinking (roughly speaking) that he or she is better than other people; similarly, to describe someone as *complimenting* implies that this person gives the impression of feeling something good towards his or her addressee.

5.1.3 Illocutionary force

Another frequently used term in speech-act studies, which also goes back to Austin, is ILLOCUTIONARY FORCE. This term can be confusing. Like gravity in physics, illocutionary force is not something which can be 'seen' directly. It shows itself only through its effects. Basically, illocutionary force is what makes a particular utterance the speech act that it is. For instance, a sentence like *It's rather cold in here* could be a bland piece of information-giving or a hint to close the window. The sentence *This gun is loaded* could be a warning, a statement of fact, or a threat. *How are you?* can be a genuine question but it can also be a greeting. In each case, we would say that the illocutionary force is different.

Illocutionary force is a property of utterances—real, situated speech acts   rather than sentences. It has something to do with the speaker's expressed or assumed motives, assumptions, and feelings. Performative verbs can be viewed as one (very explicit) means of indicating illocutionary force. Others include intonation patterns, illocutionary particles (see Chapter 6), and specialized grammatical constructions (such as the *How about*-construction, as in *How about a drink?*). Such devices are sometimes collectively termed ILLOCUTIONARY FORCE INDICATING DEVICES or IFIDs.

5.1.4 A broader view of speech acts

Though in this chapter we will confine ourselves largely to probing the meaning structure of speech-act verbs, it is important to point out that there are many (perhaps innumerable) speech acts which are not associated with any particular speech-act words.

In case our discussion of the performative vs. constative distinction may have given the wrong impression, it should be pointed out that constative utterances are certainly speech acts too. English has many speech-act verbs for distinguishing between different kinds of constative speech acts, such as *state, tell, assert, claim, insist (that), contend.*

Indeed, the position Austin himself reaches at the end of *How to Do Things with Words* is that any real, situated utterance is a speech act of some kind. This is an idea which has since been taken up and elaborated in various ways by a long line of so-called 'speech-act theorists', many of whom are also influenced by Wittgenstein's (1953) concept that utterances only have meaning within the context of the rules of the particular 'language game' in which they occur. Speech-act theorists are generally out to counter what they see as the excessively 'information-oriented' approach of much conventional thinking about language. Instead of conceiving of language as basically about the transmission of information, they emphasize that speaking is always a social action and that there are countless everyday speech acts (for example, *joking, blaming, swearing, nagging, thanking, refusing*) which are not focused on the transmission of factual information.

5.2 Searle's approach

After Austin, the biggest name in speech-act theory is that of John Searle. Like most other philosophers of language, Searle is not primarily interested in the meaning of the actual (English) words which depict speech acts. He focuses on the 'act' and asks: What conditions must be met in order for the act to have taken place? Or, putting it another way: What are the rules that govern *promising, threatening, boasting,* and so on?

Searle takes Austin's idea of felicity conditions and proposes that they are not merely ways in which a speech act can go wrong, but rather that the felicity conditions jointly constitute the illocutionary force. Furthermore, he has classified the conditions (or constitutive rules, as he prefers to see them) into four categories.

5.2.1 Searle on promising

To give an idea of Searle's work, let us consider his analysis of the 'semantical rules' for *promising*. The essentials of this analysis were originally proposed in Searle (1965). The version below has been slightly simplified and reformulated by Chierchia and McConnell-Ginet (2000: 233–4) in their popular textbook *Meaning and Grammar*.

a. The propositional content rule. P is to be uttered only in the context of a sentence (or a larger stretch of discourse) predicating some future act A of the speaker.
b. The preparatory rule. P is to be uttered only if the addressee is positively oriented toward A and the speaker so believes (and only if it is not obvious to the addressee prior to this utterance that the speaker will do A).
c. The sincerity rule. P is to be uttered only if the speaker intends to do A.
d. The essential rule. Uttering P counts as undertaking an obligation to do A.

Let's work through this analysis, rule by rule. 'Propositional content' means, essentially, what the speech act is about. Rule (a) states that in the case of a *promise* the propositional content is 'predicating some future act A of the speaker' (e.g. *I'll lend you the car on Tuesday*). However, such a propositional content will count as a *promise* only if certain other conditions are satisfied. So-called 'preparatory conditions', such as Rule (b) above, for instance, tell us what the speaker implies in the performance of the speech act. As Searle says:

To put it generally, in the performance of any illocutionary act, the speaker implies that the preparatory conditions of the act are satisfied. Thus, for example, when I make a statement I imply that I can back it up, when I make a promise, I imply that the thing promised is in the hearer's interest. When I thank someone, I imply that the thing I am thanking him for has benefited me (or at least that it was intended to benefit me), etc. (Searle 1969: 65)

For *promises* and other similar speech acts in the category of 'commissives', the main preparatory condition (or rule) is that the addressee is 'positively oriented toward A' (the future act). As well, there is the assumption that it is not already obvious that the speaker will do A. This derives from a more general requirement that illocutionary acts have 'a point'. As Searle (1969: 59) puts it: 'It is out of order for me to promise to do something that it is obvious to all concerned that I am going to do anyhow.'

Many speech acts also have 'sincerity rules', such as rule (c). These refer to a psychological state of the speaker. The expression 'sincerity rule' (or, for that matter, sincerity condition) is not perhaps the most apposite of terms, because Searle does not mean that to *promise* one must be sincere about intending to do the act. *Promises* can be sincere or insincere. Nevertheless:

> Wherever there is a psychological state specified in the sincerity condition, the performance of the act counts as an *expression* of that psychological state. This law holds whether the act is sincere or insincere, that is whether or not the speaker actually has the specified psychological state or not. Thus, ... to promise, vow, threaten or pledge (that A) counts as an *expression of intention* (to do A). (Searle 1969: 65)

According to Searle, an example of a speech-act verb without any sincerity condition is *greet*. That is, I am not expressing any psychological state by simply *greeting* someone; I am just going through a procedure, a form of words. On the other hand, if I *welcome* someone I do express a psychological state (roughly, that I am pleased this person has arrived and I want him or her to be pleased too).

Finally comes the 'essential rule', which in the case of *promising* is rule (d): 'uttering P counts as undertaking an obligation to do A.' Searle has chosen the term 'essential rule' because it is this rule which is truly constitutive of *promising* as a speech act. The concept of a CONSTITUTIVE RULE can be best understood, according to Searle, by contrasting them with regulative rules. Many of the rules of etiquette, for example, merely regulate forms of behaviour which themselves exist independently of the rules of etiquette.

> But constitutive rules do not merely regulate, they create or define new forms of behaviour. The rules of football or chess, for example, do not merely regulate, they create the very possibility of playing such games.... Regulative rules regulate a preexisting activity, an activity whose existence is logically independent of the rules. Constitutive rules constitute (and also regulate) an activity the existence of which is logically dependent on the rules. (Searle 1969: 33–4)

As Searle observes, constitutive rules seem 'almost tautological in character' for what they seem to offer is 'part of a definition'.

5.2.2 Classifying speech acts

The idea of there being four kinds of conditions or rules for speech acts provides a kind of schema for comparing and contrasting them. This can be

Table 5.1. Searlean analysis of two speech acts

	thank (for)	warn (that)
Propositional content	Past act A done by H	Future event or state, etc. E
Preparatory	S believes A benefits S	S has reason to believe E will occur and is not in H's interest
Sincerity	S feels grateful or appreciative for A	S believes E is not in H's interest
Essential	Counts as an expression of gratitude or appreciation	Counts as an undertaking to the effect that E is not in H's interest

(S: speaker, H: hearer)

seen from Table 5.1, which is excerpted, with some modifications, from Searle (1969: 66–7).

Searle (1975) later proposed that all speech acts could be grouped into five categories, based principally on the kind of essential rules they involved. For example, he grouped *promises*, *offers*, and *threats* (to do something) under the heading 'commissives' on the grounds that they commit the speaker to some future action. He grouped *thanking*, *apologizing*, *welcoming*, and *congratulating* together as 'expressives' because the essential condition in each case involves expressing a psychological state. Other categories were 'representatives', which commit the speaker to the truth of some proposition (e.g. *asserting*, *concluding*), and 'directives', which are attempts to get the hearer to do something (e.g. *request*, *order*). A final category, which has been rightly criticized as very heterogeneous, he called 'declarations'. These are acts like *christening* a child, *declaring war*, or *excommunicating*, which bring about changes in extra-linguistic 'institutional arrangements'.

There have since been many other classificatory schemes proposed for speech acts. To mention only two such schemes, Bach and Harnish (1979: ch 3) identify six general categories—constatives, directives, commissives, acknowledgements, effectives, and verdictives. Allan (1986: 190–237) identifies eight: constatives, predictives, commissives, acknowledgements, directives, effectives, authoritatives, and verdictives.

Personally, I agree with Levinson (1983: 241) that 'enthusiasm for this kind of classificatory exercise is in general misplaced', if only because the functions of language seem potentially unlimited when the diversity of cultures is taken into account. It seems unrealistic to suppose that all the speech acts in the world's languages could be fitted into any small number of discrete categories. Be that as it may, from a semantic point of view there is a more powerful objection to the approach adopted by Searle.

5.2.3 Weaknesses of the Searlean approach

The most serious problem afflicting what we may call the 'Searlean approach' (followed not only by Searle, but also by Bach and Harnish and by Allan in the works mentioned above) is its disregard for the descriptive metalanguage employed. Consider Searle's characterization of the essential rule for *promising*: 'uttering P counts as undertaking an obligation to do A.' Can you see the flaw with this formulation?

First, the expression 'undertaking an obligation' is patently complex and obscure. There is no reason to believe that either *undertaking* or *obligation* are any semantically simpler than *promise* (if anything, the opposite would appear more likely). Thus, to explain an aspect of the meaning of *promise* in terms of *undertaking* and *obligation* is to violate the principle that complex meanings should be explained in terms of simpler ones. Furthermore, the word *undertake* belongs to the same family of speech-act verbs as *promise* itself.

A similar 'obscurity critique' can be mounted against Searle's formulation of the essential conditions for *thanking* and for *warning (that)*, shown in Table 5.1 above. From a semantic point of view, where does it get us to say that *thanking* 'counts as an expression of gratitude or appreciation'? The terms *gratitude* and *appreciation* are complex and obscure. As well, listing them disjunctively either implies that *thank* has two meanings, or amounts to an admission that the factor common to both of them has not been made explicit. Likewise, explaining *warn* 'an undertaking to the effect that E is not in H's interest' would be unlikely to be very helpful to someone who did not already understand the word. The expressions *undertaking* and *interest* are too complex.

A second problem with Searlean analyses is that they are often descriptively inadequate. Suppose we ignore the obscurity, and agree that the essential condition of a *promise* is that it undertakes an 'obligation'. What kind of obligation and how does it come about? The self-imposed obligation of a *promise* is quite different, for instance, from that incurred in the making of a *vow* or a *pledge*. As Verschueren (1985: 630) points out:

'one has to recognize the existence of different kinds of obligations and of different ways in which they function in social interactions.'

Finally, the Searlean approach to speech act analysis tends to assume that English speech-act verbs designate universal or natural categories. Searle himself is on record as saying that speech acts fall into 'natural conceptual kinds'. A weaker version of this indifference to linguistic and cultural variation acknowledges in principle that the speech acts of other cultures may differ markedly from our own, but proceeds to treat the English speech act inventory as a model in terms of which everything is to be understood. This happens when, for instance, cross-linguistic studies are conducted into ways of 'complimenting' or 'apologizing' in cultures which do not themselves recognize any such speech act categories.

5.3 Reductive paraphrase of speech-act verbs

In the huge literature on speech acts, Anna Wierzbicka's (1987) *English Speech Act Verbs: A Semantic Dictionary* stands out for several reasons. It addresses over 250 separate speech-act verbs, instead of a mere handful as most others studies do. And it proposes detailed and exhaustive reductive paraphrases for every one of them, seeking to nail down the full semantic content so that the similarities and differences among them are made perfectly explicit. This section is indebted to Wierzbicka (1987), although the treatment and individual explications diverge from it considerably, especially in using a simpler and more systematic paraphrasing metalanguage.

It should be pointed out here that in this chapter we deviate from the standard treatment of speech acts by confining ourselves mainly to reportive uses of speech-act verbs. It is more usual to concentrate on performatives, but this leads to a lopsided picture. Performative verbs and utterances are the exception, not the rule, both in English and in other languages.

5.3.1 *Semantic structure of a speech-act verb:* promising

As we might expect, there are some special aspects to the semantic structure of speech-act verbs. Most importantly, they all involve the first-person format. This is particularly clear with performatives. Obviously, in saying *I order you, I dare you, I apologize, I agree,* and so on, one expresses something about one's own intentions, assumptions, and feelings. But even for reportive uses of speech-act verbs, a first-person format is still required at some level.

Suppose person P witnesses person X saying to person Y *Sit down*, and suppose that person P later describes what happened as follows: *X ordered Y to sit down*. In choosing the word *ordered* to depict X's speech act, person P is attributing a certain attitude to the original speaker X; roughly, that X appears to think: 'I know that because I say this, this someone can't not do it.' If person P were to choose another speech-act verb, such as *asked* (as in *X asked Y to sit down*), P would be attributing a different attitude to the original speaker; roughly, that X appears to think: 'it can be that this someone does it because I say this; I don't know.' The choice of *invited* (as in *X invited Y to sit down*) would attribute yet another attitude; roughly, that X appears to think: 'it will be good for you if you do this; I want you to know that you can do it now, if you want to.' Because speech-act verbs attribute an 'attitude' to a speaker, their meaning structures will always contain some attitudinal components 'in the first-person'.

Searle's rules about *promising* can be readily translated into 'first-person' paraphrases. The propositional content rule ('predicating some future act A of the speaker'), for example, could become 'X said to Y: I will do A.' Or perhaps, in view of the affiliation between *promise* and *tell* (*promising* to do A entails *telling* someone you will do A):

> X said something like this to Y:
>   I want you to know that I will do this (A) after this

(The addition of 'after this' to the second line is to make explicit that the action is a future action. This is of course implicit in the auxiliary *will*, but some languages do not have such an auxiliary.)

A component which spells out part of the semantic content directly expressed by the speaker, as 'I want you to know that I will do this (A) after this' does in the schema above, is known as a DICTUM component (from Latin 'thing said'). A dictum doesn't have to be reproduced word for word; it specifies the essential semantic 'gist' of the speaker's utterance.

Searle's preparatory rule concerns the speaker's purported beliefs that the addressee is 'positively oriented' toward the future action and that it is 'not obvious to the addressee' that the speaker will do it. To this one might add that in *promising* the speaker purports to dispel any doubts the addressee might have on this score, leading to the following components:

> I know that this someone wants me to do it
> I know that this someone can think that I will not do it
> I don't want this someone to think like this

However, there is still more to it. There is still the matter of the 'obligation' that *promising* places upon the promiser. Presumably, part of the speaker's dictum is as follows:

> I want you to know that I think about it like this: 'I can't not do it'

As Wierzbicka (1987: 207) remarked: '[T]he speaker feels that having *promised* to do something he will now have to do it (simply because he *promised*). [But] how is that possible? Why will he have to do it?' Her answer was as follows:

> the 'obligation' inherent in *promise* can perhaps be explicated as follows: 'I want us to think that if I don't, people will not believe anything that I say I will do.' In other words, by promising something, the speaker offers his personal credibility in general as a kind of guarantee that he really will perform the action in question. (1987: 207)

In my opinion, Wierzbicka's suggestion fits better the act of *giving one's word* than simple *promising*. For *promising* a much simpler component seems appropriate:

> I know that if I don't do it, this will be very bad

Now, how should these components be combined into a unified explication? For a verb like *promise*, with its complex package of sincerity conditions, one could advance the following. It follows a semantic template that is applicable to many (but by no means all) speech-act verbs. The first line is the LEXICO-SYNTACTIC FRAME. It makes it clear that *promise* is a verb of 'saying', whereby one person says something to an addressee. (The second line of this frame ('this someone wanted something to happen because of it') has been added to help account for the fact that the addressee expression appears without any preposition, as a kind of grammatical object.) The content of what is said is spelt out in the DICTUM component. The subsequent components are introduced by the line 'this someone said it like someone can say something like this to someone else, when this someone thinks like this: ——.' This APPARENT MENTAL STATE component spells out the psychological state that is being attributed to the speaker.

X promised Y (to do A) at that time:

LEXICO-SYNTACTIC FRAME

a.   someone X said something to someone else Y at that time
     this someone wanted something to happen because of it

DICTUM

b.   this someone said something like this:
     'I want you to know that I will do this (A) after this time
     I want you to know that I think about it like this now: 'I can't not do it'
     I know that if I don't do it after this, this will be very bad'

APPARENT MENTAL STATE

c.   this someone said it like someone can say something like this to someone
     else when this someone thinks like this:
     'I know that this someone wants me to do it
     I know that this someone can think that I will not do it
     I don't want this someone to think like this'

Perhaps the only point of this explication that requires further comment is the component: 'I know that if I don't do it after this, this will be very bad.' Exactly why this component seems to fit well here is not immediately clear, given that many things beyond the speaker's control can intervene. In purely logical terms it is hard to see why non-performance of the action needs to be seen as 'very bad' but in Anglo 'cultural logic' it is, i.e. the evaluation is mediated by deeply ingrained cultural attitudes.

5.3.2 Threaten

If *promise* is the standard example of a performative, then *threaten* is the standard example of a non-performative, partly on account of the similarities in meaning between the two. Palmer (1986: 115) goes so far as to say that the only difference between *threaten* and the other commissives like *promise*, *vow*, *pledge*, and *guarantee* is in 'what the hearer wants'. That is, with *promise* the hearer wants the speaker to do the future action and with *threaten* the hearer does not want it. This is a considerable overstatement, however. As Thomas Hobbes (1651: 456, quoted in Traugott 1993: 348) noticed a long time ago, there is no obligation involved in a threat: 'though the promise of good, bind the promiser; yet threats that is to say, promises of evil, bind them not.'

First, let us consider the dictum of *threatening*. Often the speaker includes an *if*-clause or an *or* construction (*If you don't do it, I'll send you to your room*; *Do it now or you'll be grounded for a week*) to make it explicit that he or she is trying to get the addressee to do (or not do). At other times, a quasi-directive motivation is implicit. For example, *I'll smack you* can be a threat, if for instance both mother and child know that the child is not supposed to touch the flowers on the dinner table, and the mother sees the child reaching for them. Nevertheless, there are some instances of *threaten* where the speaker's motivation can be unclear. For example: *Yesterday a troublemaker in my class threatened to kill me*.

In the explication below, the dictum of *threaten* is depicted simply as: 'I can do something (A) after this; if I do it, it will be very bad for you.' The wording of the dictum is compatible with sentences such as *He threatened to kill himself*.

The first line of the apparent mental state component ('I want this someone to feel something bad when this someone thinks about this') implies a menacing tone. The next two lines imply that the unpleasant prospect is being used as leverage to get the addressee to do something, but without being specific about what this might be.

X threatened to do A:

LEXICO-SYNTACTIC FRAME

a.   someone X said something to someone else Y at that time

DICTUM

b.   this someone said something like this:
    'I can do something (A) after this
    if I do it, it will be very bad for you'

APPARENT MENTAL STATE

c.   this someone said it like someone can say something like this to someone
    else when this someone thinks like this:
      'I want this someone to feel something bad when this someone thinks
        about this
      I want this someone to do something because of this
      I know that this someone doesn't want to do it'

NEGATIVE EVALUATION

d.   it is bad if someone says something like this to someone else in this way

Unlike as with *promise*, the verb *threaten* has a final NEGATIVE EVALUATION component: 'it is bad if someone says something like this to someone else in this way.' As pointed out in section 1.5, people are judgemental creatures and it stands to reason that many word meanings incorporate subjective evaluational components. Other speech-act verbs which convey negative evaluations (of various kinds) include *lie*, *slander*, *nag*, *boast*, *blackmail*, *condone*, *whinge*, and *mock*.

5.3.3 Warn

The verb *warn* (cf. Wierzbicka 1987: 177) can be used in several syntactic frames. One can *warn* someone not to do something; one can *warn* someone that something will happen (as in *She warned me that they were coming*); one can also *warn against* doing something, or *warn about* a person. For the comparison with *threaten* and *promise*, we will confine ourselves solely to the *warn not to do* (or *to do*) construction. That is, we are not considering what Searle calls the 'categorical' (*warn that*) warning as presented in Table 5.1. Searle himself observes (1969: 67) that 'Most warnings are probably hypothetical: "If you do not do X, then Y will occur".'

Probably the most salient warnings (or pseudo-warnings) are threatening ones, as for instance, when an assailant says *I'm warning you. One move and you're dead*; and certainly one of the most intriguing things about the verb *warn* is that it can be used to issue threats. True warnings, however, are protective and well-intentioned; for instance, a mother saying to a child: *Be careful, you might fall*. A warning can also be, in a sense, disinterested, i.e. the speaker need not personally want the addressee to do or not do the relevant action. For instance, my doctor can *warn* me to give up smoking without necessarily conveying the message that he or she wants me to give up smoking. The focus is rather on me. The message is that I should give up smoking for my own good.

Clearly, if someone issues me a warning they (purport to) believe that if I do something, something bad might befall me. The illocutionary purpose is to bring this to my attention. However, it would not be right to formulate the purported motive behind *warning* in terms of knowing (e.g. to assign warnings an 'informative' intention such as 'I want you to know this'), if only because warnings don't have to convey new information. A warning can be prefaced by *remember*, as in *Remember, this stuff is dangerous. Be careful how you handle it*. The point of a warning seems to be focused not on what I know but on what I am thinking about. The person *warning* me seems to want me to think about what I am going to do, to keep something in mind.

What about the dictum of *warning*? As noted by Searle, *warning* always seems to contain or imply an *if*-clause, a condition. Suppose, for example, that you tell me *You'd better be careful to lock your car. There've been lots of break-ins lately*. Have you *warned* me to lock my car? Perhaps your utterance could be viewed in that way, but it could also be seen as merely some good advice. If, on the other hand, you articulate a condition and a possible bad consequence, there can be no doubt that you have given me a *warning*. For example, both *Better lock your car. If you don't, it might not be here when you get back* and *Lock your car or it won't be there when you get back* are unambiguously warnings. Thus it can be argued that part of the dictum of *warn* should be specified as something like: 'if you do (or: don't do) something, something bad can happen to you.'

Notice that it seems more natural to cast the message behind *warn* in terms of not doing, rather than doing. Admittedly, warnings framed in the positive do occur (for instance, *Be careful, you might fall!*), but even in cases like these, there is still an implicit message not to do something (in this case, it is implicit in the word *careful*; roughly, 'Don't stop thinking about what you are doing').

These observations lead to the explication below.

X warned Y not to do A (e.g. leave the car unlocked, mention the incident):
LEXICO-SYNTACTIC FRAME

a. someone X said something to someone else Y at that time
    this someone wanted something to happen because of it
DICTUM

b. this someone said something like this:
    'I know that if you do this (A), something bad can happen to you
    it will be good for you if you think about this'
APPARENT MENTAL STATE

c. this someone said it like someone can say something like this to someone
    else when this someone thinks like this:
    'I don't want something bad to happen to this someone'

5.3.4 Order, tell, *and* suggest

It is always useful to compare a group of related words to sharpen our appreciation of the differences. In this section we look at three verbs— *order*, *tell*, and *suggest*—which are often viewed as differing merely in their 'strength' or 'directness'. In fact, we shall see that the differences involve qualitatively different illocutionary assumptions and intentions.

Let's begin with *order*, in uses where the person being addressed appears as the direct object of the verb, as in the examples below. Notice that we are not considering the more specialized use of *ordering* food or drink in a restaurant or pub; nor the syntactic frame with an action noun as its direct object, as in *She ordered an investigation/search*, etc.

> *I order you to lay down your weapons.*
> *What makes you think you can order me around?*

When someone gives an *order*, they seem to express the assumption that the addressee has no choice but to do as they are told. In addition, however, the illocutionary assumption seems to involve the addressee's recognition or acceptance of this fact. This can be seen if *order* is contrasted with *command*, a speech act which is expected to trigger an immediate, semi-automatic response. Admittedly, the difference is subtle, but it sounds more natural to speak of giving a dog or a horse a *command* than an *order*, a fact which makes sense if *order* implies an appeal to the addressee's consciousness. Even in military contexts, where both verbs can be used freely, *order* sounds better than *command* if there is any direct or implicit appeal to the subordinates' consciousness of their own subordination. For example, *That's an order, soldier!* sounds far more natural than *That's a command, soldier.*

From these considerations we arrive at the explication below. Note that in most *ordering* the explicit dictum 'I want you to do this' would be conveyed by use of a bare imperative form.

X ordered Y to do A:

LEXICO-SYNTACTIC FRAME

a.   someone X said something to someone else Y at that time
     this someone wanted something to happen because of it

DICTUM

b.   this someone said something like this:
       'I want you do this (A)'

c.   this someone said it like someone can say something like this to someone
     else when this someone thinks like this:
     'I know that because I say this, this someone can't not do it
     I know that this someone knows the same'

The verb *tell* can occur in two syntactic frames, *tell (to do)* and *tell (that)*. Here we deal only with the first of these, for the sake of the comparison with *order*. *Tell* is a common, versatile, and stylistically plain word. The speaker expresses the message something like 'I want you to know that I want you to do this (A).' This 'informative' aspect of the dictum presumably accounts for the semantic shift from *tell that* to *tell to*.

Though there is no assumption that the addressee is obliged to obey (*tell* is not power-oriented, unlike *order*), there is a certain peremptory quality to be accounted for. In the explication this is conveyed by the speaker's apparent assumption that the addressee will do it once he or she knows that the speaker wants him or her to do it.

X told Y to do A:

a.   someone X said something to someone else Y at that time
     this someone wanted something to happen because of it

b.   this someone said something like this:
     'I want you to know that I want you to do this (A)'

c.   this someone said it like someone can say something like this to someone
     else when this someone thinks like this:
     'because I say this, after this, this someone will do it'

The ostensibly 'informative' dictum of *tell*, i.e. its formulation as 'I want you to know that I want you do this', may be responsible for the fact that, unlike *order*, *tell* always requires an addressee argument. Thus, one cannot say **'Silence', he told*, in the same way that one can say *'Silence', he ordered*.

Suggest is a bit trickier than either *tell* or *order*, so to help us focus on it here are some examples showing turns of phrase which can be used to make suggestions:

'Well, then, supposing we go and call on him', suggested the Mole.
'Maybe you should just drop the whole thing and cut your losses', she suggested.

'How about going to see a doctor?' Harry suggested.
'Why don't you confide in Mark?' I suggested.

A *suggestion* is a mild, unassuming speech act. The speaker thinks (or purports to think) that it might be a good thing if the addressee does something, and therefore speaks up so that the addressee will think about doing it. There is no assumption that the addressee will necessarily follow the suggestion; on the contrary, consistent with the frequent use of interrogative forms (like *How about . . .* and *Why don't you . . .*), the speaker seems at pains to disclaim any such assumption. The implicit messages conveyed by a *suggestion* are of an essentially tentative nature. The speaker distances him or herself from any idea that he or she personally wants the addressee to do it, and also acknowledges the addressee's freedom to do as he or she wishes.

These observations can be summed up in the explication below. Note that the frame explicated here oversimplifies the possible range of roles involved in *suggesting*. It is quite possible for *X to suggest to Y that Z do A*, but for the sake of simplicity we assume that the addressee and the prospective actor are the same.

X suggested that Y do A:

LEXICO-SYNTACTIC FRAME

a.   someone X said something to someone else Y at that time
     this someone wanted something to happen because of it

DICTUM

b.   this someone said something like this:
     'it can be good if you do this (A)
     it can be good if you think about it'

APPARENT MENTAL STATE

c.   this someone said it like someone can say something like this to someone else
     when this someone thinks like this:
        'I don't want this someone to think that I think like this:
           "because I say this, after this, this someone will do it"
        I know that if this someone wants not to do it, this someone can not do it'

5.3.5 *Evaluative speech acts:* praise, criticize, compliment, insult

As mentioned, not all speech acts follow the semantic template we have been using so far. In this section we look at four examples that use a second template. One distinctive thing about verbs like these is that it is not possible to state a 'model dictum' for them, though it is possible (indeed essential) to characterize what the speaker says in evaluative terms; when one *praises* someone, for example, one says something very good about this someone; when one *compliments* someone, one says something good about this someone; when one *criticizes* someone, one says something bad about this someone.

To see this in action, consider the following explication for *praise*.

X praised Y (for . . .):

LEXICO-SYNTACTIC FRAME

a.   someone X said something very good about someone else Y at that time this someone wanted something to happen because of it

APPARENT MENTAL STATE

b.   this someone said it like someone can say something like this about someone else when this someone thinks like this about this someone else:
      'this someone did something very good
      if other people know about it, they can think something very good
      about this someone because of it
      I want someone to know this'

Notice that the reference to 'people' in the apparent mental state implies that *praising* is a speech act with an implicitly public dimension, even though particular acts of *praising* may be directed to single individuals. The prototypical praiser appears to think not only that 'this someone did something very good' but also that if people knew about it, it would bring credit to this person ('if other people know about it, they can think something very good about this someone because of it'). The final component attributes to the praising person the thought 'I want someone to know this.' This combination of components is compatible with the fact that one may praise someone with or without the praised person being present, as for example:

> *In announcing his separation from his wife, Nelson Mandela praised her for her support and sacrifice while he was in prison.*

Criticize can be seen as the negative inverse of *praise*, except that the 'strength' of the evaluation is perhaps not as great, i.e. *praise* involves 'very good', whereas *criticize* involves merely 'bad' (not 'very bad').

X criticized Y (for...):

a.   someone X said something bad about someone else Y at that time
     this someone wanted something to happen because of it

b. this someone said it like someone can say something like this about someone
     else when this someone thinks like this about this someone else:
         'this someone did something bad
         if other people know about it, they can think something bad
         about this someone because of it
         I want someone to know this'

Compliment differs from *praise* and *criticize* in that it is typically
addressed to the person concerned. In a *compliment* the speaker says
something good about the addressee, apparently to express some good
feeling about the addressee. The 'addressee orientation' of *compliment* is
reflected syntactically in the fact that the complement of *compliment* is
usually the person, rather than the thing or aspect chosen for positive
comment.

The apparent mental state includes awareness that the comment can be
pleasing to the addressee and a hint of premeditation ('if I say this, this
someone can feel something good because of it'). It also includes a wish to
please the addressee ('I want this'). It's a subtle point, but this configuration does not quite amount to saying that the complimenter says it
because he or she wants to please. Nevertheless, it is enough to distinguish
between *complimenting* someone and merely expressing appreciation.
(Incidentally, the fact that the speaker appears to assume that his or her
opinion matters to the addressee helps explain why a *compliment* can be felt
to be presumptuous.)

X complimented Y:

a.   someone X said something good about someone else Y
         to this someone else at that time
     this someone wanted something to happen because of it

b.   this someone said it like someone can say something like this to someone
     else when this someone thinks like this about this someone else:
         'if I say this, this someone can feel something good because of it
         I want this'

Finally, let's consider *insult*, which comes close to being a converse of *compliment*. As with *compliment*, it involves an awareness of the potential negative impact of speaking in this way and a wish to achieve such an effect (the strength of the effect is stronger, however: 'very bad', not just 'bad'). A difference is that *insulting* (as a kind of speech act) attracts a negative evaluation.

X insulted Y:

LEXICO-SYNTACTIC FRAME

a.   someone X said something very bad about someone else Y
      to this someone else at that time
    this someone wanted something to happen because of it

APPARENT MENTAL STATE

b.   this someone said it like someone can say something like this to someone
      else when this someone thinks like this about this someone else:
        'I want this someone to feel something very bad because I say this'

NEGATIVE EVALUATION

c.   it is bad if someone says something like this to someone else in this way

5.4 Cultural aspects of speech acts

Because the speech-act verbs in a language constitute a kind of inventory of culturally recognized ways for interacting through speech, studying them can help bring to light important aspects of the culture of its speakers. The semantic distinctions and dimensions involved can open a window onto the social values and cultural history of a people. After some reflections on the possible significance of the general English speech-act inventory, we will consider two case studies: first, some of the characteristic speech-act verbs of Australian English, and, secondly, the role and nature of 'apologizing' in Japanese, as opposed to *apologizing* and *thanking* in English.

5.4.1 Cultural aspects of English speech-act verbs

One of the most noticeable things about English speech-act verbs is that there are so many of them—hundreds rather than the dozens (or even fewer) found in many other languages. Furthermore, they are of relatively high frequency and salience for English speakers, providing as they do an elaborate framework for us to interpret verbal interaction. This applies in particular to public life, as carried on through the media. How often do news headlines consist of speech acts—of phrases such as *X accuses Y of Z*, *X condemns...*, *X offers...*, *X hails...*, and so on? As Wierzbicka (1987: 3) remarks: 'It would not be an exaggeration to say that public life can be conceived as a gigantic network of speech acts.'

This prompts one to ask where the English speech-act verbs have come from historically. Elizabeth Traugott (1994) investigated the origins of English speech-act verbs. She found that literacy and feudalism have played a big part in the evolution of the present inventory. Many performatives are first found in written feudal proclamations or court rulings, and only much later came to be used in the speech of ordinary people. Since performative verbs offer one of the most explicit and precise means of enacting speech acts, they are of special utility in such contexts. One might speculate that extensive inventories of speech-act verbs are most likely to develop in cultures which have writing.

Even within the languages of Europe, however, there are marked differences in the size of the speech-act lexicon overall, and in the concentrations of particular kinds of speech-act verbs. In some cases, cultural explanations suggest themselves. For example, English has a relative proliferation of 'directives' compared with other European languages, as can be seen by comparing the lists below, which show English and Russian directives. List (a) shows English and Russian words which are roughly equivalent in meaning. List (b) shows English words without any lexical equivalents in Russian (Wierzbicka 1988: 251–3). Of course there is room to argue over individual details, but the general point that the English inventory is much larger should be clear.

(a) *velet'*, *prikazyvat* 'order', *komandovat'* 'command', *trebovat'* 'demand', *rasporjažat'sja* 'direct', *prosit'* 'ask', *umoljat'* 'beg', *predlogat'* 'propose', *sovetovat'* 'advise', *ugovorivat'* 'persuade', *poručit'* 'charge', *predpisat'* 'prescribe'

(b) *request, implore, beseech, entreat, plead, suggest, require, instruct, urge, apply, advocate, intercede, counsel, appeal, decree, enjoin, ordain, book, authorize, commission*

Most linguists accept that lexical elaboration often betokens cultural significance. For example, the importance of kinship in Australian Aboriginal societies is connected with the highly elaborate kinship nomenclature. The importance of the seasons and the natural world to Japanese culture is reflected in the large number of Japanese terms referring to such things (cf. Inoue 1979: 296–8). So we may well ask: What aspect, if any, of the English (or 'Anglo') culture is behind the great number and specialization of English directive speech-act verbs?

An interesting, though still somewhat speculative, suggestion is that Anglo culture is particularly interested, so to speak, in different 'strategies of human interaction' and in particular with specifying the interplay between causation and volition (cf. Bally 1920; Wierzbicka 1988: 251–3). Aside from the proliferation of directive speech-act verbs, this same tendency could be seen reflected in the wealth of English causative constructions, i.e. with the subtle distinctions English draws between *making* someone do something, *getting* them to do it, *having* them do it, and so on (see Chapter 10).

5.4.2 Australian English speech-act verbs

It may have occurred to you that there are dangers in generalizing about the 'English language' and 'Anglo culture' as though these were uniform entities. Is it not true that the English language, perhaps more than any other, exists in a huge range of dialects and varieties around the world? If speech-act verbs reflect cultural categories, we should expect to find culturally relevant variation among the different varieties of English. This indeed turns out to be the case. Australian English, for example, has a number of speech-act verbs that are reflective of its traditional 'tough', anti-sentimental and anti-authoritarian ethos (Wierzbicka 1997: 202–16). These include *whinging* (looked at in detail below), *knocking* (roughly, to more or less automatically run down someone who appears to have big ideas or ambitions), *rubbishing* (roughly, heaping abuse on someone), and *dobbing* (roughly, betraying one's mates or peers by reporting bad behaviour to someone in authority).

In order to appreciate what is distinctive about *whinge*, we need to look first at the general speech-act verb *complain*. This verb is polysemous; the explication below is for the meaning *complain about* (not *complain of*), i.e. the meaning that corresponds to the noun *complaint*.

X complained to Y (about . . .):
LEXICO-SYNTACTIC FRAME

a.   someone X said something to someone else Y at that time
DICTUM

b.   this someone said something like this:
  'something bad happened to me some time before because someone
     else did something
  I feel something bad because of this'
APPARENT MENTAL STATE

c.   this someone said it like someone can say something like this to someone
     else when this someone thinks like this:
  'I want someone to do something because of this'

The explication is compatible, as required, with the different possible helpful responses to *complaining*, such as taking remedial action or doing something to help assuage the complaining person's bad feelings.

Let's look now at the Australian English *whinge*, which roughly corresponds to a blend of *complain* and *whine*. Although *whinge* is an old English word, it is today much more common in Australian English than in British English. It may also have a somewhat different meaning in the two countries. The following comments are intended to apply only to Australian English usage, as illustrated in examples like these:

  a. *Stop whinging! (frequently addressed to young children)*
  b. *Stop your whinging and get on with the job.*
  c. *Instead of whinging to the media about being shunted out of the team, he knuckled down and produced some fine performances on the field.*

Whinge differs from *complain* in several interrelated ways. To begin with, it is seen as bad and, more specifically, as weak. The underlying idea is that people should be tough enough to put up with some hardship, especially if, as the term *whinge* implies, hardships are inevitable and complaint futile. Secondly, *whinging*, like *nagging*, suggests monotonous repetition. Corresponding to *whinge*, there is the noun *whinger* (whereas there is no such noun as *complainer*). It implies a certain lack of maturity and strength, someone who complains in a semi-controlled fashion like that of a baby in distress. (Someone who demonstrates 'babyish' qualities of fearfulness, timidity, and easy vulnerability to pain can be vilified as a *sook*, another important Australianism.)

With this by way of background, one can suggest the explication below, adapted from Wierzbicka (2003a: 181–2). The verb is explicated in its most characteristic form, namely, the progressive.

X was whinging:

LEXICO-SYNTACTIC FRAME

a.   someone X was saying something to someone else Y for some time at that time

DICTUM

b.   this someone said something like this:
     'something bad is happening to me
     I feel something bad because of this'

APPARENT MENTAL STATE

c.   this someone said it like someone can say something like this to someone else when this someone thinks like this:
     'I don't want something like this to be happening to me
     because of this, I want someone else to do something
     I can't do anything'

NEGATIVE EVALUATION

d.   it is very bad if someone says something like this to someone else in this way

Aside from the different apparent mental state, the explication for *whinging* also differs from that of *complain* in its strongly negative evaluation component.

Commentators have often remarked on the value traditional Australian culture places on toughness and resilience, and on its 'anti-sentimentality' (cf. Ward 1958; Baker 1959). Horne (1986 [1964]), among others, has noted that icons such as the Anzac soldiers, the explorers, the bush-rangers, and the early settlers of the harsh Australian 'bush' exemplify such toughness, including the ability, if necessary, to suffer in silence. The semantics and the frequency of the verb *whinge* in Australian English can be seen as a lexical reflex of these characteristically Australian cultural values.

5.4.3 'Apologies' and 'thanks' in Japan

In the literature on Japanese culture and society it is often said that in Japan it is important to apologize very frequently and in a broad range of situations. For instance, Coulmas (1981: 82) writes of the difficulties that the extensive everyday usage of 'apology expressions' poses for a Western student.

Even if he has learnt the most common expressions of apology, he finds out very soon that he lacks the necessary knowledge of speech situations which would allow him to predict and use them in an appropriate way. . . . For instance, a formula such as *sumimasen* or its variants *sumimasen domo, domo sumimasen deshita*, etc. can be used as a general conversation opener; attention getter; leave taking formula; *ex ante* or *ex post* apology; and, notably, gratitude formula.

By '*ex ante* apology' Coulmas means an expression like English *Excuse me*, by which one 'apologizes' before making some imposition. An *ex post* apology is the kind of speech act we normally think of as an apology, i.e. saying you are sorry after you have done something. By 'gratitude formula', Coulmas means the kind of response appropriate upon receiving a gift. Of course, in this situation it would be very odd to say in English *Excuse me* or *I'm sorry*, but in Japanese *sumimasen* is quite appropriate. The explanation for this (to Western sensibilities) odd blurring of the distinction between thanks and apologies is that 'the Japanese conception of gifts and favours focuses on the trouble they have caused the benefactor rather than the aspects which are pleasing to the recipient' (1981: 83). As another example, Coulmas mentions that when leaving after a dinner invitation, rather than say anything like *Thank you so much for the wonderful evening*, as one might in the Western style, the Japanese guest is more likely to say something like *O-jama itashimashita* 'I have intruded on you' (1981: 83).

For a Japanese 'apology' to be called for, it is not necessary for the speaker to have done anything wrong. To illustrate this point, the Japanese psychiatrist Takeo Doi relates the experience of an American colleague who through some oversight in immigration formalities found himself being hauled over the coals by a Japanese immigration official.

However often he explained it was not really his fault, the official would not be appeased, until, at the end of his tether, he said 'I'm sorry . . .' as a prelude to a further argument, whereupon the official's expression suddenly changed and he dismissed the matter without further ado. (2000: 51)

This is consistent with Hiroko Kataoka's (1991: 64) comment in his culture manual *Japanese Cultural Encounters and How to Handle Them* that 'In Japan, one is expected to apologize . . . whenever the other party suffers in any way, materially or emotionally.'

It should be pointed out that there is a very wide range of 'apology' formulas available to the Japanese speaker, including not only *sumimasen* (lit. 'not completed'), but also *gomeiwaku wo kakemashita* 'I have caused you trouble', *shitsurei shimashita* 'I was rude', *o-wabi itashimasu* 'I offer my apologies', *mooshiwake arimasen* 'there is no excuse (to be said)', *sore-wa kyoshuku desu* 'I feel ashamed (lit. 'shrunken')', *o-kinodoku-sama (deshita)* 'I'm terribly sorry' (lit. 'this must have been poison to your soul'). These all differ in meaning, and would each be appropriate for different circumstances and different degrees of seriousness.

Here we will only address the expression *sumimasen to iu* 'to say *sumimasen*', since *sumimasen* is probably the most common and versatile of the 'apology' formulas mentioned above. The first and most obvious point to make is that we cannot expect words like *apologize, thank, regret,* and *sympathy,* which are all complex cultural constructs of the English language, to correspond to the complex cultural concepts of another language. At this level of lexical complexity it is impossible to translate precisely between English and Japanese (or any other language). However, if the meaning of the complex expressions can be broken down into much simpler concepts which do have lexical equivalents in both languages, translation (of a sort) becomes possible.

To inform our explication of what is conveyed in saying *sumimasen* we can begin with Coulmas' (1981: 88) observation that Japanese culture includes what he calls an 'ethics of indebtedness':

In Japan, the smallest favour makes the receiver a debtor. . . . Not every favour can be repaid, and if circumstances do not allow proper repayment, Japanese tend to apologize. They acknowledge the burden on the debt and their own internal discomfort about it. It is in this context that one must view the many words the Japanese have to express obligation.

This tallies with the fact that the expression *sumimasen* itself is derived from the verb *sumimasu* 'completed' in combination with the negative marker *-en,* so that, as mentioned above, it literally means 'not completed'—a reference to the need to repay the obligation to the benefactor. The other 'apology formulas' focus on the speaker's behaviour, either expressing the speaker's 'discomfort' about it (e.g. *mooshiwake arimasen* 'there is no excuse', *shitsurei shimashita* 'I was rude', *sore-wa kyoshuku desu* 'I feel ashamed') or acknowledging its effect on the addressee (e.g. *o-jama itashimashita* 'I have intruded on you', *gomeiwaku wo kakemashita* 'I have caused you trouble', *o-kinodoku-sama (deshita)* 'this must have been poison to your soul').

The explication below attempts to spell out the content of *sumimasen.* The explication format is different from that of a speech-act verb (after all, *sumimasen* is a formula word, not a speech-act verb), inasmuch as it is all 'content'.

X sumimasen to iimashita ('*X said* sumimasen'):
someone X said something like this to someone else:
   I feel something bad now because it is like this:
     I did something before
     because of this, you couldn't not do something good for me
   I think like this now because of this:
    'I can't not do something good for you after this
    I want to do it
    I can't do anything now'

The explication depicts *sumimasen* as expressing, first and foremost, a bad feeling brought about by the fact that (as the speaker portrays it) the addressee has had to do something because 'I did something'. The explication is of course terribly vague, but this is as it should be to be consistent with the very wide range of circumstances in which one might say *sumimasen*. The phrasing is intended to allow for any form of causal involvement. Along with this awareness of having been involved in causing trouble, inconvenience, etc., to the addressee, someone who says *sumimasen* is presented as feeling obliged to return the favour ('I can't not do something good for you after this'), though unable to do so at the current time. This aspect receives support from the existence of the traditional Japanese cultural concept *on*, and from the fact that Japanese commentators expressly link the need to 'apologize' with *on*. The meaning of *on* is not easy to convey in English, but it has to do with the burden of obligation to repay any debt or favour, no matter how large or small (cf. Lebra 1974; Wierzbicka 1997).

The scale of difference between 'saying *sumimasen*' and *apologizing* (the English speech-act) can be seen by comparison with the following explication for *apologize*.

X apologized to Y (for doing A):

LEXICO-SYNTACTIC FRAME

a. someone X said something to someone else Y at that time

DICTUM

b. this someone said something like this:
     'I know that you can feel something bad because I did something (A)
       before
     I want you to know that I feel something bad because of this'

APPARENT MENTAL STATE

c. this someone said it like someone can say something like this to someone else
     when this someone thinks like this about this someone else:
       'this someone can feel something bad towards me now
       I don't want this'

Comparing the two explications, the major differences are along two dimensions; first, the English verb's focus on the addressee's possible bad feelings and on the speaker's implied wish to soften any bad feelings towards him or herself; and secondly, the complete lack in the English verb of any acknowledgement of indebtedness. From a Japanese point of view, one can imagine that English *apologizing* may seem rather self-centred.

5.4.4 Cross-cultural comparisons of speech acts

Since the meanings of speech-act verbs differ from language to language, it would obviously be Anglocentric to adopt English speech-act categories as a framework for comparison across cultures. Nevertheless, a considerable body of work in contrastive pragmatics (e.g. Blum-Kulka, House, and Kasper 1989; Blum-Kulka and Kasper 1993; Pütz and Neff-van Aertselaer 2008) has done just this, i.e. it has taken English-based speech-act categories such as 'thanking', 'apology', 'compliment', 'request', 'advice', 'complaint', etc. and asked the research question: How are these speech acts 'realized' differently in different languages? Although many valuable findings have come to light in this research (about different patterns of directness or politeness, different formal means of expression, e.g. imperatives, questions, modalized sentences, etc.), treating English speech-act verbs as neutral analytical categories misrepresents the indigenous conceptualization of speech acts of other cultures and imposes an 'outsider perspective'. At the same time, failing to focus attention on the precise meanings of indigenous speech-act terms cuts off a rich source of information and insight into the speech practices of other cultures. For interesting semantic studies of speech-act verbs and related phenomena, such as conversational routines, in other languages and cultures, see Ameka (1999; 2006; 2009) on Ewe, Goddard (2002a; 2004b) on Malay, Wierzbicka (2003a; in press b) on Polish and Russian, Maher (2002) on Italian, and Pedersen (2010) on Swedish.

Key technical terms

apparent mental state	lexico-syntactic frame
constitutive rule	negative evaluation
dictum	performative verb

felicity condition

illocutionary force

illocutionary force indicating device
   (IFID)

sincerity condition

speech-act verb

Exercises and discussion questions

† next to a problem means that a solution or some commentary can be found at the end of this book.

1†. Consider the following list of verbs: *threaten, concede, believe, say, thank, convince, deny, boast, joke, nominate.* (a) Which of them are performative verbs? In each case, illustrate with a sentence which can be used performatively. (b) Of those which are not performative, which are nonetheless speech-act verbs? Again, give a sentence to justify each answer.

2†. Critically discuss the following analysis (Searle 1969: 67) of *congratulate.* Assess both its descriptive adequacy and the way it is phrased.

Propositional content: Some event act, etc. related to H.
Preparatory conditions: E is in H's interest and S believes E is in H's interest.
Sincerity condition: S is pleased at E.
Essential condition: Counts as an expression of pleasure at E.

3†. Speech-act verbs do not always correspond closely in meaning to their noun counterparts. Consider the verb *to advise,* as used in sentences like *Henry Kissinger advised the President against the meeting* and *I advise you to leave the country as soon as you can.* Compare it with the colloquial use of the noun *advice,* in contexts like *My advice would be to ...* or *If you want my advice, ...* Try to identify one or more differences in meaning between the verb *to advise* and the expressions like *my advice* and *(to give) advice.*

4†. Consider the dictum component for the verbs *recommend* and *suggest.* For each verb choose the most appropriate selection of components from the following list.

> I know that you want to do something at some time after this
> I know some things about things like this
> I know much (many things) about things like this
> I want you to know that I think like this: it will be good for you if you do this
> it can be good if you do this (A)
> it will be good for you if you do this (A)
> it can be good if you think about it
> I want to know what you think about it

5†. Try your hand at a reductive paraphrase analysis of the verb *to thank*, as used in examples like these:

To be polite I thanked him for his concern.
A spokesman for Health Minister Jim Elder yesterday thanked Mr Horan for drawing attention to the signs.
He thanked them for their efforts.
He apologized to the fans and thanked them for their prayers and their support.

First consider the dictum. That is, what kind of message does someone express verbally when they *thank*? Then try to identify the apparent mental state components. (Note: The verb *to thank* is not exactly the same in meaning as saying '*thank you*'.)

6†. Kinship plays an enormous role in Australian Aboriginal cultures. Everyone is regarded as 'related' to everyone else and so, naturally, kinship names (i.e. words with meanings like 'mother', 'auntie', 'father', or 'sister-in-law') are extended to apply to everyone. Kinship roles play a big part in regulating expectations about behaviour; for example, one is expected to provide food and assistance of all kinds to certain types of kin, to joke and kid around with certain types of kin while remaining quiet and subdued with others, and so on. Speculate a little. What kinds of special 'kinship-based' speech-act verbs do you think might be found in such cultures?

7. Studies have shown that 'compliments' are used with different frequencies, and meet with different typical responses, in England, the United States, and South Africa. Compliments are more frequent and found in a wider range of settings in the USA than in the other two countries. On the other hand, in South Africa and England a compliment is more likely to meet with an outright acceptance (e.g. *Thank you*) than in the USA, where other kinds of responses are more likely, such as disavowals or rejections, 'returning the compliment', or deflecting the praise to someone else. Can you think of any cultural factors that might help explain these facts?

8†. Malay–English dictionaries usually list several meanings for the verb *ajak*, including 'invite', 'encourage', and 'urge', but it is questionable whether *ajak* is polysemous. Consider the examples below and see if you can devise a plausible dictum for *ajak* that would be equally appropriate for all of them.

a. *'Chan pun marilah makan sama,' **ajak** ayah Arfan. 'Yalah. Marilah makan sama. Makan ramai-ramai ni lebih berselera,' emak Arfan turut **mengajak**.*
'"Chan, come eat with us," Arfan's father *urged*. "Yeah, come join us. The food tastes better when we all eat together," Arfan's mother *added encouragingly*.'
b. *Dia kata lepas exam, dia nak **ajak** Dura dan kak Muna jalan-jalan.*
'He said that he wanted to *invite* me and Muna out walking after his exams.'

c. *'Mari ke bilik Kis, kak. Salin pakaian,'* **ajak** *Balkis.*
' "Come to my room, sis. (We can) change into some fresh clothes," *suggested* Balkis.'

d. *Kerapkali juga dia* **diajak** *menaiki kereta yang dimiliki oleh lelaki-lelaki yang tidak ternampak kejujuran, dia menolak.*
'When from time to time she was *invited* to get into cars driven by men who didn't look trustworthy, she declined.'

e. *Ada juga sorang dua member* **ajak** *aku cari kerja...*
'There were two friends who *encouraged* me to go looking for work (with them)...'

6
Discourse particles and interjections

The classical grammarians used the term 'particles' for all the small, morphologically inert words which were left over after nouns, pronouns, verbs, and the other major grammatical classes had been established. On this broad definition, the class would take in most English prepositions and subordinating conjunctions, as well as words like *well*, *just*, *even*, and *too*, which are more typical examples of the way the term 'particle' (or discourse particle) is employed in modern linguistics. Interjections are words or phrases which can constitute an utterance in their own right, such as *Gosh*, *Yuck*, *Uh-oh*, *Oops*, *Shit*, and *Goodness gracious*. Sometimes the broader term 'discourse marker' is used to refer to items of both kinds.

Discourse particles and interjections interest semanticists for many reasons. For one thing, their meanings are particularly difficult to state and to translate, though fluent use of discourse particles and interjections is part and parcel of semantic competence. Ordinary conversations are peppered with them. Not surprisingly, they are often misunderstood and misused by second-language learners. Odd as it might sound, many particles have an affiliation with speech-act verbs in that they express the personal intentions, attitudes, assumptions, and feelings of the speaker.

6.1 Describing particles and interjections

Many grammars devote no more than a handful of pages to discourse particles and interjections, and some omit them entirely.

Partly this is because conventional grammatical description focuses on the sentence and often relies heavily on examples obtained from elicitation rather than natural discourse. Partly it is because most particles are usually 'optional' in the strict grammatical sense, and do not interface with the major systems of grammar. And partly it is because particle and interjection meanings are so difficult to state.

6.1.1 How to state the meaning

Aside from reductive paraphrase, there are three ways in which particles, interjections, and other discourse markers are normally described. The first approach is simply to compare the elusive meaning or function of the particle with that of a similar particle in another language, usually English. The theoretical problem with this 'translation equivalents' approach is that particles in different languages very rarely match up perfectly, even in number, let alone in meaning. For instance, corresponding to the two English particles *too* and *also*, Malay has three particles, *pun*, *juga*, and *pula*. In the case of Malay *lah*, it is hard to find any English word which can provide a consistent translation equivalent. Different authors have glossed it as 'for heaven's sake', 'I am pleading', 'of course', and 'really'.

The second approach is the use of technical or semi-technical functional labels. For instance, Halliday and Hasan (1976) describe English *too*, *moreover*, and *by the way* as 'additive', 'additive emphatic', and 'additive de-emphatic', respectively. Sometimes the labels are drawn from the fields of conversation analysis or discourse analysis. For instance, Schiffrin (1987) describes *oh* and *well* as markers of 'information management' and 'response', respectively. Functional labels are usually combined with a description of where the particle or marker occurs, i.e. its environment of occurrence. As Travis (2006) points out, this approach does not furnish a clear specification of meaning or a reliable guide to usage.

A description based solely on environment of occurrence and function fails
to capture...what it is that is shared across the range of use, how one marker
differs from others that can be used with similar functions and in similar environments,...what the relationship is between the marker and homonymic forms
in other word classes. (Travis 2006: 220)

It is particularly unhelpful to hear that a discourse particle conveys
'emphasis', a statement that could be made with equal justification of
English *too* and Malay *lah*, which we will see differ markedly in their
meanings. Aside from its vagueness, a problem with the label 'emphatic'
is that even in a single language there are usually several particles which
could fit this description. For example, in Malay the particles *pun*, *pula*, and
juga could all qualify as 'emphatic'. Obviously, different kinds of emphasis
are involved. But how can the differences be stated clearly and precisely?

A third approach is to provide a list of examples and commentary on the
various 'uses'. The theoretical objection to this procedure is that it leaves it to
the reader's linguistic intuition to infer what the various uses have in common
and how they differ, instead of making it explicit. Sometimes the same particle
will seem capable of being used in almost diametrically opposite ways. For
instance, the Malay *lah* may convey either a 'light-hearted' or an 'ill-tempered'
effect.

Even when these three methods are used in combination—as they usually
are—they rarely suffice to convey the meaning involved in a clear and
complete way, sufficient to enable someone unfamiliar with the language
to know when the particle or interjection may and may not be used.

The reductive paraphrase approach has been applied quite extensively to
particles and interjections in various languages, and with considerable success
(cf. Wierzbicka 1986b; Ameka 1992b; Travis 2006). Of course, this means
giving up the idea that such meanings are simple enough to be summed up in
a few words (like 'emphasis' or 'response marker'), and instead seeking fully
articulated and intelligibly phrased paraphrases. When we do this, we find
that many particles and almost all interjections are illocutionary, in the sense
that they express bundles of thoughts, wants, and feelings connected with the
act of speaking.

Interestingly, this approach to particles was anticipated by Locke and
Leibniz back in the seventeenth century. Locke (1976 [1690]: 245–6) remarked
in 1690 that particles encapsulate the 'postures of mind while discoursing'
and thus have 'the sense of a whole sentence contained in them'. Leibniz
added:

An abstract account . . . is not enough for a thorough explication of [the] particles: what we need is a paraphrase which can be substituted for the particle, just as a definition can be put in place of the defined expression. (Leibniz 1981 [1765]: III. vii. 332)

For most of the rest of this chapter we will explore particle and interjectional meanings using the paraphrase method. Before that, however, let's just look briefly at the distinction between discourse particles and interjections, and at some of the schemes that have been proposed for classifying different types of each.

6.1.2 Classifying particles and interjections

DISCOURSE PARTICLES and INTERJECTIONS have a lot in common. Formally, both kinds of element are morphologically invariable, and from a functional point of view, both tend to express a speaker's immediate 'here-and-now' attitudes, thoughts, and desires. The basic difference between them is grammatical. It concerns syntactic dependence. As Ameka (1992a: 108) explains:

whereas [discourse] particles are fully integrated into the syntax of utterances and cannot constitute utterances by themselves, interjections can be utterances by themselves and they are always separated by a pause from other utterances with which they may co-occur.

As one might expect from this, discourse particles usually express speaker attitudes towards a proposition (the content of the sentence of which they are a part), while interjections express 'self-contained' messages. Admittedly, particles do sometimes occur by themselves but in such cases they usually carry rising intonation (for example *And?* or *Well?*) signalling they are elliptical. In effect, the speaker is saying that there is something remaining to be said. Also, interjections can (and often do) occur as co-utterances, as for instance in *Oh, I don't know*, or *Gee, you look tired*, but this does not affect the fact that *Oh* and *Gee* can be complete utterances unto themselves.

Particles can be either words or CLITIC PARTICLES. You may not have heard the term 'clitic' before. It refers to a morpheme with an intermediate status between a word and an affix. Clitics are grammatically and semantically 'word-like', but they do not normally stand alone phonologically. Instead they attach themselves to the nearest 'normal' word, no matter what word-class it belongs to.

Interjections are by definition always phonologically independent items, but, interestingly, they are not always words, or at least not items which would be recognized as words by ordinary speakers. This is partly because interjections tend to be phonologically or morphologically anomalous. For instance, the English *tsk-tsk* (also spelt *tut-tut*) is a series of dental clicks, but clicks are not found in the phoneme inventory of English. Similarly, *Mmm*, *Psst!*, and *Shh!* don't contain vowels. Speakers tend to see such interjections simply as 'noises', without recognizing that they are conventionalized in form and almost always lack precise semantic equivalents in other languages. Ameka (1992a: 106) calls them 'conventionalized vocal gestures'. This is true even though there is often a degree of sound symbolism involved. For instance, English *Phooey!*, German *Pfui!*, and Polish *Fu!* all express a mild reaction to something unpleasant, as if blowing away an unpleasant smell, but their precise meanings and ranges of use are different.

Interjections can be divided into PRIMARY INTERJECTIONS (such as the examples mentioned so far) and SECONDARY INTERJECTIONS, which are forms identical to words of other word-classes. Swear words like *Damn!*, *Christ!*, *Fuck!*, and emotive words like *Bother!* and *Shame!* are English examples of secondary interjections. Interjections as a part of speech are also to be distinguished from interjectional phrases, such as *Dear me*, *Goodness gracious*, *Bloody hell*, *Thank God*.

Various semantic and functional schemas have been proposed to categorize particles and interjections, but, as with speech acts, such schemes are never watertight, and there is no real reason to expect that a single set of discrete categories could neatly accommodate the great variety of complex meanings expressed by discourse particles and interjections in all the world's languages. Classificatory schemes can be useful, however, to give some indication of the range of meanings involved.

Discourse particles can be grouped into the following categories (cf. Ameka 1992a): (i) connectives, such as English *and*, *or*, and *but*; (ii) information-status particles, often labelled as 'topic markers' in languages which have them; (iii) illocutionary function particles, such as questioning and exclamatory particles found in some African and Asian languages; (iv) modal particles, as in Germanic languages; (v) evidential particles, certifying the speaker's source of knowledge (see section 11.4); (vi) focus particles, which indicate how something figures in relation to other potential or real alternatives, either excluding them (like *only*, *merely*) or adding to them (like *also*, *too*, *even*).

Interjections can be divided into emotive, volitive, and cognitive (cf. Wierzbicka 2003a; Ameka 1992a) as follows.

(i) EMOTIVE INTERJECTIONS have as their primary component 'I feel something (good/bad) now'; for example, *Wow!* and *Ouch!* (ii) VOLITIVE INTERJECTIONS are primarily directed towards getting a reaction from the addressee; they contain the component 'I want you to do something now'. Examples include attention-getters such as *Hey!*, urgers to silence like *Shh!*, and signals of one's location like *Cooee!* (iii) COGNITIVE INTERJECTIONS have as their primary component 'I think like this now' or 'I now know something'. Some are self-focused such as *Aha!*, but others, such as back-channelling vocalizations (like *Mhm* and *Uh-huh*), are more-or-less 'phatic', being used primarily to acknowledge continuing communicative contact.

6.2 Three English particles—*or*, *too*, and *well*

It is impossible to attempt an exhaustive or systematic coverage of English particles here. In this section we sample three English discourse particles of rather different types, the connective *or*, the focus particle *too*, and the 'response marker' *well*.

6.2.1 The connective or

Logicians usually include the operators ∧ and ∨ as basic connectives of a logical system (see section 2.3). They tend to assume that their nearest English equivalents—*and* and *or*—are primitives (or near-primitives) and that words corresponding to them are to be found in all languages. In fact, however, languages without equivalents to *or* are not difficult to find, especially in Australia. Dyirbal and Yankunytjatjara are two of the many Australian Aboriginal languages without an equivalent to *or*. Since the meaning of English *or* is not universal, this suggests that it is not semantically 'atomic' and that we should be able to decompose it into a combination of simpler, universally attested elements. But how?

Dixon in his description of 'Dyirbal logic' (1972: 361ff.) suggests that a similar meaning can be expressed in Dyirbal by using the particle *yamba* 'maybe'. Thus, to translate 'I saw a fish, it was either a barramundi or a red bream' one could say the equivalent of 'I saw a fish, what was it?—maybe a bream, maybe a barramundi.' As Wierzbicka (1996b) points out, however, a paraphrase based on *maybe* doesn't really mimic the semantics of English *or*. One problem is that by saying *maybe* the speaker is, so to speak, putting forward a hypothesis or a conjecture; by saying *maybe* twice (e.g. 'maybe A, maybe B') the speaker is putting forward two hypotheses. Using *or* doesn't have this effect. For instance, if I say *I know that Mary is either in Canberra or in Sydney*, I am not putting forward any hypotheses (and this sentence is very hard to paraphrase in terms of *maybe*).

Another tack is as follows:

> *I saw a fish, it was either a barramundi or a red bream:*
> I saw a fish
> I don't know what kind of fish it is
> I know that it was one of these two kinds: barramundi, red bream

This presents *or* as a composite meaning built up of the semantic elements ONE (OF), THIS/THESE, and TWO. (An odd piece of historical evidence consistent with this hypothesis is that *or* derives from an Old English word which meant 'one of the two'.)

Incidentally, there are also languages without words (or other morphemes) equivalent to *and*. In a cross-linguistic survey of coordination, Mithun (1988: 336) states categorically: 'A large number of languages lack any morphological or lexical indications of conjunction whatsoever.' Within Australia, this is the case in the majority of Aboriginal languages (Dixon 1980: 458), including Dyirbal. A language may also lack an equivalent to English *and* through having two or more elements which divide the work of *and* between them, as in Yankunytjatjara (Goddard 1985), where *munu* is used to join clauses with coreferential subjects and *ka* to join clauses with different subjects.

6.2.2 The focus particle too

English *too* is one of the more studied of the English particles, cf. Green (1968; 1973), Kaplan (1984), Wierzbicka (1980a), Goddard (1986). It belongs to the category of FOCUS PARTICLES (König 1991), i.e. the class of particles which indicate how something figures in relation to potential or real alternatives. More specifically, *too* has been described as an 'additive' or 'inclusive' particle, and as a marker of 'emphatic conjunction'.

At first, it seems that *too* must be polysemous since it appears in different constructions, with different effects. These include the VP-ellipsis construction as in (a), where *too* appears in a second clause where a missing VP is understood, the 'emphatic agreement' and 'emphatic contrary' constructions shown in (b) and (c), respectively, and the stressed *too* appearing after a pause, as in (d).

a. *Mary is always late/drives a Toyota, and John is/does too.*
b. A: *You're tired.* B: *I am too.*
c. A: *John didn't take it.* B: *He did too!*
d. *Harry is considerate, and he cooks, too.*

However on closer examination this seeming polysemy turns out to be more apparent than real. The range of uses can be understood in terms of a single basic meaning (roughly, 'one more the same') which can be deployed at different levels of illocutionary structure.

In VP-ellipsis constructions the *too* forms part of the 'reduced' second conjunct, which contains only an auxiliary, like *is*, or a 'pro-verb', like *does*. Clearly, the ellipsis and the presence of the *too* allow the listener to reconstruct what the speaker has in mind. For example:

Mary is/does Z. John is/does too:
Mary is/does Z. John is/does the same

Aside from its intuitive plausibility, some evidence for this explication is provided by the fact that the intriguing phrase 'the same goes for' yields a near-paraphrase. That is, example (a) is approximately the same in meaning as *Mary is always late/drives a Toyota, and the same goes for John*. The idea that *too* contains a statement about sameness is consistent with the fact that in many languages, similar particles are identical with a word meaning 'same', e.g. Latin *idem (que)* and Russian *tože*.

However, the 'additive' element of *too* is still missing. As Halliday and Hasan (1976: 246) remark, *too* (and its negative counterpart *either*) have 'an additional element of explicitness about them, a sense of "and what is more"'. In the examples in (a) it seems that John is being added, as it were, to Mary, suggesting our explication be revised as follows:

Mary is/does Z. John is/does too:
Mary is/does Z. John is one more who is/does the same

One further refinement is needed to model the type of ellipsis in these examples, which is by no means confined to this particular construction involving *too*. For present purposes, the explication below will do. It has the desirable feature that the meaning components attributable to *too* are brought together into the final position.

> *Mary is/does Z. John is/does too:*
> Mary is/does this (Z)
> John is/does the same
> [that is] he is one more who is/does the same

A similar account can be applied to the 'emphatic agreement' construction. It is clear that the people replying in the examples below are expressing a view on what has just been said:

> A: *You'll have to take the car.* B: *I will, too.*
> A: *You're tired.* B: *I am, too.*

It is easier to grasp the special effect of the replies above by comparing them with *Yes, I will* and *Yes, I am* respectively, where B also repeats part of what A has said. The difference is that the replies with *too* explicitly comment on this fact.

What is being added, however, is not a second subject or a second proposition, but the second speaker—who adds him or herself to the first, in virtue of making an identical act of judgement, assertion, etc. Roughly:

> I say this: I will/am
> [that is] I am one more who says the same

The emphatic contrary construction, illustrated below, calls for a slightly different explication, due to the greater complexity of the presuppositions involved in the exchange. In replying, speaker B defies the effect of the first utterance. Though speaker A has sought to deny or reject something, speaker B insists on saying the very same thing; what speaker A seeks to take away, speaker B insists on adding in again.

> A: *John didn't take it.* B: *He did too!*
> A: *You're not going.* B: *I am too!*

The defiant quality results from the fact that the conflict is being made perfectly explicit (the 'same thing' component); and the insistent quality from the fact that speaker B is, equally explicitly, continuing to say it (the 'additive' component). Comparing B's replies with, for instance, *Yes, he did* or *Yes, I am*, it is easy to discern that in the former case the speaker's interest is as much focused on what is happening between the speakers as it is on what is being discussed.

A: *John didn't take it:*
   I say: one can't say this – John took it
B: *He did too!:*
   I say: he did
   [that is] I say the same thing one more time

Coming now to examples where *too* bears primary stress, we can agree with Green (1973: 205) that: 'This additional separate clause intonation on the particle seems to indicate that it is itself a separate assertion ... predicated of propositions'.

Harry is considerate, and he cooks, too.
I wouldn't have any money, and you'd have to lend me your car, too.

Comparing these sentences with versions without the *too*, it seems plain that the *too* 'seems to emphasize some logical relation between the two states of affairs, some parallelism or analogy' (Wierzbicka 1980a: 277). I would advance the explication below, according to which *too* is here a comment on the second dictum.

Harry is considerate. He cooks, too:
I say this about Harry: he is considerate
I say this about him: he cooks
this is one more thing of the same kind

6.2.3 The discourse marker well

Like *too*, the humble *well* has been the subject of a series of linguistic studies, including Lakoff (1973), Wierzbicka (1976), Schiffrin (1987: ch. 5), Jucker (1993), Schourup (2001), Aijmer and Simon-Vanderbergen (2003), Cuenca (2008), and many others. It is no doubt the single most studied discourse particle of English, and probably of any language. As with *too*, the main challenge is to explain the very wide range of uses to which *well* can be put and its 'virtually unlimited range of effects' (Schourup 2001: 1057). Many functional generalizations have been offered in the literature, usually of a rather abstract nature. For example, Schiffrin (1987: 127) claims that *well* can be used 'whenever the coherence options offered by one component of talk differ from those of another'; in a similar vein, Jucker (1993) says that *well* acts as a 'signpost' that the addressee needs to adjust some of his or her 'background assumptions'; and Aijmer and Simon-Vanderbergen (2003) propose that the general function of *well* is 'to turn the utterance into a heteroglossic one, signalling the speaker's awareness of the heterogeneity of views, positioning the utterance in the context of preceding and following texts'. Despite all the scholarly attention it has received, it is generally agreed that the meaning of *well* remains elusive.

Few researchers have been prepared to advance a first-person paraphrase for the meaning of *well*, i.e. a formulation of what a speaker is expressing when he or she prefaces an utterance with *well*. Among the few who have attempted it are Wierzbicka (1976) and Schourup (2001), and the account to be proposed here builds on both of them. Actually, Schourup does not phrase his analysis directly as a paraphrase, but it is easily adapted into paraphrase form. Essentially, Schourup's (2001: 1043) idea is that *well* displays something about the speaker's mental state in relation to the flow of discourse: specifically, it portrays the speaker as 'pausing briefly to engage in a moment of real-time consideration before going on'. The explications to be proposed below express much the same idea in the form of a paraphrase in semantic primes. They include one important addition, though, which is related to the speaker's (purported) motivation. This is the idea (adapted from Wierzbicka 1976) that the speaker wants to think very briefly about what he/she is going to say next because he/she wants to make a good job of it, i.e. because he/she wants to 'say it well'. This provides a link, albeit a loose one, between the discourse particle use of *well*, and the evaluative adverb *well* (the adverbial counterpart of *good*, as in *She sings well* or *I know him well*). We will see that three slightly different explications are called for, each adapted to a different discourse context.

The first explication applies to the use of *well* in response to something that has just been said by the addressee. The final line of the explication, in square brackets, represents the speaker's main utterance, i.e. the sentence that has been prefaced with *well*.

> *Well, —*
> you said something a short time before
> because of this I want to say something after a very short time
> I'm thinking about it now because I want to say it well
> [I say: —]

Let's see how this works with a couple of naturally occurring examples (taken from Jucker 1993). In the first two examples, the addressee's prior utterance was a question. In both cases, we can understand that the speaker has good reason to want to think for a moment before replying, and to want to signal his or her intention to do so.

A: *Are you from Philadelphia?*
B: *<u>Well</u> I grew up out in the suburbs. And then I lived for about seven years in upstate New York. And then I came back here t'go to college.*

A: *Can I just see them?*
B: *Um <u>well</u>, I'm not allowed to do that.*

In the first example, we can see that B's answer turns out to be rather complex. The message expressed by *well* in this context makes sense in terms of the speaker's need to organize his or her thoughts; cf. Halliday and Hasan's (1976: 269) remark that *well* prefacing an answer means 'I acknowledge the question and will give a considered answer.' By signalling this, the speaker also alerts the addressee that he or she may need to prepare for a bit of thought too, in order to assimilate what is to follow. In the second case, speaker B is obliged to deny the addressee's request. In this context, the message expressed by *well* makes sense as an indication to the addressee that B's reply has been well considered. (In this kind of use, *well* has been described as 'face-threat mitigator', i.e. a way of reducing a potential clash (Owen 1981). As Schourup (2001: 1052) observes, making a show of some 'consideration' helps to make the reply seem more reasoned and therefore less personal.)

The 'response-prefacing' use of *well* is not restricted to responses to questions and requests. It can also be used in response to a statement that has just been made by one's conversational partner, as in the following examples (the first two from Aijmer and Simon-Vanderbergen 2003, the third from Jucker 1993). Again, by saying *well* the speaker announces the intention of saying something very soon (i.e. after a very short time) in response, and indicates that he or she is thinking about it briefly beforehand.

A: *'Sarah, if we were in the slightest danger I'd have pulled over a long time ago'.*
B: *'<u>Well</u>, I don't know that you would have,' said Sarah.*

A: *'Oh', she said. 'You're not married.'*
B: *'<u>Well</u>, I am, but she's ... living elsewhere'.*

A: *I think they've got quite a good opinion of him.*
B: *<u>Well</u> er, I have too.*

As one can glean from the examples so far, the proposed explication can fit into a wide range of contexts, because there are many possible reasons why a speaker might want to signal that he or she is engaging in a little 'prospective consideration', to use Schourup's phrase, before going ahead with the upcoming utterance.

Even saying *well* to introduce a remark which directly conflicts with what the addressee has just said can make sense in terms of the proposed explication, especially when we compare a response with *well* to other alternatives, such as *but*. Consider the two responses shown below. The B1 version, with *but*, directly highlights the contrast between the two views being expressed. The B2 version, with *well*, seems better-natured and more well-considered, almost as if the speaker were saying, 'I'm not saying this without having thought about it.'

> A: ... *never mind. It's not important.*
> B1: *But it is important.*
> B2: <u>*Well*</u>, *it is important.*

A second discourse context for *well* is when it occurs not as part of a response to what someone else has said, but inside a single speaker's 'turn'. Sometimes it indicates a moment's thought in the interests of choosing the best word or expression, either for accuracy's sake or for rhetorical effect, as in the first and second examples (from Aijmer and Simon-Vandenberg 2003 and Watts 1986, respectively). Sometimes it introduces a so-called 'background repair', as in the third example (from Schiffrin 1987).

> a. *'I remember how punctilious he was and how thorough and*—<u>*well*</u>, *dogged.'*
> b. *It's not so bad if it's a female [cat] that's spraying, but if you have a good tomcat that's spraying,* <u>*well*</u>, *it can empty the room, it can empty the house.*
> c. ... *the only thing different I think may be with*—<u>*well*</u> *in our area, it isn't because of the school. But the only difference I would think would be maybe the better schools out there.*

For contexts like these, i.e. speaker continuation, we need a second, slightly different explication, as follows.

> ... *well,* —
> I said something a short time before
> I want to say something else about it after a very short time
> I'm thinking about it now because I want to say it well
> [I say: —]

Thirdly, as a number of scholars have pointed out, *well* is sometimes used in 'discourse-initial contexts'. For instance, Schourup (2001: 1057) gives the example of a teacher standing before a hushed classroom at the opening of a class period, and speaking as in the first example below. As he points out, examples like this pose difficulties for accounts of *well* that are based on discourse coherence or on the idea that *well* signals a divergence from listener expectations. Rather, *well* is suggesting that 'the situation at hand is actively being taken into consideration in choosing what to say next'. Another type of discourse-initial use appears in the second example below (from a written source quoted by Aijmer and Simon-Vanderberg 2003). Again the speaker appears to be reacting to a 'situation' rather than to a previous utterance.

a. <u>*Well*</u>, *as you all know, we have a guest speaker with us today.*
b. *He gazed down at the sink, and the warmth from the dishes drifted gently up into his face. '*<u>*Well*</u>*, you have to carry on. You have to carry on.'*

To accommodate these uses, a third slightly different explication is needed, as follows:

Well, —
something happened here a short time before
because of this, I want to say something after a very short time
I'm thinking about it now because I want to say it well
[I say: —]

This brief treatment has not exhausted all the uses of *well* (for example, it has not covered its use as a prompt, e.g. *Well?*), but it has covered the main ones. In broad terms, the outcome is consistent with Travis's (2005) study of discourse markers in Colombian Spanish, the most comprehensive single study so far of the semantics of discourse markers from an NSM point of view. In her analysis of the Spanish discourse marker *bueno*, Travis proposed four interrelated explications, each appropriate to a different discourse environment but sharing a partial semantic invariant. We have proposed for *well* three explications, all sharing the components 'I want to say something (about it) after a very short time' and 'I'm thinking about it now because I want to say it well'. In addition, however, each explication has some distinctive components that tailor it, or tie it, to particular discourse environments. We may say then that *well* is (at least) three-ways polysemous. It is perhaps worth noting that this kind of polysemy does not correspond perfectly with 'classical' lexical polysemy because the different meanings are associated with different discourse contexts rather than with different grammatical properties; but then again, this is only to be expected, given the nature of discourse particles.

6.3 Some discourse particles in other languages

As just mentioned, Travis (2005) gives an extended study of discourse markers in Colombian Spanish, including not only *bueño*, which can be used in ways comparable to English *well*, *good*, and *right*, but also *o sea* (roughly, 'I mean', 'that is to say'), *entonces* (roughly, 'so' or 'then'), and *pues* (no close equivalent in English, but commonly translated as 'then', 'so' or 'well'). Bromhead (2009) is a fascinating study of 'epistemic' discourse markers in sixteenth- and seventeenth-century English, such as *verily*, *in truth*, and *by my faith*. Waters (2010) looks into some French discourse particles.

In this section we explore a couple of discourse particles in non-European languages, Mparntwe Arrernte, an Aboriginal language spoken in Central Australia, and Malay (Bahasa Melayu), the national language of Malaysia.

6.3.1 Arrernte -itanye and -iknge

Wilkins (1986) begins his description of the Arrernte clitic particles *-itanye* and *-iknge* by pointing out that both are frequently used in making complaints and criticisms. To illustrate, we can consider how someone might react if they are awakened at night by a relative seeking money, an annoying but not uncommon event in the Arrernte community of Alice Springs. Note the particle *-itanye*, glossed as 'of all times', which is attached to the first phrase *ingew kngerrel* 'in the middle of the night'.

> *Ingew kngerre-le-itanye, iwenhe-ke unte petye-me,*
> night big-LOC-ITANYE, what-DAT 2sgS come-NPP
> *ingkirreke ankw-inte-rlenge?!*
> everyone asleep-lie-DS
> 'What have you come here for in the middle of the night, of all times, when everyone's sleeping?!'

(The following interlinear symbols are used in the Arrernte material: PC past completive, NPP non-past progressive, INCH inchoative, A transitive subject, S intransitive subject, O object, DAT dative, LOC locative, DS different subjects marker, REFL reflexive, ERG ergative, SEMBL semblative, Q FOCUS question focus, ABL ablative.)

If the unwanted visitor continues to press his request, the exasperated person could say the sentence below. Notice the particle *-iknge* attached to the word meaning 'I' and here glossed as 'forever'.

Arrangkwe! Th-iknge   mane   ngkwenge nthe-me. Ayenge-me   banke?
nothing   1sgA-IKNGE money 2sgDAT   give-NPP 1sgS-Q FOCUS bank?
'No way! I'm forever giving you money. What am I, a bank?'

However, neither *-itanye* nor *-iknge* are confined to criticisms or complaints, and in other contexts they seem to generate quite different effects.

Although it is associated with a sense of surprise, *-itanye* does not necessarily imply anything about the speaker's attitudes. For instance, it is quite at home in a 'matter-of-fact' simple declarative like the one below:

Lhwerrpe-k-itanye,   urinp-irre-me.
winter-DAT-ITANYE,   hot-INCH-NPP
'Even though it's winter, it's getting hot.'

Wilkins (1986: 582) sums up *-itanye* by saying that it 'cliticizes to a word or phrase denoting a prevailing or ambient condition and indicates that something is behaving unexpectedly under such conditions.' I suggest the particle can be assigned the explication below. The initial component is an attempt to capture Wilkins' notion of a 'prevailing condition'.

X-itanye, Y
at this time, it was like this: X
because of this, people could think that something like this (Y)
    couldn't happen at that time
it happened

-Itanye, then, is not inherently a particle for criticism or complaint, but when it occurs in a sentence referring to a person's action, the logical inference may be a criticism. To say of a person's action that 'people could think that something like this couldn't happen' can be tantamount to a criticism. If there are no strong cultural prohibitions involved, this inference may be mild or weak. For example, the sentence below may occur as part of a critical discourse on the poor taste of the person being talked about, or it may simply register surprise about the other person's behaviour.

Mwarre-ng-itanye   re   picture   impe-ke.
good-ABL-ITANYE   3sgA   movie   leave-PC
'Despite the fact that it was good, he left the movie.' [How could he?]

However, where the prevailing condition is widely recognized as something which should constrain behaviour, highlighting this condition with *-itanye* implies strong criticism. The prevailing condition in the sentence below is that 'there were *iperte* (holes) there'. Given this, people would not think that something like the reported action could happen.

> *Iperte-k-itanye,   mweteke   iperte-ke   kwerren-ke   (arerte-l-arteke).*
> hole-DAT-ITANYE   car   hole-DAT   insert-PC   mad-ERG-SEMBL
> 'Even though (he knew) there were holes around, he went ahead and drove into a hole (i.e. got the car bogged).'

The prevailing condition below is that 'there were *relhe mape* (women) there'. In this case, the reported action is 'unthinkable' (socially deviant) for cultural reasons.

> *Relhe   mape-k-itanye   artwe   yanhe   mantere   irlwe-lhe-ke.*
> woman   group-DAT-ITANYE   man   that   clothes   take.off-REFL-PC
> 'Even though there were women around, that man took his clothes off.'

Turning now to *-iknge*, we find that it can be appended to the end of any argument of a verb to indicate 'that the argument so marked is perceived by the speaker to be excessively involved in the verb event in whatever role it is playing and the speaker is saying s/he doesn't like that' (Wilkins 1986: 578). Depending on the context, and the kind of verb involved, the effect conveyed by *-iknge* can be akin to complaint, sympathy, or criticism, as in examples (a)–(c) respectively. Notice that the argument marked with *-iknge* may be either the undergoer of the action, as in (a) and (b), or the actor. In either case, however, this argument is the topic of the sentence, that is, what the sentence is 'about' from the speaker's point of view.

a. *Re   ayeng-iknge   twe-me.*
   3sgA   1sgO-IKNGE   hit-NPP
   'He's forever hitting me.'
b. *(Kunye)   Re   renh-iknge   ilte-me.*
   (poor-thing)   3sgA   3sgO-IKNGE   scold-NPP
   '(Poor thing.) He's always getting told off by him.'
c. *R-iknge   renhe   ilte-me.*
   3sgA-IKNGE   3sgO   scold-NPP
   'He's always telling him off.'

In the explication below, the first component establishes the argument ('X') marked by *-iknge* as the topic, regardless of the role that X plays in the event depicted in the sentence as a whole. The next two components convey the message that this event, whatever it was, 'happened many times' and that in the speaker's view 'this is not good'. These components correspond to Wilkins' comments about 'excessive involvement' in the verbal event. The final component expresses the subjective reaction of the speaker: 'I feel something bad because of this'.

> X-iknge:
> I say this about X:
>   [e.g. 'someone did this to X', or, 'X did this (to someone)']
> it happened many times
> this is not good
> I feel something bad because of this

This explication can interact with the meaning of the verb, the role and identity of the argument (X), and with the overall context, to give rise to different effects. For example, when *-iknge* is attached to a first-person undergoer (i.e. to 'me'), as in (a) above, the utterance will be interpreted as a complaint because the speaker is expressing a message which amounts to this: 'it's not good that someone keeps on doing something to me; I feel bad because of it.' If it is attached to a non first-person undergoer, as in (b), the effect conveyed is one of sympathy or compassion, because the message is: 'it's not good that this keeps happening to X; I feel bad because of it.' If it is attached to the performer of the verb, as in (c), the effect is more like criticism because the message is then 'it's not good that this person keeps doing this thing; I feel bad because of it.'

The overall effect conveyed also depends on the kind of verb involved. The examples so far have all involved verbs of 'adverse effect' (*tweme* 'hit' and *ilteme* 'scolded'). The examples below show what happens if *-iknge* is attached to the beneficiary argument of a 'verb of benefit' such as 'kiss' or 'give'. In this case, a jealous or envious effect results. Again, this effect follows from the proposed meaning of *-iknge*, because the speaker is effectively saying that 'it isn't good that this good thing keeps happening to Y; I feel bad because of it.'

a. *Re   renh-iknge   arrwantye-me.*
   3sgA   3sgO-IKNGE   kiss-NPP
   'She's always kissing him.'

b. *Unte   pwerte   relhe   yanke-k-iknge   nthe-me.*
   2sgA   money   woman   that-DAT-IKNGE   give-NPP
   'You're forever giving money to that woman.'

If -*iknge* marks a (non-first-person) argument of a verb like *angke-* 'to speak' which is neutral with respect to benefit or adversity, the utterance can be interpreted in different ways. Consider the following example, imagining the framing contexts as shown:

> *R-iknge*   *angke-me.*
> 3sgS-IKNGE   speak-NPP
> 'He's always speaking.' [When do I get my chance?]
> 'He's always speaking.' [Poor thing!]
> 'He's always speaking.' [The big-mouth.]

In other words, if the speaking in question is understood as being beneficial (leading to recognition or financial gain, for example) then one would understand the utterance as conveying a jealous complaint. If the speaking is seen as detrimental to the speaker (because it is difficult and a heavy responsibility), the effect conveyed is sympathetic. If the speaking is regarded as having an adverse effect (because it is boring and long-winded, for example), the effect is more like criticism.

6.3.2 *Malay* lah

The illocutionary particle *lah* is a salient feature of colloquial Malay, as well as of Malaysian and Singapore English (Goddard 1994). Though spelt as a separate word, *lah* is a clitic particle. It generally occurs utterance-finally, except in imperatives, where it tends to attach to the imperative word. In either case the semantic effect applies to the utterance as a whole, rather than to the particular word it is attached to.

To get an idea of its range of use, consider the following examples, which come from a well-known Malaysian cartoon novella, *Mat Som* (Lat 1989). Translations are based on the English edition of that work. In (a) and (b) we see *lah* in declarative sentences whose function may be termed 'informational', i.e. the speaker's purpose is to let the addressee know something. In (c) we see a declarative with a different function, where *lah* is used to help issue a friendly insult or jibe. (d) and (e) show its use with imperatives.

a. *Itu bukan girlfriend lah! Peminat.*
   'That's not my girlfriend *lah*. Just a fan.' (p. 101)
b. *Aku ada 'appointment' lah.*
   'I've got an appointment (i.e. a date) *lah*.' (p. 115)

c. *Engkau ni kacau saja lah!*
  'You're such a pest *lah!*' (p. 31)
d. *Kalau ya pun, jangan lah cakap kuat.*
  'Even so, no need to speak so loud *lah!*' (p. 13)
e. *Masuk lah! Aku hantar engkau.*
  'Well, get in *lah*. I'll give you a lift!' (p. 60)

In the narrow grammatical sense, *lah* is optional, in that the examples above do not become ungrammatical if *lah* is removed; but from a semantic point of view its use is virtually obligatory. Without *lah*, the utterances above would sound blunt, harsh or confrontational. The *lah* gives a 'softening' effect.

A particle *lah* (or a similar particle, also spelt *la*) is also a conspicuous feature of Malaysian and Singapore English, and has been the subject of a string of papers since the appearance of Richards and Tay (1977), who characterized it as expressing or indexing 'familiarity, informality and solidarity' in the L (or 'Low') style of Singapore English. In many cases, much the same could be said of colloquial Malay *lah*. However, *lah* by no means always conveys something like friendliness or a 'good mood'. Depending on the context and on intonation, it may give rise to quite the opposite effect. With an appropriately harsh pronunciation, the examples above can be made to sound badgering, ill-tempered, and impatient. Paradoxically, then, it might appear that the same form can express 'in precisely the same syntactic structure, diametrically opposed meanings' (Bell and Ser 1983: 8; cf. Kwan-Terry 1978).

Fortunately, it is not necessary to entertain the improbable idea that there are two 'forms' of *lah* with opposite meanings. It is possible to propose a single meaning which is versatile enough to be compatible with varying interpretations of the speaker's overall attitude. Essentially, illocutionary *lah* offers an explanation for why I am saying what I am saying. It shows a concern to correct or pre-empt a possible momentary misapprehension or misunderstanding of some kind.

> —— *lah:*
> I say this now after what happened a short time before
>   because I think that you can think something else
> it is not good if it is like this

Like *lah* itself, the explication applies as a 'tag' to another, complete utterance. Depending on the nature of that utterance, the overall effect conveyed may differ. Consider first the declarative in example (a) above. This was spoken by the character Pyan, by way of correcting Mat Som's assumption that the girl who had invited them both to a party was Pyan's girlfriend. It should be obvious that the proposed explication is highly plausible. Som clearly thinks something mistaken, and Pyan is correcting that. Now consider (b), whose English translation (without the *lah*) is 'I have an appointment (i.e. a date).' This is said by Mat Som after his friend So'ud has exclaimed on his unusually spruced-up appearance. Here too the explication is appropriate. Though Som has no reason to think that So'ud is labouring under any specific misapprehension, there is good reason, in the circumstances, for him to think that So'ud might jump to some other conclusion, e.g. that he has got a job.

Now let's consider how the explication fares when applied to a sentence like that in (c) *Kau ni kacau saja!* 'You're such a pest!' This comes from a passage of childhood reminiscences. It was said by the leader of a group of boys, to the snotty-nosed but persistent Faridah, who had managed to prevail upon the boys to let her come along with them on a search for orchid seeds. Without the *lah*, it could be quite a biting comment, as it would convey the intention to hurt the feelings of the addressee. With the *lah* it is more like a friendly jibe, not to be taken too seriously. If we substitute the explication into this context, we can see how this effect comes about. It is as if the speaker is saying:

> 'You're such a pest'. I say this now after what happened a short time before (i.e. we let you come with us) because I think that you might think something else (e.g. that we think you are OK), which would not be good.

One of the puzzling things about *lah* is that it seems to have a strengthening effect in declaratives, but a softening effect with imperatives. Can the proposed explication account for this? I believe it can, once we take account of the fact that the key meaning component conveyed by the imperative construction is 'I want you to do this'. Consider example (d). Literally *Kalau ya pun, jangan lah cakap kuat* means 'Even so, don't speak so loud', but due to the effect of *lah* the translator has chosen to render it as 'Even so, no need to speak so loud.' Som says this to his friend So'ud, who has just exclaimed loudly in a restaurant about how much money Som still owes him. Here the *lah* acts as a kind of mild reproach, a sort of reminder that of course Som wouldn't want him to talk loudly about that kind of thing, which So'ud seems to have forgotten. Making the appropriate substitution:

> 'I don't want you to talk loudly'. I say this now after what happened a short time before (i.e. you raised your voice) because I think that you can think something else (e.g. I don't care how loud you talk), which would not be good.

Example (e) is Som's friend Leman offering him a lift. It is instructive to examine the original context carefully. Som is waiting at a bus stop, working up the courage to say *hello* to his rather attractive neighbour Cik Yam, when Leman pulls up in his new car. Immediately, Leman shouts out *Masuk!* 'Get in!' Instead of doing just that, Som makes an admiring comment on the new car, and asks Leman where he got it. Leman replies that it's second-hand, and 'not bad, eh?' And then, he says (d), with *Masuk lah!* I suggest that the condition which distinguishes this second invitation (*Masuk lah!*) from the first (*Masuk!*) is precisely that Som did not respond the first time, but stayed on the kerb. Effectively, the second invitation is a kind of reminder, urging him on.

The proposed explication can also give rise to a badgering, annoyed, or impatient effect, if in the context there are reasons to think that the addressee already well knows the speaker's wishes. For instance, if we are running late and you are dawdling I could exclaim *Lekaslah! Kita tak mau lambat* 'Hurry up! We don't want to be late.' As one can see from the following substitution, the meaning proposed for *lah* is compatible with an impatient reproachful tone.

> 'I want you to hurry'. I say this now after what happened a short time before (i.e. you still aren't ready) because I think that you can think something else, which would not be good.

6.4 A fistful of interjections

In a widely read work, Erving Goffman, one of the founders of conversation analysis, had this to say about people's attitudes to expressions like *Oops!*

> We see such 'expressions' as a natural overflowing, a flooding up of previously contained feelings, a bursting of normal restraints, a case of being caught off guard. That would be what would be learned by asking the man in the street if he uses these forms, and if so, what he means by them. (Goffman 1981: 99)

Goffman was no doubt correct about ordinary people's perceptions of interjections, especially primary interjections like *Oops*, *Ow*, *Uh-oh*, and *Uh-huh*. As mentioned earlier, people usually see these as mere 'noises'— natural responses of the human animal. If this were true, however, the same noises would be found, with the same (or similar) uses, in every language, and this is simply not the case. For example, when Yankunytjatjara speakers accidentally drop something, they don't come out with anything like *Oops!* Instead a 'word-like' interjection *Munta* may be used, the same interjection which is used in situations when English speakers would say *Sorry!* or *Oh!* Nor is it difficult to find examples of interjections which lack even partial equivalents in other languages. For example, in Polish there are no interjections at all similar to English *Gee* and *Wow*. Conversely, English has no interjections like Polish *Nuże* and *Hejże*, which are used to urge someone to do something. Yiddish is famous for its ubiquitous exclamation *Oy vey!* and French for its *Oh là là!*, neither of which have English counterparts.

As these examples show, far from being natural and universal, interjections are often highly culture-specific. Even when similar forms are found in similar contexts, as for instance, English *Aha!* and Polish *Aha!*, there are usually differences in their ranges of use, betokening subtly different meanings. In this section we will compare some English interjections with their nearest counterparts in Polish. As an example of 'emotive' interjections we have *Yuck!*, to represent volitive interjections we have *Psst!* and *Shh!*, and as exemplars of cognitive interjections we will use *Oh!* and *Oh-oh!* Needless to say, this is a highly selective coverage, but it should be sufficient to show that interjections, like all other meaningful elements in a language, can be analysed semantically and assigned precise and testable explications.

6.4.1 English Yuck! vs. Polish Fu! and Fe!

With 'emotive' interjections, it is usually possible to provide a rough paraphrase using an emotion term. For example:

Yuck!   'I feel disgust.'
Ow!   'I feel pain.'
Wow!   'I feel surprise.'

But such paraphrases are not sufficient to bring out the full semantic content of the interjections, as can easily be appreciated by considering the fact that one could equally well gloss *Ugh!* as 'I feel disgust', *Ouch!* as 'I feel pain', and *Oh!* as 'I feel surprise.' Furthermore, terms like 'disgust', 'pain', and 'surprise' are complex and language-specific, and thus don't provide a good basis for explicating the meanings of related interjections in other languages.

The *Longman Dictionary of Contemporary English* (1978) describes *Yuck!* (also sometimes spelt *Yuk!*) as an 'interjection of disgust, probably imitation of the noise of retching'. This may be true historically, but these days the interjection is not confined to a reaction to stimuli which are revolting to the senses, such as confronting some gross mould in the fridge or seeing a squashed snail, but also takes in more psychological stimuli, such as the thought of being kissed by someone repulsive. According to the following explication, the interjection *Yuck!* 'gives voice', so to speak, to an immediate thought ('I don't want something like this to touch my body') and an immediate negative 'gut reaction' ('I feel something bad in my body now because of this').

> *Yuck!*
> I think like this now:
>   'I don't want something like this to touch my body'
> I feel something bad in my body now because of this

It is interesting to note that *Yuck* is on the borderline between primary and secondary interjection, as previously defined. It is not identical to any other word, but it has a word-like phonology and it participates in some compound expressions, such as *Yuck factor*, and derivations, such as *yucky*. There is a children's book character called *Mr Yuk*. These properties stand out in comparison with the primary interjection *Urgh* (also spelt *Ergh*). Perhaps its quasi word-like status helps explain some extended uses of *Yuck* that don't quite fit the explication offered above—as for example in the following quote from a letter to the editor of the *Australian* newspaper: 'FEMINISTS—YUK! As a woman I feel ashamed' (cited Wierzbicka 2003a: 303–4).

Polish has no interjection corresponding perfectly with *Yuck*. On the other hand, it has three *Fu!*, *Fe!*, and *Tfu!* which could, loosely speaking, be linked with something like disgust. We will deal only with the first two of them here.

Polish *Fu!* is more narrowly physical than *Yuck!*, being specifically focused on the mouth and the nose. One could say *Fu!* when one discovers decaying food in the refrigerator, when one is invited for the first time to eat snails, or when one sees someone else licking off a third person's plate. On the other hand, one would not say *Fu!* if some bird droppings landed on one's arm or when one saw a squashed slug on the footpath—both situations when one could easily say *Yuck!* I would propose the following explication, adapted from Wierzbicka (2003a: 303).

> *Fu!* (Polish)
> I think like this now:
>   'I don't want to touch something like this
>   I don't want something like this to be in my mouth [m]'
> I feel something very bad in my body now because of this

This explication, it should be noted, makes explicit reference only to the mouth, not to the nose. The idea is that smelling and tasting are so intimately connected that smelling something readily brings to mind a thought about what the thing would taste like. Notice also that the physical reaction is depicted as more intense than for *Yuck* (not just 'bad', but 'very bad').

Unlike *Fu!*, Polish *Fe!* is not restricted to physical sensations, but it nonetheless differs from *Yuck* in several ways. *Fe!* is always a reaction to human behaviour (typically the addressee), and it has a mildly didactic dimension. Typically it is used by adults to small children, as in collocations like *Fe, nieładnie!* 'Fe, that's not nice' and *Fe, jak pan może!* 'Fe! How can you?', but it is not restricted to this context. For example, a woman could use it flirtatiously to scold a man. *Fe!* appeals to the addressee's knowledge of social rules and sense of shame. This explication is adapted from Wierzbicka (2003a: 308):

> *Fe!* (Polish):
>
> you are doing something bad now
> I feel something now because of this
> you can know that it is bad if someone does something like this
> I want you to feel something bad when you think about it

The second component reads 'I feel something now because of this', rather than 'I feel something bad now because of this' to capture the mild and somewhat understated quality of *Fe!* The third component not only 'chides' the addressee, so to speak; the wording ('it is bad if someone does something like this') implies the existence of some kind of social consensus.

6.4.2 English Psst! and Shh! vs. Polish Pst! and Sza!

Many, perhaps most, languages have some volitive interjections which, roughly speaking, express the speaker's desire for silence. In English we have *Psst!* and *Shh!*, among others. The former is used to announce to the addressee that the speaker wants to say something to him or her without anyone else hearing it. It is private and conspiratorial.

> *Psst!*
> I want to say something to you now
> I want you to hear it
> I don't want someone else here to hear it

Shh!, on the other hand, can be addressed to a group, with the objective of calling everyone to silence. Notice that the speaker in saying *Shh!* includes him or herself in this injunction, which explains why it is that *Shh!* itself sounds most natural when spoken quietly. The interjection also seems to appeal to an assumption that it is, so to speak, in the common interest if there is silence. A typical situation for *Shh!* would be in a theatre or cinema, or while waiting to surprise the guest of honour at a surprise party. (*Shh!* differs in this respect from *Shush!* and *Hush!* which are used to quieten or to soothe children.)

> *Shh!*
> you are saying something now
> people here can hear something because of this
> this is not good
> I don't want you to do something like this now

Polish has its own *Pst!* [pst], but despite being identical in form with the English interjection, its use is different and so is its meaning. Polish *Pst!* is a kind of conspiratorial warning. It is issued to a person who is already speaking, to alert them to the fact that they can be overheard. It could be used in a classroom or a meeting to someone who is whispering to another person. It could be used when a secret is being discussed and someone approaches who is not supposed to hear it. The explication is adapted from Wierzbicka (2003a: 295):

> *Pst!* (Polish):
> I don't want you to say anything more now
>   because if you say something now, someone else can hear it
> I don't want this
> I don't want this someone else to know about this

Polish *Sza!*, pronounced [ʃɒ], resembles English *Shh!* insofar as it is an injunction to silence, but it differs in that in saying *Sza!* the speaker is not including him or herself. Thus, one can address the exclamation *Sza!* quite loudly to a group, for instance, to silence a group of noisy children. Wierzbicka (2003a: 294–5) assigns it the following explication:

Sza! (Polish):
I don't want you to say anything more now
    because I don't want people here to hear it now
I know that you can't say anything more after I say this
you know the same

Notice that the final pair of components assert the speaker's presumed authority over the people being addressed, another point of contrast with English *Shh!*

There are many other kinds of volitive interjections commonly found in the world's languages, aside from those enjoining silence. They include calls for attracting attention over a distance (e.g. English *Ahoy*, *Hello*, and Australian English *Cooee*), interjections which urge the addressee to hurry up and do something, or to be gone, and calls or 'instructions' to animals. Many languages have an interjection which is used when giving something to somebody, to urge them to take it. There are some exercises on volitive interjections at the end of this chapter.

6.4.3 *English* Oh! *and* Oh-oh! *vs. Polish* Oho!

Cognitive interjections are focused primarily on the speaker's thoughts and/or state of knowledge, with reference to feeling or wanting taking a second place. The English interjection *Oh!* is a nice example. It expresses a pretty bland message; roughly speaking, a mild reaction to some new information.

Oh!
I now know something
I didn't know it before
I feel something because of this

Perhaps naturally, in view of its blandness, *Oh* also appears in various more expressive compounds, such as *Oh dear* and *Oh my God*. These would all need to be explicated separately.

Let's compare *Oh!* with *Oh-oh!* (also spelt *Uh oh!*). It can hardly be a coincidence that in form *Oh-oh!* resembles a reduplicated version of *Oh*. *Oh-oh!* can be used when one perceives that something bad and unforeseen might well happen in the immediate future. Probably the most salient situations in which *Oh-oh!* can be used are ones which involve oneself or one's addressee, but it is not confined to such contexts. For example, I can say to you, about a third person we are watching, *Oh-oh! He's in trouble now*. Nor does there have to be an addressee present. For instance, if I reach into my bag for my car keys but can't feel them, I can say *Oh-oh!* to myself. On the other hand, the speaker is not responding in a totally immediate and unreflective way. There is time to express the view, as it were, that the impending situation will not be too serious.

All this leads to the explication below:

Oh-oh!
I now know something
because of this I know that something bad can happen a short time after this
I didn't know this before
I think about it like this: 'it will not be very bad'

The Polish interjection *Oho!* is also a reaction to new knowledge, but it differs in at least two ways from English *Oh-oh!* First, the Polish interjection is a response to a public fact of some kind, something that the speaker has just noticed or observed. For example, one could say *Oho!* on hearing remote thunder. If one says *Oho!* in response to something the interlocutor says, this treats the utterance as, in Wierzbicka's phrase, an 'observational datum'. Second, in contrast to *Oh-oh!* the Polish interjection is deliberately 'loud' and expressive. A third, but subtler, difference concerns the negative potential of the newly apprehended situation, which, according to Wierzbicka (2003a: 332), is 'hinted at rather than clearly conveyed'.

Oho! (Polish)
I now know something
I think that anyone here now can know it
I think about it like this: 'something like this can be bad'
I feel something now because of this

Key technical terms

clitic particle

discourse particle

focus particle

interjections

  cognitive interjection, emotive

  interjection, volitive interjection

  primary interjection, secondary

  interjection

Exercises and discussion questions

† next to a problem means that a solution or some commentary can be found at the end of this book.

1†. Group the elements *gee, hi, just, um, uh-huh, only, oh dear, phew, oooh, holy shit*, and *even* into the following categories: discourse particle, primary interjection, secondary interjection.

2†. The traditional generative grammar account of *too* would assign *Mary does Z and John does too* a 'deep structure' like *Mary is/does Z, and John is/does Z*. What do you think of this from a semantic point of view? How does it square up with an explication for *too* based on THE SAME?

3†. The Yankunytjatjara language has a so-called 'quotative' particle *kunyu*. It is used to cite facts which are not first-hand knowledge, to tender an opinion as belonging to some unspecified other person, to relay an order or request, among other things. Some examples follow. See if you can draft a reductive paraphrase explication for *kunyu*.

  a. *Iriti   kunyu aṉangu tjuṯa nyinangi,   ngura nyara Mimilila . . .*

    long.ago QUOT person many were.staying place that   Mimili:LOC

    'In the old days, so the story goes, people were camped at Mimili . . .'

  b. *Ka   kunyu Pitjantjatjara   kutjikiti.*

    and QUOT Pitjantjatjara   well-off

    'It can be said that Pitjantjatjara is well off.'

  c. *Pakala kunyu!*

    get.up QUOT

    'You're to get up!'

4†. In Singapore English there is a sentence-final particle which we will spell *wüt* (cf. Wong 1994: 46–63). It is also commonly spelt *what*, on the assumption that it originated from Standard English, but the Singapore English particle differs from *what* in grammar and meaning, as well as pronunciation (e.g. *wüt* is always pronounced with a low-falling tone.) Consider these examples of the *wüt* particle and draft an explication for its meaning.

a. Context: Person X asks for some pins because she wants to put a notice on the notice board. Person Y replies: *Notice board got pins wüt.*
b. Context: Person Y has been waiting outside X's office. X asks 'Why didn't you come in?' Y replies: *You told me to wait here wüt.*
c. Context: X and Y are discussing a third person who has a nickname. X says 'They call him cockroach because he is hunch (i.e. has a hunch-back).' Y replies: *But cockroaches are not hunch wüt.*
d. Context: X remarks 'I wish I were good-looking.' Y replies: *But you are wüt.*
e. Context: X and Y are watching a comedy TV show. A robber is chasing a uniformed policeman, even though the policeman's gun is in clear view. Disbelievingly, X remarks to Y: *But he (i.e. the policeman) has a gun wüt.*
f. Context: X seems surprised about the bad language of a third person; 'His language is terrible', X says. It is no surprise to Y, however, who replies: *Army wüt. (that is, he is in the Army wüt.)*

5†. Below are some translated examples of how the 'response marker' interjection *cis* can and can't be used in Language T. *Cis* is only used after someone else says something. It can be used as a self-contained utterance or be followed by a sentence, as in the examples below. Unacceptable usages are marked with an asterisk (*). Propose a plausible semantic explication for *cis*. The explication should not be more than about 50 words in length and it should be phrased entirely in semantic primes.

Cis, no one can really know that.
Cis, that could well be.
Cis, who knows?
Cis, I think it depends on how one looks at it.
Cis, I think that's a question of personal taste.
Cis, I think that's different from person to person.

*Cis, that's true.
*Cis, no doubt about that.
*Cis, how can anyone say that?
*Cis, that's great!
*Cis, how awful for you!
*Cis, that's a surprise.

6†. Here are two different explications for the English exclamation *Wow!*, adapted from Wierzbicka (2003a) and Ameka (1992a). Discuss the pros and cons of each. Propose an improved explication.

a. I now know that something happened
    I didn't think that it would happen

I think that this is very good
I feel something good because of that
b. I now know something
I didn't think I would know it
I think that this is very good
I feel something because of that

7†. Collect a number of examples of the interjections *Ow!* and *Oops!* and draft explications for them.

8†. Volitive interjections are common in many languages. Try your hand at drafting explications for the following. Admittedly, this can only be a rough exercise, since you don't have enough information to detect any subtle meaning components.

a. Mparntwe Arrernte *Me!* and Malay *Nah!* accompany the act of giving, urging the recipient to take what is being held out to them.

b. The Mayali language of Arnhem Land has an interjection *Mah!* Often it is used when the speaker wants an addressee to hurry up and do something, in which case it can be translated as 'Come on!', but it can also be used about oneself, for instance, to signal that one is about to leave. In this case it can be glossed as 'Right then'. But really (cf. Evans 1992) *Mah!* is semantically vague as to who is to carry out the action, and also as to the nature of the action itself.

9†. In Lao, most imperatives are accompanied by an utterance-final particle such as *sáa* or *mêɛ* (among others). Study the data below and propose semantic explications for these two particles.

a. A doctor has prescribed a certain pill for her patient. She tells him: 'Take two a day.' No particle is used.

b. A government minister is being chauffeured to his next appointment. He calls to the rather zealous driver: 'Drive slowly!' No particle is used.

c. Mali switches on the radio but then sees that Dang is studying, and so immediately turns it off again, apologising to Dang for disturbing him. Dang replies: 'No problem, I am about to finish here. Turn it on *mêɛ*.'

d. Kham offers sweets to his guest Phet, who politely refuses. 'Eat some *mêɛ*', says Kham.

e. Phet is about to visit Luang Prabang for the first time. Kham says: 'There are lovely caves at Pak Ou. Go and visit them *mêɛ*.'

f. Thong comes to pick up Phet from his hotel room. As they leave, Thong notices that Phet has left spare cash visible on the dresser. Thong says: 'Hey I can see your cash there. Put it away *mêɛ*.'

g. As Dang prepares to go to the market, his mother gives him money to buy her some fish. 'Buy the really nice ones, *sáa*', she says.

h. Mother wants her son to help with gardening. She plans to go out at 6 p.m. She says to her son, as he goes out earlier: 'Come back before 5pm *sáa*, then you'll have time to help me for one hour at least.'

i. Mali is working in the garden with her two sons, when she notices the youngest struggling by himself with some overfilled water-buckets. Her hands are full, so she appeals to her oldest son: 'Go help your brother *sáa*.'

j. Phet is in the back of a taxi with a rather zealous driver. A bit nervous about the speed, Phet says: 'Drive slowly *sáa*.'

10. In everyday Lebanese Arabic, interlocutors employ a great variety of interjections to signal that they are intellectually and emotionally engaged with what their conversational partner is saying (Rieschild 1996). For example, in response to a statement one may indicate agreeability by *ʔæʔ* (roughly) 'uh-huh', strong endorsement by *wællahɪ* 'by Allah' or *wæ hɪjæt ʔællæh* 'by the life of Allah', and evaluation by *sæh* 'true' or *mæʕ-æ hæʔʔ* 'truth is with you'. Paralinguistic signs such as blinking and nodding are also frequent.

In general, Lebanese Arabic conversationalists show more active involvement than is usual in mainstream English conversation. Simply to say *ʔæɪ* 'yes' would tend to convey a lack of interest; it is more usual to show interest in the topic raised by the other person by repeating part of the interlocutor's utterance. More emphatic agreement and engagement is signalled by adding to *ʔæɪ* 'yes' the word *wællæ* (a modified form of *ʔællæh* 'Allah'), and some additional comment, often containing an intensifying word such as *ktir* 'very, much'. These three different response patterns are illustrated below. For simplicity, English words are used in place of Arabic ones (except for *ʔæɪ* and *ʔæɪ wællæ*).

a. Speaker A: Have you seen Kamal lately?
    Speaker B: (a) *ʔæɪ.* (b) *ʔæɪ.* I've seen him. (c) *ʔæɪ wællæ.* I saw him yesterday.

b. Speaker A: It's cold today (isn't it?)
    Speaker B: (a) *ʔæɪ.* (b) *ʔæɪ.* It's cold. (c) *ʔæɪ wællæ.* It's very cold today.

c. Speaker A: Flats are expensive in Bas Beirut, aren't they?
    Speaker B: (a) *ʔæɪ.* (b) *ʔæɪ.* Expensive. (c) *ʔæɪ wællæ.* Very very expensive.

Assume that Speaker A, in asking the questions in examples (a)–(c) above, conveys the following illocutionary intention:

I want to know if this is true
because of this, I want you to say something
after you say it, I want to say more about this

Speculating a little, formulate semantic explications for the different messages conveyed by the three different response patterns illustrated for Speaker B. Do not use any complex words such as 'interest', 'topic', or 'involvement'.

7

Animals and artefacts

The names for kinds of living things, such as *cats*, *mice*, *dogs*, *horses*, and for so-called 'life-form' words, such as *animals*, *birds*, and *trees*, might seem unlikely places to find semantic complexity. Many people would assume that such meanings must be pretty basic, if only because they seem to correspond so directly with the facts of nature. We will soon see that any such impression is misguided. The same applies to words for everyday 'arte-facts'—manufactured items like *knives*, *cups*, *bottles*, and *brooms*. These mundane words conceal enormous semantic detail. In fact, words for living things and artefact words turn out to be far more complex in their meanings than abstract concepts like *love*, upon which far more ink has been spilt.

7.1 Semantic molecules and semantic complexity

As mentioned in Chapter 3, the NSM metalanguage includes not only semantic primes, but also so-called SEMANTIC MOLECULES. This term refers to a well-defined set of non-primitive but relatively simple meanings that function as units in the meanings of more complex concepts. Semantic molecules are ultimately reducible to configurations of semantic primes, but they are nonetheless 'semantic units' in the sense that they frequently crop up in explications for other concepts. Presumably, having recurrent semantic complexes packaged into word-like 'chunks' makes it easier for people to acquire and manipulate the huge amounts of semantic information involved (cf. Miller 1956).

We will be looking into the theory of semantic molecules in more detail in Chapter 12. In this chapter, in order to come to grips with the meanings of words for animals and artefacts, we will be using a selection of semantic molecules from several categories, as shown below. When molecules are used in explications, they are marked as such by the notation '[m]'.

BODY PARTS: head, mouth, teeth, lip, nose, hand, fingers, feet, ears, legs, arm, hair, back, tail
SOCIAL CATEGORIES AND RELATED CONCEPTS: men, women, children, home
ACTIONS, ACTIVITIES, EVENTS: hold, pick up, put down, drink, eat, play, kill, make, be born
PHYSICAL DESCRIPTORS: long, flat, round, thick, thin, straight, hard, soft, smooth, sharp, heavy
TOPOLOGICAL: front, back, end, top, middle, bottom, sides, edge, sticking out, pointed, hole
ENVIRONMENT: ground, water, day, night, light
OTHER: quickly, slowly

It is important to stress that the assertion that these words are ultimately definable in terms of semantic primes is not something that must be taken on faith. On the contrary, explications for all of them can be found in the NSM literature, and, as mentioned, we will be reviewing some of this literature in section 12.2. It is also important to emphasize that the question of whether a particular word is or isn't a semantic molecule cannot be decided quickly, on the basis of one's feelings or intuitions, or as a matter of convenience. It can only be decided after a process of disciplined semantic analysis. Some common words that seem (to English speakers) to be pretty basic, such as 'hit' and 'go', for example, are definitely not needed as semantic molecules. For the time being, however, you are being asked to accept that the meanings of the words listed above are legitimate semantic molecules.

7.2 The semantics of 'folk biology'

FOLK BIOLOGY refers to the system of names and categories (nomenclature) that ordinary people in different cultures use for talking about living things. In English, this system includes so-called 'life-form' words like *animal*, *bird*, *fish*, and *tree*, and the names of individual species such as *cat*, *sparrow*, *trout*, and *oak*. The cross-cultural study of folk biology is known as ETHNOBIOLOGY. It is a field in which there have been a host of valuable studies over the past thirty years, many of them undertaken by the well-known cognitive anthropologist Brent Berlin and his associates. Berlin (1992: 26) sums up the motivation behind this anthropological work as the conviction that: '[E]thnobiological nomenclature represents a natural system of naming that reveals much about the way people *conceptualize* the living things in their environment.'

Systems for classifying the natural world have also been studied in cognitive psychology, notably by Eleanor Rosch and others interested in the role of prototypes in human thinking. There is also a significant philosophical literature on 'natural kinds'. It would be impossible to review all this work in this book. In this section, I will introduce some of the main concepts and terminology, after which we will look into several examples. The treatment is indebted to Wierzbicka (1996a).

7.2.1 The semantic organization of the natural world

As we will see, some of the semantic issues that arise in relation to 'natural kinds' (e.g. their sheer complexity) arise also in connection with artefact words. It has been proposed, however, that there is an important structural principle which is confined to the semantic domain of living things (Atran 1990): the principle of hierarchical taxonomic ranking. This refers to a ranking in terms of 'kinds'. For example, in the English folk taxonomy, it would appear that *animals* are *creatures* of various kinds, that *dogs* are *animals* of one kind, and that *poodles* are *dogs* of one kind. Here we can see as many as four levels of ranking (*creature*, *animal*, *dog*, *poodle*).

In an elaborate taxonomy like this, the most inclusive category (in this set of terms, *creature*) is often termed the UNIQUE BEGINNER. Below this come LIFE-FORM terms, such as *animal*, *bird*, and *fish*. Life-forms are characterized by 'polytypicity'; that is, a life-form is a category which is recognized as consisting of many different kinds. Thus, we know that there are many kinds of *animal* (*cats, dogs, horses, tigers, bears,* and so on), many kinds of *bird* (*sparrows, magpies, parrots, eagles,* and so on), many kinds of *fish* (*trout, bream, perch, salmon,* and so on). The individual kinds (for example, *cats, sparrows, trout*) are often termed GENERICS or sometimes, FOLK GENERA (in the singular, genus). The generic level is generally the most stable and psychologically basic level of categorization. It is an essential property of a generic that it has an individual name which is a 'primary lexeme', i.e. a single word (including compound words like *blackbird* and *jellyfish*).

The generic *dogs* is further divided into sub-kinds, such as *poodle, terrier,* and *spaniel*. Since these terms meet the criterion of being primary lexemes, it seems logical to refer to them as SUB-GENERICS. It is important to note, however, that *dogs* are exceptional in this regard. *Dogs* is the only English folk genus which is further divided into individually named subgenerics. Cat terms like *Burmese* and *Siamese* do not qualify as sub-generics because in most people's speech they cannot stand alone as primary lexemes: normally one does not speak, except elliptically, about a *Burmese* or a *Siamese* but about a *Burmese cat* or a *Siamese cat*. 'Double-barrelled' terms (technically known as 'secondary lexemes') such as *Burmese cat, wedge-tailed eagle, rainbow trout,* and so on, usually designate distinctions within a single generic category (*cats, eagles, trout,* etc.). This further possible level of differentiation is known as the level of SPECIFICS.

Of course, things are more complicated and contentious than the simple picture just painted. First, the botanical domain doesn't seem to have any unique beginner, or at least, not in ordinary colloquial English. In 'semi-scientific' English (see below), the word *plant* has this function, but in everyday English it would sound odd to refer to an individual *tree* or *mushroom* as a *plant*. For example, one would not expect to hear an exchange like this: A: *Look at that lovely plant over there!* B: *Which one?* A: **That oak tree/That mushroom*. In fact, ethnobiological studies have shown that languages very often lack words at the unique beginner level of categorization (Berlin 1992: 190; Urban 2010).

Second, there are some terms whose status is not immediately obvious. Consider, for example, *spiders, snakes,* and *ants*. They do not seem to fall under any life-form; in ordinary English, one would not normally speak of an individual *spider, snake,* or *ant* as an *animal* (and they are obviously not *birds, fish* or *insects*, either). One suggestion is that these terms be regarded as generics which are not affiliated under any life-form (Berlin, Breedlove, and Raven 1973). Another possibility is to regard them as under-differentiated life-forms, i.e. life-forms which are not exhaustively partitioned into individually named kinds (Atran 1987a). The linguistic evidence seems to favour the second of these interpretations, if only because there are some primary lexemes which do designate individual kinds of spider (e.g. *tarantula*, *daddy long-legs*, and, in Australia at least, *redback*, *funnel-web*, and *huntsman*), individual kinds of snake (e.g. *viper*, *rattlesnake*, *python*, and, in Australia, *death-adder* and *taipan*), and individual kinds of ant (at least in Australia, where *bull ant* and *meat ant* are primary lexemes, despite being spelt with two separate words). Similarly, in the botanical realm, one could argue that *bushes*, *vines*, *ferns*, and *mushrooms* should be regarded as under-differentiated life-forms on the grounds that the existence of different kinds of bushes, vines, etc. is psychologically salient, even though not many of the different kinds have primary lexemic names.

7.2.2 Everyday colloquial English vs. 'semi-scientific English'

A great deal of confusion can result from overlooking the fact that some words for classifying living things, for example, *animal* and *plant*, have different meanings and uses in ordinary, everyday English to the meanings and uses they have in 'semi-scientific English'. I use the term 'semi-scientific' because the kind of usages in question are not confined to scientists or to strictly 'scientific-sounding' discourse. So maybe it is best to illustrate first by example. In everyday colloquial English, people do not usually refer to birds as *animals*. For example, one can hardly imagine anyone saying *What a beautiful animal!*, referring to a bird. And there are popular books with titles like *Birds and Animals of Australia* (which wouldn't make sense if birds were a kind of animal).

In what I am calling 'semi-scientific English', however, *birds* can be classified as *animals*, because in this system the natural world is partitioned into the 'animal kingdom' and the 'vegetable kingdom'. Because many English speakers have had a lot of formal education, the scientific categorization does intrude into many ordinary contexts (for instance, in the guessing game 'Twenty Questions', a common opening question is 'Is it animal, vegetable, or mineral?') But this does not affect the fact that in common usage birds are not normally referred to as *animals*. Not many people would refer to a swallow or a magpie as an *animal*. Likewise, if someone asks, about an unknown bird *What kind of animal is that?*, we would want to say *It's not an animal. It's a bird*. Similarly, insects and fish are not *animals* in the ordinary sense of the word. It would be peculiar to hear someone say *There's an animal on your collar* referring to an insect, or to say *There were some beautiful animals in the fish-tank*.

Semi-scientific English also contains quite a few terms which are not part of the folk taxonomy of everyday colloquial English at all. Probably the most notable is *mammal*. One would hardly ever hear anyone say *Look at that mammal over there!* or *What a strange-looking mammal it was!*, although these same sentences are quite all right with *animal* (or even *creature*) substituted in place of *mammal*. Nor is it true that *animal* is just a colloquial equivalent of *mammal*, as is sometimes suggested. For instance, a crocodile can be called an *animal* but not a *mammal*, and people are clearly *mammals*, but are not normally referred to as *animals*. As far as possible in this chapter, we will confine ourselves to everyday colloquial English.

7.2.3 Types of linguistic evidence

We have already been appealing to one particularly revealing type of linguistic evidence which bears on the semantics of classification, namely, common ways of referring to individual living things. It is unexceptional to refer to a particular magpie as *That bird*, or to talk about a particular dog as *That stupid animal*, showing that a *magpie* is indeed thought of as a *bird* and a *dog* as an *animal*. It makes sense then to assume that the meaning of the word *magpie* contains a component like 'a bird of one kind', and that the meaning of the word *dog* contains a component like 'an animal of one kind'. Conversely, the fact that it would sound funny to speak of a particular tree as *that plant* helps establish that semantically a *tree* is not a 'kind of plant' (i.e. the meaning of the word *tree* does not contain any component like 'a plant of one kind').

Other useful evidence is provided by ENDONYMS, i.e. words whose meanings incorporate the meaning of another 'master' word. For example, there are 'dog-words' such as *bark, growl, leash*, and *kennel*, 'cat-words' like *meow, purr*, and *mouser*, and 'horse-words' like *neigh, gallop, jockey, groom, stable, cavalry*, and so on, which provide lexical clues to aspects of the conceptualization of *dog*, *cat*, and *horse* in English. (Strictly speaking, endonymy is such a general meaning relation that it would cover hyponymy and certain part–whole relationships, e.g. *finger* and *hand*, as well as the kind of examples just listed; cf. Cruse 1986: 123. In this book, however, we will reserve the terms endonym and endonymy for relationships of semantic inclusion other than those based on 'kind of' and 'part of'.)

Common phrases and collocations can also be helpful. For example, if we want to explicate the English concept of *mouse*, words like *mousetrap* and *mousy* help highlight aspects of the concept, such as the fact that people don't like *mice* in their houses and take steps to catch and kill them, and that *mice* are seen as inconspicuous and as brownish-grey in colour. Phrases like *as quiet as a mouse* and *as poor as a church mouse* are also revealing, the first highlighting the perceived quietness of *mice* and the second that *mice* are seen to rely on people's houses for their livelihood (a church would be a poor source of food). The connection with *cats* is evidenced in sayings like *When the cat's away, the mice will play* and phrases like *a game of cat and mouse*. Some of the differences between the English concepts of *mouse* and *rat* (which are covered by the same word in some languages, such as Japanese, Malay, and Thai) are evidenced by the fact that one can say *You dirty rat!* but not *You dirty mouse!*

The importance of collocations, common sayings, endonyms and so on, as evidence for semantic structure was originally argued by the Russian linguist Jurij Apresjan, in various works (e.g. 1969; 1992 [1974]).

7.2.4 Folk biology and culture

Apresjan also insisted on the relationship between lexical meanings and cultural history:

The folk picture of the world that developed in the course of the centuries and includes folk geometry, physics, psychology, etc., reflects the material and spiritual experience of a people (native speakers of a certain language)...The task of the lexicographer (unless he wants to go beyond his discipline and turn into an en-cyclopedist) consists of discovering the naive picture of the world hidden in lexical meanings and presenting it in a system of definitions. (Apresjan 1992 [1974]: 33, 35)

Before long we will look in detail at several English 'animal concepts' (*tigers, cats, mice, rats*), but first let's consider a cross-linguistic comparison.

The Yankunytjatjara people traditionally lived a hunting and food-gathering lifestyle in arid Central Australia. Every adult Yankunytjatjara person had a detailed knowledge of all the salient and useful natural features in the environment (cf. Goddard and Kalotas 1985). This included knowing the names of, and being able to identify, all animals and all plants with any practical significance, be it for food, medicine, tool-making, or any other purpose. An adult Yankunytjatjara would know upwards of 120 different plant species. Here we can already see a culturally motivated difference from English, as very few English speakers would know a comparable number of folk biological terms. For interest, the upper limit on the number of folk generic plant terms seems to be about 500. This kind of number is attested only in cultures which are located in botanically rich tropical regions, and which, furthermore, have an agricultural base (Berlin 1992: 96–101).

It is also notable that English lumps together some species which Yankunytjatjara distinguishes, even in the domain of animals. For example, there are several species of kangaroo in central Australia, which Yankunytjatjara people know as *malu*, *kanyala*, and *kulpirpa*. Though they are distinguished in specialist English as the *red plains kangaroo* (*Macropodus rufus*), *hills kangaroo* (*Macropodus robustus*) and *western grey kangaroo* (*Macropodus fuliginous*), ordinary English labels all three species as *kangaroo*.

If we compare the Yankunytjatjara and English terms for the same kinds of living things, we notice another difference. The Yankunytjatjara terms are all primary lexemes, whereas most of the English terms are secondary lexemes. The left-hand column illustrates this with some plant names, and the right-hand column with some animal names:

apara	river red gum	*mala*	hare wallaby
kurkara	desert oak	*tjalku*	rabbit-eared bandicoot, bilby
kurara	dead-finish bush	*tarkawara*	hopping mouse
ilykuwara	witchetty bush	*tjungku*	burrowing rat kangaroo
tjanpi	porcupine grass	*waru*	rock wallaby

Among the secondary lexemes in the folk biological lexicon of Australian English, as spoken in Central Australia, a great many combine a qualifier like *bush*, *wild*, or *native* with a botanical word which originated overseas. Typical combinations are *bush tomato*, *wild fig*, and *native pine*. The few English terms which are primary lexemes, such as *mulga*, *quan-*

dong, *kangaroo*, and *emu*, have mostly been borrowed from Aboriginal languages. Here we see, embedded in the structure of the Australian English lexicon, a reflection of the relative newness of white settlement on the Australian continent.

The higher-level categories of Yankunytjatjara and English also differ markedly. There is no Yankunytjatjara word corresponding to *animal*, just as there is no English word corresponding to *kuka*. *Kuka* includes all creatures which produce meat that can be eaten, whether they be mammals, lizards, birds, or snakes; indeed, another meaning of the word *kuka* is 'meat'. Interestingly, the other higher-level general terms also involve edibility—*mai* 'edible plant' and *wama* 'edible sweet stuff'. *Mai* includes such disparate vegetable forms as fruits, roots, grains, and mushrooms. *Wama* includes such disparate things as *tjala* 'honey ant' (a species of ant which stores a sweet syrup in its distended abdomen), *kurkunytjungu*, a sweet secretion sometimes found on the branches of mulga, and *ngapari*, the sweet crusty scales sometimes found on the leaves of gum trees.

Terms like *kuka*, *mai*, and *wama* are not life-form words at all, but 'functional-collective' terms (analogous to English words like *poultry*, *game*, *fruit*, and *vegetables*). As a matter of fact, Yankunytjatjara has fewer life-forms than English, the only clear instances being *tjulpu* (roughly, 'birds of flight') and *punu* 'living things that grow out of the ground'. There are no Yankunytjatjara terms corresponding to English *lizard* or *snake*. The larger edible lizards and edible snakes (such as the rock python) are classified as *kuka*, and each has its own individual name (primary lexemes like *ngintaka* 'perentie lizard', *milpali* 'sand goanna', *kuniya* 'rock python'). Smaller lizards of the dragon variety are grouped together as *tjati*, and small skink lizards as *mulingka*. Small harmless snakes are *kuyi*, while poisonous snakes are *liru*.

Is there any cultural significance in the fact that English has more life-form words than Yankunytjatjara, whereas Yankunytjatjara has many more folk genera than English? Anthropological research has established that there is a general correlation between lexical elaboration at different levels of biological ranking and (roughly speaking) 'societal complexity'.

Folk biological taxonomies tend to decay 'from the bottom up' (from more specific classes to less specific classes) as people urbanise and become increasingly separated from direct reliance and dependence on the world of plants and animals...As a consequence, more general terms, such as life-form terms, become increasingly useful and salient ..., so much so that they tend to increase in number. Thus the growth of ethnobiological life-forms ironically indexes an overall lack of interest in and interaction with the natural world. (Brown 1979: 805)

In other words, the proliferation of life-form words in English, and the relative poverty of folk generics, is symptomatic of our increasing urban estrangement from nature.

This general observation is confirmed by research into the psychological salience of different levels of ranking in English (cf. Rosch 1978; Dougherty 1978). For the animal world, the most salient terms are at the level of folk genera. That is to say, in pairs like *animal–dog* and *animal–horse* the folk generic *dog* or *horse* is the more salient term. To put it another way, *dog* has the best claim to being a 'basic-level' term in the sense of Rosch; it is the term likely to be used first to classify a particular instance of the thing in question, and it is likely to be acquired by children earlier than either *animal* or *beagle*.

However, which members of the following pairs of terms are psychologically more salient: *tree–oak*, *bird–sparrow*, *fish–trout*? Intuitively, in these cases it is the life-form terms (*tree, bird, fish*). The reason too seems clear enough. Modern Western societies have to a large extent lost their folk knowledge of, and their folk interest in, the biological environment. They no longer conceptualize the natural world at the detailed level of individual genera. Except, that is, in the domain of higher animals.

7.3 Cats, mice, and rats

Before launching into an attempt to define English words *cats*, *mice*, and *rats*, it is worth pointing out that various linguists, psychologists, and philosophers have held that it is impossible to define folk generics, basically on account of the great complexity such definitions would require. The linguist Geoffrey Leech (1969: 85–9), for example, took the position that almost all of our shared knowledge about folk genera is non-linguistic and belongs not in the (mental) dictionary, so to speak, but in the (mental) encyclopedia. He denied even that a specification like 'it has four legs' is part of the meaning of a word like *elephant*. According to Leech, the fact that English speakers recognize something odd about an expression like *an elephant with 80 legs* is a matter of real-world knowledge and nothing to do with the meaning of *elephant*. He proposed that the best we can do by way of semantic analysis of terms like *dog, cat, elephant, rabbit*, etc., is simply to assign a distinct (and arbitrary) identifying number to each species, along with the feature –HUM (non-human); for example, –HUM 1SPE for *dog*, –HUM 2SPE for *cat*, –HUM 31SPE for *elephant*.

This proposal could find support in some philosophical writings. Saul Kripke (1972) says that the naming of natural kinds is analogous to the assignment of proper names. Just as individual people are unique and, so to speak, directly given by the world, so it is with natural kinds. We recognize that the members of a natural kind form an undifferentiated 'gestalt' (overall pattern), and we accept the name (e.g. *elephant*) as something that somebody before us has already provided. Even some anthropologists (cf. Berlin 1981: 96) have taken up this gestalt idea, and claimed that *racoon* or *tiger* is conceptualized as an unanalysed, global gestalt of 'racoonness' or 'tigerness'.

From a semantic point of view, however, there is nothing implausible about the idea that a meaning may be very complex. Nor is there any reason to think that the line between shared, linguistic knowledge and real-world, encyclopedic knowledge will turn out to be impossible to draw. As we have already seen, there are many types of evidence (including endonyms, common collocations, and proverbs) which can help us identify linguistic knowledge. Furthermore, it is not the case that all natural kinds are 'given' in the world. For example, as mentioned earlier, the English language distinguishes *mice* from *rats* while Malay and Japanese do not; Yankunytjatjara distinguishes several different kinds of kangaroo, while standard English lumps them all under the one term.

7.3.1 A preliminary example: tigers

The concept encoded in the word *cat* is semantically very complex, mainly because cats have long been important to the lifestyle of English-speaking people. To get an idea of some of the factors that may be important, it is helpful to begin with a simpler example. *Tigers* are animals which most speakers of English in Australia, the USA, and the UK do not have much to do with, and for this reason we can expect the semantic structure of *tigers* to be much simpler. The explication below is adapted from Wierzbicka (1985: 164). It is a bit rough and incomplete, and is not written in strict NSM (it uses some complex words which are not legitimate semantic molecules), but it is sufficient for present purposes.

tigers
a.   animals of one kind
b.   animals of this kind live in the jungle
c.   animals of this kind are big
      when people see them, people can think that they are like very big cats
d.   the bodies of animals of this kind are like this:
      they have yellowish fur with black stripes
      they have big sharp claws
      they have big sharp teeth
e.   they can kill animals of many other kinds
      they eat these animals after they kill them
f.   sometimes animals of this kind kill people
      because of this, people are afraid of them
      people think about them like this:
          'they are fierce, they are strong'

We can use this explication to point out some of the different kinds of component that turn up in folk generics. To begin with, the topmost component positions *tigers* as 'animals of one kind', where 'animals [m]' is a life-form word. This establishes their CATEGORY in the ranking scheme, and it also conveys a good deal of information in virtue of the semantic content of 'animal' itself. Component (b) specifies WHERE THEY LIVE (their habitat). It is usual to find such a component as the second element of an animal explication.

Component (c) indicates something about their SIZE, in the process comparing them to 'very big cats'. Obviously the reference to *cats* is specific to this explication. The components in (d) describe the distinctive BODY appearance of *tigers*. In this explication, these components are very brief, mainly because a great deal of body-related information has already been conveyed by the statement that they look like *cats*. Body components often run to a dozen or more lines. Component (e) describes characteristic BEHAVIOUR. For better-known animals, behaviour components too can be very lengthy.

Finally, under (f) are components which describe their RELATION WITH PEOPLE, including people's attitudes toward them. Some linguists would say that these are not part of the meaning of *tiger* at all, but suppose we imagine that somebody has learnt (say, from pictures or films) to distinguish *tigers* from all other animals, without having learnt that they are dangerous to humans and thought to be fierce and strong (Wierzbicka 1985: 173–4). Would we accept that this person has learnt in full the concept encoded in the ordinary English word *tiger*? Presumably not.

7.3.2 What are cats?

The explication we will discuss is adapted from Wierzbicka (1985: 167). It follows the semantic template: (a) CATEGORY, (b) WHERE THEY LIVE, (c) SIZE, (d) BODY, (e) BEHAVIOUR, including SOUND, (f) RELATION WITH PEOPLE, and (g) HOW PEOPLE THINK ABOUT THEM. Altogether the explication is over 40 lines long, so we will work through it in stages, beginning with sections (a)–(d). It would take a long time to fully discuss and justify each component in an explication like this, so we will just touch briefly on each of them.

The (a) component establishes *cats* as 'animals [m] of one kind'. The molecule 'animal' will be explicated in the next section. The (b) components claim that *cats* are conceptualized primarily as domestic animals which are cared for by people. In support of this, one can note that *cats* which don't fit this description are usually referred to in combination with a modifier; so we have *feral cats* and *stray cats*. Notice that the size component (c) is defined in relation to the human body. This kind of ANTHROPOCENTRISM (i.e. using the human body as a kind of central reference point) is a feature of size components in countless words of diverse types. In the case of *cats*, the size component mentions handling by humans, further consolidating their status as a domestic animal. The components in (d) identify the distinctive physical features of *cats* as a round head with pointed ears, a special kind of eyes, whiskers, long tail, very soft fur, and soft feet with small sharp claws. (It is no coincidence that most of these features figure prominently in cartoon representations of cats, as you will see if you examine drawings of well-known cartoon cats such as Garfield, Sylvester, Snowball, Doraemon, and Felix.) Sections (a)–(d) of the *cats* explication are as follows.

cats (partial explication):

CATEGORY

a.   animals [m] of one kind

WHERE THEY LIVE

b.   many animals [m] of this kind live in people's homes [m]
        because these people want this
     some animals [m] of this kind live in places near people's homes [m]

c.   animals [m] of this kind are not big
     someone can pick up [m] one with two hands [m]

d.   the body of animals [m] of this kind is like this:
     – they have a round [m] head [m]
     – their ears [m] are on two sides of the top [m] of the head [m], they are
         pointed [m]
     – their eyes [m] are not like people's eyes [m]
     – they have some long [m] hairs [m] near the mouth [m], these hairs [m]
         stick out [m] on two sides of the mouth [m]
     – they have a long [m] tail [m]
     – they have soft [m] fur [m]
     – they have soft [m] feet [m], they have small sharp [m] claws [m]

The behaviour sections of the explication are elaborate, reflecting the opportunity people have long had to observe the distinctive behaviour of these animals which share their lives.

cats (continued):

BEHAVIOUR

e1. – animals [m] of this kind can kill [m] small creatures [m] of many other kinds
         sometimes when they kill [m] these small creatures [m], afterwards
             they eat [m] them
     – sometimes before they kill [m] them, they do some things with them for
         some time, like children [m] often do things with some things for some
             time when they are playing [m]
     – if they want, animals [m] of this kind can be for some time in places far
         above the ground [m]
       animals [m] of many other kinds cannot be in places like this
       animals [m] of this kind can do many things in these places
     – animals [m] of this kind can move quickly [m]
     – when they move in a place, people in this place can't hear anything
         because of it
     – they can see things in the night [m] in places where there is no light [m]
     – they often sleep [m] for a short time during the day [m]
     – they often lick [m] their fur [m] for some time

SOUND

e2. at some times when animals [m] of this kind want something,
         they do something for some time with the mouth [m]

when an animal [m] of this kind does this in a place, people in this place
   can hear something of one kind because of it
when people hear this, they can think that this animal [m] wants to say
   something like: 'I want something'
   – at some times when animals [m] of this kind feel something good because
         something is happening to them, they do something else for some
            time, not with the mouth [m]
when an animal [m] of this kind does this, if someone is near this animal [m],
   this someone can hear something of one kind for some time because of it
e3.   animals [m] of another kind often live with people
   at many times it is like this:
   an animal [m] of this other kind feels something bad towards an animal [m]
      of this kind
   because of this, the animal [m] of this other kind wants to do something
      bad to the body of the animal [m] of this kind

The first part of section (e1) details the fact that *cats* can kill, and will
sometimes play with, 'small creatures of many other kinds' (e.g. mice, birds,
and insects), their climbing ability, agility, and stealthiness, and the facts they
often lick themselves and can see in the dark. Under (e1) is also found the
reference to *cats* liking to sleep during the day. Some of the linguistic evidence
in support of these components comes in the form of phrases and sayings
such as: *a game of cat and mouse, a catnap*, the belief that *cats have nine lives*
(reflecting their abilities to escape from tricky situations, and perhaps especially from high places), and the expressions *cat-burglar* (one who depends on
climbing ability) and *catwalk* (a narrow walkway for fashion models). Note
also that the word *catlike* evokes graceful motion (there is no comparable
word *doglike* or *mouselike*).

The components in (e2) describe the two distinctive sounds associated
with *cats*, namely *meowing* and *purring*. Both are endonyms of *cat*, i.e. it
would be necessary to include the word *cat* in their explications. For this
reason, it isn't possible to use the actual words *meow* or *purr* in the *cat*
explication. Finally, in (e3) there is a reference to the special relationship
cats have with another kind of animal that often lives with people (i.e.
dogs), and to the hostility or animosity they are supposed to feel towards
cats (cf. the expression *fight like cats and dogs*).

The final sections of the explication below are explicitly 'people-oriented'.
The components in (f1) and (f2) describe how *cats* figure in people's lives as
pets. Those in (f3) acknowledge their usefulness in catching mice (cf. word

mouser). Then, finally, in (g) come the attitudinal components, specifying that *cats* are generally seen as independent and inclined to be lazy.

cats (continued):

RELATION TO PEOPLE

f1. many people feel something good towards animals [m] of this kind
    in many people's homes [m], an animal [m] of this kind lives with these
       people because these people want this
    these people think about this animal [m] like this: 'this is someone'
    these people do good things for this animal [m]
    these people want this animal [m] to know that they feel something good
       towards it
    at the same time they want to know that this animal [m] feels something
       good towards them
f2. at many times people touch the fur [m] of animals of this kind with their
       hands [m]
    when someone does this, if this someone's hand [m] moves at the same time,
       this someone can feel something good in this hand [m] because of it
f3. small animals [m] of another kind can live in people's homes [m], people
       don't want this [m]
    animals [m] of this kind can kill [m] these small animals [m] of this other kind

HOW PEOPLE THINK ABOUT THEM

g. many people think about animals [m] of this kind like this:
    'if they don't want to do something, they don't do it
    at many times, they don't want to do anything
    at these times they want to feel something good for some time,
       they don't want anything else'

It is interesting that there are several English expressions linking women with *cats*, often in a negative way; for example, the adjective *catty* refers to a sharp, ill-willed remark, of a kind thought to be more typical of women than of men. One often hears the pronoun *she* used to refer to a cat, even when its sex is not known. The association between *cats* and 'femininity', in my view, tells us as much (or more) about traditional attitudes towards women as it does about *cats*. It is a topic which would consume too much space if we were to open it up here.

7.3.3 Mice *vs.* rats

As mentioned, many languages do not distinguish lexically between what are known in English as *mice* and *rats* (despite the conviction of many

English speakers that there is an obvious categorical difference between them). This makes it an instructive exercise to explicate the two words contrastively. It can be argued that the concept of *rats* is secondary to that of *mice*, in the sense that it depends in part on comparisons with *mice*; for example, that *rats* look much like *mice* except that they are very much bigger. We will therefore start with *mice*.

mice:

CATEGORY

a.   animals [m] of one kind

WHERE THEY LIVE

b.   animals [m] of this kind can live in people's homes [m]
     they can live in places near people's homes [m]
     sometimes there can be many animals [m] of this kind in one place

SIZE

c.   animals [m] of this kind are small
     if someone wants, this someone can hold [m] one in one hand [m]

BODY

d.   the body of animals [m] of this kind is like this:
     – when someone sees it, this someone can think that it has two parts
     – the head [m] is part of one of these two parts, the other part of these
        two parts is a long [m] thin [m] tail
     – the front [m] part of the head [m] is pointed [m]
     – animals [m] of this kind have small round [m] ears [m] on two sides of
        the top [m] of the head [m]
     – they have small hairs [m] near the mouth [m], these hairs [m] stick
        out [m] on two sides of the front [m] part of the head
     – they have small sharp [m] teeth [m]
     – they have very small legs [m], when they move people can't see their
        legs [m]

BEHAVIOUR

e1.   often when animals [m] of this kind are doing things in a place,
         people in this place cannot hear anything because of it
      – they can move quickly [m]
      – sometimes when they move in a place, people in this place can hear
         something of one kind like people can hear at other times, if
            someone's fingernails [m] move when they are touching
               something hard [m]
      – at some times, animals of this kind [m] can be inside a small hole [m] in a
         place

SOUND

e2. at some times when animals [m] of this kind feel something,
      they do something for some time with the mouth [m]
      if someone is very near the place where these animals [m] are at that time,
        this someone can hear something of one kind because of it
      when people hear this, they can think that these animals [m] feel
        something bad like someone can feel when this someone thinks that
          something very bad can happen to this someone's body after a short time

RELATION TO PEOPLE

f.   people don't want animals [m] of this kind to live in their homes [m],
        because they can do bad things in their homes [m]
      if many animals [m] of this kind live in people's homes [m], it can be very bad
        for these people, because in many people's homes [m] it is like this:
        – things of many kinds are in some places in these homes [m] because
            these people want this
        – they want this because they want to eat [m] these things afterwards
        – animals [m] of this kind want to eat [m] the same things
      because of this, when many animals [m] of this kind live in a place, people in
        this place often do some things with things of one kind because they want
          to kill [m] these animals [m]
      sometimes these people want an animal [m] of another kind to live in the
        same place because an animal [m] of this other kind can kill [m] animals
          [m] of this kind

HOW PEOPLE THINK ABOUT THEM

g.   many people think about animals [m] of this kind like this:
        'at all times when they are in a place, animals [m] of this kind want
            other creatures [m] not to know that they are in this place
        they want this because they don't want something bad to happen to
            them'

Now let's compare this explication with the explication for *rats* offered below. The first and most theoretically interesting point is that section (a) characterizes *rats* by reference to *mice*, as follows: 'people can think that they are like mice [m]; at the same time, people know that they are not mice [m].' A little later in the explication, in the SIZE section, *mice* again make an appearance. *Rats* are characterized as 'big', in comparison with *mice*. That is, just as 'cats [m]' functions as a conceptual ingredient in the concept of *tigers*, so 'mice [m]' is part of the concept of *rats*. From a conceptual point of view, therefore, *rats* and *mice* are not on a par with one another, even though they may be on a par from the point of view of biological classification.

Moving on, we see that the WHERE THEY LIVE section for *rats* partly overlaps with that of *mice*, but that other possible habitats for *rats* are characterized as (roughly) subterranean, dirty, dark, and wet. Linguistic evidence for these components comes from expressions such as *sewer rat*, *gutter rat*, and *water rat*, and from collocational links between *rats* and basements, caves, sewers, and the like. Section (c) characterizes *rats* as of medium size (not big, not small), but, as mentioned, adds the information that they are 'big' when compared with *mice*.

Physically the description of *rats* in section (d) has much in common with the corresponding components in the explication for *mice*. Differences include teeth that are not just 'sharp', but 'very sharp', 'big eyes' that can be seen 'in places where there is not much light', and a 'long tail' (not further described as 'thin', as with *mice*). Under BEHAVIOUR, there is reference to *rats*' reputedly voracious appetite, and to their viciousness ('they can kill small animals of other kinds'), including that they sometimes hunt in packs (notice that there are no *mice* expressions that would parallel expressions like *a pack of rats*). Nothing is provided in the way of a SOUND subsection.

In RELATION TO PEOPLE, many components are the same as for *mice*, including that people don't want them living in their homes and take steps to kill them. There are two additional details, however, both of which make the prospect of *rats* in the house much more worrying: one links *rats* with disease (i.e. the prospect that 'something very bad can happen inside these people's bodies' on account of *rats*); the other states that 'if an animal [m] of this kind bites [m] someone, it can be very bad for this someone'. Naturally, therefore, people's attitude towards *rats* is much different to their attitude to *mice*. *Rats* are thought to 'do many very bad things' and to be unclean animals, and moreover, many people find *rats* repulsive and would not want to be touched by one.

   rats:

                                                                    CATEGORY

   a.   animals [m] of one kind
        people can think that they are like mice [m]
        at the same time, people know that they are not mice [m]

                                                          WHERE THEY LIVE

   b.   animals [m] of this kind can live in places where people live,
            they can live in places below places where people live
        many animals [m] of this kind live in very dirty [m] places

many animals [m] of this kind live in places where there is no light [m]
many animals [m] of this kind live in places where is a lot of water [m]
there can be many animals [m] of this kind in one place

SIZE

c.   animals [m] of this kind are not small
animals [m] of this kind are not big
if someone thinks about mice [m] at the same time, this someone
   can think that they are big

BODY

d.   the body of animals [m] of this kind is like this:
   – their bodies are like the bodies of mice [m]
   – the head [m] is pointed [m]
   – they have small round [m] ears [m] on two sides of the top [m] of
      the head [m]
   – they have small hairs [m] near the mouth [m], these hairs [m] stick
      out [m] on two sides of the mouth [m]
   – they have very sharp [m] teeth [m]
   – they have big eyes [m], people can see their eyes [m] in places where there
      is not much light [m]
   – they have small legs [m]
   – they have a long [m] tail

BEHAVIOUR

e.   – animals of this kind [m] want to eat [m] many things
   – they can kill [m] small animals [m] of other kinds
   – sometimes many animals [m] of this kind in one place kill [m] one animal
      [m] of another kind
   – sometimes one animal [m] of this kind kills [m] another animal [m] of the
      same kind
   – animals of this kind [m] can move quickly [m]

SOUND

e2.   —

RELATION TO PEOPLE

f.   people don't want animals [m] of this kind to live in their homes [m]
      because they can do bad things in these places
   if many animals [m] of this kind live in people's homes [m], it can be very
      bad for these people
   if many of these animals [m] live in a place where people live, something
      very bad can happen inside these people's bodies because of it

in many people's homes [m] it is like this at many times:
– things of many kinds are in some places in these homes [m] because
these people want this
– they want it because they want to eat [m] these things afterwards
– animals [m] of this kind want to eat [m] the same things
because of this, when many animals [m] of this kind live in a place, people
in this place often do some things with things of one kind because they
want to kill [m] these animals [m]
if an animal [m] of this kind bites [m] someone, it can be very bad for this
someone

HOW PEOPLE THINK ABOUT THEM

g.   many people think about animals [m] of this kind like this:
'they are very dirty [m] animals [m]
they do many very bad things'
when many people think about animals [m] of this kind, they feel
something bad
many people don't want animals [m] of this kind to touch their body

It will be evident that the concept of *rats* is significantly elaborated in English, and that the *rat* represents (so to speak) the 'dark side of the mouse'. As Umberto Eco (2003: 32–3) observes in his book *Mouse or Rat?*, a perceptive set of essays on the difficulties of translation, even in languages that apparently have equivalents to the *mouse/rat* distinction, there can be subtle differences in meaning and usage between the apparent equivalents—and this is not surprising when we see the degree of complexity of meaning that is involved in such concepts. Some have suggested that the English *mouse/rat* distinction, and in particular the strongly negative attitude towards *rats*, is partly a 'cultural echo' of the Great Plague of seventeenth-century London, which was blamed on *rats*.

7.4 Taxonomic hierarchies and 'hidden essences'

In our explications for *cats*, *mice*, and *rats*, the initial category component reads: 'animals [m] of one kind', thereby establishing their position at a certain level of hierarchical ranking. What then are *animals* and *creatures*, the two higher-level categories recognized in the English ethnozoological hierarchy? For reasons that will become apparent, it will be convenient to examine an explication for *animals* in two sections.

7.4.1 *Introducing* animals

Consider first the following.

animals (partial explication):

MULTI-CATEGORY

a.   creatures [m] of many kinds
    many parts of their bodies are like parts of people's bodies

SPECIES

b.   creatures [m] of many of these kinds are born [m] like people are born [m]
    before a creature [m] of one of these kinds is born [m], for some time its
      body is inside the body of another creature [m] of the same kind
    during this time it is like part of the body of this other creature [m]

WHERE THEY LIVE

c.   creatures [m] of all these kinds live in places where parts of their bodies
      can touch the ground [m] at many times
    these places are places of many kinds
    creatures [m] of many of these kinds live in places where people don't live
    creatures [m] of some of these kinds live in places where people live

There are a number of notable points. First and foremost, the initial component presents *animals* as a multi-category concept: not as 'creatures [m] of one kind', but rather as 'creatures [m] of many kinds'. This corresponds to Berlin's observation that life-form words are characterized by 'polytypicity'.

Second, there is an immediate physical comparison with people: 'many parts of their bodies are like parts of people's bodies.' As we will see throughout the explication, the concept of *animals* involves a series of alignments and contrasts with the concept of PEOPLE. This may seem unexceptional but it underlies the particularly English-specific semantics of *animals*. If we compare the English word with its nearest counterpart in German, for example, we see that German *Tiere* (singular: *Tier*) embraces a much broader range of creatures than does *animals*: fish, birds, snakes, and even spiders and insects, can be regarded as *Tiere*, but with some exceptions it would sound strange to refer to a bird, fish, spider or snake as *an animal*.

Skipping down to section (c), the WHERE THEY LIVE section, we can see other components that help delimit the concept of *animals*: they are said to live in 'places where parts of their bodies can touch the ground [m] at many times'. This excludes fish and other aquatic creatures. Notice though that it does not exclude tree-dwelling creatures such as *squirrels* and *monkeys*; living on land, *squirrels* and *monkeys* can still be in contact with the ground at many times, even though they spend much of their time in the trees. The last two components of section (c) provide for the existence of numerous wild animals, and also for a number of animal kinds that live in association with people.

But let's go back and take a closer look at section (b).

7.4.2 The 'hidden essence' issue

The SPECIES section states (roughly put) that animals of any particular kind (*mice, tigers, horses*, etc.) 'come from' creatures of the same kind; more specifically, they are born (like people are born) from the body of 'a creature of the same kind'. This refers to the lineage of reproduction which is characteristic of natural species (*mice* come from *mice*, *tigers* come from *tigers*, *horses* come from *horses*, etc.).

Aside from capturing an inherent part of the concept of a 'species', this set of components accounts for an interesting property that philosophers discuss using the term 'essence'. To understand the issue requires a bit of background. John Locke (1976 [1690]) drew attention to an important difference between natural kinds (things like tigers, oaks, and gold) and what he termed NOMINAL KINDS (such as pencils, chairs, and cups). Locke believed that natural kinds had 'real essences', by which he seems to have meant that words like *tiger, oak*, and *gold* correspond in some way with the intrinsic make-up of the world, in a sense in which the names of artefacts do not. Artefacts like *cups, pencils*, and *chairs*, and other nominal kinds, clearly do not reflect the intrinsic nature of the world, since they exist only because people make them to suit their particular needs and purposes.

The distinction appears to be linked with a striking difference in the way people think about natural kinds as opposed to artefacts. This difference can be dramatized as follows. If we see a creature that looks and acts in every way like a *tiger*, we would naturally assume that is a *tiger*. But now suppose we are told, by someone whose judgement we trust, that this creature is not in fact a *tiger* but only looks and acts like a *tiger*. We are quite likely to accept this statement at face value. On the other hand, if we were presented with an object which looks and feels in every way like a *pencil*, but were told that it is not a *pencil*, would we accept this statement so readily? Probably not. Similarly, we would be much more ready to accept the idea that a particular unusual-looking animal could be a *tiger* (e.g. an albino tiger, lacking any stripes) than we would be to accept the idea that an unusual-looking object could be a *pencil* despite not looking like one (Atran 1987b).

Intuitively too, it seems plausible that natural kinds have 'underlying natures', in a way that artefacts don't. For example, we are not surprised to hear that scientists study *tigers* or *horses*, to find out more about their underlying natures, but if we heard of a scientist gathering some specimens of *chairs* in order to discover the nature of *chairs*, we would think that he or she was crazy. Somehow we seem to conceptualize a natural kind as having some inherent nature (or 'essence' in the traditional terminology) which makes such a thing a thing of that kind, whereas what makes something a *pencil* or a *chair* are more 'superficial characteristics such as a certain form and function' (cf. Schwartz 1978: 571–3).

Section (b) of the *animals* explication presented above contains components that can help us understand what the philosophers are getting at with their talk of 'essences'. As noted above, this section of the explication refers to creatures of any single kind of animal as being born from the body of another creature of 'the same kind' (cf. Wierzbicka 1996a: 340, 367–70). In other words, it incorporates the notion of particular 'kinds' of creatures persisting across the generations—surely a close correlate of the notion of a natural 'essence'.

7.4.3 Animals *continued*

Here is the remainder of the *animals* explication. Look through it carefully before reading the review that follows.

animals (continued):

BODY

d.   the bodies of creatures [m] of all these kinds are like this:
     – one part of their bodies is like people's heads [m]
       many parts of this part are like parts of people's heads [m]
     – some other parts of their bodies are like people's legs [m]
     – one part of their bodies is not like any part of people's bodies
       this part is at the back [m] of the body
       this part can move when the creature [m] wants it

the bodies of creatures [m] of many of these kinds are like this:
– there are two parts like people's legs [m] at the front [m] of the body
  there are two parts like people's legs [m] at the back [m] of the body
– there is something like hair [m] on many parts of their bodies
– creatures [m] of all these kinds can have bodies of two kinds, like people
  can have bodies of two kinds
some parts of the bodies of one of these kinds are like parts of women's [m]
  bodies
some parts of the bodies of the other kind are like parts of men's [m]
  bodies

BEHAVIOUR

e1. – when creatures of [m] of all these kinds want to be somewhere else,
     they do some things with parts of their bodies
   – they can do things of many other kinds

SOUNDS

e2. creatures [m] of many of these kinds can do something with their mouths
   [m] like people can do something with their mouth [m] when they
     want to say something
   when a creature [m] of one of these kinds does this, if someone is near the
     place where this creature [m] is, this someone can hear something of
     one kind because of it

HOW PEOPLE THINK ABOUT THEM

f.   people can think about creatures [m] of all these kinds like this:
     'they can do some things like people do some things
     they can feel good things, they can feel bad things'
     at the same time, people can think about creatures [m] of these kinds like this:
     'they do many things not like people do things
     they can't think like people can think
     they can't know that it is bad to do things of some kinds like people know
       that it is bad to do things of some kinds
     they can't say things like people can say things'

Note that the BODY section refers to one part 'like people's heads [m]', to other parts 'like people's legs [m]', and to one part 'not like any part of people's bodies', namely, the tail. It is stated that 'the bodies of creatures [m] of many of these kinds' have two legs at the front and back (the wording allows for exceptions such as *kangaroos* and *chimpanzees*), and fur ('something like hair [m]') on their bodies, and that, like people, their bodies come in two kinds, one with some parts 'like parts of women's [m] bodies', i.e. female, and the other with some parts 'like parts of men's [m] bodies', i.e. male.

The BEHAVIOUR section is pretty schematic, but it allows for bodily mobility and for doing 'things of many other kinds'. There is also a section providing that many animals make expressive SOUNDS with their mouths, and that this can be viewed as analogous to people saying things. Finally, there is a section HOW PEOPLE THINK ABOUT THEM, which sums up the ambivalent attitudes people have towards *animals* in general: on the one hand crediting them with feelings and recognizing that they can do many things as people can; but on the other hand, recognizing that they cannot think as people do, that they do many things that people don't do, that they lack 'moral discrimination', and that they cannot say things with words.

7.4.4 Cascading templates

All the details of the *animals* explication are interesting in themselves, and could sustain a lot of further discussion, which unfortunately limitations of space prevent us from undertaking here. Can you see, however, that there is also a general observation to be made about the semantic template for *animals*, as compared to that for *cats*, *mice*, *rats* and other individual animal names? The individual animal explications, recall, all begin with the component 'animals [m] of one kind'. In an obvious sense, then, the concept of 'animals' is part of the individual animal concepts. Less obvious, however, is that the semantic template for *animals* is, so to speak, passed down into the explications for the individual animal concepts. To put it another way, the concept of 'animal' itself sets up certain expectations: about size, about body type and body parts, and about certain ways of moving and other behaviours. It makes sense, then, that each individual animal explication will satisfy these expectations with details appropriate to the particular kind of animal in question.

7.4.5 Creatures

Finally let's have a look at an explication that has been proposed for the English word *creatures*, the topmost category in the English ethnozoological hierarchy. As one would expect, it is much less detailed than *animals*. As with *animals*, it is multi-categoric ('living things of many kinds'). The WHERE THEY LIVE section simply provides that they live in places of many kinds, the SIZE section that they are of greatly variable sizes, the BODY section that they have bodies of many kinds (but having bodies at all excludes trees, plants, algae, and the like), and the BEHAVIOUR section that they can move as they want and do things of many other kinds. Little wonder that such a schematic concept lacks equivalents in many of the world's languages. In English the word *creatures* (or *creature*) is most often used when individual species names are not known or are not relevant, e.g. to speak of *strange creatures*, *sea creatures*, *tiny* (or *microscopic*) *creatures*, and (as the hymn has it) of *all creatures great and small*.

creatures:

MULTI-CATEGORY

a.   living things of many kinds

WHERE THEY LIVE

b.   living things of these kinds live in places of many kinds

SIZE

c.   living things of some of these kinds are big, some are small
     living things of some of these kinds are very big, some are very small

BODY

d.   living things of these kinds have bodies of many kinds

BEHAVIOUR

e.   living things of all these kinds can move as they want
     living things of all these kinds can do things of many other kinds

It is notable that the *creatures* explication is composed entirely in semantic primes. Notice also that the way it is arranged lays down much of the template structure for *animals*, and (presumably) for other life-form words, such as *birds* and *fish*.

7.5 Artefact meanings

In many ways artefact words are very different from animal words, and from other natural-kind words; but the scope of the differences itself makes them an interesting counterpoint to animal words. As we have seen, there is a philosophical tradition that counterposes natural kinds and nominal kinds. A major point of similarity between these two realms of meaning, however, is that both exhibit great semantic complexity.

7.5.1 How 'simple' are everyday artefacts?

Perhaps it is not so strange that words for items of 'material culture' (as anthropologists call it) presuppose a great deal of shared cultural knowledge. Think how difficult it would be to describe a *saucepan* to someone from a culture which has no kitchens and no stoves, nothing made out of metal, and in which the boiling of water is unknown as a cooking technique (as was the case in traditional Yankunytjatjara culture). Conversely, I invite you to think how much you would need to know about the traditional culture of the Western Desert to really understand the Yankunytjatjara word *miru*, which denotes an object like that pictured in Figure 7.1. Take a good long look at the illustration before you read on.

Miru is normally glossed in bilingual dictionaries as 'spear-thrower', but people unfamiliar with the desert culture would have little idea how it is used. Most people wouldn't realize, for instance, that at one end of the *miru* (on the left in Figure 7.1) there is a sharp hook tied on with kangaroo sinew, made so as to fit into the tiny hole bored into the end of a hunting spear, so that (if you hold the spear and *miru* correctly) the *miru* can be used like a kind of lever, to launch the spear off on its way.

The complexity of the *miru* goes much further than this. For the instrument is in fact a multi-purpose tool. Embedded in the handle (on the right in Figure 7.1) is a sharp quartz chip which serves as the hunter's meat knife. And because the *miru* is so thin and made of such hard wood, it makes an ideal 'fire-saw'—that is, by rubbing the edge of it very fast back and forth over the right type of light dry wood, you can make sparks to light a fire. The translation 'spear-thrower', in other words, conveys only a fraction of the cultural 'common knowledge' taken for granted when Yankunytjatjara people use the word among themselves. (For a comparable example, imagine the term *cricket bat* being translated as, say, 'a hitting thing' or even as 'a thing to hit balls with'.)

One moral we can draw from this example is that to properly understand the meaning of an artefact word like *miru* (or *saucepan*, for that matter) we

Figure 7.1 A Yankunytjatjara *miru*

have to understand the functions of the thing in question, and (to some extent at least) how its design fits or serves those functions. Despite what one might think at first, a picture of a thing—or, more accurately, of a typical one of its kind—has quite a limited value in conveying the meaning of the word for that thing. Try to bear these points in mind, and be patient, as we set out to look in minute detail at a couple of very ordinary English words, *cup* and *mug*, which rocketed to fame as the most discussed 'simple artefact' words as a result of work by William Labov in the 1970s. As usual, we will have a methodological issue to consider.

7.5.2 The denotation conditions approach

Labov (1973) set out to apply techniques and concepts which he had pioneered in the study of speech variation. He begins with the idea that meanings will vary from speaker to speaker and occasion to occasion, just as pronunciation does. He is sceptical of the 'Aristotelian' view that categories are discrete and invariant. After all, he says, other linguistic concepts, such as phoneme and dialect, don't have perfectly clear boundaries, so why should meanings have them? Labov sees the 'meaning or significatum of a sign as the conditions which govern denotation', and he sets out to:

> introduce the study of variability in denotation, systematically displacing the categorical view which has dominated previous studies in order to discover the regularities which relate the properties of shape, function, material, etc. as they govern the conditions for the act of denotation. (Labov 1973: 347)

Labov's experiments investigate the conditions under which people are prepared to identify a drawing and description of an object as a *cup*, *mug*, *bowl*, or *vase*. The drawings depict objects with different ratios of width to depth, as shown in drawings 1–9 in Figure 7.2. The prototypical *cup*, in Labov's view, is the one at the upper left. Other drawings show *cup*-like objects which depart from the concave shape by having straight sides, or a stem, or a triangular or square shape.

In the first part of the experiment people were presented with the drawings, in random order, and asked to name them. Next, they were asked to do the same naming task, but imagining that they see a person holding the object, stirring in some sugar, and then drinking coffee from it. In a third series, they were asked to imagine seeing the object on the dinner table at someone's house, filled with mashed potatoes, and in a final fourth series

Figure 7.2 Drawings used in Labov (1973)'s *cup* experiment

they were asked to think of the object standing on a shelf with cut flowers in it. These four series were labelled 'Neutral', 'Coffee', 'Food', and 'Flower'. Another set of drawings showed objects with no handles, and in yet another series the material was specified as china, glass, metal, and paper. People's responses often came in the form of noun phrases with some modifiers, for example, *a long cup, a funny cup with a stem, a kind of cup*. Labov considered only the head noun, so that all the phrases just mentioned were classed as naming the object a *cup*.

Not surprisingly, it was found that people varied somewhat in certain cases. For instance, drawing No. 1 in Figure 7.3 was always called a *cup* and drawing No. 4 was always a *bowl*, but the intermediate ones varied. In a 'Neutral' context No. 3 was equally likely to be called a *cup* or *bowl*. This kind of effect is sometimes called REFERENTIAL INDETERMINACY.

By tabulating the responses to objects with different height–width ratios, in the different functional contexts (Neutral, Coffee, Food, Flower), Labov was able to produce diagrams showing the 'consistency profiles' for *cup*, *bowl*, *mug*, and *vase* (Figure 7.4). Both function and height–width ratio are important; for example, in the 'Food' context, people are more likely to call object No. 3 in Figure 7.3 a *bowl* than a *cup*.

As a way of summarizing the 'information about the conditions for denotation of *cup*', Labov presents the statement in Figure 7.5, which was devised with the help of a mathematician. This takes account of the

Figure 7.3 Labov cup drawings 1–4

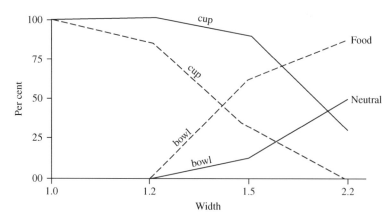

Figure 7.4 Consistency profiles for *cup* and *bowl* (Labov 1973)

influence of a set of discrete 'features' as well as of the height–depth ratio, which is non-discrete. Of the eight features, five are physical in nature ('with one handle', 'made of opaque vitreous material', 'with a saucer', 'tapering', 'circular in cross-section'), while three are functional ('used for consumption of food', 'used for the consumption of liquid food', 'used for consumption of hot liquid food'). The overlap among the functional features enables a weighting effect. In other words, if a particular object is used for drinking coffee (presumably classed by Labov as 'hot liquid food'), then it will score three functional feature points.

Overall, the formula, given in Figure 7.5, summarizes the probability that a person will use the term *cup* (with or without modifiers) to name an object with particular physical features and dimensions in a particular functional context. Labov (1973) refers to this formula as a 'definition', and compares it (favourably) with traditional dictionary definitions.

As recently as 2003, this 'beautifully simple' experiment of Labov's was adduced in a widely read textbook (Taylor 2003: 43) as proving that some of the factors used in categorization are non-discrete and that there is 'no clear dividing line' between categories: 'one category merged gradually into the other'.

7.5.3 Can 'denotation conditions' supersede meaning?

But can Labov's technique indeed replace the traditional concept of meaning, as he intends it to? Does measuring how people respond to certain

The term *cup* is used to denote round containers with a ratio of width to depth of $1 \pm r$ where $r \leq r_b$, and $r_b = \alpha_1 + \alpha_2 + \ldots \alpha_\nu$ and α_1 is a positive quality when the feature i is present and 0 otherwise.

Feature 1 = with one handle
             2 = made of opaque vitreous material
             3 = used for consumption of food
             4 = used for the consumption of liquid food
             5 = used for consumption of hot liquid food
             6 = with a saucer
             7 = tapering
             8 = circular in cross-section

Cup is used variably to denote such containers with ratios width to depth $1 \pm r$ where $r_b \leq r \leq r_t$ with a probability of $r_t - r/r_t - r_b$. The quantity $1 \pm r_b$ expresses the distance from the modal value of width to height.

Figure 7.5 Labov's 'definition' of cup (1973: 366–7)

stimuli and summarizing the results in a mathematically sophisticated formula really allow us to dispense with the conceptual notion of meaning?

There are at least two good reasons to think otherwise. First, despite Labov's claim (1973: 347) that his investigation is a study of 'knowledge or ability to apply a term to a range of objects in a way that reflects the communicative system utilized by others', it is hard to see his *cup* formula as a representation of implicit linguistic knowledge, i.e. as part of linguistic competence. At best, it is a summary of linguistic behaviour, i.e. a description of performance, not competence.

Second, it is hard to see how the DENOTATION CONDITIONS approach could apply to the meanings of many abstract words, such as *true* or *opposite*, or to discourse particles such as *but*, *merely*, or *even*, or to interjections like *hello* and *bloody hell*, or to words like *God*, *devil*, and *unicorn*. The point is that not all words 'denote' in a straightforward sense which would be amenable to external observation and measurement.

7.6 The meaning of *cup* and *mug*

We now begin our exploration of the meaning of words like *cup* and *mug* using reductive paraphrase. One important general question is how to account for prototype effects and referential indeterminacy in this area of vocabulary. Contra Labov (1973), we will see that these effects are quite consistent with a definition in discrete (i.e. verbal) terms. Paradoxical as it might sound, the vagueness of concepts like *cup* and *mug* can be captured precisely in a good explication. Our discussion will generally follow Wierzbicka's 1985 book *Lexicography and Conceptual Analysis*, but with some revision and simplification of the explications.

7.6.1 The primary importance of function

One weakness of Labov's 'definition' of *cup* is that it fails to bring out any conceptual unity among the various components such as 'with one handle', 'made of opaque vitreous material', 'used for consumption of hot liquid food', 'with a saucer', 'tapering', 'circular in cross-section'. This looks like an arbitrary collection of independent features. The point can be dramatized by a comparison of *cups* and *mugs*. Labov (1973: 357) says that 'informants agree that *mugs* are a kind of *cup*', and he implies that there is no significant difference except that *mugs* are associated with coffee. Nevertheless, a typical *cup* is quite different to a typical *mug*. For instance, *mugs* tend to be bigger and thicker than *cups*. *Cups* are typically used with a saucer, while *mugs* are not. Many *cups* have a tapering shape, the base being smaller than the top, whereas a typical *mug* has straight sides. The handle of a typical *mug* is much bigger and stronger than the handle of a *cup*. (There are even *cups* which lack handles altogether, at least if we admit that small Chinese 'cups' are indeed *cups*, but *mugs* always have handles.)

Is there really no rhyme or reason to these differences? In fact, a little reflection and observation will show that *cups* and *mugs* serve slightly different functions, and that the physical differences between them make perfect sense once we take their functions into account.

Cups are made to be used in a situation in which the people drinking are not moving around very much. We can think of a group of people sitting at or around a table, or perhaps of some people standing and chatting at a social function. Each of the people drinking will have a saucer, either on the table or in the other hand, and since the *cup* can easily be put down onto the saucer, it only needs to be held for brief periods to drink a little at a time. These facts help explain the smallness of a cup's handle, which is normally held between the fingers, and also why it is that cups can have a tapered shape. Neither of these features would be very practical if a person had to move around a lot while holding a *cup*, because there would be quite a danger of spillage. A *cup* can be quite thin (and therefore pleasingly elegant) because although the outside can get quite hot, it is not intended that the person drinking would ever put his or her hand around the *cup* itself.

Even if we don't move around much, *cups* are not the most stable of objects, hence one of the functions of the saucer is to catch any liquid that might spill and so protect the table or tablecloth. The tapered shape of a *cup* helps ensure that any spillage goes down into the middle of the saucer.

As to the relatively small size of a *cup*, this can be partly explained by the fact that in the prototypical situation of use, one is likely to have easy access to more tea or coffee from a teapot or from the kitchen. Another reason why *cups* have to be fairly small is that one has to be able to lift them up to the mouth while gripping a small handle between the fingers, so they have to be quite light even when full.

In contrast with *cups*, *mugs* are made to be usable 'anywhere', so to speak. They are made to be easy to carry around and easy to hold for a long time. This explains why *mugs* don't come with saucers (a saucer would be a nuisance), and without a saucer there is no reason for a tapering shape. The need for portability helps explain why the handle of a *mug* is big, so it can be gripped securely by putting the fingers through it for safe and easy carrying. The need to be able to hold it for extended periods explains why a *mug* is thicker than a *cup*, because this enables the person drinking to put his or her whole hand around the outside, or to put a second supporting hand under it, without risk of burning the hand. The thickness of a *mug* also makes it less prone to breakage, consistent with the idea that they are meant to be usable 'anywhere' and thus run a greater risk of being roughly handled than do *cups*. *Mugs* are bigger than *cups* because they have to be large enough to hold a decent amount, without recourse to a possible refill. To achieve the greater capacity, however, they cannot be much wider than *cups* are or else they would become awkward to handle and the contents would get cold quickly. This accounts for the fact that *mugs* are higher than they are wide.

(None of this is contradicted by the fact that one can speak of *a cup of coffee*, regardless of whether it comes in a *cup* or a *mug*. The expression *a cup of coffee* has evidently become 'lexicalized' with a meaning of its own—a meaning which is related to that of *cup* as an independent word, but which is not based directly on it.)

7.6.2 Explicating cup

Incorporating these notions about the 'functional logic' of *cups* and *mugs* into explications gives rise to explications which are long and complex.

The example below can be broken up into four parts. Section (a) specifies the primary nature of a *cup*: it is 'something of one kind' which is functional, i.e. something that people do something with; specifically, something of this kind is used when someone is drinking something hot. Section (b) spells out the physical features of a *cup*: its size, the kind of handle it typically has, its other parts, and what it is made of. Section (c) spells out the USE SEQUENCE, cf. Rosch's (1978) notion that basic-level concepts are associated with a 'motor program'. This section includes a characterization of 'something of another kind' that is often used in association with a *cup*, namely, a saucer. Section (d) specifies the ARTEFACT STATUS of *cups*: that people often want to use them to drink with and that some people make them to meet this need.

a cup:

FUNCTIONAL CATEGORY

a. something of one kind
   at many times people do something with something of this kind when
      they are drinking [m] something hot [m]
   when someone is drinking [m] something like this, before it is inside this
      someone's mouth [m], it is for some time inside something of this kind

SIZE

b. things of this kind are like this:
   – they are not big
   – someone can hold [m] one in one hand [m]

PART FOR HOLDING

   many things of this kind have a small thin [m] part on one side
   when someone is drinking [m], this someone can hold [m] this part with
      the fingers [m] of one hand [m]

OTHER PARTS

   the other parts are like this:
   – the sides [m] are like the sides [m] of something round [m]
   – they are thin [m]
   – the top [m] part of the sides has a smooth [m] round [m] edge [m]
   – the bottom [m] part of something of this kind is flat [m]
   – someone can think that the bottom [m] part is small, if this someone
      thinks about the top [m] part at the same time

MATERIAL

   things of this kind are made of [m] something hard [m]
   this something is smooth [m]

c.   when someone is doing something with something of this kind because
this someone is drinking [m] something hot [m], it happens like this:
– at some time this something is in one place for some time,
at this time the bottom [m] part is touching something flat [m]
– at this time there is something like hot [m] water [m] inside this thing
– it can be tea [m], it can be coffee [m], it can be something of another kind
– it is inside this thing because some time before someone did some things
because this someone wanted it to be like this
– after this, someone picks up [m] this something with the fingers [m] of
one hand [m]
– after this, this someone does something else to it with the hand [m]
– after this, because of this, part of the edge [m] at the top [m] of this thing
touches one of this someone's lips [m] for a short time, as this someone
wants
– during this time, this someone's fingers [m] move as this someone wants
– because of this, a little bit of something like hot [m] water [m] moves,
as this someone wants
– because of this, after this it is not inside this thing anymore, it is inside
this someone's mouth [m]
– after this, this someone puts [m] this thing down [m] on something flat [m]
– after this, this someone can do this a few more times

sometimes when someone is drinking [m] something in this way,
this someone wants not to hold [m] this thing for a short time
when it is like this, this someone can put [m] this thing down [m] on
something of another kind, in the middle [m] of this other kind of thing
these other things are made of [m] the same hard [m], smooth [m] stuff
they are round [m], they are flat [m]
the edge [m] of something of this kind is above the middle [m]

d.   many people want to drink [m] things of some kinds like this at many times
because of this, some people make [m] things of this kind

Is this explication really too long and detailed? Sections (a) and (b) are
actually quite close to Labov's definition, once we allow for the fact that
the phrasing is much simpler. The main reason that Labov's definition
appears shorter is that it does not articulate the function of a *cup* beyond
implying that, prototypically, it is used for 'the consumption of hot liquid
food'. Yet, as argued above, without a depiction of how a *cup* is actually

handled in use, as set out in the USE SEQUENCE section of the explication, the design features appear arbitrary and unmotivated.

Admittedly, the statement of physical features is a bit more elaborate than Labov's, for instance, in specifying that *cups* have a flat bottom. The reason for this is that Labov was not really trying to give a full characterization of a *cup*, but rather to identify the features which distinguish *cups* from certain other 'round containers', such as *bowls*, *glasses*, and *vases*. Since these too have flat bottoms, it did not seem necessary to mention this feature in his definition of *cup*. The explication above, however, does attempt to give a complete, positive representation of the concept. (It could also be noted that some 'round containers' do not have flat bottoms, e.g. *test-tubes*.)

The explication also refers to a 'small thin [m] part on one side' which a person can hold 'with the fingers [m] of one hand [m]' rather than relying on the word *handle*, as Labov's definition does. One could defend this simply by observing that *handle* is a semantically complex word, but such an explanation would not be fully convincing. After all, 'drink' and 'pick up' are also complex, yet they are used as semantic molecules in the explication. The real reason in favour of the treatment in the explication above is that the handle of a *cup* must indeed be small and thin, and able to be held between the fingers. The horizontal rod-like handle of a frying pan, for instance, would be quite bizarre on a *cup*.

Finally, it should be noted that the meaning of *cup* is apparently undergoing semantic change. The explication proposed and discussed above (and Labov's definition also) relates to *cup* as used by, roughly speaking, the older generation. For these older speakers, a 'handleless' and 'saucerless' *plastic cup* is not seen as a 'real cup'. For some younger speakers, however, the plastic drinking cup (as used by children for drinking juice) is apparently seen as a 'real cup' and though the traditional china cup is also for them a 'real cup', it is a marked variety, often described as a *tea-cup* or a *coffee-cup* rather than simply as a *cup* (cf. Wierzbicka 1985: 87).

7.6.3 Explicating mug

Now let's turn to *mug*. Comparing the explication below with that for *cup* gives us a clear picture of the interrelated functional and physical differences. Naturally there are many similarities and overlaps, as well as differences. The primary purpose of both *cups* and *mugs*, according to their respective explications, is for use when drinking something hot. (Admittedly there are *beer mugs*, but this is a lexicalized compound expression.) The SIZE specification given for *mug* says, essentially, that they are 'not big' and can be held for a long time in one hand, but that they are big compared with *cups*. That is, 'cups [m]' functions as a semantic molecule in the explication for *mug*, just as 'mice [m]' did in the explication of *rats*. A bit further down, 'cups' appear in a similar role, when it is stated that people can think of *mugs* as made of something thick, in comparison with *cups*.

The physical description for *mugs* includes a somewhat different kind of handle: a rounded part that someone can hold with one hand, and also that one can put one's fingers through. The *cup* handle, by contrast, was described as a 'small thin part' which someone can hold between the fingers.

The USE SEQUENCE for *mugs* mainly differs from that of *cups* insofar as there is no mention of picking it up and putting it down. And of course, there is no mention of anything comparable to a saucer. The other aspects of the explication are the same as for *cups*.

a mug:

FUNCTIONAL CATEGORY

  a. something of one kind
     at many times people do something with something of this kind when they are drinking [m] something hot [m]
     when someone is drinking [m] something like this, before it is inside this someone's mouth [m], it is for some time inside something of this kind

SIZE

  b. things of this kind are like this:
     – they are not big
     – someone can hold one in one hand [m] for a long time
     – if someone thinks about cups [m] at the same time, this someone can think that they are big

PART FOR HOLDING

     many things of this kind have a rounded [m] part sticking out [m] on one side
     when someone is drinking [m], this someone can hold [m] this part with one hand [m]
     this someone's fingers [m] can be touching this part on all sides

OTHER PARTS

the other parts are like this:
- the sides [m] are like the sides [m] of something round [m]
- they are thin [m]
- if someone thinks about cups [m] at the same time, this someone
    can think that they are thick [m]
- the top [m] part of the sides [m] has a smooth [m] round [m] edge [m]
- the bottom [m] part of something of this kind is flat [m]

MATERIAL

things of this kind are made of [m] something hard [m]
this something is smooth [m]

USE SEQUENCE

c.   when someone is doing something with something of this kind because
        this someone is drinking [m] something hot [m], it happens like this:
    - at some time there is something like hot [m] water [m] inside this thing
    - it can be tea [m], it can be coffee [m], it can be something of
        another kind
    - it is inside this thing because some time before someone did some
        things because this someone wanted it to be like this
    - after this, someone picks up [m] this something
    - after this, this someone does something to it with the hand [m]
    - after this, because of this, part of the edge [m] at the top [m] of this
        thing touches one of this someone's lips [m] for a short time, as this
        someone wants
    - during this time, this someone's hand [m] moves as this someone wants
    - because of this, a little bit of something like hot [m] water [m] moves,
        as this someone wants
    - because of this, after this it is not inside this thing anymore, it is inside
        this someone's mouth [m]
    - after this, this someone can do this a few more times

ARTEFACT STATUS

d.   many people want to drink [m] things of some kinds like this at many
        times
    because of this, some people make [m] things of this kind

7.6.4 Typical properties

A notable aspect of the above explications for *cups* and *mugs* is that some
components specify merely typical (as opposed to essential or invariable)
properties. Two such components in the *cup* explication are:

many things of this kind have a small thin [m] part on one side
sometimes when someone is drinking [m] something in this way, this someone
    wants not to hold [m] this thing for a short time
when it is like this, this someone can put [m] this thing down [m] on
    something of another kind, in the middle [m] of this other kind of thing

According to the first of these components, people think of *cups* as usually having a handle of a specific type; but the wording allows for the existence of *cups* which lack this feature. The second component, which provides for the fact that one can set a cup down for a short time in the middle of 'something of another kind', i.e. a saucer, is tagged as something which applies 'sometimes', thereby recognizing that it is not always so. Think of small Chinese *tea cups*. They do not have handles and they don't come with saucers either. Nevertheless, they serve the very same function as conventional *cups*, even to the extent that they are picked up and put down with the fingers and that they are used in a situation where they can be refilled as desired.

7.6.5 Discreteness and referential indeterminacy

We have seen that the meanings of artefact terms can be captured in verbal definitions, albeit long and detailed ones, without resort to non-discrete components such as height– width ratios or weighted features. Moreover, such verbal definitions are perfectly compatible with a degree of referential indeterminacy. To see this, we have to appreciate that there is a difference between the meaning of a word and its range of application. Just because the meaning of a word (*cup*, *mug*, *knife*, *table*, etc.) is determinate does not mean that its range of application is completely fixed and predictable. Range of application has to do with people's interpretations of the 'goodness of fit' between the underlying concept and particular objects and circumstances in the real world, which do not always coincide with the 'idealized cognitive model' (Lakoff 1987) encapsulated in the meaning.

If people are presented with an object (or a drawing of an object) contrived to be mid-way between a normal *cup* and a normal *mug*, it is no wonder that their judgements vary, especially if (as in Labov's experiment) any qualifications and caveats they offer are ignored. This does not show that people lack a clear underlying concept of *cup* or *mug*, and that 'one category merges into the other'. The existence of *mules* does not show that people's categories of *horses* and *donkeys* merge into one another. The fact that a jury may disagree as to whether a particular *killing* is a *murder* does not show that there is no clear concept of *murder*. Contra Labov, variability in range of application in 'difficult cases' is not evidence for variability in meaning.

7.7 Outstanding issues

7.7.1 'Ostension', complexity, and concept acquisition

Because of the physical nature of their referents, it has often been held that the meanings of words like *cup*, *table*, *bike* (or *cat*, *bird*, and *mouse*) can be conveyed by pure 'ostension', i.e. by pointing out instances of the kind of thing in question. And it has been noted that, as a matter of fact, examples are very important to the process whereby a child, or any language-learner for that matter, comes to pick up the meanings of such words. The philosopher Bertrand Russell (1948: 291) said that words like *bread* and *dog* are learnt by 'pointing out' in context, in contrast to words like *quadruped* which are learnt with the aid of other words, i.e. by verbal definition. The linguist Robbins Burling (1970: 80) made a similar point by contrasting what he called 'referential definitions' and 'verbal definitions'. A word like *mother*, he said, must almost always be learned in context, while an expression like *cousin* would probably call for some degree of verbal explanation.

Though one can see where these statement are coming from, so to speak, what they are doing is mixing up two things which are quite different: the content of a particular (adult) concept and the process whereby it is acquired. If Russell and Burling were correct, it would mean that a whole host of referring words would lack conceptual content altogether. It should be clear by now that such a conclusion would be misguided and untenable.

Just because the meaning of a word isn't normally explained to children in purely verbal terms does not mean that children are not constructing, unconsciously, a conceptual model of its meaning. Indeed, there is a good deal of evidence from child language acquisition studies that this is exactly what they do (cf. Keil 1989; Markman 1989; Clark 1993; 2010; Ameel, Malt, and Storms 2008). For example, very young children often use their first word for *dog* (e.g. *wau-wau*) for all four-legged animals; and *cups*, for very young children, tend to be anything you drink out of. From such simple beginnings, the child progressively adjusts and elaborates his or her conceptual models until they come into line with adult usage. A crucial part of working out the adult meanings is learning new words which contrast with already known ones, and adjusting the conceptual models for the known words accordingly.

No doubt the fact that words in a given semantic domain share a common template structure greatly aids in this process. Because the same template structure is used for all animal words, for example, the acquisition process for an animal concept can be viewed as an exercise akin to filling out a 'conceptual questionnaire' (Wierzbicka 1985: 332), putting information under various headings so as to distinguish the animal in question from its neighbours. Crucially, of course, the questionnaire is not completed once only. On the contrary, it is retained and elaborated over many years, as more and more information is assimilated. Interestingly, there is evidence emerging from studies of early lexical acquisition that English-speaking parents tend to offer information about the referents of new words in accordance with fixed formulaic frames; for example, for an animal word they mention where the animal lives, its distinctive body-parts, how it moves, what kind of noise it makes, whether or not it bites, and so on (Clark 2010; Clark and Wong 2002). The effect is to place new words into semantic fields in such a way as to highlight the similarities and differences in properties with respect to other words in the same domain. Both in its general outline and in its specifics, these findings are highly compatible with the template hypothesis that has emerged independently from empirical semantics.

For artefact words, function and use sequence are part of the template. Consistent with this, a study of children's changing concept of *cup* (Andersen 1975) showed 'a general progression from a focus on physical properties to a focus on function of the object within the socio-cultural context'. By age 6, when words like *glass*, *mug*, *bowl*, and *vase* are also well known, the children are taking account of size, shape, and material properties; by age 9 they have developed an awareness of the interdependence of these physical characteristics and of the existence of typical but optional features, such as having a handle. By age 12, their usage is comparable to adult usage, involving 'an interplay of form and culturally defined function, with increasing weight being placed on the latter' (Andersen 1975: 97– 8).

The acquisition of complex lexical concepts continues throughout middle childhood and is certainly not a simple matter of recognizing a few exemplars pointed out in context. Part and parcel of it is learning the web of associated expressions and associated common knowledge. This includes, in the case of *cups*, learning about *saucers*, learning that there are *tea-cups* and *coffee-cups*, learning that a *cup* is said to have a *lip*. In the case of *cats*, it means learning the meanings of words like *meow* and *purr*, expressions like *cat-burglar* and *catwalk*, and about *cats having nine lives*, and so on, and so on. All this knowledge is integrated into adult semantic competence. The idea that there can be simple 'referential definitions' of anything is wishful thinking.

7.7.2 Semantic complexity: how much is too much?

Above all, it should be borne in mind that the analytical difficulties posed by semantic complexity are no reason to shrink from it. We know that human society and culture are immensely complex, and it makes perfect sense that much of human language should be so too, especially those parts of it which are most heavily culture-laden.

The final word in this chapter belongs with Anna Wierzbicka, who more than anyone else has pioneered the empirical study of semantic complexity:

Looking into the meaning of a single word, let alone a single sentence, can give one the same feeling of dizziness that can come from thinking about the distance between galaxies or about the impenetrable empty spaces hidden in a single atom. . . . [But] if we don't face this complexity we shall fail to carry out some of our important professional obligations, such as that of laying the groundwork for a more effective lexicography, of developing tools which could revitalize language teaching, or of promoting cross-cultural understanding via a non-ethnocentric description of cultural variation; we shall also throw away our chance of exploring and contemplating the dazzling beauty of the universe of meaning. (Wierzbicka 1996a: 233)

Key technical terms

anthropocentrism

denotation conditions

encyclopedic knowledge

endonym

ethnobiology

folk biology

folk genus (genera)

generics

life-form

nominal kinds

referential indeterminacy

semantic molecule

unique beginner

Exercises and discussion questions

† next to a problem means that a solution or some commentary can be found at the end of the book.

1†. It is common to find artefact terms and natural kind terms treated in a completely parallel fashion so far as hyponymy relationships are concerned. For example:

animal:	*cat*	*tree:*	*oak*
	dog		*willow*
	horse		*maple*
furniture:	*chair*	*cookware:*	*saucepan*
	table		*frying pan*
	bed		*pot*

The claim is that just as the definitions of the words *cat*, *dog*, and *horse* include the concept *animal*, so the definitions for *chair*, *table*, and *bed* include the concept *furniture*. Similarly, just as *oak*, *willow*, and *maple* are semantically kinds of *tree*, so *saucepan*, *frying pan*, and *pot* are kinds of *cookware*. Critically discuss and assess this claim.

2†. As noted in the chapter, *dogs* are unusual in that there are many named sub-kinds (breeds) of dogs, such as: *terriers, Labradors, beagles, Alsatians, Dobermans, pit bull terriers, corgies,* and *greyhounds*. Assume that these individual dog breed words can be explicated using similar semantic templates and component types as discussed in the chapter. Propose the top-level sections for an explication of *terriers* or *beagles*.

3†. How do you think the SIZE component could be stated in an explication for *horses*? Try to find a way of indicating the size by comparison and/or interaction with the human body. If you use semantic molecules in your component, choose them carefully and keep the number to a minimum.

4†. An explication for *dogs* will have to include reference to various kinds of 'sound-producing' activities, including *growling* as well as *barking*. But for this exercise, just try to produce the subsection of a *dogs* explication that concerns *barking*.

5†. The lexicon of Language K, spoken in a remote region of Southern Africa, includes the following words for animals. (a) Analyse and summarize the data from a semantic point of view. (b) Can you think of any possible cultural motivations for the way the Language K animal lexicon is organized?

nombo 'lion', *gonati* 'eland', *nimbjabiko* 'elephant', *wetsaisko* 'hippo', *bongogo* 'zebra', *losho* 'rhino', *sogwamago* 'giraffe', *gwai* 'warthog', *laha* 'bush pig', *popo* 'impala', *haaneya* 'baboon', *bisogo* 'gnu', *elego* 'hartebeest', *gemangu* 'ostrich', *hubuo* 'male lion or eland carcass', *hubua* 'female lion or eland carcass', *gapulao* 'male elephant or hippo carcass', *gapulaa* 'female elephant or hippo carcass', *hamtao* 'male zebra carcass', *hamtaa* 'female zebra carcass', *huguo* 'male rhino carcass', *hugua* 'female rhino carcass', *hawao* 'male giraffe carcass', *hawaa* 'female giraffe carcass', *hachao* 'male warthog or wild pig carcass', *hachaa* 'female warthog or wild pig carcass', *lunguo* 'male impala carcass', *thungua* 'female impala carcass', *nokowo* 'male baboon carcass', *nokowa* 'female baboon carcass', *sonowo* 'male gnu or hartebeest carcass', *sonowa* 'female gnu or hartebeest carcass', *hushuwa* 'ostrich carcass'.

6†. The data is from Kayardild, the traditional language of tiny Bentinck Island in Australia's Gulf of Carpentaria. It shows the taxonomic scheme by which the Kayardild people classify various kinds of living things. Examine the data carefully and address the questions (a) and (b) below. Avoid using disjunctions (i.e. 'or') in your answers. You may have to speculate a bit on the lifestyle of the Kayardild people. If you can, it might be useful to consult an encyclopedia or other reference source about Australian marine life.

a. Describe the probable meanings of the highest-level classifiers *yarbuda*, *yakuri*, *wanku*, and *kunbulka*.
b. What are the meanings of the words *kalanda*, *barrinda*, *rajurrinda*, and *bangaa*, which are used in 'intermediate-level' classification?

HIGHEST-LEVEL	INTERMEDIATE	GENERIC
yarbuda	*kalanda yarbuda*	*wanikarra* 'pelican'
		kaarrku 'seagull'
		ngarnala 'white cockatoo'
		jirrikujirriku 'bat'
		baraburra 'black flying fox'
	barrinda yarbuda	*balangkali* 'brown snake'
		yildaa 'legless lizard'

	rajurrinda yarbuda	*warrunda* 'goanna'
		marrkaji 'frill-neck lizard'
		wardunda 'mangrove rat'
		maali 'long-necked tortoise'
yakuri	—	*ngarrawurna* 'bluefish'
		darrngkaa 'barracuda'
		buranthanda 'bonefish'
wanku	—	*kulkiji* 'tiger shark'
		darnuka 'black-tipped shark'
		dulkayirra 'fantail ray'
		kuyilda 'file stingray'
		kurdalalngka 'long black-tailed ray'
kunbulka	—	*bijarrba* 'dugong'
		kanithu 'whale'
		yakarr 'porpoise'
	bangaa	*marrkulda* 'lock-head turtle'
		yarkakarlda 'hawk-beak turtle'

7. According to the approach developed in the chapter, the semantic template for an 'animal word' contains a final section about commonly held attitudes towards that kind of animal—commonly held, that is, in the relevant community of discourse and evidenced by collocations, figurative extensions, common sayings, and the like. Such attitudes of course differ markedly between cultures.

   Choose a language other than English, do some research, and report on commonly held attitudes in that language to the following three kinds of animals: dogs, pigs, snakes. Do you agree that information of this kind should be included in semantic explications? If not, should it be accommodated in some other fashion in a comprehensive description of the language?

8†. What are some differences between a *couch* and a *sofa*? (Hint: Think of the purposes for which each is intended.)

9†. Try to devise the first and second sections of an explication for *knives*, i.e. the functional category section (which will be brief) and the physical description. Do not use 'cut' as a semantic molecule in the explication. *Knives* are used for many purposes (cutting, slicing, skinning, butchering, stabbing, peeling, spreading, etc.), which are not all easily covered by 'cutting'. On the other hand, it is fine to use 'sharp [m]'.

8

Motion

For many linguists and cognitive psychologists, motion plays a special role in human thinking. So immediate and inbuilt is our perception of motion that most people would not hesitate to include it among the most basic of human concepts. Linguists naturally expect all languages to have ways of talking about motion and ways of describing different kinds of motion (and, as far as I know, they have never been disappointed).

The psychologists Miller and Johnson-Laird (1976: 527) call motion verbs 'the most characteristically verbal of all the verbs' and the 'purest and most prototypical of verbs'. The logical extension of this view is LOCALISM. This is the hypothesis that motion provides the cognitive framework for more abstract domains of meaning such as possession, communication, and transformation. In apparent support of this, there is the fact that English 'motional' prepositions such as *to* and *from* can be used in these other domains. For instance, we speak of *taking* or *hearing* of something *from* someone; of *giving* or *saying* something *to* someone; and of traffic lights *changing from red to green*. Comparable facts are common in the world's languages. Many prominent semanticists, including Ray Jackendoff and Ronald Langacker, subscribe to a version of localism.

The popularity of localism is one good reason for us to inquire into the semantics of motion and of movement generally. The theoretical stakes are high. But there is a good practical reason as well. For despite the fact that all languages have ways of describing motion, there are fascinating differences in how they go about it. As we will see, even words as apparently simple as *come* and *go* do not have straightforward equivalents in some languages.

8.1 Approaches to space and motion

8.1.1 Pre-modern analyses

The nature of motion, and in particular its relationship with location and time, has concerned thinkers from the earliest days of philosophy. Though we can't dwell on the classical theories here, it is thought-provoking to consider one of the famous 'paradoxes' of the Greek philosopher Zeno of Elea. The paradox of the flying arrow assumes the commonsense idea that motion is a continuous change of location. A flying arrow, on this view, is in a different location at every moment of its flight. But if so, it must be at rest at every moment, and if it is always at rest, when does it move?

Over the centuries many solutions have been proposed to this brain-teaser, most recently drawing on sophisticated mathematical concepts about infinite series and infinite sets (cf. Russell 1917: 80–90). From a semantic point of view, however, one feels that since the paradox is framed in terms of ordinary concepts it ought to be possible to escape it while remaining within the realm of ordinary concepts. In this respect, Aristotle's answer to Zeno has something to offer (cf. Sorabji 1988: 332–3). His reply was that time is not truly composed of 'nows' (i.e. of moments), and that what may be true at a moment is not necessarily true over a period. According to Aristotle, it is not surprising that 'moments' are not attended by motion because one of the necessary attributes of motion is duration.

In the seventeenth century, a time of intense interest and inquiry into the fundamentals of thought and knowledge, John Locke and Gottlieb Wilhelm Leibniz held contrary views on the status of motion. In his *An Essay Concerning Human Understanding*, Locke (1976 [1690]: 84) recognized the dependence of the concept of motion on that of space, but still maintained that they were 'very distinct ideas . . . Motion can neither be nor be conceived without space, and yet motion is not space nor space motion.' In one famous passage, he decries those who attempt to define simple ideas, using motion as an example. In his critique of Locke, Leibniz (1981 [1765]) took the opposite view.

> The *atomists*, who define motion to be a *passage from one place to another*, what do they do more than put one synonymous word for another? For what is *passage* other than *motion*? And if they were asked what *passage* was, how would they better define it than by *motion*? For is it not at least as proper and significant to say *passage is a motion from one place to another* as to say *motion is a passage*, etc. This is to translate and not to define . . . (Locke 1976 [1690]: 221–2)

> [Y]ou treat as simple many ideas which are not so. Motion is one of them. I believe it to be definable, and the definition which says it is *change of place* deserves respect. (Leibniz 1981 [1765]: III. iv. 297)

Actually, Locke himself sometimes writes as if he thinks motion is definable. For example, at one point he designates 'distance' as a 'mode of space', and then speaks of 'motion being nothing but the change of distance between any two things' (Locke 1976 [1690]: 81, 85.)

Of course, to analyse motion as 'change of place' (or of distance) requires us to assume that *change* is the 'prior and more intelligible' notion. Leibniz believed that *change* was a simple and indefinable idea, but this is by no means an obvious proposition. In fact, on purely intuitive grounds the words *go* and *move* would strike most people as simpler than *change*, and children no doubt start using the words *go* and *move* well before they use *change*.

8.1.2 Modern treatments of motion: Talmy and Jackendoff

Some of the most influential modern linguistic work on motion has been done by Leonard Talmy. In Talmy (1985a; 2007) he identified four basic components of what he called a 'basic motion event'.

> The basic motion event consists of one object (the 'FIGURE') moving or located with respect to another object (the reference-object or 'GROUND'). It is analysed as having four components: besides 'Figure' and 'Ground' there are 'PATH' and 'Motion'. The 'Path' (with a capital P) is the course followed or the site occupied by the Figure object with respect to the Ground object. 'Motion' (with a capital M) refers to the presence per se in the event of motion or location . . . We will represent motion by

the form 'move' and location by 'be$_L$' (a mnemonic for 'be located'). (Talmy 1985a: 60–61; emphasis added)

Notice that Talmy treats maintenance of a stationary location as a kind of 'motion event', and many other contemporary linguists follow him in this use of terminology. The motivation for it is that the predicates 'move' and 'be located' can both be seen as fitting into the same 'Figure–Ground–Path' conceptual schema.

One difference is that where motion is involved, there can be two Grounds, normally referred to as SOURCE (the origin point of the motion) and GOAL (the destination point of the motion). The following examples show how these terms are applied. Notice that the term THEME is commonly used in place of Talmy's 'Figure' to designate something which moves.

a. _Max_   travelled   from   _Sydney_   to   _Melbourne_   via   _Canberra_.
   Figure/   Source   Goal   Path
   Theme

b. _The ball_   rolled   _down the hill_.
   Figure/   Path
   Theme

c. _We_   approached   _the village_.
   Figure/   Goal
   Theme

As you can see from example (c), a goal is not always overtly indicated by a preposition or other morphological marking, but can be implied by the meaning of the verb. _Approach_ is a transitive verb which requires a grammatical object indicating the goal. Similarly, _leave_ requires a source. In English, the path component is usually indicated by a prepositional phrase or an adverb (such as _over_ or _along_), but there are some verbs whose meanings include a specification about the path taken; for example, the verbs _enter_ and _return_ imply the same kind of paths as the composite expressions _go in_ and _go back_, respectively. This phenomenon is commonly called LEXICAL CONFLATION. Thus, you will see verbs like _approach_ and _enter_ described as 'conflating', i.e. combining, motion and ground (specifically goal), and motion and path, respectively.

In addition to the components mentioned so far, motion events (like other events) can also have a 'manner' or a 'cause' specification. Many English motion verbs encode manner, that is, the way the motion is carried out, as in the examples below.

a. *I walked/ran/rushed down the stairs.*
b. *The rock slid/rolled/bounced down the hill.*

Movement from place to place is a necessary part of the inherent meaning of the verbs in (a). As Talmy (1985a) points out, however, the verbs in (b) can all be used without any such implication. For instance, one could say *I slid on the ice, I rolled the blanket up,* and *the ball bounced twice* without implying that I, the blanket, or the ball moved along any path of motion. There is a very general pattern in English whereby a verb is construed as involving motion (as well as its primary meaning) when it is combined with a path expression. Two other examples of this are *She wore a green dress to the party* (i.e. 'she went to the party, wearing a green dress') and *I read comics all the way to New York* (i.e. 'I went to New York, reading comics all the way'). Talmy has shown that languages often seem to have preferred LEXICALIZATION PATTERNS, i.e. patterns of lexical conflation, an idea we will see more of later in this chapter.

Many of Talmy's ideas have been adapted into the treatment of motion developed by Ray Jackendoff (1983; 1990; 1996; 2010) within his theory of 'conceptual semantics' (cf. section 3.2). Jackendoff (1990) adopted GO and BE as 'basic conceptual functions' with the argument structures shown below. Notice that Jackendoff included Path as one of his major 'ontological categories' or conceptual 'parts of speech' (along with Place, Event, State, and others).

$$[_{\text{Event}}\text{GO} ([\ ], \begin{bmatrix} \text{FROM} ([\ ]) \\ _{\text{Path}}\ \text{TO} ([\ ]) \end{bmatrix})]: \textit{The bird went from the ground to the tree.}$$

$[_{\text{State}}\text{BE} ([\ ], [_{\text{Place}}\ ])]$: *The bird is in the tree.*

To account for the fact that a *be*-sentence expresses the end-state of the corresponding *go*-sentence, Jackendoff (1990) postulated a 'rule of inference':

At the termination of $[_{\text{Event}}\text{GO} ([X], [_{\text{Path}}\text{TO} ([Y])])]$, it is the case that $[_{\text{State}}\text{BE} ([X], [_{\text{Place}}\text{AT} ([Y])])]$.

As mentioned at the beginning of this chapter, many linguists subscribe to a version of 'localism'. Jackendoff explains as follows:

The basic insight of this theory is that the formalism for encoding concepts of spatial location and motion, suitably abstracted, can be generalized to many other semantic fields. The standard evidence for this claim is the fact that many verbs and prepositions appear in two or more semantic fields, forming intuitively related paradigms. (Jackendoff 1990: 25)

As examples of this last claim, there are *go*-sentences and *be*-sentences about possession like (a) and (b) below, and about the ascription of properties, like (c) and (d) below.

a. *The inheritance went to Phillip.*
b. *The money is Phillip's.*
c. *The lights went from green to red.*
d. *The light is red.*

After enumerating these and other similar examples, Jackendoff (1990: 26) remarks: 'One has the sense, then, that this variety of uses is not accidental.' His solution, as foreshadowed in the quotation above, is to regard GO and BE as designating abstract meanings, not specifically tied to their motional or locational uses. The spatial vs. possessional vs. identifica-tional meaning is to be indicated by a 'semantic field feature', notated as a subscript on the function, which 'designates the field in which the Event or State is defined'. Thus, we have $GO_{Spatial}$ (also represented simply as GO), GO_{Poss} and GO_{Ident}, and $BE_{Spatial}$, BE_{Poss} and BE_{Ident}. Jackendoff's claim is that the three semantic fields have parallel conceptual structure. 'This notation captures the lexical parallelisms . . . neatly' (1990: 26).

Jackendoff also considers motion verbs like *wiggle*, *wriggle*, *dance*, *spin*, and *wave*, which do not imply traversal of any Path, but he declines the challenge of describing the semantic differences between them. Most 'man-ner of motion' properties, he writes, are 'not the business of conceptual structure at all' (1990: 88), but instead belong to spatial-visual representa-tion. This means that all verbs which depict merely 'the internal motion of the subject, with no implications with respect to their location, change of location or configuration with respect to any other object' can be assigned a single conceptual structure, which he represents as follows (1990: 88–9):

$$[_{Event} \text{ MOVE } ([_{Thing} \ ])]$$

From the point of view of NSM semantics, the concept of 'abstract motion' confuses, rather than simplifies, the job of semantic description and explanation. Jackendoff's (1990) subscripting manoeuvre (distinguish-ing $GO_{Spatial}$, GO_{Poss}, and GO_{Ident}), for instance, may be a concise method of describing the claimed parallelism between location, possession, and ascription, but it can hardly be said to explain anything. Further, as we saw in section 3.3, 'abstracting' the meanings of GO and BE makes the semantic representations more remote from ordinary language, and therefore less susceptible to disconfirmation by reference to the facts of ordinary usage. It could also be pointed out that having GO, BE, and MOVE as distinct conceptual primitives makes it difficult to explain the interconnectedness between them. Jackendoff (1996) develops a more logically satisfying account, but at the cost of making the representations even more abstract and algebriac, and even less verifiable and cognitively plausible.

8.1.3 NSM treatment of space and motion

How can the NSM metalanguage be used to deal with notions such as source, goal, and different types of path? The semantic primes necessary for explicating motion-related concepts constitute a rather rich set, including a variety of spatial and temporal elements in addition to the posited 'fundamental' predicate of motion MOVE. It is easy to see that the locational prime BE SOMEWHERE (BE IN A PLACE), the element THIS, and the concepts of BEFORE and AFTER are all required. As Fillmore (1983: 217) once remarked, 'linear motion or locomotion' is distinguished from other types of motion such as spinning or vibrating precisely by the fact that 'the thing started out at one place at one time and ended up at another place at a later time'.

To explicate even relatively simple path-expressions such as *towards* and *away from*, it is necessary also to make use of the durational prime FOR SOME TIME, the spatial elements NEAR and FAR, and the conditional IF. Other path-expressions call for other spatial elements—*up(wards)* and *down-(wards)* involve ABOVE and BELOW; *into* involves INSIDE, and *across* involves the laterality prime ON ONE SIDE. Many expressions to do with 'manner of motion', notably speed words like *quickly* and *slowly*, rely on the 'relative time period' primes A SHORT TIME and A LONG TIME, as well as other elements. All in all, one could say that NSM analyses of motion are more elaborate than most other current approaches, but that the pay-off is a far better articulation of the relationships between motion, space, and time.

The NSM approach to source and goal can be illustrated by reference to the following schema for 'translational motion':

Something X moved from place A to place B:
something X moved for some time
before this, it was somewhere (place A)
after this, it was somewhere else (place B)

In other words, a so-called 'source' refers to the place where something was before it moved and 'goal' to another place, where it is after the movement is over. Motion of this kind is depicted as necessarily implying a period of duration. (The schema above also gives a clue as to why parallelisms between motion and transformation are so common—transformation has the same 'before-after' structure as motion. For example, *The traffic lights changed from red to green* means something like: 'something happened; before this the traffic lights were red, after this they were green.')

Of course, motion needn't have clearly defined points of origin and destination. The following explication shows the meaning of the directional (i.e. path-like) expression *towards*:

Something X is moving towards A:
something X is moving
if it moves in the same way for some time more, after this it will be near A

Notice that *towards* is linked with the concept of nearness, not with that of arrival (i.e. being at A). This allows for the fact that I can say something is moving *towards* A without implying that I think it will (or would, if it keeps going) necessarily pass through A's exact location. Of course, the term NEAR is inherently vague—just what distance qualifies as NEAR is a subjective matter. This is as it should be, since the same kind of vagueness characterizes *towards* also.

A final observation is that the explication implies that it would not make sense to speak of someone or something moving *towards* A if it were already unambiguously *near* A. Again this seems the correct result. There is nothing odd about saying *Sally sat down some distance from Harry, then she started moving towards him*, but it does sound odd to say that *?She sat down near Harry, then started moving towards him* (though *She started moving closer to him* is quite OK).

The comparable explication for *away from* is straightforward:

Something X is moving away from A:
something X is moving
if it moves in the same way for some time more, after this it will be far from A

In English, the verbs *go* and *come* are no doubt a lot more common than MOVE, and it may be wondered why *go*, for example, has not been chosen to represent motion rather than MOVE. One reason has already been mentioned, namely, the desirability of linking translational motion (i.e. moving from place to place) with other types of motion which don't imply any change of location (such as *wiggling* and *waving*). As a motion verb, *go* is confined to translational movement. Another reason to prefer MOVE is that the situation with *go* is not nearly as straightforward as it might seem at first. This is the topic we turn to next.

8.2 How to know whether you're *coming* or *going*

The heading of this section is borrowed from the title of an article by Charles Fillmore (1983), one of a string of papers in which he teases out various subtleties in the meaning and usage of English *come* and *go*. Although one often sees *come* described as meaning 'motion-towards-speaker' and *go* as 'motion-away-from-speaker' (or 'motion-not-towards-speaker'), we will see that neither verb is as simple as this.

8.2.1 The meaning of go

In Jackendoff (1990), 'abstract GO$_{Spatial}$' is predicated of all sorts of things—people, inanimate objects and natural forces alike. But ordinary English *go* is not like that. It sounds perfectly normal to speak of people and animals *going* from one place to another, but there is something curious and faintly childlike about using *go* about an inanimate object (at least, in many situations).

> *The boys are going down to the river.*
> *The horses are going down to the river.*
> ?*The clouds are going across the sky.*
> **The rock is going down the hill.*

Go is an extremely polysemous word, however, and for this effect to emerge clearly we must confine ourselves to its motional sense. In particular, we must exclude the use of the participial adjective *gone* as in *It's gone*. This can apply to anything, living or non-living (e.g. *The rock was gone, The clouds were gone*), but with no implication that the thing moved itself, so to speak. With this caveat in mind (more on this later), we can say that, by and large, motional *go* in ordinary English is confined to an animate being DOING something.

Two other interesting properties of *go* are as follows. On the one hand, it can combine directly with an indefinite or interrogative location word indicating a goal (as in *She went somewhere*, or *Where are you going?*) without the need for any prepositional *to*-phrase, which seems to imply that the idea of being somewhere is very closely tied in with the meaning of *go*. On the other hand, it seems more focused on leaving or 'moving on' than on the possibility of arriving anywhere. For example, one can say *She went yesterday* without implying that she has arrived anywhere, and it is quite possible to think of someone just *going along* without having to think of any particular destination that the person may have in mind.

To a large extent, this paradox can be resolved by the following explication.

> *Someone X went (yesterday)*:
> someone X did something for some time (yesterday)
> because of this, this someone moved during this time
> before this, this someone was somewhere
> after this, because of this, this someone wasn't in this place anymore,
>   this someone was somewhere else

Interestingly, the situation changes a bit when a *to*-phrase is added. Saying *She went to the shops* implies that she has arrived there, as can be seen from the oddity of ?*She went to the shops but she hasn't got there yet*. The explication below applies to the case where a *to*-phrase and a *from*-phrase are both present.

> *Someone X went from A to B (yesterday)*:
> someone X did something for some time (yesterday)
> because of this, this someone moved during this time
> before this, this someone was in place A
> after this, because of this, this someone wasn't in this place anymore,
>   this someone was in place B

Notice that this explication incorporates components which constitute the explication for *X moved from A to B* (see section 8.1.3), consistent with the fact that *X went from A to B* entails *X moved from A to B*.

8.2.2 A cross-linguistic perspective on go

People often think that *go* is such a simple word that it must have equivalents in all languages. It is not uncommon even for linguists to put forward GO (in capital letters to show its technical status) as a linguistic universal, sometimes explaining that what is meant is a verb of 'translational motion'. But although words approximating English *go* are indeed found in many languages, there are plenty of languages which lack an exact semantic equivalent to English *go*. Such a language is German, which has two everyday words for 'translational motion': *gehen* (roughly) 'go on foot' and *fahren* (roughly) 'go by vehicle'. To say in German the equivalent of *She went to the shops*, one has in fact to say a little more than this—because in choosing between *gehen* and *fahren* one must indicate whether she went under her own steam or not.

A similar situation is found in Polish, which has *iść* 'move from one place to another on foot' and *jechać* 'move from one place to another in a vehicle' (verbs cited in infinitive form). In Polish, furthermore, these verbs can occur either in the imperfective form or with various perfective prefixes. For example, *X szedl* (imperfective) means roughly 'X was walking', *X po-szedl* means roughly 'X went', and *X przy-szedl* means roughly 'X came'. *Po-* and *przy-* are perfective aspectual prefixes. Another two perfective prefixes, *do-* and *od-*, are used to form verbs meaning roughly 'reach (a place)' and 'leave'; compare *X do-szedl do miejsca A* 'X reached (to) place A' and *X od-szedl z miejsca A* 'X left (from) place A'. In other words, different verbs will be used for 'was going along', 'went', and 'went from place-A': *szedl*, *po-szedl*, and *od-szedl*, if we are on foot; and *jechal*, *po-jechal*, and *od-jechal*, if we are in a vehicle.

Still another situation is found in Longgu, one of the languages of the Solomon Islands (Wilkins and Hill 1995). The English word *go* can be translated into Longgu in at least two ways, depending on the situation and on the speaker's perspective. If the motion is seen as simply 'moving from one place to another', without any focus on the source (or on the goal), the word *la* 'move along' will be used. But if the movement is seen as being away from the speaker or other reference point, a directional particle *hou* 'thither' will be used in combination with *la*; that is, there is a contrast between two 'go expressions', *la* and *la hou*. (The same verb *la* 'move along', in combination with another directional particle *mai* 'hither', is used to form the Longgu expression closest in meaning to English *come*, namely *la mai* 'come to (this place)'.)

From these facts about German, Polish, and Longgu, it is clear that *go* is not a viable candidate as a semantic universal.

8.2.3 Deictic conditions on English come

How does *come* differ from *go*? One dimension of contrast is that *come* is 'goal-oriented'. As Miller and Johnson-Laird (1976: 531) put it: 'someone who is coming will not have come until he has reached the destination (although someone who is going will have gone before he gets there).' Notice also that in asking *When did he come?* we are asking about the time of arrival (though *When did he go?* asks about the time of departure). *Come* also implies or takes for granted that the goal of the motion is a known place. Thus, it sounds strange in normal circumstances to ask *?Where did he come to?*, though there is nothing odd about *Where did he come from?*

Most discussions, however, concentrate on another—more intriguing—property of *come*—the way in which it imparts a particular perspective or point of view upon the motion event being reported. The most obvious situation in which *come* sounds more appropriate than *go* is when the speaker is at the destination AT ARRIVAL TIME. For example, if I work at a shop in town and I learn that John is intending to visit this shop tomorrow, it would sound quite odd if I reported this fact to you by saying *?John's going to the shop tomorrow*. To put it this way would be, in effect, to ignore the fact that I will be there when he arrives. It would be more natural to say, in this situation, *John's coming to the shop tomorrow*. (For the same reason, *Come here!* sounds fine, but *Go here!* sounds peculiar.) *Come* is also preferred to *go* if the speaker is at the destination AT THE TIME OF SPEAKING. For example, if I am at the shop talking with you over the telephone I can say *John's coming to the shop tomorrow*, even if we both know that I will not be there tomorrow. Examples like this can be brought under the heading of 'motion towards the speaker' (or more precisely, 'towards the speaker's location'), provided this is understood as referring either to the speaker's current location or to his or her location at arrival time.

As mentioned earlier, it is often assumed from examples like these that the basic meaning of *come* is 'motion towards the speaker'. But English *come* is also possible, and sometimes even preferred over *go*, in a wide range of other contexts. This fact is usually put down to so-called DEICTIC PRO-JECTION, referring to a speaker's ability to imaginatively 'project' to some remote location. Before we examine this notion more carefully, let us review some of the different 'deictic conditions' under which *come* can be used. The exposition roughly follows Fillmore's (1966; 1971; 1975a) classic series of articles on the subject.

Come can be used in relation to the ADDRESSEE'S LOCATION. Suppose that you work at the shop (and that I do not). I could tell you that *John's coming to the shop tomorrow* on the assumption that you will be there when he arrives, or, regardless of the situation at arrival time, if you are there at the time of speaking. If I were to use the word *go* in such contexts, it would sound as if I don't know (or don't care) where you are.

Regardless of the speaker's and the addressee's locations, *come* is often preferred over *go* if what Fillmore calls the HOME BASE FACTOR is at work, i.e. if the destination is one's literal home or another place one identifies with, such as a workplace or homeland. For example, if you and I both work at the shop, one of us could utter example (a) below while we were at the pub after work. It might be thought that this example is accounted for by an inference that John is expecting one of us to be there, but consider example (b). One can easily imagine the Vice-Chancellor not being interested in lowly individuals such as you and me, but even so the sentence remains acceptable.

a. *It's a pity John's coming to the shop tomorrow, when neither of us will be there.*
b. *It's a pity the Vice-Chancellor is coming to the Department tomorrow, when neither of us will be there.*

The examples we have seen so far illustrate the fact that *come* is preferred over *go* if the so-called 'deictic centre' is the location of the speaker or of the addressee (at speech time or at arrival time), or the home base of the speaker or of the addressee. *Come* can also be found in discourse about 'third persons', i.e. where neither speaker nor addressee is a participant in the events being related. For instance, example (a) below could occur in a public lecture about America as a nation, regardless of the speaker's own nationality and regardless of where the lecture takes place. Fillmore (1975a) attributes this to the fact that America, in this context, is 'the subject of the narrative' and as such can function as a deictic centre. Example (b) could occur in a discussion of a crime. Fillmore describes such examples as 'motion toward the central character' (or toward the central character's 'home base').

a. *People come to America with all manner of hopes and dreams.*
b. *The thief came into her bedroom.*

To complete this review of uses of *come*, it should be pointed out that there are certain contexts in which either *come* or *go* may be used equally felicitously—but with subtly different effects. For example, in (a) and (b) below the versions with *come* seem more sensitive to the expected location of the speaker or addressee.

a. *She came/went to the corner as we'd arranged, but I'd got stuck in the traffic and didn't make it.*
b. *I came/went to the front door to let you in, but you had already left.*

Both *come* and *go* may be embedded under a speech-act verb, such as *tell* in (c), or under a verb of 'subjective experience' such as *wonder*, as in (d) (other similar verbs include *think*, *hope*, and *wish*). From the overall context, we understand that Lucy will be at her own party and at her graduation. Intuitively, the versions with *come* are somehow more sensitive to this fact about the location of the 'central character'.

c. *Have you told Lucy that you're coming/going to her party?*
d. *Lucy wonders if he'll come/go to her graduation.*

Finally, it should be mentioned that *come* can be used for 'accompaniment', as in *Can I come with you?* This should probably be analysed in terms of the phrasal expression *come with*, however (even when a *with*-phrase is not included, as in *Do you want to come?*, it is 'understood').

8.2.4 A cross-linguistic perspective on come

Although *come* can be used in many situations aside from 'motion towards the speaker', it would seem curious to say that it has a different meaning in each of these situations (e.g. motion towards addressee, motion towards central character, motion towards speaker's, addressee's or central character's 'home base'). Intuitively, the meaning is the same in all these situations. As mentioned, one widely accepted explanation is that 'motion towards the speaker' is the basic (or prototypical) meaning and that the other uses are simply the result of the ability, which we all have, to adopt another person's point of view—to put ourselves into someone else's shoes.

As simple and appealing as it may seem, however, this explanation faces several difficulties. One of these difficulties, noted by Lyons (1977: 579) at the time he coined the term 'deictic projection', is the existence of unexplained restrictions on a speaker's power of 'projection' to remote spatio-temporal coordinates. Why should deictic projection be possible with *come*, for example, but not with *here* and with *now*?

Perhaps more pressing is the fact, also noted by Lyons, that apparent equivalents of *come* in other languages, even European languages such as French (*venir*) and Italian (*venire*), do not allow deictic projection as freely as English *come*. Levinson (1983: 83) makes a similar observation about Japanese *kuru*—using *kuru* one cannot 'project' even to an addressee's location. For example, to say the equivalent of 'I'm coming (to you)' in Japanese, one must say the equivalent (or near equivalent) of 'I'm going (to you)'. Differences in the range of use of putative equivalents of *come* and *go* have also been reported for Spanish, Turkish, and Hindi (Gathercole 1977, cited in Wilkins and Hill 1995; Sinha 1972). If the flexibility of *come* is the result of an inherent human capacity for deictic projection, these facts seem rather strange: Why should the exercise of this capacity vary so much from language to language?

An alternative explanation is that the differences in the behaviour of '*come* verbs' across languages are the result of differences in the lexical semantics of the verbs involved. Why, after all, should we assume that English *come*, French *venir*, Japanese *kuru*, and so on are precise semantic equivalents? If *come*, *venir*, *kuru*, and so on have somewhat different lexical meanings, then their different ranges of use would make perfect sense (cf. Wilkins and Hill 1995). This line of reasoning brings us to the following idea. If one of the most distinctive properties of English *come* is its capacity to support deictic projection—that is, to suggest a point of view of someone other than the speaker him or herself—then perhaps this property has its roots in the meaning of *come* itself; in other words, that the meaning of *come* is not simply 'motion towards the speaker', but something more complex.

8.2.5 The meaning of English come

Let us take another look at *come*. Is it possible to find an explication which would be consistent with its range of use, as reviewed above? Consider the following explication.

Someone X came to place-A (yesterday):
someone X did something for some time (yesterday)
because of this, this someone moved during this time
after this, because of this, this someone was in place-A
someone in this place could think about it like this:
   'this someone is in the place where I am'

The first three components are quite similar to those proposed for *go*, which is as it should be given that an act of *coming* can be seen (from another point of view) as an act of *going*. A slight difference from *go*, necessary to account for the 'goal orientation' of *come*, concerns the temporal perspective. When we speak of X *coming* at some time, we view X's motion as the prior condition which has led to X being at the destination at this time. This temporal perspective differs from that involved with *going*, which views X's motion as the cause of X's departure from a particular place.

However, these differences in temporal perspective are minor compared to the final component in the explication above, which is primarily responsible for the special quality of *come*. This component acknowledges the possibility of an 'egocentric' interpretation of X's final location by an unidentified 'someone in this place': this unidentified person could interpret X's final location as 'this someone is in the place where I am'. In effect, this component installs a reference to a subjective point of view into the meaning of *come* itself. Notice also that the subjective component appears without any specific time reference; it depicts a potential interpretation, not tied to any specific time.

It may seem odd that the potential interpretation 'X is in the place where I am' is attributed to an unidentified 'someone in this place'. But this is the only phrasing which is compatible with the fact that the implied person whose point of view is being taken into account may be the speaker, the addressee, or even a third person. According to the explication, the actual identity of the person is left open, to be inferred from the context. Let's run through some examples to see how this works, starting with our favourite example *John's coming to the shop tomorrow*. As we have seen, this sentence is compatible with the situation of either speaker or hearer being at the shop. It is also compatible with the point of view of a third person (for example, if Lucy works at the shop one may well say *Does Lucy know John's coming to the shop tomorrow?*) All these possibilities are sanctioned by the explication. (Of course, a sentence like *Come here!* strongly implies that the identity of the implied person is the speaker him or herself, since the choice of the word *here* implies that the speaker is in the particular place which is being indicated. However, even with *come here*, it is possible to find contexts in which the imputed viewpoint belongs to someone other than the speaker; e.g. *Come here, your mother wants to speak with you*.)

As Fillmore pointed out, a sentence like *John's coming to the shop tomorrow* is also possible if the person whose potential point of view is being recognized works at or owns the shop. In this connection it is important to take account of the fact that the meanings of many English place-nouns (like *shop, house, room, school, office*, and so on) refer to the possibility of someone being there. It is arguably this property, rather than the fact of a place being someone's 'home base' in a literal sense, which accounts for the acceptability of *come* in sentences of this kind.

Further, because the component 'someone in this place could think about it like this: this someone is in the place where I am' refers to a POTENTIAL interpretation, it is even compatible with hypothetical or imagined situations. This explains the effect of *I came to the front door, but you had already left*. In choosing the verb *came* (rather than *went*) the speaker alludes to his or her expectation that someone (evidently the addressee, in this case) would be able to think 'X is in the place where I am'—even though in reality this expected situation never came to pass.

In sentences like *People come to America with all manner of hopes and dreams* the effect of *come* is to allude, rather vaguely, to a potential 'someone else in this place' recognizing the immigrants as being 'in the place where I am', thus accounting for the faintly 'welcoming' quality of the sentence. This appears to be an improvement on Fillmore's claim that such sentences are possible because the place (*America*, in this case) is the 'subject of the narrative'. (Fillmore's explanation would predict that *come* could be used with equal ease about remote, unpopulated places.)

8.2.6 Come *and* go *with inanimate 'movers'*

The explications proposed above for *go* and *come* have been tailored to suit people and animals—beings capable of 'doing' something. This strategy was justified, in the early part of section 8.2, by appealing to the fact that in many situations it sounds odd to speak about inanimate objects *coming* or *going*. Nevertheless, there are contexts in which *go* and *come* can be used to describe the motions of inanimate bodies without any trace of semantic anomaly, and this remains to be explained.

At least three different categories of 'problem uses' (if we may call them that) can be identified. First, *come* and *go* are often used about vehicles, as in:

> *When does the bus come?*
> *Where does the train go?*
> *The plane was going to Sydney.*

Such sentences are consistent with a kind of imputed 'as if' intentionality, because it is part of our understanding of *buses*, *trains*, and *planes* (and, presumably, part of the lexical meaning of the words) that people are in control of them and that people use them to move about in. Indeed, it is acceptable to overtly attribute purposes of various kinds to such vehicles, for example, to say *The train stopped to unload*, or *The bus was speeding because it was running late*.

Second, *come* and *go* can be used about natural phenomena like the tides, rain, and sun.

> *The tide was going out.*
> *The floodwaters came right up to the front fence.*
> *The sun went down/came up.*

Curiously, sentences of this kind are acceptable only when the complement is either a 'path'-complement (e.g. *The tide went out*, *The sun came up*) or contains a 'path-like' expression (compare *?The floodwaters came to the front fence* with *The floodwaters came up to the front fence*).

Presumably such uses are possible because the meanings of words like *sun*, *tide*, and *rain* refer to the fact that these things move by themselves. In this connection, it is interesting to note the phenomenon of 'childhood animism' (Piaget 1973 [1929]; Astington 1993: 9–12). Essentially, children pass through a series of stages before arriving at the adult view of the world in which movement, life, and consciousness are clearly separate. At an early age they attribute consciousness to anything that moves: the sun and a bicycle are conscious, a table and a stone are not. Even after discovering that objects like bicycles move only because of outside agents, they continue for some time to over-attribute volition to things which apparently move of their own accord, such as the sun and wind. In a developmental perspective, therefore, one can think of the use of *come* and *go* with natural phenomena as an echo of earlier animistic conceptions. These observations do not in themselves provide a semantic account of adult uses of *come* and *go* with natural phenomena, but they make it plausible that polysemy is involved. I suspect that the picture will only become clear after a detailed analysis of the meanings of words like *rain, sun, flood,* and *tides* has been carried out, and this remains a task for the future.

Finally, it has to be acknowledged that *come* and *go* can be used with inanimate objects where it is clear that the objects moved because of intentional human action. For example:

> *It's a fault if the ball goes out of the court.*
> *The ball came down at her feet.*

Once again, such uses apparently require that a 'path' be indicated (as one can see by comparing the last cited example with **The ball came to her feet*). I know of no linguistic literature on this topic, and it too must be designated as an unsolved puzzle.

We will examine 'manner of motion' verbs, like *walk, run,* and the like in the next chapter.

8.3 Motion verbs in Arrernte

In this section we sample some facts about motion verbs in a language very different from English, namely the Arrernte language of Central Australia. You probably remember this language, as we looked at some of its particle meanings in Chapter 6. We won't be able to go into the same degree of semantic detail as we have for English *go* and *come*, but even so we will be able to see that Arrernte has a radically different system of motion meanings.

8.3.1 Coming and going in Arrernte

In Arrernte, the exponent of the most basic of all motion verbs MOVE appears to be *aname-irreme* (Henderson and Dobson 1994: 125), but, as in English, movement from place to place is not normally described directly in terms of MOVE, but by means of more specific translocational verbs. The nearest equivalents to English 'go' and 'come' are *lhe-* and *petye-*, respectively. As with *go* in English, *lhe-* appears to be the semantically less complex of the two. It can be used to ask a general question about where someone is going, as in (a) below, or to canvass various possible destinations (even when these include 'here'), as in (b), which could be given as an answer to (a). The Arrernte suffix *-werne* means 'to'. It is glossed as ALLATIVE, which is the technical label for a suffix with this meaning. (The other glossing symbols used in the Arrernte examples are explained in section 6.3.)

a. *Nthenhe-werne   re   lhe-me?*
   where-ALLATIVE   3sg   go-NPP
   'Where is she going?'
b. *Ayenge   kutne   pmere   nthenhe-werne   re   lhe-tyeke,*
   1sg   don't.know   place   where-ALLATIVE   3sg   go-PURPOSIVE
   re   apeke   petye-me   nhenhe-werne.
   3sg   maybe   come-NPP   here-ALLATIVE
   'I don't know where she's going. Maybe she's coming here.'

From this, it might seem safe to assume that *lhe-* could be used much as English *go* is, but this is not so. One of the commonest mistakes made by English speakers learning Arrernte is to use *lhe-* for situations where Arrernte speakers normally would use *petye-*. How does this come about? The answer lies in the semantics of *petye-*. As Wilkins and Hill (1995: 224) explain:

All that *petye-* 'come' requires is that the figure move along a path 'towards' the place where the speaker is, and there is no implication of movement 'to' that place ... So, any time a figure moves from its point of origin to another place which is closer to the place where the speaker is, then *petye-* 'come' is the felicitous choice, and *lhe-* 'go' is not.

In other words, Arrernte speakers normally keep track of all motions in terms of whether or not they bring a moving figure closer to the deictic reference point and register the fact by the choice of *petye-*, even if the motion is known to terminate a long way from where we are. For example, an Arrernte sentence like:

   Re   petye me   store-werne.
   3sg   'come'-NPP   store-ALLATIVE
   'She's "coming" to the store.'

does not imply in the slightest that we are at the store or have any special affiliation with the store. All it implies is that moving to the store brings her closer to us. Thus, we can see that 'come' is really quite a misleading translation for *petye-*, and that 'move nearer to here' or 'move this way' would be more accurate. (Strictly speaking, all this applies not to *petye-* alone, but to the combination of *petye-* along with an NP marked with allative case *-werne*, but nothing serious hinges on this detail.)

8.3.2 More Arrernte motion verbs

Two other morphologically basic Arrernte motion verbs are *unte-* 'hurry, go speedily' and *knge-* 'take, carry', both of which may be suffixed with *-tye* to indicate motion in the direction of the deictic centre. Notice that *untetye-* and *kngetye-* are like *petye-*, insofar as they require motion only towards the deictic centre, not necessarily right up to it.

(*pe-)	*unte-* 'hurry'	*knge-* 'take, carry'
petye- 'move this way'	*unte-tye-* 'hurry this way'	*knge-tye* 'carry this way'

The existence of the *-tye* suffix makes one wonder whether the verb *petye-* could be derived historically from an earlier motion verb **pe-*, and there is evidence to support this; for instance, the neighbouring and closely related language Kaytetye has a stem *ape-* for 'go'. However, in contemporary Arrernte the older form **pe-* has been replaced by *lhe-*.

Each of the three 'move-this-way verbs' can be compounded with *alpe-* 'go back':

pety-alpe 'move back this way'	*unte-ty-alpe-* 'hurry back this way'	*knge-ty-alpe-* 'carry back this way'

To get a sense of how these verbs work together as a system, let's bring back our old faithful example about going to the store, but to complicate matters a little, let's imagine that after visiting the store the person we're talking about comes in our direction. If going to the store itself is already a step in our direction, then as one would expect from what we know about *petye-* 'move this way', the sentence describing her movements will contain two instances of *petye-*. A situation like this is shown in Figure 8.1(a).

Re	*petye-me*	*store-werne,*	*ikweripwerre*	*nhenhe-werne*
3sg	'come'-NPP	store-ALLATIVE	after.which	here-ALLATIVE

petye-tyenhenge
'come'-subsequently
'She's 'coming' to the store, after which she's coming towards here.'

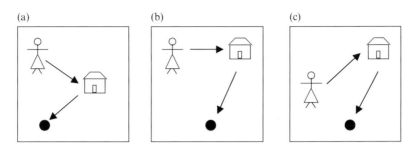

Figure 8.1 Arrernte motion diagrams

As we might also expect, if going to the store doesn't bring the person we're talking about either nearer to or further from us, i.e. if the moving person's path goes laterally from our point of view, *lhe-* 'go' replaces *petye-* in the first clause. A situation like this is shown in Figure 8.1(b).

If going to the store takes the moving person further away from us, we will again have *lhe-* 'go' in the first clause, but in the second clause *petye-tyenhenge* 'subsequently come' will be replaced by *petyealpa-tyenhenge* 'subsequently come back', because any path from the store towards where we are will necessarily involve a degree of returning towards where the moving person was earlier. A situation like this is shown in Figure 8.1(c).

> *Re   ilh-me   store-werne,   ikweripwerre   nhenhe-werne*
> 3sg 'go'-NPP store-ALLATIVE after.which   here-ALLATIVE
> *petyalpa-tyenhenge*
> 'come.back'-subsequently
> 'She's going to the store, after which she's coming back towards here.'

If the moving person was hurrying, then *unte-* 'hurry', *untetye-* 'hurry this way', and *untetyalpa-* 'hurry back this way' would be used in a parallel fashion to *lhe-* 'go', *petye-* 'come', and *petyalpa-* 'come back this way', respectively. If the person was carrying something, the three verbs would be *knge-* 'carry', *kngetye-* 'carry this way', and *kngetyalpe-* 'carry back this way'.

8.3.3 Grammatical and cultural importance of motion to the Arrernte people

Overall, we can see this system of motion verbs as reflecting an interest in keeping track of people's movements, and, in particular, how far away they are from a reference point. It is not difficult to see how functional such a system would have been in the traditional lifestyle of the desert-dwelling Arrernte people.

In fact, motion plays an important part even in Arrernte grammar, through an elaborate and unusual grammatical category known as 'associated motion' (Wilkins 1989: ch. 4; 2004). Basically, what this means is that almost all verbs can be (and frequently are) marked with special suffixes to indicate that the event or action depicted by the verb takes place against a background of a specific kind of motion. There are fourteen of these suffixes, some indicating simultaneous motion of a particular kind, others indicating prior or subsequent motion. Examples include:

> *-intye* 'do while moving this way', *-intyalpa* 'do while coming back', *-intyelhe* 'do while coming through', *-tyantye* 'do while moving upwards', *-tyekerle* 'do while moving downwards', *-tylhe* 'go and do', *-rlelhe* 'do and go', *-artnelhe* 'do and quickly go', *-artnalpa* 'do and quickly go back', *-tyalpe* 'go back and do', and *-rlalpe* 'do and then go back'

As you can see, the semantic dimensions involved include the same parameters of 'moving this way', 'moving back', and 'moving quickly' as are found in the simple motion verbs, and some of the same forms (e.g. *-tye*, *-alpa*, and *-lhe*) are involved as well. This suggests that the system probably arose through compounding with the motion verbs or through verb serialization. In the contemporary language, however, the associated motion suffixes function as a separate and fully productive system. In other words, ordinary verb roots like *irrpe-* 'go into', *tnye-* 'fall', *twe-* 'hit', or *ne-* 'sit' can all be marked in fourteen different ways to indicate associated motion. For instance, *irrp-intye* means 'go into while coming this way', *twe-tyantye-* 'hit while moving upwards', and *tnye-rlalpe-* 'fall then go back'.

Ordinary discourse in Arrernte makes heavy use of associated motion marking, so much so that one is regarded as speaking like a child (or as being deliberately 'uncooperative') if one omits relevant associated motion markings when the relevant facts are known. Needless to say, this is tough going for English-speaking language-learners, who are not used to continuously updating and registering spatial and orientational information. The whole system is consistent with the conclusions of the anthropologist David Lewis, who investigated the remarkable orientational abilities of Aboriginal hunters. Based on non-linguistic evidence, he concluded:

It would appear then, that the essential psychophysical mechanism was some kind of *dynamic image* or *mental 'map'*, which was *continually updated* in terms of time, distance and bearing, and more radically *realigned at each change of direction*, so that the hunters remained *at all times* aware of the precise direction of their base and/or objective. (Lewis 1976: 262; emphasis in original)

It is also instructive to consider the cultural importance of travel and spatial orientation to Aboriginal people. The anthropologist Fred Myers (1986: 54) made the following comments about the nearby Pintupi people, and, as Wilkins (1989: 298) observes, the same applies to the Arrernte people:

Orientation in space is a prime concern for the Pintupi. Even their dreams are cast in the framework of spatial co-ordinates. It is impossible to listen to any narrative, whether it be historical, mythological, or contemporary, without constant reference to where events happened. In this sense, place provides the framework around which events coalesce... Not temporal relation but geography is the great punctuator of Pintupi story telling.

8.4 Motion verbs in other languages

As mentioned earlier, Talmy (1985a; 2007) has argued that languages tend to have a preferred lexicalization patterns concerning what kinds of semantic components are found in a typical colloquial motion verb. In English, the predominant pattern is to combine a specification for 'manner' along with motion, for example in verbs like *walk*, *run*, *crawl*, *fly*, *swim*, and *ride*. Also, in English we can freely use many verbs, such as *float*, *roll*, and *bounce*, in ways which incorporate a sense of movement from place to place. This is known as MOTION+MANNER CONFLATION. In this section we will take a brief look at a selection of facts from some non-English languages with different lexicalization patterns. The coverage is necessarily rather superficial.

8.4.1 Spanish 'motion+path' verbs

The most common alternative pattern to MOTION+MANNER is MOTION+PATH CONFLATION, the preferred pattern in the Romance languages of Europe, and also in Semitic and Polynesian languages. In Spanish, for example, one cannot use a verb like *float* or *roll* to convey motion, as in English sentences like *The bottle floated out of the cave*, or *I rolled the keg into the storeroom*. Instead of being conveyed by the verb, the manner specification must be expressed as a separate phrase, as shown below.

a. *La botella entró a la cueva, flotando.*
    The bottle moved-in to the cave, floating.'
b. *Metí el barril a la bodega, rodándolo.*
    'I moved-it-in the keg to the storeroom, rolling it.'

However as examples (a) and (b) above also show, Spanish has many motion verbs which incorporate specific path specifications. *Entrar* means 'to move inside' and *meter* 'to make move inside'. Other Spanish verbs of this type include the following:

> *salir* 'move-out', *pasar* 'move-by/through', *subir* 'move-up', *bajar* 'move-down', *volver* 'move-back', *cruzar* 'move-across', *andar* 'move-about', *ir* 'move along'.

Actually, English also has a good number of such verbs, mostly words of Latin origin, such as *enter, exit, ascend, descend, traverse*. These don't affect Talmy's generalization because they do not represent the most numerous or most colloquial pattern in English.

8.4.2 Atsugewi 'motion+figure' verbs

According to Talmy (1985a; 2007), a small number of languages have the peculiar characteristic of regularly encoding facts about the kind of figure which is involved in motion. English has only a few verbs like this (e.g. *flow* and *ooze* specify that the figure is liquid), but in Atsugewi (Hokan, northern California), typical verbs of motion contain comparable specifications about the nature of the moving figure.

Atsugewi is a polysynthetic language, meaning that it combines into a single word many kinds of grammatical elements which in other languages would be conveyed by separate words. In a polysynthetic language, what would be a whole English sentence can often be expressed by a single, very complex word. As far as I know, it is only in polysynthetic languages that MOTION+FIGURE CONFLATION has been reported as the typical pattern for motion verbs. The following are examples of Atsugewi verb roots (Talmy 1985a: 73). In a sense, one could say that Atsugewi has a classifier system (see section 11.3) built into its motion verbs.

-síaq̓- 'runny icky material (e.g. mud, manure, rotten tomatoes, guts, chewed gum) to move/be located'

-lup- 'small shiny spherical object (e.g. a round candy, an eyeball, a hailstone) to move/be located'

-caq- 'slimy lumpish object (e.g. a toad, cow dropping) to move/be located'

-i̓- 'small planar object that can be functionally affixed (e.g. a stamp, a clothing patch, a button, a shingle, a cradle's sunshade) to move/be located'

-swal- 'limp linear object suspended at one end (e.g. a shirt on a clothesline, a hanging dead rabbit, a flaccid penis) to move/be located'

Notice that each can be used to indicate either motion or static location, depending on whether it co-occurs with a directional suffix (such as -ič̓t- 'into liquid' or -cis- 'into fire') or with a stative locational suffix (such as -ik·- 'on the ground'). For example, the one-word sentences in (a) and (b) below have the same verb root, namely -síaq̓- 'runny icky material move/be located', but in (a) it is combined with a locative suffix and in (b) with a directional suffix. Notice that both examples also contain a so-called 'instrumental prefix' indicating the cause of or reason for the situation being described. (The examples are framed by the affix set '-w- -ᵃ which indicates a third-person subject and factual mood; these affixes are left unglossed. The phonetic form is given first, then a morphophonemic breakdown.)

a. [ẇosta̓q̓ík·a]

'- w- uh- síaq̓ -ik·-ᵃ

from gravity runny icky material (be located) on the ground

Free translation: 'Guts are lying on the ground.'

b. [č̓wasta̓q̓íč̓ta]

'- w- ca- síaq̓ -ič̓t-ᵃ

from wind runny icky material (move) into liquid

Free translation: 'The guts blew into the creek.'

c. [č̓wasẃálmič̓]

'- w- ca- swal -mič̓

from wind limp material (move) onto the ground

Free translation: 'The clothes blew down (from the clothesline).'

I have reproduced some of Talmy's Atsugewi data and his interpretation of it because it is well known, but I must say that a few questions remain in my mind about the assertion that motion+figure is the preferred semantic pattern in this language. We have already seen reasons for supposing that the most prototypical motion scenes involve animate (especially human) actors, but all Talmy's examples are for inanimate figures. There is not really enough data here to draw conclusions about the favoured semantic pattern across the whole language.

It can also be asked whether Talmy and the few other linguists who have described such systems have exaggerated their peculiarity by using exotic translations. After all, many English manner+motion verbs could also be recast into exotic formulations; for example, *slide* could be glossed as 'rigid planar object move laterally' and *roll* as 'tubular or spherical object move with rotation'. Croft (1994: 156–61) argues that the whole category of 'figure classifying' motion verbs is 'probably illusory'. Finally, it is not clear that the roots listed above deserve to be called verbs, given that the 'motional' sense is signalled by the directional suffix. On the face of it, the directional suffix has as good a claim to be designated as the verb.

Key technical terms

deictic projection

figure

goal

ground

lexical conflation

lexicalization pattern

localism

motion+figure conflation

motion+manner conflation

motion+path conflation

path

source

theme

Exercises and discussion questions

† next to a problem means that a solution or some commentary can be found at the end of this book.

1. In William Frawley's (1992: 171) textbook *Linguistic Semantics* the following passage occurs. How could this characterization of motion be criticized from the point of view of semantic theory?

   Motion entails the *displacement* of some entity, or positional change... The elemental structure of a motion event is abstractly *Displace(x)*.

2. Talmy's description of a 'basic motion event' (see section 8.1) seems to assume that a place is a kind of 'Object'. Do you think that a place is a kind of 'thing'?

What is the relationship between being at a place (e.g. *at the beach*) and being (say) at the car (as in: *See you at the car*)?

3†. In English the pronoun *we* can have either an 'inclusive' or an 'exclusive' interpretation. Inclusive means 'including the addressee', as in *We study linguistics* as spoken by one linguistics student to another. Exclusive means 'not including the addressee', as in *When my flatmate and I went shopping yesterday, we bought some nice posters*. Consider the sentences below and explain why the version with *go* allows either an inclusive or exclusive interpretation of *we*, but *come* requires an exclusive reading.

We'll go there right away.
We'll come there right away.

4. The English verb *go* can be followed directly by an indefinite pronoun; thus, one can speak of *going somewhere*, *going nowhere*, and *going anywhere*. Most specific destinations, however, must be introduced by means of a *to*-phrase; for example, the sentences *They went to the market* and *She went to Lismore* would be ungrammatical without *to*. On the other hand, it is acceptable to speak of *going home*, whereas **going to home* is no good. Can you explain this?

5†. Fillmore (1975a) gives the following description of the 'deictic conditions' for *come* and *bring*: Why would it not be desirable to accept this statement as a partial description of the meaning of *come* and *bring*?

motion toward either the speaker or the addressee at either coding time or reference time or toward the home base of either the speaker or the hearer at reference time.

6. How would you describe the difference between (a) and (b) below? Do you agree with the explanation given in this chapter?

a. *She told him I'd come right over.*
b. *She told him I'd go right over.*

7†. Consider the sets of motion verbs given in (a)–(c) below. Decide in each case whether there is a dominant pattern of lexical conflation, and if so, state what it is. Also, identify any apparent exceptions to the dominant pattern in each set.

a. Japanese: *aruku* 'walk, go forward using the legs', *tobu* 'fly, jump, move above the ground', *hashiru* 'speed along, go fast', *hau* 'crawl, move forward lying on the stomach'
b. Malay: *masuk* 'enter, go in', *turun* 'go down', *lompat* 'leap, jump', *naik* 'climb, ascend, go up', *keluar* 'go out'
c. Yankunytjatjara: *pakaṇi* 'get up, come out', *parpakaṇi* 'fly', *kalpanyi* 'climb', *tjarpanyi* 'go in, enter', *wirtjapakaṇi* 'run', *punkaṇi* 'fall'.

8†. Malay *lari* is usually glossed as 'run' and can certainly be used in similar contexts to English *run*, as in (a) and (b) below. However, *lari* is also possible in contexts like (c) and (d). How does *lari* differ from English *run*? Can you suggest a reductive paraphrase explication for *lari*?

a. *Lari! Lari!* 'Run! Run!'
b. *Ben Johnson lari pecut.* 'Ben Johnson runs like a flash.'
c. *Ikan/burung tu sudah cepat lari.* 'The fish/birds have already got away.'
d. *Kereta tu sudah cepat lari.* 'That car went off quickly.'

9†. In Danish, the directional adverb *hen*, roughly 'over', is often found in combination with motion verbs. The construction consists of a motion verb such as *tog* 'went' or *gik* 'walked', the directional adverb *hen*, and a destination phrase (a preposition and noun phrase). For example: *Hun gik hen til købmanden* 'She went over (*hen*) to the grocer's'. Here is a list of typical noun phrases which can occur as destinations in such constructions:

skolen 'the school', *banken* 'the bank', *brugsen* 'the local (co-operative) shop', *kirken* 'the church', *børnehaven* 'the kindergarten', *bageren* 'the bakery', *tanken* 'the petrol station', *kiosken* 'the kiosk', *hjørnet* 'the (street) corner', *svømmehallen* 'the (public indoor) swimming pool', *torvet* 'the town square', *biblioteket* 'the library', *legepladsen* 'the playground', *posthuset* 'the post office'

On the other hand, when people are talking about going from one town or city to another, they would not normally use *hen*; for example, **hen til København* 'over to Copenhagen' is semantically anomalous (as is **hen til Sverige* 'over to Sweden', even if one goes there over the bridge that connects the two countries). Some other odd-sounding expressions are *?hen til skoven* 'over to the woods', *?hen til stranden* 'over to the beach', and *?hen på landet* 'over to the countryside'. Using reductive paraphrase, what would you hypothesize about the meaning of *hen*?

9

Physical activity verbs

It is not too difficult to accept that words from some domains, such as social categories and value terms, can embody different culturally-based conceptualizations. In relation to the physical world, however, it is tempting to assume that everybody walks, everybody eats, everybody cuts, chops, and digs from time to time, and, correspondingly, that there is little scope for variation in this realm of meaning. In fact, however, there are substantial differences, mainly because words do not simply label external realities, but rather represent ways of construing or interpreting reality. In this chapter we will look into the semantics of three kinds of verbs of physical activity: bodily motion (like *walk* and *run*), ingestion (*eat*, *drink*, and the like), and complex activities, such as *cut*, *chop*, and *dig*, that typically involve using a purpose-built instrument such as a knife, axe, or shovel.

Verbal semantics is relevant to many aspects of sentence structure, because, as linguists have long been fond of saying, the verb is the grammatical heart of a sentence. It sets the ground plan for the clause as a whole, determining the number, character, and (to a large extent) the grammatical status of the noun-phrases in the sentence. Towards the end of the chapter we will be looking at a number of so-called syntactic alternations involving physical activity verbs, i.e. special grammatical constructions in which a verb adopts a modified meaning.

Bodily motion verbs like *walk* and *run*, though surprisingly complex in some ways, are actually among the semantically simplest verbs of human bodily activity. This makes them a good place to start our investigation into this area.

9.1 'Manner-of-motion' verbs: *walk* vs. *run*

Ever since Leonard Talmy (1985a) introduced the idea of lexicalization patterns using verbs of motion as his premier example, linguists have taken a special interest in how different languages depict human motion. As we know from Chapter 8, Talmy's key observation was that some languages, like English, tend to package a lot of information about manner of motion into their motion verbs. The difference between *walk* and *run*, for example, involves not just speed but some details about how the feet and legs move with respect to the ground. Other languages tend instead to build in information about the direction or 'path' being taken by the person whose motion is being described; for example, whether the person is moving upwards or downwards, or into or out of something. In such languages, to convey the same kind of manner details as we have in English, one has to add an extra word, e.g. Spanish *entra caminando* '(he) enters walking'. Many studies have been conducted with a view to deciding how consistent languages are in terms of their lexicalization patterns, how the movements of people (and animals) in such languages are described in real discourse, whether other aspects of lexical or grammatical structure correlate with lexicalization patterns, and other related questions (Papafragou, Massey, and Gleitman 2002; Slobin 2000; 2004; Bohnemeyer, Eisenbeiss, and Narasimhan 2006; Malt et al. 2008; Malt, Gennari, and Imai 2010; Taylor 1996; Gennari et al. 2002). Much less attention has been given to analysing what exactly is involved in the 'manner' semantics of motion. This will be our focus in this section, which is based on Goddard, Wierzbicka, and Wong (forthcoming).

Let's begin with the question of the appropriate semantic template. While verbs of locomotion like *walking*, *running*, and *climbing* have different meanings, they exhibit a lot of semantic and syntactic similarities and it is the job of the semantic template to capture these. Semantically, these verbs involve physical displacement and voluntary movement of the legs by an animate human subject. Syntactically, they can combine with words that are associated with location (e.g. *here*, *in the garden*), duration (e.g. *for some time*), and displacement (e.g. *from place A to place B*).

According to NSM research, the semantically simplest frame for these verbs is the progressive or imperfective, e.g. *He is walking*, *She is running*. For this frame, the semantic template has three sections: LEXICO-SYNTACTIC FRAME, PROTOTYPICAL MOTIVATIONAL SCENARIO, and MANNER. The lexico-syntactic frame embodies components that identify all intransitive words of locomotion in English and distinguishes them from other verbal classes. It has a mandatory actor (someone doing something), which distinguishes these verbs from non-agentive verbs of movement, such as *slip* and *fall*. It has a durative component ('for some time') and it captures the aspect of controlled bodily movement in a place.

> LEXICO-SYNTACTIC FRAME for *walking* and *running*:
>   someone X is doing something somewhere for some time
>   because of this, this someone's body is moving at the same time
>   as this someone wants

Notice that the frame is couched in the progressive or IMPERFECTIVE, i.e. as something that is ongoing ('walking'), rather than as a completed or perfective act ('walked'). As we'll see later, in section 9.4, it is easier to do it this way because completing an activity means bringing in some additional elements of meaning (for example, reaching a destination). As well as this, 'activities' are inherently durative in nature, i.e. they take some time and effort, and from an experiential point of view one often sees people undertaking the activity. These considerations favour adopting an imperfective perspective in the basic lexico-syntactic frame for verbs of bodily motion. Incidentally, this has long been the favoured position in the Russian lexicological tradition.

The second part, PROTOTYPICAL MOTIVATIONAL SCENARIO, tells us what prototypically motivates people to do this. In general, human activities are goal-directed, purposeful; and to understand why they are conducted as they are, one has to take account of the actor's intentions. I hasten to add that we are talking about a prototypical motivation. People can *walk* for many reasons aside from wanting to get to somewhere not too far away, and they can *run* for other reasons than to get somewhere far away quickly;

for example, a person can go *walking* or *running* for exercise. However, anyone who *walks* for whatever reason can be likened to someone who walks for the prototypical reason, which is, roughly speaking, to get from one point to another without urgency.

> PROTOTYPICAL MOTIVATIONAL SCENARIO for *walking*:
> at many times when someone does this, this someone does it because it is
>   like this:
> – this someone is somewhere
> – this someone wants to be somewhere else after some time
> – this other place is not far from the place where this someone is

Prototypically, a person who *runs* wants to get from one place to another in as short a time as possible. There is a distinct sense of urgency, as evidenced in expressions such as *run for your life* or *I've gotta run*. Also, while a person might *walk* slowly, it is difficult to think of a context in which one might want to *run* slowly. As Taylor (1996: 27) writes: 'Typically, you run to a place because you need to get there quickly. The desire to reduce the time needed to get to a destination can become the very point of running.'

> PROTOTYPICAL MOTIVATIONAL SCENARIO for *running*:
> at many times when someone does this, this someone does it because it is
>   like this:
> – this someone is somewhere
> – this someone wants to be somewhere else after a short time
> – this other place is far from the place where this someone is

Next in the template comes MANNER. For words like *walk* and *run*, the manner components need to be able to reflect the repetitiveness and regularity of specific movements of the legs and feet. The introductory part of this section, for both verbs, is as follows:

> when someone does this, this someone does something with the legs [m]
>   many times
> because of this, this someone's legs [m] move at many times in the same way
>   it happens like this:

Now let's look further into the MANNER section. The interesting thing about English *walk* and *run* is that both verbs imply quite a bit of detail about the movements of the legs and feet. You might like to look back at Nida's (1975: 120) analysis, which was presented in section 2.5. As he put it, both verbs depict the feet moving alternatively (in a 121212 order), with *walk* implying that 'one foot (is) always on surface' and *run* implying 'one foot not always on surface'. Nida's terminology is compressed. In NSM phrasing we will use the phrase 'touching the ground [m]', rather than 'on surface'. Here 'ground' is a semantic molecule. Nida has also not specified that the typical pattern of foot movement in *walking* and *running* involves motion in a forwards direction, i.e. when each foot goes down onto the ground, it touches in a spot which is in front of the person. In our explication we will use the molecule 'in front [m] of'.

We are now in a position to review the proposed manner section for English *walk*. For convenience, I have divided it into two sections labelled (a) and (b).

> MANNER section for *walking*:
> a.   when someone does this, this someone does something with the legs [m]
>   many times
>   because of this, this someone's legs [m] move at many times in the same way
>   when this is happening, this someone's feet [m] touch the ground [m] at
>   many times in many places
> b.   it happens like this:
>   – at some time, one foot [m] is touching the ground [m] somewhere for a
>   short time
>   – during this time the other foot [m] moves
>   – when it is moving, it is not touching the ground [m]
>   – after this, it is touching [m] the ground [m] in another place
>   – this other place is in front [m] of this someone
>   – at the same time, this someone's body moves
>   – after this, the other foot [m] moves in the same way
>   – because of this, after this, this someone's body is in front [m] of the place
>   where it was before
>   the same thing happens many times

The components in (a) introduce the idea of repeated actions with the legs and repeated foot contact with the ground. The components in (b) elaborate on this, indicating that in each case one foot stays on the ground while the other one moves forwards briefly and touches the ground in front of the person. After the same sequence is repeated, the person's body has advanced to be in front of the place where it was before.

If we compare this with the corresponding manner for *running*, we see that many components are identical. This is as it should be, since *walking* and *running* have much in common (compared even with other English human motion verbs, such as *crawling*, *skipping*, *swimming*, etc.). One difference is that for *running*, the legs are described as moving 'quickly [m]' and the contact between foot and ground is said to last only 'for a very short time'. Another concerns how the pattern of foot and leg movement is described. For *running*, the "mechanics" part starts with one foot moving forward and touching the ground very briefly in front of the person, after which the other foot moves in the same way. A third difference is that with *walking*, the moving foot is described as 'not touching the ground [m]', whereas with *running* the phrase 'moves above the ground [m]' is used. This is connected with the different "visualisation" and phraseology associated with *running*.

> MANNER section for *running*:
> a. when someone does this, this someone does something with the legs [m]
>   at many times
>   because of this, this someone's legs [m] move quickly [m] at many times
>   in the same way
>   when this is happening, this someone's feet [m] touch the ground [m] at
>   many times in many places
> b. it happens like this:
>   – at some time one foot [m] moves quickly [m] above the ground [m]
>   – because of this, after this, this foot [m] is in front [m] of this someone
>   – after this, this foot [m] touches the ground [m] for a very short time
>   – after this, the other foot [m] moves in the same way
>   – because of this, after this, this someone's body is in front [m] of the place
>   where it was before
>   the same thing happens many times

The full explication for English *walking* is given below. You can easily substitute the corresponding sections for *running* to compile the full explication for that word. (The only other difference, not mentioned so far, concerns the prototypical motivation for *running*. While the prototypical situation for *walking* involves someone wanting to be somewhere else (not far away) 'after some time', the corresponding situation for *running* involves wanting to be there 'after a short time'.)

> *Someone X is walking*
>
> LEXICO-SYNTACTIC FRAME
>
> someone X is doing something somewhere for some time
> because of this, this someone's body is moving at the same time as this
>   someone wants
>
> PROTOTYPICAL MOTIVATIONAL SCENARIO
>
> at many times when someone does this, this someone does it because it is
>   like this:

– this someone is somewhere
– this someone wants to be somewhere else after some time
– this other place is not far from the place where this someone is

MANNER

when someone does this, this someone does something with the legs [m]
    at many times
because of this, this someone's legs [m] move at many times in the same way
when this is happening, this someone's feet [m] touch the ground [m] at
    many times in many places
it happens like this:
– at some time, one foot [m] is touching the ground [m] somewhere for a
    short time
– during this time the other foot [m] moves
– when it is moving, it is not touching the ground [m]
– after this, it touches [m] the ground [m] in another place
– this other place is in front [m] of this someone
– after this, the other foot [m] moves in the same way
– because of this, after this, this someone's body is in front [m] of the place
    where it was before
the same thing happens many times

9.1.1 Extended uses of running, with dogs and other animals

Obviously, the proposed meaning of *running* given above cannot apply to
sentences like *The dog is running*, which has a living but non-human subject.
Like most animals, dogs have four legs instead of two; and *run* can also be
used in relation to many other kinds of animals (horses, cheetahs, etc.) and
to some birds (ostriches, chickens, etc.). Goddard et al. (forthcoming) propose that the meaning expressed in these uses can be represented as follows.
Essentially this identifies the meaning of *run* when used about a dog or a
chicken, as an analogical extension 'from the basic sense of rapid motion by
a two-legged human' (Taylor 1996: 29).

A *living thing of one kind (e.g. dog, chicken) is running (somewhere)*:
a.   a living thing of one kind X is doing something somewhere for some time
      because of this, its body is moving in this place at the same time as it wants
b.   this living thing is doing this like people do something in a place
      when they are running [d] in this place

The extended meaning comprises only two parts. The first part is the lexico-
syntactic frame, which is very similar to the one for the basic meaning of

the word: it specifies an activity involving controlled bodily motion in a place. The second part likens this motional activity to the human act of 'running'. The word 'running' is (of course) semantically complex. In this explication it is functioning, in effect, as a kind of derivational base. To acknowledge this, instead of the normal molecule notation [m] we use the notation [d], for derivational base.

9.1.2 Language-specific ways of thinking about 'gaits'

The fact that the semantics of *walk* and *run* are complex and language-specific does not mean that 'anything goes' in the world's languages when it comes to describing modes of human locomotion. As in many areas of the lexicon, how languages divide up the world is partly (but only partly) constrained by external realities. In relation to human locomotion, it so happens that from a biomechanical point of view, i.e. how the limbs, muscles, joints, etc. are configured and function, there is a significant discontinuity between what we call, in English, *walking* and what we call, in English, *running* (Malt et al. 2008). That is, if someone is moving along on foot at increasing speed, there will be an abrupt transition between two gaits.

This doesn't mean that all or most languages have words like the English ones. On the contrary, we know that this simply isn't so, since many languages do not have verbs with the same amount of manner detail built into them as the English verbs do. It does make it likely, however, that all languages will have well-adapted lexical resources for recognizing the difference. We can expect, and available evidence seems to bear this out, that few languages will be blind to the bodily and experiential realities of human movement to the extent that their words and phrases would cross-cut the biomechanical distinction altogether.

From a semantic point of view, the important thing not to lose sight of is that even in relation to the physical world, meanings are not simply labels or names for what is 'out there'. Rather they are (or represent) ways of thinking about what is out there; in the case of human movement, ways of thinking about how people can, and usually do, move from place to place.

Somewhat surprisingly, we do not yet have a big portfolio of fine-grained semantic studies about human motion verbs across a range of languages.

True, there have been many cross-linguistic studies but they have been at best conducted at a 'moderate' level of semantic analysis that often glosses over matters of detail. Deep and detailed semantic analysis will no doubt bring to light many new and valuable findings. To give a sense of what is 'out there'—not in the external world but in the world of meaning—here are a sample of observations about how routine ways of human movement are dealt with in different languages.

Russian has a batch of words that occupy a similar lexical space to English *go*, *walk*, and *run*. *Idti* (roughly) 'go/walk' is the most common, but as in Polish (see below) it is not as specific in terms of manner as English *walk*. To get closer to *walk* from a manner point of view, there are two alternatives—*xodit'* (roughly) 'walk' and *guljat'* (roughly) 'go for a walk', and the same goes for *run*—*bežat* (roughly) 'run' and *begat'* (roughly) 'run (to)'. In each case the distinction is between more purposeful, goal-directed movement vs. more 'procedural' depiction of the movement.

Now consider Polish. Does it have semantic equivalents of English *walk* and *run*? Polish *biec* is a close counterpart to *run*, but the situation with *walk* is more complex, because the most common Polish word used in the appropriate contexts, namely *iść*, has a more general meaning than *walk*. This is linked with the fact, mentioned in Chapter 8, that Polish does not have general verbs like English *come* and *go*, which can apply both to movement on foot and to movement by vehicle. Rather, in Polish, as in German and many other languages, there is an obligatory lexical distinction between (roughly speaking) 'going somewhere on foot' and 'going somewhere by vehicle'. At the same time, a question like 'When are you going?' would frequently be translated into Polish as *Dokąd idziesz?*, i.e. with the verb *iść*. Likewise, Polish *iść* is used very widely in figurative ways that are more suggestive of English *go* than *walk*; for example, in sentences like 'The path was "walking" through the woods' and 'New times are "walking" [towards us]'. In short, Polish *iść* and *biec* are more different from one another than *walk* and *run* are, because *walk* and *run* are on a par in terms of descriptive specificity, whereas Polish *biec* 'run' is more specific in its manner components than *iść*.

The implication seems to be that in Polish, the activity usually described in English as *walking* is seen as the norm, whereas that described in English as *running* is seen as a departure from the norm and more deserving of specific description. Many languages, however, appear to have a verb for (roughly speaking) 'deliberate rapid movement' without any particular specification of how the legs and feet move. For example, Yankunytjatjara has *walaringanyi* (morphologically related to *wala* 'fast') and Malay has *lari*. Both can be used equally freely about people, birds, and animals.

Despite the impression one may get from the literature that verbs of motion is a field well studied in lexical typology, there is still great scope for cross-linguistic semantic research.

9.2 'Eating' and 'drinking' across languages

From an English speaker's point of view, 'eating' and 'drinking' might seem to represent activities which are so natural and universal that all languages must have corresponding words. But this is not so. Some languages—a surprising number, actually—don't have separate words for these two activities. These include Kalam from Papua New Guinea, Shanghainese (the Sinitic language/dialect spoken in and around Shanghai, China), and Warlpiri from Central Australia. It also seems that even in languages which do distinguish between something like 'eating' and something like 'drinking', it is not necessarily the case that all the semantic details are exactly the same as in English. As we will see, this appears to be the case for Mandarin Chinese.

In this section we look into several of these verbs, concentrating on the differences between them. We will draw especially on Wierzbicka (2009b; 2010c) and Ye (2010). An extremely valuable overview of studies on eating and drinking is Newman (2009).

To begin with, let's consider the following lexico-syntactic frame, which is arguably shared by them all.

> LEXICO-SYNTACTIC FRAME for 'eating' and 'drinking' verbs:
>   someone X is doing something to something Y for some time
>   because of this, something is happening to this something at the same time
>   [at the same time, this someone can feel something in the body because
>   of this]

The key ideas are that the actor does something to something (with parts of his or her body, most particularly, the mouth), and that this has a concurrent effect on that thing. It might seem that the second component amounts to recognizing *eat* and *drink* as canonical transitive verbs (which they are not; cf. Næss 2007; 2009), but this is not really so: the

lexico-syntactic frame for canonical transitive verbs (such as *cut* or *chop*—
see below) has this component capped off with an additional phrase ('as
this someone wants'), which explicitly focuses the actor's intention on the
effect upon the object. *Eating* and *drinking* (and related verbs in other
languages) are not like this. Though what is being consumed is of course
being affected in the process, this fact is not likely to be of particular interest
to the actor. Possibly there is a third component in the lexico-syntactic
frame, recognizing a concurrent associated feeling in the actor's own body.

Another shared component of verbs of *eating* and *drinking* (in English
and in other languages) concerns the prototypical motivational scenario;
namely, that the prototypical actor is doing something to the object with
the mouth because he or she wants this thing, or at least part of this thing,
to be inside his or her body. That is the point of ingestion.

From here on, however, it seems that different languages can conceptualize the nature of the activity and how it is carried out in somewhat
different ways. One dimension of difference depends on whether the
nature of the object or substance consumed is taken into account. If it
is, the most common differentiation is between things like water (i.e.
liquids) for *drinking* vs. things not like water (i.e. solids) for *eating*.
Connected with this is a further possible difference concerning the manner in which the activity is carried out. The conceptualization of *eating*
tends to involve some reference (roughly speaking) to chewing, which is
not necessary or appropriate for *drinking*. Interestingly, both verbs also
tend to conjure up an image of an item being transported to the mouth
with the use of the hands.

As we will see shortly, in some languages the existential importance, i.e.
the life-sustaining function, of *eating* and *drinking* can also find a place in
the semantic structure of the relevant verbs.

9.2.1 English drinking *and* eating

It is easier to start with *drinking*, because the mechanics are less complex.
Note that the prototypical motivational scenario includes two components:
first, that the object is 'something like water [m]', and second, that the actor
'wants this something to be inside their body'. As for the manner component, it provides for an iterative structure (as with *walk* and *run*, in this
respect); specifically, it involves doing something with the mouth that

causes some of the 'water-like' substance to be inside the mouth for a very short time, following which a further action of the mouth causes it to be somewhere else inside the person's body. The manner section also involves some preliminary action with the hands.

Someone X is drinking something Y:

LEXICO-SYNTACTIC FRAME

a.   someone X is doing something to something Y for some time
     because of this, something is happening to this something at the same time

PROTOTYPICAL MOTIVATIONAL SCENARIO

b.   at many times when someone does this to something, this someone does
        it because it is like this:
     – this something is something like water [m]
     – this someone wants this something to be inside their body

MANNER

c.   when someone does this to something, the same thing happens many times
        it happens like this:
     – this someone does something to something with the hands [m]
     – at the same time, this someone does something to this something
        with the mouth [m]
     – because of this, after this, part of this something is for a very short time
        inside this someone's mouth [m]
     – after this, this someone does something else to it with the mouth [m]
     – because of this, after this, it is not inside this someone's mouth [m]
        anymore, it is somewhere else inside this someone's body for some
        time

Now let's consider how this explication would need to be modified to produce a suitable explication for English *eat*, the natural counterpart and partner word for *drink*. First, we will need a slightly different prototypical scenario, because with *eat* the nature of the object is '*not* something like water [m]'. Related to this, the manner section of the *eat* explication is more elaborate. There are more details about actions of parts of the mouth (related to chewing) and how these actions affect the substance in the mouth.

Someone X is eating something Y:

LEXICO-SYNTACTIC FRAME

a.   someone X is doing something to something Y for some time
     because of this, something is happening to this something at the same time

PROTOTYPICAL MOTIVATIONAL SCENARIO

b. at many times when someone does this to something, this someone does
       it because it is like this:
       – this something is not something like water [m]
       – this someone wants this something to be inside their body

MANNER

c. when someone does this to something, the same thing happens many times
       it happens like this:
       – this someone does something to something with the hands [m]
       – at the same time, this someone does something to it with the mouth [m]
       – because of this, after this, part of this thing is for a short time
             inside this someone's mouth [m]
       – when this part is inside this someone's mouth [m],
             this someone does something to it with some parts of the mouth [m]
       – because of this, something happens to it at this time
       – after this, this someone does something else to it with the mouth [m]
       – because of this, after this, it is not inside this someone's mouth [m]
             anymore, it is somewhere else inside this someone's body for some
             time

9.2.2 Kalam ñb 'eat/drink'

The Papuan language Kalam (Pawley and Bulmer in press) has no words
equivalent in meaning to English *eat* and *drink*. Instead, both activities (as it
seems from an English point of view) are designated by the verb *ñb* (which is
pronounced *ñəb*, by the way). According to Pawley and Bulmer's dictionary, *ñb* is general in its semantics, rather than ambiguous. A sentence like
Tap etp nbsay? 'What are they eating/drinking?' is genuinely vague.

The explication below shows how such an undifferentiated 'eat/drink'
meaning can be constructed (Wierzbicka 2009b).

Someone X is ñb-ing something Y: [Kalam]

LEXICO-SYNTACTIC FRAME

a. someone X is doing something to something Y for some time
       because of this, something is happening to this something at the same time

PROTOTYPICAL MOTIVATIONAL SCENARIO

b. at many times when someone does this to something, this someone does
       it because it is like this:
       – this someone wants this something to be inside their body

c. when someone does this to something, the same thing happens many times
    it happens like this:
    – this someone does something to something with the mouth [m]
    – because of this, after this, part of this something is for a short time
        inside this someone's mouth [m]
    – after this, this someone does something else to it with the mouth [m]
    – because of this, after this, it is not inside this someone's mouth [m]
        anymore, it is somewhere else inside this someone's body for some
        time

The explication above follows the same semantic template as for English *eat* and *drink*. Many of the details also remain the same, while others differ. Notably, the prototypical motivation does not characterize the substance either as 'something like water [m]' (as with *drink*) or as 'not something like water [m]' (as with *eat*). Relatedly, the period of time for which each mouthful of the substance remains in the mouth is described as 'a short time' (rather than 'a very short time', as with *drink*). Naturally, no elaborate manner details are appropriate.

Why is this better than just saying that *ñb* means 'eat or drink'? Because to do this would be to present a Kalam meaning as a disjunction of two English concepts. This would violate the ideal of representing meanings from an indigenous perspective, from the insider's point of view. Plus, it would fail to present a unitary meaning (since a disjunction effectively means polysemy). Furthermore, it would hardly amount to an analysis at all to simply substitute two complex unanalysed words in place of the Kalam original. On the other hand, by decomposing the Kalam meaning down into semantic primes and simple molecules such as 'mouth [m]', we can give a fine-grained depiction of a unitary meaning and at the same time show its similarities and differences with both English *drink* and *eat*.

9.2.3 Mandarin Chinese

Even in languages which apparently have separate verbs for 'eat' and 'drink', there are sometimes reasons to believe that the meanings of these verbs do not exactly match those of the English verbs. This is the case in Mandarin Chinese. This section is based closely on the work of Zhengdao Ye (2010). Ye argues that the demarcation between Mandarin *chī* and *hē* cannot be neatly drawn along the line of solids vs. liquids, because while the kind of substances introduced into the mouth for *hē* are indeed things like water, those for *chī* cannot be characterized simply as 'things not like water'.

First, corpus materials show that it is not uncommon to have prototypical liquid substances, such as water, beverages, soy or cow's milk, as the objects of *chī*; for instance, in phrases like *chīshuǐ* [eat water] and *chījiǔ* [eat alcoholic.beverage] (cf. Tao 2000). However, *hēshuǐ* and *chīshuǐ* imply a very different construal of the mouth-related event. *Hēshuǐ* [drink water] emphasizes the manner of consumption, where the water moves through the mouth in a continuous, smooth and unimpeded way (in order to quench thirst). In contrast, *chīshuǐ* [eat water], in its basic meaning, focuses on the drinking activity as a 'basic need in life' (Ye 2010), as in a phrase like *chīshuǐ nán* 'the difficulty in finding water to drink'. *Chī* can also go with various watery substances, such as *xīfàn* 'rice or millet gruel' and *zhōu* 'congee, porridge', that are a regular part of the Chinese diet. Using *chī* in this way places emphasis on the eating event as a whole and on having these foodstuffs as a source of nourishment.

Second, nouns which refer to pills and capsules always collocate with *chī* in Mandarin, which seems to suggest that the process of chewing may not have the same status in the Chinese conceptualization as it does in English *eat*. Third, breast milk always collocates with *chī*, but not with *hē*. The lexicalized item *chīnǎi* [eat milk] 'suck breast' once again places the emphasis on the life-sustaining role of the consumption, since for babies, mother's milk can be thought of as the sole source of nourishment.

In support of her contention that *chī* is undifferentiated between solid and liquid, but on the other hand emphasizes the life-sustaining function, Ye (2010) adduces evidence from figurative expressions. In this, she is taking a lead from Newman (1997), who argued that many figurative uses of English *eat* originated in the destructive implications of chewing as a semantic component. Ye points out that such extensions are rare in Mandarin Chinese, while, on the other hand, the language has a wealth of compounds and fixed expressions connecting *chī* with life and with 'making a living'. One cluster involves *chī* in combination with *fàn* 'cooked rice' or 'meal'. *Chīfàn* can also mean 'make a living', 'keep alive', and 'live on/off'. Hence, *yǒu/méi fàn chī* [have/not.have rice eat] can mean 'have/not have means for living' and *chī fàn nán* [eat meal difficult] can mean 'it's difficult to make a living'. Some more specific examples include: *kào dǎliè chīfàn* [rely hunting eat.meal] 'rely on hunting for a living'; *chī xiànchéngfàn* [eat ready-made.meal] 'enjoy the fruits of somebody else's labour'. The verb *chī* can also take words for non-edible things, or even people, as objects where they specify the very means for making a living. For example: *chī láobǎo* [eat labour.insurance] 'depend on welfare benefits'; *chī láoběn* [eat old.capital] 'rest on one's laurels'; *chī fùmǔ* [eat parents] 'live off one's parents'.

The following is based closely on Ye's (2010) explication for *chī*. Compared with English *eating*, it has a number of interesting features, which are commented on below.

Yǒurén X zài chī dōngxi Y *'Someone X was 'eating' something Y':*

LEXICO-SYNTACTIC FRAME

a.   someone X was doing something to something Y with the mouth [m] for some time

because of this, something was happening to this something at the same time

at the same time, this someone could feel something in the body because of this

PROTOTYPICAL MOTIVATIONAL SCENARIO

b.   at many times when someone does this to something, this someone does it because it is like this:

– this someone wants this something to be inside their body because this someone does not want to feel something bad in their body

c.   – people know that if someone does not do something like this for a long time, this someone cannot live

MANNER

d.   when someone does this to something, the same thing happens many times it happens like this:

– this someone does something to this something with the hands [m]

– at the same time, this someone does something to it with the mouth [m]

– because of this, after this, part of this something is for a short time inside this someone's mouth [m]

– after this, this someone does something else to it with the mouth [m]

– because of this, after this, it is not inside this someone's mouth [m] anymore, it is somewhere else inside this someone's body for some time

This explication for *chī* differs from that of English *eat* in that it does not contain the component 'this something is not something like water'. On the other hand, it adds a component to the prototypical motivation, that the actor has a bodily based motivation—'this someone does not want to feel something bad in their body.' An even greater difference is an entirely different component, labelled as (c) in the explication: 'people know that if someone does not do something like this for a long time, this someone cannot live.' This reflects the special status of the *chī* act, highlighting its life-sustaining function. In the 'manner bundle', *chī* does not contain a 'chewing' component, and the absence of any such component, Ye (2010) argues, reflects a more total interpretation of the 'eating' experience for Mandarin *chī*.

Incidentally, Ye's (2010) study also addresses the situation in another Sinitic language, Shanghai Wu, also known as Shanghainese. This is spoken in the metropolitan area of Shanghai by approximately 14 million native speakers. In Shanghai Wu, a single lexical item *chyq*, a cognate of *chī*, is used to describe any activity involving the intake of foodstuffs, liquid and non-liquid, and it also applies to smoking tobacco, etc. In effect, any activity where substances are introduced into the mouth, go down the throat, and end up inside the body can be described as *chyq*. To account for this, Ye (2010) postulates that the prototypical motivation is to ingest 'parts' of the consumed object. But this is another story.

9.3 Complex physical activities: *cutting* and *chopping*

So far the physical activity verbs we've looked at have been purely bodily, in the sense that one can perform them with one's body alone, without the aid of any tools, instruments, or the like. In this section, we take on these more complex physical activity verbs, choosing for the sake of example English *cut* and *chop* and their nearest counterparts in several other languages. Needless to say, we are not interested in the specific verbs *cutting* and *chopping* alone: they stand for a whole class of complex physical activity verbs, with dozens or hundreds of members. The involvement of an 'instrument' (as it is termed in linguistics) in activities like these means that the semantic template needs to be elaborated: to characterize the nature of an appropriate instrument (e.g. something with a sharp edge, something heavy, something with a long handle), how the instrument is used (e.g. how it is held, whether it is used repetitively, what degree of control the agent can exercise over its movements), and how the instrument exercises its ongoing effect on the object. The treatment largely follows Goddard and Wierzbicka (2009).

Not surprisingly, perhaps, it turns out that the details of the instrument and how it is used are analogous to the manner section of the template for purely bodily activity verbs; i.e. instead of describing what an actor does with parts of the body, we need to describe what the actor does with an instrument that is suitable for the purpose at hand. As shown in Figure 9.1, the three-part macro-structure remains the same, except that in place of the manner section, there are three subsections titled INSTRUMENT, USING THE INSTRUMENT, and WHAT IS HAPPENING TO THE OBJECT.

But we are getting ahead of ourselves. Before getting to the instrument-related sections of the template, we ought to consider the lexico-syntactic frame and prototypical motivational scenarios for complex physical activity verbs. It turns out that these sections too are more complex than the corresponding sections of the explications we have seen so far.

> LEXICO-SYNTACTIC FRAME for *cut, chop,* and many other complex physical activity verbs:
>   someone X is doing something to something for some time
>   because of this, something is happening at the same time to this something
>   as this someone wants
>   this someone is doing it with something else Z

Note the presence of the instrument item (Z) in the third line. From a technical point of view, this must be characterized not just as 'something', but as 'something else', in order to avoid it getting confused with the object.

Purely bodily activities, e.g. *walk, run, eat, drink*	Complex physical activities involving instruments, e.g. *cut, chop, grind*
LEXICO-SYNTACTIC FRAME	LEXICO-SYNTACTIC FRAME
PROTOTYPICAL MOTIVATIONAL SCENARIO	PROTOTYPICAL MOTIVATIONAL SCENARIO
MANNER	• INSTRUMENT, INCL. USING THE INSTRUMENT AND WHAT IS HAPPENING TO THE OBJECT

Figure 9.1 Template structure for two subclasses of physical activity verbs

The second part of the frame says that there is a resulting concurrent effect on the object, and furthermore, that this takes place 'as this someone wants'; that is, the effect on the object is controlled.

The prototypical motivational scenario characterizes the activity as something people typically do because they have formed the intention of achieving a certain effect on a particular object that they have in front of them—to divide it into two pieces, to separate off a number of small pieces, or to reduce it entirely to small pieces, and so on. A schematic representation is given below.

> PROTOTYPICAL MOTIVATIONAL SCENARIO for *cut*, *chop*, and many other
> complex physical activity verbs:
>> at many times when someone does this to something, this someone does it
>> because it is like this:
>>> a short time before, this someone thought like this about it:
>>>> 'I don't want this something to be one thing anymore, I want it to
>>>> be two things
>>>> . . .'

The structure is more complex than the corresponding prototypical motivational scenarios for *walk*, *run*, *eat*, *drink*, and the like. For these other verbs, it was enough to indicate what a prototypical actor wants to achieve, but with *cut*, *chop*, and others, it seems necessary to set out an intention; and the notion of intention involves thinking as well as wanting— something like a conscious wanting.

9.3.1 English cut

Let's see how this works out with English *cut*, as in examples like: *She was cutting the cake* or *He was cutting some meat*. I will present the full explication, then we can review some of its significant features.

*Someone X is **cutting** thing Y (e.g. some paper, a cake) with thing Z:*
LEXICO-SYNTACTIC FRAME

a.   someone X is doing something to something Y for some time
    because of this, something is happening at the same time to this some-
      thing as this someone wants
    this someone is doing it with something else Z

b.   at many times when someone does this to something, this someone does
     it because it is like this:
       a short time before, this someone thought like this about it:
         'I don't want this something to be one thing anymore, I want it to
           be two things
         because of this, I want to do something to this something for some
           time
         when I do this, I want something to happen to this something all
           the time as I want'

c.   when someone does this to something, it happens like this:
     – this someone holds [m] part of something else with one hand [m] all
       the time
     – some parts of this other something are sharp [m]
     – the sharp [m] parts of this other thing touch this thing for some time
     – during this time this someone's hand [m] moves as this someone wants
     – because of this, the sharp [m] parts [m] of this other thing touch this
       thing in some places as this someone wants

d.   because of this, something happens to this thing in these places as this
     someone wants
     because of this, after this, this thing is not like it was before

As one can see, the prototypical motivation starts with the actor's
thought that:

'I don't want this something to be one thing anymore, I want it to be two things'

The second part of this statement might meet with the objection that
(obviously) one can *cut* an object into more than two pieces, but this
objection does not seem to be valid. For one thing, the reference to 'two
things' is embedded in a prototypical frame ('at many times when someone
does this . . .'), so there is no claim that *cutting* is always intended to
produce two pieces. But just as importantly, even when cutting something
into multiple pieces, the first 'cut' would normally separate the object into
two, and the same can be said about every subsequent 'cut'.

As well as the intention of wanting to divide something into two things,
the explication presents the prototypical actor as envisaging an operation
that takes some time, and as wanting a high degree of control over the
separation process:

because of this, I want to do something to this something for some time
when I do this, I want something to happen to this something all the time as I
want

Cutting is very different in this respect from *tearing*, for example, which
might also result in separate pieces but which normally does not allow the
agent control over the exact form of these pieces.

Now look at section (c) in the explication, which deals with the instrument and how it is used. It says that the instrument must have some sharp
parts, and that the instrument can be held in such a way that as the agent's
hand moves under the agent's control, so the instrument as a whole moves
under the agent's control. The wording here is compatible with different
kinds of cutting tools, including both knives and scissors. This arrangement
means that when the sharp parts of the instrument are in contact with the
object, the agent can exercise control over the movement of the sharp part.
Finally, section (d) makes it clear that the moving contact with the sharp
part of the instrument has an ongoing and, so to speak, permanent effect on
the object.

You may have noticed that this explication for *cutting* does not cover
every use of *cut*. In particular, since it deals with intentional and controlled cutting, it does not cover examples such as *I cut my foot on a rock*
or *He cut himself shaving*, which are non-intentional and do not imply
any potential result of division into two or more parts; nor does it cover
sentences which have an inanimate object as subject, e.g. *The glass cut his
hand*. In fact, there is ample formal and semantic evidence that these uses
are instances of distinct (albeit related) meanings and they will be covered
in section 9.5.

Before that, however, it is useful to compare *cut* with a closely related
verb, such as *chop*. To make matters more interesting, we will look not only
at English *chop* but also at its nearest equivalents in two other languages:
Polish and Japanese.

9.3.2 English chop, Polish rąbać, Japanese kizamu

Chop differs from *cut* first of all in the prototypical motivational scenario,
which can be stated as below. Notice that the prototypical intention is to
produce, not two things, but 'many small things' from something that

starts off, at least from the prototypical actor's point of view, as 'something big'. There is also no intention to maintain a high degree of control over the division process.

'I don't want this something to be one thing any more
I want this one big thing to be many small things'

Turning to the INSTRUMENT, unlike as with *cutting*, where the instrument could be simply a piece of sharp rock or glass, with *chopping* it has to be something with two parts: a long part (typically, a handle) and a part with a sharp edge. As for the manner of using the instrument, the agent holds the long part, such that when the person's hand moves, the instrument moves accordingly.

From here on, yet more differences between *chopping* and *cutting* become apparent. To begin with, the action of *chopping* is repetitive, i.e. the same thing happens many times, and this is obviously connected with the intention to produce many pieces. You will see in the explication below that the iterative aspect is dealt with in the same fashion as the iterative movements of *walking* and *running*. The trajectory of the instrument is then described: it first moves for a very short time in such a way that it comes to be briefly 'far above' where it started from. The specification 'far above' indicates that the instrument is raised relatively high. Then it moves in another way so that it is no longer above that place, and after that the sharp edge of the instrument comes into contact with the object.

After this, the sharp edge penetrates into the object for a very short time and this produces an effect on the object concerned. This effect takes place (or rather, is thought of as taking place) each time in a single moment.

The way in which this process and its effect are depicted—in particular, the quick movement of the instrument up and down, and the penetration of the sharp edge of the instrument into the hard object—implies considerable force. Nothing is said here about a lack of precision in the action or about a lack of control over the form of the resulting pieces, but the absence of components indicating such precision and control accounts for the differences in this respect between *chopping* and *cutting*.

Here then is the full explication of *chopping*.

*Someone (X) is **chopping** thing Y (e.g. some wood) with thing Z:*
LEXICO-SYNTACTIC FRAME

a. someone X is doing something to something Y for some time
    because of this, something is happening at the same time to this something
        as this someone wants
    this someone is doing it with something else Z
PROTOTYPICAL MOTIVATIONAL SCENARIO

b. at many times when someone does this to something, this someone does it
        because it is like this:
    this something is something hard [m]
    a short time before, this someone thought like this about it:
        'I don't want this something to be one thing anymore
        I want this one big thing to be many small things'
INSTRUMENT

c. when someone does this to something, this someone holds [m] something
        else all the time
    this other something has two parts: one of these two parts has a sharp [m]
        edge [m], the other part is a long [m] part
    this someone holds [m] the long [m] part
    at the same time this someone does the same thing with this other thing
        many times
    it happens like this:
    – this other thing moves for a very short time in one way
    – after this, it is for a very short time far above the place where it was before
    – after this, it moves for a very short time in another way
    – after this, it is not above this place anymore
    – at this time, the sharp [m] part of this thing touches something in one
        place
    – after this it is for a very short time inside this thing
    the same thing happens many times
WHAT IS HAPPENING TO THE OBJECT

d. because of this, something happens to this thing many times
    when it happens, it happens in one moment
    because of this, after this, this other thing is not like it was before

One possible objection to this explication concerns the appropriateness
of characterizing the object in the prototypical motivational scenario as
'something hard [m]'. Isn't this inconsistent with the fact that *chopping*
often occurs in culinary contexts, where the things being chopped can be

rather soft, such as tomatoes, mushrooms, garlic, various herbs, and meats, such as chicken? Such usages in themselves do not necessarily pose a problem, however, because the relevant component ('at many times when someone does this to something, this someone does it because it is like this: ... this something is something hard [m]') does not restrict *chopping* to hard items. It merely characterizes *chopping* by way of a frequently occurring 'reference situation' involving hard items. The real question is: given that *chopping* in culinary contexts frequently collocates with soft items, how can one be sure that the reference situation spelt out in the prototypical motivational scenario is indeed centred on 'something hard [m]'?

Three points can be raised. The first relates to the internal logic of the explication. The fact that the object in the prototypical scenario is 'something hard [m]' is what motivates and ties together several other aspects of the explication, such as the need for an instrument with a long handle and the fact that this instrument is raised relatively high above the object being chopped. Both of these provisions enable more force to be brought to bear on the object. A second argument is more subjective and intuitive. In culinary contexts, one would often have a choice between using the word *chopping* and other expressions, such as *cutting up*, *mincing*, *dicing*, etc. In some cases, the very same activity could be described in different ways. Choosing the word *chopping* seems to imply greater attention to the 'forcefulness' of the activity—and this property has its semantic roots in the reference situation in which the object is 'something hard [m]'. A third point is that the collocation with *wood* (*chopping wood*) appears to be most psychologically salient of all collocations, which testifies to its prototypicality from a cognitive point of view. In this connection, note the existence of the derivate *wood-chopping*, and the absence of any comparable words such as **tomato-chopping*, **herb-chopping*, etc.

Another objection to the *chopping* explication—more a gut reaction than a principled objection—is that it must be too long. How can all that detail be part of the meaning of a single verb? One response is to point out that every detail appears to be motivated by the requirements of internal consistency and logic and/or by links to the range of use of the word *chop* in comparison with other semantically similar words (*cut*, *slice*, *hack*, etc.). Another justification for the degree of semantic detail comes from comparing *chop* not with other English words, but with its equivalents or near-equivalents in other languages. These comparisons show how small details of semantic content explain slightly but discernibly different ranges of use. We will first consider the Polish verb *rąbać* and then the Japanese verb *kizamu*. Both are the normal dictionary equivalents to English *chop*.

English *chop* and Polish *rąbać* are very similar in meaning, yet there are subtle differences in their respective ranges of use and typical collocations. The Polish verb is used above all in relation to wood and ice. It cannot be used to translate phrases like *chopping vegetables* or *chopping onions*, and while it can be used to translate *chopping meat*, this is only in relation to very big chunks of meat attached to bones (normally with reference to a butcher). The action of *rąbać* can be done with an axe or with a heavy butcher's knife, but not with an ordinary kitchen knife.

To account for these similarities and differences, Goddard and Wierzbicka (2009) assigned both words the same lexico-syntactic frame, as given above. The prototypical motivational scenario for both words is nearly identical. It involves the prototypical actor forming the thought 'I don't want this something to be one thing anymore, I want this one big thing to be many small things.' The nature of this goal is of course linked to the iterative manner of *chopping* as an activity.

An important difference between the English and Polish motivational scenarios is that for English the prototypical object is characterized as 'something hard [m]', whereas for Polish it is 'something very hard [m]'. The INSTRUMENT section is also very similar, referring (roughly speaking) to a long-handled object with a sharp edge, but the Polish version includes an additional component, specifying that the instrument is 'something heavy [m]'. The MANNER section too is very similar (referring, essentially, to repeatedly raising and bringing down the edge of the axe, etc. onto the object). The significant difference is that for *chop* the instrument is described as being raised 'far above' the object, whereas for *rąbać* the corresponding specification is 'very far above', thus depicting the more extreme 'swing' of *rąbać*.

Turning now to the Japanese verb *kizamu*, we can note firstly that its prototypical and most frequent uses are in relation to food preparation. Indeed, though *kizamu* can be used to translate phrases like *chopping vegetables*, it cannot be used to translate phrases like *chopping wood*, i.e. its range is restricted in the opposite direction from Polish *rąbać*. This suggests that the desired outcome of *kizamu* is more accurately described as 'very small', rather than simply 'small', and also, that the raising of the instrument should be described as bringing it simply 'above' where it started from, rather than 'far above' (as with *chopping*) or 'very far above' (as with *rąbać*).

Furthermore, the types of instrument with which one can perform the more small-scale action of *kizamu* are not quite as specific as with English *chopping* and *rąbać:* it is not necessary to describe the prototypical instrument as having a 'long part' which is grasped by the agent's hand. Rather, it is enough (as with English *cut*) to state that one part has a sharp edge, and that the agent controls the instrument by grasping 'another part'.

One further difference between Japanese, on the one hand, and English and Polish, on the other, may concern the nature of the impact. In both English and Polish it is envisaged that the sharp edge of the instrument will penetrate into the object—a description which implies a considerable force (greater in Polish than in English, because in Polish the instrument is heavy and the arm is raised higher, but nonetheless in both cases quite considerable). In Japanese, on the other hand, it appears that the contact between the sharp edge of the tool and the object can be quite superficial. This conjecture is supported by the fact that *kizamu* can be extended to paper (i.e. if some paper is being 'chopped' into very small pieces with a sharp-edged instrument, this too can be described with the verb *kizamu*) and also by the fact that *kizamu* is often used in relation to flat thin things like *nori* 'seaweed'.

At this point, it can be seen that the overall semantic structure of *chop*, *rąbać*, and *kizamu* is very similar. They all involve an intention of transforming something relatively big into many small things, an instrument with a sharp edge, a repeated movement of a hand holding this instrument, the raising and lowering of the instrument, and the repeated momentary contacts of the sharp edge with the object. The differences mainly concern details about the prototypical object and instrument, and the manner of using the instrument.

The cultural underpinnings of the semantic differences between *chop*, *rąbać*, and *kizamu* are not too difficult to see. In Poland, with its long, cold winters, the need to chop wood for the fire is extremely salient in living memory, and so is the need to 'chop' ice, in particular, in order to create a *przerębel*, where fishing can be done in winter under a surface covered by ice. On the other hand, the type of activity described in English as 'chopping vegetables' was relatively unknown in Poland until recent times, since apart from cabbage, the only vegetables which were commonly eaten in traditional times were potatoes, beetroots, and carrots, which are usually cooked whole, and there is no tradition of mixed salads which might involve 'chopping'. Thus, a concept like *rąbać*, which implies the use of great physical force, is (so to speak) more worthy of lexicalization than one like English *chop*, which implies only a modicum of force.

As for the Japanese verb *kizamu*, it seems to reflect Japanese culinary traditions, where a wide variety of elegant and aesthetically pleasing dishes involve the use of very small pieces of food which can be held daintily between finger and thumb or elegantly lifted to the mouth with chopsticks. Given such traditions, a concept like *kizamu* is more useful in the Japanese lexicon than one like *rąbać*, or even *chop*. (Given that Japan also has cold winters with snow, it may well be asked: what words and expressions do the Japanese use to speak about chopping wood? Obviously, *kizamu* would not be suitable. It seems that chopping wood is not often done in Japan. Even in remote mountain areas, people generally collect dead branches on the ground (or, these days, buy wood at the store). The verb normally used in Japanese for chopping logs is *waru* 'break (something hard)'.)

These examples, and others in Goddard and Wierzbicka (2009), indicate how the semantics of similar 'cutting and chopping' verbs in several languages can be captured in a similar systematic fashion: i.e. using a common semantic template, with some identical components, some similar-yet-different components, and some additional components.

9.4 Perfective uses of physical activity verbs

As mentioned earlier, the standard view in Russian lexicology is that the imperfective uses of physical activity verbs are semantically prior to their perfective uses. NSM research concurs. Of course, this issue presents itself in a particularly pressing fashion in Russian and other Slavic languages, because in these languages most verbs (including all physical activity verbs) exist in two morphologically distinct forms: imperfective and perfective. Semantic analysis shows, however, that the basic issue is equally relevant to English and other languages without such a clear-cut morphological division. Imperfective *cutting* (cutting-in-progress) and *chopping* (chopping-in-progress) are semantically simpler than perfective uses of *cut* and *chop*. Why? Because the imperfective merely implies a potential outcome, whereas perfective uses go further in specifying that a certain outcome has been achieved.

If we take the imperfective or durative forms of physical activity verbs as basic, we can devise non-circular explications for them, as shown above. It is then not too difficult to explicate perfective uses in terms of imperfective *cutting*, and other elements. The explication below shows how this can be done for the so-called Simple Past tense in English. The sentence being explicated is *She cut the apple (into four pieces)*. As one can see, the explication relies on 'cutting [d]' as a derivational base. The agent's action is depicted as involving a process of 'cutting'—component (b). This process produces an effect, i.e. 'because of this, something happened to this thing at the same time'—component (c). Equally integral to the Simple Past (perfective) usage is the accomplishment of an overall result, which is given in component (d): 'because of this, after this, this thing was not one thing anymore (it was four things).'

She cut the apple (into four pieces):
a. she did something to something (the apple) at this time
b. she did it to this something like this: she was cutting [d] it for some time
c. because of this, something happened to this something (the apple) at the same time as she wanted
d. because of this, after this, it was not one thing anymore, (it was four things)

As one would expect, the same pattern works for past tense uses of *chop*, as in the explication below. In fact, it would be appropriate to see these explications as examples of a semantic template for Simple Past uses of English physical activity verbs.

She chopped the wood:
a. she did something to something (the wood) at this time
b. she did it to this something like this: she was chopping [d] it for some time
c. because of this, something happened to this something (the wood) at the same time as she wanted
d. because of this, after this, it wasn't many big things anymore, it was many small things

The basic pattern shown in the two explications above applies to most—but not all—Simple Past sentences with physical activity verbs, providing that the subject is a volitional human agent. There are also some non-prototypical examples, such as *She cut the thread*, where due to the nature of the patient the action is carried out more or less instantaneously. In cases like this, it wouldn't make sense to say that the subject had performed some 'cutting' for some time. A slightly different structure is needed, as shown below. It describes the process not as literal 'cutting', but as LIKE what one does when one cuts something.

She cut the thread (at this time):
a.   she did something to something (the thread) at this time
b.   she did it to this something like someone does something to something
     when this someone is cutting [d] this something
c.   something happened to this something at the same time because of it
    it happened in one moment
d.   because of this, after this, it was not one thing anymore, it was two
    things

The same pattern can explain Simple Past tense sentences like *She chopped the onion in two* and *She chopped the onion in half*. Recall that the explication for *chopping* includes a reference to a prototypical actor wanting to produce 'many small things' and it also depicts *chopping* as a repetitive activity. How can this be reconciled with sentences like those just mentioned, where only two pieces are produced in a single 'go'? It can be done as shown below. In component (b), the actor's action is depicted as similar to what someone does when someone is chopping something.

She chopped the onion in two:
a.   she did something to something (the onion) at this time
b.   she did it to this something like someone does something to something
     when this someone is chopping [d] this something
c.   something happened to this something at the same time because of it
    it happened in one moment
d.   because of this, after this, it was not one thing any more, it was two
    things

Thus, although a perfective sentence with *chopped* in the Simple Past can include a specification that it resulted in only two pieces, it nonetheless implies that the process which led to that result was akin to the process of *chopping*—i.e. akin to a process conceptualized in terms of a prototypical scenario involving a transformation of one big thing into many small things.

Similarly, for a sentence like *He chopped the tree down*, the result may entail not only that the tree is not one thing any more, but also that most of the tree is down on the ground, below where it was before. Likewise, a sentence like *He chopped the onion up* (with particle *up*) may imply that the whole onion was involved and that the resulting pieces were very small. These added effects and nuances come from the particles associated with the verb (*chop down*, *chop up*, etc.).

In short, Simple Past (perfective) uses can be explicated in terms of the imperfective. To attempt to proceed in the opposite direction, however— e.g. to explicate imperfective *cutting* in terms of perfective *cut*—leads to circularity and confusion. Why? Because *cutting* presents a certain action-in-progress but it does not presuppose a final result. Perfective *cut*, on the other hand, presupposes the previous action-in-progress (*cutting*) and adds the notion of an accomplished result. For this reason, analyses which take the non-durative *cut* as basic usually end up with blatantly circular definitions such as 'to cut = to produce a cut (on something)' (cf. Guerssel et al. 1985; Hale and Keyser 1986). The question 'What does *a cut* mean?' is then not asked, and the meaning of the durative form *cutting* is not raised either. Presumably, few would claim that *He was cutting meat* means 'he was producing a cut on some meat'.

To judge by linguistic evidence, physical activities—focused on a goal and extended in time—seem to be more salient in human experience than physical acts with an immediate result. Examples of the former type include activities such as 'cutting', 'chopping', 'grinding', 'mowing', 'kneading', 'cooking', 'digging', 'painting', 'slicing', 'peeling', and so on, while examples of the latter type include acts like 'killing' and 'breaking'. It can hardly be an accident that human languages tend to have extensive sets of verbs designating physical activities; while those areas of the verbal lexicon which designate 'acts' in a strict sense are chiefly directed at people or at other living things, rather than at physical objects. For example, many languages have extensive sets of verbs designating speech acts (rather than 'speech activities') or other interpersonal acts (e.g. 'kill', 'hit', 'kiss'). Presumably, the underlying reason is that to achieve a desired impact on the physical world one usually has to engage in activities of some duration ('doing something to something for some time'), often involving an instrument. It is often much simpler, in terms of time and effort, to make an impact on a person or other living thing.

9.5 Constructional variants (syntactic alternations)

In addition to ordinary Simple Past (perfective) sentences, there are also certain Simple Past uses in English with distinctive semantic and grammatical properties, such as those exemplified in the three examples below. It must be emphasized that we are dealing specifically with an English verb, because the following frames do not necessarily have equivalents in other languages. Since Fillmore (1968), sentences like these have been much studied in the literature on SYNTACTIC ALTERNATIONS (also termed 'argument alternations' and/or 'valency alternations'); for reviews, see Levin and Rappaport Hovav (2005) and Tenny and Pustejovsky (2000).

> *She cut herself on the hand.*
> *I cut my face while shaving.*
> *He cut his foot on a rock.*

These three sentences belong to three separate, albeit closely related lexico-grammatical constructions, but they all share two properties which decisively set them apart from the basic meaning of *cutting* as explicated above. First, they do not normally occur in imperfective versions, e.g. **She was cutting herself on the hand, *I was cutting my face while shaving, *He was cutting his foot on a rock*. Second, sentences like those shown above normally imply unintentional or accidental actions. These two properties (syntactic and semantic) of course make perfect sense together, because as we have seen, imperfective *cutting* implies controlled activity ('as this someone wants') and this would be inconsistent with an unintentional act.

We will now consider each of the three sentence types individually. In addition to the properties just mentioned, sentences like *She cut herself on the hand* are characterized by the presence of the reflexive pronoun in object position and by the optional presence of a 'locus of bodily contact' phrase with preposition *on*. The implication is that the subject was doing something for some time, and that on account of this, something happened to him or her, because something sharp came into contact with part of the subject's body, not as the subject wanted. These aspects are spelt out in components (a)–(c) in the following explication. The unintended sharp contact has an effect ('because of this, something happened to this part of this someone's body'), as stated in (d). The direct connection with *cutting* is provided by component (e): 'it happened to it like something happens to something when someone is cutting [d] this something.' That is, the manner in which the body-part is affected is likened to the manner in which something happens to something when it is being cut. 'Cutting [d]' functions as a derivational base in the explication.

She (X) cut herself on the hand (while …):
a. someone (X) was doing something for some time
b. because of this, something happened to this someone during this time
c. it happened because something sharp [m] touched part of this someone's body not as this someone wanted
d. because of this, something happened to this part of this someone's body at this time
     it happened in one moment
e. it happened to it like something happens to something when someone is cutting [d] this something

Though similar in many respects, sentences like *I cut my face while shaving* are formally different in that the affected body-part appears as the direct object and there is no reflexive pronoun. Another example is: *I cut my finger when I was grating the carrots.* Verbs like *shave* and *grate* imply the use of something sharp in an instrument-like fashion:

He (X) cut his face while shaving:
a. someone (X) was doing something for some time with something sharp [m]
b. at some time during that time, this sharp [m] thing touched part of this someone's body not as this someone wanted
c. because of this, something happened to part of this someone's body at this time it happened in one moment
d. it happened to it like something happens to something when someone is cutting [d] this something

We also have to deal with the third construction, as illustrated above with *He cut his foot on a rock.* Another example is: *He cut his hand on the barbed wire.* As with the other two constructions, it normally implies an accidental event, but in this case the *on*-phrase indicates a sharp object present in the physical situation, which happens to come into contact with part of the subject's body. It is not an instrument or 'quasi-instrument' under the control of the actor. Nor, relatedly, does the sharp thing have to move in order to produce the reported result; typically it is the person's body-part which moves. Nevertheless, the event is similar enough in

manner and effect that it can readily be likened to what happens to
something when someone is cutting it, as specified in component (d).

He (X) cut his foot on a rock:
a. someone (X) was doing something for some time in a place
    where there was something sharp [m]
b. at some time during that time, part of this someone's body touched this
    sharp [m] thing not as this someone wanted
c. because of this, something happened to this part of this someone's body
    at this time
    it happened in one moment
d. it happened to it like something happens to something
    when someone is cutting [d] this something

Finally we look briefly at sentences like those below, in which an inanimate object appears in the subject position.

*As she pushed through the dense bush, the razor-sharp leaves cut her face
terribly.*
I was clearing the pieces away and one of them cut my hand.

Compared with the previous examples, such sentences are even vaguer
and more unspecified as to the nature of the causing situation, i.e. how
exactly it comes about that the sharp thing denoted by the subject comes
into contact with part of the patient's body. It could be that something
present in the physical environment moves so as to touch the patient's
body, or it could be that the person is handling or otherwise using the sharp
item. The scenario encapsulated in this construction, as explicated below,
simply takes off from the proposition that 'something sharp [m] touched
part of this someone's body, not as this someone wanted', as in component
(a). This leads to a consequent effect on that body-part, as per component
(b), which can be likened to what happens to something when someone is
cutting it, as in component (c).

The glass cut her (X's) hand:
a. something sharp [m] touched part of this someone's (X's) body,
    not as this someone wanted
b. because of this, something happened to this part of this someone's body
    at this time
    it happened in one moment
c. it happened to it like something happens to something
    when someone is cutting [d] this something

In summary, in addition to its normal transitive frame, the English verb *cut* can appear in a number of other constructional frames, each expressing a different and somewhat specialized meaning. On account of the semantic particularities of each construction, it is impossible to cover the full range of use of *cut* with a single explication. On the contrary, descriptive adequacy demands that each specifiable lexico-grammatical frame be assigned its own distinct semantic explication, so that the similarities and differences between them can be made fully explicit. When this is done, however, it becomes apparent that the productive imperfective frame with a physical substance or thing as the direct object, functions as a derivational base in the other explications, by way of the analogy clauses which feature in the explications shown in this section.

The NSM approach on this issue is broadly consistent with constructional accounts of syntactic alternations in the works of Rappaport Hovav and Levin (1998), Goldberg (1995), Croft (1998; 2001), Jackendoff (2002), and others. The main differences are, first, that NSM researchers insist that the imperfective functions as the root meaning vis-à-vis the other constructions, and second, the use of an analogy structure as a way of incorporating an imperfective meaning into schemas for the other constructional frames.

Key technical terms

[d] derivational base	manner
imperfective	prototypical motivational scenario
instrument	syntactic alternations
lexico-syntactic frame	

Exercises and discussion questions

† next to a problem means that a solution or some commentary can be found at the end of this book.

1†. Discuss the semantics of the English verb *nibble*, as used in sentences like: *How come you're only nibbling at your food?*. Try to identify some semantic components that differentiate *nibbling (at)* from *eating*.

2†. In English, the normally transitive verb *eat* can also be used without any explicit object, in a so-called 'pseudo-intransitive' construction, e.g. *He was eating*. Most transitive verbs do not permit this, e.g. **He was breaking*. Discuss what is going on with pseudo-intransitive uses of *eat*. Does the verb have the same meaning in this construction as in its regular transitive uses? Are there any constraints on the pseudo-intransitive use?

3†. As you know, Kalam and Warlpiri are languages that have a single verb whose meaning does not differentiate between what are categorized in English as distinct activities ('eating' and 'drinking'). Something similar is found in Shanghainese. Can you think of any possible cultural and/or lifestyle reasons that may help account for this phenomenon, at least in some instances?

4†. Danish has three basic verbs that can be used, in different contexts, to translate English 'cut': *skærer, klipper, hugger*. Examine the following characteristic collocations for each of them and hypothesize about how their explications may differ:

Skærer is used with words like: *løg* 'onions', *tomater* 'tomatoes', *gulerødder* 'carrots', *kager* 'cakes', *kød* 'meat'.
Klipper is used with: *hår* 'hair', *hæk* 'privet hedge', *julehjerter* 'christmas hearts' (Christmas decorations made from glazed paper or cardboard), *purløg* 'chives', *karse* 'garden cress', *roser* 'roses', *papir* 'paper'.
Hugger is used with: *brænde* 'wood', *sten* 'stone', *is* 'ice'.

5†. Try your hand at stating the prototypical motivational scenario for the English verb *to dig* (as in *He was digging in the garden* or *She was digging a hole*).

6†. Now try to formulate a set of MANNER components for *digging*.

7. Many languages lack verbs that correspond to common generic physical activity or physical action verbs of English—such as *carry*, *break*, and *hit*. Do some research on a language other than English and report your findings. In stating the meanings of the verbs involved, don't use any words that you know do not have equivalents in the language concerned.

For example, if you find a language with four 'verbs of carrying' (but without any general verb corresponding to 'carry'), try to gloss the meanings of the four verbs without using 'carry'. Do not resort to other even more abstract words, such as 'transport' or 'convey'.

10

Causatives

A causative is an expression in which an event (the caused event) is depicted as taking place because someone does something or because something happens. As in many languages, causatives in English fall into three broad divisions on formal grounds. Analytic causatives are syntactic constructions with separate verbs such as *make* (*I made him do it*), *get* (*I got him to do it*), and *have* (*I had him do it*). Morphological causatives are created by processes such as suffixation by *-en* and *-ify* (e.g. *widen*, *blacken*, *nullify*). Lexical causatives are words like *kill*, *send*, and *feed* which seem to be related in meaning to other words (such as *die*, *go*, and *eat*), without there being any visible sign of the meaning relation in the morphological make-up of the causative word itself.

As we pass from analytic to morphological to lexical, we find increasing 'semantic cohesion', in some sense, between the causing event and the caused event; for example, the analytic expression *cause to die* suggests a looser and more indirect causal link than that conveyed by the lexical causative *kill*. One of the challenges for a good account of causatives is to articulate and explain such subtle distinctions in a clear and verifiable way. Another is to explain the equally subtle differences between the causatives of different languages.

10.1   How basic is BECAUSE?

Although linguists have tended to treat causation as a primitive in their descriptive work, there have been various attempts to decompose it into simpler notions.

10.1.1 Classical attempts to analyse causation

Many philosophers have contended that whatever causation is, it is created by the mind rather than being a matter of fact in the external world. David Hume (1902 [1777]), in his *Enquiries Concerning the Human Understanding* (sections 4–7), insisted that causes and effects are merely events which we find, in our experience, to be 'constantly conjoined'. He maintained that our impression that there is a 'necessary connection' between one thing and another is an illusion. J. S. Mill (1960 [1843]) also tried to explain causation away in terms of 'invariable sequence', arguing that to say that *A causes B* is just to say that B is immediately followed by A and that all things similar to A are always immediately followed by things similar to B.

From a semantic point of view, these attempts to define causation in terms of invariable sequence run into serious problems. First, in some cases B always and invariably follows A without being caused by A; for example, death invariably follows birth but it would be foolish to say that birth causes death. Second, a causing event may take place at exactly the same time as the caused event; for example, a pencil may be moving because the person holding it is moving his or her hand. Third, both Hume's and Mill's accounts are geared to explaining 'causal laws' rather than everyday uses of the word *because*, and it is hard to see how they could apply to sentences like *He left because she insulted him* or *I married her because I love her*.

Another, more promising, approach is to try to define causation by way of the counterfactual construction, i.e. the grammatical construction in a sentence like *If X hadn't happened, Y wouldn't have happened*. The linguist

Masayoshi Shibatani (1976), for example, first characterizes a 'causative situation' as a relation between two events such that one occurs at t_1 and the other at t_2, after t_1, and the occurrence of the second event is 'wholly dependent' on the occurrence of the first event. He continues:

the dependency of the two events here must be to the extent that it allows the speaker to entertain a counterfactual inference that the caused event would not have taken place at that particular time if the causing event had not taken place, provided that all else had remained the same. (Shibatani 1976: 1)

Essentially, Shibatani is proposing that the notion of 'because' can be decomposed in terms of the counterfactual construction and negation.

Event-Y happened because event-X happened:
if event-X had not happened,
    event-Y would not have happened

The idea of causation as *conditiones sine quibus non* has also been adopted by philosophers such as H. L. A. Hart and A. J. Ayer (cf. Hart and Honoré 1959). Modern logicians like David Lewis (1973) have tried to formalize the notion using the concept of counterfactual implication in the 'closest possible world'.

Anna Wierzbicka once advocated a counterfactual analysis of causation, which is why BECAUSE was not among the semantic primitives which she proposed in the 1970s and 1980s (Wierzbicka 1972; 1980a). She has since rejected this analysis, however, pointing out that even if it is true that *If Mary hadn't met John, she wouldn't have married him*, it does not follow that *Mary married John because she met him*. In other words, a necessary condition is not the same thing as a cause (Wierzbicka 1989: 321). Conversely, it can also be observed that a causal relation may exist without a negative counterfactual necessarily following from it. For example, if my doctor explains that I have developed lung cancer because of smoking, he or she isn't necessarily committed to the claim that if I hadn't smoked I would now be cancer-free.

Lacking an adequate paraphrase for this apparently indispensable notion, NSM researchers have now accepted BECAUSE as a semantic primitive. One notable predecessor, in this respect, was the philosopher Immanuel Kant (1934 [1781]). He included causation, along with time and space, among his 'transcendental notions', insisting that such ideas could not be derived from experience but, on the contrary, are imposed by the mind upon experience.

10.1.2 Talmy and Jackendoff on causation

There have also been attempts to decompose causation from another quarter. The cognitive linguist Leonard Talmy (1985b; 1988; 2000) has developed a scheme for a 'fundamental notional system' which he calls 'force dynamics'. This is supposed to be 'a generalization over the trad-itional linguistic notion of "causative"'' which analyses "causing" into finer primitives' (Talmy 1988: 1–2).

The system is based on the idea of an opposition between two entities which manifest an intrinsic 'force'. One of these entities (the 'Agonist') is foregrounded, that is to say, singled out for focal attention. Opposed to the Agonist is a second, or background, force element (the 'Antagonist'). The salient issue in any force-dynamic scenario is whether the Agonist will be able to 'manifest its force tendency', or whether it will be overcome by a stronger Antagonist. A 'force tendency' may be either toward motion (or, more generally, action) or toward rest (or, more generally, inaction). Talmy depicts force-dynamic scenarios by means of schematic diagrams, the basic elements of which are shown in Figure 10.1.

The most basic force-dynamic patterns, which do not involve change over time, are shown in Figure 10.2. The illustrative sentences are chosen from the domain of motion, but, according to Talmy, they could equally have been drawn from the psychological or social domains. Notice that diagrams (a) and (d) correspond to sentences containing the word *because*. They depict an Agonist with an intrinsic tendency toward rest or motion being overcome by a stronger Antagonist.

Adding another factor—change through time—gives rise to further force-dynamic patterns. In one of these types, the Antagonist, rather than

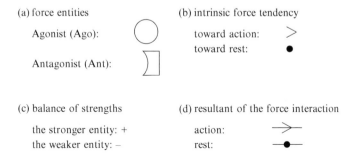

Figure 10.1. The basic elements of Talmy's (1988) 'force dynamics' diagrams

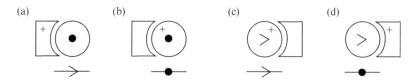

Figure 10.2. Basic force-dynamic patterns: (a) *The ball kept rolling because of the wind blowing on it.* (b) *The shed kept standing despite the gale wind blowing against it.* (c) *The ball kept rolling despite the stiff grass.* (d) *The log kept lying on the incline because of the ridge there*

impinging steadily on the Agonist, enters or leaves this state of impingement. Figure 10.3 shows two such patterns in situations where the Antagonist is stronger. The shifting in time is indicated by the conventions of an arrow for the Antagonist's transition into or out of impingement, and a slash on the resultant line separates the 'before' and 'after' states of activity.

These diagrams are an excellent illustration of a basic semiotic point: that a visual representation cannot—in and of itself—convey a meaning. In order to understand the diagrams, we have to be able to understand the symbolic conventions they use: that the circle represents the Agonist, that > means a 'force tendency towards action', that —•— means a 'resultant of rest', and so on. As argued in Chapter 3, from a semiotic point of view, a diagram never stands alone; it always depends on a system of verbal captions, whether these are explicit or implied.

Actually, Talmy himself demonstrates this point when he explains a generalization about four force-dynamic patterns (Fig. 10.2(a) and (d), Fig. 10.3 (a) and (b)) which can be seen to 'constitute the general causative category':

The four patterns...have in common one property, absent from all other force-dynamic patterns, that emerges from force-dynamic analysis as definitional of the

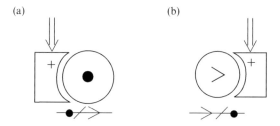

Figure 10.3. More complex force-dynamics diagrams: (a) *The ball's hitting it made the lamp topple from the table.* (b) *The water's dripping on it made the fire die down*

concept of causation. This property is that the AGONIST'S RESULTANT STATE OF ACTIVITY IS THE OPPOSITE OF ITS INTRINSIC ACTIONAL TENDENCY. (Talmy 1988: 57; emphasis added)

It should be clear that this 'definition' of causation leaves a good deal to be desired. First, the proposed definition includes the expression *resultant*, whose own meaning presumably already contains the concept BECAUSE. Second, even if the problem just noted can be corrected, the entire system still rests on a semantically obscure concept of 'force', a notion which comes from physics but which Talmy applies metaphorically to all sorts of non-physical situations. Explaining 'force' in terms of an 'intrinsic tendency' toward action or rest does not improve the situation. (Incidentally, Talmy's notion of 'intrinsic tendency' is similar to the old metaphysical notion that anything which moves or produces an effect is manifesting a 'power' to do so.)

Ray Jackendoff (1990; 2010) adapts Talmy's ideas to produce his own proposed decomposition of CAUSE, an element which he used to regard as primitive. To see how Jackendoff's decomposition works, we first have to appreciate his semantic function AFF ('affect') which is used to represent the action dimension of verbal concepts. AFF has two argument-slots, the first corresponding to the semantic role of actor and the second to patient. Jackendoff proposes that Talmy's Agonist–Antagonist dyad can be viewed as a patient–agent dyad: the Agonist is the person on whom the force is being applied (the patient) and Antagonist is the person applying it (the agent).

Of course, something more is needed to capture the range of outcomes in force-dynamic configurations. Jackendoff therefore introduces a new function, CS, which contains a 'success parameter'. CS^+ depicts the application of force with a 'successful outcome', CS^u the application of force with an 'undetermined outcome', and CS^- an 'unsuccessful outcome'. The previous notation CAUSE has been replaced by CS^+, as in the representation below (Jackendoff 1990: 130–3). This shows that Antagonist *Harry* is successfully affecting Agonist *Sam*, and that the effect is that Sam undertakes the action of going away.

Harry forced Sam to go away.

$$\left[\begin{array}{l} CS^+ \text{ ([HARRY],} \left[\begin{array}{l} GO \text{ ([SAM], [AWAY])} \\ AFF \text{ ([SAM],)} \end{array} \right]) \\ AFF \text{ ([HARRY], [SAM])} \end{array} \right]$$

If CS^u is substituted in place of CS^+ in the representation above, we would have a representation for *Harry pressured Sam to go away*, because in this case the outcome (whether or not Sam does go away) is left undetermined by the sentence.

Jackendoff's system deserves a much more detailed treatment than space allows here. For present purposes it is enough to note that it goes astray in just the same ways that Talmy's system does—obscurity and circularity. Clearly, the expression CS^+ is less readily intelligible than the expression CAUSE, which it is replacing. And, crucially, the CS function is explained in terms of the word *outcome*, a term which itself already contains the meaning BECAUSE.

We can conclude that Talmy and Jackendoff have not succeeded in expurgating causation from semantics.

10.1.3 'Cause' or 'because'?

Though many discussions of causatives are conducted in terms of the English abstract noun *causation* and/or the English verb (*to*) *cause*, it is important to note that both these expressions are relatively complex compared with the connective *because* (*of*). This intuitively obvious fact is reinforced by the fact that *because* (or *'cos*) is acquired by children much earlier than either of the other terms—as early as age two in many cases (cf. section 12.3). Furthermore, though there are many languages (e.g. Hindi, Yankunytjatjara, Japanese) which lack a term corresponding to the English verb *to cause*, all languages, as far as we know, have a word or bound morpheme which can express the semantically primitive meaning BECAUSE (see section 10.5).

10.2 Conventional descriptions of causatives

Standard descriptions of causatives are based on formal distinctions as to how the meaning element of 'causing' is indicated, and on a smallish set of descriptive labels (like 'direct', 'indirect', 'directive', and 'coercive') indicating semantic distinctions.

10.2.1 Formal distinctions

In an ANALYTIC CAUSATIVE (or PERIPHRASTIC CAUSATIVE), there is a separate verb associated with the causative meaning; usually this verb is capable of functioning also as a main verb with a different (but often related) meaning. For instance, English *make* can occur as the causative verb in a construction like *I made him work*, or as a main verb in its own right, as in *I made a cake*. Typically, analytic causative constructions are productive; that is, numerous verbs or adjectives may combine with the causative word to form complex expressions. There may be several such constructions in the same language, with fine semantic distinctions between them, as is the case with the English *make* causative, *get* causative and *have* causative (compare *I made him wash the car, I got him to wash the car, I had him wash the car*).

A MORPHOLOGICAL CAUSATIVE consists of a single word in which the causative meaning is conveyed by a special morpheme or morphological process. In English the suffixes *-en* and *-ify* form morphological causatives (such as *blacken, sweeten, thicken, nullify, liquify, verify*). There are also many causative verbs in English which are derived, without overt morphological modification, from adjectives or nouns (for example, *clean, empty,* and *open* are derived from adjectives, and *mop, dust,* and *knife* are derived from nouns).

The analytic/morphological distinction is not always as clear-cut as I have just presented it. For instance, the French *faire*-construction, as in *J'ai fait courir Paul* 'I have made Paul run', at first seems like an analytic causative, with *fait* (infinitive form *faire*) expressing cause, and *courir* 'to run' expressing effect. But closer examination shows that the two verbs do not behave like fully separate, independent verbs. Instead, for most purposes, a combination like *faire courir* behaves as a single predicate. For instance, if *faire* and *courir* were fully separate we might expect the noun-phrase *Paul* to be either the object of *faire* or the subject of *courir*, which in either case would mean that it should be possible to place *Paul* between the two verbs; but this is not possible. In fact *Paul* behaves as though it were the object of the combination *faire courir* (cf. Comrie 1989: 169).

Analytic causatives and morphological causatives are often grouped together as PRODUCTIVE CAUSATIVES (though languages often have some morphological causatives which are not very productive). A third type of causative is the LEXICAL CAUSATIVE. This category takes in words like *kill* and *feed*, which appear to be in a direct semantic relationship with other verbs, such as *die* and *eat*, but where the causative relation receives no formal expression at all. Some linguists would go so far as to call the *kill–die* relationship one of suppletion.

In the late 1970s causatives were one of the most hotly contested battle-grounds between two rival approaches to generative grammar (cf. Harris 1993). The conflict focused on the best analysis of morphological and lexical causatives. The generative semantics school claimed that these causative words derived from underlying phrases which were like analytic causatives; in essence, that a verb like *widen* or *kill* originated in deep structure as a phrase like 'cause to become wide' or 'cause to become dead'. The interpretive semantics school (which won out in the end) claimed that this didn't work because there were too many syntactic and semantic differences between the lexical and analytical versions.

10.2.2 Semantic labels for causatives

The most common semantic distinction drawn is that between DIRECT CAUSATION and INDIRECT CAUSATION (or mediated causation). Lexical causatives like *kill* and *break* imply more direct causation than the nearest analytic versions such as *cause to die* or *make (it) break* (cf. Fodor 1970; Wierzbicka 1980a). Some analytic causatives (e.g. the English *have* causative, as in *She had Jeeves wash the car*) imply that verbal communication has passed from causer to causee; the term DIRECTIVE CAUSATION is some-times used about such constructions. Because they tend to imply indirect causation, analytic causatives are often impossible where the causee is inanimate, or else they suggest that the causer has magical powers, as in *I caused the books to leave the room* or *I made the tree fall*.

Facts like these are found in many languages. They seem to reflect a principle of ICONICITY, in which the formal make-up of an expression reflects something about its meaning (Haiman 1985: 109): the greater the 'linguistic distance' between the elements representing the cause and the effect, the greater the 'conceptual distance' between them also.

The difference between alternative causative constructions is sometimes described in terms of 'degrees of coercion'. For instance, in the Japanese morphological causative, formed with suffix *-(s)ase*, the causee may be marked either with the direct object postposition *o* or with the indirect object postposition *ni* (glossed OBJ and INDIR.OBJ respectively). According to Comrie (1989), the semantic difference is that postposition *o* implies greater coercion than postposition *ni*. According to Comrie, example (a) below means something like 'Taroo forced Ziroo to go', whereas (b) implies less coercion, for example, 'Taroo persuaded Ziroo to go' or 'Taroo got Ziroo to go by asking nicely'.

a. *Taroo ga   Ziroo o   ik-ase-ta.*
        SUBJ   OBJ   go-CAUSE-PAST
b. *Taroo ga   Ziroo ni   ik-ase-ta.*
        SUBJ   INDIR.OBJ go-CAUSE-PAST

Though useful up to a point, conventional labels like 'direct', 'indirect', 'directive', 'coercive', and so on suffer from certain weaknesses. They are obscure in the sense that they do not clearly and fully articulate the meaning structures involved, and their predictive power is not very great: learning that a causative in a particular language is 'indirect' or 'directive' does not give one enough information to correctly predict its range of application. The small inventory of technical labels also tends to suggest that there is a small inventory of language-independent 'types' of causation, which individual languages may or may not instantiate; for instance, that there is a single semantic package called 'indirect causation' which is realized by the analytic causatives of English, Spanish, and French, for example. On closer examination, however, it turns out that different conditions and restrictions apply in different languages.

10.3 Productive causatives across languages

In this section we look into some productive causatives, of both the analytical and morphological types, attempting to unpack their semantic content into explications composed of simple and intuitively understandable components.

10.3.1 The English have causative

For reasons which will become apparent, it is useful for us to begin with an English causative construction which, though semantically complex, is rather restricted in its scope: the *have* causative. It is illustrated by examples like these:

> *She had her secretary type the letters.*
> *He had his driver bring the car round.*
> *They had her sing at the party.*
> *He had his tailor make up an exact copy of the suit.*
> *I had them wait outside.*

As suggested by the technical label often used for the *have* causative (i.e. 'directive'), sentences like those above imply the existence of some kind of well-established power relationship between the causer and the causee. According to the explication below, the causative scenario conveyed by the *have* construction begins with the causer X wanting the causee Y to do something. The causer X knows that if Y learns of X's wish, then Y will do it. Because of this, X conveys this message 'to someone'. The wording tends to imply an intermediary, but is also compatible with the immediate recipient of the instruction being Y him or herself. In any case, as stated in the final component, the result is that Y does as X wishes.

> *Someone X had someone Y do something:*
> someone X wanted someone Y to do something
> X knew that if someone said to Y something like 'X wants you to do this',
>   Y would do it because of this
> because of this, X said something like this to someone
> because of this, after this Y did it as X wanted

As one would expect from this explication, the *have* causative is normally incompatible with a non-human causee; cf. **The trainer had the lion dance.*

10.3.2 The family of English make causatives

It is sometimes said that 'the English *make* causative' conveys a meaning of 'coercive causation'. Such a statement is misleading, not only because the term 'coercive' is often not particularly appropriate, but also because of the implication that there is only a single *make* causative (with a single 'coercive' meaning). In fact it is necessary to distinguish a half dozen or so semantically distinct *make* constructions depending on the nature of the causer (e.g. whether the causer is a person or an event) and on the nature of the complement (e.g. whether it depicts an intentional action, an involuntary action, or an event which happens to the causee), among other factors (Wierzbicka 2003b; 2006d: 180–2).

The simplest *make* causative scenario (which we can dub the '*make* of induced thought') is where an event or someone's actions causes a person to think something which he or she otherwise wouldn't have thought. For example:

(i) *It made me realize how lucky I was.*
   The smell of shrimp paste made me remember my time in Malaysia.
(ii) *He made me realize I was wrong.*

Two slightly different explications are needed, depending on whether the causal trigger is an event or a person's actions. In both cases, the experiencer's thought is causally attributed to the event or action, and moreover the triggering event or action is identified as the exclusive cause ('Y didn't think like this at that time because of anything else').

Event-X made someone Y think like this:
something happened (event X) (at that time)
because of this, Y thought like this: '– –' (e.g. 'I'm very lucky' or 'I was wrong')
Y didn't think like this at that time because of anything else

Someone X made someone Y think like this:
someone X did something (at that time)
because of this, Y thought like this: '– –' (e.g. 'I'm very lucky' or 'I was wrong')
Y didn't think like this at that time because of anything else

Note that these explications have been revised from the versions presented in Wierzbicka (2003b; 2006d), which contained counterfactual components.

A second *make* causative can be dubbed the '*make* of induced feeling'. Again, two slightly different explications are called for, depending on whether the causal trigger is an event or a person's actions.

(i) *It made me feel a lot happier.*
   It made her feel proud of her background.
(ii) *She made me feel special.*
   He made her feel sick (i.e. disgusted).

Event-X made someone Y feel like this:
something happened (event X) (at that time)
because of this, Y thought something at that time
at the same time Y felt something because of it
Y didn't think like this at that time because of anything else

Someone X made someone Y feel like this:
someone X did something (at that time)
because of this, Y thought something at that time
at the same time Y felt something because of it
Y didn't think like this at that time because of anything else

None of the *make* constructions we have seen so far would warrant the label 'coercive'. But of course, there is a '*make* of coercion' which is found in examples like those below. In these examples the complements designate actions (*eating fish, repeating the story, going, apologizing*) which can be done intentionally.

She made him eat fish.
They made me repeat the story over and over.
You can't make me go.
Maria made Pedro apologize.

If we tried to bring these examples under the explications we have seen so far, we would fail to capture the richness of the 'coercive' causative scenario. The *make* sentences above clearly imply that the causee (Y) does something unwillingly, in response to some kind of pressure (threats, parental authority, nagging, etc.) from the causer (X). They also imply that X acts deliberately to bring about this result; that X realizes that some 'coercive' action is necessary to bring about the desired effect (because otherwise Y will not do it).

Teasing out the exact nature of the scenario conveyed by the '*make* of coercion' is no simple matter, and requires a more detailed treatment than we can afford here. However, if we compare *X made Y do Z* with *X forced Y to do Z*, we can discern that X's will is not completely overridden in the '*make* of coercion' construction. When we *make* someone do something, we achieve the outcome by making them realize that they have no choice but to do it. This effect can be captured in the following explication.

Someone X made someone Y do something:
X wanted Y to do something
because of this, X did something
because of this, Y thought something like this: 'I can't not do this'
Y did it because of this, not because of anything else

Notice that this explication correctly predicts certain implications of the '*make* of coercion' construction, which are not conveyed by the other *make* constructions already mentioned; for example, that X acted intentionally, and that Y complied 'under protest', as it were.

Already we have seen four semantically distinct *make* constructions. There are several more; for example, the '*make* of unwanted happening' (*You made me fall!*), the '*make* of involuntary emotional reaction' (*She made him cry*), the '*make* of necessity' (*The rain made him go inside*). Each of these constructions is characterized by distinctive restrictions and implications which prevent it from being merged with one of its 'siblings' in the *make* family. Though it is not possible for us to review them adequately here, it should be abundantly clear that it is misleading and simplistic to say that 'the' *make* construction indicates 'coercive causation'. It is worth noting that English seems especially rich in analytic causatives in the area of 'interpersonal relations' (cf. section 10.5). Aside from the *make* and *have* causatives, there are also various causative constructions with *get* (e.g. *She got him to type the letters*, *He got him to change his mind*, *He got the sauce to thicken*) and with *let* (as in *They let me borrow the car*, *Let me try it*). Some of these are explored in the Exercises at the end of the chapter.

10.3.3 The Spanish hacer causatives

Spanish has a common analytic causative based on the verb *hacer*. Since as a main verb *hacer* means 'make' or 'do', one might expect that the *hacer* causative would be much the same as the English *make* causative, but in fact the *hacer* causative has a broader range of use, reflecting a different semantic structure. We will confine ourselves to complements which contain intentional verbs, i.e. to examples which are comparable to the English '*make* of coercion'. The presentation follows Curnow (1993). The dialect being described could be called 'general spoken South American Spanish'.

In the *hacer* causative, the complement verb usually appears in the infinitive. *Hacer* (in the appropriately inflected form) and the infinitive verb constitute a close-knit unit, as can be seen from the fact that the 'causee' normally appears in front of the verb *hacer*, rather than in front of the infinitive verb. The construction is not restricted to human causees. The causee in example (a), for instance, could be an animal such as a horse or dog. (In the Spanish examples, INF means infinitive and REFLEX means reflexive. The symbol PREP is used for the versatile Spanish preposition *a*.)

a. *Le   hice   irse   de   aquí.*
   to-him   hacer:1sgPAST   go:INF:REFLEX   from   here
   'I made him leave.'

b. *Me   hicieron   leer   el   libro.*
  to-me   hacer:3plPAST   read:INF   the   book
  'They made me read the book.'

Bilingual dictionaries usually gloss the *hacer*+infinitive construction as 'make', and sometimes as 'force', 'oblige', or the like, as if to emphasize its coercive aspect, but there are examples, such as those below, for which an English *make* causative is not a viable translation. Though these examples suggest that the causee did not have much choice in the matter, they do not imply that he or she acted unwillingly. Notice that, as shown in (c), the causee need not appear explicitly, unlike as in English.

c. *Hizo   construir   una   entrada   separada.*
  hacer:3sgPAST   build:INF   an   entrance   separate
  'He/she had (someone) build a separate entrance.'
d. *Le   hago   lavar   la ropa   a   una   vecina.*
  to-her   hacer:1sgPRES wash:INF   the clothes   PREP   a   neighbour
  'I have my clothes washed by a neighbour.'

There is a notable semantic difference between the *hacer*+infinitive construction and the nearest corresponding English causatives. Both the '*make* of coercion' and the *have* causative imply that the causer intended to bring about the particular result; so sentences like **Harry unintentionally made John eat the meat* and **Harry made John eat the meat without wanting to* sound peculiar. But comparable sentences with the *hacer*+infinitive construction are quite acceptable. The following example could be used to describe a situation in which José intends to deceive Juan into eating vegetables, but something goes wrong and the outcome is that José ends up eating meat instead. Alternatively, it could be that Juan intended to get Nancy to eat meat, but it didn't work out and it was Juan who ended up eating it.

José le   hizo   comer   carne   a   Juan   sin   querer.
  José to-him   hacer:3sgPAST   eat:INF   meat   PREP Juan without   want:INF
  'José made Juan eat meat without wanting to.'

(Actually, in this sentence *sin querer* 'without wanting to' is syntactically ambiguous. It could refer to either Juan or José, but we consider only the reading where it applies to the causer, José.)

The acceptability of sentences like the one above could be accommodated by an intention component which is vague about the identity of the causee (e.g. 'X wanted someone to do something'), but there are other *hacer*+infinitive sentences which do not imply any intentionality at all. For example:

> Con llegar   tarde nos   hiciste   postergar la   reunión.
> with arrive:INF late   to-us hacer:2sgPAST   delay:INF the   meeting
> 'By arriving late you made us delay the meeting.'

Taking all this into account, one could propose the explication below.

> *X hacer Y do Z (infinitive verb):*
> X did something
> because of this, someone Y did Z
> Y didn't do it because Y wanted to do it

This does not, of course, preclude the possibility that X acted intentionally. Indeed, without evidence to the contrary, it is only natural to assume that X's action was intentional. But this is only a pragmatic implication, since it can be overridden by linguistic or contextual information to the contrary.

In addition to the *hacer*+infinitive construction, it is also possible (though much less common) for the complement verb to appear in the subjunctive form in a finite clause introduced by the complementizer *que* 'that'; for example:

> Hice   que lo   hiciera.
> hacer:1sgPAST   that it   do:3sgSUBJ
> 'I made him/her do it.'

We will not consider this less common construction here. Curnow (1993) argues that, unlike the infinitival construction, it implies conscious intention by the causer.

10.3.4 Japanese -(s)ase *causatives with* o *and* ni

As mentioned earlier, Japanese causative verbs formed with the suffix *-(s)ase* can take an object (the causee) marked either with the direct object postposition *o* or with the indirect object postposition *ni*. Comrie (1989) explains the semantic difference as due to different 'degrees of coercion' but, as Wierzbicka (1988: 238–40) points out, this explanation cannot be reconciled with the fact that both constructions can sometimes be translated by English *let*. She cites the following sentence, from Kitagawa (1974: 50), which shows that coercion is not part of the meaning of the *o* causative.

*Moo uma o turete kaeru zikan datta ga, amari yukaisoo ni kakoi no naka o hashitte
iru no de Taroo wa sono mama moo shibaraku uma o hashiraseta.*
'The time had come to take the horse back, but, because the horse was running so
joyously in the arena, Taroo let (*made) the horse run for a little while more.'

It is also a fact that both causatives can be used to ask for permission (cf.
Iwamoto 1987), as shown below. It would hardly make sense to say that the
difference is that the speaker is asking to be strongly coerced in (a) and
weakly coerced in (b).

a. *Watashi o ikasete kudasai.*
   'Please let me go (don't prevent me from going).'
b. *Watashi ni ikasete kudasai.*
   'Please let me go (permit me to go).'

Both Kitagawa and Iwamoto suggest that the *o* causative attributes
'total responsibility' to the causer—so much so that the causee's volition
or non-volition becomes irrelevant. This idea can be captured very directly,
as follows:

X ga *someone-Y* o *Verb*-aseta:
X did something
someone Y did something (Verb) because of this, not because of anything else

The *o* causative can also be used with inanimate causees; for example,
Taroo go yasai o kusaraeta 'Taroo caused/let the vegetables rot'. This
represents a different (but related) subconstruction which can be explicated
as follows:

X ga *something-Y* o *Verb*-aseta:
X did something
something happened (Verb) to something Y because of this, not because of
   anything else

When the causee (Y) is marked with the indirect object postposition *ni*,
the implication is quite different, namely, that Y performed the action
willingly.

X ga *someone-Y* ni *Verb*-aseta:
X did something
because of this, someone Y did something (Verb)
Y wanted to do this

Notice that Y may want to do the action for many reasons. Sometimes it
may be inherently desirable from Y's point of view (as in the above example

of the horse being allowed to run longer), and sometimes Y is merely eager
to do whatever X wants him or her to do.

10.4 Some causative verbs in English

For linguists, the prototypical lexical causative is undoubtedly *kill*. Since
McCawley (1968) it has been the subject of a long line of articles debating
the pros and cons of analysing *kill* as 'cause to die' (or as 'cause to become
not-alive'). Many other causative verbs are apparently susceptible to a
similar analysis. In this section, we first take a brief overview and then
examine some English lexical and morphological causatives in more detail.

10.4.1 The causative/inchoative alternation

The term CAUSATIVE/INCHOATIVE ALTERNATION refers to a situation in which
there are two verbs, one transitive and one intransitive, which are identical
in form, and where V-transitive can be roughly paraphrased as 'cause to V-
intransitive'. Some representative examples are shown in (a). The term
causative/inchoative alternation is often extended to cover situations in
which the resultant state is indicated by an adjective, as in the examples
in (b) and (c). The transitive verbs are usually said to depict a 'change of
state' or a 'change of position' (cf. Levin 1993: 27–30).

a. $break_{trans}$ — $break_{intrans}$ Juanita *broke* the vase. The vase *broke*.

   $melt_{trans}$ — $melt_{intrans}$ The sun *melted* the snow. The snow *melted*.

   $hurt_{trans}$ — $hurt_{intrans}$ You *hurt* my leg. My leg *hurt*.

   $drop_{trans}$ — $drop_{intrans}$ Kwan *dropped* the keys. The keys *dropped*.

   $move_{trans}$ — $move_{intrans}$ Sasha *moved* the chair. The chair *moved*.

b. *sharpen* — *sharp* The boy *sharpened* the pencil. The pencil was *sharp*.

   sweeten — *sweet* Who *sweetened* my coffee? My coffee is *sweet*.

   thicken — *thick* Katya *thickened* the sauce. The sauce was *thick*.

c. $clean_{verb}$ — $clean_{adj}$ I *cleaned* the car. The car was *clean*.

   $shut_{verb}$ — $shut_{adj}$ Naomi *shut* the door. The door was *shut*.

   $warm_{verb}$ — $warm_{adj}$ Chris *warmed* the soup. The soup was *warm*.

The verbs in (b) are morphologically derived from the corresponding
adjectives by adding -en. Since the verbs in (c) appear to be in a parallel
semantic relationship with the corresponding adjectives, they are often said

to be ZERO-DERIVED. The idea is that in either case the adjective is semantically simpler than the verb, and that the verb is derived from the adjective
regardless of whether or not an explicit morpheme (such as -*en*) is involved.

10.4.2 Killing the cat

If we compare *X killed Y* with *X caused Y to die* or *X caused Y's death*, we
can observe several ways in which *kill* appears to be more 'direct' than its
closest phrasal counterparts. From *X killed Y*, we can infer that X actually
did something to Y, whereas no such inference follows from *X caused Y's
death* (which, if anything, implies a certain indirectness). Recall, in this
connection, the Wild West scenario mentioned towards the end of section
3.2: a gunsmith fails to service the sheriff's six-shooter properly, as a result
of which the weapon jams and the sheriff is shot down. Katz (1970: 253)
made the point that although the gunsmith *caused the sheriff's death*, the
gunsmith did not *kill* the sheriff. The outlaw who shot the sheriff had this
honour.

Because a sentence like *X caused Y to die* is, at some level, a combination
of two clausal units, one embedded within the other (*X caused [Y to die]*), it
is possible to add two incompatible adjuncts of time, in a way which is
impossible with *kill*. For example, there is nothing odd about *John caused
Bill to die on Sunday by stabbing him on Saturday*, but a sentence like *?John
killed Bill on Sunday by stabbing him on Saturday* is anomalous (Fodor
1970). The point here is a subtle one. If John stabs Bill on Saturday and Bill
dies the next day, we can freely say that *John killed Bill*. What we cannot do
is to specify the time of the killing in a way which separates it from the time
of death; that is, we cannot say either that *?John killed Bill on Saturday* or
that *?John killed Bill on Sunday*, though it remains open to us to say
something like *John killed Bill last week*. In this sense it can be said that
kill (unlike *cause to die*) requires a perceived temporal unity of the action
and the resulting death.

As a first approximation, consider the explication below. This assigns *kill*
a structure involving three interrelated events. The first component recognizes that *killing* Y implies doing something to Y. The second says that X's
action has an immediate effect on Y, which would typically be a fatal event
in Y's body. The third says that this effect brings about an outcome ('after
this Y died'), which could occur some time later.

Someone X killed Y (e.g. John killed the cat):
someone X did something to Y
because of this, something happened to Y at this time
because of this, after this Y died

In support of a 'three-event' structure like this, McCawley (1968) argued that a sentence like *I almost killed the fly* can be used in relation to three different situations: (i) I almost did something which would have killed the fly (but I missed my chance), (ii) I did something which almost killed the fly (e.g. hit it glancingly, not causing enough damage to come close to killing it), (iii) I did something which brought the fly to the point of death (i.e. inflicted a potentially fatal injury), but it survived. That is, it would appear that *almost* can potentially interact with the meaning of *kill* in three ways, in what Cruse (1986: 67–8) would call a 'quasi-syntactic ambiguity'. For a similar analysis of *kill*, see Parsons (1994: ch. 6).

Despite the attractions of the above explication, there are reasons to think that it is not quite right. They centre on the explicit statement, in component (c), that 'Y died'. The difficulty is that the word *die* appears to be subject to some restrictions which are not shared by *kill*. In particular, whereas it sounds perfectly normal to speak of *killing* insects, snails, and even viruses, there is something slightly unusual about speaking of a moth, a snail, or a virus *dying*. I don't mean that using *die* in this way is ungrammatical—it isn't. But it carries a certain 'weighty', almost anthropomorphic tone which is lacking in comparable sentences with *kill*. (Even examples like *Moths die if they fly too close to a flame* have a slightly weighty tone which is totally absent from e.g. *The cat killed the moth*. And sentences such as *The moth died in the flame* sound almost comically solemn.) Interestingly, the words *live, alive,* and *dead* also lack the gravitas of *die*. Consider examples like *Butterflies live for only a few weeks, I've swatted that fly twice but it's still alive,* and *I found a dead moth on the table.*

These and other considerations have led NSM researchers to reject the usual assumption that *die* can be explicated as an inchoative verb based on 'live' (e.g. *Y died at time t* = 'before t, Y was living; something happened to Y at t; after this, Y was not living'), and to argue that, paradoxical as it may sound, DIE is a semantic prime in a complementary relationship with LIVE. Bearing in mind the difference in tone between *kill* and *die*, it is interesting to observe that it is possible to rephrase the explication of *X killed Y* so as to get rid of the component 'X died'. The same effect can be obtained using the two final components in the following explication, which depict the termination of Y's life.

Someone X killed someone else Y (e.g. John killed the cat):
someone X did something to someone else Y
because of this, something happened to Y at this time
because of this, something happened to Y's body
because of this, after this Y was not living anymore

This formulation would have the advantage of explaining why there is no gravitas or hint of anthropomorphism when we speak of *killing* lowly creatures like insects, snails, or viruses. This seems intuitively better in relation to people as well. If I describe an event as *John killed Bill*, I seem to be concerned with the fact that John did something to Bill which brought Bill's life to an end. There is something 'matter-of-fact' about the perspective implied by *kill*, which is at odds with the more experiential tone suggested by *Bill died*.

Any account of the meaning of *kill* must also sort out the situation with sentences like those below. They show that inanimate objects and event-nouns may appear as the subject of *kill*, even though it would sound peculiar to speak of a bullet, explosion, or disease 'doing something to someone'.

The explosion killed the cat.
The plague killed thousands of people.
A stray bullet killed Bill.

The only apparent solution is to posit polysemy—that is, to say that the sentences above exemplify a distinct meaning *kill₂*, which has an event, not an action, as the causal 'trigger' (cf. Parsons 1994: ch. 6). Nouns like *explosion* and *plague* depict events or occurrences directly; a subject NP like *a stray bullet* makes an elliptical reference to the event of a bullet hitting someone. One piece of grammatical evidence that *kill* is polysemous in this way is the fact that *kill₁* can take an instrument phrase (*John killed the cat with a knife*), whereas *kill₂* cannot (**The explosion killed the cat with a piece of flying rock*). This is consistent with the hypothesis that *kill₁* contains the semantic component DO (which may take an instrument phrase) while *kill₂* does not.

Event-X killed₂ Y (e.g. the explosion killed the cat):
something happened (in this place)
because of this, something happened to Y at this time
because of this, something else happened to Y
because of this, after this Y was not living anymore

10.4.3 Breaking the window, bending a spoon

It is sometimes assumed that 'verbs of physical affect' like *break* and *bend* are fully semantically parallel to *kill*, but there are some subtle differences. The explications below highlight the fact that with *break* and *bend* the resultant state applies more or less immediately. In the case of *killing*, the cessation of life can occur some time after the initial impact on the victim's body, but with *breaking* or *bending* something, the outcome is virtually co-terminous with the agent's action.

Bend has the simpler structure. Consider the following:

> *Someone X bent Y (e.g. Karla bent the spoon):*
> someone X did something to Y
> because of this, something happened to Y at this time
> because of this, after this Y was not straight [m] anymore

Break is an interesting verb because, as mentioned in Chapter 1, many languages do not have a verb with such a broad range of application, i.e. one that disregards, for example, whether the affected object becomes two separate pieces or many pieces (Majid and Bowerman 2007). We can capture the outcome of English *breaking* with the component: 'because of this, after this Y was not one thing anymore.' *Break* differs from *bend* not only in its outcome, but also in its inherent aspect. In conventional terminology, it is a punctual verb, i.e. the breaking event 'happens in one moment'.

Arguably the explication still needs a bit more detail, if it is to adequately predict the range of use of *break* (in the intended sense). Consider a tower of blocks, for example, the sort of thing a young child often makes, and suppose someone knocks it over. The verb *break* would not be perfectly appropriate to describe this event, and the reason is that we can easily imagine the blocks all being put back together again. This suggests that an explication for *break* should include a 'subjective' component indicating that the result (namely, that 'Y was not one thing anymore') is seen as irrevocable or irreversible. These considerations lead us to the following:

> *Someone X broke Y (e.g. Howard broke the window):*
> someone X did something to Y
> because of this, something happened to Y at this time
> it happened in one moment
> because of this, after this Y was not one thing anymore
> someone could think about it like this: 'it can't be one thing anymore'

Incidentally, it should be noted that *break* is a polysemous verb. The explication above applies only to the sense found in examples like: *to break a stick, an egg, a lightbulb, a vase,* or a *model plane.* It doesn't cover examples where X's action doesn't cause physical separation but rather disrupts the functionality of a machine or other device; e.g. *She broke my TV (my phone,* etc.).

Like *kill* in this respect, it would appear that transitive *break* and *bend* have secondary 'event-based' meanings, as seen in sentences like:

> *The explosion broke our front window.*
> *The impact bent the pole.*

> *Event-X broke Y (e.g. the explosion broke the window):*
> something (event X) happened in this place
> because of this, something happened to Y at this time
> it happened in one moment
> because of this, after this Y was not one thing anymore
> someone could think about it like this: 'it can't be one thing anymore'

10.4.4 Cleaning the table, warming the soup

In this section, we will confine ourselves to 'change of state' causatives derived from adjectives for physical or material properties (such as *clean, warm, cool, thick, thin, wide, sweet,* and *rough*), reserving the possibility that a slightly different story may be appropriate for verbs like *open, shut,* and *empty,* which involve a change of position or location.

The verbs *clean* and *warm* are usually held to be zero-derived from the adjective describing the resulting state; i.e. *clean* means roughly 'cause to become clean', and *warm* means roughly 'cause to become warm'. Such verbs do not, however, imply the occurrence of an event in the same way that *break* and *bend* do. If someone *breaks* something, for example, there has been an event of 'breaking'. But to speak of someone *cleaning* or *warming* something does not imply an event of 'becoming clean' or 'becoming warm'.

There are also some other interesting differences between verbs like *clean* and *warm,* on the one hand, and those like *kill* and *break,* on the other. First, *clean* and *warm* are intentional verbs; one can *kill* or *break* something unintentionally, but it would sound odd to say that *?Harry unintentionally* *cleaned the table* or *?Juan unintentionally warmed the soup*. Second, *clean* and *warm* are activity verbs, and more specifically, accomplishment verbs. They necessarily imply some duration, and so readily accept progressive aspect. These observations are incorporated in the following explication. The same schema would apply to other verbs based on physical state adjectives.

> *Someone X cleaned Y (e.g. Harry cleaned the table):*
> someone X wanted Y to be clean [d]
> because of this, X did something to Y for some time
> because of this, after this Y was clean [d]

An interesting property of accomplishment verbs is that the progressive aspect does not entail that the change of state has come about: the table is not *clean* until one has finished *cleaning* it, the soup is not *warm* till one has finished *warming* it. This property, which is sometimes called the 'imperfective paradox', can be modelled in the following explication.

> *Someone X was cleaning Y:*
> someone X wanted Y to be clean [d]
> because of this, X was doing something to Y for some time
> someone could think like this at this time:
> 'if this someone does this for some time more, after this Y will be clean [d]
>   because of it'

In other words, it appears that for accomplishment verbs like *clean* and *warm*, progressive aspect implies a conditional statement; whereas no such component is necessary for progressives of verbs such as *wipe*, *sweep*, or *wash* which focus on the manner in which the action was done rather than on the result (cf. Vendler 1967; Levin and Rappaport Hovav 1991).

10.5 Causation and culture

In this section we will consider two angles on the connection between causation and culture. The first is the extreme suggestion that certain non-Western peoples simply don't have the concept of causation as we (Westerners) know it, and that this can be seen from the supposed fact that their languages don't have any word for 'because'. The second is the more moderate idea that different languages exhibit different degrees of grammatical elaboration of causative meanings.

10.5.1 The translatability of because

The claim that tribal non-Western peoples don't have any clear notion of causation belongs to a long tradition of commentary on 'primitive mentality', a tradition which also holds that such people lack logical concepts such as IF and ALL, and are incapable of abstract reasoning (cf. Lévy-Bruhl 1926). Though this tradition is largely discredited, it has not been completely laid to rest.

As far as causality is concerned, the usual assertion is that indigenous people, such as Papua New Guineans or Australian Aborigines, blur the distinctions between causation and temporal succession, and between causation and simultaneity. That is, that they don't distinguish clearly between one thing happening BECAUSE of another, and one thing happening AFTER or AT THE SAME TIME as another. This proposition, or something very similar, has been argued by Margaret Bain in relation to the Pitjantjatjara people of Central Australia (Bain and Sayers 1990; Bain 1992). How credible are such claims?

At first glance there is indeed no ready equivalent for BECAUSE in Pitjantjatjara, and bilingual speakers usually 'draw a blank' if asked outright for one. There are no subordinate clause constructions which are unambiguously causal. In simple clauses, there are two case-markers (ABLative and LOCative) which can be used to indicate a causal relationship, as illustrated below, but the contrast between them appears to be based on the distinction between prior cause (ablative) and concurrent cause (locative); furthermore, both markers appear to be primarily locational in function.

a. *Ngayulu pikatjararingu,   kapi   kura-nguṟu.*
   1sg   sick:INCHO:PAST water   bad-ABL
   'I got sick, because of (from) bad water.'
b. *Ngayulu puṯu kunkunaringi,   muntur-ta.*
   1sg   can't   sleep:INCHO:P.IMPF   noise-LOC
   'I couldn't get to sleep because of (in) the noise.'

Though it might seem that there is no Pitjantjatjara exponent of causality 'pure and simple', this impression disappears when we look into the matter more closely (Goddard 1991a). To begin with, we find that causal uses of the ablative and locative markers differ in frequency. The locative is infrequent and restricted to 'ambient' or 'environmental' causes, whereas the causal use of the ablative is relatively frequent. More importantly, we can find plenty of examples, such as those below, where the causal ablative is used without the cause-factor being unambiguously prior in time.

a. *Tjinguṟu ... mukulya wiya-nguṟu tjana pitulu panṯini.*
   maybe   love   NEG-ABL   3pl   petrol   sniff:PRES
   'Maybe ... it's because of a lack of (parental) care that they sniff petrol.'

b. *Kata pika-nguṟu nguṯuly-nguṯulypa pakalpai.*
   head   sore-ABL   glands   get.up:CHAR
   '(The) glands swell up from (having) a sore head.'

c. *Ngayulu tjiṯuṟu-tjiṯuṟu nyinanyi nyuntula-nguṟu.*
   1sg   discontent   sit:PRES   2sg-ABL
   'I'm discontented on account of you.'

A clinching argument which establishes causation as distinct from temporal notions emerges when we ask how (if at all) the two could be explicitly distinguished. How could one say in Pitjantjatjara things like: 'Sure, Y happened during (or, after) X, but not because of X'? For example, if there is truly no unambiguous way of indicating causality as opposed to simultaneity, the final sentences in the passage below ought to be impossible to express in Pitjantjatjara because both the potential 'cause-factors' (the kids making noise and me having worrying thoughts) are concurrent with the effect (not being able to sleep).

A: *I couldn't get to sleep last night.*
B: *Yes indeed. The kids were making a lot of noise.*
A: *No, it wasn't the kids. I was thinking about my grandfather—you know how sick he is. That's why I couldn't sleep.*

However, there is a natural way of rendering the final part of the exchange, as shown below, and, not surprisingly, it relies on *-nguṟu*.

Wiya. Tjitji tjuṯa-na kulintja   wiya. Panya   ngayulu puḻkaṟa
no   child PL-1sg   listen:NOML   NEG   you.know   1sg   really
kuliningi,   ngayuku tjamu.   Panya   paluṟu pikatjara ngarinyi.
think:P.IMPF   my   grandfather you.know   DEF   sick   lie:PRES
Pala palula nguṟu-na puḻu   kunkun   ngaringi.
that   DEF-ABL-1sg   in.vain   asleep   lie:P.IMPF
'No. I wasn't listening to the kids. I was thinking about my grandfather. You know how sick he is. Because of that I couldn't sleep.'

In the phrase *pala palula-nguṟu*, *pala* 'that' is a deictic, the middle element of a set of three (*nyanga, pala, nyara*) which are roughly differentiable on the basis of proximity. So far as this construction is concerned, however, there does not seem to be anything special about *pala*: *nyanga palula-nguṟu* and *nyara palula-nguṟu* are also well-formed, and carry the meanings one might expect, namely, 'because of this' and 'because of that'. The element glossed as DEF (oblique stem form *palula-*) indicates an anaphoric reference; when it functions adnominally, it signals that a referent is the same as one previously mentioned or understood.

Essentially, then, the overall construction works as follows: the immediately preceding clause depicts a situation or event, the deictic *pala* (or *nyanga* or *nyara*) in combination with the DEFinite stem *palula-* enables an anaphoric reference to this situation or event, and *-nguṟu* makes the causal relation explicit. Two other examples of causal meanings expressed by this construction with *-nguṉu* are below (Eckert and Hudson 1988: 154).

a. *Tjitji   puḻka   tatinu   ka   pala   palula-nguṟu   kaṯakatingu.*
   child   big   climb:PAST   CONTR   that   DEF-ABL   break:PAST
   'A big child rode it and because of that it broke.'

b. *Aṉangu   tjuṯa   pikaringanyi.   Nyara   palula-nguṟu-ṉa   ankunytja*
   person   PL   fight:INCHO:PRES   that   DEF-ABL-1sg   go:NOML
   wiya   wantinyi.
   NEG   don't:PRES
   'People are fighting. Because of that I won't go.'

Similar arguments and examples can be adduced to show that the causal use of Pitjantjatjara *-nguṟu* is distinct from temporal succession.

Two other Australian Aboriginal languages which have been carefully examined for exponents of causation are Arrernte (Harkins and Wilkins 1994) and Kayardild (Evans 1994). In both cases, the conclusion has been that the languages have perfectly adequate means of expressing the causal relation, albeit that at first glance this is obscured by the fact that the exponents are polysemous and may express, in other constructions, meanings of a spatial or temporal nature. At present, there are no known cases of languages which lack an exponent for BECAUSE (cf. Goddard and Wierzbicka 1994b).

10.5.2 Grammatical elaboration of causal concepts

All languages have numerous complex words, especially lexical causatives, whose meanings include the notion BECAUSE (e.g. words with meanings

like 'kill', 'break', 'send', and so on). However, languages differ markedly
in the grammatical elaboration of causality. At one extreme, there are
languages like Kayardild which have no causative constructions, either
morphological or analytic (Evans 1994). At the other, there are languages
like English with a wide range of causative constructions, especially in the
area of human interaction. Wierzbicka (1988: 251) tabulates the following
set of causative patterns for English, and one does not have to agree with
every detail of this list to be impressed by its size.

X made Y $V_{intentional}$-INF	*X made Y wash the dishes.*
X made Y $V_{non-intentional}$-INF	*X made Y cry.*
X made Y ADJ	*X made Y furious.*
X had Y $V_{intentional}$-INF	*X had Y wash the dishes.*
X had X's Z $V_{intentional}$-ed	*X had her boots mended.*
X got Y to $V_{intentional}$-INF	*X got Y to wash the dishes.*
X got Y Y ADJ	*X got Y furious.*
X got herself $V_{intentional}$-ed	*X got herself kicked out.*
X $V_{intentional}$-ed Y into doing Z	*X talked/tricked Y into doing Z.*
X $V_{aspectual}$-ed Y V-ing	*X kept Y waiting.*

Most languages appear to fall somewhere between the extremes of
English and Kayardild. Among European languages, for instance, English
has more analytic causatives than French, French more than German, and
German more than Russian. These differences are very intriguing and one
is tempted to ask whether they are related in any way to cultural interests
and preoccupations. One suggestion in this regard comes from Charles
Bally's (1920) pioneering study of semantic typology of European languages,
Impressionisme et grammaire. Bally identified two 'psychological tendencies'
manifested in the syntax of different languages: an impressionistic one,
focusing on phenomena as they present themselves to human beings, most
prominent in Russian, and an analytical one, focusing on presumed relations
between causes and effects, most prominent in English.

The range of English causatives seems to be focused on subtleties of
causation in human interaction, and in particular on the interplay of
causation and volition. The same putative 'cultural preoccupation' can
also be observed in lexical elaboration; as noted in section 5.4, English
exhibits a proliferation of directive speech-act verbs (like *request, suggest,
direct, demand, recommend*) which enable speakers to categorize aspects of
social interaction with much greater delicacy than is possible, for instance,

in Russian. It can be argued that the wealth of 'human interaction' causatives in English is linked with the Anglo-Saxon cultural emphasis on the autonomy and rights of the individual (Wierzbicka 2006d). Though some researchers till shun the topic, the scope for investigating connections between grammar and culture is great, so long as precise and culture-neutral descriptive tools can be employed to safeguard against subjectivity and ethnocentrism.

Key technical terms

analytic causative	indirect causation
causative/inchoative alternation	lexical causative
direct causation	morphological causative
directive causation	productive causative
iconicity	zero-derived

Exercises and discussion questions

† next to a problem means that a solution or some commentary can be found at the end of the book.

1. What are some of the differences between *I opened the door* and *I made the door open*?

2†. Hofmann (1993: 241) presents the following table, in which BCM stands for 'inchoative' (roughly, 'become') and COZ for 'causative'. Hofmann is suggesting that the verbs in the top row all bear the same semantic relationship to their counterparts in the bottom row. Critically discuss.

BCM:	X *dies*	X *gets* Y	X *learns* Y	X *falls*
COZ-BCM:	Z *kills* X	Z *gives* X Y	Z *teaches* X Y	Z *drops* X

3†. In Italian there is an analytic causative based on the verb *fare* 'make/do' which has an extremely wide range of use. It can often be translated into English as a *make* causative, a *have* causative, or a *get* causative. For example, sentence (a) below is compatible with all three translations shown.

 a. *Allora, la faccio venire domani, la mia Elena, a pranzo?*
    'So should I make/have/get my Elena (to) come to lunch tomorrow?'

With this in mind, and considering the following examples (drawn from Ginzburg 1976), propose a semantic explication for the *fare* + Verb-infinitive construction.

    b. *Non mi fa mai dormire quel bambino.*
       'This baby doesn't let me sleep at all.'
    c. *Quello nuovo lo farai dormire con la segretaria.*
       'I will have this new (baby) sleep with the secretary (i.e. in the secretary's room).'
    d. *Fai venire qui Edoardo subito perché la sua ragazza si è suicidata.*
       'Get Edward here immediately because his girlfriend has committed suicide.'

4†. Consider the English '*make* of necessity' construction, as shown in examples (a)–(c). Suggest a reductive paraphrase explication.

    a. *The rain made him go inside.*
    b. *The arrival of the police made me run for my life.*
    c. *Murdoch was annoyed. Not with the expansion of (...) Not with the development of (...) What made him reach for the phone at around midday on September 5 were four paragraphs on page two of the Daily Telegraph's business section.*

5†. Consider the English *get* causative construction, illustrated in sentences like:

    a. *Libby got Jeff to type the letters.*
    b. *Clancy got Phoebe do his work homework for him.*
    c. *I might get you to sign this.*

What would be some of the weaknesses of characterizing the meaning of this *get* construction as 'indirect causation'? What are some of the differences between *get* causatives and the corresponding *make* causatives? See if you can devise an explication for *get* causatives like those shown above.

6†. Yankunytjatjara has several morphological causatives. One of them, the suffix -*nta*, occurs only in association with a small number of roots, some of them nouns, as in (a), and some of them adjectives, as in (b). What kind of semantic specifications are conveyed by the -*nta* causative? (Note that the final suffix -*ṉu* is the past tense marker.)

    a. *nguntintaṉu* 'broke (its) neck, e.g. of rabbit' [*ngunti* 'back of neck']
       liṟintaṉu 'strangled' [*liri* 'throat']
    b. *iluntaṉu* 'killed' [*ilunytja* 'dead']
       kaṯantaṉu 'broke (solid object)' [cf. *kaṯaly* 'broken']
       piluntaṉu 'staved in, crushed' [cf. *piluny* 'collapsed, caved in']
       tjaḻantaṉu 'made burst open, so liquid inside flowed out'
            [cf. *tjaḻaly* 'having liquid inside']

7†. English has many causative verbs which are zero-derived from nouns, e.g. *to butter*, *to skin*, *to paint*, *to knife*. They are not semantically homogeneous, but fall into various subclasses. For this exercise, just try to find explications for the three verbs in the examples below. Do not feel obliged to stick solely to semantic primes, but do try to avoid using any blatantly obscure or complex terms.

  a. *Samantha watered the lawn.*
  b. *Nick buttered the toast.*
  c. *Maxine powdered her nose.*

8†. Dixon (1991: 291–3) carried out a small survey of speakers' attitudes to verbs which can be used both transitively and intransitively. He reports that for most verbs, speakers generally consider the intransitive uses to be more basic; some examples are listed in (a) below. However, for others, such as those listed in (b), the transitive uses are judged to be the more basic. Can you think of any explanation for this phenomenon?

  a. *trip, burst, hurt, melt, burn*
  b. *spill, break, drop, stretch*

9†. The following pairs of sentences show a transitive/intransitive alternation involving bodily postures. Propose semantic explications for the transitive constructions. Confine yourself to examples in which the grammatical object is human, as in these examples.

  a. *We laid Bill down on the bed (and took off his shoes).*
  b. *Bill was lying down on the bed.*

  a. *Maxine sat the baby up.*
  b. *The baby was sitting up.*

11

Grammatical categories

What is the relationship between grammatical semantics and lexical semantics? Oddly enough, this important question has generally been avoided by both syntacticians and lexical semanticists. Till recently the lexicon has seemed too large, messy, and language-specific for most syntacticians, while lexical semanticists have generally contented themselves with word-level or lexical field studies and have not intruded into the domain of syntax. Though there are signs of change, there is still a widespread assumption that lexical semantics and grammatical semantics are essentially different domains, calling for different descriptive toolkits.

In this chapter we will see that the meanings of language-specific grammatical categories and constructions can be stated in clear and testable formulations using the same reductive paraphrase approach that 'works' for lexical meanings. Our examples will be drawn from languages in many parts of the world, and include some grammatical phenomena, such as minimal-augmented pronoun systems, numeral classifiers, elaborate locational deixis, and evidential systems, which may seem somewhat exotic. But 'exotic' grammatical categories frequently don't look that way when seen from a semantic point of view.

There is second theme to the chapter as well. A distinctive aspect of the NSM approach is the close attention it pays to the meta-terminology of grammatical description, and in particular the need to achieve greater clarity and consensus about the meanings and operational criteria for grammatical terms such as dative, causative, relative clause, adverbial clause, and so on. The NSM approach is to identify for each such term a semantic prototype which can be used as a standard for the cross-linguistic identification of constructions of a given kind. In this way, the practice of linguistic typology can be anchored in semantic terms. Within a single language, NSM research indicates that many grammatical constructions are polysemous, i.e. there is a family of interrelated lexico-grammatical constructions with a prototype-plus-extensions structure.

11.1 Pronominal systems

The universality of the so-called 'first-person singular' and 'second-person singular' pronouns is taken for granted by typologists, and rightly so. No language is known which lacks equivalents to I and YOU. True, in some languages there are several different variants of each, the choice between them signalling solidarity, social distance, respect, intimacy, or the like, but even in languages of this kind, such as Thai, Japanese, and Malay, it is possible to identify primary, semantically unmarked exponents for I and YOU (cf. Diller 1994; Onishi 1994). The meanings I and YOU are among the best established semantic primes. Other pronominal categories, however, differ markedly from language to language. For example, some languages have dual pronouns, i.e. pronouns reserved for groups of two people only. Some languages make a distinction between inclusive and exclusive 'we', depending on whether the addressee is included in or excluded from the set of people being referred to. In this section we see how language-specific pronominal categories can be semantically decomposed. For convenience, we will concentrate on 'first-person non-singular' pronouns, i.e. on words for 'we' in various languages. But before we can settle down to this, there is a question to be resolved about the English pronoun *you*.

11.1.1 Are 'you' singular or plural?

The NSM primes I and YOU are regarded as inherently singular (so really it is misleading to refer to them as 'first-person singular' and 'second-person singular', as though 'singularity' were a separable semantic component). As far as is known, all of the world's languages have a unique and inherently singular exponent of I. The great majority also have a unique and inherently singular word for YOU; for example, French has *tu*, Mandarin Chinese *ni*, Yankunytjatjara *nyuntu*. English, however, is unusual in using the same form *you* for both singular and plural contexts. This raises the question: Are there two homonymous words *you$_{sg}$* and *you$_{pl}$*, as assumed in traditional grammar (the homonymy analysis)? Or is there a single *you* which is semantically 'number-neutral' and interpreted as either singular or plural depending on context (the generality analysis)?

Grammarians traditionally recognize homonymy where grammatical processes indicate the existence of separate words with the same word-form (cf. section 1.4). Bloomfield (1933: 224) says, for instance, that the fact that the same phonetic form *sheep* is substitutable for both singular *lamb* and plural *lambs* forces us to regard *sheep* as 'a set of homophones, a singular noun *sheep* ... and a plural noun *sheep*'. Few contemporary linguists would disagree. Applied to English *you*, the same reasoning favours the homonymy analysis.

Consider the implications of the existence of the two reflexive forms *yourself* and *yourselves* (cf. Lyons 1968: 277). In (a) below *myself* is singular because it is the reflexive counterpart of its antecedent subject *I*, which is singular; in (b) *ourselves* is plural in number because its antecedent *we* is plural. What then of *yourself* vs. *yourselves* in (c) and (d)? To preserve the generalization that a reflexive pronoun agrees in number with its antecedent, we must recognize grammatically distinct words *you$_{sg}$* and *you$_{pl}$*. Consider also the examples given in (e) which show that with reciprocal and relational-symmetric predicates it is possible to substitute *you* in place of *we* (though *I* and other singular pronouns are excluded). Again, this is sufficient evidence for the existence of a plural word *you$_{pl}$*, homonymous with its singular counterpart.

a. *I saw myself in the mirror.*
b. *We saw ourselves in the mirror.*
c. *You saw yourself in the mirror.*

d. *You saw yourselves in the mirror.*
e. *We/you looked at each other.*
    We/you are sisters.
    We/you are a team.

It is also worth noting that many non-standard varieties of English have distinct forms, such as *youse* and *y'all*, for 2pl.

We can conclude that there are two distinct English words—*you$_{sg}$*, which is semantically primitive, and *you$_{pl}$*, which is not. When we use the term YOU in this chapter, we always mean the inherently singular, semantically primitive meaning.

11.1.2 Who are 'we'?

What's wrong with saying that *we* means 'I and some other people'? Though intelligible, and effective for pedagogical purposes, from a reductive paraphrase point of view there are problems with this. To begin with, *and* is a complex word and stands in need of further explication. As well, do we really want to say that plural pronouns are literally coordinate structures? Aside from the inherent implausibility of this, there are languages which lack an additive conjunction akin to English *and* (Mithun 1988), but have plural pronouns nonetheless. But worst of all, a paraphrase like 'I and some other people' fails to predict that English *we* can refer to just two people. Introducing a disjunction into the paraphrase, viz. 'I and another person or some other people', solves this problem but at the cost of claiming that *we* is polysemous.

The alternative is an analysis based on inclusion, something like: 'the group of people of which I am a part'. Though appealing in that it is number-neutral, this paraphrase cannot be accepted as it is. 'Group' is not a readily cross-translatable word, and in any case it seems counter-intuitive to say that every instance of *we* contains a literal reference to a 'group'. Certainly the people referred to as *we* need not constitute a group in any spatio-temporal sense. (Consider, for instance: *What do Lady Gaga and I have in common?* Answer—*We both dislike broccoli.*) There is a sense in which the referents are 'brought together' by being referred to as *we*, but this action seems to take place in the speech act itself.

The explication schema below is essentially a reformulation of the 'group' paraphrase.

we:
some people
I am one of these people

(In the expression 'these people', the form 'these' can be regarded as an allolexic variant of 'this', because '*this people' is not well-formed in English and because plurality is fully implicit in 'people'. For an explanation of allolexy, see p. 67.)

Notice that the explication is noncommittal as to whether or not the addressee (i.e. YOU) is included in the collective reference, and also on the number question. The wording remains applicable even in contexts where it is obvious that, aside from the speaker, there is only one other person involved (as in *Suzie and I went to the shops, and on the way we got lost*).

Some cross-linguistic evidence for this analysis comes from the fact that in languages whose *we* pronoun is formally analysable, morphological exponents of I, ALL, and PEOPLE are commonly involved. This is clearest in newly stabilized pidgins, where there has been no time for historical change to obscure the etymology. For instance, Samoan Plantation Pidgin had *mi ol* 'we', where quantifier *ol* < English 'all', and early Tok Pisin had *mi-pela* 'we', where the form *-pela*, from English *fellow*, can be regarded as an exponent of the concept PEOPLE.

11.1.3 The dual/plural and inclusive/exclusive distinctions

Now let's look at the nearest equivalents to English *we* in a language with a DUAL/PLURAL distinction such as Yankunytjatjara, whose first- and second-person pronouns are shown in Table 11.1 (Goddard 1985).

The explications below are modified versions of those for English *we*. The lead component for *ngali* takes the form 'these two people'. Characterizing the number category of the plural is more difficult. We can reject 'three or more' on the grounds that it is counter-intuitive to say that the plural pronouns depend on the number 'three'. A better candidate might be

Table 11.1.   Yankunytjatjara first- and second-person pronouns

	Singular	Dual	Plural
1st	*ngayulu*	*ngali*	*nganana*
2nd	*nyuntu*	*nyupali*	*nyura*

'more than two', but the presence of 'more than' seems to imply—wrongly—that a kind of grading process is involved in using the pronoun *nganana*. I suggest its meaning is simpler than that, involving merely an opposition to the dual (i.e. a denial that the number is two), not an amendment to it (to the effect that the number is 'more than two').

ngali (1 dual):   *nganana* (1 plural):
two people   some people, not two people
I am one of these people   I am one of these people

Now let's look at a language with an INCLUSIVE/EXCLUSIVE distinction, such as Malay, where the relevant forms are *kita* 'we (incl)' and *kami* 'we (excl)'. The meanings of such terms must involve YOU, including or excluding it respectively.

kita (1 plural incl):   *kami* (1 plural excl):
some people   some people
I am one of these people   I am one of these people
you are one of these people   you are not one of these people

Many languages have both the dual/plural distinction and the inclusive/exclusive distinction. A much cited example is Palaung (Burma), whose first-person pronouns are shown in Table 11.2.

The four non-singular Palaung pronouns can be explicated as follows:

ar (1 dual incl):   *yar* (1 dual excl):
two people   two people
I am one of these people   I am one of these people
you are one of these people   you are not one of these people

ε (1 plural incl): $y\varepsilon$ (1 plural excl):
some people, not two people   some people, not two people
I am one of these people   I am one of these people
you are one of these people   you are not one of these people

Table 11.2. Palaung first-person pronouns (Burling 1970: 17)

Singular	Dual	Plural	
$\mathupsilon$	*ar*	ε	Inclusive
	yar	$y\varepsilon$	Exclusive

Table 11.3. Rembarrnga first- and second-person pronouns arranged according to traditional categories

	Singular	Dual	Trial	Plural
1 Incl	*ngunu*	*yukku*	*ngakorrbbarrah*	*ngakorru*
Excl		*yarrbbarrah*		*yarru*
2	*ku*	*nakorrbbarrah*		*nakorru*

11.1.4 Minimal-augmented pronoun systems

MINIMAL-AUGMENTED pronoun systems are found in the Philippines (Conklin 1967), in Africa (Wiesemann 1986), and in northern Australia. As our example, we will take the Australian language Rembarrnga (McKay 1978; Dixon 1980). As can be seen from Table 11.3, the Rembarrnga pronoun paradigm looks asymmetrical if it is laid out according to traditional categories. There seems to be a special first-person 'trial' inclusive (where 'trial' designates a pronoun reserved for groups of three people). Even more suspicious—except for 1 dual inclusive, the duals are marked by -*bbarrah*, but -*bbarrah* also appears in the 1 trial inclusive.

Symmetry and morphological transparency can be restored if the paradigm is rearranged as shown in Table 11.4 (McKay 1990: 429f.). This arrangement assumes that the 1+2 pronoun *yukku* (formerly called the 'first-person dual inclusive') is functionally parallel to the 1sg and 2sg pronouns, in serving as a basic (or 'minimal') category which is subject to two kinds of number modification: 'unit-augmented' (i.e. plus one other person) and 'augmented' (i.e. plus more-than-one persons). This interpretation explains why *yarrbbarrah* and *nakorrbbarrah* refer to groups of two in number ('I and one other', and 'you and one other'), whereas the morphologically parallel form *ngakorrbbarrah* ('I and you and one other') refers to a group of three people.

Despite the intuitively satisfying layout of the paradigm shown in Table 11.4, many people find the semantic aspects of the description rather

Table 11.4. Rembarrnga pronouns arranged by minimal/augmented categories

	Minimal	Unit-augmented	Augmented
1	*ngunu*	*yarrbbarrah*	*yarru*
2	*ku*	*nakorrbbarrah*	*nakorru*
1+2	*yukku*	*ngakorrbbarrah*	*ngakorru*

difficult to follow. The terms 'unit-augmented' and 'augmented' are far from self-explanatory, and the exact semantic content of the '1+2' form is unclear, if we assume that it does not include the specification 'two' (because the Rembarrnga system does not include any true 'dual' pronouns). Plausible explications for Rembarrnga pronouns can be given in NSM, however. The 1+2 form can be explicated as shown below.

> *yukku* (1+2):
> some people
> I am one of these people
> you are one of these people
> there are no more

The final component ('there are no more') provides a way of restricting the referents to 1sg and 2sg, without using the specification 'two'. As we will see, components involving 'more' (corresponding to the technical term 'augmented') are key ingredients of the Rembarrnga system.

The unit-augmented forms involve a reference to 'one other someone', as illustrated below. On the left is the 1+2 unit-augmented pronoun. Notice that the net effect of the set of components shown is that the pronoun has three referents, including 'I' and 'you', i.e. it is referentially equivalent to a '1st person trial inclusive'. The 1 unit-augmented pronoun can be explicated in similar fashion, as shown on the right. Notice that because 'you' is excluded (rather than included), the net effect is to indicate reference to two people, as required. ('You' must be excluded from *yarrbbarrah* since the 'I, you' combination is covered by *yukku*, the 1+2 form.)

> *ngakorrbbarrah* (1+2 unit-aug):   *yarrbbarrah* (1 unit-aug):
> some people   some people
> I am one of these people   I am one of these people
> you are one of these people   you are not one of these people
> one other someone is one   one other someone is one
>   of these people   of these people
> there are no more   there are no more

The augmented forms can be economically analysed as shown below. In each case, the explication exactly matches its unit-augmented counterpart, except for one crucial difference. The final component ('there are more') indicates that the referents itemized in the bulk of the explication are not exhaustive. The net effect is that the minimum number of referents for *ngakorru* is four, while the minimum number of referents for *yarru* is three, as required. Either pronoun can of course have an unlimited number of additional referents.

ngakorru (1+2 aug):	*yarru* (1 aug):
some people	some people
I am one of these people	I am one of these people
you are one of these people	you are not one of these people
one other someone is one	one other someone is one
of these people	of these people
there are more	there are more

It should be noted that these explications have not been checked with native speakers of Rembarrnga. They also assume that the expression 'there are more' and its converse 'there are no more' are valid NSM combinations, which is not altogether clear at the present time. Nevertheless, the explications represent a clear and coherent hypothesis about the semantics of the minimal-augmented pronouns of Rembarrnga and other languages with similar systems.

11.2 Locational deixis

In English, when we wish to point out an object we can indicate something about where the referent is by choosing between the two basic deictics available to us—namely, *this* or *that*. But in many other languages speakers have a choice of three, four, or five LOCATIONAL DEICTICS (or even more). In a typological survey of 149 languages, Hyslop (1993) isolated eight 'parameters of meaning' which are involved in such systems. In this section we explore how they can be stated in the Natural Semantic Metalanguage. Not surprisingly, the main terms needed for this purpose are the spatial primes NEAR, FAR, ABOVE, BELOW, SIDE, and INSIDE, along with the 'visual' prime SEE.

According to Hyslop, by far the most common semantic categories in locational deixis are distance, visibility, and elevation (in that order). In relation to distance, the most frequently drawn distinction is between 'proximal' and 'distal', which are technical variants of NEAR and NOT NEAR. To be more explicit, 'proximal' normally means NEAR ME since in fully two-thirds of Hyslop's sample, locational deixis was structured exclusively according to relative distance from the speaker. In some languages, however, distance from the addressee also comes into the picture. For example (note that & is a vowel symbol in the Marshallese orthography):

Georgian (Vogt 1971):

es	'near speaker'
eg	'near addressee'
is/igi	'near neither'

Marshallese (Bender 1969: 76):

y&y/yih&h	'close to speaker'
yin	'close to speaker, close to addressee'
ney/neyney	'not close to speaker, close to addressee'
yen/yiyen	'not close to speaker, not close to addressee'

For Georgian and Marshallese, the contrast between NEAR and NOT NEAR may be sufficient, but for languages with more than two degrees of distance, it is almost certain that FAR is grammaticalized as well. Hyslop found 11 languages with four degrees of distance. Kusaiean is one such. It seems clear from Lee's glosses that the last two forms involve the meaning FAR. Possibly *ngoh* encodes FAR FROM HERE (or FROM ME) and *ngi* encodes VERY FAR FROM HERE (or FROM ME).

Kusaiean (Lee 1975: 129):

nge	'this'
ngacn	'that'
ngoh	'that over there'
ngi	'that way over there'

Other languages reported to have more than three 'degrees of distance' are Malagasy (with six) and Koasati (with seven). In general, the 'distal pole' tends to be more differentiated than the proximal, which makes good sense: the practical difference between FAR and VERY FAR is likely to be more important than that between NEAR and VERY NEAR.

Coming now to visibility, it is sometimes difficult from the available descriptions to decide whether a term truly refers to referents which are 'out of sight', or merely to something which is 'extremely distal' (VERY FAR). Even when visibility is involved it can be hard to decide on the best formulation in particular cases; for instance, to decide between a subjective orientation, as in 'I can't see this', or a more objective 'someone can't see this from here'. Nevertheless, some languages have been described in enough detail to make it quite plain that visibility is a factor. For instance, coastal Yidiny (Dixon 1977: 180f.) has a demonstrative stem *yu-* which can only be used for referents that are both distant and visible; in Kabardian (Colarusso 1989: 296) the term *a* indicates a referent that is not visible to the speaker though it could be any distance away.

Hyslop (1993) found the parameter of elevation in eight different language families, always in languages spoken in mountainous regions. For example, Paamese has a set of location nouns which indicate that a referent is located above or below the position of the speaker.

Paamese (Crowley 1979: 127):

kèmai	'over here'	*kèva*	'over there'
kema	'up over here'	*kevina*	'up over there'
kemita	'down over here'	*kevita*	'down over there'

In some languages, the elevation parameter is usually described in terms of 'uphill' vs. 'downhill' (or 'upriver' vs. 'downriver'). Some languages also distinguish more than one 'degree of elevation' above and below the speaker. Presumably, in such cases NEAR and FAR combine with ABOVE and BELOW to produce contrasts like 'above here' (or 'above the place where I am'), 'far above here' (or 'far above the place where I am'), 'very far above here' (or 'very far above the place where I am').

The remaining semantic categories found in locational deixis are rare, being attested chiefly in languages of the Eskimo-Aleut and Paleo-Asiatic families. Most of them seem to be based on the prime ON (THIS) SIDE. For example, West Greenlandic has a demonstrative *qanna* which indicates that a referent is 'on the other side ... of some intervening surface, usually a wall or door' (Fortescue 1984: 260). West Greenlandic also has a number of demonstratives which indicate on which side of the settlement a referent is located: seaward (or west) side, inland (or east) side, north side, or south side. There are additional specifications for elevation and distance, where appropriate. Reinterpreting somewhat the data from Fortescue (1984: 259–63), these can be listed as follows:

West Greenlandic:

kanna	'not far down on the seaward side'
sanna	'far down on the seaward side (e.g. out to sea)'
pinnga	'not far up on the inland side (e.g. higher up in the settlement)'
panna	'far up on the inland side (e.g. on a mountain behind the settlement)'
anna	'on the north side'
qanna	'on the south side'

There were two languages in Hyslop's (1993) sample—Aleut and West Greenlandic—which have locational deictics whose meanings involve IN-SIDE. For example, Geoghegan (1944) describes Aleut *sadán* as indicating a referent 'outside the house', and *ukán* as indicating a referent 'inside the house'. This fact (if it is a fact) may have its rationale in the importance of the shelter of the igloo to the Arctic lifestyle; but it must be said that the original data is not especially clear.

11.3 Classifier systems

Generally speaking, we say that a language has a CLASSIFIER SYSTEM when it has grammatical devices which, in certain contexts, oblige speakers to categorize a referent along specific semantic dimensions. For living things, these dimensions may include whether or not the referent is human, and, if not, what kind of life-form (e.g. animal, fish, plant) or functional category (e.g. edible, dangerous) it belongs to. For inanimates, semantic dimensions may include the physical properties (e.g. shape, size, material) and functions (e.g. vehicle, tool) of the item. From the point of view of grammar, up to six different types of classifier construction can be distinguished, though the distinctions are obscured by the fact that in most languages the same classifiers participate in several different constructions (Aikhenvald 2000).

We will concentrate on the two most common types: noun classifiers and numeral classifiers. In either case, the classifier, which may be a word or an affix, is a noun-phrase element. NOUN CLASSIFIERS can occur with ordinary nouns in a broad range of contexts. They are found in languages from all parts of the world. An example of a language with noun classifiers is Yidiny (North Queensland, Australia), which has twenty of them. Ordinary nouns in Yidiny are often preceded by a noun classifier focusing on the essential nature or potential use of the referent, for example, *jarruy durrgu* 'CL:BIRD owl', *buri birmar* 'CL:FIRE coal', *mayi badil* 'CL:EDIBLE plant ricketty-nut' (Dixon 1977: 480ff.).

NUMERAL CLASSIFIERS are more grammatically restricted than noun classifiers, appearing mainly next to numerals and other quantifying expressions, and sometimes also with demonstratives. Numeral classifiers are common in the languages of Asia, Central America, and South America. In such languages, one cannot refer, for example, to a specific number of teachers, cats, cigarettes, or houses, without including a numeral classifier along with the noun and the numeral. As shown below in (a)–(d), the resulting phrases have a structure analogous to that found in English expressions like *two sheets of paper*, *three head of cattle*, and *four members of the family*. (Words like *sheet*, *head*, and *member* are not true classifiers, however, but are better termed 'measures' or 'unit counters'.)

a. *sensei*   *san-nin* (Japanese)
    teacher   three-CL:PEOPLE
b. *empat*   *ekor*   *kucing* (Malay)
    four   CL:ANIMAL   cat
c. *bùrì*   *sɔ́.ŋ*   *muan*   (Thai)
    two   CL:STICK-LIKE   cigarettes
d. *géi*   *gāan*   *ngūk*   (Cantonese)
    several   CL:BUILDING   house

There is, no doubt, a deep semantic reason for the association of classifiers with counting, namely, that before we can count anything we must identify the referents as being 'of the same kind'.

Historically, both noun and numeral classifiers originate from ordinary nouns with concrete meanings. In some languages, many or most classifiers are still identical in form with ordinary nouns. For example, in Malay the classifier *ekor*, which is used with animals, fish, and birds, is identical with an ordinary noun meaning 'tail'. On the other hand, there are languages in which all the classifiers are completely opaque in form.

It might head off potential misunderstandings to point out the main difference between a classifier system and a system of GRAMMATICAL GENDER, such as we find in German, French, and many other European languages, and in many African languages. A gender system is essentially a classification of nouns (i.e. of words). There is always a semantic basis for parts of a gender system (e.g. for words referring to humans), but the majority of the system is not semantically based. Gender is also intimately connected with the grammatical process of 'agreement', i.e. the phenomenon whereby other words in the clause adopt different forms to 'agree with' the gender of a noun. The number of genders is usually fairly small and quite fixed.

Classifiers, however, do not classify nouns but the referents of nouns—the actual things in the world which the speaker 'picks out' to say something about on a particular occasion. The basis for the system is always predominantly, if not exclusively, semantic. Because of this, it is usual in some circumstances to have a choice of classifiers, depending on how one is viewing the referent in question. Classifiers are not normally involved in grammatical agreement processes. They are often found in sizeable numbers, and sometimes form a 'semi-open' class, lacking clear boundaries. Classifier systems differ according to whether they are exhaustive or partial (i.e. do all nouns receive classifiers, or only some?), and according to whether the use of classifiers is obligatory or not. The formal status of classifiers can vary on a continuum from more-or-less 'lexical' to more-or-less 'grammatical'.

11.3.1 Classifier systems young and old

A quick way to develop a feel for the variety in classifier systems is to compare a system in the early stage of development, such as the noun classifier system of Jacaltec (Guatemala), with a very old and elaborated system, such as the numeral classifier system of Cantonese. Jacaltec (Craig 1986) has twenty-four classifiers, neatly divided between those for the social world (people, spiritual beings) and those for the inanimate world (natural and manufactured things). Most of the Jacaltec classifiers are identical in form with ordinary nouns. The system is semantically transparent, and, as we will see, the categories identified by the classifiers are all motivated by the concerns of traditional Mayan culture.

Some typical Jacaltec sentences illustrating classifier use are given below. In (a) we see the classifiers *naj* and *no7* preceding nouns, and in (b) we see the same forms acting as anaphoric (i.e. pronoun-like) elements. (Note that the digit 7 is used as a letter in the Jacaltec alphabet.)

a. *Xil   naj   Pel   hune7 hin   no7   txitam   tu7.*
   saw CL:MAN Pedro   one   my   CL:ANIMAL pig   that
   'Pedro saw that one pig of mine.'

b. *Xil   naj   no7.*
   saw CL:MAN CL:ANIMAL
   'He saw it (an animal).'

Among the Jacaltec social classifiers the major divide is between those for the high deities and those for human beings. Most of the major categories have separate classifiers for male and females. Thus, high male deities (classifier *cuman*, lit. *cu-man* 'our-father') include *cumam dios* 'God' and *cuman tz'ayic* 'the sun god'; high female deities (classifier *cumi7*, lit. *cu-mi7* 'our-mother') include *cumi7 virgen maria* 'Virgin Mary' and *cumi7*

x'ahaw 'the moon goddess'. With human beings, the most neutral classifiers are *naj* (for men) and *ix* (for women). They are generally used when
addressing or referring to people outside one's own immediate family who
are about the same age or not very much older than oneself. Thus, one
could say things like *naj winaj* 'the man', *naj Antun* 'Antonio', *ix ix* 'the
woman', and *ix Ros* 'Rosa'. The male classifier *naj* is also used with the
designations for minor deities (such as wind) and spirits embodying afflic-
tions (such as disease, poverty, and sadness) which are said to live among
humans; so there are expressions like *naj cak'e* '(spirit of) wind', *naj ya7b'il*
'(spirit of) disease'. Inside the family, different classifiers are used: *ho7* for
male family members and *xo7* for female family members.

There are further options to express the speaker's recognition of the
social standing of the person being addressed or referred to. To show
high respect, for instance, for a much older person or for one's father or
mother, one can use the special classifier *ya7*. At the other end of the social
scale there is a special classifier for infants, *unin*. Interestingly, these two
classifiers are indifferent to the male/female distinction which runs through
the rest of the system.

The social classifiers reflect the organization of the 'powers that be' in the
Jacaltec world, in recognizing two orders of higher powers (one of a god-
like nature, and the other of a more human-like nature). At the level of
community organization, the system reflects the importance of gender and
the nuclear family (Craig 1986: 272).

Turning now to classifiers for things outside the social world, there is a
versatile classifier *no7* used for animals, such as *no7 mis* 'cat' and *no7 lab'a*
'snake'. It is also used for products which come from animals, such as *no7
lech* 'milk' and *no7 xañab'* '(leather) sandal'. Here we see an instance of
regular polysemy, commonly found in classifier languages, whereby the
same classifier is used for both the source or material and for products
which come from or are made out of this source or material. In Jacaltec
there are many other instances of the same pattern. For example, the
classifier for corn, *ixim*, is also used to classify tortillas, and the classifier
for cloth, *k'ap*, is also used to classify garments.

There are four classifiers which identify other major categories of things in
the natural world: *te7* 'plant', *k'a7* 'fire', *ha7* 'water', *ch'en* 'rock'. In addition,
there are seven more specific classifiers, all of which seem 'keyed' to items of
particular cultural and economic importance in traditional Jacaltec life.
These are: *metx'* 'dog', *ixim* 'corn', *atz'am* 'salt', *tx'otx'* 'soil, clay', *tx'añ*

'rope', *k'ap* 'cloth', and *tx'al* 'thread'. Craig (1986) argues that the specific classifiers can be seen as 'metaphors for the life sustaining functions of the Jacaltec community'. Pre-eminent among these is corn, which not only is the main crop of the Mayan people but also has deep religious significance. The dog is the only pet animal of Mayan culture (non-domestic dogs, such as the coyote, are classified with other animals as *no7*). In the old Mayan culture, salt was one of the main trading items and pottery-making (which used clay) was one of the main crafts. Rope-making, cloth-weaving, and thread-weaving are still the three major specialized crafts in the Jacaltec community (rope-making is done only by men, cloth-weaving by mature women, and thread-weaving by unmarried women and girls).

From its semantic transparency, and the fact that almost all its classifiers correspond to nouns which are still in use in the language, it is a safe bet that the Jacaltec system is of recent origin. What, then, do older systems look like? Consider the following data, adapted from Matthews and Yip (1994: 101–5), on numeral classifiers for inanimates in Cantonese. There are a dozen-plus common classifiers based on physical properties such as shape, orientation, and size, as in (a)–(f) below. Some of these can also be used as 'measures' or unit counters, when combined with mass nouns. A smaller number of common classifiers are based on function, as in (g) and (h).

a. *lāp* for round, small things
   e.g. *yāt lāp láu* 'a button', *géi lāp yeuhkyún* 'a few pills'
b. *jēung* for objects with a flat side which typically faces upwards
   e.g. *jēung tói* 'table', *jēung dang* 'seat, bench', *jēung jí* 'sheet of paper'
c. *fūk* for thin flat things with four sides
   e.g. *fūk wá* 'painting', *fūk séung* 'photograph'
d. *gauh* for things which are lump-like or have no fixed shape
   e.g. *gauh sehk* 'stone', *gauh chaatgāau* 'rubber, eraser'
e. *jī* for things which are long, round in shape, and thin
   e.g. *jī bāt* 'a pen', *jī dék* 'flute', *yāt jī fā* 'a single flower'
f. *tiuh* for things which are long and thin
   e.g. *tiuh tàuhfaat* 'a strand of hair', *tiuh louh* 'road', *tiuh sèh* 'snake'
g. *ga* for vehicles and largish machines with moving parts
   e.g. *ga chē* 'car', *ga fēigēi* 'aeroplane', *ga yī-chē* 'sewing machine'
h. *bá* for tools, weapons, and implements
   e.g. *bá jē* 'umbrella', *bá dōu* 'knife', *bá só* 'lock'

As often happens in classifier languages, there are circumstances in which a speaker will have a choice of classifiers depending on how he or she views the object involved. For example, *chēung* 'gun' could be classified as *jī* (by its cylindrical shape) or as *bá* (by its function as a weapon); *syùhn* 'sailing vessel' could be classified as *ga* (large vehicle) or as *jek* (small object), yielding the meanings 'ship' vs. 'boat', respectively. An extreme case is the word *yéh* 'thing' which can take almost any classifier, according to the kind of thing being referred to.

In Cantonese, unlike Jacaltec, most of the classifiers cannot be used as independent nouns (though historical studies show that they started out that way). Many have meanings which seem rather schematic and which cannot be correlated with culturally significant items. Furthermore, aside from general classifiers which can be used with a wide range of objects, like those listed in (a)–(h) above, there are more than twenty more specialized classifiers; for example, *bouh* for sophisticated books and mechanical devices (e.g. *bouh síusyut* 'novel', *bouh jihdín* 'dictionary', *bouh séunggēi* 'camera'), *gāan* for buildings where people live or gather (e.g. *gāan nguk* 'house', *gāan jáuhlàuh* 'restaurant'), *sáu* for songs and poems. All these characteristics are symptomatic of the antiquity of the Cantonese system.

11.3.2 Classifiers, prototypes, and polysemy

Probably most classifiers are polysemous. Sometimes, as in Jacaltec, the polysemy is fairly regular; for instance, it is easy to state a general rule that a classifier with the primary meaning 'X' may also express the meaning 'something made of X'. But in many languages there are classifiers with a veritable maze of interrelated meanings which can only be understood in terms of a 'prototype and polysemy' analysis. The most celebrated example of an analysis of this kind is Lakoff's (1987: 104–7) description of the Japanese numeral classifier *-hon*. To illustrate the complexities involved, we too will examine *-hon*, in the light of a later and more detailed study by Matsumoto (1993). Notice that Japanese numeral classifiers are suffixes to numerals.

In Japanese, there are only four commonly used classifiers whose meanings are based on physical properties. Aside from *-hon* for longish thin things, these are *-ko*, a 'general' classifier for discrete objects, *-mai* for thin, flat things (such as leaves and pieces of paper), -*tsubu* for very small items (such as beans, tablets, and grains). The other common Japanese classifiers are based on function. Matsumoto (1993) lists thirteen of them, including -*dai* for largish machines, -*ki* for aircraft, -*ken* for buildings where people live or do business (such as houses and shops), -*seki* for large sea vessels, -*soo* for small sea vessels, -*choo* for tools, -*satsu* for books.

The most typical uses of -*hon* are with long-thin things such as pencils, sticks, fingers, needles, carrots, bananas, ropes, strings, and cords. Note that both rigid and flexible items are covered. Some examples are given below; notice that -*hon* has several allomorphs, including -*pon* and -*bon*.

empitsu ni-hon	*kyuuri ip-pon*	*himo san-bon*
pencil two-CL:HON	cucumber one-CL:HON	string three-CL:HON
'two pencils'	'one cucumber'	'three strings'

Aside from prototypical long-thin referents, Matsumoto (1993) discusses -*hon*'s use with a disparate range of other items. Like Lakoff (1987), Matsumoto argues that it is best analysed in terms of a so-called 'radial polysemy' structure. There are two sets of extended uses pertaining to concrete objects. The first relates to things like cassette tapes, typewriter ribbons, and camera films—objects that can be seen as consisting of a 'hon-like' item which is rolled up. Some speakers also apply -*hon* to rubber bands and tyre tubes, objects which are normally in a 'circular' shape but which, if cut, would assume a more typical *hon*-like shape. The second concerns fluids which come in 'closed long-shaped containers' such as bottles, cans, long cartons, tubes, and syringes. Not only the container but also the fluid inside (be it whisky, coke, milk, paste, or a medical injection) can be classified as -*hon*.

Three further uses of -*hon* relate to non-physical referents. As suggested by Lakoff (1987), the use of -*hon* with home runs, hits and fouls in baseball, passes and shots in soccer and basketball, serves in volleyball, rallies in pingpong, and so on seems explicable in terms of a ball travelling along a narrowly defined 'trajectory'. The extended use is based on a likeness between the image of a long thin object and the trajectory of a moving object. According to Matsumoto (1993), a similar principle explains why telephone calls and letters can sometimes be classified as -*hon*, since they can be seen as involving communication which travels from one place to another. He notes that -*hon* is acceptable when it refers to telephone calls being connected or received, but not when it refers to telephone conversations (even though the same noun *denwa* 'telephone' is used for both). Similarly, *-hon* is acceptable when speaking of sending a letter, but not when speaking about writing a letter. The key factor seems to be point-to-point transmission.

A third set of non-physical uses is based on what Matsumoto calls 'experiential length'. Theses, TV serials, movies, and play scripts 'form a continuum when we experience (read, write, watch) them in real time, and can therefore be regarded as one dimensional' (1993: 678). This explanation cannot be quite right, however, because it would predict that *-hon* can be applied to a long telephone conversation, which is incorrect. From the range of acceptable referents, however, we might speculate that what is involved is a narrowly focused 'story' or an extended examination of a particular topic.

Though this does not exhaust all possible uses of *-hon*, it should be clear that its apparently bewildering variety of possible referents is not as bizarre and arbitrary as it seems at first. As with so many semantic phenomena, the key to developing a clear picture is to work patiently through the language-specific facts. Unfortunately, there are relatively few careful studies of individual classifiers to be found in the sizeable classifier literature. Scholars have generally concerned themselves either with describing the entire classifier system of a particular language (which limits the attention that can be given to any individual classifier) or with the syntax or historical development of classifiers, or with attempts to generalize about universals in the semantic organization of classifier systems.

11.3.3 Semantic organization of classifier systems

Various schemes have been proposed to sum up universal tendencies in the semantic organization of classifier systems from unrelated and geographically separated languages. A seminal example is Allan's (1977) scheme of seven 'categories of classification', based on his survey of more than fifty classifier languages. Allan's four main categories are shown below, along with their major sub-categories. Similar schemes are often found in textbooks and in the secondary literature on classifiers.

Material:	(1a) animacy
	(1b) abstract and verbal nouns
	(1c) inanimacy
Shape:	(2a) saliently one-dimensional
	(2b) saliently two-dimensional
	(2c) saliently three-dimensional
Consistency:	(3a) flexible
	(3b) hard or rigid
	(3c) non-discrete
Size	

As Allan acknowledges, there are several difficulties with this system. First, some of the subcategories are heterogeneous. For example, 'human-ness', 'social status', and animacy in a literal sense are all placed under the (1a) heading 'animacy'. Classifiers for such disparate categories as trees, vehicles, food, body-parts, and tools are all placed under the (1c) heading 'inanimacy'. Second, most of the categories intermesh. For example, shape and consistency are very often combined, e.g. one-dimensional+rigid ('stick-like'), two-dimensional+flexible ('fabric-like'), as are shape and size (e.g. three-dimensional+small). The question is: Why?

A problem with universal schemes is that there is a tendency for infor-mation to get lost if it doesn't fit neatly, especially as successive authors reinterpret and simplify the work of their predecessors. For example, aside from three 'shape' categories based on dimension, Allan (1977: 301–2) mentions a further three non-dimensional sub-categories: 'prominent curved exterior' (for hills, humps, heaps, horns, rising smoke, fingernails, ribs, bowlike objects, floats, etc.), 'hollow' (for container-like and pipe-like objects), and 'annular', i.e. ringlike (for rings, garlands, and garments that encircle the body). But other commentators who have drawn on Allan's work tend to forget about these. For this reason, the picture of classifier systems one finds in textbooks and in much of the secondary literature is over-simplified.

With this caveat in mind, it is interesting to review the typological semantics of classifiers from an NSM point of view. The most widespread distinction is between humans, i.e. PEOPLE, and non-humans (Croft 1994). Classifiers for non-human 'beings', such as deities and spirits, presumably involve a direct contrast with PEOPLE. If there is more than one human classifier in a particular language, the most common distinction is male vs. female. Also common are social meanings connected with relative age, status, and family or group membership. These will presumably involve universal or near-universal semantic molecules such as 'men [m]', 'women [m]', 'children [m]' (see Chapter 12), and components associated with social meanings (such as 'this someone has lived for a very long time', 'people like this are above people like me', and 'these people are like parts of one thing').

The meanings that underlie classifiers for 'living things' of various kinds, such as animals, birds, fish, and plants, is probably not different in any fundamental way from the semantics of words like 'animal', 'bird', 'fish', and 'tree'. (This is not to say that such classifiers have exactly the same meanings as these English words, only that similar types of semantic components are involved.)

We now come to classifiers for inanimate things. As noted, such systems always seem to include one general or 'neutral' classifier (similar or identical in meaning to SOMETHING/THING) which can be used with just about anything. For example, in Cantonese there is *go*, in Burmese *khu*, in Vietnamese *cai*. These classifiers are used to count 'mixed groups' (e.g. a collection of a couple of pens, a few marbles, and a knife) or objects whose specific nature is unknown or irrelevant to the speaker.

Most inanimate classifiers seem to rely heavily on semantic molecules for shapes and physical properties, especially: 'long', 'flat', 'round', 'thick', 'thin', 'pointed', 'sticking out', 'straight', 'hard', 'soft', 'sharp'. Many classifiers for inanimates seem to be connected with the notion of 'handling' (cf. Denny 1976), but this observation is fully consistent with this list of semantic molecules, since their meanings too crucially involve manipulation with the hands (see Chapter 12; Wierzbicka 2006c; Goddard and Wierzbicka 2007).

If concrete objects tend to be classified according to how they can be handled by a human being, this would explain the common intermeshing of shape, consistency, and size components, as well as being consistent with the covert anthropocentrism of many lexical items for physical objects and living things. Function-based classifiers (e.g. for houses, vehicles, tools, clothing) are, of course, obviously connected with human activities, i.e. with things PEOPLE DO WITH other things. In short, despite the fact that classifiers are often presented in the secondary literature as exotic and mystifying, there is no reason to think that they are any less amenable to reductive paraphrase analysis than words of other kinds.

11.4 Evidentials and experiencer constructions

11.4.1 Evidentials

EVIDENTIALS are grammatical markers which spell out the grounds for what one says (cf. Chafe and Nichols 1986; Palmer 1986: 51–77; Aikhenvald 2004). The English language does not have evidentials in the form of a coherent grammatical system, though somewhat similar meanings can be expressed by 'epistemic' (i.e. knowledge-related) uses of modal verbs (e.g. *He must be ill, She should be there by now*) and by sentence adverbs such as *probably, certainly, apparently,* and *presumably* (Wierzbicka 2006a: ch. 8). True evidentials are found in a wide range of languages around the world, but are especially well known in native American languages. The examples used in this section come from a dialect of Quechua spoken in Central Peru, and from the Californian language Kashaya, which has one of the richest systems of evidential marking known.

Most evidential meanings appear to be based around a component involving KNOW, THINK, or SAY. We will see examples of each of these broad types in turn, drawing heavily on the interpretation of Wierzbicka (1996a: ch. 15). Evidentials indicating 'how I know' often specify personal experience as the basis, and in many cases specify the precise mode. For instance, in Kashaya there are three suffixes labelled by Oswalt (1986) 'Performative', 'Factual-Visual', and 'Auditory'. The 'Performative' suffix *-mela* is described by Oswalt as signifying 'that the speaker knows of what he speaks because he is performing the act himself or has just performed it' (p. 34). The Factual-Visual suffix *-yă* indicates that 'the speaker knows of what he speaks because he sees, or saw, it' (p. 36). The Auditory suffix *-Vnnă* signifies that 'the speaker knows of what he speaks because he heard the sound of the action' (p. 37). Examples are given in (a)–(c) below.

a. *qowá°q-mela* (phonetically: *qowáhmela*)
    pack-PERFORM
    'I just packed.'
b1. *qowá°q-yă* (phonetically: *qowahy*)
    pack-VISUAL
    '(I just saw) he packed.'
b2. *mo-ma°c-yă* (phonetically: *momá·y*)
    run-in-VISUAL
    '(I just saw) he ran in.'

c. *mo-maᵒc-V̂nnă* (phonetically: *momá·cin*)
run-in-AUDITORY
'(I just heard) someone ran in.'

Apparently, the meanings of these three Kashaya evidentials can be stated as follows:

a. *-mela*   Kashaya Performative (perfective)
I know this because I did it
b. *-yă*   Kashaya Factual-Visual (perfective)
I know this because I saw it
c. *-V̂nnă*   Kashaya Auditory
I know this because I heard it

Aside from 'personal experience' evidentials, it is also common to find evidentials which specify that the speaker's knowledge derives from inference. This too can be exemplified from Kashaya. The 'Inferential I' suffix *-qă* can be used, for example, by someone entering a house and detecting the odour of baking bread. Equally, it could be used by someone making a deduction about future performance based on present experience, as in the example below.

mu   *cohtoc-qă* (phonetically: *mu cohtocʰqʰ*)
that   leave-INFERENTIAL I
'He must have left.'

The only formula general enough to fit these (and other) contexts of use appears to be as below:

-qă   Kashaya Inferential I:
I know this because I know something else

Coming now to evidentials based on THINK in contrast to KNOW, the most prominent type indicates the speaker's lack of complete certainty. For example, in Tarma Quechua (Weber 1986) there is a contrast between three evidential suffixes, *-shi*, *-mi*, and *-chi*. The first of these is a 'hearsay' evidential (see below), but the other two encode a contrast between 'conviction' and 'conjecture'. This distinction can be captured as:

a. *-mi*   Tarma Quechua 'conviction':
I know this
b. *-chi*   Tarma Quechua 'conjecture':
I can think that it is like this, I don't know it

Finally, there is a class of evidentials usually called QUOTATIVES or 'hearsay particles', by which a speaker attributes his or her dictum to someone else. For example, the Quechua suffix *-shi* indicates that 'the speaker has obtained the information that he is supplying through hearsay' (Adelaar 1977: 79, quoted in Weber 1986: 138). A similar evidential is found in Kashaya.

> *-shi*   Tarma Quechua 'hearsay':
> I say this because someone else said it
> I don't say: I know it

Interestingly, the usage of *-mi* 'conviction' vs. *-shi* 'hearsay' is influenced by the cultural attitudes of the Quechua people. As Weber (1986: 138) says, in Quechua culture '(only) one's own experience is reliable' and the cultural norm is 'Avoid unnecessary risk, as by assuming responsibility for information of which one is not absolutely certain.' This helps explain why *-shi* is used to mark a wide range of sentences, ranging from cases where the speaker is highly sceptical of the reported information (as in the case of 'The moon is made of cheese') right through to cases where the speaker has every reason to be sure that the sentence is true (as in 'My mother's grandfather's name was John').

Sometimes, a language can have what is, in effect, an 'anti-hearsay' evidential. This appears to be the case in the Huanuco dialect of Quechua, which differs in this respect from the Tarma dialect mentioned above. In Huanuco Quechua, the *-mi* suffix doesn't just convey 'conviction', as in Tarma. It specifies that the conviction arises not from information provided by someone but from direct experience, as it were (Weber 1986; Wierzbicka 1994a).

> *-mi*   Huanuco Quechua 'anti-hearsay':
> I say this not because someone else said it
> I know it

This has been far from an exhaustive survey of evidential marking. There are many other similar, but subtly different, meaning configurations attested in the world's languages. Even so, it should be clear that the meanings encoded in such categories can be pinned down with precision in paraphrase formulas.

11.4.2 Experiencer constructions

Some writers use the term 'experiencer' to designate a case-role associated
with the principal argument of some or all of the following predicate types:
perception (e.g. *see, hear*), intellection (e.g. *think, know*), emotion (e.g. *hate,
fear*), sensation (e.g. *hunger, itch*). Characterized in this way, the category
of 'experiencer' is a very variable and heterogeneous one. Here we confine
the term to constructions whose prototypical predicate is one of emotion or
sensation, i.e. a predicate which crucially involves the semantic prime FEEL.
For such predicates, many languages offer their speakers a range of constructions encoding alternative perspectives on how someone comes to
have the feeling in question, such as whether it is controllable, wanted or
unwanted, externally caused or self-generated. These components involve
WANT, THINK, BECAUSE, CAN (and NOT), and often discriminate between
GOOD and BAD feelings. In some respects, the range of EXPERIENCER CON-
STRUCTION meanings is analogous to that of evidential meanings, except
that evidentials involve KNOW, THINK, and SAY, whereas experiencer constructions involve FEEL. English has some experiencer constructions, as
shown by the contrast between pairs of sentences like *That surprised me*
and *I was surprised at that*, or *I really liked your performance* and *Your
performance really pleased me*. In this section, however, we will concentrate
on languages in which experiencer constructions are more abundant and
productive, Ewe (West Africa) and Polish.

In Ewe (Ameka 1990), emotion and sensation predicates are found in
numerous distinct grammatical frames. Some predicates, by virtue of their
lexical semantics, are confined to a single construction, but others are
compatible with several alternatives. For instance, with the verbs *tsri-*
(roughly) 'avoid, abstain, hate' and *hiá* 'need, want', the experiencer may
appear as subject, as in (a) and (b), or as object, as in (c) and (d):

a. *Me-tsri   aha.*
   1sg-hate   alcohol
   'I hate/quit alcohol.'
b. *Kofi   hiá   ga.*
   Kofi   need   money
   'Kofi needs money.'
c. *Aha   tsri-m.*
   alcohol   hate-1sg
   'I am allergic to alcohol' (lit. 'alcohol hates me').

d. *Ga*   *hiǎ*   *kofí.*
   money   need   Kofi
   'Kofi is in need of money' (lit. 'money needs Kofi').

Ameka (1990) argues that the Experiencer Object is conceptualised as a passive, non-volitional participant. Consistent with this, it is notable that predicates which designate emotional reactions (like *dzi dzɔ* 'feel happy', *dzi kú-* 'feel angry') only appear in the object experiencer construction. The same applies to predicates designating uncontrollable physiological experiences (like *dɔ wu-* 'be hungry', *aɖuɖɔtó-* 'have urge to urinate'). The object experiencer construction appears to encode the meaning stated below, which includes components of 'non-volition' and 'uncontrollability':

> Ewe 'object experiencer' construction:
> someone X felt something not because X wanted it
> X couldn't not feel this

In two other Ewe constructions, the experiencer appears with the preposition *ná* 'to'. The grammatical subject can then be either the abstract 'stimulus' for the emotion, as in (a); or, if the main verb is the causative verb *dó* 'put on, cause' with an emotion term as its complement, the subject may be a person responsible for provoking or inducing the emotion, as in (b).

a. *É-dzɔ*   *dzi*   *ná*   *m.*
   3sg-straighten   heart   to   1sg
   'It pleased me.'
b. *Ðeví-á*   *dó*   *dzidzɔ*   *ná*   *m.*
   child-DEF   put.on   happiness   to   1sg
   'The child caused me pleasure.'

From Ameka's (1990) discussion, the meanings encoded by these two constructions appear to be as follows:

> Ewe 'emotional stimulus' construction:
> someone X felt something
>   because X thought something about something ('stimulus')
> not because X wanted to feel this

> Ewe 'emotional causer' construction:
> someone X felt something
>   because someone else ('person responsible') did something
> not because of anything else

In Polish (Wierzbicka 1988: 390–433), emotions may be presented in three different grammatical constructions. It is possible to present an emotional experience 'neutrally', i.e. simply to say that a person 'felt something'. The emotion word is then a verb in the 'passive' form bearing a prefix indicating imperfectivity, as in:

> *Adam był uradowany (zmartwiony, zasmucony).*
> 'Adam was pleased (worried, saddened).'

More common, and more characteristically 'Polish' in cultural terms, are the active and the impersonal constructions. 'Active' emotions which are subject to some control are depicted by active verbs with a nominative experiencer subject, and often with a reflexive particle (*się*) as in (a) below. The impersonal construction, as in (b) below, has the experiencer in the dative case, and the predicate takes the form of an adverbial with a copula (which is usually deleted in present tense).

> a. *Adam żałował (cieszył się, martwił się, smucił się).*
>   'Adam regretted (rejoiced, worried, was sad).'
> b. *Adamowi było żal (wstyd, smutno).*
>   'Adam felt regret (felt ashamed, felt sad).'

The emotion verbs which participate in the active construction all have a markedly cognitive dimension. The construction depicts the experiencer as engaged in thoughts which sustain a certain feeling. The impersonal construction, by contrast, starts with a feeling and indicates that the thoughts underlying it were involuntary.

> Polish active emotion construction:
> someone X thought about something for some time
>   because X wanted to think about it at that time
> because of this, X felt something at that time
>   like someone can feel when they think like this

> Polish 'impersonal' emotion construction:
> someone X felt something for some time
>   because X thought about it at that time
> X thought about it at that time
>   not because X wanted to think about it at that time

Experiencer constructions have been reported in a very wide range of languages. It may even be that every language, if examined closely, would turn out to make available to its speakers alternative grammatical frames for conveying different perspectives on 'feelings'.

11.5 Diminutives

Grammatical labels such as 'causative', 'inceptive', 'instrumental', 'adversative', 'passive', 'relative clause', and the like can be deceptive. Though it is widely agreed that each term makes reference to some kind of semantic or functional prototype, around which individual languages allow language-specific extensions, there is still much room for disagreement and misunderstanding about the nature of the semantic or functional prototype. Even in cases where one would imagine that the prototype is intuitively fairly clear, as with the category DIMINUTIVE, a contrastive examination of several languages shows that there are many semantic differences which are concealed or glossed over by the use of a single global label. In this section we illustrate by comparing some of the meanings conveyed by 'diminutives' in Spanish and in Australian English.

11.5.1 Two meanings of the Spanish diminutive

The Spanish diminutive is multifunctional and highly polysemous (quite aside from the existence of multiple forms and regional variants). Certainly it is not just a matter of literal 'smallness'. As Gooch (1970: 1) remarks, diminutive morphology is frequently used 'to convey those things which belong more to the warmth of the heart than to the coolness of the head', i.e. to convey good feelings, especially in personal interaction. The diminutive in Spanish (and in many other languages) is linked with children, both conceptually and in usage, i.e. one uses a lot of diminutives when speaking about and to children. Incidentally, diminutive morphology often derives historically from the word for 'child', as well as from 'small' (Jurafsky 1996). Travis (2004) explicates a set of similar-yet-different, i.e. polysemous, meanings of the Spanish diminutive. We will consider only two of these here.

Most titles of children's tales use the diminutive; for example, *Blanca-nieves y los 7 enanitos* ('Snow White and the seven dwarves'), *Los tres cerditos* ('The three pigs'). A word like *cerdito* [pig-DIM] brings to mind two contexts of use, both linked with children; namely, when talking to a child about a pig, or when referring to a baby pig. Similarly, *abriguito* [coat-DIM] will be used when talking to a child about a coat or when referring to a child's coat (and also to refer to a cute women's coat). Travis (2004) proposes that the meaning can be captured in the following explication. Notice the presence of the semantic molecules 'child [m]' and 'children [m]'.

> *animalito/lobito* 'animal/wolf-DIM':
> an animal/wolf
> I think about it like this: 'this thing is something small,
>   like a child [m] is someone small'
> when I think about it like this, I feel something good
>   like people can feel when they think about small children [m]

In a smaller proportion of uses, the diminutive can be used about literal small size. The following examples from Travis (2004) are in Colombian Spanish. Sentence (a) is about a miniature microphone being used for the recordings; (b) refers to a small bug that destroys an otherwise very strong material used to make houses; and (c) refers to small black spots that Angela sometimes sees in her kitchen.

a. Santi*: Eso es un micrófono? Sí.* Angela: *Sí, eso es un microfonito.*
   'Santi: "That is a microphone? Right?" Angela: "Yes, that is a microphone-DIM." '
b. *Claro que es que el problema de la – de la= guadua es la plaga.*
   .. hay un cucarroncito escarabajo, así chiquitico, yo no sé cómo se llama.
   'Of course, the problem with the – with the *guadua* (a variety of bamboo) is the plague. There's a beetle-DIM, small-DIM like this, I don't know what it's called.'
c. *Yo a veces veo unos punticos, .. negritos, en las cosas,… Y yo creo que son de mosca.*
   'I sometimes see some black-DIM spots-DIM, on things… And I think they're from a fly.'

Of course, the diminutive is not the only way of referring to small size: there are the adjectives *pequeño* and *chiquito* 'small', for example, and this fact in itself indicates that even the 'literal smallness' uses of the diminutive are not solely about smallness as such. In (b) above, *chiquito* 'small' is used itself in the diminutive (*chiquitico*), and the noun it modifies also takes the diminutive. Commenting on this example, Travis (2004: 263–4) says:

Thus, the diminutive appears to express something other than small size alone, namely 'good feelings' on the part of the speaker. In this case, it is certainly not good feelings TOWARDS the referent (for example, the speaker does not feel good towards the bug or the spots left by cockroaches), but in thinking of the referent as something small, the speaker feels something good, in a similar way to how they feel when thinking about children.

This meaning of the diminutive can be explicated as follows:

microfonito 'microphone-DIM':
when I say this about this thing, I think about this thing like this:
  'it is a small thing of its kind'
when I think about it like this, I feel something good
  like people can feel when they think about small children [m]

11.5.2 The Australian English 'diminutive'

The range of semantic variation expressible by so-called 'diminutives' across languages is starkly illustrated when the Spanish diminutive is contrasted with the hypocoristic diminutive of Australian English. Its characteristic derivational diminutive (actually, a family of them) is a notable feature of Australian English, identified as such by linguists like Roland Sussex (2004a, 2004b), and by language commentators in the popular media.

No other English runs Australian English even close when it comes to creativity and usage of hypocoristics, which are pushing ever more vigorously into the written language as well. (Sussex 2004a)

Examples follow. Sussex (2004a) says that they express solidarity, good mood, and familiarity. Wierzbicka (1992a) says that they express 'convivial good humour'. There is an important similarity with nicknaming.

Chrissy prezzies (Christmas presents), *brekkie* (breakfast), *barbie* (barbecue), *cozzies* (swimming costume), *pozzie* (position, in a cinema, when parking etc.), *trannie* (transvestite), *firies* (fire-fighters), *tantie* (tantrum), *rellies* (relatives), *veggies* (vegetables), *lippy* (lipstick), *footie* (football), *piccies/pickies* (movies, or pictures of any sort), *biccies/bickies* (biscuits), *postie* (postman), *sunnies* (sunglasses), *undies* (underwear), *mushies* (mushrooms), *kindy* (kindergarten), *eccies/ekkie* (ecstasy tablet), *salties* (salt-water crocodiles), *freshies* (fresh-water crocodiles).

The same formation extends to place names, such as *Brissie* (Brisbane), *Tassie* (Tasmania), *Kossie/Kozzie* (Mt Kosciuszko), *Rocky* (Rockhampton), *The Newie* (New England Hotel), and hundreds of others (Simpson 2001).

These distinctively Australian examples are very different from the regular English diminutive in *-ie*, e.g. *birdie*, *horsie*: formally, because the regular diminutive does not involve any abbreviation, and semantically, because the regular diminutive conveys a childish effect. In relation to the latter point, note that the Australian formation can readily occur in adult sentences with a somewhat annoyed tone, as in (a), while a comparable sentence with a regular *-ie* diminutive, as in (b), would sound ridiculous.

a. *Those bloody maggies!* (i.e. magpies—aggressive birds which attack pedestrians and cyclists in spring)
b. *?Those bloody birdies!*

Far from being a feature of children's speech, the Australian English diminutive is often used by men, and many of them have a 'male flavour'. For example:

a. *Once I have established with a mechanically gifted friend that I know enough about a carburettor to call it a <u>carbie</u>, it would be inconsistent to use the full form carburettor.* (Sussex 2004a)
b. *Instead of scunging for freebies, I might even spend whatever bucks are required to get a good <u>pozzie</u> [i.e. position] at Albert Park next March.*

At the same time, whatever the matter being discussed, the use of an Australian English *-ie* form brings with it a certain lightness of touch and a sense of easy familiarity. For the speaker, things such as this are, to put it colloquially, 'no big deal'. For example, the speaker venting his or her annoyance with the magpies at the same time conveys the impression that he or she is well familiar with the problem and is not too worried about it. As the comment in the first example above indicates, men who know about motor mechanics invariably call a carburettor a *carbie*. And the sports fan quoted in the second example conveys casual familiarity with the business of securing a good position at the match. In contrast with the Spanish diminutive, there is no sense whatsoever of endearment.

When the term abbreviated and appended with the *-ie* denotes something dangerous or scary, the meaning conveyed can seem quite curious. The first example below is about fresh-water crocodiles, found in rivers and waterholes of the Northern Territory of Australia. They are not as dangerous as salt-water crocodiles, but they are still responsible for a number of serious injuries, and the occasional death, each year. By referring to these dangerous creatures as *freshies*, the writer conveys a casual familiarity and a distinctly 'unimpressed' quality. Salt-water crocodiles, by the way, are referred to in the same style as *salties*. As a reminder of more mundane uses, consider the second example below about *mozzies* (mosquitoes). Both examples also show that such terms are acceptable in professional discourse.

They do not prey on people but will bite in self-defence. Since some large <u>freshies</u> take wallabies, children should always be supervized near freshwater crocodiles. (Information briefing by the Environmental Protection Agency)
'We've had quite a bit of rain during November, it's time to clean up around the home to ensure you aren't providing a breeding ground for mozzies,' Dr Dalton said.

All these observations bear on the explication given below. Notice the attitudinal component 'it is not something big', which conveys an 'unimpressed' or 'undaunted' attitude. This is followed by a component directly linked with this: 'when I say something about it, I don't want to say it with a big word.' In a sense this component spells out the effect of 'cutting something down to size', by using an abbreviated word rather than a 'big word'. The next component specifies the assumed sense of ease ('people here don't have to think much about things like this') due to their familiarity with the topic ('because they know about things like this well'). Notice that these properties are not specific to the speaker but are extended to 'people here': in this way, they include the other significant company and, potentially, the hearer as well. Finally, there is a component expressing the speaker's good feeling, not directed in this case towards the object or topic in question, but connected with the casual attitude just attributed to the people around.

> Explication for Australian English 'diminutive' (*barbie, pozzie, carbie, maggies, freshies, mozzies,* etc.):
> something
> when I say this about it, I think about it like this:
>   'it is not something big
>   when I say something about it, I don't want to say it with a big word
>   people here don't have to (i.e. can not) think much about things like this
>   because they know about things like this well'
> when I think about it like this, I feel something good

To summarize, contrastive semantic analysis brings to light a number of similarities and differences, including a subtle but important contrast between the semantic specification 'small' (involved in the Spanish diminutive) and the semantic specification 'not big' (involved in the Australian English diminutive). A second difference is that the Australian English form, but not the Spanish one, conveys a distinctive kind of 'easy familiarity' and a deliberate avoidance of a 'big word' for a familiar thing of this kind. Perhaps the central point of difference between the two is whether or not there is a prototype or reference point involving 'children', as there is in Spanish, but not in Australian English. Both formations express the speaker's 'good feeling'.

With clear and detailed semantic descriptions in hand, it becomes possible to draw out the cultural connections. Spanish culture is well known for its emphasis on interpersonal warmth, i.e. the expression of good feelings towards other people. Spanish diminutives provide a compact and versatile grammatical means to service this need (Travis 2004; 2006). Traditional Australian (Aussie) culture is known for its anti-sentimentality, good-natured humour, love of informality, and dislike for 'long words' (Wierzbicka 1992a; Goddard 2006a). The semantic content of the Australian 'diminutive' is congruent with all these themes.

11.6 Concluding remarks

Though this chapter has surveyed a range of grammatical categories, the coverage has been highly selective. In fact, it can be argued that every semantic prime is found as a part of a grammaticalized meaning in some of the world's languages. Table 11.5 lists some other grammatical phenomena and the primes they involve.

Table 11.5. Some morphosyntactic construction types and associated semantic primes (Goddard 1997b)

ONE, TWO, SOME, MUCH~MANY	number-marking systems (incl. duals, paucals)
THE SAME, OTHER	switch-reference, obviation, reflexives, reciprocals
WANT	imperatives, purposives, 'uncontrolled' marking
KNOW, SEE, HEAR, SAY	evidential systems
WORDS	delocutive verbs, logophoricity, proper nouns
DO, HAPPEN	case marking and transitivity, passive voice, inchoatives
FEEL, THINK	experiencer constructions, interjections
GOOD, BAD	benefactives, adversatives
BIG, SMALL	diminutives, augmentatives
VERY	superlatives, expressives
NOW, BEFORE, AFTER, A LONG TIME, A SHORT TIME, FOR SOME TIME, MOMENT	tense (incl. degrees of remoteness), aspect
HERE, ABOVE, BELOW, SIDE, NEAR, FAR	elaborate locational deixis
PART	inalienable possession
KIND	classifier constructions

The natural semantic metalanguage was devised primarily from investigations of lexical semantics, but it now seems that every element of it can also be found in grammatically encoded meanings. If this is so, there is no fundamental gulf between grammatical semantics and lexical semantics.

Key technical terms

classifier system	inclusive/exclusive distinction
diminutive	locational deictic
dual vs. plural pronouns	minimal-augmented pronoun system
evidential	noun classifier
experiencer construction	numeral classifier
grammatical gender	quotative

Exercises and discussion questions

† next to a problem means that a solution or some commentary can be found at the end of the book.

1†. (a) The Australian language Dyirbal (Dixon 1972) has a future vs. non-future tense system. For example, the verbs *balgaŋ* 'will hit' and *baniŋ* 'will come' can only be used about the future, whereas *balgan* 'hit, is hitting' and *baniɲu* 'came, is coming' can be used about either the present or the past. (If it is necessary to differentiate present from past, this can be done using time adverbs, such as *ŋumbuŋga* 'yesterday', *ŋudaŋga* 'recently', or *dyada* 'now'.) How can the meaning conveyed by the Dyirbal 'future' and 'non-future' tenses be stated in simple terms from the natural semantic metalanguage?

(b) The Amazonian language Hixkaryana has three past tense categories, which have been given the grammatical labels 'immediate past', 'recent past', and 'distant past'. Derbyshire (1985: 196–7) says that the 'immediate past' is used for events which took place on the same day or on the previous night, the 'recent past' is used for events of the previous day or any earlier time up to a few months, while the 'distant past' is used for anything earlier than that. Derbyshire notes, however, that this is 'relative to the total situation, and sometimes an event of only a few weeks ago will be expressed with the distant past suffix.' Try to state a plausible hypothesis about the meanings of the Hixkaryana 'recent past' and 'distant past' categories.

2†. It is often said that the English word *this* is a 'spatial deictic' and that its meaning involves a component like 'close to the speaker'. Assess the validity of this claim, by considering the range of use of *this*.

3. Consider the reflexive construction as in the examples below. From a semantic point of view, what condition must be met for a reflexive pronoun (like *myself*, *yourself*, *himself*) to be used? What does this imply about the meaning encoded in the reflexive construction?

   a. *I cut myself.*
   b. *You shouldn't think too much about yourself.*
   c. *He looked at himself in the mirror.*

4†. Consider English constructions like those illustrated in (a) and (b) below, where an animate subject does something to a person. Compare these sentences with corresponding versions where the body-part appears as direct object (e.g. *A bee stung Norm's finger, Mary kissed Juanita's forehead*). What meaning components are conveyed by the *on*-phrase constructions?

   a. *A bee stung Norm on the finger.*
      The puppy bit John on the leg.
   b. *Mary kissed Juanita on the forehead.*
      Maxine patted John on the shoulder.

   Although the examples in (a) share some components with the examples in (b), there is also a subtle meaning difference between the two types of example. Can you pin it down? (Hint: Consider the types of verb involved.)

5†. Consider the following phrases from Language Z. Figure out the meanings of each of the words. You will find that there are several different word-classes involved. List the words in each class, together with their meanings.

a.	*bayi yuri garbu*	'a few kangaroos'
b.	*balan ngamun*	'breast'
c.	*bayi yara bulgan*	'big man'
d.	*balam binara yunggul*	'one peanut'
e.	*bayi gubi*	'wise man'
f.	*balan ngalban*	'father's younger sister'
g.	*balan jugumbil garbu*	'a few women'
h.	*balam jugur bulgan*	'big yam'
i.	*balam laymun buga*	'rotten lemon'
j.	*bayi guya buga garbu*	'a few rotten fish'
k.	*bayi wangal bulgan*	'big boomerang'
l.	*bayi wir*	'husband'
m.	*balan gajin bulgan*	'big girl'
n.	*balan guynggun*	'spirit of a dead woman'
o.	*bayi yugaba*	'small rat'

6. Examine the data below, which show some examples of the numeral classifier construction in Malay. Work out the semantic basis for the classification.

   a. *sehelai kain* 'a piece of cloth', *dua helai kertas* 'two sheets of paper', *tiga helai kemeja* 'three shirts', *empat helai kain* 'four pieces of cloth'
   b. *sebiji guli* 'one marble', *dua biji* 'two seeds', *tiga biji telor* 'three eggs', *empat biji mata* 'four eyes'
   c. *seekor ikan* 'one fish', *dua ekor anjing* 'two dogs', *tiga ekor ayam* 'three chickens', *empat ekor tikus* 'four mice'
   d. *sebatang rokok* 'one cigarette', *dua batang pencil* 'two pencils', *tiga batang pokok* 'three trees', *empat batang kayu* 'four sticks'
   e. *sekeping surat* 'one letter', *dua keping kayu* 'two planks', *tiga keping kertas* 'three sheets of stiff paper', *empat keping syiling* 'four coins'

7†. In Lakhota (Sioux), there are two different prefixes which can be used to indicate that the subject of a verb is first-person singular (i.e. 'I'). One prefix is *wa-*. Examples of verbs which take this prefix are given in (a). The other prefix is *ma-*. Examples are given in (b). All the examples are of intransitive verbs. Examine the data and propose a semantic explanation for the choice of prefix. (Sometimes the prefixes are not the very first elements in the word. Ignore this.)

   a. *wapsíča*   'I jumped'
      wapšá   'I sneezed'
      ináwaxme   'I'm hiding'
      iyówaya   'I yawn'
      iwáye   'I spoke'
      wat^{h}i   'I live, dwell'
      waškáte   'I'm playing'
      blowákaska   'I hiccough'
   b. *mayázą*   'I'm in pain'
      mahį́xpaye   'I fell'
      mawášte   'I'm good'
      mat'é   'I fainted'
      malák^{h}ota   'I'm Sioux'
      amákisni   'I got well'

12

Developments, extensions, and applications

In this final chapter we review the developmental trajectory of NSM semantics, then spend some time on the relatively new theory of semantic molecules. After that we will look briefly into how the NSM approach can be extended to the study of language acquisition, cultural discourse analysis, and non-verbal communication.

12.1 The trajectory and ongoing development of the NSM system

Anna Wierzbicka's interest in the pursuit of non-arbitrary semantic primitives was triggered by a 1965 lecture on the subject by Andrzej Bogusławski, who in his turn had been inspired by Leibniz's vision of discovering the 'alphabet of human thoughts' through linguistic analysis (Bogusławski 1970; Wierzbicka 1992b). Wierzbicka's book *Semantic Primitives*, which appeared in English in 1972, inaugurated the NSM programme.

Since then, the history of the NSM approach can be outlined as follows. The 1970s to mid-1980s was the 'early development' period. The key publications (Wierzbicka 1972; 1980a; 1980b) worked with a very austere set of 13 or 14 semantic primes (then termed 'semantic primitives'). Even so, valuable analytical work was done on emotion terms, body-parts, stage-of-life terms, speech-act verbs, case constructions, and a number of other areas. Wierzbicka (1985) was an unprecedented investigation into the semantics of concrete vocabulary. The mid-1980s to late 1990s has been dubbed the 'expanding set' phase. Over this period the inventory of semantic primes was expanded more than fourfold, approaching its current number of 64. A new emphasis on cross-translatability and lexical universals entered the programme. From the mid-1990s onwards, the focus shifted to the grammar of the metalanguage and to 'whole metalanguage' studies embracing both lexicon and grammar. Key publications include the two-volume *Meaning and Universal Grammar* (Goddard and Wierzbicka 2002) and *Cross-Linguistic Semantics* (Goddard 2008). More recently one can discern a trend towards increased systematization, as the theory of semantic molecules and semantic templates has been developed (though in some ways this trend can be seen as a return to the earlier descriptive work on areas of great semantic complexity). Other trends include new work on culture-historical semantics (Wierzbicka 2006a; 2010a; Bromhead 2009), and the uptake and application of corpus techniques to semantic research (Goddard 2009a; Wierzbicka 2009c).

In terms of acceptance and recognition, NSM semantics has experienced a notable upswing in the current century (cf. Lehrman 2006), though it remains true to say that it is often ignored or marginalized by proponents of rival approaches. Within linguistics, increasing interest and acceptance has been aided by the tide slowly turning against the narrow English-based 'syntacticocentrism' (Jackendoff 2002) which predominated for most of last century. At the same time, the NSM approach has attracted favourable attention in adjacent disciplines such as anthropology (D'Andrade 2001; Geertz 2000: 208–9), cultural psychology (Shweder 2004), evolutionary psychology (Jones 1999), and semiotics (Eco 1999: 150–3).

In addition to Anna Wierzbicka, Cliff Goddard, Jean Harkins, Bert Peeters, Felix Ameka, and other 'old hands', there is a new generation of NSM researchers, such as Catherine Travis, Rie Hasada, Marie-Odile Junker, Uwe Durst, Kyung-Joo Yoon, Zhengdao Ye, Jock Wong, Anna

Gladkova, Yuko Asano-Cavanagh, Adrian Tien, Helen Bromhead, Carol Priestley, Carsten Levisen, Sophia Waters, and Sandy Habib.

12.1.1 Innovation and change in the NSM programme

The key conviction of NSM semantics has remained stable over its 40-year life to date, namely, that ordinary natural languages are adequate to represent their own semantics via language-internal paraphrase. This belief in the METASEMANTIC ADEQUACY of natural languages entails the view that every language has an irreducible semantic core with a language-like structure: a mini-lexicon of indefinable expressions (semantic primes) and their associated syntax.

This is not to say, however, that NSM semantics has been static. Many new ideas have entered the programme over the years. To illustrate, we can briefly sample some of the changes. Many of course concern the shape of the metalanguage itself. Each and every prime has its own biography, so to speak, explaining how its claim to indefinability emerged, how its entry into the system affected the system as a whole, and (usually) how new applications of the prime became apparent over time. Most of the changes resulted from the realization that analyses for the domains of time, space, quantification, and cognition from the 'early development' period needed improvement. For example, Wierzbicka (1980a) had analysed tense and other temporal phenomena in terms of 'worlds becoming worlds', an idea akin to the treatment of time in some systems of logic. This analysis has been gradually replaced by a more intuitively appealing set of temporal primes, including WHEN~TIME, NOW, BEFORE, and AFTER, as well as the time-period primes A SHORT TIME and A LONG TIME, the durational prime FOR SOME TIME, and the 'anti-durational' MOMENT.

In the early 1990s, a couple of the erstwhile proposed primes ('world' and 'imagine') were discarded on account of non-translatability. The interrelationship between different elements of the prime inventory can be illustrated as follows. In the early days Wierzbicka had explicated existence as 'being part of the world', but this option closed off when 'world' was struck from the primitive inventory. THERE IS was consequently added to the list and subsequent cross-linguistic testing seems to show that it has a lexical foothold in all languages. Similarly, the superseded prime 'imagine' had previously been used to explicate conditional constructions, but with this option closed off, IF was added to the inventory of primes; and again, cross-linguistic testing suggests that all languages can express IF meanings.

For a couple of years in the mid-1990s, it was hypothesized that a bi-clausal counterfactual construction (IF . . . WOULD) was a semantic prime, in addition to the plain conditional IF (Wierzbicka 1996a). The rationale was that counterfactual sentences, e.g. *If we hadn't found water, we would have died*, appeared to resist explication in terms of the conditional IF alone. Subsequent work showed, however, that some languages lack full equiva-lents of the counterfactual (Hasada 1997), and after renewed effort a plausible line of explication for counterfactual meanings was discovered (Goddard 2002b: 303–6).

Over the 'expanding set' phase, the NSM conception of primitive mean-ings changed in one important respect. Like Leibniz (cf. Ishiguro 1972: 45–6), Wierzbicka used to believe that primes should be intuitively inde-pendent, because if two concepts have something in common they could not both be semantically indivisible—or so it seemed. The changing shape of the prime inventory forced a revision of this stance, since there are many intuitive connections among primes which cannot be factored out as dis-crete components. Such connections are now known as NON-COMPOSITIONAL RELATIONSHIPS. Most obvious are the affiliations between primes which form pairs of opposites or converses, such as GOOD and BAD, NEAR and FAR, and BEFORE and AFTER. Though the primes in such pairs are mutually related, it is impossible to extract any common feature from them. Abstract terms such as 'evaluation', 'distance', and 'temporal sequence' are more obscure and difficult to translate across languages than simple basic terms like GOOD, BAD, NEAR, FAR, BEFORE, AFTER, and so on, and could not possibly replace the latter in a universal semantic metalanguage. Other, subtler non-compositional relationships apply between SOMEONE and OTHER, between DO and SAY, and between IF and MAYBE, among others.

One of the biggest innovations in NSM thinking came with the idea (taken for granted in this book, see section 3.1) that many primes, espe-cially the predicate primes, have a number of different valency options. In terms of timing, this idea can be dated to the mid-1990s (Wierzbicka 1996a: 113–14; Goddard 1998: 333–6).

Returning to the prime inventory, a relatively recent entrant is WORDS, which supplements SAY in the domain of speech and language. In its favour are, on the one hand, its resistance to non-circular definition (in contexts like 'He said one word' or 'She said the same thing in/with other words'), and on the other, its apparent indispensability for adequate explication of names and naming (words for identifying persons, places, etc.), counting (words for keeping track of 'how many' things there are somewhere), speech formulae, e.g. *Goodbye* and *How do you do?*, honorific words, and magical formulae, as well as for concepts such as *language* and *paraphrase*. Despite some claims to the contrary, evidence indicates that WORDS is lexicalized in all or most languages (Goddard 2011b).

The most recent proposal is that there is a prime LITTLE~FEW, which is a counterpart of MUCH/MANY. The main arguments in its favour are its resistance to explication and the apparent need for it in the explication of other concepts. How could one explicate an expression like 'a little water', for example? The obvious suggestion would be 'some water, not much' but this putative paraphrase doesn't make the grade, because it would be compatible with, so to speak, a medium-sized amount of water. Another possibility would be to use an expression like 'small part', but there is seemingly no way to work this into a plausible paraphrase. From the point of view of practical explication, a prime like LITTLE~FEW seems to be needed in explicating concepts that involve 'small amounts', e.g. words like *drip*, *drop*, and *sip*. The putative prime LITTLE~FEW remains to be tested cross-linguistically, so its current status is provisional. If it proves itself in cross-linguistic testing, the prime inventory will reach 64 in number.

From a theoretical point of view, the biggest new idea in NSM semantics is the theory of semantic molecules, dealt with in the next section.

Though such developments over time may puzzle or frustrate some observers, they are inevitable in view of the empirical character of the NSM approach. It would be suspicious if hypotheses about the shared lexicogrammatical core of all languages did not change in response to continued semantic analysis and cross-linguistic research.

12.2 The theory of semantic molecules

Semantic primes can be regarded as the 'atoms' of meaning. In recent years NSM researchers have been developing and refining an additional theoretical construct: semantic molecules. As we know from earlier chapters, semantic molecules are non-primitive meanings (hence, ultimately decomposable into semantic primes) that function as units in the semantic structure of other, yet more complex words. In this section we review the theory of semantic molecules in more detail. Along the way we will see explications for some of the common molecules that have been used earlier in the book.

The NSM notion of semantic molecules is similar to that of 'intermediate-level concepts' in the Moscow School of Semantics (Apresjan 1992; 2000; Mel'čuk 1989). The Moscow School linguists see semantic explication as a step-wise process. At the bottom level the entire explication would be composed of semantic primitives. As we ascend through intermediate levels, chunks of primitives are replaced, wherever possible, with semantically equivalent words (the Maximum Block Principle). There is one crucial difference between the NSM concept of semantic molecules and the Moscow School notion of intermediate-level concepts: the constraint that NSM semantic molecules must be meanings of lexical units in the language concerned. Along with this constraint there is a corresponding cognitive claim: that when semantic molecules appear in explications, this represents something conceptually 'real', i.e. a real conceptual dependency between concepts of different levels of complexity.

12.2.1 Nesting and chains of semantic dependency

As we have seen in Chapters 7–9, the meanings of words for concrete objects and for physical activities and actions usually involve a number of semantic molecules. There are some items of concrete vocabulary, however, that can be paraphrased directly into semantic primes. Two very important words of this kind are the body-parts 'hands' and 'mouth'. The explications below are based on Wierzbicka (2007a), a study that proposes explications for over 40 body-part words from English and from other languages.

hands:
two parts of someone's body
they are parts of two other parts on two sides of this someone's body
these parts of someone's body can move as this someone wants
these parts of someone's body have many parts
these parts can move in many ways as this someone wants

because people's bodies have these parts, people can do many things
   with many things as they want
because people's bodies have these parts, people can touch
   many things as they want

mouth:
one part of someone's body
something can be inside this part
when people want things of some kinds to be inside the body,
   they do something to these things with this part

Though 'hands' and 'mouth' can be explicated without resort to any semantic molecules, the same does not apply to most other body-part words. Wierzbicka (2007a) found that body-part explications generally require specifications of three different kinds: the location of the body-part, a partial characterization of its shape, and an indication of its function. The aspect of interest at this moment is the need for a shape specification, because shape descriptors are semantic molecules, not semantic primes. For example, the explication for *legs* requires 'long [m]' and the explication for *head* requires 'round [m]'.

legs (someone's legs):
two parts of someone's body
these parts are long [m]
these parts are below all the other parts of the body
these parts of someone's body can move as this someone wants
because people's bodies have these parts, people can move
   in many places as they want

head (someone's head):
one part of someone's body
this part is like something round [m]
this part is above all the other parts of the body
when someone thinks about something, something happens in this part
   of this someone's body

(Note that since they are framed in terms of 'someone's body', these explications do not apply to the body-parts of animals. The NSM view is that body-part words when applied to animals involve an analogical extension from an anthropocentric prototype. For example, *head₂* (e.g. *a cat's head* or *a snake's head*) can be explicated as: 'one part of the body of a living thing of one kind; this part is like one part of people's bodies; this part of people's bodies is the head [m]'.)

Now the critical thing: shape concepts—including 'long', 'round', 'flat', and 'straight'—include the concept of 'hands' in their semantic structure (Wierzbicka 2006c). This is because shape descriptors designate properties that are both visual and 'tangible', and to spell out the nature of the latter concept requires both semantic prime TOUCH (contact) and semantic molecule 'hands [m]' (cf. Fig. 12.1). The two explications below show how it can be done. It has to be noted, though, that words like *long* and *round* are highly polysemous. The explications below only apply to the shape descriptor uses, i.e. when the adjectives combine with 'something' in a classifier-like fashion to describe the overall shape of an item; as for example, when we describe a *cucumber* as 'something long' or an *orange* as 'something round'. (This usage is distinct from the 'relative' or dimensional use, in which *long*, for example, contrasts with *short*; cf. Wierzbicka 2006c: 118–19).

> *something long (e.g. a cucumber, a tail, a stick):*
> when someone sees this thing, this someone can think about it like this:
>> 'two parts of this thing are not like any other parts,
>> because one of these two parts is very far from the other'
> if someone's hands [m] touch this thing everywhere on all sides,
>> this someone can think about it in the same way

> *something round (e.g. an orange):*
> when someone sees this thing on all sides, this someone can think about it
>> like this:
>> 'all parts of this thing are like all the other parts'
> if someone's hands [m] touch this thing everywhere on all sides,
>> this person can think about it in the same way

Since 'hands' can be explicated directly into semantic primes, using it as a semantic molecule does not incur any circularity. Neither is it circular to use 'long' and 'round' in the explications for 'legs' and 'head'. What we can see, however, is that there is a chain or hierarchy of semantic dependency which can be represented as follows:

$$\{\text{'legs', 'head'}\}_3 < \{\text{'long', 'round'}\}_2 < \{\text{'hands'}\}_1 < \{\text{semantic primes}\}$$

This diagram is intended to indicate that each word set enclosed in curly brackets depends semantically on all the word sets to the right of it. Notice the subscript notation, designating the 'level' of words of a particular group. In a similar vein, it is convenient to speak of a LEVEL-ONE MOLECULE or a LEVEL-TWO MOLECULE, etc.

Let us work through a second example, this time from the domain of social categories (Goddard and Wierzbicka to appear). The following explication shows how 'children' can be explicated directly into primes.

children:
people of one kind
all people are people of this kind before they can be people not of this kind
when someone is someone of this kind, this someone has lived for a short time,
     not a long time
the bodies of people of this kind are small
when people are like this, they can do some things, they can't do many other
     things
because of this, if other people don't do some good things for them,
     bad things can happen to them

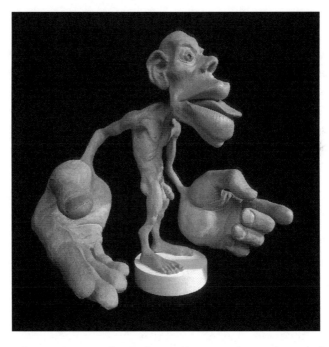

Figure 12.1. Sensory homunculus: body parts in proportion to the area of the cortex concerned with sensory perception. From a neurological point of view, there is nothing controversial about the idea that 'human hands mediate, to a large extent, between the world and the human mind' (Wierzbicka 2007b). The presence of 'hands [m]' as a hidden semantic molecule in many physical quality concepts presents a remarkable alignment between semantics and neurophysiology

Now consider the following explication for 'women', noting that in the final line the word 'child' appears as a semantic molecule. Essentially, the idea is that the concept of 'women' is based on the assumption that there are two kinds of people's bodies, 'women' being people of the kind whose body type allows them to have children. In other words, the concept of 'women' depends semantically on the concept of 'child'. (The explication for the singular 'child [m]' is the same as for 'children [m]', except that the initial component is 'someone of one kind', rather than 'people of one kind'.)

women:
people of one kind
someone can be someone of this kind after this someone has lived for some
    time, not for a short time
there are two kinds of people's bodies, people of this kind have bodies
    of one of these two kinds
some parts of bodies of this kind are not like parts of bodies of the other kind
the bodies of people of this kind are like this:
    at some times there can be inside the body of someone of this kind
      a living body of a child [m]

Taking the analysis a step further, Goddard and Wierzbicka (to appear) argue that the meaning of 'men' incorporates 'women' as a semantic molecule. Subsequently, all three of these basic social categories, i.e. 'men', 'women', and 'children', are needed in the explications of numerous other words—for example, in the domain of kinship (Wierzbicka to appear a). Once again, there is a chain of semantic dependencies:

{'father', 'mother', 'husband', 'wife'}$_4$ < {'men'}$_3$ <{'women'}$_2$
    < {'children'}$_1$ < {semantic primes}

Clearly, many complex concepts have multiple nestings of molecule within molecule. At least five nestings are known to occur. In the explication for *chairs* and *tables*, for example, the most complex molecules are bodily action verbs like 'sit [m]' and 'eat [m]'. They contain body-part molecules such as 'legs [m]', 'bottom [m]', 'back [m]', and 'mouth [m]'. These in turn contain shape descriptor molecules, which in turn harbour the molecule 'hands [m]', composed purely of semantic primes. An additional nesting occurs when natural kind terms function as semantic molecules at a shallow level of semantic structure. For example, words for unfamiliar species such as *tigers* and *zebras* contain a likeness-reference to familiar natural kinds, such as 'cats' and 'horses', respectively. Endonyms like *purr* and *saddle* also contain references to 'cats' and 'horses', respectively (cf. Chapter 7).

As we have already seen in Chapters 7 and 9, explications for many concepts require numerous semantic molecules, which can be of different levels. For example, to explicate the concept 'sun' we need to employ both 'sky [m]' and 'round [m]', which are level-one and level-two molecules, respectively. To explicate 'blue', we need four molecules: 'colour [m]', 'sky [m]', 'sea [m]', and 'sun [m]' (the latter is needed to indicate that the visual prototype for English *blue* is the sky during the day, not at night) (Goddard 2010a; Wierzbicka 2008; in press a). Some further examples of chains of semantic dependency are shown in Table 12.1.

The theory of semantic molecules is still in an early stage of development. It is already clear, though, that many of the semantic molecules required for explicating the English lexicon are language-specific (albeit that ultimately they can all be resolved into universal semantic primes). On the other hand, it also appears that some semantic molecules may be universal. The molecule 'hands' is a prime candidate, and cross-linguistic surveys appear to support this position, once sufficient attention is focused on questions of language-specific polysemy (Wierzbicka 2007a). The same goes for 'children' and other basic social categories, like 'men' and 'women', and some basic kin concepts, such as 'mother' and 'father' (Goddard and Wierzbicka to appear; Wierzbicka to appear a).

Table 12.2 itemizes some of the most important semantic molecules of English, with possible universal molecules indicated as such (Goddard 2010a).

Table 12.1.   Chains of semantic dependency and levels of nesting

{'sun'}$_3$	< {'round'}$_2$ < {'hands'}$_1$ < {primes}
	< {'sky'}$_1$ < {primes}
{'eat', 'drink'}$_3$	< {'water'}$_2$ < {'mouth', 'hands'}$_1$ < {primes}
	< {'hands'}$_1$ < {primes}
{'sweet', 'sour'}$_4$	< {'eat', 'drink'}$_3$ < {'water'}$_2$ < {'mouth', 'hands'}$_1$ < {primes}
	< {'mouth'}$_1$ < {primes}
{'blue'}$_4$	< {'sea'}$_3$ < {'water'}$_2$ < {'mouth', 'hands'}$_1$ < {primes}
	< {'sky'}$_1$ < {primes}
	< {'sun'}$_2$ < {'sky'}$_1$ < {primes}
	< {'colour'}$_1$ < {primes}

Universal semantic molecules obviously have a profound relevance to cross-cultural communication, comparable to that of semantic primes. Presumably, they also bear a heavy epistemological significance: as foundational concepts in knowledge structures, and/or as pivot points around which human knowledge is organized.

The fact that semantic molecules can be highly language-specific also has important cognitive and linguistic implications, sometimes in non-obvious ways. Wierzbicka (2008; in press a) argues, for example, that English 'colour [m]' functions as a semantic molecule in English words like *red*, *blue*, *green*, etc., but that many non-European languages lack 'colour words' in the true sense, because their visual descriptor words do not

Table 12.2. Selection of important semantic molecules of English (possible universal molecules marked with *)

Body-parts and products	*hands, *mouth, *eyes, *head, ears, face, nose, arms, legs, feet, teeth, fingers, fingernails, lips, tongue, back, bottom, breasts, hair, skin, *blood, poo
Animal body-parts	tail, wings, horns, claws, fur
Topological	top, bottom, side, front, back, edge, ends, hole, sticks out
Social categories and family	*children, *men, *women, *mother, *father, *wife, *husband, *be born
Physical	*round, long, flat, straight, hard, soft, thick, thin, sharp, heavy
Visual	light, colour, white, black, red, green, yellow, blue, brown
Environmental and ambient	*sky, *ground, *sun, *fire, *water, *day, *night, rain, wind, snow, sea, grass, sand, hot, cold
Life-forms and related words	*grow, creature, animal, bird, fish, tree, flower, egg
Materials	wood, stone, paper, metal, glass, leather, wool, thread, material (fabric)
Food, household, domestic animals	sweet, sour, bread, meat, bed, dog, cat, horse, sheep, cow, pig, mouse
Transport, mechanical parts, technology	car, plane, boat, train, road, wheel, pipe, wire, engine, machine, electricity, computer
Times and places	year, day_2, month, week, country, home, school, church, bank, building, room
Activities	*hold, sit, stand, lie, sleep, eat, drink, fly, dig, pull, make
Actions	*kill, jump, kick, bite, scratch, pick up, buy
Communication and expression	*laugh, write, read, draw, sing
Miscellaneous general	quickly, slowly, sick, name, sound
Miscellaneous cultural	game, book, language, dance, number, doctor, soldier, scientist, king, God, money, music, ball, gun

involve any comparable molecule. The semantic molecule 'number [m]' also has huge significance in English (and in many other languages), both in helping to constitute the productive lexical domain of number words (Goddard 2009b) and, less obviously, in contributing to diverse other concepts connected with quantification and measurement, such as categories like *age, temperature, weight*, units of measurement, words for measuring devices, or arithmetical concepts.

To judge from the reactions of English speakers, language-specific molecules such as 'colour' and 'number' can be so deeply ingrained in everyday thinking that native speakers can find it hard to believe that they are not lexical universals. Confronted with the counter-evidence, speakers often fall back on the claim that they nevertheless must be conceptual universals, even though this move has the dubious consequence of implying that English is a 'gifted' language (possessing a one-to-one correspondence between its lexical items and universal conceptual categories, a privilege denied to other languages).

Intermediate between precise universal molecules and highly language-specific molecules, there appears to be a set of approximate or near-universal molecules. Certain taxonomic supercategories—'bird', 'fish', and 'tree', for example—seem to more or less correspond across many languages (albeit with discernible differences). Where such near-equivalents exist, the semantic differences between them may well be fairly inconsequential for most purposes. At the present time, we do not know much about the scope, nature, and significance of 'near-universal' semantic molecules.

12.2.2 Wider implications

The exploration of semantic molecules promises to contribute much to a general theory of vocabulary structure, as well as to shed new light on conceptual structure. It leads to new ways of understanding semantic complexity in the lexicon, new ways of depicting semantic dependencies and interrelationships, and new ways of thinking about the structuring of lexical concepts. As emphasized at various points in this book, semantic molecules enable an enormous compression of semantic complexity, by embedding or telescoping lexical units, one inside the other. From a cognitive point of view, it appears that, once established, molecules can be processed as single units, thereby enabling the mind to manipulate and manage vast amounts of semantic content.

The notion of chains of semantic dependency provides a liberating alternative to the rigid taxonomic hierarchy model that still dominates semantic thinking in many other approaches. It emerges from NSM research that many semantic structures have a kind of 'gangly and lumpy' texture: lengthy strings of simple semantic primes interspersed with semantically dense molecules. Though NSM practitioners tend to take this kind of texture (or architecture) for granted, it is unlike anything envisaged in structuralist or generativist approaches to lexical semantics.

12.3 Language acquisition

Noam Chomsky has rightly identified language acquisition as one of the fundamental challenges facing linguistic theory. How can a young child, in a few short years, master the intricacies of language, intricacies which continue to baffle linguistic science? This is especially puzzling in view of the fact the 'data' to which the child is exposed, i.e. the speech of adults and other children, does not seem to contain enough information to support the task. This argument (sometimes called the 'poverty of the stimulus') has convinced many researchers that children are born predisposed to learn language—that humans have, in Steven Pinker's (1994) catchy phrase, a 'language instinct'. With Chomsky, some researchers assume that the biological endowment which enables us all to acquire a language is fundamentally syntactic, while others see the basic organizational principles of child language as fundamentally semantic or conceptual.

Perhaps the greatest impediment to exploring such issues in child language studies has been the lack of a well-founded and rigorous semantic methodology. Some investigators have relied on Fillmore's (1968) semantic case roles, while others (such as Roger Brown, M. A. K. Halliday, Steven Pinker) have devised their own set of semantic labels to categorize the meanings or functions which they attribute to the young child. The abstractness and obscurity of such labels (e.g. 'agentive', 'dative', 'factitive', 'instrumental', 'regulative', 'implication', and 'recurrence') makes it open to question whether different researchers are applying them in the same way.

12.3.1 Innate concepts in language acquisition

One argument that has led many scholars to conclude that the child embarks on language learning pre-equipped with some basic concepts is that it is hard to see how certain concepts could be learned purely from experience. Logical operators and seemingly abstract concepts such as 'not', 'all', and 'the same' are the classic examples.

The discovery that there are many striking regularities in the early 'child grammars' of different languages also suggests that there is a prelinguistic conceptual basis for language learning, consisting of basic notions which are essential to all languages. As Melissa Bowerman (1985: 1284) once put it: 'children's starting semantic space is not a tabula rasa … children are conceptually prepared for language learning.' Admittedly, Bowerman and colleagues have also documented ways in which the language-specific semantics of the adult language is an important influence on early child grammar (Bowerman and Choi 2001; 2003), but there is no real conflict between these findings and the notion that language acquisition rests on a universal conceptual base. As the esteemed cognitive psychologist Jerome Bruner (1990: 72) writes:

how we 'enter language' must rest upon a selective set of prelinguistic 'readiness for meaning'. That is to say, there are certain classes of meaning to which human beings are innately tuned and for which they actively search. Prior to language, these exist in primitive form as protolinguistic representations of the world whose full realization depends upon the cultural tool of language.

12.3.2 NSM primes in child speech

As far as one can tell from the literature, exponents of most semantic primes are attested in early child speech, at least in English (see below) and in Mandarin Chinese (Tien 2005; 2010). All appear to be well in evidence by the age of 5.

Three important provisos are as follows. (i) A child's exponent of the prime may vary from those of adults; for example, young children use *little* instead of *small*; (ii) There may be distinctive kinds of polysemy in young children's speech; for example, *no* may be used for NOT (e.g. *no wet*), and also for NOT + WANT (e.g. *no mama* for 'I don't want to go to mama') and

THERE IS + NOT (e.g. *no pocket* for 'there is no pocket here on Mommy's shirt'); cf. Braine (1976), Bloom (1991); (iii) The presence of a lexical exponent does not mean that a prime is fully acquired, because the child may have active command over only a small part of the prime's syntactic possibilities. For example, though the word *do* appears early in the third year in English-speaking children it is some time before the child is able to use it with the full range of complement and valency options, e.g. 'do something to something,' 'do something to someone else', 'do something to something with something'. Nevertheless, the presence of the lexical item, used with apparently the same meaning as its adult counterpart, is concrete linguistic evidence that the corresponding concept has some foothold, so to speak, in the child's mind.

The early emergence of exponents of some primes, such as WANT, SEE, BIG, SMALL, NOT, MORE, and HERE, will be self-evident to anyone familiar with young children. Questions with *what*, *who*, and *where* occur very early, testifying to the presence of the concepts SOMETHING, SOMEONE, and WHERE/PLACE (cf. Ervin-Tripp 1970; Tyack and Ingram 1977). Several investigators have proposed that the category 'humans' (i.e. PEOPLE) is a particularly important one for children. Carey (1985) found that children initially organize biological knowledge around humans as a prototype. Jackendoff (1992: 74) refers to the finding that children as young as 17 months know that proper names can be applied to people and to people-like objects such as dolls, but not to inanimate objects such as boxes. He comments: 'they seem predisposed to make a cognitive distinction between persons and everything else... and to find a linguistic distinction that encodes this difference.'

The verb *do* is found early, as are 'actor–action' patterns like *Kendall swim*, *Kimmy eat*, *hug Mommy*, and *Daddy break it* (Braine 1976). All child language researchers concur that the concept of movement (MOVE) is fundamental to early child cognition (cf. Bloom 1991); the verb *go* often appears among the very earliest words. There is less acquisition data on the emergence of HAPPEN, though questions like *What happened it?* and *What happened horse?* are well-attested in the third year (Moerk 1992: 78–96; Corrigan 2004; see also Tien 2009 on Mandarin Chinese exponents of HAPPEN in child speech).

There is a sizeable literature on children's use and understanding of mental predicates, in the context of the debate on children's 'theory of mind' (e.g. Lewis and Mitchell 1994; Farrar and Maag 2002; Astington

2000). The general picture is that mental verbs appear and develop strongly over the third year, with *know* and *think* being by far the most common (Shatz, Wellman, and Silber 1983; Furrow et al. 1992). Though *say*, and the use of reported speech generally, has received less attention, it seems that many children spontaneously use direct quotation in the third year (Ely and McCabe 1993).

In the spatial domain, as Slobin (1985: 1180) says, 'All cross-linguistic acquisition data point to an initial salience of topological notions of containment, support and contiguity', i.e. presumably INSIDE, TOUCH, and NEAR. Both *up* and *down* are found early in the developmental sequence (cf. Johnston 1985; Nelson 1973, cited in Ingram 1989; Smiley et al. 2007), implying ABOVE and BELOW in the context of motion. In the temporal domain, the evidence indicates that exponents of the concepts WHEN/TIME, BEFORE, and AFTER are all present before the end of the third year, although BEFORE is often realized initially as *first*, and AFTER as *and then* (i.e. 'after this'). Though less is known about children's use of time-period and durational expressions, it appears that exponents of the time-period primes A LONG TIME and A SHORT TIME are apparent by the middle of the fourth year, with A SHORT TIME being often realized as *a little while* (cf. French and Nelson 1985; Peterson 1990).

Most of the 'logical' concepts are solidly represented in the speech of young children. Far from being a late development, the concept of 'existence' (THERE IS) emerges in infant speech, combined with negation in expressions such as *allgone*. BECAUSE (as *'cause*) is well in evidence at age 3, despite its abstract and 'non-empirical' nature, and IF is solidly attested at age 4.

It is not clear when the word PART occurs first in children's speech, although 'part–whole' utterances like *Mummy hand* and *cow tail* are attested at a very early stage. Braine (1976: 7) includes the combinations *other part* and *other piece* in his record of one child's earliest two-word utterances. As for KIND OF, questions like *what kind of* occur relatively early, though not as early as simple *wh-* questions (cf. Clancy 1985).

As food for thought, Table 12.3 presents a selection of utterances which illustrate semantic primes in the speech of children under 5 years old.

Table 12.3.   Child utterances illustrating the use of exponents of semantic primes in early child speech in English

2 years old and before:

 I CAN'T... WANT THIS (David 1;9); WHAT HAPPEN (David 1;10); BAD BAD boy baby... Boy IN (looking at a picture of a boy in a house) ... THERE'S A LITTLE ball (Gia 1;10)... Spider MOVE... Melissa walk... Daddy HERE (Kendall 1;11)... ALL GONE BIG stick... OTHER hand... TWO cup... ALL wet (Jonathon 2;0)... WHERE A LITTLE one... WHAT'S IN THIS (Kathryn 2;0)... HAPPEN down there (Todd 2;6).

3 years old:

 There MORE (meaning 'there's more'; Jonathon 2;1)... SEE UNDER there... WHAT THIS (Eric 2;1)... I HEAR Kevin!... CAN'T reach it (Gia 2;1)... I DO it... THERE'S a tape IN there (Peter 2;1)... YOU CAN'T SEE IT CAUSE it's way INSIDE.... Get them CAUSE I WANT IT (unnamed)... I DON'T KNOW WHAT KIND of bed that (Adam, about 3)... I think you have sugar (Adam 3;4)... AFTER the birthday, they go home (age 3;1).... I had one BEFORE we came HERE (age 3;10)... Eat the green PART FIRST (unnamed 3;7).

4 years old:

 DIS is a different KIND of airplane (Adam, 4)... And we wait FOR A LITTLE WHILE, but not too LONG, then we go back... Fire's aren't ALIVE, silly... Then IF a whale came, they would get eated. But IF they hided, the whale MAYBE COULDN'T find them.... Mom SAID, 'SAY, SAY something'. And I SAID: 'No, I wanta go home' (unnamed)... Now she KNOWS that I KNOW. She used to THINK that I don't KNOW when really I did (Ross 4;8).

Sources: The utterances of the youngest children are taken from corpus materials in Braine (1976), except for Todd's which comes from Peterson (1990). The unnamed 3-year-olds are from Bloom (1991) and French and Nelson (1985: 109), respectively; Adam from Bodin and Snow (1994: 102) and Wellman and Bartsch (1994). The unnamed 4-year-olds are from French and Nelson (1985: 106–7), Kuczaj and Daly (1979: 573), and Ely and McCabe (1993), respectively. The utterances by Adam and Ross come from Bodin and Snow (1994: 103) and Wellman and Bartsch (1994), respectively.

12.3.3 'Implicit' conceptual primes

Notwithstanding that exponents of many primes appear relatively early in child speech, it is still a 'stand out' fact that most of a child's early words are *not* exponents of semantic primes. For example, in one young child's speech (Goddard 2001), early words (under 24 months) included: *mama, papa, bath, bird, duck, nana* (banana), *ball,* and *oh-oh,* and (slightly later) *mouth, hand, wheel, door, off, broke, made,* and *noise.* Even though the meanings of these early words must be simpler than the corresponding words in an adult's vocabulary, it is obvious that they cannot be explicated in terms of the small set of primes which already have exponents in the child's own vocabulary. Evidently, then, the child is making use of a larger set of primes, many of which are present conceptually but which still lack lexical exponents. (The language of young children is therefore not yet meta-semantically adequate, i.e. it does not include sufficient lexical resources to enable language-internal paraphrase of all its semantic content.)

This situation offers an interesting, though challenging, research opportunity: the prospect that we can discern aspects of the child's implicit conceptual vocabulary by semantic analysis of his or her non-primitive words (Tien 1999; 2005; 2010; Goddard 2001). The task is a daunting one, but it is not altogether different from that which faces a field linguist who undertakes semantic analysis of an unknown adult language from an unfamiliar culture. In either case we have to begin with close naturalistic observation of usage: documenting the range of contexts in which a certain expression is used—and not used—and comparing the usage of alternative expressions which can be found in different contexts. Then we experiment to discover the most economical semantic explications which match the attested range of usage. Obviously one must guard against the assumption that the child's meaning for a particular form corresponds fully to the adult meaning—i.e. against 'adultcentrism', the child language analogue of ethnocentrism.

It is not possible here to review research findings in this area, which (it must be admitted) is still in its infancy. Here are a couple of examples, though. One of the earliest child words is *oh-oh*, which seems clearly to imply the concept HAPPEN, well before *happen* appears as an independent word. Many young children have an early word that expresses a meaning like that of the adult word 'hot' (in relation to physical objects). Presumably its meaning must involve TOUCH, FEEL, and BAD, yet typically TOUCH and FEEL do not yet have independent lexical exponents. Similarly, most young children start to use many 'animal sound words' (*quack-quack*, *bow-wow*, and the like) well before they start to use the word HEAR.

Linked with the notion of an implicit 'conceptual vocabulary' is the fact that a child's active production vocabulary constitutes only one part of the potential evidence of his or her semantic competence. Communication is a two-way street, and comprehension is just as important as production. If anything it is more important, since, as every parent (and every L2 language learner) knows, comprehension (receptive vocabulary) always runs far ahead of production. Synthesizing results from various studies, Ingram (1989: 140–3) suggests that, as a norm, about 100 words are understood (in some fashion) even in the so-called proto-linguistic period, before the first recognizable words are produced.

The real test of whether or not a given semantic prime exists as a conceptual element in a young child's mind is therefore not production, but comprehension—what the child can understand, rather than what it can express. Tapping into comprehension in a systematic way presents methodological problems, however, which explains why comprehension testing is still a relatively underdeveloped area in child language research (Crain and Thornton 1998; Houston-Price, Mather, and Sakkalou 2007). New techniques are emerging, but as with research into production, optimal outcomes will only be achieved when experimental design is guided and informed by a sound overall semantic theory.

Though dialogue between acquisition studies and NSM semantics has barely begun, one can expect that the NSM system, as a comprehensive, independently established framework for semantic analysis, will eventually be of great value to language acquisition research.

12.4 Cultural scripts

It is a truism that in different societies people not only speak different languages, but use them in radically different ways. In some societies, for example, conversations bristle with disagreement, voices are raised, and emotions are conspicuously vented, while in others people studiously avoid contention, speak in mild and even tones, and guard against any exposure of their inner selves. In this section we will see how such culture-specific 'ways of speaking' can be described by means of 'cultural scripts' written in universal semantic primes.

12.4.1 Ethnography and ethnocentrism

The most influential approach to discourse and culture studies is the 'ethnography of communication' (Hymes 1968 [1962]; Gumperz and Hymes 1986 [1972]; Bauman and Sherzer 1974; Carbaugh 2005). It emphasizes that to be a competent speaker calls for much more than knowledge of words and grammar alone. It means knowing how to speak in culturally appropriate ways to different people about different things in different settings. Ethnographers of communication have documented the patterning of speech events in a wide range of cultures, often finding that they differ very markedly from mainstream Western ways of speaking. To describe and explain such phenomena, ethnographers usually posit culture-specific NORMS OF INTERACTION and interpretation.

Describing cultural norms of speaking is no easy task. The normal practice is to use technical (or semi-technical) labels such as 'direct' vs. 'indirect' and 'formal' vs. 'informal', but these terms are used with different meanings in different contexts. For instance, when Japanese speech patterns are contrasted with English ones, the Japanese are described as 'indirect' and the English as 'direct', but when English is compared with Hebrew, it is the English speech patterns which are 'indirect' and the Hebrew 'direct'. It is not a simple matter of different 'degrees of (in)directness' either. The differences are not merely quantitative but qualitative: cultures differ on what to be 'indirect' about, on how to be 'indirect', and, most importantly perhaps, on why to be 'indirect'. A similar critique applies to the notions of 'formality', 'politeness', and 'involvement' (Irvine 1979; Janney and Arndt 1993; Besnier 1994).

Terms like 'directness', 'politeness', 'deference', 'face', 'hierarchy', and so on make our analyses vulnerable to ethnocentrism because the concepts designated by these specialist English words cannot be translated easily into the languages involved. They therefore cannot disclose what anthropologists call an INSIDER PERSPECTIVE, i.e. an interpretation from the point of the view of the people concerned. Ethnographic studies often attempt to overcome this problem by incorporating indigenous terms (e.g. Malagasy *tsiny* 'guilt', Japanese *enryo* 'restraint', Yankunytjatjara *kunta* 'shame') into their descriptions, but then the difficulty of translation arises in reverse.

The metalanguage of semantic primes can help overcome these problems by providing a precise and culture-independent way of formulating cultural rules for speaking, known as CULTURAL SCRIPTS (Wierzbicka 1994b; 1994c; 1994d; Goddard 2006b; Goddard and Wierzbicka 1997; 2004).

The next two sections demonstrate the cultural scripts method by comparing two unrelated cultures (Japanese and Malay) which are often described as favouring an 'indirect' discourse style, at least in the public sphere. How similar are they really? And what is the 'cultural logic' behind the discourse preferences?

12.4.2 Some cultural scripts of Japanese

Japanese culture is often characterized by its suppression or distrust of verbalism. For instance, Doi (1988: 33) contrasts the Western emphasis on 'the importance of words' with traditional Japanese values, saying that the latter are 'more conscious of matters that words do not reach'. Other writers have pointed to the Zen Buddhist emphasis on the 'inutility' of linguistic communication and to the Japanese preference for non-verbal communication in traditional pedagogy and even in mother–child interaction.

One cultural source of verbal restraint is the Japanese ideal of *enryo*, usually translated as 'restraint' or 'reserve.' As pointed out by Smith (1983: 44–5), 'much of the definition of a "good person" involves restraint in the expression of personal desires and opinions.' Often *enryo* inhibits Japanese speakers from saying directly what they want, even in response to direct questions, and it also makes it culturally inappropriate to ask others directly what they want. Mizutani and Mizutani (1987: 49) explain that except with family and close friends it is impolite to say such things as *Nani-o tabetai-desu-ka* 'What do you want to eat?' and *Nani-ga hoshii-desu-ka* 'What do you want to have?' A guest in Japan is not constantly offered choices by an attentive host, as in the United States. It is the responsibility of the host to anticipate what will please the guest and simply to present items of food and drink, urging that they be consumed, in the standard phrase, 'without *enryo*'.

As with one's wants, so with one's thoughts and feelings. It is not only a question of when to express them, but whether one should express them at all. Barnlund (1975) gives statistical data showing enormous differences between Japanese and Americans not only in the range of topics they are prepared to talk about, but also in the range of persons to whom they are prepared to reveal their thoughts and intentions. If one is to speak, it is important to premeditate in order to avoid saying anything which could hurt or offend somebody or which could embarrass the speaker him/herself.

All these observations suggest that among the cultural scripts of Japan are the following. Notice that cultural scripts are introduced with the framing expression 'many people think like this'. In effect, this says (in semantic primes) that what follows represents a widespread social attitude.

Some Japanese cultural scripts connected with 'verbalization':
many people think like this:
at many times it is good not to say anything to other people

many people think like this:
at many times it is not good to say things like this to other people:
  'I want this', 'I don't want this'
  'I think like this', 'I don't think like this'
if I say things like this to someone, this someone can feel something bad
  because of this

many people think like this:
before I say something to someone, it is good if I think about it for some time
I don't want someone to feel something bad because I say something

Another Japanese ideal relevant to discourse preferences is *omoiyari*, which is one of the key personal virtues of Japan (cf. Travis 1998). Lebra (1976: 38) describes it as 'the ability and willingness to feel what others are feeling...and to help them satisfy their wishes...without being told verbally'. It is not hard to find evidence to support Lebra's characterization of Japanese culture as a whole as an *'omoiyari* culture'. For instance, in a reader's column in the newspaper *Shikoku Shimbun*, where readers place a photo of their child and state their hopes and expectations, one of the most common is *Omoiyari no aru hitoni nattene* 'Please become a person with *omoiyari.*' In education guidelines for teachers, the first one is *Omoiyari no kokoro o taisetsuni shimashoo* 'Let's treasure the mind/heart of *omoiyari*'. The ideal of wordless empathy is carried over into everyday interaction. For example, speaking of the 'ingroup' Nakane (1970: 121) says that 'among fellow-members a single word would suffice for the whole sentence'. Mutual sensitivity goes so far that each easily recognizes the other's slightest change in behaviour and mood and is ready to act accordingly.

This high sensitivity to other people's feelings is linked with the tendency for the Japanese to withhold explicit displays of feeling. Honna and Hoffer (1989: 88–90) observe that Japanese who cannot control their emotions are considered 'immature as human beings'. This applies not only to negative or unsettling emotions such as anger, fear, disgust, and sorrow. Even the expression of happiness should be controlled 'so that it does not displease other people'.

These complementary attitudes can be captured as below. According to these scripts, Japanese cultural attitudes discourage one from verbalizing about one's own emotions while encouraging emotional sensitivity toward other people.

> *Some Japanese cultural scripts connected with 'verbalizing' feelings:*
> many people think like this:
> at many times when I feel something, it is not good if say something
>   about it to someone else
> if I do this, this other someone can feel something bad because of it
> at many times I can't say what I feel
>
> many people think like this:
> at many times when I am with someone else, I can know what
>   this other someone feels
> this other someone doesn't have to say something about it to me
> it is good if it is like this

A great deal has been written about Japanese communication style, much of it of variable quality. A selection of worthwhile references includes Maynard (1997), Hasada (1997; 2006), Minami (2002), Kita and Ide (2007).

12.4.3 Some cultural scripts of Malay

The traditional culture of the Malay people places great emphasis upon *patut* 'proper' and *sesuai* 'appropriate' conduct and, as an integral part of this, upon speaking in the proper way. Observers describe Malay culture as valuing 'refined restraint', cordiality, and sensitivity, and Malays themselves as courteous, easygoing, and charming. The norms of refined (*halus*) speech in Malay somewhat resemble those of Japanese, but on closer examination the similarities turn out to be superficial.

One concept fundamental to Malay interaction is the social emotion of *malu*. Though it is usually glossed as 'ashamed', 'shy', or 'embarrassed', these translations don't convey the fact that Malays regard the capacity to feel *malu* as a social good, akin to a sense of propriety. Swift (1965: 110) describes *malu* as 'hypersensitiveness to what other people are thinking about one' (note the ethnocentric perspective reflected in this phrasing). Desire to avoid *malu* is the primary force for social cohesion—not to say conformism—in the Malay village. Two related social concepts are *maruah*, roughly, 'dignity, honour', and *harga diri* 'self-respect' (*harga* 'value, *diri* 'self'), both of which are threatened by the prospect of being disapproved of by others, that is, by *malu* (cf. Goddard 1996a; 1997a; 2000).

Vreeland et al. (1977: 117) emphasize the importance of these concepts for Malay behaviour generally:

The social value system is predicated on the dignity of the individual and ideally all social behaviour is regulated in such a way as to preserve one's own *amour propre* and to avoid disturbing the same feelings of dignity and self-esteem in others.

As in Japan, one is expected in Malay society to think before one speaks. There is a common saying to this effect: *Kalau cakap fikir lah sedikit dulu* 'If you're going to speak, think a little first.' But the underlying cultural attitude is somewhat different to that in Japan. As well as sensitivity to other people's feelings (cf. the saying *jaga hati orang* 'mind people's feelings'), Malay verbal caution is motivated by wanting to avoid the addressee's thinking anything bad about one.

Malay cultural script enjoining 'verbal caution':
many people think like this:
before I say something to someone, it is good if I think like this:
   'I don't want this someone to feel something bad because I say something
   I don't want this someone to think something bad about me'

Another difference is the value Malay culture places on verbal skill. A refined (*halus*) way of speaking is universally admired, bringing credit to oneself and one's upbringing. It is a skill learnt in the home, and not necessarily connected with wealth, noble birth, or formal education. As Asmah (1987: 88) remarks: 'A rice farmer with only six years of primary education may be found to speak a more refined language than a clerk in a government department.' Aside from courtesy and considerateness, the linguistic features of *halus* speech include use of elegant phrases instead of mundane vocabulary, careful attention to forms of personal reference (e.g. avoiding direct address and self-reference), and recourse to the large inventory of traditional sayings (*peribahasa*) to allude to any potentially sensitive matters. A soft (*lembut*, also 'gentle, tender') voice is also important.

Halus speech is especially valued in formal situations, or when talking with *orang lain* 'other/different people', i.e. people outside the immediate family circle. One always feels such people are liable to be watching and passing judgement, ready to disparage those without verbal finesse as *kurang ajar* 'uncouth (lit. 'under-taught')'. On the other hand, a cultivated way with words wins admiration. The overall complex of cultural attitudes can be captured as follows.

> *Malay cultural script recognising widespread 'judgemental attitudes' to how to speak:*
> many people think like this:
> when someone says something to someone else,
>   sometimes people think about it like this:
>   'this someone knows how to say things well to other people, this is good'
>   sometimes people think about it like this:
>   'this someone doesn't know how to say things well to other people,
>   this is not good'

Malay culture discourages people from verbally expressing how they feel, the ideal demeanour being one of good-natured calm *senang hati* (lit. 'easy heart'), but in contrast with the situation in Japan, it is alright to express feelings through one's facial expressions and other actions, and there is an underlying assumption that people can be relied upon to be sensitive to such non-verbal manifestations.

The use of 'meaningful looks' (*pandangan bermakna*) is a favoured non-verbal strategy. For instance, the verb *tenung* (cf. *bertenung* 'to divine') depicts a kind of glare used to convey irritation with someone else's behaviour, e.g. a child misbehaving or someone in the room clicking a pen in an irritating way. Widening the eyes *mata terbeliak* (lit. 'bulging eyes') conveys disapproval. Lowering the eyes and deliberately turning the head away (*jeling*) without speaking can convey that one is 'fed up' with someone. Pressing the lips together and protruding them slightly (*menjuih-kan bibir*) conveys annoyance. Non-verbal expression is critical to the closest Malay counterpart of English 'angry', namely *marah* 'offended, angry' (cf. Chapter 4), which is associated not with scenes of 'angry words' but with the sullen brooding performance known as *merajuk*.

The relevant cultural script can be written as below.

> *Malay cultural script for relying on non-verbal communication of feelings:*
> many people think like this:
> when I feel something, it is not good If I say something like this to someone
>   else:
>   'I feel like this'
> if this other someone can see me, this other someone can know how I feel

12.4.4 Reprise

It should be evident from the comparison of Japanese and Malay that speech patterns which are superficially similar (for instance, a preference for 'verbal restraint') may spring from different cultural values and be associated with different social meanings in different cultural settings. To bring these connections to light, and even to describe the speech patterns themselves without ethnocentric distortion, requires careful attention to the metalanguage of description and analysis. Formulating our accounts of cultural rules in terms of the natural semantic metalanguage allows the precision to distinguish between apparently similar speech styles, while helping to safeguard against the danger that our account will be distorted by the linguistic and conceptual baggage we bring with us from own culture.

12.4.5 Anglo cultural scripts as an antidote to Anglocentrism in pragmatics

One of the key concerns of much work in the cultural scripts framework is to de-naturalize the pragmatics of English, which is often taken (or mistaken) as culturally unmarked; cf. Wierzbicka (2003a; 2006a; to appear b), Peeters (2000b); Goddard (2006a; to appear a; to appear b). It therefore seems important to adduce at least one cultural script of mainstream Anglo culture. In doing so we can also take the opportunity to show how cultural scripts (or rather, recurrent patterns of expression influenced by cultural scripts) can exert an influence on language structure.

A wide range of sociological, historical, and culture-analytical literature indicates that something like 'personal autonomy' is one of the primary ideals of Anglo culture. The following script is intended to capture an important aspect of this ideal.

Anglo cultural script for 'personal autonomy':
many people think like this:
when someone does something, it is good if this someone can think about it
  like this: 'I am doing this because I want to do it'

It is not difficult to see that this ideal can inhibit speakers of mainstream English from using the bare imperative when they want someone else to do something (because a bare imperative includes a message like: 'I want you to do this; I think that you will do it because of this'). It is well known that in most social situations Anglo speakers prefer to frame their directives in a more elaborated fashion, using 'interrogative directives' such as *Will you...?*, *Would you...?*, *Can you...?*, *Could you...?*, *Would you mind...?*, and the like. Although these constructions clearly convey the message 'I want you to do this', they acknowledge the addressee's autonomy by embedding the potentially confronting message into a question-form, as if inviting the addressee to say whether or not he or she will comply. Another favoured strategy is the use of 'helpful suggestions', such as *Perhaps you could ...*, *You might like to ...*, and *I would suggest ...* (Wierzbicka 2006b: 51f.).

In a similar fashion, it can be argued that Anglo cultural values encourage speakers to express something like 'epistemic caution' when saying what they think, and to routinely acknowledge the possible existence of differing opinions (Wierzbicka 2003a; 2006a). This, it is argued, is linked with the high-frequency English formula *I think*, with phrases like *in my opinion* and *as I see it*, with hedges such as *kind of* and *a bit*, and also with the frequency and grammatical elaboration of tag questions in mainstream Anglo English (Wong 2008).

Explaining these ways of speaking in terms of Anglo cultural scripts and Anglo cultural values is quite different from explaining them as manifestations of supposed 'universals of politeness' or other universals of human interaction (Brown and Levinson 1987; Levinson 2000; 2006). NSM scholars have long been critical of universalist approaches to pragmatics, charging them with semantic naivety, explanatory inadequacy, and thinly disguised Anglocentrism. The alternative paradigm, which gives priority to culture-internal explanation of speech practices, using cultural scripts and semantic explication as its key tools, is known as ETHNOPRAGMATICS (cf. Goddard 2006a).

12.5 Non-verbal communication

Language is not the only way in which people communicate. Facial expressions, postures, and gestures are also meaning-bearing and they also vary cross-culturally, to a greater or lesser extent. In this section we see how the natural semantic metalanguage can be applied to the study of non-verbal communication.

12.5.1 Facial expressions and 'basic emotions'

Since facial expressions reflect and communicate feelings, it is not surprising that many of the controversies in the scholarly literature about facial expressions mirror the controversies surrounding the nature of emotions. Psychologists who believe in the existence of a small set of biologically inbuilt basic emotions (see section 4.1) also believe that there is a corresponding set of universal facial expressions (cf. Ekman 1993; 2004). Their main evidence comes from experiments which supposedly show that certain expressions are interpreted the same way by people all over the world, regardless of their cultural backgrounds.

The methodology of these experiments has been called into question on three counts. First, the stimuli used are often not candid shots of real-life emotions but posed photographs of exaggerated expressions that have been designed to exemplify the presumed 'basic emotions' as unequivocally as possible (cf. Scherer 1992: 144). Second, the experimenters usually assume that other languages have adequate equivalents to English words like *anger*, *disgust*, *fear*, *joy*, *surprise*, and *sadness*, and do not take proper account of the difficulties of translation (cf. Wierzbicka 1995a; 2009a). Third, in the most widely used method people are shown a series of photographs and asked to match them with a small set of terms preselected by the researcher; they are not allowed to volunteer their own interpretations.

Criticizing this method, Russell (1991: 435) asks us to put ourselves in the shoes of a test subject:

You are shown a photograph of a young woman with a bright smile. You are asked to describe how she feels by selecting one word from the following list: *sad, angry, disgusted, afraid, surprised, happy*. Most likely, you'd select *happy*. But now suppose that *happy* had been replaced on the list with *elated*. Given the alternatives, you'd have no choice but to select *elated*. If *happy* were successively replaced with *serene, satisfied, excited, grateful*, and *triumphant*, you'd again select any of these words in turn. … Indeed, substitute for *happy* any clearly positive word … and the conclusion remains the same.

Russell concludes that, at best, 'forced-choice' experiments can show that facial expressions receive similar (but not necessarily identical) interpretations in different cultures (cf. Russell and Fernández-Dols 1997).

12.5.2 Reading human faces

Vying with the dominant Ekman position is another approach, represented by Ortony and Turner (1990) and Scherer (1992). According to these scholars, facial expressions are best viewed, not as global 'gestalts', but as configurations of components such as: smile, compressed lips, clenched teeth, raised lip, widened eyes, raised eyebrows, furrowed brow, wrinkled nose, and so on. They suggest that each of these 'components of facial expression' can be linked with a corresponding component of emotion. Wierzbicka (1993; 1995c; 1999: ch. 4) argues that the natural semantic metalanguage provides a suitable framework for analysing the semantics of facial 'gestures', as well as of words. We will illustrate with three examples—the smile, raised eyebrows, and the 'puckered brow'.

One can hypothesize that the basic or prototypical meaning expressed by smiling is as below. (Notice that the lack of the illocutionary expression 'I say: —' indicates that this is not an explication of a linguistic utterance.)

> \<smiling\>
> I feel something good now

Why is this better than saying that a smile conveys the message 'I feel happy'? First, it is phrased in terms which are universally translatable, which the word *happy* is not. Second, though the meaning stated above is closely related to that of *happy*, it is not identical to it (cf. section 4.3). The proposed 'smile message' is semantically simpler. This is as it should be, because not all smiling faces would be interpreted as showing happiness; other compatible emotions include amusement, tenderness, and gratitude.

Of course, it would be foolish to say that the explication represents the actual mental state of someone who is smiling. A smile may be 'put on' for social reasons, to cover bad feelings, to convey an impression of friendliness, or whatever. What the explication represents is the meaning conveyed by (and ascribed to) such expressions, not the person's real psychological state.

Needless to say, different cultural norms may operate to encourage or discourage particular facial expressions (as implied in section 12.4). For example, in Japanese society people are expected to show a smile in public when actually they feel negative emotions, as for example when confronted with news of the death of a family member (Hearn 1992 [1893]; Morsbach 1973). A Japanese smile can also be used to display a kind of 'powerless-ness' to others, for example, when telling one's superiors about one's mistakes or requesting a favour (cf. Leathers 1992: 86–90; Hasada 1997). Cultural rules of this type, known in the psychological literature as DISPLAY RULES (Ekman and Friesen 1969), are of great interest and importance to cross-cultural communication. We will look at some examples shortly, but for the moment let's continue to focus on components of facial expression as they function in the English-speaking world.

Consider raising of the eyebrows, a feature found in some of the facial expressions associated with 'surprise'. Ortony and Turner (1990: 322) follow Charles Darwin's lead in proposing that raising the eyebrows is 'a manifestation of the fact that the person is devoting considerable attention to the visual environment'. Similarly, Peck (1987) in his *Atlas of Facial Expression* points out that the natural explanation for widening the eyes and raising the brows is 'to see better'. On the other hand, raised eyebrows are also characteristic of expressions of incredulity or disbelief, i.e. they are not necessarily associated with anything visible.

With this in mind, we can hypothesize that the basic meaning of the raised eyebrows is heightened attention to what is going on:

<raising eyebrows>
(I think) something is happening here now
I want to know more about it

As a final example, we can take the kind of frown which involves 'puckering' the brow. Many researchers have suggested cognitive correl-ates. Ekman (1979: 196, cited in Scherer 1992: 142) says that it is found during 'concentration, determination, or when some difficulty is encoun-tered'. Peck (1987: 51) says that it represents 'trouble'. One could suggest the following representation:

<puckering brow>
I want to do something
I don't know what it is good to do
I can't not think about it now

This is compatible with the fact that the puckered brow is found associated with worry and distress, as well as with concentration.

12.5.3 Reading American faces, reading Chinese faces

As mentioned, even advocates of universal facial expressions recognize the need for culture-based 'display rules', though typically they seem to think of them as something that 'other' cultures have. In fact, it seems likely that all cultures have cultural scripts related to the expression of feelings, and many of these scripts can have implications for facial expressions. American culture is no exception in this regard.

In many parts of the world there is a stereotype of Americans as typically wearing a 'smiley' positive face. A great range of evidence suggests that American culture encourages displays of cheerfulness and a 'positive attitude', as part of a general cultural value set that promotes positivity and valorizes *happiness*, *fun*, and *enjoying yourself* (Wierzbicka 1999: 241–51; McMahon 2006; Ehrenreich 2009). Consider the following cultural scripts. The first is rather general: an endorsement of a positive, optimistic attitude. The second and third are more specific. They encourage people to have good feelings when they can and to show their good feelings publicly; and in particular, to try to give the impression of feeling good during verbal interaction.

Anglo-American cultural scripts favouring having a 'positive attitude' and projecting positive feelings:
many people think like this:
it is good if someone can think at many times that something good will happen
it is good if someone can feel something good at many times because of this

many people think like this:
it is good if someone can feel something good at many times
at many times when someone feels something good,
   it is good if other people can know it

many people think like this:
at many times when I say something to someone else,
   it is good if this someone thinks that I feel something good at this time

Needless to say, a full treatment of facial expression in any culture would be a very large undertaking and it is not possible here to do more than scratch the surface. To get a sense of what would be involved, it is helpful to briefly compare the American 'culture of facial expression' with that of China.

In Chinese culture, according to Ye (2006), attitudes towards disclosure and display of one's feelings are very different. Generally speaking it is considered normal to keep one's feelings, especially one's deepest feelings, to oneself. In relation to expression of positive feelings, there are specific restrictions on visible expression of feeling very good. Ye proposes the following cultural script:

> *Chinese cultural script for concealing displays of feeling very good:*
> many people think like this:
> when someone feels something very good because something very good
>   happens to this someone,
> it is not good if other people can know this when they see this someone's
>   *liǎn* 'face' [m]

In relation to smiling, many Western observers over the years have noted with puzzlement that Chinese people may smile in some situations in which such a reaction would be unexpected from Westerners; especially, when a subordinate is dealing with the potential displeasure of someone in a superior position.

Ye (2006) proposed the following Chinese cultural script for 'compensation by a smile', an expression that corresponds to the Chinese phrase *péi xiào*. For ease of reference, the script is presented in two sections. Section (a) says that a Chinese person generally recognizes the existence of some people who are in a superior social position to themselves and with whom one has an asymmetrical relationship in terms of 'power' (these people can issue directions to oneself, but one can't do likewise to them). When one is with such people, according to section (b) of the script, one should conceal from them any bad feelings that one may have; in fact, it is preferable to give the impression that one is feeling something good at that time. Smiling provides one vehicle to convey this impression.

Chinese cultural script for 'compensation by a smile':
    many people think like this:
a.   I can think about some people like this:
      'these people are people above me
      these people can say things like this to me:
         'I want you to do this', 'I don't want you to do this'
      I can't say things like this to these people'
b.   when I am with someone like this, if I feel something bad,
      it is not good if this someone knows it
    it is good if this someone thinks that I feel something good at this time

(Section (b) of the script above is a generalization across two scripts proposed by Ye (2006: 149), both more specific than the one above.)

Up to this point we have been assuming that the physical details of the facial expression (i.e. smiling) are much the same across cultures. The differences we have been discussing are not about the expression itself, but about its interpretation in particular cultural settings. But though some expressions (such as smiling) may—perhaps—be universal in the physical sense, there are also culture-specific facial expressions, i.e. particular configurations of facial gestures that are codified, named, and endowed with a particular interpretation in some cultures, but not others. Ye (2004) draws attention to the importance of lexical evidence in establishing what is going on from a culture-internal point of view. 'Linguistic descriptions of facial expressions', she writes, represent 'a local facial encoding system', which, if appropriately analysed, can provide 'valuable resources for us to gain a culture-internal view of the face' (Ye 2004: 195). Let us see two examples.

Consider Ye's analysis of the meaning conveyed by a Chinese facial expression known as *piě zuǐ* 'corner of the mouth falls to one side':

<*piě zuǐ* ('corner of the mouth falls to one side')>
I now know that this someone did something
I think like this about it:
   'this is not good
   I want to say something because of this
   I don't want to say any words now'

Ye (2004) argues that the *piě zuǐ* expression has no counterpart, either physically or in its expressive value, in the Anglo system of facial expressions. Physically, *piě zuǐ* is a little reminiscent of a 'sneer', but it differs from a sneer because it does not expose the teeth, and from an expressive point of view, the message is subtler and less intense. The speaker shows that he or she considers the other person's action or speech to be incorrect or un-acceptable and has an urge to say something. Instead, however, the speaker refrains from saying anything and instead (via the *piě zuǐ* expression) shows something like disdain.

A second Chinese facial gesture without any counterpart in English involves a rapid sticking out of the tongue, often accompanied by wide-open eyes and sometimes by a tuck of the head. Many cultures have similar gestures from a physical point of view, which often seem to involve, one way or another, something like surprise or disbelief; but the precise mes-sages expressed can vary significantly from culture to culture. For Chinese, Ye (2006) proposes the following. It combines, roughly speaking, some-thing like disbelief, a negative reaction, and 'speechlessness' ('I want to say something because of this, I don't know what I can say now').

<*tǔ shétou* ('put out one's tongue')>
I now know something
I didn't know before that something like this could happen
I feel something bad because of this
I want to say something because of this
I don't know what I can say now

In addition to these and other examples of Chinese-specific facial ex-pressions, many of which would be missed or misinterpreted by Westerners unfamiliar with Chinese culture, Ye (2006) has a striking suggestion about a more 'global' difference between Chinese and Western styles of facial expression. From a Chinese point of view, she tells us, Western faces appear extremely mobile in the eyes, brows, and forehead. Chinese phrase-ology has a large vocabulary for facial expressions involving the eyebrows: see Table 12.4.

Generically the expressions listed in Table 12.4 can be grouped together as *méi fēi sè wǔ* ('eyebrows fly, facial expression dances') and, in Chinese thinking, they indicate spontaneous and unregulated expression of good feelings that can accompany speech—as if the speaker cannot contain him or herself. As one might suspect from our discussion so far, such unregulated and effusive expression is not generally admired in mainstream Chinese culture. Ye quotes from a compendium of Chinese etiquette: 'when one speaks, one generally should not move their eyebrows and their eyes, other-wise, they risk being considered as frivolous' (Hao and Sun 1991: 24). The

Table 12.4.   Commonly used Chinese expressions involving the eyebrows (*méi*)

xǐ shàng méi shāo (lit. 'delight/joy to the tip of the brows'), *yáng méi tǔ qì* (lit. 'raise eyebrows, utter breath', 'to feel elated'), *méi lì* (lit. 'eyebrows standing (on their inner tips)'), *shùqǐ liǎngdào méimao* (lit. 'erect two eyebrows'), *é méi dào lì* (lit. 'moth-like eyebrows stand upside down'), *chóu méi kǔ liǎn* (lit. 'sad/worried eyebrows, bitter face'), *zhòu méi/zhòuzhòu méi* (lit. 'wrinkle eyebrows'), *méi mù chuán qíng* (lit. 'eyebrows and eyes convey feelings'), *méi lái yǎn qù* (lit. 'eyebrows fro, eyes to', 'to converse with eyes and brows'), *jǐ méi nòng yǎn* (lit. 'squeeze the brows, play with the eyes'), *méi gāo yǎn dī* (lit. 'eyebrows high, eyes low', 'adopt different attitudes and measures under different circumstances'), *méi kāi yǎn xiào* (lit. '(the space between) the eyebrows are open, and the eyes are smiling'), *lì méi lì yǎn* (lit. 'erect brows, erect eyes'), *lì méi chēn mù* (lit. 'standing eyebrows, angry eyes'), *sǐ méi dèng yǎn* (lit. 'dead brows, staring eyes'), *méi fēi sè wǔ* ('eyebrows fly, facial expression dances')

implication is that Western faces, as read by the Chinese, often seem overly expressive and dramatic.

Westerners trying to read Chinese faces often experience the opposite impression. The Chinese face seems unexpressive—'inscrutable', as the stereotype has it. Ye's (2006) interpretation is that Western viewers are, so to speak, not looking in the right place for facial cues of emotion, and are not appropriately sensitized as to what to look for.

in Chinese people's perception, the upper part of the face plays an important role in conveying feelings and emotions. However, culture discourages them from having very expressive and dramatic facial expressions. Hence, it follows that the lower part of the Chinese face is where most of the culturally prescribed facial movements occur... in stark contrast to most Western cultures, where the expressivity of the face is registered in its upper part. (Ye 2006: 143)

12.5.4 Bodily actions and gestures

Like facial expressions, bodily actions like hugs, bows, kisses, and handshakes also convey meanings; and as with facial expressions, their meanings cannot be analysed and compared insightfully without a rigorous semantic framework. A further similarity between these two domains of non-verbal communication is that, paradoxical as it may sound, linguistic descriptions of actions and gestures can provide valuable clues to the culture-internal point of view. Interestingly, one can often discern an iconic basis (e.g. 'lowering oneself' in the case of bowing) to communicative bodily actions, and this helps explain why similar bodily actions tend to be associated with similar meanings across cultures. 'Similar' does not mean identical, however, as we will see.

We will consider examples of two broad semantic types or modes: overtly 'symbolic' gestures, such as shaking hands, bowing, or exchanging ritual kisses (e.g. in greetings or partings), and more expressive-spontaneous gestures, such as kissing, hugging, or slapping someone on the back. Gestures of both types are like 'saying' something in a non-verbal way, but those of the second type present themselves as more impulsive and less 'situation-bound'.

Consider first a more or less ritualized 'gesture', namely, *shaking hands*. Handshakes do not occur unexpectedly and in the middle of a conversation, but as 'declarations' at significant moments: during an introduction, upon leave-taking, to seal a contract or a bet, at a prize-giving, to make up after a disagreement. The performance is evidently undertaken to convey some kind of message appropriate to the situation.

What, then, is the message expressed by *shaking hands*? Is it possible to postulate a single meaning which would be compatible with its broad range of use, or do we have to posit two or more related meanings (polysemy)? Although the question is not usually posed in these terms, one can find conflicting interpretations in the literature. For example, *Webster's Third New International Dictionary* (1971) implies a polysemy interpretation when it says that the *handshake* is 'a sign of friendship, affection, or good wishes or as a mere polite formality'. On the other hand, Schiffrin (1981) implicitly favours a monosemy interpretation when she describes the *handshake* as a ritual which functions as 'a sign of access and solidarity'.

The formula below presents *shaking hands* as a socially recognized two-person routine in which each person conveys the same set of messages to the other (cf. Wierzbicka 1995b: 230). The gesture is depicted as, in a sense, a substitute for words—doing it is saying something 'not with words'.

<shaking hands>
when two people do this, they say the same thing, not with words
they say something like this:
   'I think something good about you now
   I do this now because I want you to know it
   at the same time, I want you to know that I think like this:
     "it is good if I can do some things with you"
   I feel something good because of this'
it is good if two people do this at times of some kinds

The reciprocal and mutual aspect of the message expressed by *shaking hands* is, of course, congruent with the physical nature of the routine, in which the two people cooperate in doing the same thing at the same time. In some contexts, this can be a powerful symbol (see Figure 12.2).

Needless to say, it is not being claimed that this formula applies everywhere outside the Anglo cultural world. Nor is it being claimed that when people shake hands they are necessarily sincere about the social messages which are exchanging. The same applies to the exchange of 'hello' and 'goodbye' *kisses*, which is normal and expected in some parts of the Anglo world (and in many other European settings).

Like shaking hands, exchanging mutual kisses is a symmetrical performance and one that requires precise coordination in time and space. It is a more 'personal' gesture than hand-shaking, however, first because it brings the actors much closer together, often into brief cheek to cheek contact, and secondly because the ritual kiss echoes, so to speak, the more intimate message of a spontaneous kiss (see below).

Figure 12.2. The power of a handshake, the power of a kiss. Israeli PM Yitzhak Rabin and Palestinian leader Yasser Arafat shake hands on the White House lawns after the signing of the Oslo Agreement in 1993. According to Tyler (2008), President Clinton was obsessed with the possibility that Arafat would kiss him in front of the camera at the signing and enlisted the help of Saudi Ambassador Bandar to prevent this. Arafat protested that he wanted to show the affection of the Palestinian people for the new American president, but Bandar prevailed. AP: Ron Edmonds

when two people do this, they say something like this, not with words:
  'I feel something good towards you now
  I do this now because I want you to know it
  I know that you feel the same towards me'
it is good if two people do this at times of some kinds

What then of giving someone a spontaneous kiss? Wierzbicka (1995b) calls it a 'momentary movement of affection'. Of course there are many ways in which one person can kiss another, and kissing someone (transitive) has to be distinguished from mutual (reciprocal) kissing. We will consider transitive uses, such as the following:

He kissed her warmly/passionately (cf. *a warm kiss, a passionate kiss*).
She gave him a kiss.

Though not necessarily passionate or sexual, there is a sensuous element for both parties, making a kiss akin to a caress. The involvement of the lips has a special significance, since as Wierzbicka (1995b: 222) puts it, 'the lips are so delicate, sensitive, and soft, they can be seen as a very fine and trustworthy instrument of self-disclosure.'

<a kiss>
when someone does this to someone else, this someone says something like
  this, not with words:
  'I feel something good towards you now
  I want to do this now because of it
  I want you to know what I feel now
  I know that you can feel something good because I do this
  I want you to feel something good because of it'

As a final example, let us consider *hugging*; specifically, let us compare 'hugging' in Anglo and Russian cultures (Monahan 1983; Wierzbicka 1995b). From an English speaker's point of view, Russians *hug* a great deal, so it may come as a surprise to many English speakers to hear that the Russian language does not have an exact equivalent to *hug*. The nearest words, *obnjat'* (verb) and *ob"jatie* (noun), are much closer to the English word *embrace*. What then is the difference between *hugging* and *embracing*? One difference is that *hugging* implies putting one's arms around the upper part of another person's body and squeezing briefly, whereas *embracing* could involve the entire body and it could go on for some time. (This helps explain why *embrace* (like *ob"jatie*) can be used about erotic situations, whereas *hug* cannot.) So when we see two Russians warmly greeting each other on TV and interpret this as the famous Russian 'bear hug', really we are imposing an Anglocentric point of view. The Russians themselves do not think they are *hugging*, because they do not have a word with the same conceptual content as English *hug*.

If we stick with English *hugging*, then, what can we say about the kind of meaning it expresses? One thing expressed is akin to affection; a *hug* displays a swell of 'good feeling' toward the other person. More specifically, one could argue that a *hug* conveys a caring or protective message (as if putting one's arms around the other person conveys an intention to provide protection from cold and from harm). A *hug* is also intended to make the other person feel something good. This leads to the following formula for the meaning conveyed by a *hug*:

> <a hug>
> when someone does this to someone else, this someone says something like
>   this, not with words:
>   'I feel something good towards you now
>   I want good things to happen to you
>   I don't want bad things to happen to you
>   I want to do this to you now because I want you to know this
>   I want you to feel something good because of this'

12.5.5 Cautionary remarks

Our discussion of non-verbal communication has barely scratched the surface of a huge and strikingly underdeveloped field of study. The handful of explications presented above are merely indications of how linguistic semantics can be extended to other realms of expressive behaviour. Two important issues we have not considered in adequate detail are: How extensive is the iconic basis of non-verbal communication? How do cultural values and priorities encourage, suppress, elaborate, or restrict the uses and social functions of gestures and facial expressions?

Answers to questions like these will require a great deal of detailed descriptive work in a variety of cultures. We can be sure, however, that many of the methodological and analytical questions that will arise are the same as those facing linguistic semantics; for example, the issue of poly-semy vs. generality, the discreteness (or non-discreteness) of semantic components, the distinction between meaning and use. It would be a shame if insights into these matters from linguistic semantics were to be ignored in the emergent field of non-verbal communication studies.

Key technical terms

cultural script

display rules

ethnopragmatics

insider perspective

level-one (level-two, etc.) semantic
   molecule

metasemantic adequacy

non-compositional relationship

norms of interaction

Discussion questions

1. Some Russian semioticians say that natural language is the 'primary modelling system' for human understanding (cf. Lucid 1977). Sebeok (1991: 50) explains what they mean as follows: 'Natural language, in brief, is thus posited as the primary, or basic, infrastructure for all other (human) sign systems.' Discuss. What other 'human sign systems' do you think they have in mind? Do you agree that language is the primary vehicle for human understanding?

2. Noam Chomsky (1991: 30) has drawn a remarkable conclusion from certain facts about language acquisition and semantic complexity. The facts are, first, that 'lexical items are acquired by children at an extraordinary rate, more than a dozen a day at peak periods of language growth' and, secondly, that the concepts behind even simple words like *persuade*, *chase*, or *murder* are extremely difficult to describe: '[d]ictionary definitions do not even come close; like traditional grammars they only provide hints for the reader who already has tacit know-ledge of most of the answer.' Chomsky concludes: 'Barring miracles, this means that the concepts must be essentially available prior to experience, in something like their full intricacy. Children must be basically acquiring labels for concepts they already have...'. Discuss this issue in the light of what we know about semantic variation between languages.

3. In a discussion of clashes in the social attitudes and communicative styles of Americans and Australians, Renwick (1980: 22–4) claims that:

For Americans, if someone is similar to them, they assume that person is apt to like them. Wanting Australians to like them, Americans tend to see Australians (and others) as similar to them . . .

Americans tend to like people who agree with them. Australians are more apt to be interested in a person who disagrees . . .

An Australian, when trying to get a sense of a person, looks for qualities within and is especially alert to interesting personal characteristics. An American is more apt to look at what the person does and has done.

Assuming that these statements are more or less valid, what predictions could one make from them about differences in conversational style between Americans and Australians?

4. In her book *Lost in Translation* Eva Hoffman (1989) relates her experiences as a Polish teenage immigrant adjusting to life in America. Among many observations about differences in interpersonal style between Polish and American culture, there is this one:

I learnt that certain kinds of truth are impolite. One shouldn't criticize the person one is with, at least not directly. You shouldn't say 'You are wrong about that' though you might say, 'On the other hand, there is that to consider'. You shouldn't say, 'This doesn't look good on you', though you may say, 'I like you better in that other outfit'. (Hoffman 1989: 146)

Try to write a cultural script summing up the 'Anglo' restriction on saying negative and potentially hurtful things. Remember to use only semantically simple words in your script.

5. What sort of messages are conveyed by 'laughing' and by 'crying'? Can you capture the expressive content in words?

6. What is the physical difference between a *hug* and a *cuddle*? Can you pinpoint the meaning conveyed by *cuddling* someone?

7. Discuss the uses of each of the hand gestures pictured in Figure 12.3 (Morris et al. 1979). See if you can come up with a single meaning for each which would be compatible with its range of use.

8. Look at the drawings in Figure 12.4. What meanings do you think can be ascribed to each of these bodily behaviours? What are you taking into account in coming to your conclusions?

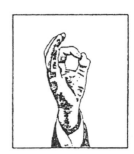

Figure 12.3. Hand gesture diagrams

Figure 12.4. Body posture/movements

Solutions to selected exercises

Chapter 1

1. (a) Sense. (b) Reference. (c) Reference. (d) Sense.

2. (a) Homonymy. (b) Polysemy. (c) Polysemy. (d) Homonymy.

3. (a) Homonymy. The two meanings are unrelated. (b) Polysemy. Both meanings involve becoming aware of (i.e. coming to know) something. It is not quite as good to say that both involve 'perceiving', because *perceive* is a fairly abstract word, and also because it seems somewhat metaphorical to speak of *perceiving* things mentally. (c) Polysemy. Both involve a kind of clothing, one being more specific than the other. (d) Homonymy. One meaning is something like 'to presume to treat someone like a child'; the other something like 'to favour a commercial venue'. This is an interesting example because the words are etymologically (i.e. historically) related, both deriving from Latin *pater* 'father'. Historical facts are not evidence for contemporary meanings, however, because ordinary speakers do not know the etymologies.

6. (a) Gradable antonyms. (b) Complementary antonyms. It is true that the outcome may be a draw, but this still doesn't make the words gradable antonyms because we cannot speak of degrees of *winning* and *losing*, as we can with true gradable antonyms like *hot* and *cold*. (c) Converses. (d) Complementary. (e) Gradable antonyms. (f) Converses. (g) Gradable antonyms.

7. (a) Taxonomic. (b) Collective. (c) Collective. (d) Taxonomic. (e) Collective. (f) Collective.

8. This problem is adapted from one devised by Felix Ameka. In the $z\partial$ set there are two words; the noun $z\partial_1$, which is three-ways polysemous, and the verb $z\partial_2$. The two words $z\partial_1$ and $z\partial_2$ are related in meaning.

   $z\partial_1$ (i) heel (ii) butt end (iii) clay container set in ground, used for storing palm wine and water.
   $z\partial_2$ to walk.

   One meaning for $z\partial_1$ is 'heel'. The meaning 'butt end' is related by shape and position. The 'clay container' meaning may be related to 'heel' by the common connection with the ground, but is even more plausibly related to the meaning 'butt end', since the container is fixed ('butted') into the ground. The verb zo_2 'to walk' is related in meaning to the noun via the connection between the foot and walking.

In the *nya* set, there are only two words, but one of them is three-ways polysemous.

nya₁ word.
nya₂ (i) to chase (away) (ii) to wash (clothes), to purge of dirt (iii) to knead/mould.

The meaning 'chase' is related to 'to wash (clothes), to purge of dirt' because both share the idea of making something go away from somewhere. The second meaning is related to the third because the hands are used in a similar way in both cases. Here we have a set of interrelated meanings, and as such it satisfies the definition of polysemy, but it is interesting to note that there is no meaning component which is common to all three meanings.

'To knead/mould' can be plausibly regarded as a single general meaning, something like 'to work at (something) with the hands, changing the shape of it'. However, it would be going too far to say there is a single general meaning which could cover 'wash, knead, mould'. Why? Because although it might be possible to state such a meaning, it is not particularly plausible to think that when Ewe people talk of washing their clothes the word they use means nothing more than, for instance, 'to work the clothes, changing their shape'.

In the *to* set there are five words, three of which are polysemous.

to₁ mountain
to₂ (i) ear (ii) father-in-law
to₃ (i) edge (ii) quarter, section (of a town) (iii) clan
to₄ (i) to pass through (ii) to be in vogue
to₅ to pound

It is safest to regard the 'mountain' meaning as belonging to a separate, unrelated word. Possibly the meaning 'mountain' is related to 'ear' by the notion of something jutting out, but this seems tenuous. Linking 'edge' and 'mountain' also seems far-fetched. To establish a case for polysemy it is not enough to note some vague association, e.g. that mountains have edges, or to speculate vaguely, e.g. that perhaps mountains mark the edge of Ewe territory. What is necessary is to actually state some component which can be plausibly regarded as part of both meanings.

The noun *to₂* has the meanings 'ear' and 'father-in-law'. They are related because in Ewe culture the father-in-law is the one who 'lends an ear' to married couples, to help them with their problems. The noun *to₃* is three-ways polysemous. Its first two meanings both involve the notion of 'a part'—of either a place or an object. These meanings presumably cannot be reduced to a single general meaning, because it would be possible to have a 'quarter' or 'section of a town' which was not on the 'edge' of the town. The meaning 'clan' is related because the members of a clan typically live together in the same section of a town.

The verb to_4 has two meanings: 'to pass through' and 'to be in vogue'. They are related because something that comes into vogue is by definition transitory, i.e. it will pass and go out of vogue. If you missed this, it is probably because you were distracted by the high stylistic tone of the gloss 'be in vogue'. If the meaning had been given as 'be a passing fad' the connection would have been obvious.

The verb to_5 'to pound' has an unrelated meaning.

Chapter 2

2. The definitions are not good, but there is no circularity. *Bold* is defined in terms of *courageous*, and *courageous* in terms of *brave*, but *brave* is defined in terms of other words (*endure*, *danger*, *pain*, etc.), without reference to *courageous* or *bold*. All three definitions can be seen as obscure, because the defining words used (*brave*, *courageous*, *endure*, *danger*, etc.) are of comparable complexity to those being defined.

Taken as a set, the definitions effectively claim that the three words *bold*, *brave*, and *courageous* all mean the same thing. This is descriptively inadequate because they do not have the same range of use. For example, one could say that a child who spoke out of turn was *bold*, but not *courageous* or *brave*. One could say that a public servant who spoke out against corruption was *courageous*, without necessarily being *brave* or *bold*. The definition for *brave* is not descriptively adequate either, since the mere ability to withstand pain does not amount to bravery.

3. (a) The definitions for *chase* and *pursue* are flawed by obscurity, but that of *follow* is not. Using *pursue* in the definition of *chase* is clearly a bad move, since it is obviously of similar semantic complexity to *chase* itself. As well, both definitions contain *overtake*, and other complex words like *seize*, *capture*, and *kill*. The phrases *in order to* and *with a view to* could also be more simply phrased, e.g. as *wanting*.

Essentially, *chase* is defined in terms of *pursue*, and *pursue* in terms of *follow*. There is no circularity here.

(b) Descriptive adequacy criticisms include: (i) The *etc.* is inexplicit and therefore open-ended. (ii) The element of 'speed' is missing from *chase* (a turtle could *pursue* a snail, but hardly *chase* it). (iii) For *pursue*, the desire of the pursued to get away is missing (one can *chase* a ball, but hardly *pursue* it), as is the determination of the pursuer to continue as long as necessary. (iv) *Chase* and *pursue* involve simultaneous movement of the two parties, but *follow* doesn't.

4. Your answer to the first part of this question depended on the dictionary you used. *The Australian Concise Oxford Dictionary* does a pretty poor job. It defines the relevant sense as follows: '3. body of persons travelling or working together (*fishing, reading, -party*); social gathering, esp. of invited guests at a private house (*birthday, dinner, tea, -party*).' This fails on descriptive adequacy, first, because it effectively merges two different senses of *party*, and second, because even the second part of the definition is too broad: there are social gatherings that are not parties. The expression 'social gathering' probably qualifies as obscure, in the sense that it is likely to be no simpler than the word *party* itself. The definition is not circular, because neither of the words *social* or *gathering* will require *party* in their own definitions.

As for improvements, I would be in favour of referring to some people being in a place for some time, doing some things together, with a certain kind of motivation, roughly, to have fun or enjoy themselves.

5. It is not easy to give a fully satisfactory answer to this question, but one important aspect (relevant to the difference between *Good evening* and *Good night*) is that *night* is thought of as a time when the sun is not in the sky (in opposition to *day*), a time when many people sleep. *Evening*, on the other hand, is a time after the sun has gone down, when many people are still doing many things.

6. The truth-tables for *but* and *and* are the same. This means first, that the meaning difference between *and* and *but* is not captured in any way by truth-tables. Logicians say that the difference is not 'truth-conditional'. Secondly, since *and* and *but* are both truth-conditionally equivalent to the logical connective ∧, we can conclude that the connective ∧ does not correspond to any word in ordinary English.

7. To distinguish each object from the others in the most economical way, using binary features, means using two features only. There are various possible solutions, depending to some extent on how we chose to identify the 'objects' in the first place. The features (call them A and B) must be chosen so that diagrammatically:

	+A	−A
+B	object1	object3
−B	object2	object4

There is no point in having features such as +LIVING, +ADULT, or +ANIMAL which apply to all the objects equally, and hence do not serve any distinguishing function.

One economical solution uses the features ± FOUR-LEGGED and ± MEAT-EATING. Another uses the features ± PATTERNED and ± WHISKERS.

8. (a) Since there are four words, the most economical solution would use two binary features. For instance, [± WATER] and [± THICK], like so:

mist [+WATER, −THICK];   *haze* [−WATER, −THICK]
fog [+WATER, +THICK];   *smog* [−WATER, +THICK]

Variants of these feature-labels, such as [± AQUEOUS] and [± OPAQUE], would be equally acceptable.

9. A sibling relationship between P and Q can be analysed as follows. P is Q's *sibling:* PARENT OF P = PARENT OF Q. (a) *Cousins* are people who share a grandparent, so to begin with we could write the following formula. X is Y's *cousin:* PARENT OF (PARENT OF X) = PARENT OF (PARENT OF Y). This formula is too broad as it stands, however, since it would apply also to siblings. For X and Y to be *cousins*, we have to rule out the possibility that they have the same parents, so we have to add the proviso: PARENT OF X ≠ PARENT OF Y. (b) If X is Y's *nephew*, then X is male and one of X's parents is a sibling of Y, that is: X is MALE and PARENT OF X = SIBLING OF Y. Substituting in the analysis of the sibling relationship gives—X is Y's *nephew*: X is MALE, & PARENT OF (PARENT OF X) = PARENT OF Y. An additional specification is needed to rule out the possibility that Y is one of X's parents: Y ≠ PARENT OF X.

10. The extreme obscurity of 'earth-protuberance' is bizarre, and could hardly be taken to represent the cognitive reality of any ordinary language user. On a different tack, the definitions misleadingly imply that the four words are all on a par with one another, differing only in size; but *mountain* and *hill* are clearly a kind of pair—both are ordinary landscape categories. *Mound* seems quite different; it implies something made by people or animals, rather than a natural feature of the landscape. In my dialect, the word *hillock* is rare or non-existent. I imagine it has some fairly direct relationship with *hill* (a 'mini' hill), but if so, this is not reflected in the definitions. Finally, there is (arguably) a lot more to words like *mountain* and *hill* than mere 'largeness'. Factors such as height (elevation) and visibility (i.e. that people can see them from a distance) are also involved (Bromhead 2011). Because Cruse's analyses are componential analyses, however, it is not strictly fair to raise this objection. Componential analysis, as you remember, does not aim at giving a full portrait of a word's meaning, only at identifying the minimal set of binary oppositions that will distinguish it from other closely related words.

11. As with the previous question, there are numerous faults. At a general level, there is surely something rather ridiculous about features such as +FRYING PAN and +FAT. More specifically, how would the feature 'frying pan' be explained or defined (without using *fry*, that is)? The feature +RACK, SIEVE, ETC. is highly problematical on account of the 'etc.'—without further explanation, it is not obvious what other items would qualify. Finally it is hardly satisfactory to stipulate that the feature [LIQUID] does not include *fat*.

Chapter 3

1. *Abnormal* implies a negative evaluation, something like 'this is bad', or perhaps (in order to model the somewhat objective or scientific sound of the word) 'people can know that this is bad'.

2. (a) Examples of acceptability contrasts between *cried* and *wept* include sentences like the following.

   *The baby was crying/*weeping.*
   *He wept/*cried silently/in a dignified way.*
   *He cried/*wept loudly.*
   *The poor thing cried/*wept herself to sleep.*
   *She was crying/*weeping inside.*

   Some of the differences between *crying* and *weeping* are that *crying* involves making a sound (but not necessarily producing tears); whereas *weeping* involves tears (but not necessarily sound). *Weeping* is compatible with a degree of control, but *crying* seems involuntary. *Weeping* also seems to call for some 'thought': you need to know what you are *weeping* about, and it cannot be a response to mere physical pain. It is possible to *weep tears of joy*, so it would not be correct to say that *weeping* is always a response to sadness.

   (b) Examples of acceptability contrasts between *horrified* and *terrified* include:

   *I was horrified/*terrified to discover that my enrolment had been cancelled.*
   *I felt terrified/*horrified as the truck thundered toward me.*

   Horrified is a bad feeling you have when you realize that something unexpectedly very bad has happened (not necessarily to yourself). It is akin to *shock*. *Terrified* is a very bad feeling you have when you are certain that something very bad and painful is about to happen to you personally. It is like intense fear.

3. Both words are highly resistant to reductive paraphrase. For 'know', people sometimes think of words like *certain* and *sure*, but these do not provide a satisfactory basis for a reductive paraphrase for several reasons. First, they do not seem to be any simpler than the word *know* itself. If anything, the opposite is the case (young children start using *know*, for example, well before they learn *sure* or *certain*). Second, even if *sure*, for example, did mean the same as *know*, simply substituting one word for another is not paraphrasing, because it does not break down the meaning of the original word into constituent parts. Third, and most importantly, *I am sure (of it)* does not mean the same as *I know (it)*; for example, one can be subjectively sure of something without necessarily knowing it; and the two sentences *I don't know* and *I'm not sure* are intuitively quite different in meaning. The only plausible line of explication for *know* is via

say. Many years ago, Wierzbicka entertained the idea that 'I know that such-and-such' can be paraphrased as 'I can say that such-and-such', but from an intuitive point of view the two sentences do not mean the same thing. Furthermore, their range of use is not the same; for example, one can say about a dog or a chicken that it *knows* where something is, but not that it 'can say' where something is.

As for *good*, putative equivalents such as *positive* or *valued* are obviously non-starters on account of their relative obscurity, and as well, they do not match the range of use of *good*; for example, *a good person* does not mean the same as *a positive person* or *a valued person*. The most promising line of explication is probably via 'want', e.g. 'something good happened to me' = 'something happened to me, I wanted this'; 'a good person' = 'a person, people want a person to be like this'. But 'good' and (roughly) 'wanted' do not correspond in meaning. It is not contradictory to say *something good happened that I didn't want*, or to say *I want to do something that is not good*. One might think that the situation could be saved by bringing in 'people', i.e. by paraphasing *good* as 'people want it like this', but there are many uses of *good* which wouldn't lend themselves to such a move, e.g. for example, 'I felt something good'.

Because 'know' and 'good' resist (non-circular) paraphrase in this way, they are good candidates for the status of semantic primes.

4. Except for *gaze*, all the definitions are marred by obscurity. It is obscure and complex to define *glare* in terms of *stare*, and *stare* in terms of *gaze*; not to mention defining *watch* in terms of *observation*. *Look*, on the other hand, is indeed relatively less obscure and complex than *gaze*, *glare*, *stare*, and *watch*. So defining *gaze* in terms of *look* is moving in the right direction, i.e. explaining a complex meaning in terms of others which are relatively simpler. Words such as *angrily*, *fiercely*, *astonishment*, and *observation* are also all obscure to varying degrees, in the sense that each is itself quite complex and requires further explication.

There is a messy web of interrelationships among the words defined and those used in definitions, but strictly speaking there is no circularity. The real problem with the definitions is their descriptive inadequacy. All the definitions overlook some discernible aspect of meaning. *Gazing* requires not only some duration and steadiness, but some 'good feeling' being experienced, e.g. wonder, interest, fondness. It would be odd to say *He was gazing at her with hatred*.

Glaring does indeed imply a bad feeling toward the person being glared at, but it could be hatred, contempt, spite etc., as well as 'angrily' or 'fiercely'. *Glaring* also seems to imply an intended message. Finally, it isn't quite true that *glaring* must be 'long and steady' (implied by use of *stare* in the definition). It is acceptable to say *She turned and glared at him*. The idea that *staring* involves looking 'fixedly, long and steadily' seems all right, but the phrase 'with the eyes open' is either redundant (one can hardly look at anything if the eyes are closed) or, if it means 'open wider than usual' it is incorrect.

The definition of *watching* doesn't make explicit that something being 'watched' must be subject to change or capable of action. One can *watch* a person or film but not a statue or a painting (unless one thinks something might happen to it, e.g. that it might be stolen). There is an intention behind watching—to see what happens. This is probably what the definition is getting at with the phrase 'keep under observation', but *observation* is more complex and obscure than *watching*.

5. This problem is based on Stanwood (1993). (a) Looking first at the nature of the movement, you could have observed such things as the following: the moving things (bat, flag, tail) don't move away from the actor; they move from one side to another, travelling in a plane or sweeping motion; the end of the thing closest to the person's body moves much less than the other end does. As for the actions performed by the subjects, in all cases they involve doing something by moving part of the body (arm, hand, tail).

(b) One difference is whether or not the movement is repetitious, and if so, the number of times an individual movement must or may occur. *Swung* in the first example sentence depicts a single movement. *Waved* could refer either to a single movement or to several. *Wagged* requires several distinct movements. *Swinging* an object typically involves holding something in the hand while moving the whole arm, or at least from the elbow down (admittedly, *swinging* one's arms or legs doesn't involve holding anything else). *Waving* can also involves holding something, as well as the hand moving, though it could involve part or all of the arm moving as well. *Wagging* is narrowly restricted to the tail of a dog or a person's finger. Another difference is how vigorous the motion typically is.

(c) We *swing* things like bats, rackets, axes, and swords. The typical purpose seems to be so that the thing hits something else and affects it in some way. We *wave* things like flags or our hands. The typical purpose seems to be so that someone else can see it, because we want to communicate something to that other person, typically to attract their attention or to show how we feel.

(d) The tail must be a distinct part (unlike the case of a fish or a worm), but this still doesn't explain why horses and elephants are not said to *wag* their tails. For a dog the important thing seems to be that *wagging* the tail expresses something, e.g. that it feels good or excited.

6. Terms like *contest, amusement, pastime,* and *rules* are just as complex and difficult as the word *game*. Reliance on these relatively obscure terms undermines the definitions. By the way, beware of using the length of a word as the sole evidence of its obscurity—short doesn't necessarily mean simple. When you think about it, a short word like *rules* has a rather complex meaning.

In assessing descriptive adequacy, it is not correct to say (as newcomers to semantics sometimes do) that the definitions are satisfactory because they 'cover' all the uses of the word *game*. The notion of descriptive adequacy is more specific than that. It is a question of whether or not the definitions predict the range of use, and that means excluding inappropriate uses as well as including the appropriate ones. Definition (1) seems to say that any 'amusement or pastime' is a *game*, which hardly seems right. What about listening to the radio, or knitting, or taking long walks in the country? The example given for this definition is *a children's game*, suggesting that the point of separating out this meaning is to cope with the fact that children's games do not necessarily have the same kind of fixed, set-in-advance rules as adults' games as defined under (2). However, this is not made explicit, and as it stands, definition (1) is quite misleading.

As for definition (2), one could ask whether games like solitaire and patience really fall under the heading of *contests* (especially if *contest* is defined, as it is in many dictionaries, in terms of 'competition'). We could also wonder whether guessing games, knowledge and/or trivia games, and odd games like charades can fit within the definition of 'chance, skill or endurance'. The definition also seems to imply that any *contest for amusement* would qualify as a game. What about a kids' potato sack race? It is a contest. Its goal is primarily amusement; but nonetheless there is something not quite right with calling this kind of activity a *game*. And what about a debate? And so on.

It is also unclear what is meant by *set rules*—what other kind of rules are there? On the reasonable assumption that what the dictionary means is something like widely known, highly codified rules of the sort that exist for football and golf, then this too would be a source of descriptive inadequacy, for even as adults we can improvise rules for casual, more or less private *games*. A further criticism would be that the definition does not show the link between the concept of a *game* and the concept of *playing*.

As for whether a general explication of *game* is possible, Wierzbicka (1990a) suggested that a reductive paraphrase should include the following ideas: Cf. Alexander (2006).

(1) human action (animals can play, but they don't play games) (2) duration (a game can't be momentary); (3) aim: pleasure; (4) 'suspension of reality' (the participants imagine that they are in a world apart from the real world); (5) well-defined goals (the participants know what they are trying to achieve); (6) well-defined rules (the participants know what they can do and what they cannot do); (7) the course of events is unpredictable (nobody can know exactly what is going to happen).

8. Lakoff and Johnson (1980) say that the most general conceptual metaphor in this realm is IDEAS ARE ORGANISMS. I would not have expected you to come up with a particular formulation. The appropriateness of the term ORGANISM is questionable, if the metaphor is intended to faithfully represent people's real cognitive processes. It would be more satisfactory to use wordings like IDEAS ARE ALIVE or IDEAS ARE LIVING THINGS. Of the nine examples given in the question, a couple sit rather awkwardly under the proposed metaphor IDEAS ARE ORGANISMS (or: LIVING THINGS);

for example, *Where'd you dig up that idea?* Perhaps Lakoff and Johnson had in mind the notion of exhuming a dead body. If so, it is a pretty loose connection.

Several of the expressions seem to cohere around a more specific theme connected with childhood (the reference to *giving birth* to an idea, being *father* of a theory, to a field of study being in its *infancy*, to an idea being someone's *brainchild*). To recognize this, Lakoff and Johnson (1980) propose a sub-metaphor IDEAS ARE PEOPLE, but again, the wording is probably not optimal. It would be preferable to state the conceptual metaphor as IDEAS ARE CHILDREN. A weakness of both the proposed conceptual metaphors is that they would license a much broader range of expressions than is actually found.

Chapter 4

1. All four terms describe a feeling one has in response to an evaluation of a person (be it of the person's character or of something the person has done). One dimension of contrast is whether this person is oneself or someone else. *Admiration* and *contempt* are focused on someone else; *pride* and *shame* on oneself. One could use a feature like [± SELF-FOCUSED]. A second dimension of contrast is whether the attribute in question is evaluated as good or bad. *Admiration* and *pride* concern a favourable evaluation; *contempt* and *shame* an unfavourable evaluation. One could use a feature like [± POSITIVE]. This analysis is based on Ortony et al. (1988: 134–46). Of course there are other factors involved in addition to these two, which taken alone, would not enable us to differentiate *shame* from *guilt*, *contempt* from *disdain*, or *admiration* from *respect*.

2. These explications are not necessarily the optimal explications for the words in question. Nonetheless, for the purposes of the 'matching' exercise, it is clear that *terrified* matches best with explication (c). *Terrified* is clearly the most intense of the three emotions, and this corresponds to the fact that explication (c) describes the feeling as 'very bad' (as opposed to simply 'bad' in the other two explications. Explication (c) includes the prototypical thought 'something very bad can happen to me now', where the presence of the element 'now' corresponds to something like immediacy. The combination 'I want to do something, I can't do anything' suggests a sense of helplessness.

   Comparing explications (a) and (b) against *afraid* and *frightened*, the key differentiator is the first component in the cognitive scenario. *Frightened* implies greater immediacy than *afraid*, so this makes explication (b) a better match. Notice that it is perfectly normal to say *I'm afraid that something bad will happen tomorrow*, whereas *?I'm frightened that something bad will happen tomorrow* sounds odd.

3. Clearly it is either *jealous* or (perhaps) *envious*. The complicating—and discussable—aspect of the choice is that the word *jealous* is apparently in the process of

shifting in its meaning, and taking over some of the range of the older use of *envious*. To put it another way, many people apparently no longer use the word *envious* much in their everyday speech, i.e. they don't respect the contrast that many dictionaries still want to draw between the two meanings. The final component of the explication ('because of this, this someone feels something bad towards this other someone') indicates a 'directed' bad feeling, which also seems more suited to *jealous* than to *envious*.

4. The best combination is (iii). *Jubilant* has an expressive quality, implying something like a public celebration. There is a sense of having overcome some difficulty, of having achieved a long-sought-after goal 'against all odds', as it were. Typical examples: *The whole crowd was jubilant when they heard the election results*; and *The team was jubilant after winning the grand final*.

   Combination (i) is too focused on the speaker's action. Many examples of *jubilant* would be excluded by this. The same point applies to combination (ii), and as well, the public or social aspect of *jubilant* is left out. Combination (ii) would be more suited to something like *joyful* or *exultant*, than to *jubilant*. Combination (iii) doesn't cohere because components (a) and (f) do not work well together. Combination (iv) does not make good sense, since components (i) and (j) clash. Combination (vi) is not too bad, but it leaves the aspect of 'overcoming' out of the picture, i.e. it would be more suited to a word like *rejoice* than *jubilant*.

5. *Someone X was ashamed at this time:*
   someone X thought like this at this time:
     'people can know something bad about me
     I don't want people to know this
     if people know this, they can't not think something bad about me
     when I think about it, I can't not think the same'
   because of this, this someone felt something bad at this time
     like someone can feel when they think like this

   The first component of the cognitive scenario allows for the fact that one can be *ashamed* about a personal attribute such as one's poverty or ugliness, as well as of something one has done. Using a hypothetical construction in the second component is consistent with the fact that *shame* is often associated with wanting to cover up the relevant attribute.

   Someone X was embarrassed at this time:
   someone X thought like this at this time:
     'something is happening to me now, not because I want it
     someone else knows about it
     this someone is thinking about me now
     I don't want people to think about me like this'
   because of this, this someone felt something bad at this time
     like someone can feel when they think like this

Very few languages have a word quite like *embarrassed*. It's an interesting thing that you can be *embarrassed* by unwanted personal attention at any time, even in situations where the onlookers are thinking and feeling good things about you; for example, when you receive a prize or when your friends all sing 'Happy Birthday' for you. For an engaging discussion of *shame, embarrassment*, and related emotions in other cultures, see Harkins (1996).

6. (a) There are two main aspects that must be adjusted. (i) 'Make' is an English-specific causative verb, so it can't be used in NSM. The basic idea can be rephrased as 'because of this/it'. (ii) 'Feel bad' is not allowable in NSM syntax. It has to be rephrased as 'feel something bad'. Strictly speaking, *person* is not ideal NSM either. In an older version of NSM it was used as an allolex of SOMEONE, but it is now thought that 'person' introduces some subtle English-specific semantics. It is best to replace it with 'someone', even though the combination 'this someone' sounds a bit unnatural. The optimal rewrites are therefore: 'this someone feels something bad because of it/this', or: 'because of this/it, this someone feels something bad'.

(b) 'Feel about' is not a permissible expression in NSM. To put it another way, semantic prime FEEL does not have a valency option with 'about'. The construction is possible in English, but it is language-specific and expresses a complex meaning, based on FEEL and THINK together. Interestingly, once we decompose the English 'feel about' construction into two parts, we can see that the 'about' extension actually belongs with the THINK part: 'when I think about this someone, I feel something good (because of it).'

Notice that FEEL itself cannot combine in pure NSM directly with GOOD, i.e. instead of 'feel good', the correct expression is 'feel something good'. The rewrite 'I feel something good because of this someone' may look like good NSM, but it is elliptical. To make sense of it, we have to fill in some missing material, e.g. 'I feel something good, because this someone did something'.

7. *Surprise* is a reaction to something immediate and unexpected, in the sense that the experiencer didn't think that it would happen. It is not necessarily either a good or a bad feeling (one can be pleasantly or unpleasantly surprised). Admittedly, 'nice surprises' may be more salient (e.g. birthday parties), but this is probably a pragmatic effect resulting from the fact that the word *shocked* is confined to unpleasant surprises.

X was surprised at that time:
someone X thought something like this at that time:
  'something happened now
  I didn't think that this would happen'
because of this, this someone felt something at that time
  like someone can feel when they think like this

English recognizes a 'stronger' kind of *surprise*, i.e. *amazement*, for a person's reaction to a situation which he or she didn't know could happen.

X was amazed at that time:
someone X thought something like this at that time:
  'something happened now
  I didn't know that this can happen'
because of this, this someone felt something at that time
  like someone can feel when they think like this

Feeling *shocked* is a reaction to coming face to face with something so bad that it strikes one as hard to believe. It throws one into something akin to confusion, lost for words and/or thoughts. It is unpleasant.

X was shocked at that time:
someone X thought something like this at that time:
  'I now know that something very bad happened
  I didn't think that something like this can happen
  I don't know what I can think'
because of this, this someone felt something bad at that time
  like someone can feel when they think like this

8. *X feels disappointed (at this time):*
   X feels something bad at this time
     like people can feel when they think something like this:
     'I thought before that something good will happen
     now I know that it will not happen'

   X feels relief (at this time):
   X feels something good at this time
     like people can feel when they think something like this:
     'I thought before that something bad will happen
     now I know that it will not happen'

9. This exercise is based on the work of Rie Hasada (cf. Hasada 1994). Below I give a model explication and some supporting comments. Given the limited data, there is room for some variation in your explications. For an excellent answer, the main requirements are that your explication is not inconsistent with any of the examples given and that it is phrased in simple terms, and, most importantly of all, that you have a supporting argument for each component.

   X feels MUT:
   a. someone X thinks like this at this time:
   b.   'someone did something
   c.   I don't want this
   d.   I want to say something now (to this someone) because of this
   e.   I can't say it now'
   f. because of this, this someone feels something bad at this time
         like someone can feel when they think like this

In the prototypical scenario, the feeling of *mut(to)* is triggered by someone doing something—component (b). The wording here assumes that saying something can be regarded as doing something. This act is unwanted, as stated in component (c). It would not be completely plausible to see the speaker's interpretation of the act as 'doing something bad (to me)', in view of example (iv).

Components (d) and (e) reflect the aspect of inhibition or suppression which is clearly evident in all the examples (except example (iv), and even here it is plausible). The experiencer has an urge to say something, presumably to speak up and voice his or her displeasure. The component given in (d) is the minimum that is required by the logic of the explication, but it is quite possible, even plausible, that it should be continued along the following lines: 'because I want to say how I feel'. Likewise with component (e). It is given here in minimal form, but it would be plausible to add a continuation as follows: 'because if I say something, something bad can happen', or 'because I know that it will be bad if I say something about it'. Notice that the reaction must be a verbal one, as we can see from the ungrammatical option of 'hitting' in example (vi). When we say that an explication should match the range of use of a word, this of course includes matching with how the word cannot be used, as well as with how it can be used. There is no evidence to motivate a component like 'I want to do something bad to this someone.'

X feels KAT:
a.   someone X thinks like this at this time:
b.   'someone did something (very) bad
c.   I don't want this
d.   because of this, I want to do something bad to this someone now'
e.   because of this, this someone feels something (very) bad at this time
        like someone can feel when they think like this

Component (b) of the prototypical scenario presents the triggering stimulus as the thought that someone has done something '(very) bad'. Notice that, as shown by example (xii), the action does not have to be directed at the experiencer personally, so it would be incorrect to phrase component (b) as 'someone did something bad to me'. Component (c) presents it as unwanted. Component (d) depicts the experiencer as feeling an urge to 'do something bad to this someone now'. Examples (ix) and (x) describe the experiencer actively doing something, and the translations used in (vii) and (viii) also imply an urge to act. It would be possible to add a component like 'this someone does something because of this' at the end of the explication; but this is not advisable on the data given, because it is not clear from the data that the feeling of *kat(to)* necessarily translates into action.

The instructions for this question noted that the uses of *mut(to)* and *kat(to)* for physical sensations are relevant to the emotional senses, but asked you to ignore this for the sake of the exercise. According to Hasada (1994), these Japanese words, and many others like them, incorporate a physical or sensory image in addition to a prototypical cognitive scenario. The physical sense of *mut(to)* describes a person's feelings when surrounded by stench and heat, a situation in which one feels that one cannot open one's mouth. This image is linked with the inhibition which an emotionally *mut(to)* person feels against uttering any words. The physical sense of *kat(to)*, which describes intense heat, is also linked with the emotional *kat(to)* feeling. A person feeling emotional *kat(to)* often actually feels physically hot, with a rush of blood to the head or in the body. Hasada includes a physical image of being a hot place (or of being hot) in the explication for emotional *kat(to)*. Emotion words which include sensory images or physical scenarios (in addition to cognitive scenarios) are sometimes called psychomimes.

Chapter 5

1. (a) *Concede, say, thank, deny,* and *nominate* are performative verbs, as shown by their capacity to occur with a first-person subject, in 'present-tense' form, with performative effect; for example:

    I concede we have made some mistakes.
    I say this whole project stinks.
    I thank you and everyone else who's supported me.
    I deny that completely.
    I nominate Oscar.

    (b) *Threaten, boast,* and *joke* are not performatives, but they are nonetheless speech-act verbs because it is possible to place them in a sentence like 'In saying that, I was X-ing'. They can also function as verbs of report; for example:

    'Don't even think about it', he threatened.
    'I am the greatest', she boasted.
    'Looks like a real live wire', he joked.

    (c) *Believe* does not satisfy the above criteria and is not a speech-act verb. It is perfectly true, of course, that one can say *I believe* ... and that by doing so one professes one's belief. But it is not the case that saying *I believe* ... actually constitutes believing (whereas saying *I deny it* or *I thank you* actually is denying or thanking).

2. One weakness of Searle's description is its use of complex and obscure terms such as 'in H's interest'. Another weakness is that the description does not predict the range of use of *congratulate* very well. On the one hand, one might question whether it correctly predicts that we can *congratulate* someone on the birth of a child. (Does it really make sense to view this kind of event as 'in H's interest'?) On the other hand, there are events which do seem to be 'in H's interest' that it would be odd to *congratulate* someone about; for example, receiving one's immunization shots, or recovering from an illness.

3. Unlike *My advice would be* . . . , the verb *to advise* sounds somewhat 'official', and it implies something like specialized knowledge on behalf of the adviser (as does the noun *adviser* itself, actually). The noun *advice*, in the relevant sense, is far more informal and it does not imply any special status or specialized knowledge. For example, a sentence like *My advice is, don't rush into it* can come from a friend who is not claiming any special knowledge on the subject (a new relationship, job prospect, or whatever). Notice also that offering *advice* in English is often done with the help of the formula *If I were you,* . . . ; but this formula would be quite out of place for someone *advising* someone to do something (Wierzbicka in press b).

4. (a) For *recommend*:
   this someone said something like this:
      'I know that you want to do something at some time after this
      I want you to know that I think about it like this:
         "it will be good for you if you do this (A)"
      I know much (many things) about things like this'

   (b) For *suggest*:
   this someone said something like this:
      'it can be good if you do this (A)
      it can be good if you think about it'

5. *X thanked Y (for* . . . *):*

LEXICO-SYNTACTIC FRAME

   a.   someone X said something to someone else Y at that time
        this someone wanted something to happen because of it

DICTUM

   b.   this someone said something like this:
        'I know that you did something because you wanted to do something
           good for me'

APPARENT MENTAL STATE

   c.   this someone said it like someone can say something like this to someone else
        when this someone thinks like this:
        'I feel something good towards this someone at the same time'

6. Two types of kin-based Aboriginal speech-act verbs have been reported in the literature. (a) A verb expressing a kin-based 'request', i.e. conveying a message like 'I want you to do this, I think that you will do it because of how you are related to me'. Hudson (1986) describes such a verb *japirlyung* in the Walmajarri language. (b) A verb meaning 'to call someone by a kinship term', either to address them or to refer to them. Yankunytjatjara *walkuṉi* and Arrernte *anperneme* are verbs like this (Goddard 1996b: 211; Henderson and Dobson 1994: 149).

8. The following seems a plausible dictum for these examples of Malay *ajak*. The speaker expresses the wish that the addressee does something with him or her, at the same time expressing the idea that 'it will be good if you do it'. In many cases the prospective action is a pleasant one, such as eating together, but this is not always the case, so no component about 'feeling something good' is included.

Someone X ajak *Y to do something (A):*
someone X said something like this to Y:
  'I want you to do something (A) with me after this
    it will be good if you do it'

Chapter 6

1. Discourse particles: *just, only, even*. Primary interjections: *gee, hi, um, uh-huh, phew, oooh*. The remaining items (*oh dear*, and *holy shit*) are interjectional phrases. Strictly speaking, interjectional phrases are not secondary interjections, since the latter are by definition single words.

2. From a semantic point of view, the main problem with deriving *John does Z and Mary does too* from *John does Z and Mary does Z* is that it changes the message. First, it adds something which the speaker left unexpressed (i.e. the explicit statement that *Mary does Z*). Secondly and more importantly, it removes something that the speaker did express, namely, the statement of identity ('same-ness'), cf. Wierzbicka (1980a: 275).

3. There were several ways to approach this question. The following is one possible explication:

  —— *kunyu:*
someone else said this before
I say this to you now because I want you to know what it was

4. According to Wong (1994: 56–7), by 'tagging' a statement with *wüt* the speaker signals that he or she is contradicting an apparent presupposition of the previous proposition.

  In example (a) X's question presupposes that there are no pins available on the notice board. In (b), X's question presupposes that X has not told Y to wait. In (c), the apparent presumption behind the nickname *cockroach* is that cockroaches are 'hunched' (i.e. have a hunchback). Notice that in this case, the presupposition in question isn't necessarily the addressee's: it applies to the group of people being discussed, who use the nickname *cockroach*.

  In (d), X's remark 'I wish I were good-looking' presupposes that he is not good-looking. Example (e) differs from all the others in that there is no preceding utterance. In this case, the presupposition which the speaker has in mind is that someone (anyone) would believe such an unlikely scenario as a robber chasing an armed policeman. In (f), the apparent assumption is that the person's bad language is remarkable or surprising. Y does not think so and gives the reason for it (i.e. the person in question comes from the army).

An explication like the following can accommodate all these uses:

—— *wüt*:
something happened now
because of this, I think like this now:
   'someone here thinks something about something
    it is not true'
I say this because I want you to know this

The first component presents the triggering event as 'something happened now' (rather than 'you said something now' or 'someone said something now') to allow for *wüt* utterances in response to third-party statements, as in (c), and for non-verbal situations, as in (e). The second component spells out the speaker's inference that 'someone here thinks something about something'. Again, the wording has to allow that the 'someone' in question is not necessarily the addressee. However, the final component specifies that the speaker's illocutionary intention is directly focused on the addressee.

5. In using *cis* the speaker appears to be expressing a non-committal and non-judgemental attitude towards what the other person has said. The interjection is compatible with neutral and opened-ended continuations, but incompatible with definitive ones. At the same time, the speaker appears to be expressing something like a calm or non-emotional state of mind. We can infer this because *cis* is incompatible with expressions of feeling (positive, negative, or neutral).

Possible components are as follows: 'maybe it is like this, maybe it is not like this.' Plus something like: 'I don't feel anything now when I think about it.' And perhaps something like: 'people can think about it in many ways.' By the way, this problem is a disguised form of Danish. *Cis* is based on the Danish response marker *tja*. This problem was devised by Carsten Levisen.

6. A notable difference between (a) and (b) is that (a) characterizes the feeling that goes with *Wow!* via the component 'I feel something good because of that', whereas (b) has the comparable component as simply 'I feel something because of that.' A drawback of (a) is that it doesn't include the element 'now'. Explication (b) does include a 'now', but only in the first component, where it relates to the 'immediacy' of the experiencer's knowledge state ('I now know something').

An improved explication is shown below. It would be incompatible (as required), with using *Wow* in contexts like: **Wow, that's terrible.*

Wow!
I now know something
I didn't know before that it can be like this
I can think something good about something now because of this
I feel something now because of this

7. *Ow!* expresses a negative reaction to a sudden pain—*Ow, that hurts.* In the explication below the 'pain' aspect is depicted as a 'bad feeling' due to 'something bad happening now to one part of my body'. There is an element akin to protest ('I don't want this'). A minimizing component also seems necessary; one can hardly imagine someone saying *Ow!* if an injury is serious.

Ow!
I feel something bad now in one part of my body
because something bad is happening in this part
I don't want this
I don't want to think like this: 'it is something very bad'

One says *Oops!* as a kind of acknowledgement of having just done something which has caused something bad, while at the same time avowing that it wasn't intentional and minimizing (or seeking to minimize) the extent of the damage done.

Oops!
I did something in one moment a very short time before (ago)
I know that something bad happened because of it
I didn't want this to happen
I don't want to think that it is very bad

It's possible that there is an additional 'minimizing' component, which brings in the semantic element 'small': i.e. 'I think about it like this: "it is something small". This kind of component has been proposed for some 'minimizer' modifiers, such as English *a bit* (in sentences like *It was a bit awkward*). Such a component has not yet been proposed in published work for any interjections, but intuitively it seems to fit quite well. Another interjection that could use such a component would be *Ouch!*. It could help with differentiating *Ouch!* from *Ow!*.

8. (a) For the Mparntwe Arrernte *Me!* and Malay *Nah!*, we could consider the following:

I want you to have thls
because of this, I want you to do something now

(b) Mayali *Mah!* is not easy to explicate on the data given, but we could consider the following. As stated in the question, the key thing is to remain vague about who is the potential performer of the action. The explication below is written with the idea that someone who says *Mah!* is expressing their wish for a certain 'outcome'.

I want something to happen
it can happen if someone does something now
I want this

9. This problem was devised by Nick Enfield (cf. Enfield 1994). He assigns the Lao particles *mêế* and *sáa* the following semantic explications:

Verb *mêế:*
I want you to know that you can do Verb
I say this because I think that it will be good for you if you do it

Verb *sáa:*
I want you to do Verb
(I think) it will be good for me if you do it
I don't know if you will do it

Chapter 7

1. As we saw in Chapter 1, words like *furniture* and *cookware* are not taxonomic category words, but collective words: i.e. they designate 'things of many kinds'. Further, they are complex: while the explication of *oak* must contain 'a tree [m] of one kind', it would be counter-intuitive and would lead to circularity to try to define *a saucepan*, for example, as 'cookware of one kind'. There is also a grammatical reason why such a move would be awkward. *Furniture* and *cookware* are not 'count nouns', i.e. they do not have singular forms, but instead use a 'unitizer' constructions, e.g. *a piece of furniture, an item of cookware*.

2. The following applies the same kind of approach to characterizing 'breeds' as was used in the chapter to characterize individual species: essentially, that a *beagle, terrier*, etc. is a 'dog [m] of one kind' born of another dog of the same kind. Subsequent sections of the explication will indicate the distinctive physical and behavioural features.

a beagle, terrier, Labrador, etc.:
a. a dog [m] of one kind
b. before a dog [m] of this kind is born [m], its body is part of
        the body of another dog [m] of the same kind
c. dogs [m] of this kind are small (very small, big, very big)
d. the bodies of dogs [m] of this kind are not like the bodies of other
        dogs [m], they are like this:

        ... ...
        ... ...

3. How an animal can be handled (picked up, held, etc.) seems to work as a standard of reference for small domestic animals like *mice*, *cats*, and *dogs*, but it is obviously inapplicable to *horses*. The most plausible approach would be to use someone standing next to the animal as a standard of reference. Perhaps something like this:

> if someone is standing [m] near an animal [m] of this kind, on one side of this animal [m], this someone's head [m] is not far above this animal's back [m].

There might be a case for an extra component too:

> this animal's [m] head [m] can be above this someone's head [m], if this animal [m] wants it

The only semantic molecules needed for this way of stating it (i.e. 'stand', 'head', and 'back') are independently needed for other purposes. This is preferable to using words such (say) 'tall' or 'high', which may not warrant molecule status. Although horse breeders and the like measure the size of horses using 'hands' (hand widths), this practice is not widely known and it would hardly be plausible to embed such a perspective in an explication for the ordinary person's meaning of the word *horses*.

4. This was a difficult question. The components below try to capture the ideas of an 'expressive' and (so to speak) 'rapid' sound produced by the mouth, which is loud, and which can be interpreted (sometimes at least) as intended to express 'attention-getting' messages: either to draw attention to the dog's own location in a place or to draw attention to someone else's location in a place.

> at many times, when animals [m] of this kind feel something, they do something with the mouth [m]
> when they do this, parts of the mouth [m] move quickly [m]
> at the same time people can hear something of one kind because of this
> when an animal [m] of this kind does this in a place, people far from this place can hear it
> when people hear something of this kind, sometimes they can think that this animal [m] wants to say something like this to someone: 'I am here now', sometimes they can think that it wants to say something like: 'someone else is here now'

5. Language K is a disguised and probably somewhat distorted form of Hadza, a Khoisan language spoken in Tanzania, based on data from Parkvall (2006). (i) The Language K lexicon is unusual in several ways: (a) It includes a set of distinct words for the 'carcasses' of various large animal species. Notice that the gloss 'carcass' is not the same in meaning as 'meat'. English of course has specific words for various kinds of meat that come from certain species (*pork* from pigs, *mutton* from sheep, etc.). (b) Several of the the 'carcass' words are not tied to a single species, but rather group together pairs of species: lion and eland, elephant

and hippo, hartebeest and gnu, warthog and wild pig. (c) On the other hand, unlike the individual species words, the carcass words are differentiated by gender: male marked with suffix -*o* and female with suffix -*a*.

(ii) It is logical to speculate that all these species are eaten for food—hence the existence of distinct words for the carcasses. As it happens (and you could not be expected to come up with this), the people who speak this language not only hunt, but also scavenge on the found carcasses of these animals. Why do some of the Language K words lump together carcasses of two distinct species? Several suggestions come to mind: perhaps the meat tastes similar, perhaps the hides or general body shapes are similar, perhaps the carcasses are found in similar locations. As for the gender distinction, this too is mysterious, but perhaps has something to do with different body shapes and/or food tastes.

6. This problem was devised by Nicholas Evans. Remember that the instructions asked you to avoid disjunctions (i.e. using 'or') and complex terms, e.g. 'cartilageous'.

(a) The highest-level classifiers are:
yarbuda: creatures that don't live in the sea
yakuri: fish; creatures that live in the sea, do not breathe air, and have scales and hard bones
wanku: creatures that live in the sea, do not breathe air, without hard bones and without scales; (and/or) dangerous sea creatures
kunbulka: creatures that live in the sea, and breathe air; (and/or) big creatures that people catch and eat

(b) The words used for intermediate classification are:
kalanda: flying (can move through air, having wings, etc.)
barrinda: crawling (moves along ground without legs)
rajurrinda: walking (moves along ground using four legs)
bangga: turtle; *kunkulka* with a hard shell, which comes onto land and lays eggs

8. Lehrer (1970: 93) says that *sofa* and *couch* are 'virtually synonymous', except that *sofa* has an optional component 'with arms' and *couch* an optional component 'without arms'. Wierzbicka (1985: 68) gives a more convincing account based on a difference in function:

sofas are made for a few people to be able to sit on comfortably, whereas couches are made to meet a double purpose: they should be comfortable for a few people to sit on and for one person to lie on. There is a reason why the sofa-like piece of furniture in a psychoanalyst's office is generally called a couch, not a sofa—even by those people who might call an identical piece of furniture in a living-room a sofa. In fact, the partial difference in function between couches and sofas entails also another probable difference in appearance: sofas tend to have backs, whereas couches (especially psychoanalysts' couches) are more likely not to have a back. (Wierzbicka 1985: 61)

9. The following are plausible sets of components for the first two sections of an explication for *knives*.

   a. something of one kind
      people can do something to many things with something of this kind
   b. things of this kind are like this:
      – they have two parts
      – one of them has a long [m] sharp [m] edge [m]
      – this part is made [m] of something very hard [m]
      – it can have a sharp [m] point [m] at one end [m]
      – the other part is not sharp [m]
      – someone can hold [m] it with one hand [m]
      – because of this, when someone is holding [m] it, if this someone's hand [m] moves as this someone wants, the sharp [m] part moves at the same time as this someone wants

Chapter 8

3. In *We'll come there right away*, the verb *come* implies moving to where the addressee is. This wouldn't make any sense if the addressee were one of us, so the interpretation of *we* in this context must be 'exclusive'. In *We'll go there right away*, the verb *go* doesn't imply anything about the location of the addressee, and so it can be used regardless of whether the addressee is with us or is somewhere else.

5. The list of deictic conditions is a string of disjunctions (motion toward the speaker OR toward the addressee OR toward the home base of the speaker OR toward the home base of the addressee). There is nothing wrong with this as a description about when *come* can be used, but if it were taken as a description of the MEANING of *come*, it would be claiming that the word is four-ways polysemous. It would be much preferable to posit a single meaning compatible with these four contexts of use.

7. (a) In the Japanese set the dominant pattern is MOTION+MANNER (*aruku* 'walk, go forward using the legs', *hashiru* 'go fast', *hau* 'crawl, move forward lying on the stomach'). The verb *tobu* 'fly, jump, move above the ground' appears to be an exception to this pattern.
(b) In the Malay set the dominant pattern is MOTION+PATH (*masuk* 'enter, go in', *turun* 'go down', *naik* 'climb, ascend, go up', *keluar* 'go out'). *Lompat* 'leap, jump' is an exception.
(c) There is no real dominant pattern among the Yankunytjatjara verbs given. *Pakaṉi* 'get up, come out', *tjarpanyi* 'go in, enter', and possibly *punkaṉi* 'fall' could be regarded as examples of MOTION+PATH conflation, but *kalpanyi* 'climb', *parpakaṉi* 'fly', and *wirtjapakaṉi* 'run' show MOTION+MANNER conflation.

8. Malay *lari* does not contain any 'manner of motion' component (unlike English *run*). The essential thing about *lari* seems to be rapidity of motion. The explication captures this idea in terms of being able to travel far in a short time.

Someone X lari *(Malay):*
someone X does something in a place for some time
because of this, this someone moves for some time
because of this, after a short time, this someone can be far from the place
    where this someone was before

The explication incorporates the hypothesis that *lari* involves not just moving, but 'doing'. Admittedly, a car can *lari*, but presumably this is possible because we understand that someone inside the car is doing something.

9. This problem was devised by Carsten Levisen. It seems that this use of Danish *hen* encodes movement towards a place which is both nearby and familiar to local people.

this other place is near here
people here know this place well

Chapter 9

1. There are many differences between *nibbling* and *eating*. (i) *Eating* is in some sense a normal, typical, and routine activity, whereas *nibbling* isn't. For *eating*, one can introduce a prototypical motivational scenario with the component 'at many times someone does something like this to something when it is like this: …'; but for *nibbling*, such a component wouldn't make sense. Perhaps though, the first phrase could simply be changed to: 'at some times'. (ii) Unlike as with *eating*, someone who is *nibbling* is not simply wanting to get something inside their bodies via the mouth. At most they are wanting to get some 'little bits' of it into their bodies, and perhaps not even into their bodies as such, so much as into the mouth. (iii) So far as manner is concerned, it seems clear that *nibbling* involves 'smaller' (briefer) movements; and also that the teeth are rather salient. The manner component for *eating* does not mention 'teeth' as such, though they are included, by allusion, in the reference to 'parts of the mouth'. For *nibbling*, however, one could make a case that the manner section should mention 'someone doing something to this something for a short time with the teeth [m]', or 'for some time, this someone's teeth [m] are touching this something, the teeth [m] are moving at this time'; or some such. (iv) *Nibbling* seems strongly associated with the image of 'mice'. One could make a case that the explication of *nibbling* should include some kind of analogy referring to mice or (perhaps) to 'small animals of one kind'. For example: 'at many times mice [m] (or, small animals [m] of one kind) eat [m] something in this way.'

2. The construction is called 'pseudo-intransitive' for a very good reason. Although there is no explicit object, the nature of eating implies some affected 'stuff', and hearing a sentence like *He was eating* we understand that he was eating something (or perhaps, some things). From a grammatical point of view, we could say that an indefinite object has been elided or deleted. Interestingly (and this is a rather subtle point) the nature of the 'understood' indefinite object is constrained. It has to be the kind of thing that is normally eaten (i.e. food). To see this, consider that regular transitive *eat* can be extended to cover *eating* of non-canonical substances. For example, a sentence like *Oh my God, the baby's eating grass* is perfectly acceptable, but the same situation could not be described simply as *The baby was eating*. The generalization seems to be that the 'pseudo-intransitive' use of *eat* is suitable only for prototypical situations of *eating*. This being the case, it seems fair to say that *eat* in the 'pseudo-intransitive' construction has a slightly different meaning from its meaning in the regular transitive construction.

3. The question asked you to speculate about 'possible cultural and/or lifestyle' reasons for a language not differentiating between two modes of 'consumption'. The most obvious line of speculation is that it may have to do with whether or not there is a sharp line between two such modes of consumption in the culture concerned. In the 'Western' lifestyle, for example, most dishes consist of solid items. Furthermore, in many settings they are presented to the eater in more or less big pieces, i.e. the individual eater usually has to cut them up with knife and fork into smaller pieces, and then once in the mouth one has to chew these pieces a little to make them easy to swallow. Of course, there are also soups and stews and ice-cream, and some kinds of food require less cutting and chewing than others, but overall these are in the minority. In other cultures, however, things may be less clear-cut. Much Chinese food is based on rice or noodles, for example, which require less chewing than most Western foods, and, as well as that, the other ingredients are often presented in smaller pieces, suitable for picking up with chopsticks. Some regional cuisines have a great many dishes that combine solid and 'watery' foods, such as dumpling soups, steamed fish and chicken, stews, and noodle dishes.

   Whether factors like these are or are not relevant, and if so, to what extent, is unclear at this time. In other words, we are engaging here in speculation or conjecture. Any simple hypothesis about a causal relation between 'food practices' and the lexicon has to take account of many apparent counter-examples. For example, Cantonese cooking also has a lot of combined solid-plus-watery foods, and yet Cantonese has distinct words for 'eating' and 'drinking'. Likewise, as Wierzbicka (2009b) observes, the Warlpiri language has a single verb *ngarni*, while other Aboriginal groups in similar ecological conditions (and presumably, similar eating practices) have separate verbs for 'eating' and 'drinking'.

4. This question was devised by Carsten Levisen. To begin with *skærer*, one might think at first that it is much like English *cut*, except for two things: (i) there are no

examples of its use with things like paper and thread, and (ii) the only examples provided concern food items. When we consider that many of the examples provided for Danish *klipper* would be expressed in English with *cut*, the possibility of a close correspondence between *skærer* and *cut* seems even less likely.

Examining the range of use of *klipper* brings up an interesting possibility, because it would seem that its uses all involve instruments that bring two long sharp edges together in a 'sideways' action, i.e. instruments such as (to use English words for them): scissors, garden clippers, secateurs, and shears. This being the case, we could hypothesize that *skærer* implies an instrument with one long sharp edge (like a knife), while *klipper* implies an instrument with two long sharp edges that 'work' together.

In fact, though you were not to know this, Danish has a single word (*saks*) for all the various 'bipartite' sharp-edged tools that English distinguishes as scissors, clippers, shears, and the like. It is therefore possible that 'saks' functions as a semantic molecule in the Danish concept of *klipper*. Certainly the association between *klipper* and *saks* is very salient for Danes—even more salient than the association between 'chop' and 'axe' is for English speakers. It is easy to think of uses of *chop* that do not require an 'axe' (e.g. chopping vegetables in the kitchen), whereas in Danish almost all uses of *klipper* involve a *saks*.

Returning to *skærer*, and assuming that it requires an instrument with a single long, sharp edge (like a knife), the question arises: what else can we hypothesize about its meaning? One possibility would be that its prototypical motivational scenario involves food preparation. This would be a reasonable conjecture from the examples provided. Another possibility would be a component related to a high degree of control over the separation process, but there is insufficient evidence in the data provided.

Coming now to *hugger* (used with wood, stone, and ice), it looks as if this word could be close in meaning to Polish *rąbać* (roughly, 'chop with heavy axe'), i.e. a verb implying an object that is 'hard' or 'very hard', and (therefore) an instrument that is not only sharp, but also 'heavy'. Together, these requirements imply forceful blows. It would also be plausible to hypothesize that (like *chop*) *hugger* requires multiple repeated blows, at least in imperfective uses.

5. The following seems like a reasonable prototypical motivational scenario for *digging*. The basic idea is that the digging person does something to the ground in a place because they want to 'shift' some of the ground there, to some extent at least. The wording is deliberately vague, so that it is compatible with just 'turning the soil', as one does when one *digs* ground in a garden, and with moving some of the ground up and away to the side, as one does when *digging* a hole.

   at many times when someone does something like this in a place, this
       someone does it because it is like this:
           a short time before this someone thought like this about the ground [m] in
               this place:
           'I want some parts of the ground [m] in this place not to be in the places
               where they are now
           because of this I want to do something to the ground [m] in this place'

6. The following seems like a reasonable MANNER for *digging*.

when someone does something like this in a place, it happens like this:
– parts of this someone's body move for some time as this someone wants
– because of this, parts of something touch some parts of the ground [m] in this place for some time as this someone wants
– during this time, these parts of this something move as this someone wants
– because of this, at the same time something happens to these parts of the ground [m] in this place

Chapter 10

2. Hoffman's table implies that there is a constant relationship between the words in the two rows. If we interpret COZ as 'cause' and BCM as 'come to', we could recast it as follows:

(a) *kill* = cause to die (come to be not alive), (b) *give* = cause to get (come to have), (c) *teach* = cause to learn (come to know), (d) *drop* = cause to fall (come to be moving downwards)

This table implies at least two questionable claims. (i) The validity of the BCM element is not equally apparent in all four cases. It may make sense, for example, to interpret the result of 'dropping X' as 'X comes to be moving downwards', because 'moving downwards' is a dynamic predicate and all that is required for an action to qualify as 'dropping' is that the object begins to move downwards. It is not at all clear, however, that the same goes for the other verbs, where the result is a state. It would be more economical and more intuitive to define the result-state of 'Z gives X Y' as simply 'X has Y', rather than as 'X gets Y' (X comes to have Y). (ii) 'Z kills X' definitely entails that 'X dies', and no agency or actions on X's part are required or implied, but things are not so simple with 'Z teaches X Y' and 'X learns Y'. For Y to learn requires some agency or effort on behalf of the learner and this is left out. (There are also some examples where the entailment does not go through, e.g. *He taught me geography in school* does not entail *I learnt geography*, but these may be due to a separate meaning of 'teach'.)

It is also fair to say (though this was not precisely the point of the question) that none of Hoffman's 'equations' is justified if we interpret them as strict statements about semantic compositionality. The most plausible one is no doubt 'kill = cause to die'. We have seen that even this equation is suspect, but many linguists continue to assume that 'die' is a semantic component of *kill*; to argue that it isn't requires some subtlety and attention to detail. On the other hand, it is not at all obvious that 'learn' is a semantic component of *teach*, that 'get' is a semantic component of *give*, or that 'fall' is a semantic component of *drop*.

3. In view of the very wide range of use of the Italian *fare* construction and the apparent lack of any semantic constraints on its use, a very broad and unconstrained explication is required. For example (cf. Wierzbicka 1988: 247):

X ha fatto Y do Z (infinitive verb):
X did something
because of this, Y did something (Verb)

4. In the '*make* of necessity' construction, an event leads the causee to a realization that an action is necessary. The following explication is adapted from Wierzbicka (2006d).

Event-X (in place P) made someone Y do Z (e.g. The rain made her go inside):
someone Y was in place P
something (event X) happened in this place
because of this, someone Y thought: 'I can't not do something Z'
because of this, Y did Z (e.g. *go inside*) at this time, not because of anything else

5. The trouble with the term 'indirect causation' is its vagueness. Describing something in this way does not tell us much about when it would be appropriate to use the construction. As well, there are other causatives that could equally well receive the same designation, e.g. the English *have* causative. Finally, the term 'indirect causation' has been used by linguists to describe many causatives in many languages, and it is highly unlikely that they are all the same in terms of their meanings and range of use.

Comparing the *get* causative with the *make* causative (and confining ourselves to verbs that are subject to voluntary control), we can say that *get* implies the use of persuasion, inducements, even manipulation, but it falls short of anything like coercion, as implied by the *make* causative. The *get* causative implies that the doer does the act willingly, while at the same time implying that he or she wouldn't have wanted to do it except for some action by the causer (cf. Wierzbicka 2006d: 177–9).

Someone X got someone Y do something:
someone X wanted someone Y to do something
X knew that Y would not do it if Y did not want to do it
because of this, X did something
because of this, after this Y wanted to do it
because of this, Y did it, as X wanted

6. For both sets of verbs, the effect on the causee is negative or 'adverse'; i.e. something bad happens to the object. For the two verbs in (a), it is plausible to suppose that more is implied than this, because both verbs describe a situation where the 'victim' ends up dead (no longer living), and in both cases this is brought about by physical contact with a particular part of the body (the back of the neck or the throat). The body-part word (*ngunti* or *liri*) is the root of the causative formation.

With the words in set (b), the root of the causative usually appears to be an adjective (in a slightly modified form) that describes the resultant condition brought about by the causative action: 'dead', 'broken', or 'staved in'. The root *tjalaly* appears not to follow this pattern, because it is glossed as 'having liquid inside', i.e. it apparently designates the prior state rather than the resultant state. This may be an exception or it may be an anomaly in the data. (Actually the revised second edition of *The Pitjantjatjara/Yankunytjatjara to English Dictionary* (Goddard 1996b) gives this word the meaning 'easily broken so that the contents flows or runs out, e.g. eggs'.)

In any case, from a semantic point of view all the verbs seem to indicate a disruption of a prior state that otherwise would have continued, i.e. like English *break* and *kill*, they imply someone doing something to something (or to someone else) and something happening to this something or someone because of it; as a result of this, the affected something or someone is no longer as it was before (e.g. 'it is not living any more', 'it is not one thing any more', 'it is not hollow any more', 'it no longer has liquid inside it any more'); and overall, this outcome can be seen as bad.

7. These verbs depict someone doing something which has the effect of causing a substance (such as *butter*, *powder*, or *water*) to be distributed 'all over' the thing in question (i.e. *the toast*, *the nose*, *the lawn*, etc.). We wouldn't say that Samantha had *buttered the toast* if she had just put some butter on the middle of the lawn. This effect is difficult to capture. We could consider:

Someone X buttered something Y (e.g. toast):
someone X did something to something Y for some time
this someone did it with something like butter [d]
she did it because she wanted this something to be touching all parts of Y
because of this, after this, this something was touching all parts of the toast

You may have noticed that it is possible to *butter toast* with something other than butter, namely, margarine. This may mean that the verb *butter* is not based directly on the noun *butter*, or that the noun *margarine* semantically includes the noun *butter* (roughly, it is like butter and used for the same things as butter) and this licenses the extension of the verb *butter* to margarine.

8. Dixon's (1991: 291–3) explanation is that if a thing 'often gets into the state described by the activity on its own, without outside assistance, then the verb is thought to be basically intransitive. But if one would normally expect there to be a Causer (even if one might not know who or what it is) then the verb is thought to be basically transitive'. A person can *trip* without anyone else being around, so *trip* tends to be thought of by speakers as basically intransitive, whereas if a liquid *spills* it is normally somebody's fault, so *spill* is thought of as basically transitive. Similarly, things may *burst* without human intervention, but for most instances of *breaking* a human agent is involved.

9. Roughly speaking, *lay* means 'cause to be lying', and transitive *sit*, as in *Maxine sat the baby up*, means 'cause to be sitting'. These relationships can be captured using the first three components in the explication below. They state that transitive verbs like these depict a scenario in which the causer wants the causee to be in a certain bodily posture (lying down, sitting up, etc.), and because of this does something to that person, as a result of which the causee winds up in the desired position. But there is more to it than this, because the conditions on *lay*, and on transitive *sit*, are quite restricted. A sentence like *We laid Bill down on the bed*, for example, tends to imply that Bill is unconscious, ill, or drunk, so that he can be handled as if he were an inanimate object. Likewise, *Maxine sat the baby up* is felicitous because we assume that babies can be manipulated in this fashion (Levin 1993: 31). With this in mind, we can consider the following explication.

We laid Bill down on the bed:
we wanted Bill to be lying down on the bed
because of this, we did something to Bill
when we did this, we did it like people do things like this to things, not to
   other people
because of this, after this Bill was lying down on the bed

Chapter 11

1. (a) The Dyirbal 'future tense' encodes the meaning AFTER NOW. The 'non-future' encodes NOT AFTER NOW. Interestingly, most tense systems work on a two-way opposition, rather than the three-way 'past–present–future' scheme we are more used to hearing about. Aside from a 'future' vs. 'non-future' opposition, as in Dyirbal, the other common system is 'past' (BEFORE NOW) vs. 'non-past' (NOT BEFORE NOW).

(b) It seems plausible that the Hixkaryana 'distant past' encodes the meaning A LONG TIME BEFORE NOW, and the 'recent past' encodes the converse meaning, that is, NOT A LONG TIME BEFORE NOW. It would not be very plausible to suppose that the Hixkaryana language would have grammatical categories referring to weeks or to months.

2. It is difficult to square the claim that *this* is a 'spatial deictic' (having the meaning 'close to the speaker') with the fact that in ordinary usage *this* occurs in countless non-spatial contexts; e.g. *this time, this song, this word, this day*. Even when physical things are being referred to, there are contexts in which the choice between *this* vs. *that* doesn't indicate anything about relative distance. For instance, if I am pointing out a tooth which is hurting I can say *Not that one, this one*; yet obviously both teeth are the same distance from me.

To maintain the view that *this* is 'basically' spatial, one would have to claim that its other uses are metaphorical; but without independent justification this move would merely beg the question.

4. Body-part constructions like these have been much discussed in the literature on syntactic alternations and argument structure, and not only in relation to English. Analogous constructions exist in many European, and non-European, languages. Wierzbicka (1988) is a foundational early study. Chappell and McGregor (1996) is a large collective volume on this and similar issues across many languages. The usual observation about the English *on*-construction is that it presents the action as 'affecting' the person by way of the contact with the specified body-part. This is clearer if we compare, say, *The puppy bit John on the leg* with *The puppy bit John's leg*. In the latter sentence, *John's leg* is the grammatical object and seems to be, as it were, a full-blown participant in the event being described. In *The puppy bit John on the leg*, however, the grammatical object and (it would seem) the focus of the speaker's attention is *John*. Furthermore, there is an implication that the person wasn't just affected physically, but also that this person felt something, usually something unpleasant and hurtful. That will help explain why we don't normally hear things like *The puppy bit the table on the leg* or *Mary kissed the Bible on the cover*. As for the *on*-phrase, its role seems to be to identify the 'locus' or place of bodily contact.

So from a semantic point of view, we could say that the *on*-constructions imply components such as: 'X did something to part of Y's body', 'when X did it, X touched this part of Y's body' and 'Y felt something (bad) because of it'. The examples in (b) arguably imply a bit more than this, mainly because the verbs (*kiss* and *pat*) are verbs that depict 'expressive' actions. That is, they don't just depict a certain kind of contact with the body, they also imply, at least in the prototypical case, that the actor intended to convey a certain kind of attitude or message to the person.

5. Dyirbal (north Queensland, Australia) is one of the languages most often mentioned in discussions of noun classification, partly because it figures in George Lakoff's (1987) widely read *Women, Fire and Dangerous Things*. In fact, the title of this book is inspired by the fact that one of the four Dyirbal noun classes is used for women (and things associated with women), fire (and things associated with fire), and dangerous things. The original analysis of Dyirbal noun classifiers, on which Lakoff based his work, is Dixon (1972: 306–12).

Dyirbal nouns often occur with a determiner. There are four different determiners, the choice between them indicating the category of the noun (or, more precisely, of the referent of the noun). The data supplied for this question shows only three of these classifying determiners: *bayi*, *balan*, and *balam*. On the data given, they can be glossed as follows:

bayi 'something to do with men or edible creatures (i.e. kangaroos, fish)'
balan 'something to do with women'
balam 'vegetable food'

(The fourth element *bala* indicates a 'residue class', i.e. it is used for nouns which do not fit into any of the other three categories.)

The other words are as follows. Nouns: *yuri* 'grey kangaroo', *ngamun* 'breast', *yara* 'man', *binara* 'peanut', *gubi* 'wise man', *ngalban* 'breast', *jugumbil* 'woman', *jugur* 'yam', *laymun* 'lemon', *guya* 'fish', *wangal* boomerang', *wiru* 'husband', *gajin* 'girl', *guynggun* 'spirit of a dead woman', *yugaba* 'small rat'. Adjectives and quantifiers: *buga* 'rotten', *bulgan* 'big', *yunggul* 'one', *garbu* 'few'.

7. The principle for choosing between *wa-* and *ma-* is simple. Verbs which depict the subject DOING something take *wa-*. Notice that it doesn't matter if the action is unintentional or beyond the control of the actor; even involuntary bodily actions like sneezing and yawning take *wa-*. Verbs which do not involve DOING take *ma-*. Mithun (1991), from whom the data is taken, says that the distinction is between 'performers and non-performers'.

Although the examples provided are all of intransitive verbs, the same prefixes are used with transitive verbs too. With transitive verbs *wa-* indicates a first-person singular agent (i.e. a 'doer') and *ma-*, a first-person singular patient. Grammatical systems of this general kind are known as 'active' case systems, though the semantic basis of many other active case systems is more complex than that of Lakhota.

References

ADELAAR, WILLEM F. H. (1977). *Tarma Quechua*. Lisse: Peter de Ridder.

ADZOMADA, J. K. (1969). *Dictionary of Ewe Homonyms*. Accra: Waterville.

AIJMER, KARIN and SIMON-VANDENBERGEN, ANNE-MARIE (2003). 'The discourse particle *well* and its equivalents in Swedish and Dutch'. *Linguistics*, 40(6): 1123–61.

AIKHENVALD, ALEXANDRA Y. (2000). *Classifiers: A Typology of Noun Categorization Devices*. Oxford: Oxford University Press.

—— (2004). *Evidentiality*. Oxford: Oxford University Press.

AITCHISON, JEAN (1987). *Words in the Mind: An Introduction to the Mental Lexicon*. Oxford: Blackwell.

—— (2003). *Words in the Mind: An Introduction to the Mental Lexicon*, 3rd edn. Oxford: Blackwell. Original edition 1987.

ALEXANDER, DENNIS (2006). 'Literal, figurative, metaphorical: a semantic inquiry into the semantic field of game and play in English'. PhD thesis, University of New England, Armidale.

ALLAN, KEITH (1977). 'Classifiers'. *Language* 53(2): 285–311.

—— (1986). *Linguistic Meaning* (2 vols). London: Routledge & Kegan Paul.

ALLWOOD, JENS, ANDERSSON, LARS-GUNNAR, and DAHL, ÖSTEN (1977). *Logic in Linguistics*. Cambridge: Cambridge University Press.

AMEEL, EEF, MALT, BARBARA, and STORMS, GERT (2008). 'Object naming and later lexical development: from baby bottle to beer bottle'. *Journal of Memory and Language* 58: 262–85.

AMEKA, FELIX (1990). 'The grammatical packaging of experiencers in Ewe: a study in the semantics of syntax'. *Australian Journal of Linguistics* 10(2): 139–81.

—— (1992a). 'Interjections: the universal yet neglected part of speech'. In Ameka (1992b: 101–18).

—— (ed.) (1992b). Special issue on 'Interjections'. *Journal of Pragmatics* 18(2/3).

—— (1999). ' "PARTIR, c'est mourir un peu": universal and culture specific features of leave-taking'. In J. Mey and A. Bogusławski (eds.), *'E Pluribus Una': The One in the Many (RASK, International Journal of Language and Communication* 9/10). Odense: Odense University Press, 257–84.

—— (2006). ' "When I die, don't cry": the ethnopragmatics of "gratitude" in West African languages'. In Goddard (2006b: 231–66).

—— (2009). 'Access rituals in West African Communities: an ethnographic perspective'. In G. Senft and E. Basso (eds.), *Ritual Communication*. Oxford: Berg, 127–51.

ANDERSEN, ELAINE S. (1975). 'Cups and glasses: learning that boundaries are vague'. *Journal of Child Language* 2: 79–103.

APRESJAN, JURIJ D. (1969). 'O jazyke dlja opisanija znacenij slov'. *Izvestija Akademii Nauk SSSR, Serija Literatury i Jazyka* 28: 415–28.

——(1992[1974]). *Lexical Semantics: User's Guide to Contemporary Russian Vocabulary*. Ann Arbor: Karoma. (Orig. published in 1974 as *Leksiceskaja Semantika—Sinonimeceskie Sredstva Jazyka*, Moscow: Nauka.)

——(2000). *Systematic Lexicography*. Translated by K. Windle. Oxford: Oxford University Press.

ARISTOTLE (1928). ' "Of Definitions": extracts from *Topica* Book VI, Ch 1–4'. In W. D. Ross (ed.), *The Works of Aristotle*. London: Oxford University Press.

ARNAULD, ANTOINE, and NICOLE, PIERRE (1996[1662]). *Logic or the Art of Thinking*. Translated by J. V. Buroker. Cambridge: Cambridge University Press.

ASMAH HAJI OMAR (1987). *Malay in its Sociocultural Context*. Kuala Lumpur: Dewan Bahasa dan Pustaka.

ASTINGTON, JANET WILDE (1993). *The Child's Discovery of the Mind*. Cambridge, MA: Harvard University Press.

——(2000). 'Language and metalanguage in children's understanding of mind'. In J. W. Astington (ed.), *Minds in the Making: Essays in Honour of David R. Olson*. Oxford: Blackwell, 267–84.

ATKINS, B. T. S. (1992/1993). 'Theoretical lexicography and its relation to diction-ary-making'. *Dictionaries* 14: 4–43.

ATRAN, SCOTT (1987a). 'Ordinary constraints on the semantics of living kinds: a commonsense alternative to recent treatments of natural-object terms'. *Mind and Language* 2: 27–63.

——(1987b). 'The essence of folk biology: a reply to Randall and Hunn'. *American Anthropologist* 89: 149–51.

——(1990). *Cognitive Foundations of Natural History*. Cambridge: Cambridge University Press.

AUSTIN, J. L. (1975). *How to Do Things with Words*, 2nd edn. Cambridge, MA: Harvard University Press. (Original edition 1962.)

Australian Concise Oxford Dictionary, The (1987). Edited by G. W. Turner. Mel-bourne: Oxford University Press.

Australian Oxford Dictionary (2004). Edited by B. Moore (2nd edn). Melbourne: Oxford University Press. (Original edition 1999.)

AVERILL, JAMES R. (1980). 'A constructionist view of emotion'. In R. Plutchik and H. Kellerman (eds.), *Emotion: Theory, Research and Experience*. New York: Academic Press, 305–39.

BACH, KENT, and HARNISH, ROBERT M. (1979). *Linguistic Communication and Speech Acts*. Cambridge, MA: MIT Press.

BAIN, MARGARET S. (1992). *The Aboriginal-White Encounter in Australia: Towards Better Communication*. Darwin: Summer Institute of Linguistics.

BAIN, MARGARET S. and SAYERS, BARBARA J. (1990). 'Degrees of abstraction and cross-cultural communication in Australia'. Paper presented at the Sixth International Conference on Hunting and Gathering Societies, University of Alaska, Fairbanks.

BAKER, SYDNEY J. (1959). *The Drum: Australian Character and Slang*. Sydney: Currawong.

BALLY, CHARLES (1920). 'Impressionisme et grammaire'. In *Mélanges d'histoire litteraire et de philologie offerts à M. Bernard Bouvier*. Geneva: Société anonyme des éditions Sonor, 261–79.

BARCELONA, ANTONIO (ed.) (2003). *Metaphor and Metonymy at the Crossroads: A Cognitive Perspective*. Berlin: Mouton de Gruyter.

BARDON, GEOFF (1979). *Aboriginal Art of the Western Desert*. Adelaide: Rigby.

BARNLUND, DEAN (1975). *Public and Private Self in Japan and the United States: Communicative Styles of Two Cultures*. Tokyo: Simul.

BARRETT, LISA FELDMAN, MESQUITA, BATJA, OCHSNER, KEVIN N., and GROSS, JAMES J. (2007). 'The experience of emotion'. *Annual Review of Psychology* 58: 373–403.

BATTIG, WILLIAM F., and MONTAGUE, WILLIAM E. (1969). 'Category norms for verbal items in 56 categories'. *Journal of Experimental Psychology Monograph* 80.

BAUMAN, RICHARD, and SHERZER, JOEL (eds.) (1974). *Explorations in the Ethnography of Speaking*. London: Cambridge University Press.

BÉJOINT, HENRI (1994). *Tradition and Innovation in Modern English Dictionaries*. Oxford: Clarendon Press.

BELL, ROGER T., and PENG QUEE SER, LARRY (1983). ' "To-day *la*?" "Tomorrow *lah*!": the *LA* Particle in Singapore English'. *RELC Journal* 14(2): 1–18.

BENDER, BYRON (1969). *Spoken Marshallese: An Intensive Language Course with Grammatical Notes and Glossary*. Honolulu: University of Hawaii Press.

BERLIN, BRENT (1981). 'The concept of rank in ethnobiological classification: some evidence from Aguaruna folk botany'. In R. Casson (ed.), *Language, Culture and Cognition*. New York: Macmillan, 92–113.

——(1992). *Ethnobiological Classification: Principles of Categorization of Plants and Animals in Traditional Society*. Princeton, NJ: Princeton University Press.

—— BREEDLOVE, DENNIS E., and RAVEN, PETER H. (1973). 'General principles of classification and nomenclature in folk biology'. *American Anthropologist* 75: 214–43.

BESEMERES, MARY, and WIERZBICKA, ANNA (eds.) (2007). *Translating Lives: Living with Two Languages and Cultures*. St Lucia: University of Queensland Press.

BESNIER, NIKO (1994). 'Involvement in linguistic practice: an ethnographic appraisal'. *Journal of Pragmatics* 22: 279–99.

BLACKBURN, PATRICK, and BOS, JOHAN (2005). *Representation and Inference for Natural Language: A First Course in Computational Semantics*. Stanford, CA: CSLI.

BLOOM, LOIS (1991). *Language Development from Two to Three*. Cambridge: Cambridge University Press.

BLOOMFIELD, LEONARD (1933). *Language*. New York: Holt, Rinehart & Winston.

BLUM-KULKA, SHOSHANA, HOUSE, JULIANE, and KASPER, GABRIELE (eds.) (1989). *Cross-Cultural Pragmatics: Requests and Apologies*. Norwood, NJ: Ablex.

——and KASPER, GABRIELE (1993). *Interlanguage Pragmatics*. Oxford: Oxford University Press.

BOAS, HANS C. (2009a). 'Semantic frames as interlingual representations for multilingual lexical databases'. In H. C. Boas (ed.), *Multilingual Framenets in Computational Lexicography*. Berlin: Mouton de Gruyter, 59–100. (Original published in *International Journal of Lexicography* 1995, 18(4), 445–78.)

——(ed.) (2009b). *Multilingual Framenets in Computational Lexicography*. Berlin: Mouton de Gruyter.

BODIN, LAURA, and SNOW, CATHERINE (1994). 'What kind of a birdie is this? Learning to use superordinates'. In J. L. Sokolov and C. E. Snow (eds.), *Handbook of Research in Language Development Using CHILDES*. Hillsdale, NJ: Erlbaum, 77–109.

BOGUSŁAWSKI, ANDRZEJ (1970). 'On semantic primitives and meaningfulness'. In A. Greimas, R. Jakobson, M. R. Mayenowa, and S. Zolkiewski (eds.), *Sign, Language and Culture*. The Hague: Mouton, 143–52.

BOHNEMEYER, JÜRGEN, EISENBEISS, SONJA, and NARASIMHAN, BHUVANA (2006). 'Ways to go: methodological considerations in Whorfian studies on motion events'. *Essex Research Reports in Linguistics* 50: 1–19.

BOWERMAN, MELISSA (1985). 'What shapes children's grammars?'. In D. I. Slobin (ed.), *The Crosslinguistic Study of Language Acquisition*, vol. 2: *Theoretical Issues*. Hillsdale, NJ: Erlbaum, 1257–1320.

——and CHOI, SANG-CHIN (2001). 'Shaping meanings for language: universal and language-specific in the acquisition of semantic categories'. In M. Bowerman and S. C. Levinson (eds.), *Language Acquisition and Conceptual Development*. Cambridge: Cambridge University Press, 475–511.

————(2003). 'Space under construction: language-specific spatial categorization in first language acquisition'. In D. Gentner and S. Goldin-Meadow (eds.), *Language in Mind: Advances in the Study of Language and Thought*. Cambridge, MA: MIT Press, 387–427.

BRAINE, MARTIN D. S. (1976). 'Children's first word combinations'. *Monographs of the Society for Research in Child Development* 41: 1–97.

BRIGGS, JEAN L. (1995). 'The study of Inuit emotions: lessons from a personal retrospective'. In J. A. Russell, J. M. Fernández-Dols, A. S. R. Manstead, and J. C. Wellenkamp (eds.), *Everyday Conceptions of Emotion: An Introduction to the Psychology, Anthropology and Linguistics of Emotion*. Dordrecht: Kluwer Academic, 203–20.

——(2000). 'Emotions have many faces: Inuit lessons'. *Anthropologica* 42(2): 157–64.

BROMHEAD, HELEN (2009). *The Reign of Truth and Faith: Epistemic Expressions in 16th and 17th Century English*. Berlin: Mouton de Gruyter.

—— (2011). 'Ethnographical categories in English and Pitjantjatjara/Yankunytjatjara'. *Language Sciences* 33(1): 58–75.

BROWN, CECIL (1979). 'Folk zoological life forms: their universality and growth'. *American Anthropologist* 81: 791–817.

BROWN, PENELOPE, and LEVINSON, STEPHEN C. (1987). *Politeness: Some Universals of Language Usage*. Cambridge: Cambridge University Press. (Original edition 1978.)

BRUNER, JEROME (1990). *Acts of Meaning*. Cambridge, MA: Harvard University Press.

BURLING, ROBBINS (1970). *Man's Many Voices: Language in its Cultural Context*. New York: Holt, Rinehart & Winston.

CANN, RONALD (1993). *Formal Semantics*. Cambridge: Cambridge University Press.

CARBAUGH, DONAL (2005). *Cultures in Conversation*. Mahwah, NJ: Erlbaum.

CAREY, SUSAN (1985). *Conceptual Change in Childhood*. Cambridge, MA: MIT Press.

CHAFE, WALLACE L., and NICHOLS, JOHANNA (eds.) (1986). *Evidentiality: The Linguistic Coding of Epistemology*. Norwood, NJ: Ablex.

CHAPPELL, HILARY, and MCGREGOR, WILLIAM B. (eds.) (1996). *The Grammar of Inalienability: A Typological Perspective on Body Part Terms and the Part Whole Relation*. Berlin: Mouton de Gruyter.

CHIERCHIA, GENNARO, and MCCONNNELL-GINET, SALLY (2000). *Meaning and Grammar: An Introduction to Semantics*, 2nd edn. Cambridge, MA: MIT Press. (Original edition 1990.)

CHOMSKY, NOAM (1965). *Aspects of the Theory of Syntax*. Cambridge, MA: MIT Press.

—— (1991). 'Linguistics and cognitive science: problems and mysteries'. In A. Kasher (ed.), *The Chomskyan Turn*. Oxford: Blackwell, 26–53.

CIENKI, ALAN (1998). 'STRAIGHT: an image schema and its metaphorical extensions'. *Cognitive Linguistics* 9(2): 107–49.

CLANCY, PATRICIA (1985). 'The acquisition of Japanese'. In D. I. Slobin (ed.), *The Crosslinguistic Study of Language Acquisition*, vol. 1: *The Data*. Hillsdale, NJ: Erlbaum, 373–524.

CLARK, EVE V. (1993). *The Lexicon in Acquisition*. Cambridge: Cambridge University Press.

—— (2010). 'Learning a language the way it is: conventionality and semantic domains'. In B. C. Malt and P. Wolff (eds.), *Words and the Mind: How Words Capture Human Experience*. Oxford: Oxford University Press, 243–65.

CLARK, EVE V. and WONG, ANDREW D.-W. (2002). 'Pragmatic directions about language use: offers and words and relations'. *Language in Society* 31: 181–212.

COLARUSSO, JOHN (1989). 'East Circassian (Kabardian dialect)'. In B. G. Hewitt (ed.), *The Indigenous Languages of the Caucasus*, vol. 2: *The North-West Caucasian Languages*. Delmar, NY: Caravan Books, 261–355.

COMRIE, BERNARD (1989). *Language Universals and Linguistic Typology*, 2nd edn. Oxford: Blackwell. (Original edition 1981.)

Concise Oxford Dictionary (2000). Edited by J. Pearsall. Oxford: Oxford University Press.

CONKLIN, HAROLD C. (1967). 'Lexicographical treatment of folk taxonomies'. In F. W. Householder and S. Saporta (eds.), *Problems in Lexicography*. Bloomington: Indiana University Press, 119–42.

CORRIGAN, ROBERTA (2004). 'The acquisition of word connotations: Asking "What happened?"'. *Journal of Child Language* 31(1): 381–98.

COULMAS, FLORIAN (1981). ' "Poison to your soul": thanks and apologies contrastively viewed'. In F. Coulmas (ed.), *Conversational Routine: Explorations in Standardized Communication Situations and Prepatterned Speech*. The Hague: Mouton, 131–48.

CRAIG, COLETTE (1986). 'Jacaltec noun classifiers'. In C. Craig (ed.), *Noun Classes and Categorization*. Amsterdam: Benjamins, 263–93.

CRAIN, STEPHEN, and THORNTON, ROSALIND (1998). *Investigations in Universal Grammar: A Guide to Experiments on the Acquisition of Syntax and Semantics*. Cambridge, MA: MIT Press.

CROFT, WILLIAM (1994). 'Semantic universals in classifier systems'. *Word* 45(2): 145–71.

——(1998). 'Event structure in argument linking'. In M. Butt and W. Geuder (eds.), *The Projection of Arguments: Lexical and Compositional Factors*. Stanford, CA: CSLI, 1–43.

——(2001). *Radical Construction Grammar: Syntactic Theory in Typological Perspective*. Oxford: Oxford University Press.

CROWLEY, TERRY (1979). 'The language of Paama (New Hebrides)'. PhD thesis, Australian National University, Canberra.

CRUSE, D. A. (1986). *Lexical Semantics*. Cambridge: Cambridge University Press.

CUENCA, MARIA-JOSEP (2008). 'Pragmatic markers in contrast: the case of *well*'. *Journal of Pragmatics* 40(8): 1373–91.

CURNOW, TIMOTHY JOWAN (1993). 'Semantics of Spanish causatives involving *hacer*'. *Australian Journal of Linguistics* 13(2): 165–84.

DALE, PETER K. (1986). *The Myth of Japanese Uniqueness*. London: Croom Helm.

D'ANDRADE, ROY (2001). 'A cognitivist's view of the units debate in cultural anthropology'. *Cross-Cultural Research* 35(2): 242–57.

DENNY, J. PETER (1976). 'What are noun classifiers good for?' *Papers from the Twelfth Regional Meeting, Chicago Linguistic Society*. Chicago: CLS, 122–32.

DERBYSHIRE, DESMOND C. (1985). *Hixkaryana and Linguistic Typology*. Arlington: Summer Institute of Linguistics and University of Texas.

DILLER, ANTHONY (1994). 'Thai'. In Goddard and Wierzbicka (1994b: 149–70).

DIXON, R. M. W. (1972). *The Dyirbal Language of North Queensland*. Cambridge: Cambridge University Press.

——(1977). *A Grammar of Yidiny*. Cambridge: Cambridge University Press.

——(1980). *The Languages of Australia*. Cambridge: Cambridge University Press.

——(1991). *A New Approach to English Grammar, on Semantic Principles*. Oxford: Clarendon Press.

DOI, TAKEO (1974). '*Amae*: a key concept for understanding Japanese personality structure'. In T. S. Lebra and W. P. Lebra (eds.), *Japanese Culture and Behavior*. Honolulu: University of Hawaii Press, 145–54.

——(1988). *The Anatomy of Self*. Tokyo: Kodansha.

——(2002). *The Anatomy of Dependence: The Key Analysis of Japanese Behavior*, revised edn. Translated by J. Bester. (Original English edn 1973). Tokyo: Kodansha International. (First published 1971 as *Amae no Kōzō* by Kōbundō, Tokyo.)

DOUGHERTY, J. W. D. (1978). 'Salience and relativity in classification'. *American Ethnologist* 5: 66–80.

ECKERT, PAUL, and HUDSON, JOYCE (1988). *Wangka Wiru: A Handbook for the Pitjantjatjara Language Learner*. Underdale: South Australian College of Advanced Education.

ECO, UMBERTO (1999). *Kant and the Platypus: Essays on Language and Cognition*. Translated by A. McEwen. London: Secker & Warburg.

——(2003). *Mouse or Rat? Translation as Negotiation*. London: Weidenfeld & Nicolson.

EHRENREICH, BARBARA (2009). *Bright-Sided: How the Relentless Promotion of Positive Thinking has Undermined America*. New York: Metropolitan Books, Holt.

EKMAN, PAUL (1979). 'About brows: emotional and conversational signals'. In M. E. Cramnach, K. Foppa, M. Lepenies, and D. Ploog (eds.), *Human Ethnology*. Cambridge: Cambridge University Press, 169–249.

——(1992). 'An argument for basic emotions'. *Cognition and Emotion* 6(3/4): 169–200.

——(1993). 'Facial expression and emotion'. *American Psychologist* 48(4): 384–92.

——(2004). *Emotions Revealed*. New York: Holt.

—— AND FRIESEN, W. V. (1969). 'The repertoire of nonverbal behavior: categories, origins, usage and coding'. *Semiotica* 1: 49–98.

ELY, RICHARD, and MCCABE, ALLYSSA (1993). 'Remembered voices'. *Journal of Child Language* 20: 671–96.

ENFIELD, NICK (1994). 'Aspects of Lao Syntax: Theory, Function and Cognition'. Honours thesis, Australian National University.

ENFIELD, NICK and WIERZBICKA, ANNA (eds.) (2002). *Pragmatics and Cognition* (special issue on 'The body in the description of emotion'), 10(1).

ERVIN-TRIPP, SUSAN (1970). 'Discourse agreement: how children answer questions'. In J. R. Hayes (ed.), *Cognition and the Development of Language*. New York: Wiley, 79–107.

EVANS, NICHOLAS (1992). '"*Wanjh! Bonj! Nja!*": sequential organization and social deixis in Mayali interjections'. *Journal of Pragmatics* 18: 225–44.

——(1994). 'Kayardild'. In Goddard and Wierzbicka (1994b: 203–28).

FARRAR, M. J., and MAAG, L. (2002). 'Early language development and the emergence of a theory of mind'. *First Language* 22: 197–213.

FILLMORE, CHARLES J. (1966). 'Deictic categories in the semantics of *come*'. *Foundations of Language* 2: 219–27.

——(1968). 'The case for case'. In E. Bach and R. T. Harms (eds.), *Universals in Linguistic Theory*. New York: Holt, Rinehart & Winston, 1–88.

——(1970). 'Subjects, speakers, and roles'. *Synthèse* 21: 251–74.

——(1971). 'Types of lexical information'. In D. D. Steinberg and L. A. Jakobovits (eds.), *Semantics: An Interdisciplinary Reader in Philosophy, Linguistics, and Psychology*. Cambridge: Cambridge University Press, 370–92.

——(1975a). *Santa Cruz Lectures on Deixis 1971*. Bloomington: Indiana University Linguistics Club.

——(1975b). 'An alternative to checklist theories of meaning'. *Berkley Linguistics Society* 1: 123–31.

——(1977). 'The case for case reopened'. In P. Cole and J. M. Sadock (eds.), *Grammatical Relations*. New York: Academic Press, 59–83.

——(1983). 'How to know whether you're *coming* or *going*'. In G. Rauh (ed.), *Essays of Deixis*. Tübingen: Narr, 219–27.

——and ATKINS, BERYL T. (1992). 'Toward a frame-based lexicon: the semantics of RISK and its neighbours'. In A. Lehrer and E. F. Kittay (eds.), *Frames, Fields and Contrasts: New Essays in Semantics and Lexical Organization*. Hillsdale, NJ: Erlbaum, 75–102.

——KAY, PAUL, MICHAELIS, LAURA A., and SAG, IVAN A. (2010). *Construction Grammar*. Stanford, CA: CSLI.

FODOR, JERRY (1970). 'Three reasons for not deriving "kill" from "cause to die"'. *Linguistic Inquiry* 1(4): 429–38.

FORTESCUE, MICHAEL (1984). *West Greenlandic Eskimo*. London: Croom Helm.

FRAWLEY, WILLIAM (1992). *Linguistic Semantics*. Hillsdale, NJ: Erlbaum.

FRENCH, LUCIA A., and NELSON, KATHERINE (1985). *Young Children's Knowledge of Relational Terms: Some Ifs, Ors, and Buts*. New York: Springer.

FURROW, DAVID, MOORE, CHRIS, DAVIDGE, JANE, and CHIASSON, LORRAINE (1992). 'Mental terms in mothers' and children's speech: similarities and relationships'. *Journal of Child Language* 19: 617–31.

GATHERCOLE, VIRGINIA C. (1977). 'A study of the comings and goings of the speakers of four languages: Spanish, Japanese, English and Turkish'. *Kansas Working Papers in Linguistics* 2: 61–94.

GEERAERTS, DIRK, and CUYCKENS, HUBERT (2007a). 'Introducing cognitive linguistics'. In Geeraerts and Cuyckens (2007b: 3–24).

——— (eds.) (2007b). *The Oxford Handbook of Cognitive Linguistics*. New York: Oxford University Press.

GEERTZ, CLIFFORD (1975). *The Interpretation of Cultures*. London: Hutchinson.

—— (2000). *Available Light: Anthropological Reflections on Philosophical Topics*. Princeton, NJ: Princeton University Press.

GENNARI, SILVIA P., SLOMAN, STEVEN A., MALT, BARBARA C., and FITCH, W. TECUMSEH (2002). 'Motion events in language and cognition'. *Cognition* 83: 49–79.

GEOGHEGAN, R. H. (1944). *The Aleut Language*. Seattle: U.S. Department of the Interior.

GINZBURG, NATALIA (1976). *Ti ho sposato per allegria: e altre commedie*. Turin: Einaudi.

GLADKOVA, ANNA (2010a). 'A linguist's view of "pride"'. *Emotion Review* 2(2): 178–9.

—— (2010b). ' "Sympathy", "compassion", and "empathy" in English and Russian: a linguistic and cultural analysis'. *Culture and Psychology* 16(2), 267–85.

—— (2010c). *Russkaja kul'turnaja semantika: ėmocii, cennosti, žiznennye ustanovki* [*Russian Cultural Semantics: Emotions, Values, Attitudes*]. Moscow: Languages of Slavic Cultures.

GODDARD, CLIFF (1985). *Yankunytjatjara Grammar*. Alice Springs: Institute for Aboriginal Development.

—— (1986). 'The natural semantics of TOO'. *Journal of Pragmatics* 10(5): 635–44.

—— (1991a). 'Testing the translatability of semantic primitives into an Australian Aboriginal language'. *Anthropological Linguistics*, 33(1): 31–56.

—— (1991b). 'Anger in the Western Desert: a case study in the cross-cultural semantics of emotion'. *Man* 26(2): 265–79.

—— (1994). 'Semantic theory and semantic universals'. In Goddard and Wierzbicka (1994b: 7–30).

—— (1996a). 'The "social emotions" of Malay (*Bahasa Melayu*)'. *Ethos* 24(3): 426–64.

—— (ed.) (1996b). *Pitjantjatjara/Yankunytjatjara to English Dictionary*, revised 2nd edn. Alice Springs: IAD Press.

—— (1997a). 'Cultural values and "cultural scripts" in Malay (*Bahasa Melayu*)'. *Journal of Pragmatics* 27(2): 183–201.

—— (1997b). 'Semantic primes and grammatical categories'. *Australian Journal of Linguistics* 17(1): 1–42.

—— (1997c). *Studies in the Syntax of Universal Semantic Primitives* (special issue of *Language Sciences* 19(3)).

—— (1998). *Semantic Analysis: A Practical Introduction*. Oxford: Oxford University Press.

GODDARD, CLIFF (2000). '"Cultural scripts" and communicative style in Malay (*Bahasa Melayu*)'. *Anthropological Linguistics* 42(1): 81–106.

——(2001). 'Conceptual primes in early language development'. In M. Pütz, S. Niemeier, and R. Dirven (eds.), *Applied Cognitive Linguistics I: Theory and Language Acquisition*. Berlin: Mouton de Gruyter, 193–227.

——(2002a). 'Directive speech acts in Malay (Bahasa Melayu): an ethnopragmatic perspective'. *Cahiers de praxématique* (special issue on 'Langue, discours, culture', edited by Christine Béal et al.), 38: 113–43.

——(2002b). 'The on-going development of the NSM research program'. In C. Goddard and A. Wierzbicka (eds.), *Meaning and Universal Grammar: Theory and Empirical Findings*. Amsterdam: Benjamins, 301–21.

——(2004a). 'The ethnopragmatics and semantics of "active metaphors"'. *Journal of Pragmatics* (special issue on 'Metaphor', edited by Gerard Steen), 36: 1211–30.

——(2004b). 'Speech-acts, values and cultural scripts: a study in Malay ethnopragmatics'. In R. Cribb (ed.), *Asia Examined: Proceedings of the 15th Biennial Conference of the ASAA, 2004, Canberra*. Canberra: Asian Studies Association of Australia & Research School of Pacific and Asian Studies, Australian National University.

——(2006a). '"Lift your game Martina!": Deadpan jocular irony and the ethnopragmatics of Australian English'. In Goddard (2006b: 65–97).

——(ed.) (2006b). *Ethnopragmatics: Understanding Discourse in Cultural Context*. Berlin: Mouton de Gruyter.

——(2007). 'A culture-neutral metalanguage for mental state concepts'. In A. C. Schalley and D. Khlentzos (eds.), *Mental States*, vol. 2: *Language and Cognitive Structure*. Amsterdam: Benjamins, 11–35.

——(ed.) (2008). *Cross-Linguistic Semantics*. Amsterdam: Benjamins.

——(2009a). '*Not taking yourself too seriously* in Australian English: semantic explications, cultural scripts, corpus evidence'. *Intercultural Pragmatics* 6 (1): 29–53.

——(2009b). 'The conceptual semantics of numbers and counting: an NSM analysis'. *Functions of Language* 16(2): 193–224.

——(2010a). 'Semantic molecules and semantic complexity (with special reference to "environmental" molecules)'. *Review of Cognitive Linguistics* 8(1): 123–55.

——(2010b). 'Universals and variation in the lexicon of mental state concepts'. In B. C. Malt and P. Wolff (eds.), *Words and the Mind: How Words Capture Human Experience*. Oxford: Oxford University Press, 72–92.

——(2011). 'The lexical semantics of *language* (with special reference to *words*)'. *Language Sciences* 33(1): 40–57.

——(in press). 'Semantic primes, semantic molecules, semantic templates: key concepts in the NSM approach to lexical typology'. *Linguistics* (special issue on 'Lexical typology', edited by Maria Koptjevskaja-Tamm and Martine Vanhove).

GODDARD, CLIFF (to appear a). 'Early interactions in Australian English, American English, and English English: cultural differences and cultural scripts'. *Journal of Pragmatics* (special issue on 'Impoliteness in English', edited by Michael Haugh and Klaus Schneider).

—— (to appear b). 'Cultural scripts and communication style differences in three Anglo Englishes'. In B. Kyrk-Kastovsky (ed.), *Intercultural Miscommunication*. Amsterdam: Benjamins.

—— and KALOTAS, ARPAD (eds.) (1985). *Punu: Yankunytjatjara Plant Use*. Alice Springs: IAD Press.

—— and WIERZBICKA, ANNA (eds.) (1994). *Semantic and Lexical Universals: Theory and Empirical Findings*. Amsterdam: Benjamins.

———— (1997). 'Discourse and culture'. In Teun A. van Dijk (ed.), *Discourse as Social Interaction*. London: Sage, 231–57.

———— (eds.) (2002). *Meaning and Universal Grammar: Theory and Empirical Findings*, vols 1 and 2. Amsterdam: Benjamins.

———— (eds.) (2004). *Cultural Scripts* (special issue of *Intercultural Pragmatics* 1(2)).

———— (2007). 'NSM analyses of the semantics of physical qualities: *sweet, hot, hard, heavy, rough, sharp* in cross-linguistic perspective'. *Studies in Language* 31 (4): 765–800.

———— (2008). 'Universal human concepts as a basis for contrastive linguistic semantics'. In M. d. l. Á. Gómez-Gonzáles, J. L. Mackenzie, and E. Gonzáles Álvarez (eds.), *Current Trends in Contrastive Linguistics: Functional and Cognitive Perspectives*. Amsterdam: Benjamins, 205–26.

———— (2009). 'Contrastive semantics of physical activity verbs: "cutting" and "chopping" in English, Polish, and Japanese'. *Language Sciences* 31: 60–96.

———— (to appear). '*Men, women* and *children*: the conceptual semantics of basic social categories'. In *Words and Meanings: Lexical Semantics across Domains, Languages, and Cultures*.

———— and WONG, JOCK (forthcoming). '"Walking" and "running" in English and German: the cross-linguistic semantics of verbs of human locomotion'.

GOFFMAN, ERVING (1981). *Forms of Talk*. Oxford: Blackwell.

GOLDBERG, ADELE (1995). *Constructions: A Construction Grammar Approach to Argument Structure*. Chicago: University of Chicago Press.

GOOCH, ANTHONY (1970). *Diminutive, Augmentative, and Pejorative Suffixes in Modern Spanish*, 2nd edn. Oxford: Pergamon Press.

GRADY, JOSEPH E. (1997). 'Theories are buildings revisited'. *Cognitive Linguistics* 8(4): 267–90.

GREEN, GEORGIA (1968). 'On *too* and *either*, and not just *too* and *either*, either'. In *Papers from the 4th Regional Meeting, Chicago Linguistics Society*: 22–44.

—— (1973). 'The lexical expression of emphatic conjunction: theoretical implications'. *Foundations of Language* 10: 197–248.

GRUBER, JEFFREY (1970). *Studies in Lexical Relations*. Bloomington: Indiana University Linguistics Club.

GUERSSEL, MOHAMMED, HALE, KENNETH L., LAUGHREN, MARY, LEVIN, BETH, and WHITE EAGLE, JOSIE (1985). A cross-linguistic study of transitivity alternations. In W. H. Eilfort, P. D. Kroeber, and K. L. Peterson (eds.), *Papers from the Parasession on Causatives and Agentivity at the Twenty-first Regional Meeting*. Chicago: Chicago Linguistic Society, 48–63.

GUMPERZ, JOHN J., and HYMES, DELL H. (eds.) (1986). *Directions in Sociolinguistics: The Ethnography of Communication*, 2nd edn. Oxford: Blackwell. (Original edition 1972.)

HAIMAN, JOHN (1985). *Natural Syntax: Iconicity and Erosion*. Cambridge: Cambridge University Press.

HALE, KENNETH L., and KEYSER, SAMUEL JAY (1986). 'Some transitivity alternations in English'. *Lexicon Project Working Papers #7*. Cambridge, MA: MIT Press.

HALLIDAY, M. A. K., and HASAN, R. (1976). *Cohesion in English*. London: Longman.

HAO, MINGJIAN, and SUN, WEI (eds.) (1991). *Zhōngguó Yìngyòng Lǐyí Dàquán* [The Compendium of Chinese Social Etiquette]. Shanghai: Wénhuà Chūbǎnshè.

HARKINS, JEAN (1996). 'Linguistic and cultural differences in concepts of shame'. In D. Parker, R. Dalziell, and I. Wright (eds.), *Shame and the Modern Self*. Melbourne: Australian Scholarly Publishing, 84–96.

——and WIERZBICKA, ANNA (eds.) (2001). *Emotions in Crosslinguistic Perspective*. Berlin: Mouton de Gruyter.

——and WILKINS, DAVID P. (1994). 'Mparntwe Arrernte and the search for lexical universals'. In Goddard and Wierzbicka (1994b: 285–310).

HARRÉ, ROM (ed.) (1986). *The Social Construction of Emotions*. Oxford: Blackwell.

HARRIS, RANDY ALLEN (1993). *The Linguistic Wars*. New York: Oxford University Press.

HARRIS, ROY (1983): see Saussure.

HART, H. L. A., and HONORÉ, A. M. (1959). *Causation in the Law*. Oxford: Clarendon Press.

HASADA, RIE (1994). 'The Semantic Aspect of Onamatopoeia: Focusing on Japanese Psychomimes'. Master's thesis, Australian National University, Canberra.

——(1997). 'Some aspects of Japanese cultural ethos embedded in nonverbal communicative behaviour'. In F. Poyatos (ed.), *Nonverbal Communication in Translation*. Amsterdam: Benjamins, 83–103.

——(2006). 'Cultural scripts: glimpses into the Japanese emotion world'. In Goddard (2006b: 171–98).

HASER, VERENA (2005). *Metaphor, Metonymy, and Experientialist Philosophy: Challenging Cognitive Semantics*. Berlin: Mouton de Gruyter.

HAWKINS, BRUCE (1984). 'The semantics of English spatial prepositions'. PhD Dissertation, University of California, San Diego.

HEARN, LAFCADIO (1992 [1893]). 'The Japanese smile'. In L. Allen and J. Wilson (eds.), *Lafcadio Hearn: Japan's Great Interpreter*. Sandgate: Japan Library, 71–9.

HENDERSON, JOHN, and DOBSON, VERONICA (1994). *Eastern and Central Arrernte to English Dictionary*. Alice Springs: IAD Press.

HOBBES, THOMAS (1996 [1651]). *Leviathan*. Edited with an introduction by J. C. A. Gaskin. Oxford: Oxford University Press.

HOFFMAN, EVA (1989). *Lost in Translation: A Life in a New Language*. London: Minerva.

HOFMANN, T. R. (1993). *Realms of Meaning: An Introduction to Semantics*. London: Longman.

HOLLIER, FIONA, MURRAY, KERRIE, and CORNELIUS, HELENA (2008). *Conflict Resolution Trainer's Manual: 12 skills*, 2nd edn. Chatswood, NSW: The Conflict Resolution Network.

HONNA, NOBUYUKI, and HOFFER, BATES (eds.) (1989). *An English Dictionary of Japanese Ways of Thinking*. Tokyo: Yuhikaku.

HORNE, DONALD (1986). *The Lucky Country: Australia in the Sixties*, 3rd edn. Melbourne: Penguin. (Original edition 1964.)

HOUSTON-PRICE, CARMEL, MATHER, EMILY, and SAKKALOU, ELENA (2007). 'Discrepancy between parental reports of infants receptive vocabulary and infants' behaviour in a preferential looking task'. *Journal of Child Language* 34(4): 701–4.

HUDSON, JOYCE (1986). 'An analysis of illocutionary verbs in Walmatjari'. In G. Huttar and K. Gregerson (eds.), *Pragmatics in Non-Western Perspective*. Dallas: Summer Institute of Linguistics and University of Texas at Arlington.

HUMBOLDT, WILHELM VON (1988 [1936]). *On Language: The Diversity of Human Language-Structure and Its Influence on the Mental Development of Mankind*. Translated by P. Heath. Cambridge: Cambridge University Press.

HUME, DAVID (1902 [1777]). *Enquiries Concerning the Human Understanding, and Concerning the Principles of Morals*, 2nd edn. Oxford: Clarendon Press.

HURFORD, JAMES R., and HEASLEY, BRENDON (1983). *Semantics: A Coursebook*. Cambridge: Cambridge University Press.

HYMES, DELL H. (1968). 'The ethnography of speaking'. In J. Fishman (ed.), *Readings on the Sociology of Language*. The Hague: Mouton, 99–138. (Originally published 1962.)

HYSLOP, CATRIONA (1993). 'Towards a typology of spatial deixis'. Honours thesis, Australian National University, Canberra.

ILSON, R. F. (ed.) (1986). *Lexicography: An Emerging International Profession*. Manchester: Manchester University Press.

INGRAM, DAVID (1989). *First Language Acquisition: Method, Description and Explanation*. Cambridge: Cambridge University Press.

INOUE, KYOKO (1979). 'Japanese: a story of language and their people'. In T. Shopen (ed.), *Languages and Their Speakers*. Cambridge, MA: Winthrop, 241–99.

IORDANSKAJA, LIDIJA N. (1974). 'Tentative lexicographic definitions for a group of Russian words denoting emotions'. In J. Rozencvejg (ed.), *Machine Translation and Applied Linguistics*. Frankfurt: Athenäum, 88–117.

IRVINE, JUDITH T. (1979). 'Formality and informality in communicative events'. *American Anthropologist* 81(4): 773–90.

ISHIGURO, HIDE (1972). *Leibniz's Philosophy of Logic and Language*. London: Duckworth.

IWAMOTO, ENOCH (1987). 'Syntax and semantics of Japanese causative constructions'. MS, Australian National University, Canberra.

IZARD, CARROLL E. (1977). *Human Emotions*. New York: Plenum Press.

——(2009). 'Emotion theory and research: highlights, unanswered questions, and emerging issues'. *Annual Review of Psychology* 60: 1–25.

JACKENDOFF, RAY (1983). *Semantics and Cognition*. Cambridge, MA: MIT Press.

——(1990). *Semantic Structures*. Cambridge, MA: MIT Press.

——(1991). 'Parts and boundaries'. In B. Levin and S. Pinker (eds.), *Lexical and Conceptual Semantics*. Cambridge, MA: Blackwell, 9–47.

——(1992). *Languages of the Mind: Essays on Mental Representation*. Cambridge, MA: MIT Press.

——(1996). 'The proper treatment of measuring out, telicity, and perhaps even quantification in English'. *Natural Language and Linguistic Theory* 14: 305–54.

——(2002). *Foundations of Language: Brain, Meaning, Grammar, Evolution*. Oxford: Oxford University Press.

——(2006). 'On conceptual semantics'. *Intercultural Pragmatics* 3(3): 353–58.

——(2007). *Language, Consciousness, Culture: Essays on Mental Structure*. Cambridge, MA: MIT Press.

——(2010). *Meaning and the Lexicon: The Parallel Architecture 1975–2010*. Oxford: Oxford University Press.

JANNEY, RICHARD, and ARNDT, HORST (1993). 'Universality and relativity in cross-cultural politeness research: a historical perspective'. *Multilingua* 12(1): 13–50.

JOHNSON, MARK (1987). *The Body in the Mind: The Bodily Basis of Meaning, Imagination, and Reason*. Chicago: University of Chicago Press.

JOHNSTON, JUDITH R. (1985). 'Cognitive prerequisites: the evidence from children learning English'. In D. I. Slobin (ed.), *The Crosslinguistic Study of Language Acquisition*, vol. 2: *Theoretical Issues*. Hillsdale, NJ: Erlbaum, 961–1004.

JONES, DOUG (1999). 'Evolutionary psychology'. *Annual Review of Anthropology* 28: 553–75.

JUCKER, ANDREAS H. (1993). 'The discourse marker *well*: a relevance-theoretical account'. *Journal of Pragmatics* 19: 435–52.

——(2009). 'Speech act research between armchair, field and laboratory: the case of compliments'. *Journal of Pragmatics* 41: 1611–35.

JURAFSKY, DANIEL (1996). 'Universal tendencies in the semantics of the diminutive'. *Language* 72(3): 533–78.

KANT, IMMANUEL (1934[1781]). *Critique of Pure Reason*. Translated by J. M. D. Meiklejohn (2nd edn). London: Dent.

KAPLAN, JEFF (1984). 'Obligatory *too* in English'. *Language* 60: 510–18.

KATAOKA, HIROKO C. (1991). *Japanese Cultural Encounters and How to Handle Them*. Chicago: Passport Books.

KATZ, JERROLD J. (1970). 'Interpretive semantics vs. generative semantics'. *Foundations of Language* 6: 220–59.

——(1972). *Semantic Theory*. New York: Harper & Row.

——(1987). 'Common sense in semantics'. In E. Lepore (ed.), *New Directions in Semantics*. London: Academic Press, 157–233.

——and FODOR, JERRY A. (1963). 'Structure of a semantic theory'. *Language* 39: 170–210.

——and POSTAL, PAUL M. (1964). *An Integrated Theory of Linguistic Descriptions*. Cambridge, MA: MIT Press.

KEIL, FRANK C. (1989). *Concepts, Kinds, and Cognitive Development*. Cambridge, MA: MIT Press.

KEMPSON, RUTH (1977). *Semantic Theory*. Cambridge: Cambridge University Press.

Kenkyusha's New Japanese-English Dictionary (1974). Edited by K. Masuda (4th edn). Tokyo: Kenkyusha.

KERTÉSZ, ANDRÁS, and RÁKOSI, CSILLA (2009). 'Circular vs. cyclic argumentation in the Conceptual Metaphor Theory'. *Cognitive Linguistics* 20(4): 703–32.

KITA, SOTARO, and IDE, SACHIKO (2007). 'Nodding, *aizuchi*, and final particles in Japanese conversation: how conversation reflects the ideology of communication and social relationships'. *Journal of Pragmatics* 39(7): 1242–54.

KITAGAWA, CHISATO (1974). 'Case marking and causativization'. *Papers in Japanese Linguistics* 3: 43–57.

KOJIMA, SETSUKO, and CRANE, GENE A. (1987). *A Dictionary of Japanese Culture*. Singapore: Chopmen.

KÖNIG, EKKEHARD (1991). *The Meaning of Focus Particles: A Comparative Perspective*. London: Routledge.

KÖVECSES, ZOLTÁN (1995). 'American friendship and the scope of metaphor'. *Cognitive Linguistics* 6(4): 315–46.

——(2002). *Metaphor: A Practical Introduction*. Oxford: Oxford University Press.

KRIPKE, SAUL (1972). 'Naming and necessity'. In D. Davidson and G. Harman (eds.), *Semantics of Natural Language*. Dordrecht: Reidel, 253–355.

KUCZAJ, STAN A., and DALY, MARY J. (1979). 'The development of hypothetical reference in the speech of young children'. *Journal of Child Language* 6: 563–79.

KWAN TERRY, A. (1978). 'The meaning and the source of the "la" and the "what" particles in Singapore English'. *RELC Journal* 9(2): 22–36.

LABOV, WILLIAM (1973). 'The boundaries of words and their meanings'. In C.-J. Bailey and R. Shuy (eds.), *New Ways of Analyzing Variation in English*. Washington, DC: Georgetown University Press, 340–73.

Lakoff, George (1972). 'Linguistics and natural logic'. In D. Davidson and G. Harman (eds.), *Semantics of Natural Language*. Dordrecht: Reidel, 545–665.

——(1987). *Women, Fire and Dangerous Things*. Chicago: University of Chicago Press.

——(1988). 'Cognitive semantics'. In U. Eco, M. Santambrogio, and P. Violi (eds.), *Meaning and Mental Representations*. Bloomington: Indiana University Press, 119–54.

——and Johnson, Mark (1980). *Metaphors We Live By*. Chicago: University of Chicago Press.

————(2003). *Metaphors We Live By*, 2nd edn. Chicago: University of Chicago Press.

——and Kövecses, Zoltán (1987). 'The cognitive model of anger inherent in American English'. In D. Holland and N. Quinn (eds.), *Cultural Models in Language and Thought*. Cambridge: Cambridge University Press, 195–221.

Lakoff, Robin (1973). 'Questionable answers and answerable questions'. In B. B. Kachru, R. B. Lees, Y. Malkiel, A. Pietrangeli, and S. Saporta (eds.), *Issues in Linguistics: Papers in honor of Henry and Renée Kahane*. Urbana: University of Illinois Press, 453–67.

Langacker, Ronald W. (1987). *Foundations of Cognitive Grammar*, vol. 1. Stanford, CA: Stanford University Press.

——(2010). 'Cognitive grammar'. In B. Heine and H. Narrog (eds.), *The Oxford Handbook of Linguistic Analysis*. Oxford: Oxford University Press, 87–110.

Lat (1989). *Mat Som*. Petaling Jaya: Kampung Boy.

Leathers, Dale G. (1992). *Successful Nonverbal Communication: Principles and Applications*, 2nd edn. New York: Macmillan. (Original edition 1986.)

Lebra, Takie S. (1974). 'Reciprocity and the asymmetric principle: an analytic reappraisal of the Japanese concept of *On*'. In T. S. Lebra and W. P. Lebra (eds.), *Japanese Culture and Behavior: Selected Readings*. Honolulu: University of Hawaii Press, 192–207.

——(1976). *Japanese Patterns of Behavior*. Honolulu: University of Hawaii Press.

Lee, Kee-dong (1975). *Kusaiean Reference Grammar*. Honolulu: University of Hawaii Press.

Leech, Geoffrey N. (1969). *Towards a Semantic Description of English*. Harlow: Longman.

——(1981). *Semantics: The Study of Meaning*. Harmondsworth: Penguin.

Lehrer, Adrienne (1969). 'Semantic cuisine'. *Journal of Linguistics* 5 (1): 39–55.

——(1970). 'Indeterminacy in semantic description'. *Glossa*, 4 (1): 87–110.

Lehrman, Alexander (2006). 'Meaning as grammar'. *Language Sciences* 28: 553–75.

Leibniz, Gottfried Wilhelm (1973[1679]). *Philosophical Writings*. Translated by M. Morris and G. H. R. Parkinson; edited by G. H. R. Parkinson. London: Dent.

LEIBNIZ, GOTTFRIED WILHELM (1981[1765]). *New Essays On Human Understanding*. Translated and edited by P. Remnant and J. Bennet. Cambridge: Cambridge University Press.

LEVIN, BETH (1993). *English Verb Classes and Alternations*. Chicago: University of Chicago Press.

——and RAPPAPORT HOVAV, MALKA (1991). 'Wiping the slate clean: a lexical semantic exploration'. In B. Levin and S. Pinker (eds.), *Lexical and Conceptual Semantics*. Cambridge, MA: Blackwell, 123–51.

——— (2005). *Argument Realization*. Cambridge: Cambridge University Press.

LEVINSON, STEPHEN C. (1983). *Pragmatics*. Cambridge: Cambridge University Press.

——(2000). *Presumptive Meanings: The Theory of Generalized Conversational Implicature*. Cambridge, MA: MIT Press.

——(2003). *Space in Language and Cognition: Explorations in Cognitive Diversity*. Cambridge: Cambridge University Press.

——(2006). 'On the human "interaction engine"'. In N. J. Enfield and S. C. Levinson (eds.), *Roots of Human Sociality: Culture, Cognition and Interaction*. Oxford: Berg, 39–69.

——and WILKINS, DAVID P. (eds.) (2006). *Grammars of Space: Explorations in Cognitive Diversity*. Cambridge: Cambridge University Press.

LEVISEN, CARSTEN (2010). 'The Danish universe of meaning: semantics, cognition and cultural values'. PhD thesis, University of New England, Armidale.

LÉVY-BRUHL, LUCIEN (1926). *How Natives Think* [*Les fonctions mentales dans les sociètiés inférieures*]. Translated by L. A. Clare. London: Allen & Unwin. (Reprinted 1979, New York: Arno Press.)

LEWIS, CHARLIE, and MITCHELL, PETER (eds.) (1994). *Children's Early Understanding of Mind: Origins and Development*. Hove: Erlbaum.

LEWIS, DAVID (1973). 'Causation'. *Journal of Philosophy* 70: 556–67.

——(1976). 'Observations on route finding and spatial orientation among the Aboriginal peoples of the Western Desert Region of Central Australia'. *Oceania* 46(4): 249–82.

LINDNER, SUSAN J. (1983). *A Lexico-Semantic Analysis of English Verb Particle Constructions with OUT and UP*. Bloomington: Indiana University Linguistics Club.

LOCKE, JOHN (1976 [1690]). *An Essay Concerning Human Understanding*. Abridged and edited with an introduction by John W. Yolton. London: Dent.

Longman Dictionary of Contemporary English (1978). Edited by H. Gay et al. Harlow: Longman.

Longman Dictionary of Contemporary English (1987). Edited by H. Gay et al. (2nd edn). Harlow: Longman.

LUCID, DANIEL P. (ed.) (1977). *Soviet Semiotics: An Anthology*. Baltimore: Johns Hopkins University Press.

LUTZ, CATHERINE A. (1988). *Unnatural Emotions: Everyday Sentiments on a Micro-nesian Atoll and Their Challenge to Western Theory*. Chicago: University of Chicago Press.

LYONS, JOHN (1968). *Introduction to Theoretical Linguistics*. Cambridge: Cambridge University Press.

——(1977). *Semantics* (2 vols). Cambridge: Cambridge University Press.

——(1995). *Linguistic Semantics*. Cambridge: Cambridge University Press.

Macquarie Dictionary, The (1987). Edited by A. Delbridge (2nd edn). Sydney: Macquarie Library. (Original edition 1981.)

MAHER, BRIGID (2002). 'Natural semantic metalanguage theory and some Italian speech act verbs'. *Studies in Pragmatics* 4: 33–48.

MAJID, ASIFA, and BOWERMAN, MELISSA (eds.) (2007). *'Cutting and Breaking' Events: A Cross-Linguistic Perspective* (special issue of *Cognitive Linguistics* 18(2)).

MALT, BARBARA C., GENNARI, SILVIA P., and IMAI, MUTSUMI (2010). 'Lexicalization patterns and the world-to-words mapping'. In B. C. Malt and P. Wolff (eds.), *Words and the Mind: How Words Capture Human Experience*. Oxford: Oxford University Press, 29–57.

————————AMEEL, EEF, TSUDA, NAOAKI, and MAJID, ASIFA (2008). 'Talking about walking: biomechanics and the language of locomotion'. *Psychological Science* 19(3): 232–40.

MARKMAN, ELLEN M. (1989). *Categorization and Naming in Children: Problems of Induction*. Cambridge, MA: MIT Press.

MATSUMOTO, YOSHIKO (1993). 'Japanese numeral classifiers: a study of semantic categories and lexical organization'. *Linguistics* 31(4): 667–713.

MATTHEWS, STEPHEN, and YIP, VIRGINIA (1994). *Cantonese: A Comprehensive Grammar*. London: Routledge.

MAYNARD, SENKO K. (1997). *Japanese Communication: Language and Thought in Context*. Honolulu: University of Hawaii Press.

McCAWLEY, JAMES D. (1968). 'The role of semantics in a grammar'. In E. Bach and R. T. Harms (eds.), *Universals in Linguistic Theory*. New York: Holt, Rinehart & Winston, 124–69.

——(1970). 'Semantic representation'. In P. M. Garvin (ed.), *Cognition: A Multiple View*. New York: Spartan Books, 227–47.

——(1972). 'A program for logic'. In D. Davidson and G. Harman (eds.), *Semantics of Natural Language*. Dordrecht: Reidel, 498–544.

——(1993). *Everything that Linguists have Always Wanted to Know about Logic**But Were Ashamed to Ask*, 2nd edn). Chicago: University of Chicago Press. (Original edition 1981.)

McKAY, GRAHAM R. (1978). 'Pronominal person and number categories in Rembarrnga and Djebbana'. *Oceanic Linguistics* 17: 27–37.

——(1990). 'The addressee: Or, is the second person singular?' *Studies in Language* 14(2): 429–32.

McMahon, Darrin M. (2006). *Happiness: A History*. New York: Atlantic Monthly Press.

Mel'čuk, Igor A. (1989). 'Semantic primitives from the viewpoint of the Meaning–Text Linguistic Theory'. *Quaderni di semantica* 10(1): 65–102.

Mill, John Stuart (1960 [1843]). *A System of Logic, Ratiocinative and Inductive: Being a connected view of the principles of evidence and the methods of scientific investigation* (8th edn). London: Longman.

Miller, George (1956). 'The magical number seven, plus or minus two: some limits on our capacity for processing information'. *Psychological Review* 63(2): 81–97.

—— and Johnson-Laird, Philip N. (1976). *Language and Perception*. Cambridge: Cambridge University Press.

Minami, Masahiko (2002). *Culture-Specific Language Styles: The Development of Oral Narrative and Literacy*. Clevedon: Multilingual Matters.

Mitchison, Naomi (1985). *Memoirs of a Spacewoman* (new edn). London: Women's Press. (Original edition 1962.)

Mithun, Marianne (1988). 'The grammaticization of coordination'. In J. Haiman and S. A. Thompson (eds.), *Clause Combining in Grammar and Discourse*. Amsterdam: Benjamins, 331–59.

—— (1991). 'Active/agentive case marking and its motivations'. *Language* 67(3): 510–46.

Mizutani, Osamu, and Mizutani, Nobuko (1987). *How to be Polite in Japanese*. Tokyo: Japan Times.

Moerk, Ernst L. (1992). *A First Language: Taught and Learned*. Baltimore: Brookes.

Monahan, Barbara (1983). *A Dictionary of Russian Gesture*. Ann Arbor, MI: Hermitage.

Morgan, Lewis Henry (1871). *Systems of Consanguinity and Affinity of the Human Family*. Washington, DC: Smithsonian Institution.

Morris, Desmond, Collett, Peter, Marsh, Peter, and O'Shaughnessy, Marie (1979). *Gestures: Their Origins and Distribution*. London: Cape.

Morsbach, Helmut (1973). 'Aspects of nonverbal communication in Japan'. *Journal of Nervous and Mental Disease* 157(4): 262–77.

Munn, Nancy D. (1973). *Walbiri Iconography*. Ithaca, NY: Cornell University Press.

Myers, Fred R. (1986). *Pintupi Country, Pintupi Self: Sentiment, Place and Politics among Western Desert Aborigines*. Washington, DC/Canberra: Smithsonian Institution/Australian Institute of Aboriginal Studies.

Næss, Åshild (2007). *Prototypical Transitivity*. Amsterdam: Benjamins.

Næss, Åshild (2009). 'How transitive are EAT and DRINK verbs?' In J. Newman (ed.), *The Linguistics of Eating and Drinking*. Amsterdam: Benjamins, 27–43.

Nakane, Chie (1970). *Japanese Society*. London: Weidenfeld & Nicolson.

NASIR, LILY HASLINA (1989). *Rindu Yang Tidak Tertuai*. Kuala Lumpur: "K" Publishing & Distributors.

NELSON, KATHERINE (1973). 'Structure and strategy in learning to talk'. *Monographs of the Society for Research in Child Development* 38. Ann Arbor, MI.

NEWMAN, JOHN (1997). 'Eating and drinking as sources of metaphor in English'. *Cuadernos de Filología Inglesa* (special issue on 'Cognitive linguistics') 6(2): 213–31.

——(ed.) (2009). *The Linguistics of Eating and Drinking*. Amsterdam: Benjamins.

NIDA, EUGENE A. (1975). *Language Structure and Translation*. Stanford, CA: Stanford University Press.

OATLEY, KEITH, and JOHNSON-LAIRD, PHILIP N. (1987). 'Towards a cognitive theory of emotions'. *Cognition and Emotion* 1: 29–50.

ONISHI, MASAYUKI (1994). 'Semantic primitives in Japanese'. In Goddard and Wierzbicka (1994b: 361–86).

ORTONY, ANDREW, CLORE, GERALD L., and COLLINS, ALLAN (1988). *The Cognitive Structure of Emotions*. Cambridge: Cambridge University Press.

——AND TURNER, TERENCE J. (1990). 'What's basic about basic emotions?' *Psychological Review* 97(3): 315–31.

OSWALT, ROBERT L. (1986). 'The evidential system of Kayasha'. In W. Chafe and J. Nichols (eds.), *Evidentiality: The Linguistic Coding of Epistemology*. Norwood, NJ: Ablex, 29–45.

OVERING, JOANNA, and PASSES, ALAN (2000). *The Anthropology of Love and Anger: The Aesthetics of Conviviality in Native South America*. London: Routledge.

OWEN, MARION (1981). 'Converstional units and the use of "well"'. In P. Werth (ed.), *Conversation and Discourse*. London: Croom Helm, 99–116.

Oxford Advanced Learner's Dictionary (1995). Edited by J. Crowther (5th edn). Oxford: Oxford University Press.

Oxford Australian Junior Dictionary, The (1980). Edited by R. Sansome and A. Ridsdale. Melbourne: Oxford University Press.

Oxford Paperback Dictionary (1979). Edited by J. Hawkins. Oxford: Oxford University Press.

PALMER, FRANK R. (1981). *Semantics*, 2nd edn. Cambridge: Cambridge University Press. (Original edition 1976.)

——(1986). *Mood and Modality*. Cambridge: Cambridge University Press.

PANTHER, KLAUS-UWE, and RADDEN, GÜNTER (eds.) (1999). *Metonymy in Language and Thought*. Amsterdam: Benjamins.

PAPAFRAGOU, ANNA, MASSEY, CHRISTINE, and GLEITMAN, LILA (2002). 'Shake, rattle, 'n' roll: the representation of motion in language and cognition'. *Cognition* 84: 189–219.

PARKVALL, MIKAEL (2006). *Limits of Language*. London: Battlebridge.

PARSONS, TERENCE (1994). *Events in the Structure of English: A Study in Subatomic Semantics*. Cambridge, MA: MIT Press.

PAVLENKO, ANETA (2005). *Emotions and Multilingualism*. Cambridge: Cambridge University Press.

PAWLEY, ANDREW, and BULMER, R. N. H. (in press). *A Dictionary of Kalam with Ethnographic Notes*. Canberra: Pacific Linguistics.

PECK, S. R. (1987). *Atlas of Facial Expression*. New York: Oxford University Press.

PEDERSEN, JAN (2010). 'The different Swedish *tack*: an ethnographic investigation of Swedish thanking and related concepts'. *Journal of Pragmatics* 42(5): 1258–1265.

PEETERS, BERT (2000a). 'Setting the scene: recent milestones in the lexicon-encyclopedia debate'. In B. Peeters (ed.), *The Lexicon Encyclopedia Interface*. Amsterdam: Elsevier, 1–52.

——(2000b). '"S'engager" vs. "to show restraint": linguistic and cultural relativity in discourse management'. In S. Niemeier and R. Dirven (eds.), *Evidence for Linguistic Relativity*. Amsterdam: Benjamins, 193–222.

——(ed.) (2006). *Semantic Primes and Universal Grammar: Empirical Evidence from the Romance Languages*. Amsterdam: Benjamins.

PEIRCE, CHARLES S. (1932). 'Speculative grammar'. In C. Hartshorne and P. Weiss (eds.), *Collected Papers of Charles Sanders Peirce*, vol. 2: *Elements of Logic*. Cambridge, MA: Harvard University Press, 129–269.

PETERSON, CAROLE (1990). 'The who, when and where of early narratives'. *Journal of Child Language* 17: 433–55.

PETRUCK, MIRIAM R. L. (1996). 'Frame semantics'. In J. Verschueren, J.-O. Östman, J. Blommaert, and C. Bulcaen (eds.), *Handbook of Pragmatics*. Amsterdam: Benjamins, 1–13.

PIAGET, JEAN (1973 [1929]). *The Child's Conception of the World*. Translated by J. Tomlinson and A. Tomlinson. St Albans: Paladin.

PINKER, STEVEN (1994). *The Language Instinct: The New Science of Language and Mind*. London: Allen Lane.

POTTIER, B. (1963). *Recherches sur l'analyse sémantique en linguistique et en traduction méchanique*. Nancy: Université de Nancy.

POWER, MICK, and DALGLEISH, TIM (2008). *Cognition and Emotion: From Order to Disorder*, 2nd edn. Hove: Psychology Press. (Original edition 1997.)

PÜTZ, MARTIN, and NEFF-VAN AERTSELAER, JOANNE (eds.) (2008). *Developing Contrastive Pragmatics: Interlanguage and Cross-Cultural Perspectives*. Berlin: Mouton de Gruyter.

RAPPAPORT HOVAV, MALKA, and LEVIN, BETH (1998). 'Building verb meanings'. In M. Butt and W. Geuder (eds.), *The Projection of Arguments: Lexical and Compositional Factors*. Stanford, CA: CSLI, 97–134.

REDDY, MICHAEL J. (1979). 'The conduit metaphor: a case of frame conflict in our language about language'. In A. Ortony (ed.), *Metaphor and Thought*. Cambridge: Cambridge University Press, 284–324.

RENWICK, GEORGE W. (1980). *Interact: Guidelines for Australians and North Americans*. Chicago: Intercultural Press.

RICHARDS, JACK C., and TAY, MARY W. J. (1977). 'The *la* particle in Singapore English'. In W. Crewe (ed.), *The English Language in Singapore*. Singapore: Eastern Universities Press, 141–56.

RIESCHILD, VERNA ROBERTSON (1996). 'Lebanese-Arabic discourse: adult interaction with young children (with reference to Australian-English situations)'. PhD thesis, Australian National University, Canberra.

ROSALDO, MICHELLE (1980). *Knowledge and Passion: Ilongot Notions of Self and Social Life*. Cambridge: Cambridge University Press.

ROSCH, ELEANOR (1977). 'Human categorization'. In N. Warren (ed.), *Advances in Cross-Cultural Psychology*, vol. 1. London: Academic Press, 1–49.

——(1978). 'Principles of categorization'. In E. Rosch and B. Lloyd (eds.), *Cognition and Categorization*. Hillsdale, NJ: Erlbaum, 27–48.

RUPPENHOFER, JOSEF, ELLSWORTH, MICHAEL, PETRUCK, MIRIAM R. L., JOHNSON, CHRISTOPHER R., and SCHEFFCZYK, JAN (2006). 'FrameNet II: Extended Theory and Practice'. http://framenet.icsi.berkeley.edu/index.php?option=com_wrapper &Itemid=126. Accessed 14/9/09.

RUSSELL, BERTRAND (1917). *Mysticism and Logic and Other Essays*, 2nd edn. London: Allen & Unwin.

——(1948). *Human Knowledge: Its Scope and Limits*. New York: Simon & Schuster.

RUSSELL, JAMES A. (1991). 'Culture and the categorization of emotions'. *Psychological Bulletin* 110(3): 426–50.

——(1994). 'Is there universal recognition of emotion from facial expression? A review of the cross-cultural studies'. *Psychological Bulletin* 115(1): 102–41.

——and FERNÁNDEZ-DOLS, JOSÉ-MIGUEL (eds.) (1997). *The Psychology of Facial Expression*. Cambridge: Cambridge University Press.

SAUSSURE, FERDINAND DE (1983 [1922]). *Course in General Linguistics*. Translated by R. Harris. London: Duckworth.

SCHEFFLER, HAROLD W. (1978). *Australian Kin Classifications*. Cambridge: Cambridge University Press.

SCHERER, K. R. (1992). 'What does facial expression express?' In K. T. Strongman (ed.), *International Review of Studies on Emotion*, vol. 2. Chichester: Wiley, 139–65.

SCHIFFRIN, DEBORAH (1981). 'Handwork as ceremony: the case of the handshake'. In A. Kendon (ed.), *Nonverbal Communication, Interaction and Gesture*. The Hague: Mouton, 237–50.

——(1987). *Discourse Markers*. Cambridge: Cambridge University Press.

SCHOURUP, LAWRENCE (2001). 'Rethinking *well*'. *Journal of Pragmatics* 33(7): 1025–60.

SCHWARTZ, STEPHEN P. (1978). 'Putnam on artifacts'. *Philosophical Review* 87(4): 566–74.

SEARLE, JOHN (1965). 'What is a speech act?' In M. Black (ed.), *Philosophy in America*. London: Allen & Unwin, 221–39.

SEARLE, JOHN (1969). *Speech Acts: An Essay in the Philosophy of Language*. Cambridge: Cambridge University Press.

——(1975). 'Indirect speech acts'. In P. Cole and J. L. Morgan (eds.), *Speech Acts*. New York: Academic Press, 59–82.

SEBEOK, THOMAS A. (1991). *A Sign Is Just a Sign*. Bloomington: Indiana University Press.

SELLS, PETER (1985). *Lectures on Contemporary Syntactic Theories*. Stanford, CA: CSLI.

SHATZ, MARILYN, WELLMAN, HENRY M., and SILBER, SHARON (1983). 'The acquisition of mental verbs: a systematic investigation of the first reference to mental state'. *Cognition* 14: 301–21.

SHIBATANI, MASAYOSHI (1976). 'The grammar of causative constructions: a conspectus'. In M. Shibatani (ed.), *The Grammar of Causative Constructions*. New York: Academic Press, 1–40.

SHWEDER, RICHARD A. (2004). 'Deconstructing the emotions for the sake of comparative research'. In A. S. R. Manstead, N. Frijda, and A. Fischer (eds.), *Feelings and Emotions: The Amsterdam Symposium*. Cambridge: Cambridge University Press, 81–97.

SIBLY, ANNE (2008). 'The semantics of physical contact verbs: lexicographic sketches of *caress, fondle, kit, kick, punch, slap, smack, stroke,* and *touch*'. BA (Hons) sub-thesis, Australian National University, Canberra.

——(2010). '*Harry slapped Hugo, Tracey smacked Ritchie*: the semantics of *slap* and *smack*'. *Australian Journal of Linguistics* 30(3), 323–48.

SIMPSON, JANE (2001). 'Hypocoristics of place-names in Australian English'. In D. Blair and P. Collins (eds.), *English in Australia*. Amsterdam: Benjamins, 89–112.

SINHA, ANJANI KUMAR (1972). 'On the deictic uses of "coming" and "going" in Hindi'. *Papers from the Eighth Regional Meeting of the Chicago Linguistics Society*: 351–8.

SLOBIN, DAN I. (1985). 'Crosslinguistic evidence for the language-making capacity'. In D. I. Slobin (ed.), *The Crosslinguistic Study of Language Acquisition*, vol. 2: *Theoretical Issues*. Hillsdale, NJ: Erlbaum, 1157–256.

——(2000). 'Verbalised events: a dynamic approach to linguistic relativity and determinism'. In S. Niemeier and R. Dirven (eds.), *Evidence for Linguistic Relativity*. Amsterdam: Benjamins, 107–38.

——(2004). 'The many ways to search for a frog: linguistic typology and the expression of motion events'. In S. Strömqvist and L. Verhoeven (eds.), *Relating Events in Narrative: Typological and Contextual Perspectives*. Mahwah, NJ: Erlbaum, 219–57.

SMILEY, PATRICIA, and HUTTENLOCHER, JANELLEN (1995). 'Conceptual development and the child's early words for events, objects, and persons'. In M. Tomasello and W. E. Merriman (eds.), *Beyond Names for Things: Young Children's Aquisition of Verbs*. Hillsdale, NJ: Erlbaum, 21–61.

SMITH, ROBERT J. (1983). *Japanese Society: Tradition, Self and the Social Order.* Cambridge: Cambridge University Press.

SOLOMON, ROBERT C. (1984). 'Getting angry: the Jamesian theory of emotion in anthropology'. In R. A. Shweder and R. A. LeVine (eds.), *Culture Theory: Essays on Mind, Self and Emotion.* Cambridge: Cambridge University Press, 238–54.

SORABJI, RICHARD (1988). *Matter, Space and Motion.* Ithaca, NY: Cornell University Press.

STANWOOD, RYO E. (1993). 'The hitchhiker's guide to *shake, wave, swing*, and *wag*'. *Working Papers in Linguistics* 22(2): 141–7.

SUSSEX, ROLAND (2004a). 'Australian hypocoristics: putting the *-ie* into *Aussie*'. *Australian Style*: available at: http://www.shlrc.mq.edu.au/style/dec2004.htm

——(2004b). 'Lexical and social aspects of diminutives/hypocoristics in Australian English'. Paper presented at the Biennial Australex Conference, July, Sydney.

SWIFT, M. G. (1965). *Malay Peasant Society in Jelebu.* London: Athlone Press.

TALMY, LEONARD (1985a). 'Lexicalization patterns: semantic structure in lexical forms'. In T. Shopen (ed.), *Language Typology and Syntactic Description*, vol. 3: *Grammatical Categories and the Lexicon.* Cambridge: Cambridge University Press, 57–149.

——(1985b). 'Force dynamics in language and thought'. In W. H. Eikfont, P. D. Kroeber, and K. L. Peterson (eds.), *Papers from the Parasession on Causatives and Agentivity at the Twenty First Regional Meeting of the Chicago Linguistics Society.* Chicago: CLS, 293–337.

——(1988). 'Force dynamics in language and cognition'. *Cognitive Science* 12: 49–100.

——(2000). *Toward a Cognitive Semantics.* Cambridge, MA: MIT Press.

——(2007). 'Lexical typologies'. In T. Shopen (ed.), *Language Typology and Syntactic Description*, vol. 3: *Grammatical Categories and the Lexicon*, 2nd edn. Cambridge: Cambridge University Press, 66–168. (Original edition 1985.)

TAO, H. (2000). 'Cóng "chī" kàn dòngcí lùnyuán jiégòu de dòngtài tèzhēng' ['Eating' and emergent argument structure]. *Zhōngguó Yǔwén* 3: 21–38.

TAYLOR, JOHN R. (1996). 'On running and jogging'. *Cognitive Linguistics* 7(1): 21–34.

——(2003). *Linguistic Categorization*, 3rd edn. Oxford: Oxford University Press. (Original edn 1989.)

TENNY, CAROL, and PUSTEJOVSKY, JAMES (2000). 'A history of events in linguistic theory'. In C. Tenny and J. Pustejovsky (eds.), *Events as Grammatical Objects: The Converging Perspectives of Lexical Semantics and Syntax.* Stanford, CA: CSLI, 3–37.

TIEN, ADRIAN (1999). 'Early lexical exponents and 'related' lexical items as manifestation of conceptual/semantic primitives in child language'. MA thesis, Australian National University, Canberra.

TIEN, ADRIAN (2005). 'The semantics of children's Mandarin Chinese: the first four years'. PhD thesis, University of New England, Armidale.

—— (2009). 'Semantic prime HAPPEN in Mandarin Chinese: in search of a viable exponent'. *Pragmatics and Cognition* 17(2): 356–82.

—— (2010). *Lexical Semantics of Children's Mandarin Chinese during the First Four Years*. Munich: LINCOM.

TRAUGOTT, ELIZABETH C. (1993). 'The conflict promises/threatens to escalate into war'. *Proceedings of the 19th Annual Meeting of the Berkeley Linguistics Society*: 348–58.

—— (1994). 'Subjectification and the development of modal meanings'. Paper presented at the Australian Linguistics Institute, La Trobe University, Melbourne (July).

TRAVIS, CATHERINE E. (1998). '*Omoiyari* as a core Japanese value: Japanese-style empathy?' In A. Athanasiadou and E. Tabakowska (eds.), *Speaking of Emotions: Conceptualization and Expression*. Berlin: Mouton de Gruyter, 55–82.

—— (2004). 'The ethnopragmatics of the diminutive in conversational Colombian Spanish'. *Intercultural Pragmatics* 1(2): 249–74.

—— (2005). *Discourse Markers in Colombian Spanish: A Study in Polysemy*. Berlin: Mouton de Gruyter.

—— (2006). 'The natural semantic metalanguage approach to discourse markers'. In K. Fischer (ed.), *Approaches to Discourse Particles*. Amsterdam: Elsevier, 219–41.

TYACK, D., and INGRAM, D. (1977). 'Children's production and comprehension of questions'. *Journal of Child Language* 4: 211–24.

TYLER, PATRICK (2008). *A World of Trouble: The White House and the Middle East? From the Cold War to the War on Terror*. New York: Farrar, Straus & Giroux.

URBAN, MATTHIAS (2010). 'Terms for the unique beginner: cross-linguistic and cross-cultural perspectives'. *Journal of Ethnobiology* 30(2): 203–230.

VENDLER, ZENO (1967). *Linguistics in Philosophy*. Ithaca, NY: Cornell University Press.

VERSCHEUREN, JEF (1985). *What People Say They Do With Words*. Norwood, NJ: Ablex.

VOGT, HANS (1971). *Grammaire de la langue géorgienne*. Oslo: Universitets Forlaget.

VREELAND, NENA, DANA, GLENN B., HURWITZ, GEOFFREY B., JUST, PETER, MOELLER, PHILIP W., and SHINN, R. S. (1977). *Area Handbook for Malaysia (Microform)*, 3rd edn. Glen Rock, NJ: Microfilming Corporation of America.

WARD, RUSSEL (1958). *The Australian Legend*. Melbourne: Oxford University Press.

WASOW, THOMAS (1985). 'Postcript'. In Sells (1985: 193–205).

WATERS, SOPHIA (2010). 'The semantics of French discourse particles *quoi* and *ben*'. In Y. Treis and R. De Busser (eds.), *Selected Papers from the 2009 Conference of the Australian Linguistic Society*, available at: http://www.als.asn.au.

WATTS, RICHARD J. (1986). 'Relevance in conversational moves: a reappraisal of "well"'. *Studia Anglica Posnaniensia* 19: 37–59.

WEBER, DAVID J. (1986). 'Information perspective, profile, and patterns in Quechua'. In W. Chafe and J. Nichols (eds.), *Evidentiality: The Linguistic Coding of Epistemology.* Norwood, NJ: Ablex, 137–55.

Webster's Third New International Dictionary (1971). Edited by P. B. Gove. Springfield, MA: Merriam.

WELLMAN, HENRY M., and BARTSCH, KAREN (1994). 'Before belief: children's early psychological theory'. In C. Lewis and P. Mitchell (eds.), *Children's Early Understanding of Mind: Origins and Development.* Hove: Erlbaum, 331–54.

WIERZBICKA, ANNA (1972). *Semantic Primitives.* Translated by A. Wierzbicka and J. Besemeres. Frankfurt: Athenäum.

——(1976). 'Particles and linguistic relativity'. *International Review of Slavic Linguistics* 1(2/3): 327–67.

——(1980a). *Lingua Mentalis: The Semantics of Natural Language.* Sydney: Academic Press.

——(1980b). *The Case For Surface Case.* Ann Arbor: Karoma.

——(1985). *Lexicography and Conceptual Analysis.* Ann Arbor: Karoma.

——(1986a). 'Human emotions: universal or culture-specific?' *American Anthropologist* 88(3): 584–94.

——(ed.) (1986b). Special edition on 'Particles'. *Journal of Pragmatics* 10(5).

——(1987). *English Speech Act Verbs: A Semantic Dictionary.* Sydney: Academic Press.

——(1988). *The Semantics of Grammar.* Amsterdam: Benjamins.

——(1989). 'Semantic primitives: the expanding set'. *Quaderni di semantica* 10(2): 309–32.

——(1990a). '"Prototypes save": on the uses and abuses of the notion of "prototype" in linguistics and related fields'. In S. L. Tsohatzidis (ed.), *Meanings and Prototypes: Studies in Linguistic Categorization.* New York: Routledge & Kegan Paul, 347–67.

——(1990b). 'The semantics of emotions: *fear* and its relatives in English'. *Australian Journal of Linguistics* 10(2): 359–75.

——(1992a). *Semantics, Culture, and Cognition: Universal Human Concepts in Culture-specific Configurations.* Oxford: Oxford University Press.

——(1992b). 'The search for universal semantic primitives'. In M. Pütz (ed.), *Thirty Years of Linguistic Evolution: A Festschrift for René Dirven.* Amsterdam: Benjamins, 215–42.

——(1993). 'Reading human faces: emotion components and universal semantics'. *Pragmatics and Cognition* 1(1): 1–23.

——(1994a). 'Semantics and epistemology: the meaning of "evidentials" in a cross-linguistic perspective'. *Language Sciences* 16(1): 81–137.

WIERZBICKA, ANNA (1994b). '"Cultural scripts": a semantic approach to cultural analysis and cross-cultural communication'. In L. F. Bouton and Y. Kachru (eds.), *Pragmatics and Language Learning*. Urbana: Division of English as an International Language, University of Illinois, 1–24.

—— (1994c). '"Cultural scripts": a new approach to the study of cross-cultural communication'. In M. Pütz (ed.), *Language Contact and Language Conflict*. Amsterdam: Benjamins, 69–87.

—— (1994d). 'Emotion, language, and "cultural scripts"'. In S. Kitayama and H. R. Markus (eds.), *Emotion and Culture: Empirical Studies of Mutual Influence*. Washington, DC: American Psychological Association, 130–98.

—— (1995a). 'Emotion and facial expression: a semantic perspective'. *Culture and Psychology* 1(2): 227–58.

—— (1995b). 'Kisses, handshakes, bows: the semantics of nonverbal communication'. *Semiotica* 103(3/4): 207–52.

—— (1996a). *Semantics, Primes and Universals*. New York: Oxford University Press.

—— (1996b). 'The semantics of "logical concepts"'. *Moscow Linguistics Journal* (Festschrift for E. V. Paducheva, edited by T. Yanko) 2: 104–29.

—— (1997). *Understanding Cultures Through their Key Words*. New York: Oxford University Press.

WIERZBICKA, ANNA (1999). *Emotions across Languages and Cultures: Diversity and Universals*. Cambridge: Cambridge University Press.

—— (2003a). *Cross-Cultural Pragmatics: The Semantics of Human Interaction*, 2nd edn. Berlin: Mouton de Gruyter. (Original edition 1991.)

—— (2003b). 'The semantics of English causative constructions in a universal-typological perspective'. In M. Tommasello (ed.), *The New Psychology of Language: Cognitive and Functional Approaches to Language Structure*. Mahwah, NJ: Erlbaum, 113–53. (Original edition 1998.)

—— (2005). 'There are no "color universals", but there are universals of visual semantics'. *Anthropological Linguistics* 47(2), 217–44.

—— (2006a). *English: Meaning and Culture*. New York: Oxford University Press.

—— (2006b). 'Anglo scripts against "putting pressure" on other people and their linguistic manifestations'. In Goddard (2006b: 31–63).

—— (2006c). 'Shape in grammar revisited'. *Studies in Language* 30(1): 115–77.

—— (2006d). 'The English causatives: causation and interpersonal relations'. In Wierzbicka (2006a: 171–203).

—— (2007a). 'Bodies and their parts: an NSM approach to semantic typology'. *Language Sciences* 29(1): 14–65.

—— (2007b). 'Shape and colour in language and thought'. In A. C. Schalley and D. Khlentzos (eds.), *Mental States*, vol. 2: *Language and Cognitive Structure*. Amsterdam: Benjamins, 37–60.

WIERZBICKA, ANNA (2008). 'Why there are no "colour universals" in language and thought'. *Journal of the Royal Anthropological Institute* 14: 407–25.

——(2009a). 'Language and metalanguage: key issues in emotion research'. *Emotion Review* 1(1): 3–14.

——(2009b). 'All people eat and drink: does this mean that "eat" and "drink" are universal human concepts?' In J. Newman (ed.), *The Linguistics of Eating and Drinking*. Amsterdam: Benjamins, 65–89.

——(2009c). 'Exploring English phraseology with two tools: NSM semantic methodology and Google'. *Journal of English Linguistics* 37(2): 101–29.

——(2010a). *Experience, Evidence and Sense: The Hidden Cultural Legacy of English*. New York: Oxford University Press.

——(2010b). 'The "history of emotions" and the future of emotion research'. *Emotion Review* 2(3): 269–273.

——(2010c). '"Eating" and "drinking" in Kalam'. In J. Bowden, N. Himmelmann, and M. Ross (eds.), *A Journey through Austronesian and Papuan Linguistic and Cultural Space: Papers in Honour of Andrew K. Pawley*. Canberra: Pacific Linguistics, 651–662.

——(forthcoming). 'Why not "happiness studies"? The cultural semantics of *happiness, bonheur, Glück* and *sčas'te*'. In L. Iomdin et al. (eds), *A Festschrift for Jurij Apresjan*. Moscow: Jazyki Russkoj Kultury.

——(in press a). 'How much longer can the Berlin and Kay paradigm dominate visual semantics? English, Russian and Warlpiri seen "from the native's point of view"'. In D. Young (ed.), *Re-materialising Colour*. Wantage: Kingston.

——(in press b). 'Advice: a contrastive and cross-cultural perspective'. In H. Limberg and M. Locher (eds.), *Discourse of Advice*. Amsterdam: Benjamins.

——(to appear a). 'Seven universal of kinship: overcoming the Eurocentrism of kinship semantics through seven universal semantic molecules'. *Anthropological Linguistics*.

——(to appear b). 'When cultural scripts clash: Miscommunication in "multicultural" Australia'. In B. Kryk-Kastovsky (ed.), *Intercultural Miscommunication*. Amsterdam: Benjamins.

WIESEMANN, URSULA (ed.) (1986). *Pronominal Systems*. Tübingen: Narr.

WILKINS, DAVID P. (1986). 'Particles/clitics for criticism and complaint in Mparntwe Arrernte (Aranda)'. *Journal of Pragmatics* 10(5): 575–96.

——(1989). 'Mparntwe Arrernte (Aranda): studies in the structure and semantics of grammar'. PhD thesis, Australian National University, Canberra.

——(2004). 'The verbalization of motion events in Arrernte'. In S. Strömqvist and L. Verhoeven (eds.), *Relating Events in Narrative: Typological and Contextual Perspectives*. Mahwah, NJ: Erlbaum, 143–57.

——and HILL, DEBORAH (1995). 'When "go" means "come": questioning the basicness of basic motion verbs'. *Cognitive Linguistics* 6(2/3): 209–59.

WITTGENSTEIN, LUDWIG (1953). *Philosophical Investigations*. Translated by G. E. M. Anscombe. Oxford: Blackwell.

WONG, JOCK (1994). 'A Wierzbickan approach to Singlish particles'. Master's thesis, National University of Singapore.

——(2008). 'Anglo English and Singapore English tags: their meanings and cultural significance'. *Pragmatics & Cognition* 16(1): 88–117.

YE, ZHENGDAO (2004). 'The Chinese folk model of facial expressions: a linguistic perspective'. *Culture and Psychology* 10(2): 195–222.

——(2006). 'Why the "inscrutable" Chinese face? Emotionality and facial expressions in Chinese'. In Goddard (2006b: 127–69).

——(2010). 'Eating and drinking in Mandarin and Shanghainese: a lexical-conceptual analysis'. In E. Christensen, E. Schier, and J. Sutton (eds.), *ASCS09: Proceedings of the 9th Conference of the Australasian Society for Cognitive Science*. Sydney: Macquarie Centre for Cognitive Science, 375–83.

ZADEH, LOFTI A. (1965). 'Fuzzy sets'. *Information and Control* 8: 338–53.

Language Index

General Index

reference 4–5, 7, 10, 25, 29, 50
referential indeterminacy 223, 225, 233–4
relational predicates 54–6
Renwick, G. W. 411
Richards, J. C. 181
Rieschild, V. R. 193
Rosaldo, M. 100
Rosch, E. H. 25, 196, 203, 228
Ruppenhoffer, J. 79
Russell, B. 234, 241
Russell, J. A. 100, 399, 400

sad 100, 111–12
Sakkalou, E. 390
Saussure, F. 9, 10
Sayers, B. J. 328
scenarios 84–5, *see also* prototypical cognitive scenario, prototypical motivational scenario
Scheffczyk, J. 79
Scheffler, H. W. 55
Scherer, K. R. 399, 400, 401
Schiffrin, D. 163, 171, 174, 407
Schourup, L. 171, 172, 173, 174
Schwartz, S. P. 217
semi-scientific English 198–9
scripts, see cultural scripts
Searle, J. 129, 133–8, 139, 143, 144, 159
Sebeok, T. A. 411
secondary interjection 166, 185
secondary lexeme 197, 201
Sells, P. 3
semantic competence 1, 37, 46, 62, 236, 389
semantic field/domain 51, 53, 54, 56, 58, 95, 235, 245
semantic change 27
semantic metalanguage 13, *see also* Natural Semantic Metalanguage

semantic molecule 71–2, 95, 194–5, 375–83
semantic primes 13, 65–71, 367, 372–5, 385–90
semantic primitive 13, 65, 66, 305, 391, 372, 376, *see also* semantic prime
semantic representation 4, 12, 26, 246
semantic template 95, 105–6, 107, 140, 147, 206, 219, 271, 285, 296, 372
semantic universals, *see* universals
semiotic 12, 91, 308
Simon-Vanderbengen, A-M. 171, 173, 174, 175
sense 5, 29
Ser, L. P. Q. 181
set intersection 50–1
set theory 50–1, 83
set union 50
shaking hands 407–8
Shatz, M. 387
Sherzer, J. 390
shh 187
Shibatani, M. 306
Shinn, R. S. 395
Shweder, R. A. 100, 372
Silber, S. 387
sincerity conditions (rules) 135–366, 159
Sibly, A. 72
Simpson, J. 364
Sinha, A. K. 254
situation semantics 46
Slobin, D. I. 270, 387
Sloman, S. A. 270
Smiley, P. 387
Smith, R. J. 372
Snow, C. 388
Solomon, R. C. 100
Sorabji, R. 241
source 243, 246–8, 250
space 246–8

Made in United States
Troutdale, OR
09/11/2023

12818958R00283